PLANNING IN
INTELLIGENT SYSTEMS

PLANNING IN INTELLIGENT SYSTEMS

Aspects, Motivations, and Methods

Edited by

WOUT VAN WEZEL
RENÉ JORNA
ALEXANDER MEYSTEL

WILEY-
INTERSCIENCE

A JOHN WILEY & SONS, INC., PUBLICATION

Published by John Wiley & Sons, Inc., Hoboken, New Jersey.
Published simultaneously in Canada.

For general information on our other products and services or for technical support, please contact our Customer Care Department within the United States at (800) 762-2974, outside the United States at (317) 572-3993 or fax (317) 572-4002.

Wiley also publishes its books in a variety of electronic formats. Some content that appears in print may not be available in electronic formats. For more information about Wiley products, visit our web site at www.wiley.com.

Library of Congress Cataloging-in-Publication Data:

Planning in intelligent systems: aspects, motivations, and methods/edited by Wout van Wezel, Rene Jorna, Alexander Meystel.
   p.cm
  Includes bibliographical references and index.
  ISBN 0-471-73427-6 (cloth)
 1. Expert systems (Computer science). 2. Intelligent control systems. 3. Artificial intelligence. I. Wezel, Wout van. II. Jorna, Rene. III. Meystel, A. (Alex)
  QA76.76.E95P533 2006
  006.3′3- -dc22

2005021353

Printed in the United States of America

10 9 8 7 6 5 4 3 2 1

CONTENTS

CONTRIBUTORS

Erwin Abbink, Department of Logistics, NS Reizigers, NL-3500-HA, Utrecht, the Netherlands

Michael H. Bowling, Computer Science Department, Carnegie Mellon University, Pittsburgh, PA 15213–3891

C.W. Duin, Faculty of Economics and Econometrics, Universiteit van Amsterdam, P.O. Box 19268, 100066, Amsterdam, the Netherlands

Pieter-Jan Fioole, Department of Logistics, NS Reizigers, NL-3500-HA Utrecht, the Netherlands

Henk W.M. Gazendam, Faculty of Public Administration, Twente University, NL-7500-AE, Enschede, the Netherlands; and Faculty of Management and Organization, University of Groningen, NL-9700-AV Groningen, the Netherlands

R. Hajema, Faculty of Economics and Econometrics, Universiteit van Amsterdam, P.O. Box 19268, 100066, Amsterdam, the Netherlands

Jean-Michel Hoc, Centre National de la Recherche Scientifique et Université de Nantes, F-44321 Nantes, France

Bernhard Hommel, Cognitive Psychology Unit, Department of Psychology, Leiden University, 2300-RB Leiden, the Netherlands

Rune M. Jensen, Computer Science Department, Carnegie Mellon University, Pittsburgh, PA 15213–3891

René Jorna, Faculty of Management and Organization, University of Groningen, NL-9700-AV Groningen, the Netherlands

Derk Jan Kiewiet, Faculty of Management and Organization, University of Groningen, NL-9700-AV Groningen, the Netherlands

Leo G. Kroon, Rotterdam School of Management (RSM), Erasmus University Rotterdam, NL-3000-DR Rotterdam, the Netherlands; and Department of Logistics, NS Reizigers, NL-3500-HA Utrecht, the Netherlands

Ramon M. Lentink, Rotterdam School of Management (RSM), Erasmus University Rotterdam, NL-3000-DR Rotterdam, the Netherlands

Kenneth N. McKay, Department of Management Sciences, University of Waterloo, Waterloo, Ontario, Canada N2L 3G1

Alexander Meystel, Electrical and Computer Engineering Department, Drexel University, Philadelphia, PA 19104

J. Riezebos, Faculty of Management and Organization, University of Groningen, NL-9700-AV

Jürgen Sauer, Department of Computer Science, University of Oldenburg, D-26121 Oldenburg, Germany

N.M. van Dijk, Faculty of Economics and Econometrics, Universiteit van Amsterdam, P.O. Box 19268, 100066, Amsterdam, the Netherlands

Wout van Wezel, Faculty of Management and Organization, University of Groningen, NL-9700-AV Groningen, the Netherlands

Cor van't Woudt, Department of Logistics, NS Reizigers, NL-3500-HA Utrecht, the Netherlands

Manuela M. Veloso, Computer Science Department, Carnegie Mellon University, Pittsburgh, PA 15213–3891

Vincent C.S. Wiers, Institute for Business Engineering and Technology Application (BETA), Eindhoven University of Technology, Eindhoven 5600-MB, the Netherlands

Rob A. Zuidwijk, Rotterdam School of Management (RSM), Erasmus University Rotterdam, NL-3000-DR Rotterdam, the Netherlands

PREFACE

To be able to plan, one needs intelligence. To act intelligently, however, one needs to plan. The questions that this paradox raises express the goal of this book. The abilities to anticipate and plan are essential features of intelligent system, whether they are human or machine. We might even go further and contemplate that a better planning results in higher achievements. As a consequence, understanding and improving planning is important. So, how do intelligent systems make plans? What are their motivations? How are the plans executed? What is the relation between plan creation and plan execution? Are planning and intelligence as connected as the paradox suggests? Many questions that are studied by a manifold of research disciplines for various kinds of intelligent systems employ a wealth of planning goals, methods, and techniques. Our goal is to investigate whether planning approaches in the different fields share more than merely the word *planning*. If so, knowing of the various planning paradigms might lead to a better understanding of planning in general and to cross-fertilization of ideas, methods, and techniques between the different planning schools in, for example, cognitive psychology, organizational science, operations research, computer science, and robotics.

In September 1999, we (Wout, René, and Alexander) organized a session on planning at the International Congress of the IASS-AIS (International Association for Semiotic Studies) in Dresden. At that meeting, we discussed the lack of a general planning theory, and we decided that a book discussing and comparing the various (scientific) fields that deal with planning would be a good start. The ideas about a geography, a landscape, of planning were further explored at a session at the INFORMS (Operations Research) meeting in Philadelphia in November 1999. There, we invited a number of people with the prospect to further discuss and explore the ideas about the book.

The conferences at which we discussed the book and the people involved in writing the chapters are emblematic for the broad scope of planning approaches that exist. Our own backgrounds resemble this as well. The throughput time of six years might very well be ascribed to the different disciplines in which our individual backgrounds can be found. Discussions between a control theorist and expert in cybernetics, a cognitive scientist, and a production management and organizational scholar that should lead to a single comprehensive book on planning are prone to lead to intense discussions about the approaches in particular. We are convinced that broadening the scope as we did is necessary as a first step in finding a unified theory of planning.

We are indebted to several people that helped us in various ways in the creation of the book. The Netherlands Railways—in particular, Tjeu Smeets and Leo Kroon—provided ample opportunities for valuable empirical research in a stimulating and challenging environment. Jan Riezebos and Herman Balsters reviewed some of the mathematical chapters. Sonja Abels provided operational support and René Jorna thanks NIAS (Netherlands Institute for Advanced Studies; KNAW), where he stayed the academic year of 2004/2005, for providing support and facilities.

Groningen July 8, 2005   WOUT VAN WEZEL
                                                          RENÉ JORNA
                                                  ALEXANDER MEYSTEL

1

INTRODUCTION

WOUT VAN WEZEL AND RENÉ JORNA

Faculty of Management and Organization, University of Groningen,
NL-9700-AV Groningen, the Netherlands

1.1. INTRODUCTION

No living thing seems to be conscious of the future, and none seems concerned to design for that future, except Man. But every man looks ahead and attempts to organize for tomorrow, the future of the next day or of the next generation. Whatever he has to do or proposes to do, he plans; he is a planner. He seems to be distinguished from all other forms of life by this faculty, this necessity. Man plans to rebuild employment, or to increase his company's volume of business, or to win an election, or to write a letter, or to build a bridge, or to buy a cigar, or to get his hair cut, or to put alcohol in the radiator of his car against the prospect of sub-zero weather, or to give the baby paregoric against the prospect of a sleepless night, or to build a city—he plans all the time. By his very nature every man plans constantly.

> —Jacob L. Crane, Planning organization and the planners, paper presented at the Annual Meeting of the American City Planning Institute, Washington D.C., January 19, 1936.

In his paper, Crane provides us with an analysis of the differences between individual personal planning and city planning by governmental agencies. He concludes there are similarities, but there are sharp differences as well. For example, a human planning for himself both determines the course of action, and he acts himself. In contrast, a city planner in a government will only make the plan, not execute it. Furthermore, coordination and integration of plans is more important for city planning than for personal planning. In the decades following Crane's observations,

Planning in Intelligent Systems: Aspects, Motivations, and Methods, Edited by Wout van Wezel, René Jorna, and Alexander Meystel
Copyright © 2006 John Wiley & Sons, Inc.

much research has been done on planning. We now know of the physical and cognitive functions that humans use to make plans for themselves. Furthermore, planning is a formalized function in almost all organizations, and much literature has been written about how plans in organizations can or should be made.

An important event for planning that could probably not be foreseen in the beginning of the twentieth century, when Crane wrote about planning, is the widespread use of computers. Computer programs can make plans as well as individuals and organizations. Examples are algorithms in advanced planning systems that create schedules for all kinds of organizational processes (e.g., production schedules, staff schedules, routing schedules), and planning algorithms that are used by robots to play soccer or to collect stones on Mars.

Research in planning has mainly been categorized by taking both the creator of the plan and who it is created for as a starting point. For example, how a human makes a shopping list is investigated in academia other than that for a human who makes a production schedule or an unmanned air vehicle that determines its own route. In this book we explore various planning approaches and we try to determine whether planning can be a self-sufficient area of research where scholars from different disciplines can exchange ideas and share research results. Sharing research methodologies, planning methods, and solution techniques will improve our understanding of planning and scheduling in general, and it can result in improvements in each of the individual planning research schools.

In this introductory chapter, we will present our conviction that different planning fields share many characteristics. Each of the subsequent chapters will describe and discuss a specific kind of planning. In the concluding chapter, we will formulate the similarities and, of course, the differences and we will show the prospects of a common research agenda.

In this chapter we start in Sections 1.2, 1.3, and 1.4 with discussions about what planning is and how it can be modeled. Sections 1.5 and 1.6 describe a number of characteristics of planning. These characteristics can be used as a first starting point to compare planning approaches. Section 1.7 outlines the structure of the book.

1.2. DEFINITION OF PLANNING

Where will we go and how do we get there? This question is an inherent part of the functioning of humans and organizations. The ability to anticipate and plan is usually seen as a required and perhaps even essential feature of intelligent systems. It is the fundament of goal-directed behavior; systems that pursue goals need to take the future into account. In this book, we will compare different planning research fields. To be able to compare and analyze differences and similarities, we need a common, abstract conceptualization of planning. As a starting point, we presume that all intelligent systems use anticipation to plan (van Wezel and Jorna, 2001). An anticipatory system is "a system containing a predictive model of itself and/ or its environment, which allows it to change a state at an instant in accordance with the model's predictions pertaining to a later instant" (Rosen, 1985). Our definition of planning will be built around this definition of anticipatory systems, by distinguishing three main elements of planning.

First, it is important to acknowledge that some entity must make the plan. Note that all kinds of entities—for example, humans, robots, computer programs, animals, organizations, and so on—can make plans. Important features of the planning entity are (a) the model of the future that the planning entity has and (b) the process characteristics of making the plan:

a. The planning entity needs some kind of model of the future, since the future is essentially nonexistent. This model should include states, possible actions of the executing entities and the effect of actions on the state they reside in, constraints, and goals. Planning and anticipation presume that such a predictive model is available; otherwise, the chance that a plan can be executed as intended becomes a shot in the dark.

b. Planning is a process. It consists of all kinds of activities that ultimately result in the plan. Information must be collected, there might be communication about constraints, difficult puzzles must be solved, and so on. The kinds of processes are determined by the kind of entity that makes the plan, but there are many generic characteristics as well.

Second, someone or something must execute the plan; that is, the intended future must somehow be attained. Again, this can be done by all kinds of entities, and the planning entities need not necessarily be involved in plan execution themselves.

The *third* element of planning is the plan itself. The plan is the main communication mechanism between the planning entity and planned entity. The plan signifies the belief that the planning entity has in the model of the future: The implicit or explicit actions in the plan will lead to the desired or intended future state. It can never be a full specification of the future itself because it can never be specified more precisely than the model of the future allows. It can, of course, be specified with less detail than the model of the future. Two kinds of plans are possible. First, the plan can specify the intended future state. The executing entity itself must determine how to get there. Second, the plan can specify the actions that the executing entity must perform. Although the desired future state is then not specified in the plan as such, it will, ceteris paribus, be reached by performing all specified actions.

The following five factors will be recurring themes throughout this book: planning entity, model of the future, planning process, executing entity, and plan. We will see that this definition provides a sound basis with which planning approaches can be described and compared. The following sections will describe some more generic aspects of these elements.

1.3. PLANNING COMPLEXITY AND PLANNING HIERARCHIES

A widely accepted characteristic of planning is that it is complex. This book would not be necessary if planning were trivial and easy to understand. But then, what is so complex about planning? Humans plan their errands continuously, production planners schedule whole factories, automatic vehicles find their destination, and even microprocessors plan the execution of computer code to increase speed. Apparently, something strange is going on. On the one hand, plans are made all the time. On the other hand, we find it difficult to understand the way that humans make plans and to design systems or computer programs that plan. The partial answer to this, of course, is that planning problems do not exist by themselves, but are perceived by the planning entity. This entity, which we presume intelligent, will not formulate unsolvable problems for itself, or, as Simon (1981, p. 36) states: "What a person cannot do he will not do, no matter how much he wants to do it." In addition, the model of the future is full of uncertainties, and even for a problem that the planning entity itself has formulated, good-enough alternatives will be accepted, "not because he prefers less to more but because he has no choice" (op. cit.). This is inevitably the case for planning, because time is not only a part of the plan, it is also something that is used up during plan creation. The moment of plan execution is getting nearer and nearer while the planning entity is seeking the solution. At some point in time, whether the planning entity is happy with it or not, the plan must be executed. Somehow, intelligent systems know how to make planning simple enough to be manageable but complex enough to attain advantageous goals.

Simon (1981) notes that complex systems are usually somehow ordered hierarchically in order to manage complexity. He uses the term hierarchy in the sense that a system is "composed of interrelated subsystems, each of the latter being in turn hierarchic in structure until we reach some lowest level of elementary subsystems" (op. cit., p. 196). Note that this does not necessarily mean hierarchic in the sense of an authority relation; it means an ordering of parts in wholes, and these wholes are, in turn, parts of other wholes. We will argue that planning is no exception; setting aside trivial planning problems, planning always takes place hierarchically. Even more, we will argue that much of the differences between planning approaches can be contributed to the way in which these approaches partition the planning problem in independently solvable subproblems. Therefore, a sound understanding of the hierarchical nature of planning is a prerequisite for understanding the differences and similarities between planning approaches.

There are two main reasons to take planning decisions in a hierarchy (Starr, 1979). First, some decisions *must* be made hierarchically due to a lack of information. This means that a decision is needed before all the required input for that decision is available. The input must then somehow be predicted. An example is that a company must order raw materials before their own customers place their orders. They do this on the basis of an expectation about the total amount of orders, which is a different hierarchical level than the individual order. Second, decisions *can* be taken hierarchically because it reduces the amount of information that a planning entity must process. Planning problems are often transcomputational, which means that the amount of plan alternatives is so large that even a computer that is the size of the earth cannot assess all possibilities in millions of years (Klir, 1991). As an example, consider the simple task of determining the sequence of 20 tasks. If the planning entity (for example, a computer program) can assess 1 billion sequences (plans) per second, it will take 77 years to check all possible sequences and will take 1620 years with 21 operations. For that reason, most planning problems cannot be solved by assessing all possible plans and choosing the best. In order to limit the work, a plan can be created in a hierarchical way.

A plan consists of statements about the future. As we saw, a plan can either specify a future state description or actions that lead to that state. Notwithstanding the manifestation of the plan, the creation of it always involves decision-making. If we view the process of plan creation as a system, every decision that somehow determines a part of this future can be regarded as a subsystem. An example of such a hierarchy of planning is the creation of a plan that assigns orders to machines. If making the total plan is seen as a system, then the assignment of an order to a machine for Tuesday between 12 AM and 3 PM can be seen as a subsystem (Meystel and Albus, 2002). This assignment itself can also be seen as a system, which is composed of subsystems or subdecisions. With the use of this paradigm, we can use system theories for analyses of planning decisions by intelligent systems. The view of planning as a hierarchy of decisions provides a common ground for all planning decisions that are made regardless of the level of detail.

A consequence of the view that a hierarchy exists in decision making is that a hierarchy also exists in the things that are planned. More specifically, the model that the planning entity has of the planned entity and its environment must allow hierarchical decision making. This implies that the model of the future must also allow descriptions at hierarchical levels. In the next section, we will elaborate on this by discussing generic models of decision behavior and the planning domain.

1.4. BASIC MODELS OF PLANNING

There are two kinds of basic models for all planning situations. The first is a model of the decision behavior of the planning entity, and the second is a model of the results of the decision behavior (the plan). We will discuss both in greater detail.

1.4.1. Making the Plan: Decisions of the Planning Entity

In Section 1.2 we have discussed that planning involves a planning entity. In Section 1.3, we specified that such a planning entity makes decisions, and that these decisions are ordered hierarchically. In this section, we propose a generic decision model that is based on these principles. A consequence of the generic nature of this model is that it does not describe in detail how planning decisions are related to other kinds of decisions. In Chapter 4, Jorna goes into this issue by analyzing and discussing the differences between planning, decision making, and problem solving.

As stated in the previous section, we view the planning process as a hierarchy of decision-making activities. At each hierarchical level, the task is to find a solution within the constraints that are specified by the higher level. A constraint is a rule that restricts the possible plan alternatives. Constraints can be determined beforehand as inherent parts of the model of the future, but they can also be determined during the process of plan creation. Often, the higher level also specifies the goals that should be attained as good as possible. There are two kinds of constraints and goals:

1. *Content Constraints and Goals.* These constraints and goals relate to the solution itself. They can specify aggregates (e.g., the average number of hours that employees can work, the minimum utilization rate of the machines, the amount of food I must buy for next week at the grocery, etc.) or specific rules (e.g., John and Jack may not be in the same shift, I must buy exactly one loaf of bread, etc.).

2. *Process Constraints and Goals.* These restrain the way in which the planning entity makes the plan. This can be about the maximum throughput time for making the plan, about the maximum amount of information processing capacity that may be used (for example, the number of planners that is involved), about the tools that can be used, whether a factory planner may negotiate directly with customers about due dates or not, and so on.

The solution at a given hierarchical level specifies the constraints and goals for the lower level(s). In this way, using multiple hierarchical levels, the plan can be made stepwise. An important feature of a hierarchical decision-making system is that decision levels should be able to handle feedback. If a constraint is too severe and the lower level cannot find a solution, constraints must be relaxed.

The decisions at the lowest level are not specified in greater detail by the planning entity. The solution at the lowest level specifies when, what, and how the planned actions must be executed. However, most often the plan must be specified further during the execution of the plan. For example, a plan can specify that the production of a batch in a factory starts at 4 PM. Usually, this does not mean that it will start at exactly 4 PM. In factory settings, it usually will start when the batch that was scheduled as its immediate predecessor (e.g., the one starting at 3 PM) is finished.

Figure 1.1 depicts the discussed elements. It shows three decisions with their relations, and reveals the following characteristics:

- A hierarchical planning decision is defined as a decision that constrains another decision (arrow 1). Therefore, the hierarchical relation between two decisions is based on the fact that a decision's solution space is restricted by the other decision.
- It might be difficult or impossible to make a decision within the imposed restrictions. Then, somehow this must be fed back to the decision that imposed the constraint (arrow 2).
- Decisions that share constraints must somehow be coordinated because their combined decisions determine whether the constraint is violated or not (arrows 3 and 4).

Figure 1.2 shows an example of a decision structure that is based on this model.

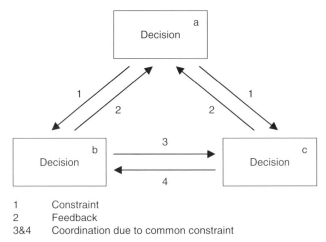

1   Constraint
2   Feedback
3&4   Coordination due to common constraint

Figure 1.1. Basic hierarchic decision model.

Figure 1.3 shows a decision structure at the individual level for the shunting problem in the Netherlands Railways. An individual planner has to go through a (structured) hierarchy of decisions to produce a plan for trains at the shunting yard.

A collection of decisions with their hierarchical relations constitutes the way that
a planning problem is tackled. The model in Figure 1.1 shows the basic elements
that can be used to model the structure of planning levels. This view on planning
implies that relations between planning decisions are always structurally the same
regardless of the decision level and regardless of the entities that make and execute
the plan. In Section 1.5, we will describe in greater detail more general characteristics of planning decisions. First, however, we will discuss what it is that planning
decisions decide about.

1.4.2. Modeling the Plan: States of the Planning Entity

As stated in the previous subsection, planning decisions differ from other kinds of
decisions. We can now describe (at least partly) what planning decisions are by
describing the decision domain. *First*, planning is a synthetic rather than an analytic
(diagnosis) or modification (repair) task (Clancy, 1985; Schreiber, Wielinga, and
Breuker, 1993). *Second*, planning involves decisions about the future and not the
execution of these decisions. *Third*, an important feature of planning is that it is
about choosing one alternative out of a huge number of alternatives that are structurally similar. Determining why a motor does not work is not planning (it is a diagnosis task), building a house is not planning (it is also a synthetic task: however, it
concerns not only a decision, but also the realization of the plan), but routing trains,
making a production schedule, making a staff schedule, and determining the trajectory of an automatic vehicle are planning tasks (these are synthetic tasks and concern
choosing one out of a number of similar alternatives of future states).

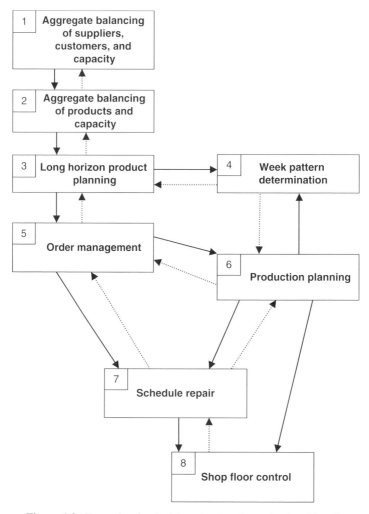

Figure 1.2. Example of a decision structure (organizational level).

With this demarcation, we can further define planning, by explaining what is meant by "structurally similar alternatives." The vague connotation of the word "similar" already indicates that it is not inherently clear whether a problem is a planning problem or not, but that in itself is not important. We propose to model a planning problem as follows. *A planning problem consists of groups of entities, whereby the entities from different groups must be assigned to each other. The assignments are subject to constraints, and alternatives can be compared on their level of goal realization.* For example, production scheduling is a problem where orders must be assigned to machines, in a shift schedule people are assigned to shifts, and in task planning tasks are assigned to time slots and resources. Now we can

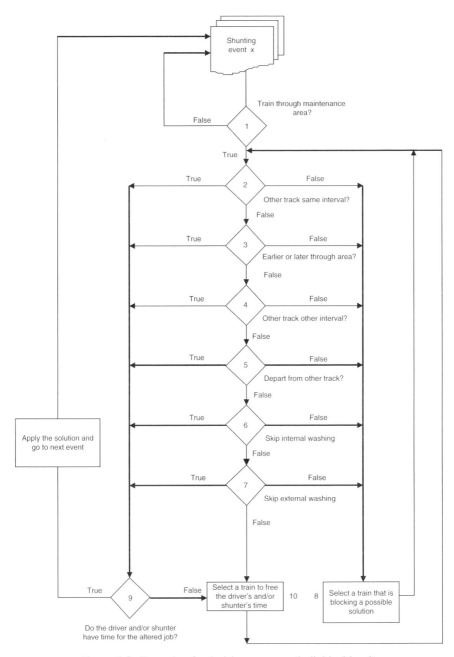

Figure 1.3. Example of a decision structure (individual level).

also specify what we mean by "similar"; it means that plan alternatives have the same structure (e.g., orders are assigned to machines), but a different content (e.g., in plan alternative A, "order 1" is assigned to "machine 1," and in plan alternative B, "order 1" is assigned to "machine 2"). This definition also precludes some areas that are commonly regarded as planning—for example, strategic planning and retirement planning. Although the boundaries are debatable, such planning problems do not exhibit the third feature of planning—that is, alternatives are structurally similar.

Not by coincidence, the view on planning as just described fits in nicely with the decision models, where basic decisions are setting constraints and assigning entities. The link to decision models, however, shows an additional requirement. If decisions at hierarchical levels are distinctive, then there should also be models of domains at multiple hierarchical levels. For example, in Figure 1.2, each decision deals with either (a) other kinds of planned entities or (b) planned entities at different levels of abstraction or resolution. Furthermore, the planning entity can be an aggregate of planning entities itself. Most apparently, this is the case in organizational planning, where a planning department can be said to make a plan, but where individual human planners make the subplans, as is the case in Figure 1.2.

Two types of subplans can be distinguished in a planning hierarchy: aggregation and decomposition. In *aggregation*, the dimensions that exist in the planning problem stay the same, but individual entities of a dimension are grouped. For example, a plan that contains the assignment of individual orders to production lines for a certain week can be aggregated to a plan that contains the assignment of orders per product type to production lines in that week. Aggregation can be used to establish boundaries or constraints for individual assignments of entities that fall within an aggregated group. For example, it is first decided how much caramel custard will be made next week. Then individual orders that fall in this product family can be assigned to a specific production time. In this way, several stages of aggregation can be sequentially followed whereby each stage creates boundaries for the next stage.

In the second type of subplan, *decomposition*, a subset of the entities that must be planned is considered as a separate planning problem. Decomposition can deal with all entities of a subset of the dimensions, all dimensions with a subset of the entities, or a combination of subsets of dimensions and entities. For example, if we attune orders, machines, and operators, we could first assign orders to machines and then operators to the chosen order/machine combinations. Or, we can first assign all customer orders, after which we assign all stock orders.

The decision models and the state models of planning together can be used to depict the decision behavior of planning entities. In the next subsection, we will recapitulate the elements that form our basic model of planning.

1.4.3. Conclusion

In Sections 1.2 and 1.3, we have described what planning is:

- Planning means that a *planning entity* determines a future course of actions for an *executing entity*. These actions should lead to a desired future state. The belief that the actions lead to the state is based on the *model of the future* of the planning entity. The future course of actions or the desired future state is expressed by the *plan*.

- Planning is a complex activity and often involves reasoning with incomplete information. Plans are usually made hierarchically.

Then, in this Section (1.4), we have further explored generic features of planning, by proposing how decisions of the planning entity can be modeled:

- A plan contains the assignments of entities of different categories.
- The assignments are subject to constraints.
- Alternatives can be compared on their level of goal realization.
- During the process of plan creation, subplans can be created at hierarchical levels other than the final plan.
- Constraints and goals are distinct at each hierarchical level.
- Decisions determine constraints for lower-level decisions.
- Grouping takes place by aggregation.
- Partitioning takes place by disaggregation or by decomposition.

Figure 1.4 summarizes the elements of planning.

In this book a number of planning approaches are discussed by various authors (Table 1.1). Although the approaches at first sight do not always seem to have much in common, our generic planning model provides the means to compare the approaches and analyze where they differ. Thus, we can show that different approaches share more than they differ.

The aim of this book is to show that planning approaches can be categorized along other dimensions than their research field. In the next section, we will describe a number of generic characteristics that can be derived from this model. The approaches and their relation to these generic characteristics will be discussed in more detail in the individual chapters of the book. The diversity in the planning approaches will become clear by stating questions that are based on the model in Figure 1.4, for example:

1. What is the planning entity? Is it a natural entity (i.e., human) or an artificial entity? How does it make decisions? How is the planning decomposed? What are the partitioning criteria? In what order are the decisions made?
2. What is the executing entity? Is it an organization or an individual? Is it perhaps the planning entity itself? Do multiple executing entities have to coordinate or are they independent?
3. What kind of model of the future does the planning entity have? How flexible is the model with respect to adjustment?

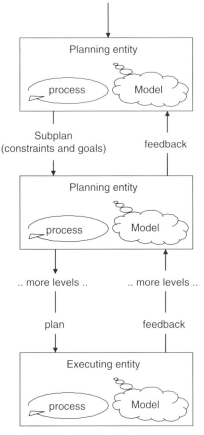

Figure 1.4. Overview of planning.

The following sections describe a number of generic characteristics of planning entities that can be used to formulate answers to these kinds of questions.

1.5. GENERIC PLANNING CHARACTERISTICS

In this section, we describe a number of information processing characteristics of the planning entity and its relation to the environment. The characteristics that will be discussed are: (a) closed versus open world assumptions; (b) the information processing mechanism and its architectural components, such as memory or attention; (c) (internal) representations; (d) communication, meaning, and interpretation; (e) characteristics of coordination; and (f) aspects of execution of the plan.

"Closed World" Versus "Open World". As we already indicated, the planning task itself can be called a synthetic or configuration task. It is well known that these kinds

TABLE 1.1. Planning Approaches Discussed in This Book

Authors	Approach	Example
Hommel (Chapter 2)	Neuropsychological aspects of human planning	Catching a ball
Hoc (Chapter 3)	Cognitive psychological aspects of human planning	Flying a fighter aircraft
Jorna (Chapter 4)	Cognitive psychological aspects of humans planning for organizations	Making a staff schedule
Gazendam (Chapter 5)	Planning in organizational multi-actor systems	Two people that give a different meaning to a plan
McKay and Wiers (Chapter 6)	Planning processes in manufacturing organizations	The relations between planning and functional departments like purchasing, sales, and production
van Wezel (Chapter 7)	Planning support in organizations	The trade-off between goal maximization and usability of an algorithm
Kroon and Zuidwijk (Chapter 8)	Mathematical algorithms for planning support in organizations	An algorithm to generate a time table for a railway operator
Sauer (Chapter 9)	Artificial Intelligence algorithms for planning support in organizations	Algorithms that make schedules that coordinate activities in multiple sites of a factory
Bowling, Jensen, and Veloso (Chapter 10)	Artificial Intelligence algorithms for planning by robots	Two robots that play soccer and create a coordinated plan
Meystel (Chapter 11)	Planning as part of a multiresolutional control hierarchy	The role of planning in the reasoning process of an intelligent actor

of tasks are very difficult to complete, by humans alone as well as with the support of software. In the previous section, we described a way to model plans and planning decisions. Each assignment problem consists of choosing from alternatives that are structurally the same. In classical terms this means searching through a problem space to find an acceptable solution, which is usually called problem solving. From a decision perspective, realizing a suitable plan or solving a planning problem requires three nearly decomposable phases. In state space descriptions the first phase is the design of a complex initial state, of goal states, and of admissible operations to change states. Note that we are talking here about the states in the search process of the planning entity and not about the states that the planned domain (or the planned entity) can be in. The second phase is, given the admissible operations, to search for an optimal solution. The search process may be done by exhaustive computation or by adequate heuristic evaluation functions in combination with sophisticated computations. In many cases, search does not give an optimal solution. The most one may get is a satisfying solution, and even that is often not possible. Then, the third phase starts in which one goes back to the initial state and the admissible operations. Another route is chosen in the hope that a solution is found. In other words, the phases of (1) initial state, (2) search, no solution, and (3a) start again with initial state follow the so-called "closed world" assumption. This is the necessary sequence if algorithms are applied. However, there is another way of dealing with the third phase which is more usual, especially if humans have to make a planning. If, given the constraints and goal functions, the second phase does not give an optimal or satisfactory outcome, the planner is already so much involved in the planning process that because he has a glimpse of the solution given the constraints, he takes his "idea" of a solution for compelling. He therefore changes the initial state(s) and admissible operations—that is, the constraints—in such a way that they fit the preconceived solution. This order of phases can be named the "open world" approach. It consists of (1) initial state, (2) search, including not finding a real or established fixed solution, and (3b) adjustment of initial state according to the "fixed" solution reality. In other words, the model of the future is not fixed because rules are adjusted. This sequence of activities is what human planners—whether in the industry, in transportation planning, or in staff scheduling—frequently and with great success do. However, formalizing such knowledge for use in a computer program or robot is very tricky. In AI this kind of practice is also known as the reformulation problem. It remains an open issue how and from which perspective the planning entity adjusts his initial state and/or operations.

Information Processing Mechanism. During problem solving, the planning entity has to process information. An information processing mechanism operationalizes the way information is selected, combined, created, and deleted. The mechanism itself needs a physical or physiological carrier. Examples are the brain as our neurological tissue, the layered connection system of a chip in a computer, a human individual in an organization, or a group of interconnected individuals in an organization. This is of course relevant when we realize that the contents of the model of the future can be restricted by the physical, physiological, or functional properties of the carrier.

The most relevant distinction is the one in internal and external mechanism. By internal we mean that there is no direct access to the system from outside. Internally controlled, but not directly visible, processes—not cognitively penetrable as Phylyshyn (1984) called it—take place in the system. The cognitive system and the chip are internal, but they differ in the sense that the latter is designed, which means that its operations are verifiable. External are information processing mechanisms such as groups of individuals or organizations. With respect to planning, this distinction is of course relevant if one realizes that if the plan needs to be communicated, a translation is necessary between the physical carrier and the receiver, which must be taken into account during planning. This is the case when a planning entity makes a plan that is executed by (many) others.

Architectural Components. An architecture is a set of components of which the arrangement is governed by principles of form or function (Curry and Tate, 1991). A cognitive architecture consists of memory components, of attention processors, of sensory and motor components, and of various kinds of central processors. The division is by function, and the components are all implemented in neurological structures in the brain. Two other material structures for architectural layout are the chip and the constellation of a group of individuals. The same kind of components can be discerned for the computer (e.g., a robot), consisting of memory, sensory and motor components, and central processors. For a group of individuals the architecture is different because although the constituting elements are similar as for the individuals, the roles and tasks are different. Again, the discussion about the character of the architecture boils down to a discussion about internally or externally defined. Internal are chips and the cognitive architecture, whereas groups of people and organizations can be dealt with externally.

(Internal) Representations. In cognitive science the conceptual framework to deal with representations can be found in the approaches of classical symbol systems, connectionism, and situated action (Posner, 1989; Newell, 1990; Dölling, 1998; Smolensky, 1988; Jorna, 1990). The basic idea in classical symbol systems theory is that humans as information processing systems have and use knowledge consisting of representations and that thinking, reasoning, and problem solving consist of manipulations of these representations at a functional level of description. A system that internally symbolizes the environment is said to have representations. Representations consist of sets of symbol structures on which operations are defined. Examples of representations are words, pictures, semantic nets, propositions, or temporal strings. A representational system learns by means of chunking mechanisms and symbol transformations (Newell, 1990). A system is said to be autonomous or self-organized if it can have a representation of its own position in the environment. This means that the system has self-representation. Connectionism and situated action are attacks on missing elements within the classical symbol system approach. Connectionism criticizes the neglect of the neurological substrate within the symbols approach and defends the relevance of subsymbolic processing or parallel distributed processing. Situated action criticizes the neglect of the environment within the symbol approach and emphasizes the role of actions, situatedness, and "being in the world."

Mostly, plan execution takes place in the environment of an entity. An entity that makes a plan for itself can of course misinterpret its position in the environment—for example, because it cannot represent its environment (e.g., the primitives of the model of the future have not enough expressive power) or because it cannot manipulate its representation of the environment adequately. Furthermore, an entity that makes a plan for others can additionally have this problem with respect to the entities that must execute the plan. Representations are also immediately relevant for anticipation. A description of a future state in whatever symbol system or sign system is the core of any discussion about anticipation.

Communication, Meaning, and Interpretation. Communication means the exchange of information between different components. Depending on whether we are talking about internal or external information processing entities, communication means possibilities for and restrictions on the kinds of symbols or signs (the codes) that are used for information exchange. If we relate this to the aforementioned discussion about representations, the various kinds of signs have different consequences. Clearly, sign notations are more powerful (allow less ambiguity), but also more restricted than sign systems, which in turn are more powerful than just sign sets (Goodman, 1968; Jorna, 1990; Jorna and van Heusden, 1998). Unambiguous communication requires sign notations (reducing ambiguity as much as possible), but we know that all communication between humans is not in terms of notations. If computers require sign notations and humans work with sign systems, then if the two have to communicate, they have to adjust to each other. Until recently, most adjustments consist of humans using notations. Now, interfaces are designed that allow computers to work with less powerful (allowing more ambiguity) but more flexible sign systems. This means that computers can now better deal with ambiguity. For mental activities no explicitness (channels, codes, etc.) is necessary; for planning as an external activity, managing others in organizations, it is essential.

Coordination. Coordination concerns attuning, assigning, or aligning various entities that are not self-evident unities. Information processing in a cognitive system is a kind of coordination mechanism (with no direct access). It is internal or mental. The coordinating processor is cognition itself. No explicit code is necessary. If the code is made explicit and obeys the requirements of a notation, we can design an artificial intelligent actor that in its ultimate simplicity could be a chip. In case of a set of entities that are not by themselves a coherent unity—for example, individuals in an organization—various coordination mechanisms can be found, such as a hierarchy, a meta-plan, mutual adjustment, a market structure, and many others (Thompson, 1967; Gazendam, 1993). The important difference with single human actors is that these coordination mechanisms are external and of course with direct access.

Planning, Execution, and Control. Making a plan, executing it, and monitoring the outcomes in reality are valued differently in planning your own actions compared to planning actions of others (i.e., organizational processes). Planning in organizations usually is decoupled from the execution of the plan. There are two main reasons why the planner is someone other than the one who executes the plan. First, planning is a difficult job that requires expertise and experience. This is the organizational concept of task division. Second, a planner must be able to weigh the interests of many parties. Therefore, he must have knowledge about things that go beyond the limits of the individual tasks that are planned. The consequence of this decoupling is almost always inflexibility with respect to adaptation. For simple tasks such as doing errands, the possible division in terms of subtasks may be interesting, but can in reality be intertwined with flexible adaptation after unforeseen events. If the controlling entity is itself a unity, discussions about transfer, communication, sign systems to do the communication, and representations are almost trivial. This does not make the planning task itself simpler; it only prevents the explicitly formulated occurrence of ambiguity, interpretation, and meaning variance.

Our starting point in this book is that planning is always in essence about the same thing: anticipating on the future and determining courses of action. The above-discussed characteristics allow us to determine the similarities and dissimilarities of the various planning approaches and perspectives. This will become more evident in the next section and later in the consecutive chapters.

1.6. CONSOLIDATION: FROM DIFFERENT PLANNING WORLDS TO DIFFERENT PLANNING WORDS

In this chapter, we proposed a generic model of planning. Someone or something creates a plan, and someone or something executes that plan. Both are acting in an environment, and the planning entity, planned entity, and environment have a number of characteristics with which a planning situation can be described. The characteristics can be used for all planning fields and thereby they can be used to compare planning approaches. The following list summarizes the characteristics:

Planning Environment. Different planning approaches have different environments. Even within approaches different environments can be distinguished. Some characteristics are:

1. The predictability of the environment. (Is the plan executed in a closed world in which the presumptions will not change, or is it executed in an open world?)
2. Kinds of events that trigger planning:
   a. Time-based: For example, a plan needs to be made each week.
   b. Event-based: A plan must be made after an event, for example a rush order in a factory.
   c. Disturbance-based: A plan must be adjusted because a disturbance occurs that renders the plan invalid—for example, a shop that is closed when I do my shopping.
3. Goals and constraints. The goals and constraints are often determined by the planning environment. They can be about the plan itself—for example, the time at which the actions that are specified in the plan must be finished or the amount of resources that are used. They can also be about the process of making the plan—for example, when the plan must be available or how much people may be involved in making the plan. Goals and constraints

can be about time, materials, remaining life span of the system, energy, the degree of fault-tolerance, money, capacity usage, and so on. Making the constraints and goals explicit is often the hard part in planning.

Planned Entities. The actions in the plan must be performed by someone or something. Several aspects are important:

1. Is the planned entity the same as the planning entity?
2. Does the plan deal with actions of individuals or actions that are performed by groups of individuals?
3. Is the planned entity a natural entity (e.g., human) or an artificial entity (e.g., a machine, a robot, or a computer program)?
4. Does the planned entity possess intelligence itself? That is, can it interpret the plan and change it if necessary?
5. What kind of constraints do the planned entities impose on the plan?
6. Does the planned entity use scarce resources that also have to be planned?

Planning Entities. Someone or something must make the plan—that is, search for alternative plans and choose one. Important aspects of the planning entity are as follows:

1. Does the planning entity execute the plan itself or is the plan executed by others?
2. Is it a natural entity (human) or is it an artificial entity (computer program)?
3. What kind of planning methods does it use?
4. What is the planning strategy? That is, how does it choose an appropriate planning method?
5. What kind of information processing mechanism does it have?
6. What are the architectural components?
7. What kinds of representations does it use?
8. How does it communicate?
9. How does it coordinate with other planning entities and with planned entities?

Plan. The plan itself is the specification of future actions.

1. Horizon: What time span does the plan cover?
2. Frequency: How often is the plan created or adapted?
3. Level of detail: Does the plan need more detail in order to be executed? Does the executing entity have to fill in the details, or is the plan used as a template for another planner?
4. Structure: What is actually planned—for example, human actions, machines, time, locations, vehicles, movements, and so on.

A plan that contains explicit temporal assignments on an interval or ratio level of measurement is usually called a schedule.

5. (Re)presentation: How is the plan represented or depicted? Does it specify the end state, or does it provide a process description that leads to the end state?

Planning Methods. The planning method depicts the decision process of the planning entity. A planning entity can have multiple planning methods to choose from. Some generic issues with regard to planning methods are as follows:

1. How does the planning entity deal with combinatorics, for example?
   a. Plan partitioning: Divide the plan in multiple subplans and treat the subplans independently.
   b. Multiresolutional planning: Make a plan with less detail (and less complexity), and use that plan as a template for a plan with more detail (at a higher level of resolution).
   c. Learning: Use (and possibly adapt) a previously found solution for a problem that was equal or similar.
   d. Opportunistic planning: Apply the first feasible solution that is found without looking whether there are better solutions (e.g., when planning under strict time constraints).
2. How much does the use of a planning method cost? Methods can, for example, be costly in terms of the information processing capacity that is needed, or in the tools that are used, or in the throughput time that is needed.
3. What is the starting point? For example:
   a. An empty plan
   b. An existing plan that must be supplemented
   c. An existing plan with errors that must be corrected
   d. A previous plan that can be used as a template
4. How are conflicts during the solution process solved (i.e., when the planning entity gets stuck)?
   a. Backtracking
   b. Repair
   c. Adjustment of constraints to make the plan valid
5. Does the method search for an optimal solution or state, or does it search for a satisfactory solution?

In the various parts of this book, we will refer to these generic characteristics in order to be able to show common aspects of different planning approaches. Thus, our presumption is that those different planning approaches are not as different as they appear. The structure of this book in which the planning approaches are discussed will be described in the next section.

1.7. STRUCTURE OF THIS BOOK

There are two parts in this book: Part A is theoretical and part B is practical. Part A contains 10 theoretical chapters. The chapters are not meant to be introductions to the respective research fields. Rather, each chapter explores one or more issues in its research field in detail. Thereby exposing different planning issues, languages, models, and methods. The respective theoretical contributions will be introduced briefly.

Hommel (Chapter 2) gives a psychophysiological analysis of planning. He shows that planning and plan execution are very much interrelated by discussing three planning steps that humans take during an action. Thus, his contribution deals with humans that plan their own future actions. However, the planning horizon is very short, less than one second.

Chapter 3, by Hoc, contains cognitive analyses of the planning behavior of human operators in dynamic environments where there is no clear-cut distinction between plan generation and plan execution and where the human operator does not fully control the environment and hence faces uncertainty—for example, in industrial process control and in anesthesiology. In contrast to Hommel, Hoc uses a functional level of description rather than a physiological one. As with Hommel, Hoc is a typical example of an analysis of humans that plan their own future behavior.

In Chapter 4, Jorna analyzes the behavior of 34 planners in three planning domains (staff scheduling, production planning, and transportation planning) in two countries (The Netherlands and Indonesia). Each planner had to solve a simple planning problem that was structurally the same for all planners but modified for each domain so the terminology was always comprehensible. The contribution of Jorna exemplifies traditional (cognitive) task analyses (e.g., see the contribution by Hoc), but since the objects of study are planners and their problem-solving processes, this study deals with humans that plan for or take part in organizational processes.

Gazendam (Chapter 5) takes a broader perspective on planning by looking at organizations as multi-actor systems. In his view, planning is a form of coordination that takes place by negotiation and coordination. Thus, his contribution can be classified as one in which humans plan organizational processes, be it that Gazendam does not study individuals but rather groups of individuals.

Following Gazendam's line of reasoning, one would expect theories and methodologies that can be used to evaluate or even design the organization of the planning function in organizations. In Chapter 6, however, McKay and Wiers note that most planning research looks at planning in isolation from other organizational functions, disregarding cognitive aspects of human planners and the organizational context in which human planners work. As a starting point to further enhance our knowledge on the role of planning in organizations, McKay and Wiers propose a framework with which the interconnections between planning and other organizational functions can be depicted.

Complementing the line of reasoning of McKay and Wiers, van Wezel looks at computer support of planning in organizations. Noting that the essential problems in computer support have not changed in the past 30 years, van Wezel proposes a structure for reuse in scheduling system development, and a framework for using algorithms in scheduling support systems.

Kroon and Zuidwijk show in Chapter 8 how techniques from Operations Research are applied to a multitude of planning problems in the Netherlands Railways (in Dutch: NS). Clearly, this is a typical example of artifacts that make plans for organizational processes. They also stipulate that plan generation is important but not enough for full planning support.

Sauer (Chapter 9) applies techniques from Artificial Intelligence to production scheduling. He, therefore, deals with artificial planning actors that plan organizational processes. In particular, he looks at problems that occur when schedules of different factories must be attuned.

Similar to Sauer, Bowling et al. (Chapter 10) also apply techniques from Artificial Intelligence to attune the actions of multiple actors. Unlike Sauer, however, the kinds of actors they investigate are robots or simulated robots that on the one hand plan for themselves but on the other hand have to cooperate with or work against others.

Meystel considers in Chapter 11 the planning process as part of the control process. He shows that a view on planning as a nested system of state-space search processes can yield efficient computational algorithms that are similar to those obtained by human planning strategies. Thus, his work can be classified as artificial agents that plan for themselves.

Table 1.2 provides an overview of the theoretical contributions.

TABLE 1.2. Theoretical Book Chapters

	Planning Entity = Executing Entity	Planning Entity $\neq$ Executing Entity
Planning Entity = Natural	• Neuropsychological analyses of planning (Hommel, Chapter 2) • Planning in cognitive psychology (Hoc, Chapter 3)	• Cognitive aspects of planning in organizations (Jorna, Chapter 4) • Planning in organizational science (Gazendam, Chapter 5; McKay and Wiers, Chapter 6)
Planning Entity = Artificial	• Planning by robots (Bowling et al., Chapter 10) • Planning in complex autonomous systems (Meystel, Chapter 11)	• Artificial Intelligence in production planning (Sauer, Chapter 9) • Planning support and reuse (van Wezel, Chapter 7) • Planning in operations research (Kroon and Zuidwijk, Chapter 8)

TABLE 1.3. Application-Oriented Chapters

Kiewiet et al. (Chapter 13)	(Cognitive) task-oriented approach
Abbink (Chapter 14)	Constraint Satisfaction Programming
Lentink et al. (Chapter 15)	Mixed Integer Programming
Haijema et al. (Chapter 16)	Dynamic Programming
Riezebos and van Wezel (Chapter 17)	Mixed initiative support approach

Part II of this book contains descriptions of different planning approaches that are applied to one case study, namely the shunting of trains at a station of the Netherlands Railways. Passenger trains that enter a station at the end of the day must leave the following morning, often in another configuration. This requires that the trains have to be separated in carriages, the carriages have to be parked at shunting tracks, and the following morning they have to be combined again to passenger trains. This problem is not only challenging from a mathematical perspective, but also interesting from a (cognitive) task and organizational perspective, since dozens of planners at the Dutch Railroad Company work on this problem. After describing the shunting problem in Chapter 12, the respective case study chapters will discuss how the problem was tackled from the different approaches (Table 1.3).

In the conclusions (Chapter 18), we assess the various planning approaches that are discussed in this book with the framework that is depicted in this introductory chapter. We will show that planning approaches are comparable and that often different planning words are used to describe the same phenomena. In Chapter 18 we also propose a research agenda to make use of the generic elements of planning and scheduling.

PART I

THEORETICAL

INTRODUCTION TO CHAPTER 2

Hommel's chapter describes a kind of planning that may not be planning at first sight. In Hommel's studies, subjects get a task they have to carry out after some kind of event. For example, subjects must press the left button when a green light switches on, and they must press the right button when a red light switches on. Hommel takes a cognitive neuropsychological point of view, where the planning horizon is extremely short and where the planning frequency is so high that planning and execution seem very much integrated.

Can we speak of planning here? When we observe the action behavior of a human, we cannot observe a planning process as such. Planning and action are almost simultaneous. The planning process stays internal and is hard to analyze because the subject performs it subconsciously. However, a robot may possess the same characteristics. The only difference might be that we know we have programmed the robot's behavior with some kind of planning algorithm, whereas the way in which a human plans his or her actions is largely unknown. To settle this for Hommel, we will analyze how human actions score on the definition of planning discussed in the introduction. There we stated that planning is a synthetic task in which an alternative from a large set of structurally similar alternatives has to be chosen based on constraints and goals.

First, an action is the synthesis of a number of underlying activities, so determining the action is a synthetic task. Second, the planning phase must be discernable from the action phase. Although not apparent while observing human actions, Hommel shows on the basis of experiments that such a distinct planning phase

Planning in Intelligent Systems: Aspects, Motivations, and Methods, Edited by Wout van Wezel, René Jorna, and Alexander Meystel

exists. Third, planning means choosing from a large number of structurally similar alternatives. On the one hand, choosing between the left or right button after seeing a green or red light results in a very low number of structurally similar alternatives. On the other hand, however, we should note that pressing the button is an experimental task for research purposes. More involved actions such as riding a bicycle or driving a car are much more complex, but essentially the same as choosing the button to press on the basis of a visual cue. Fourth, human actions are subject to constraints and goals when choosing one of the alternative courses of action. For example, consider a ball that someone has to catch. The movement that we want to make is limited by constraints such as objects that block the movement, the flexibility and inertia of our muscles and bones, and the fact that the palm of our hand must be toward the ball at the end of the movement. The goal is to maximize the chance that we catch the ball, which can be a trade-off between the speed with which we move our arm and the accuracy with which we move it.

Overall, human actions do possess all the characteristics that make up planning. In his chapter, Hommel will extensively discuss issues such as the development of planning methods by infants, the way in which we focus our attention in action planning, and the hierarchy of control and movement that can be found in the stimulus–response cycle. In the concluding chapter (18), we will compare human actions planning with the other planning approaches, and there we will analyze why humans are able to make complicated planning decisions within a few milliseconds, whereas making a planning decision with a computer can take hours and a planning decision in an organization can take days.

2

HOW WE DO WHAT WE WANT: A NEUROCOGNITIVE PERSPECTIVE ON HUMAN ACTION PLANNING

BERNHARD HOMMEL

Cognitive Psychology Unit, Department of Psychology, Leiden University, 2300-RB Leiden, the Netherlands

2.1. INTRODUCTION

The present chapter approaches the issue of action planning—that is, the preparation and implementation of goal-directed movements—from a cognitive psychology and, to some degree, cognitive neuroscience point of view. It will focus on actions that are much simpler than most of those discussed in the other chapters of this book and will consider empirical findings from both behavioral experiments and neuro-physiological studies. Accordingly, the chapter deals with the *how*, rather than the *why*, of action planning and, thus, will be concerned more with the transformation of behavioral goals into overt behavior than with the issue where those goals are coming from and why they have been chosen.

On first sight it may not be self-evident that bodily expressions as simple as pressing a key, moving one's hand, or uttering a syllable—the typical responses used in cognitive labs—really deserve to be called actions. One may also tend to doubt that they are planned the same way as the often more complex, multistep actions performed in everyday life, such as baking a cake. It is especially the required sequencing of action steps that makes the need for advanced planning obvious; indeed, efficiently sequencing one's behavior in tasks like the Tower of London problem is considered to be an important aspect of people's action-planning abilities in clinical

Planning in Intelligent Systems: Aspects, Motivations, and Methods, Edited by Wout van Wezel, René Jorna, and Alexander Meystel

psychology (e.g., Shallice, 1982). In contrast to more complex action sequences, the elements of these sequences are often understood as mere movements—in the service of an overarching action goal—or reactions to a triggering stimulus.

However, I shall provide evidence that even the most primitive element of an action chain needs to be, and actually is, planned much like any other, more complex and extended action or action sequence. That is, even elementary "reactions" as used in standard experimental tasks carry the signature of, and therefore count as, planned intentional actions. The three following sections will elaborate in more detail on what this signature looks like. In particular, I shall argue that (i) actions are planned in terms of their perceptual effects, (ii) action plans are not monolithic units but are, instead, integrated assemblies of action-effect codes, and (iii) action planning can be characterized as preparing a cognitive reflex.

2.2. ACTIONS ARE PLANNED IN TERMS OF THEIR EFFECTS

It is fair to say that modern cognitive psychology has put much more emphasis on the receptive than on the productive side of human behavior (e.g., Rosenbaum, 1991)—presumably a swing-back reaction to behaviorism. Indeed, almost any cognitive psychology textbook covers the topics of perception, attention, memory, reasoning, and decision making (almost always in that very order), while the issue of how all these processes are transformed into coherent, goal-directed action is commonly neglected altogether or dealt with in passing. Implicitly, action is often seen as a consequence of, and as actually caused by, stimulus processing (Prinz, 1997), as obvious from the standard information-processing model depicted in Figure 2.1: Action is conceived of as a stimulus-induced reaction, even though filtered and constrained by internal, cognitive processes. In a sense, acting is just another, rather late step of stimulus processing. Unfortunately, however, this view does not capture the goal-directed nature of intentional action, as the following example illustrates.

2.2.1. A Case Example

Take a typical experimental reaction-time task as sketched in Figure 2.2. The example task requires a speeded press of a left versus right key in response to a

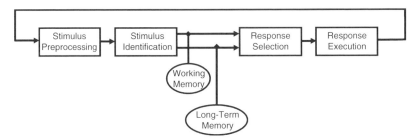

Figure 2.1. A standard stage model of human information processing.

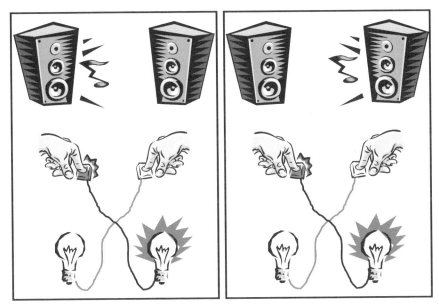

Figure 2.2. Sketch of a reaction-time task. It requires a left-hand keypressing response to a low tone (shown in this example), as well as a right-hand response to a high tone (not shown). The location of the tone varies randomly (i.e., is presented via the left or right loudspeaker, as shown in the left and right panel, respectively), and subjects are asked to ignore it. As a less typical design feature, each key is connected with a light source on the opposite side, so that pressing the left key switches on a right light while pressing the right key switches on a left light (see Hommel, 1993). Note that the tone precedes and signals the response, whereas the light flash follows it.

low or high tone, respectively (the lights come into play only later). Because the mapping of tone pitch to response location is arbitrary, performing the task presupposes some instruction and some kind of maintenance of the instructed stimulus–response mapping rules (low → left, high → right) in working memory. With respect to the model shown in Figure 2.1, this means that the transition from stimulus identification to response selection is mediated by working memory, which can be thought of as "containing" the mapping rules (e.g., Anderson, 1982).

If this were the whole story, any stimulus–response mapping should yield equally good performance, provided that the number of rules (and, thus, the required capacity) is held constant. However, this is not what experimental evidence shows. What it does show, instead, is that performance is sensitive to the similarity between stimuli and responses, so that mapping a left response onto a left stimulus and mapping a right response onto a right stimulus produces considerably faster reactions and fewer errors than mapping a right response onto a left stimulus and mapping a left response onto a right stimulus (e.g., Broadbent and Gregory, 1962). This benefit of stimulus–response feature overlap affects performance even if the overlap is task-irrelevant. With regard to our example, this means that responses will be faster to stimuli that spatially correspond (as in the left panel of Figure 2.2) than to stimuli that do not (as in the right panel)—the so-called *Simon effect* (Simon and Rudell, 1967; for an overview, see Lu and Proctor, 1995).

Apparently, then, the translation of stimulus information into responses does not strictly obey the task-defining mapping rules, but is also affected by background knowledge and hard-wired or overlearned stimulus–response routines. This insight has led to the formulation of dual-route models of information processing, in which response tendencies can be triggered by both intentionally applied mapping rules and long-term associations between stimulus and response codes (de Jong, Liang, and Lauber, 1994; Hommel, 1993; Kornblum, Hasbroucq, and Osman, 1990). The general idea underlying these models is built into our processing model in Figure 2.1, where two pathways lead from stimulus to response processing, one supported by short-term requirements and another by long-term procedural knowledge.

Processing models of this sort have been quite successful in accounting for a wide range of observations and phenomena, as well as in generating new predictions in many fields of cognitive psychology. Indeed, one or another variant of such models can be found in almost any introductory textbook—and predecessors were with us from the beginnings of experimental psychology (Ach, 1910). And yet, they do not tell us much of interest about how an intentional action is actually planned. Indeed, planning is confined to a single, not further specified process: the implementation of mapping rules into working memory. What is lacking, however, is any consideration of the role that intentions and goals play in the planning process—possibly a reflection of the fact that in experimental tasks, goals are commonly externally defined by the instruction given to the subjects.

But goals do have an effect, as can be demonstrated by means of a slight modification of the standard Simon task. Consider, again, the task depicted in Figure 2.2, but assume that each key is connected with a light source on the opposite side. Thus, pressing the left key switches on a light on the right side, while pressing the right key flashes a light on the left side. If one describes the task goal as "pressing the left (right) key in response to a low (high) tone," the result is a normal Simon effect; that is, people are faster to press the left key if the tone appears on the left than on the right side, and vice versa (Hommel, 1993, Exp. 1: key condition). Hence, subjects find the situation depicted in the left panel of Figure 2.2 easier than that shown in the right panel. However, consider the very same task is described differently, namely as "switching on the right (left) light in response to a low (high) tone." In this case, people are much faster to press the left key if the tone appears on the right than on the left side, and vice versa (Hommel, 1993, Exp. 1: light condition). That is, they prefer the situation shown in the right panel of Figure 2.2.

This observation shows that the way a task and the stimulus–response rules it comprises are planned, depends on the goal the actor has in mind. Apparently, this goal determines how responses are cognitively coded and represented—that is, what those responses mean and what effects they produce. If it is "pressing a key" that is intended, the response is coded in terms of the location of the key and/or the finger performing the press, so that a stimulus sharing this feature facilitates selecting it. However, if it is "flashing a light" that is intended, the very same response is coded in terms of the location of the light the finger movements affects. In other words, responses are coded and selected in terms of the intended effects they produce (Hommel, 1996, 1997).

2.2.2. Ideomotor Approaches to Action

The emphasis on action effects in action control echoes the ideomotor approaches of Lotze (1852), Harless (1861), and James (1890). Deeply rooted in the introspective tradition of theorizing, these authors found it rather natural to think of actions set up by personal intentions, not as evoked by instructed target stimuli. Accordingly, the theoretical problem they had to deal with consisted of the question of how motor patterns can be brought under intentional control, an issue commonly not addressed by information-processing models. The answer they proposed is sketched in Figure 2.3. Without any experience with one's own body, along with its possible artificial extensions, there is no connection between the content of the cognitive system and the motor system responsible for executing movements. However, performing (at first, mostly random) movements produces specific effects that can be perceived and cognitively coded. Due to an associative mechanism (presumably rather primitive), the motor codes that just produced a given movement and the cognitive codes that represent the movement's perceptual consequences get connected, so that a kind of cross-domain, sensorimotor structure emerges (Figure 2.3, left panel). Once such a structure is acquired, it can be used either way, which means that the individual has acquired a "mental cue" (to use the words of James) to access motor patterns to achieve intended goals. From now on, the previously involuntarily experienced

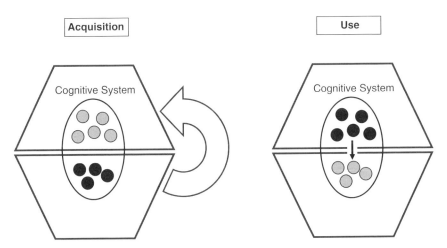

Figure 2.3. A two-stage model of the emergence of action control (after Elsner and Hommel, 2001). At the first stage, shown on the left side, the motor pattern producing a particular, perceived effect becomes integrated with the cognitive codes representing that effect. At the second stage, shown on the right, the motor pattern is intentionally executed by activating the cognitive codes that represent its anticipated effect.

movement effects can be produced intentionally by activating the codes of these effects, which then spread their activation to the associated motor codes. In other words, actions are planned by (literally) anticipating their effects.

Probably because they fit so nicely with the phenomenal experience of an acting individual, ideomotor approaches to action control were almost common wisdom during the heyday of introspective psychology (see overviews by Greenwald, 1970; Prinz, 1987; Scheerer, 1984) but were almost forgotten thereafter, even "officially" discredited by both behaviorists (Thorndike, 1913) and early information-processing theorists (Miller, Galanter, and Pribram, 1960). This does not mean that action effects would not have played an important role in explaining the acquisition of action control. However, this role was commonly confined to providing information about an action's success or failure, as in closed-loop models of motor-skill learning (Adams, 1971; Schmidt, 1975), but did not capture the function of a mental cue used in action planning as considered in ideomotor approaches (Hommel, 1998a). And yet, ideomotor concepts have seen a renaissance in the last decade or so, and empirical evidence in their support is steadily increasing. Interestingly, this support comes from four different, but converging, lines of investigation: the study of acquired, remote action effects, studies on the development of action planning, the discovery of so-called "mirror neurons," and the investigation of somatic markers.

2.2.3. Remote Action Effects

The ideomotor approach of James (1890) distinguishes between "natural" sensory effects of a movement and more remote effects. In some cases such a distinction is very clear and easy to draw, such as with switching a room light on. Performing that action produces all sorts of feedback from the hand and finger movements involved, but it also changes the visual conditions in another, more remote part of the room, and in some sense one may even tend to see the former to cause the latter. In other cases, however, the distinction is less clear, such as when steering a bike or dancing with a partner. Indeed, it is quite often difficult to say exactly where one's own body ends and one's tool or one's physical or social environment begins; indeed, subjects have a hard time to tell whether an observed movement is performed by their own hand or the hand of an otherwise invisible confederate (Daprati et al., 1997). From a developmental standpoint the distinction between more and less natural action effects is even more obsolete. After all, if the ideomotor approach is correct in assuming that infants first need to learn what effects their movements have, the only thing that should count is the contingency between movement and effect but not the sensory channel registering the effect or whether the effect is more proximal or distal (Hommel, 1997, 1998a; Wolff, 1987).

Giving up the conceptual distinction between body-related and remote action effects opens the door for a wide range of empirical investigations, simply because external, remote effects can be much better experimentally manipulated than proximal, body-related effects. Indeed, manipulating the latter would require blocking of one or more sensory channels, a rather dramatic intrusion, or studying human patients or animals that suffer from the loss of one or more channels, problems which often come with other deficits of unpredictable impact (e.g., Aschersleben, Stenneken, Cole, and Prinz, 2002). Working with remote action effects is much easier and has shown to yield promising results. The probably first study to demonstrate the role of remote action-produced events in human action planning, the one of Hommel (1993), was already introduced above. As described above and shown in Figure 2.2, responses were consistently followed by light flashes in the opposite location. The fact that performance depended on the instructions given to the subjects—with the stimulus facilitating actions with spatially corresponding goals—has two implications: First, subjects apparently associated their responses with the remote effects and, second, they somehow made use of these associations when selecting the responses.

The observation that action–effect associations are used for selecting intended actions is consistent with the ideomotor approach, but it covers only part of its predictions. What remains to be shown is that such associations are established automatically, a prediction that can only be tested if subjects are not instructed to attend to the novel action effects or rewarded for using them. To provide such a test, Hommel (1996) had subjects run through two different experimental phases, which were designed to mirror the natural sequence of acquisition and use of action–effect associations, respectively. In the first, acquisition phase subjects were to press a response button once or twice, as signaled by a visual stimulus. The two actions produced different auditory effects so that, for instance, a single key press would result in a low-pitched tone and a double press would produce a high-pitched tone (see Figure 2.4, left panel). Subjects were told that there would be tones sounding, but it was pointed out that these would not be important or informative in any sense and that they should be ignored. Nevertheless, it was expected that subjects would acquire associations between the cognitive tone representations and the actions the tones accompanied. This was tested in the second, test phase by presenting randomly chosen low- or high-pitched tones together with the visual stimulus (see right panel). Again, it was pointed out that these tones were not informative and could safely be ignored. However, if tones and actions really became associated in the acquisition phase, presenting a tone should prime (i.e., pre-activate) the associated action, thereby facilitating performance if the primed action is to be carried out (upper part of right panel) and impairing it if the other, alternative response is actually required (lower part). Indeed, this was observed in a series of experiments with varying stimuli, responses, and action effects, suggesting that events that accompany particular responses are really picked up and integrated with those responses in an automatic fashion.

A recent study of Elsner and Hommel (2001) shows that action–effect associations can affect not only the speed of response selection but also its outcome. In the acquisition phase, their subjects were also presented with response-contingent tones much like the ones sketched in the left part of Figure 2.4. In the test phase, however, subjects performed free-choice reactions to low- and high-pitched tones. The question of interest was not how quickly people react under these conditions but whether they tend to select and carry out the response that is "suggested" by

Figure 2.4. Sketch of the experimental design used by Hommel (1996). In the first phase, the acquisition phase (*left panel*), subjects pressed a reaction key once or twice, thus triggering a low- and high-pitched tone, respectively (for one example). In the second phase, the test phase (*right panels*), randomly selected tones were also presented as task-irrelevant, to-be-ignored primes. The prime tones matched the tone the correct response would produce in some trials (*upper panel*) but not in others (*lower panel*).

the acquired action effect. If so, we had direct evidence for the notion that action–effect representations play a crucial role in action planning. Indeed, Elsner and Hommel observed a pronounced tendency to perform actions that previously produced the tone that now appeared as stimulus. Importantly, this tendency remained unchanged in size and direction when the free-choice task was carried out under heavy mental load induced by a secondary task, which rules out any strategic use of action–effect associations. A follow-up study combining Elsner and Hommel's task with positron electron tomography (PET) revealed that this effect-induced action tendency is directly reflected in the activation of neural assemblies in the supplementary motor area (Elsner et al., 2002), which is known to play a central role in action planning (Decety et al., 1994).

Converging evidence for the use of action–effect codes comes from a recent study of Kunde (2001). He used a four-alternative choice-reaction time task, in which each of two effect tones was mapped onto two responses (4 : 2 mapping). In each trial, one response was precued; that is, it was indicated which response would be the most likely in this trial. As one would expect, valid cues facilitated performance; that is, subjects performed much better if the precued response was actually asked for than if another response was required. However, performance in these latter conditions depended on the action effects. Although responses were slowed, the slowing was reduced if the required response shared its effect tone with the precued, prepared response. Apparently, then, preparing a response was associated with activating the acquired effect-tone code, which then also primed the other response associated with it.

2.2.4. Development of Action Planning

An important implication of the idea that actions are planned in terms of their effects is that intentional planning presupposes and, thus, follows the acquisition of movement-related consequences. As discussed in the previous section, this hypothesized sequence can be successfully simulated in adults by confronting them with novel, arbitrary response-contingent events. But it is as interesting to see whether comparable, or at least consistent, evidence can be found in the cognitive development of infants and children. Indeed, there are indications that bilateral response–effect associations are formed from the first months of age on, whereas the development of action-planning abilities is much slower and much more extended in time.

To investigate the acquisition of response–effect associations, Watson and Ramey (1972) hung rotating "contingency mobiles" over the cribs of 2-month-old infants. If the mobile's movement was contingent on the pressure the infant exerted on his/her pillow, pillow responses were more frequent than if the mobile moved noncontingently, or not at all. Comparable results were observed by Rovee and colleagues (Rovee and Rovee, 1969; Fagen and Rovee, 1976), who had only slightly older infants manipulate mobile movements by means of strings attached to their feet. Interestingly, infants showed mobile-related behavior even after retention delays of two days or longer (Butler and Rovee-Collier, 1989; Fagen, Rovee-Collier, and Kaplan, 1976). Thus, not only do perceived action effects motivate infants to show the critical behavior more often, but also their representations become integrated with the behavior they accompany. Using a different method, Rochat and Striano (1999) found increased sucking behavior in 2-month-olds if the pressure the infant applied to his or her pacifier systematically modified the pitch of a tone. Likewise, Kalnins and Bruner (1973) reported that even 5- to 12-week-old infants adapt their sucking behavior if that increases the optical clarity of a film presented to them.

These findings show that infants can pick up movement–effect relationships very soon after birth, and just a little experience is sufficient for the acquisition of relatively durable memory traces. However, it takes much longer to learn how to make efficient use of these traces—that is, to plan goal-directed actions. Sure enough, some degree of action control will develop during the first months, the most obvious being saccadic eye movements. And yet, most action-related executive functions emerge at considerably higher age, as does the organization of brain structures presumably mediating those functions. There is evidence for at least two major steps in the development of action control.

The first step can be roughly located around 7–10 months of age. During that time, infants exhibit considerable improvement with regard to inhibiting counter-productive grasp and withdrawal reflexes (Diamond, 1990), ignoring alternative goals (Diamond and Gilbert, 1989), and suppressing inefficient strategies (Diamond, 1990) during goal-directed reaching. There is also evidence for the improvement of action-related working-memory or task-set functions, such as needed in Piaget's A-not-B task. In this task, subjects are first rewarded for reacting toward an object hidden in location A. Then the object is placed in A again and then visibly moved to B, an adjacent location. A common finding is that infants (Gretch and Landers, 1971; Fox, Kagan, and Weiskopf, 1979) and monkeys with lesions in the dorsolateral prefrontal cortex (Diamond and Goldman-Rakic, 1986) have considerable problems with this task, the more so the longer the delay between hiding the object in B and the response. However, infants show dramatic improvements between 7 and 12 months, with an increase of the tolerated delay from 1 second to about 10 seconds (Diamond, 1985). The basis for these developmental trends is not clear; they may be related to the observation that metabolic activity in the frontal cortex lags behind other cortical areas and approaches adult values not before 8–12 months of age (Chugani and Phelps, 1986; Chugani, 1994).

A second major step in the development of action control seems to take place at about 5–6 years of age. There are several indications suggesting considerable gains in the ability to inhibit prepotent responses around that time. Children of 4 years or younger are unable to wait for a more preferred or bigger reward in the presence of a less preferred or smaller, but immediately available, reward, whereas children of 5–6 years commonly manage to wait (Mischel and Mischel, 1983). Likewise, children of 3–4 years often fail to inhibit their responses in no-go trials of go/no-go tasks, whereas 5 to 6-year-olds have little problems (Bell and Livesey, 1985; Livesey and Morgan, 1991). A similar observation was made by Luria (1959, 1961). He reported that preschool children were able to squeeze a bulb in response to a light flash, but they failed to refrain from squeezing when the light was extinguished, even though they did recall and understand their instructions to do so. Even more interesting in the present context, children of 5 years or older show strong improvements with regard to the ability to switch between S-R rules and to perform stimulus-incompatible actions. If children of 2.5–3 years are asked to sort drawings according to one criterion and then to switch to another, they often fail and show perseverance of the old sorting rule—even though they have no difficulty remembering and verbalizing the new, correct rule (Zelazo, Reznick, and Piñon, 1995). Failures of young children in inhibiting inappropriate but stimulus-compatible responses have been reported by Diamond and colleagues. Gerstadt, Hong, and Diamond (1994) asked children between 3.5 and 7 years of age to perform a Stroop-like task that required saying "day" in response to a card showing a moon and stars, and saying "night" to a card showing a bright sun. While children younger than 5 performed close to chance, performance of the older children improved dramatically and approached that of the oldest age group. In a very similar task, Diamond and Taylor (1996) asked 3.5 to 7-year-olds to perform Luria's tapping task, which requires tapping once when the experimenter taps twice, and vice versa. Again, children younger than 5 performed badly, while 6-year-olds reached an accuracy of 95%.

Even though the detailed mechanisms underlying this developmental leap are not yet unraveled, there is consensus that the (slow) maturation of the frontal cortex plays a major role (e.g., Diamond, 1990; Fuster, 1989; Johnson, 1999; Shallice and Burgess, 1998). Indeed, patients with frontal-lobe damage tend to exhibit executive deficits very similar to those in children younger than 5–6 in having difficulties to suppress stimulus-induced or stimulus-compatible actions in Stroop-like tasks (Drewe, 1975; Luria, 1966; Perret, 1974), spatial-compatibility tasks (Décary and Richer, 1995), or everyday life (Lhermitte, 1983). In view of the fact that the frontal cortex shows the longest period of development of any brain region (Chugani and Phelps, 1986; Huttenlocher, 1990), this suggests that executive functions mature relatively late in ontogenesis. Thus, the ability to acquire action–effect associations does indeed seem to precede the capacity to make intentional use of them.

2.2.5. Mirror Neurons

According to the ideomotor approach to action planning, we learn to master our actions by means of self-observation. That is, we move, observe ourselves while moving, and thereby connect the codes of what we do (i.e., motor patterns) with the codes of what we perceive (i.e., action effects). As argued above, this mechanism should work independent of whether the observed action effects are proximal, body-related sensations or distal, remote events, and I have already discussed evidence supporting this assumption. Moreover, there is evidence that perceiving action effects tends to prime the corresponding action, which is in agreement with the idea of a close coupling of perceptual and motor codes. Such a view opens an interesting possibility with respect to the effect of social perception: Observing the behavior of others should tend to invoke comparable behavior in the observer, just as implied by the old idea of "behavioral contagion" and empathy (e.g., McDougall, 1908/1923).

Recent neurophysiological findings provide strong support for the assumption of integrated perception–action codes. Di Pellegrino, Fadiga, Fogassi, and Rizzolatti (1992) measured single-cell activity in the rostral part of the inferior premotor cortex of a macaque monkey while he was either performing particular goal-directed actions himself or watching an experimenter doing so. It turned out that the same cells were active in both cases. Control experiments showed that very specific conditions need to be met to trigger the firing of these so-called "mirror neurons." They only (or at least most strongly) react to the experience of interactions of an agent and a goal object, but are insensitive to either objects alone or objectless pantomimes (Gallese, Fadiga, Fogassi, and Rizzolatti, 1996).

More recently, progress has been made in extending these insights to humans. Interestingly, watching actions activates the human homologue of that part of the macaque brain where the mirror neurons were detected (Grafton, Arbib, Fadiga, and Rizzolatti, 1996). And these structures also seem to share their functional characteristics, especially the sensitivity to goal-directed, meaningful action. That is, human subjects show premotor activity while watching a familiar, purposeful action but not when facing a novel, meaningless movement (Decety et al., 1997). Indeed, this is what the ideomotor account would lead one to expect, because only familiar actions should be represented by integrated clusters of perceptual and motor codes. Once an action is acquired, observing it primes the same muscle groups that one would use to carry it out oneself (Fadiga, Fogassi, Pavesi, and Rizzolatti, 1995).

The discovery of mirror neurons had and still has a huge impact on many fields of cognitive psychology and the cognitive neurosciences. Indeed, it provides a source of inspiration for all sorts of speculations on the basis of empathy, human sociability, imitational skills, or the origin of language, the validity of which needs to be carefully investigated. What is clear, however, is that they (or their human homologues) are ideal neural examples of integrated structures connecting perceived action effects and the motor patterns producing them, and therefore prime candidates to mediate effect-based action planning.

2.2.6. Somatic Markers

Human decision making is influenced by many factors, such as background knowledge, logical reasoning, situational biases, and emotions. However, not all of those factors are equally appreciated by experts and advisors on skilled decision making, or researchers investigating the decision process. Indeed, it seemed obvious for centuries that cognitive, rational contributions are much more helpful in reaching an appropriate decision than emotions and personal preferences. And yet, this widely shared view came under increasingly heavy attacks in the recent years. There are both logical and empirical arguments challenging the superiority of cognitively based decisions.

For one, cognitive processes, and especially the integration of all relevant knowledge, have been argued to take too long under many circumstances in everyday life, so that some kind of short-cutting full-fledged reasoning is often essential for efficient action (Gigerenzer and Goldstein, 1996). Moreover, there are many simple, "fast-and-frugal" heuristics available that not only allow for much faster decisions, but also provide solutions the quality of which can be surprisingly high. For instance, if asked to judge which of two cities has more inhabitants (e.g., San Antonio or San Diego), people often prefer the city whose name is more familiar to them—with rather good success (Goldstein and Gigerenzer, 1999). That is, reasonable decisions need not be, and often actually are not, based on exhaustive reasoning.

The same line of thought has led Damasio (1994) and his colleagues to postulate a guiding role of emotions in decision making. In a nutshell, he assumes that performing actions produces positive or negative somatic states, which then become associated with the actions' representations. If so, people can retrieve the somatic markers of possible actions when making their mind up which one to perform. That is, they can anticipate which somatic states each action would create and base their decision on this quickly available "gut feeling." Damasio assumes that a whole neural network is responsible for acquiring and using the hypothesized links between actions and somatic markers, with the interaction of the prefrontal cortex and the amygdala playing a major role (e.g., Damasio, Tranel, and Damasio, 1991). Accordingly, Damasio's approach predicts a breakdown of efficient decision making in case of lesions or disorders in prefrontal brain areas. Indeed, the approach was originally motivated by an attempt to make sense of the sad story of Phineas Gage, a previously likable railroad worker whose personal and social decline began when an explosion drilled an iron rod into his forebrain (Damasio, 1994). The hypothesis that efficient decision making is based, and perhaps even dependent on, prefrontally mediated associations between actions and somatic markers finds support in a number of observations.

First, patients suffering from lesions in the ventromedial part of their frontal cortex perform particularly badly in experimental card-drawing games with complicated contingencies between the deck the cards were drawn from and financial gains and losses. Bechara et al. (1994) had frontal patients, patients without frontal lesions, and healthy controls play such a game. There were two advantageous card decks, with small gains but few losses, and two disadvantageous decks, with high gains but frequent losses, to draw from. All three groups would start drawing randomly from all four decks. However, whereas nonfrontal patients and controls then gradually started to prefer the more advantageous decks, frontal patients continued to frequently draw cards from the disadvantageous deck, suggesting that they did not realize the overall loss. In fact, they lost their entire game budget and needed to take loans.

Second, taking an unfavorable decision seems to be accompanied by particular emotional states, indeed, at least in individuals with intact frontal lobes. This is suggested by findings of Bechara et al. (1996), who measured galvanic skin conductance responses (GSCRs) of frontal patients and healthy controls while playing the card-drawing game. Of particular interest were the GSCRs during the decision interval—that is, the few seconds before a card was drawn. Whenever, they were about to draw from the disadvantageous deck, controls exhibited increases in GSCR (i.e., sweated more), and they did more the more experience they had. This did not occur in frontal patients, who showed comparable, nonincreasing GSCRs before drawing from "good" and "bad" decks. That is, an intact frontal lobe seems to enable people to emotionally anticipate loss, and it is not unreasonable to assume that it is this ability that underlies good performance in the card-drawing game.

Although developed on a more motivational than cognitive background, it is interesting to note that the somatic-marker account follows the same line of thought as the ideomotor approach: On both accounts, people acquire information about the consequences of their actions and use anticipations of these consequences to select appropriate actions. Indeed, there is empirical evidence suggesting that the mechanisms underlying the integration of perceptual and emotional action effects are at least comparable. Beckers, de Houwer, and Eelen (2002) used basically the same paradigm as Hommel (1996) and Elsner and Hommel (2001). In an acquisition phase, subjects performed binary-choice responses to the grammatical category of neutral words. One response was consistently followed by a mild electroshock—that is, accompanied by an unpleasant action effect. In the following test phase, the stimulus words were chosen to possess positive or negative emotional valence. As expected, subjects performed better when the valence of the stimulus matched the pleasantness of the response; that is, negative words were responded to more quickly with the response followed by a shock, and the opposite was true for positive words. Apparently, then, the actions acquired the emotional valence of their consequences.

A similar conclusion is suggested by findings of van der Goten et al. (submitted), who had subjects perform two overlapping keypressing tasks. The two responses in the secondary task triggered the presentation of a smiley or a grumpy, respectively. Results show that preparing smiley-producing responses facilitated the processing of emotionally positive words in the primary task, while preparing grumpy-producing responses primed words with a negative valence. That is, the responses must have been integrated with the emotional valence of their effects, thereby emotionally "marking" them.

To summarize, there is strong, increasing evidence that actions are planned in terms of their effects. In particular, perceived and felt effects of movements are acquired in a presumably automatic fashion and from infancy on, and they become integrated with the motor patterns that evoke (or at least accompany) them. Complex neural networks have been suggested to underlie the integration of actions and consequences, with the prefrontal and premotor cortices playing a central role.

2.3. ACTION PLANS ARE INTEGRATED ASSEMBLIES

Human action planning has often been likened to writing and compiling a computer program—that is, likened to creating an ordered list of instructions that is later read out by the motor machinery (e.g., Miller et al., 1960). Indeed, most work on planning-related issues in the artificial intelligence domain has implicitly or explicitly employed this interpretation of the planning term. With regard to long-term projects like writing a book or raising one's children, this is certainly a reasonable approach that is likely to capture the essence of the presumably rather abstract cognitive representations involved. However, it is important to see that such high-level descriptions only solve part of the problem, which makes them an unlikely candidate if it comes to more concrete planning processes as discussed in this chapter. True, instruction lists do solve the sequencing part of the planning problem by specifying the necessary steps in the order in which they need to be carried out. But how the symbols specifying a given step are actually translated into "motor language"— that is, how the planning symbols are "grounded" (Harnad, 1990)—remains a mystery.

In contrast to symbolic accounts, ideomotor approaches provide an obvious solution to this translation or grounding problem. It is assumed that with increasing experience, more and more motor patterns become connected with cognitive "cues" or "markers," which makes them available to planning processes. On this view, concrete planning consists of anticipating the features of the intended action goal, which means priming the corresponding cognitive codes. Because these codes are associated with the motor patterns producing them, activation will spread to the motor system where the required movements are then ready to go. If we would only be busy with one plan and one action at a time, this sketch would be perfectly plausible and it may therefore well capture the planning processes going on under such circumstances. Unfortunately, however, these circumstances are rare. Typically, the action plans we have prepared strongly overlap in time and we often carry out more than one plan concurrently, such as when talking while walking or driving. This overlap of plans creates what is commonly called a "binding problem."

2.3.1. The Binding Problem in Action Planning

Concurrently held and carried out action plans introduce a serious problem that symbolic accounts commonly overlook. Consider the left panel of Figure 2.5, which sketches the way the cognitive codes of the intended goal translate into motor activity. Now consider the situation that two plans are maintained and/or translated into behavior at about the same time, as depicted in the right panel. Note that on both the cognitive and the motor level there is no way to tell members of one plan from members of the other—there is just a bunch of codes being active. Given the representational structure of the human brain, this is a real problem.

Indeed, there is converging evidence that the primate brain uses different neural populations in various cortical areas to represent and control different features of an action. For instance, distinct cell assemblies have been shown to code the direction (Alexander and Crutcher, 1990; Georgopoulos, 1990), force (Kalaska and Hyde, 1985), and distance (Riehle and Requin, 1989) of arm movements in monkeys. Likewise, human subjects exhibit different electrophysiological brain patterns [so-called Bereitschaftspotentials (Deecke, Grozinger, and Kornhuber, 1976)] depending on the duration (Vidal, Bonnet, and Macar, 1991) and force (Bonnet and MacKay,

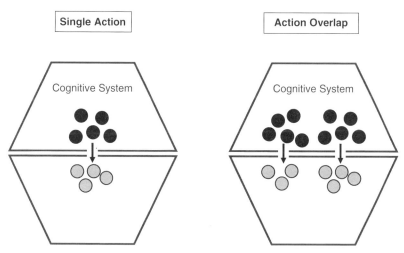

Figure 2.5. Illustration of the feature-binding problem in action planning. No problem arises if only a single action is planned, or a single plan is maintained, at one time (*left panel*). However, if more than one action is planned, the relationship between plan elements and plans become undetermined (*right panel*).

1989; Kutas and Donchin, 1980) of a planned action, as well as depending on the to-be-used hand (Osman et al., 1992). These observations suggest that action planning involves the coordination of multiple codes distributed across a wide range of brain areas. In fact, even in the rhesus monkey, preparing an action activates a whole neural network including the posterior parietal cortex, the premotor cortex, and the primary motor cortex (Requin, Lecas, and Vitton, 1990). Correspondingly, a simple grasping movement activates the superior parietal cortex, the premotor cortex, the basal ganglia, and the cerebellum of the human brain, as studies with PET have revealed (Rizzolatti et al., 1996).

Given this preference of brains to represent action plans in a distributed fashion, the question arises of how they are able to coordinate all the elements belonging to a given plan. And, even more pressing, we need to ask how brains can distinguish between the elements belonging to one plan and those that belong to another, concurrently maintained plan—the so-called "binding problem" sketched in Figure 2.5. Let us now consider how this problem might be solved and what the cognitive implications of the solution are.

2.3.2. Integration of Action Features

Logically, there are at least two possibilities to deal with binding problems: hierarchical command structures and coordinative structures (see Singer, 1994). The first solution presupposes a strictly hierarchical representation of action elements, much like in an army. Thus, there is a command neuron or neural assembly that governs a subordinate layer of elements, which again may rule another, even more subordinate layer, and so forth. A given action plan would therefore be defined and coordinated by its chief, so to speak, which is directly responsible for its immediate subordinates and indirectly responsible for lower layers. The problem with this view is that such types of structures are very vulnerable to cell loss and dysfunction, especially if their "chiefs" are concerned. Moreover, one would need to assume a distinct command neuron or assembly for each possible course of action, a not overly parsimonious solution in particular if one thinks of action sequences.

An alternative solution would be to somehow "tag" or "mark" all the elements belonging to a particular plan, so that all plan members would share the same tag. According to the current state of the discussion, the prime candidate to represent such a tag is the temporal behavior of cells. That is, the firing of neurons or networks of neurons belonging to the same action plan may become synchronized, so that the integrated elements are rhythmically coupled (Abeles, 1991; Singer, 1994; von der Malsburg, 1981).

Indeed, experimental animal data have been accumulated over the last decade supporting the view that temporal synchronization serves as a neural mechanism to functionally link neurons within and between cortical areas and subcortical structures (for reviews see MacKay, 1997; Singer, 1994). Most of these studies have investigated the role of synchronization in visual feature binding, but there is also evidence for some role in action control. For instance, action-contingent synchronization of cell groups has been observed in the motor cortex of monkeys (Sanes and

Donoghue, 1993), between motor and somatosensory areas of the monkey (Murthy and Fetz, 1992, 1996), and across the visual and parietal cortex and the parietal and the motor cortex of the cat (Roelfsema et al., 1997).

In humans, the presence and functional significance of neuronal synchronization has been investigated mainly by using electroencephalography (EEG) and magneto-encephalography (MEG). Most importantly, recent studies provide evidence for a relation between the temporal coherence among cell assemblies and the planning and initiation of action. For instance, Pfurtscheller et al. (1994) and Salenius et al. (1996) observed that the onset of gamma oscillations in the primary motor cortex is time-locked to the initiation of finger, toe, and tongue movements. But synchronization may also mediate the coupling of primary motor cortex and spinal motor neuron pool—that is, the transfer of action plans to the periphery. Indeed, significant coherence can be observed between EEG/MEG signals from the primary motor cortex and the rectified EMG of various muscles (for review see Hari and Salenius, 1999). Thus, there is evidence that the cortically distributed neural elements that make up an action plan are integrated by coordinating their temporal behavior, thereby "tagging" all the ingredients belonging to the same plan.

2.3.3. Occupation of Feature Codes

The integration of action features into coherent action plans has a few consequences. Most of them are, of course, positive in unequivocally marking each feature code and thereby allowing for the concurrent maintenance of multiple plans. Given that feature codes are also open to and affected by perceptual information (see above), there are even more positive implications that will be discussed in the following section. However, there are also drawbacks. Ironically, it was these drawbacks that turned out to be particularly diagnostic in experimental analyses of the integration process.

Assume, for instance, that some action plan A is created and that the relevant action-feature codes are integrated, as indicated on the left side of Figure 2.6. Now assume that the given individual is willing to create another plan B before carrying out A. If there is no overlap in features between the two plans, there is no obvious hindrance for that, apart from possible (and likely) capacity limitations of the cognitive system with respect to the number of plans to be concurrently entertained (cf. Raffone and Wolters, 2001). However, consider the situation if there is some feature overlap. For instance, the two planned actions may be intended to be performed with the same effector—the right hand, say. If so, the features RIGHT and HAND should have been integrated into plan A already, so that they are less available for—that is, more difficult to integrate into—plan B. Thus, feature overlap between an already created and a to-be-created action plan should impair forming the latter, because the overlapping feature codes are, in some sense, occupied by the former (Stoet and Hommel, 1999).

Indeed, there are a number of findings that support this rather counterintuitive prediction. A first hint comes from studies on verbal planning by Meyer, Gordon, and colleagues (Meyer and Gordon, 1985; Yaniv et al., 1990). They had subjects

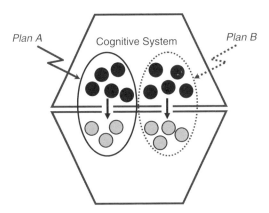

Figure 2.6. Sketch of the implications of sequential action planning. Planning action A leads to the integration of the corresponding feature codes. Later planning of action B is unaffected if there is no feature overlap between A and B. However, if features already integrated into plan A are needed for plan B as well, a *code-occupation* problem arises.

prepare one of two utterances, such as the syllable "up," and to utter it as soon as a go signal appeared. In some trials, however, another signal would appear and call for the alternative utterance, the idea being that the corresponding delay of reaction time reflects the amount of the re-planning required. Interestingly, the delay increased with the similarity between the prepared and the eventually uttered syllable. For instance, switching from one voiced to another voiced syllable (up → ut) took more time than switching from an unvoiced to a voiced syllable (ub → ut), as if binding the feature VOICED to a syllable would somehow block access to this feature by another utterance.

A similar observation was made by Rosenbaum et al. (1986). They had subjects recite letter strings of different length with alternating stress (e.g., AbCdAbCd...). Curiously, strings of an uneven number of letters were more difficult to perform than strings with even numbers, irrespective of the overall length. For instance, subjects found it harder to perform the string AbCaBc... than AbCdAbCd.... Again, it seems that integrating a particular letter with the feature STRESSED or UNSTRESSED interferes with (re-)combining it with another feature.

Even stronger evidence for code-occupation effects comes from a recent study by Stoet and Hommel (1999). They used an ABBA design, in which subjects were asked to create an action plan A and then to create and carry out another plan B, before eventually performing the planned action A after B was completed. In some trials there was a feature overlap between the two plans, such as if subjects carried out a simple movement with the index finger of their left (or right) hand while holding in mind a plan of a more complex action with the same hand. In other trials the two plans did not overlap, such as when the finger movement and the more complex action were carried out with different hands. Results showed that feature overlap impaired performance, so that moving the left-hand index finger, say, was slowed down by holding in mind an action plan referring to the same as compared to a different hand. Again, it seems that considering a particular feature in creating an action plan occupies the corresponding cognitive code of that feature. Interestingly, Stoet and Hommel (1999) found competition between plans even if the two actions were carried out with different effectors sharing egocentric location only—that is, planning to perform an action with the left hand impaired responses with the left foot. This suggests that occupied action features need not refer to an effector but apparently can be of any kind.

In the previous section, I have argued that actions are planned in terms of their perceptual effects and that the medium of those planning activities are acquired perceptuomotor structures (see Figure 2.3). Accordingly, what is integrated and what gets bound in the process of creating an action plan is actually not a single motor code but a perceptuo-motor assembly, so that an action plan is actually an integrated assembly of (previously) integrated assemblies. Because the latter are perceptuo-motor structures, they have a dual function in both controlling a particular action feature (i.e., making sure that the planned action possesses the corresponding feature) and registering perceptual information about that feature (see Section 2.2.5). Hence, these structures mediate both the production and the perception of the feature they represent (Hommel et al., 2001a, 2001b).

A particularly provocative prediction from this view is that planning an action should actually affect the perception of a feature-overlapping event the same way that it affects the planning of a feature-overlapping action. For instance, creating the plan to perform a left-hand action should interfere with perceiving a "left" event. To test this prediction, Müsseler and Hommel (1997a) had subjects prepare a left or right key-pressing action and perform it at leisure. However, before pressing the intended key, subjects were asked to "signal" the upcoming response by means of a double key-press, which served as an indicator of when subjects had completed action planning. This double press triggered the brief presentation of a pattern-masked left- or right-pointing arrow, the direction of which was to be indicated at leisure at the end of the trial. Hence, subjects were presented with a "left" or "right" stimulus while maintaining a feature-overlapping or not overlapping action plan. As predicted, arrow perception was drastically affected by action planning: The accuracy of reporting a left- or right-pointing arrow was much lower if the arrow appeared while maintaining a feature-overlapping action plan than if arrow direction and keypress location did not correspond. In a follow-up study, Müsseler and Hommel (1997b) even found the detection of stimuli to be impaired by planning a feature-overlapping action. Thus, creating an action plan occupies not only codes needed to plan other feature-overlapping actions, but also codes that mediate the perception of feature-overlapping events. This provides strong support for the idea that action plans are integrated assemblies of sensorimotor structures.

2.4. ACTION PLANNING CREATES A PREPARED REFLEX

Having discussed the *how* of action planning, let us now turn to the *when*. In information-processing models of human performance, planning an action is commonly equated with selecting a response. Accordingly, the time point of planning is often assumed to follow the perception of action-relevant situational circumstances—that is, after the left part of the model shown in Figure 2.1 has been run through. Indeed, we sometimes do encounter situations in which we first realize a particular action opportunity, then make up our mind how to proceed, and eventually perform the apparently most appropriate action—shopping would be an example.

And yet, most situations do not really fit this example, not even in laboratory experiments. Commonly, we have planned how to react long before the relevant stimulus conditions occur, as Sigmund Exner had already noted in 1879. In his chapter on attention, he mentions the example of a speeded hand movement that he carried out in response to a visual stimulus. Exner noticed that long before the stimulus came up, he had already set himself into some kind of state that ensured that the response would be carried out as intended. Evoking that state, he considered, must be a voluntary, attentional act. However, once the state was created, he felt that the eventual response became involuntary in the sense that no further effort of will was needed to perform it. In a way, Exner concluded, the cognitive system works like a prepared reflex (see Hommel, 2000).

Exner was not the only one to challenge the seemingly self-evident notion that the will intervenes between stimulus processing and response execution. In a series of reaction time experiments, Münsterberg (1889) found evidence that even with unpracticed stimulus–response pairs, motor responses are often initiated long before their trigger stimulus is completely identified and consciously perceived. This made him doubt that stimulus–response translation depends on a mediating decision or act of will—a position nicely supported by recent investigations of Neumann and Klotz (1994), Eimer and Schlaghecken (1998), and others. Similar considerations were put forward by Marbe (1901) and his Würzburg colleagues from a more phenomenological perspective. To study acts of response-related decision, Marbe had his subjects respond to all sorts of questions, ranging from weight judgments to arithmetic problems. However, when he asked them to describe the processes that intervene between hearing the question and giving the response, the answers were not very informative: They gave some description of the stimulus or the response, but nothing that would refer to a decision. Among other things, it was this outcome that led adherents of the then-evolving Würzburg school to believe that task instructions are transformed into a cognitive task set before, but not as a result of, stimulus presentation.

Only recently, the general issue of how people set themselves to perform a task has seen a renaissance in cognitive psychology and the cognitive neurosciences (for overviews, see Hommel, Ridderinkhof, and Theeuwes, 2002; Monsell and Driver, 2000), although most research efforts are devoted to handling, or switching between, multiple tasks and the side effects that are produced, rather than to the mechanisms underlying the prepared reflex Exner observed. However, there is evidence that at least three functions serve to prepare the cognitive system to act in a reflex-like, apparently effortless fashion: (i) the increased attention to appropriate context or trigger conditions for the planned action; (ii) the implementation of then automatically working stimulus–response associations defining the task; and (iii) the delegation of control to lower-level movement routines. All three functions basically serve to delegate parts of action control to the environment, thereby keeping the action plan flexible and the cognitive load of the planning individual at a minimum. Let me discuss these functions in turn.

2.4.1. Enabling Automatic Detection of Appropriate Context Conditions

Although there are situations in which we carry out an action as soon as the planning process is completed, most actions are planned for the future—be it near, as in an experimental task with trials occurring every few seconds, or far, as when preparing for a journey. However, planning for the future requires some sort of specification of the appropriate action context—that is, of the stimulus conditions that are supposed to trigger the prepared action plan. Accordingly, action plans must include information about the context and the stimulus conditions under which the planned action is to be carried out. Such information may refer to particular stimulus–response rules that specify how situational parameters are translated into action parameters—an issue I will get back to in the next two sections. But there also needs to be some information that, in a more general sense, defines the circumstances appropriate to execute the plan. An example might be the sign or visual characteristics of a particular underground station that signals to you to leave the train right now—that is, to launch your behavioral "exit routine." Obviously, the identification of appropriate trigger conditions is a crucial precondition for successful performance, which is why several authors have suggested that action planning may lead to the automatic (i.e., effortless) detection of such conditions (Bargh and Gollwitzer, 1994; Lewin, 1926; Patalano and Seifert, 1997). Indeed, there is converging evidence that associating a planned action with particular, anticipated stimulus conditions facilitates the detection of trigger conditions, or of stimuli related to them.

For instance, Gollwitzer and Mertin (reported in Bargh and Gollwitzer, 1994) asked subjects to name actions they intended to carry out in the near future and then had them perform a dichotic-listening task. In this task, subjects monitored one of two auditory channels for target words, to which they responded as soon as possible. As to be expected, presenting words in the unattended channel slowed down performance considerably. However, performance was particularly impaired if these words were related to the action plans the subjects had mentioned before. Apparently, the plan-related words attracted attention automatically and thereby drew it away from the task-relevant channel.

Further evidence for the prioritized processing of plan-related stimuli comes from Goschke and Kuhl (1993). Their subjects were instructed to either perform a particular set of actions themselves or to watch an experimenter performing it. Before carrying out or observing the actions, they were presented with to-be-recognized words that were either related to the respective actions or neutral. If subjects expected to observe an action, reaction times to action-related and neutral words were equivalent. However, if they expected to perform an action themselves, action-related words were recognized considerably faster than neutral words. Importantly, this advantage for action-related words was only obtained if the recognition test preceded performance of the action but not if the action was completed before the test. These findings were replicated and extended by Marsh, Hicks, and Bryan (1999), who demonstrated that canceling an action plan has the same effect as carrying it out. Hence, maintaining an action plan sensitizes the individual to stimuli related to it.

A final example for the attentional consequences of action planning has been reported by Craighero et al. (1999). In their study, participants planned to grasp a bar that was rotated 45 degrees to the left or right. The initiation of the movement was signaled by a picture of a bar that appeared on a monitor. The orientation of the pictured bar was entirely irrelevant to the task and varied randomly, and subjects were urged to ignore it. Nevertheless, the planned movements were initiated faster if its orientation matched the bar's orientation. To test whether this was a true perceptual effect, the authors included trials in which the visual bar also appeared while a manual grasp was planned, but where it signaled a foot response. Foot responses were still faster if the visual bar was congruent with the manual action plan, showing that the plan really facilitated perceptual processes.

2.4.2. Enabling Automatic Stimulus–Response Translation

Having detected that a particular action can be carried out does not necessarily tell the individual how this is to be done. For instance, even if I have successfully approached a supermarket and recognized that this provides me with an opportunity to carry out my plan to buy the ingredients for my favorite dish, I still need to recall those ingredients, recall or figure out where to find them, put them into my shopping kart, and so forth. Thus, to carry out an action plan requires not only the detection of trigger stimuli, but also the use of if–then or stimulus–response rules that define how to deal with particular situational stimuli and constraints (e.g., Allport, 1980; Anderson, 1982; Meyer and Kieras, 1997).

Although this assumption is uncontroversial, it is controversial whether the implemented rules can be used as automatically as the prepared-reflex metaphor suggests. On first sight there are reasons to doubt that they can, especially in view of what has come to be known as the psychological refractory period (PRP) effect (Telford, 1931). This term is used to describe the common observation that performance on the second of two tasks decreases with increasing temporal overlap between the tasks; hence, people have difficulty to carry out more than one task at a time. Considerable research effort has been devoted to find out where this difficulty comes from, and there is consensus that it has to do with stimulus–response translation (for recent overviews, see Meyer and Kieras, 1997; Pashler, 1994). In particular, it has been claimed that humans are unable to apply more than one stimulus–response rule at a time, so that applying the rules of a secondary task needs to await the completion of the primary task (e.g., McCann and Johnston, 1992; Pashler, 1994; Welford, 1952). If this were so, it implied that stimulus–response translation—that is, the application of stimulus–response rules—draws on cognitive resources. If so, the prepared-reflex metaphor would be seriously misled, because it rests on the idea that once a rule is implemented in the cognitive system, its application is entirely stimulus-driven and, hence, effortless.

Interestingly, recent studies have challenged the belief that the PRP effect reflects a problem with stimulus–response translation. In fact, there is increasing evidence that stimulus–response translation is fully automatic (once the rules are implemented), thus lending credit to the prepared-reflex metaphor. The basic logic underlying these studies is shown in Figure 2.7. For instance, in Hommel's (1998b) experiments, subjects performed two tasks in a row: a manual response to the color of a visual stimulus followed by a vocal color-word response to the shape of that stimulus. That is, if a red H appeared, subjects would press a left key and then say "red," if a green H appeared they would press a right key and then say "red," and so forth. Note that the colors red and green are involved here as both stimulus colors of the primary stimulus (i.e., stimulus for Task 1) and meanings of the secondary response (i.e., the response in Task 2), but that secondary responses were associated with stimulus *shape*, not stimulus *color*! Hence, subjects were *not* to name the color of the stimulus.

Now, consider that the secondary stimulus would be translated into the secondary response only after the primary response is selected, as the claim of a stimulus–response translation bottleneck implies. Then the primary task should not be affected by the identity of the secondary response—that is, by whether this response is compatible or incompatible with the color of the primary stimulus. However, if both sets of task rules were applied concurrently, as the prepared-reflex account predicts, one might expect the processing of the colors in the primary task to be affected by the meaning of the secondary response, as indicated by the dotted lines in Figure 2.7. Indeed, it turned out that responses to red stimuli in the primary task were faster

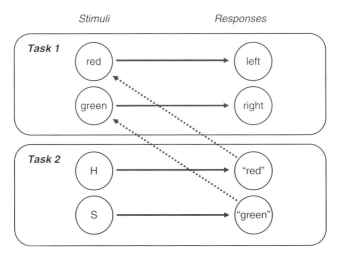

Figure 2.7. Sketch of the dual-task design employed by Hommel (1998b) and Hommel and Eglau (2002). Subjects first perform a manual left–right keypress response to the color of the stimulus, followed by a vocal color-word response to the shape of the stimulus (i.e., the letter). Note that with some combinations the secondary response feature overlaps with the primary stimulus.

if the secondary response was "red" rather than "green," and the opposite was true for green stimuli (Hommel, 1998b). More recent studies (Logan and Delheimer, 2001; Logan and Schulkind, 2000) replicated and extended these findings in a variety of tasks, suggesting that more than one stimulus can be translated into an instructed response at a time.

Even more direct evidence for the effortlessness of stimulus–response translation has been gathered by Hommel and Eglau (2002). In one experiment they had subjects perform the above-described dual task of Hommel (1998b) in the context of a third task that was considered to draw on working-memory capacity. Before being presented with the red or green Hs or Ss, subjects memorized the order of a randomly assembled string of two (low load) or eight (high load) digits, which they would try to recall at the end of the trial. Yet, the effect of the secondary response on the processing of the primary stimulus was virtually identical in the two load conditions, suggesting that stimulus–response translation does not depend on working memory. In another experiment of the Hommel and Eglau study, subjects performed Hommel's (1998b) dual task for half a session before being asked to drop the secondary, vocal task and to proceed with the manual part of the task only. Interestingly, the compatibility between the (no longer performed) secondary response and the primary (and now only relevant) stimulus continued to matter, and it did so until the end of the session. Apparently, then, stopping to carry out the secondary task did not prevent subjects from translating the no longer relevant secondary-task stimulus into the no longer emitted secondary-task response—a particularly strong demonstration of the automaticity of implemented stimulus–response rules.

2.4.3. Delegating Control to Sensorimotor Loops

Planning is a double-edged sword. On the positive side, it makes creative use of anticipations, expectations, and future possibilities and thereby strongly enhances the temporal operation space of purposeful action. On the negative side, however, planning an action strongly relies on the accuracy of those predictions of future events and, thus, is likely to fail if some of them turn out to be invalid. The latter may be less of a problem in typical laboratory situations, where the tasks are often simple and well-defined, stimuli and responses are few, and distraction is absent. However, these characteristics do commonly not apply to everyday situations, which makes them much harder to predict. Accordingly, it would seem to be an optimal strategy to plan as much as necessary to reach an intended goal—but no more. Indeed, not all parameters of an action are relevant for its success: If one intends to take a sip of juice, it does not matter exactly how the glass is grasped and moved toward the mouth—if one only gets that drink. Action plans could therefore afford to be incomplete in specifying only what is important for reaching the intended goal and what can reliably be predicted before the limbs begin to move. Accordingly, several authors have argued on both theoretical and empirical grounds that action planning underspecifies the intended action and leaves open "slots" to be filled by on-line sensory information (Jeannerod, 1984; Schmidt, 1975; Turvey, 1977).

Indeed, the available evidence suggests that the planning process is restricted to the molar aspects of the action. For instance, Prablanc and Pélisson (1990) asked subjects to move their hands to a goal position that was indicated by a light. In some trials the goal light was shifted by about 2–4 cm after the movement began. Cleverly, the shift was carried out while subjects moved their eyes, so that they were entirely unaware of it. Nevertheless, the hand almost always moved to the new goal location, and it did so without any hesitation or signs of correction in the speed or acceleration profiles. That is, the action plan was adapted to the changed situation in the absence of any conscious awareness that a change was taking place (cf. Bridgeman et al., 1979; Goodale, Pélisson, and Prablanc, 1986). The molar, goal-relevant aspects of the action (i.e., moving the hand to the light) were apparently included in the plan while the more incidental features (i.e., the exact movement path) were not.

Based on these and other empirical observations, Milner and Goodale (1995) have proposed a neurocognitive model of visuo-motor manual action, in which off- and on-line channels of information processing are considered. In their model, on-line sensorimotor processing proceeds along the dorsal visuo-motor pathway that begins to segregate in the primary visual cortex and then connects to the motor cortex via relay stations in the posterior parietal cortex. This channel is assumed to deliver information about grasp- and reaching-relevant visual information, such as location and size, that directly feeds into systems responsible for hand control. Milner and Goodale claim that information processed along this route is not available to consciousness, which, apart from the double-step studies mentioned above, fits with the observation that patients suffering from form agnosia are able to properly grasp objects they at the same time are unable to identify (Goodale et al., 1991). The other, off-line channel is assumed to run from primary visual areas straight to the infero-temporal cortex—that is, to areas responsible for object recognition. It has access to memory and is accessible by consciousness, and its main function is proposed to be restricted to perception. If this channel is impaired, as in optic ataxia, people may be able to identify an object but at the same time be unable to grasp it properly (Perenin and Vighetto, 1988).

Milner and Goodale's two-pathway model has been widely discussed and in some cases challenged. For instance, the authors assume that manual grasping is not affected by visual illusions (because the former is processed dorsally, the latter ventrally), but such effects do occur under some circumstances (Bruno, 2001; Franz, 2001). Moreover, the model has not much to say about how the two streams interact to produce coherent action, and it seems to underestimate the degree to which they interact (Jackson, 2000). Action planning is ignored altogether (Hommel et al., 2001b), so that the model seems to attribute most of the action control to the stimulus. However, taken more generally, Milner and Goodale's distinction between a memory-less on-line channel that provides ongoing actions with the most up-to-date sensory information and a memory-based off-line channel that is more sensitive to the thoughts and intentions of the individual is in good agreement with, and provides a useful summary of, the data available so far (Hommel et al., 2001b; Rossetti and Pisella, 2002). This leaves us with a picture along the lines of

Figure 2.8, which sketches the complementary functions of an off-line perception–action pathway setting up general plans for goal-directed action and an on-line sensorimotor channel filling in the slots left open by the planning process.

Taken together, there is increasing evidence suggesting that planning an action leads to the implementation of direct stimulus–response associations and of the delegation of some aspects of control to lower-level sensorimotor systems. Although the implementation of such routines is undoubtly an intentional and presumably attention-demanding process, the implemented processes seem to live pretty much their own life. Thus, planning results in a kind of self-automatization in the sense that the trigger conditions defined in the plan automatically call up the action elements needed to deal with the situational constraints at hand—sometimes even outside the actor's awareness.

2.5. UPSIDES AND DOWNSIDES OF HOW WE PLAN OUR ACTIONS

According to the findings and arguments discussed thus far, human action planning takes place in terms of the perceivable effects of the planned action, the plans emerging from the planning process are integrated assemblies of action-feature codes and trigger information, and the function these plans have consists in some sort of self-automatization of the acting individual. Why does it work like this? Why, for instance, has human evolution provided us with distributed representations of action plans, rather than, say, ordered lists of symbol strings as used by the computer this chapter was prepared with? What sense does it make to first create a binding problem and then solve it by a relatively complicated neural mechanism? Although any attempt to address these questions is obviously speculative, it makes sense to briefly compare the benefits and the disadvantages of action planning and the way it seems to work in humans.

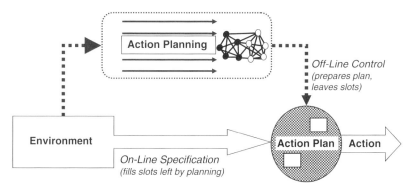

Figure 2.8. The interaction of sensorimotor processing and action planning. Action plans are worked out off-line and then, after completion, specified by on-line sensorimotor processing.

2.5.1. Effect-Based Planning

Planning an action in terms of its expected effects has a number of apparent draw-backs. Perhaps the most obvious drawback is that it leaves the actual realization of the action underspecified: For instance, planning to grasp a visible cup of coffee in terms of effects is likely to include information about the location of the cup while at the same time failing to fully specify the hand to be used, the kinematics of its move-ment, and the time–force function of the final grasp. Because some effector has to move eventually, to travel a particular path, and to exert a particular force on the cup, the question is where this information is coming from.

However, once we take into consideration the planning individual, her learning history, the structural constraints her body imposes, and the situational context she is acting in, it becomes clear that there is an abundance of information available. For instance, people are commonly right- or left-handed, which implies that hand selection is usually determined by hand preference. The visible object and its spatial relation to one's body and hand provide further constraints for kinematic-related choices, while the cup's shape specifies the kinematics of the grasp (e.g., Jeannerod, 1997). The exerted force may be determined by (a) stored knowledge about the cup's stability and weight or (b) visually derived estimations of these parameters, or it may be controlled by tactile information that is generated by touching the cup. Because the information available from on-line vision and tactile channels is lawfully related to muscle movements, there is every reason to leave the control of the action's motor parameters to these channels. The action plan proper thus can afford to focus on what is relevant, namely, the goal of the action and the effects it is intended to produce.

An obvious virtue of this strategy is to open up the temporal horizon for planning. The less detailed a plan is, the less its execution will suffer from inaccurate predic-tions, simply because less had to be predicted when creating it. In other words, the strategy to restrict action planning to the general level and to delegate the control of action details to the current situational constraints allows humans (and, presumably, some infrahuman species as well) to develop action plans that are much more flex-ible and resistant to situational changes than a more detailed planning would.

Another advantage of effect-based action planning is that it facilitates transfer. For instance, consider the ability of people to write their signature not only with their preferred hand, but also with the other hand, their feet, and even their mouth (Raibert, 1977). Although this ability, as well as the quality of the signature, no doubt improve with practice, the transfer from one effector to another takes surpris-ingly little time. This would not be possible if the underlying action plan would entirely consist of low-level, muscle-specific routines. Rather, the plan seems to be in terms of size-scalable spatial relations of the to-be-produced action effect, so that it can be used to control different effectors. Effect-based planning also allows the transfer of action between people—that is, learning by imitation. Indeed, recent research has revealed strong links between action perception and action planning (see Bekkering and Wohlschläger, 2002, for an overview), and some authors have speculated that the above-mentioned mirror neurons may represent the physiological substrate of this link (see Rizzolatti, Fogassi, and Gallese, 2001).

2.5.2. Distributed Planning

Action plans are represented in an anatomically and functionally distributed fashion. This calls for binding mechanisms—that is, mechanisms that integrate the distributed elements of an action plan into a coherent structure, namely, the action plan. Obviously, distributed representations create considerable processing problems and computational costs. Apart from inviting erroneous bindings, a major drawback of the requirement to integrate action features before carrying out the corresponding action is that this may be responsible for the type of dual-task costs discussed earlier: To make sure that only the relevant codes are bound to a given action plan, it seems necessary to temporally block or suppress other codes, which implies that only one action can be planned at a time (Jolicœur et al., 2002; Stoet and Hommel, 1999). Moreover, maintaining an action plan may create crosstalk effects such as evident from the above-mentioned code-occupation phenomena. In view of all these problems, it is reasonable to ask what the advantages of distributed representations might be.

One advantage becomes obvious when considering the phylogenetic development of man or other animals making use of distributed representations. In the course of this development, there must have been gross changes with respect to the anatomical and functional potential to perform actions: The body posture changed to upright, hands and feet changed in structure and flexibility, and vocal abilities emerged and developed. These developments considerably enlarged the action repertoire and, thus, increased the number and types of brain codes representing and controlling all those actions and their characteristics. Instead of restructuring the action-related parts of the brain every time new action features became available, the strategy to code those features in a distributed fashion must have facilitated this task enormously.

On an ontogenetic scale, distributed representations reduce the impact of brain lesions produced by injuries, illness, or genetic defects, because at least smaller lesions are unlikely to eliminate an entire class of actions (cf. Bach-y-Rita, 1990; Evarts, 1980). A further, more functional advantage of distributed action plans is that they facilitate adapting and modifying them. For instance, people are able to specify and program some features of an action before all of its features are known (Rosenbaum, 1980) and modify particular parameters without replanning the whole action (Rosenbaum and Kornblum, 1982).

All taken together, the difficulties that distributed representations create seem to be outweighed by the opportunities they provide. Moreover, there are reasons to think that some of the difficulties can be overcome by practice. Assume that particular feature codes are integrated into the same plan over and over again. Would that not suggest to create some more enduring memory trace that can be retrieved as a whole? Systematic studies of the transition from integration to retrieval are still lacking, but there is some evidence that supports a retrieval-based consideration. For instance, even though combining two tasks is known to produce considerable costs in performance, recent studies have indicated that having highly motivated subjects practice the tasks for an extended period of time can actually eliminate those costs (Schumacher et al., 2001). This might suggest that relying on stored "bindings"—hence, retrieving already integrated action plans—is a way to circumvent time-consuming on-line integration processes.

2.5.3. Delegating Control

We have seen that the human brain delegates control to lower-level sensorimotor routines and to the environment in a number of ways. This has obvious advantages by (i) restricting the computationally expensive planning phase proper to one brief period in time, thereby minimizing interference with other ongoing processes; (ii) confining the plan to relevant aspects, thereby minimizing its extent and complexity; (iii) automatizing the detection of trigger conditions, thereby minimizing cognitive load; and (iv) maximizing the plan's sensitivity to the environmental conditions on execution, thereby minimizing errors due to inaccurate predictions. However, these advantages come with a cost.

Indeed, even though plans can automatize a number of processes, they can only do so if they are properly maintained. Maintenance, however, does seem to require capacity. For instance, de Jong (2000) argues that switching to a new task presupposes a sufficiently high activation of the corresponding intention or action goal, and he discusses evidence suggesting that if performance on a new task is worse, the less likely the action goal had been activated in advance. Altmann (2002) shows that even performance within a particular task gets worse from trial to trial, and he attributes this effect to goal forgetting. The ability to maintain action goals depends on the integrity of the frontal lobe of the human brain, as evident from the frequent observation of "goal neglect" in patients suffering from frontal lesions (Duncan et al., 1996). This might explain why aging, which is known to affect the frontal lobes in particular, impairs the ability to switch between tasks (Kray and Lindenberger, 2000) and to recall that a planned action is to be carried out—at least if environmental support is limited (Maylor, 1996). Even age-independent individual differences modulate goal maintenance, as indicated by the strong (negative) correlations between IQ and goal forgetting obtained by Duncan et al. (1996). In other words, what appears to us as intelligent behavior may reflect to a large degree the ability to actively maintain one's action goals.

2.6. CONCLUSIONS

The purpose of this chapter was to characterize action planning from a cognitive and cognitive neuroscience point of view and, hence, from a level of analysis laying at the most molecular end of the range represented in this book. Accordingly, the type of actions investigated in the studies reported and discussed are often rather simple and artificial, and many would tend to call them mere movement or reaction rather than true voluntary action. Nevertheless, it was my intention to show that even these, however undemanding, acts share central, defining characteristics with the most complex expressions of human behavior. In particular, even the most primitive behavioral acts can be shown to be prospectively controlled by cognitively represented goals. Not only are their features assembled in a way to reach the intended behavioral outcome, the feature codes themselves are meaningful, behaviorally grounded representations of anticipated future action effects. To become a functioning and "maintainable" action plan, these codes need to be integrated and linked to the stimulus conditions that ought to trigger the action later on. Code integration has negative effects, such as difficulties to code similar perceptual events or action plans, but the host of the effects is positive. In particular, creating a plan is associated with (a) the implementation of stimulus–response rules and sensorimotor routines and (b) sensitizing the cognitive system for the detection of appropriate action conditions. In a sense, action planning is like arming the cognitive system to behave like a reflex machinery. All these characteristics are shared by more complex behavioral acts, which supports the idea of a continuum between "true" action and apparent reaction (Hommel et al., 2001a; Prinz, 1997). After all, what counts for acting humans is the satisfaction provided by reaching relevant goals, not the number and size of muscles employed to reach them.

AUTHOR NOTES

Correspondence concerning this chapter should be addressed to Bernhard Hommel, Leiden University, Cognitive Psychology Unit, P.O. Box 9555, 2300 RB Leiden, The Netherlands; Hommel@fsw.LeidenUniv.nl.

INTRODUCTION TO CHAPTER 3

Where Hommel investigates cognitive neuropsychological aspects of planning at the millisecond level, Hoc analyzes planning from a functional cognitive perspective and with a more than 5-seconds time horizon. As with Hommel, Hoc deals with humans that plan for themselves (however, in operator and controller settings), but the differences are that planning in this chapter is a conscious activity rather than a programmed (unconscious) stimulus–response action. This uses other information processing mechanisms and other architectural components. Still, the functions are physiologically embedded, as is shown by the famous case of Phineas Gage, a foreman that had a tragic accident:

> It appears from his own account, and that of the bystanders, that he was engaged in charging a hole, preparatory to blasting. He had turned in the powder, and was in the act of tamping it slightly before pouring on the sand. He had struck the powder, and while about to strike it again, turned his head to look after his men (who were working within a few feet of him), when the tamping iron came in contact with the rock, and the powder exploded, driving the iron against the left side of the face, immediately anterior to the angle of the inferior maxillary bone. Taking a direction upward and backward toward the median line, it penetrated the integuments, the masseter and temporal muscles, passed under the zygomatic arch, and (probably) fractured the temporal portion of the sphenoid bone and the floor of the orbit of the left eye, entered the cranium, passing through the anterior left lobe of the cerebrum, and made its exit in the median line, at the junction of the coronal and sagittal sutures, lacerating the

Planning in Intelligent Systems: Aspects, Motivations, and Methods, Edited by Wout van Wezel, René Jorna, and Alexander Meystel
Copyright © 2006 John Wiley & Sons, Inc.

longitudinal sinus, fracturing the parietal and frontal bones extensively, breaking up considerable portions of brain, and protruding the globe of the left eye from its socket, by nearly one half its diameter. (Harlow, 1848; cited by Neylan, 1999)

The significance of the case of Gage—who survived the horrible accident—is that it contributed to the debate in neurology at the time (Barker, 1995). The recovery of Gage seemed to contradict the then emerging theories of cerebral localization which state that cognitive functions are localized in certain parts of the brain. Gage's consequential change in behavior seemed in favor of the localization hypothesis:

His contractors, who regarded him as the most efficient and capable foreman in their employ previous to his injury, considered the change in his mind so marked that they could not give him his place again. He is fitful, irreverent, indulging at times in the grossest profanity (which was not previously his custom), manifesting but little deference for his fellows, impatient of restraint or advice when it conflicts with his desires, at times pertinaciously obstinate, yet capricious and vacillating, *devising many plans of future operation, which are no sooner arranged than they are abandoned in turn for others appearing more feasible.* In this regard, his mind was radically changed, so decidedly that his friends and acquaintances said he was "no longer Gage." (Harlow, 1868; cited by Neylan, 1999; emphasis added)

Sadly bud interestingly, Gage had trouble making and executing plans after suffering brain damage. Compared to the cognitive neuropsychological domain discussed by Hommel, the planning horizon in the kind of planning that Hoc discusses is longer (measured in seconds) and the time lapse between planning and execution is larger. Therefore, other research methods can be used to analyze such planning processes. In the following chapter, this kind of planning is analyzed from a functional cognitive perspective rather than a physiological one. Within the broad area of cognitive aspects of planning, Hoc focuses on dynamic supervisory control tasks like, among others, air traffic control and anesthesiology.

In dynamic supervisory control tasks, the planning phase cannot always be clearly separated from the action phase. Planning is one of the ways to keep the situation under control. As Hoc argues, this involves cognitive activities in tasks such as diagnosis, prognosis, decision making, and decision evaluation. In the tasks that Hoc has analyzed, these activities are integrated in tight loops with plan implementation, because the human can only partly control the situation and reaction times are very short. Hoc especially examines abstraction and anticipation as mechanisms that humans use in the different phases of planning in dynamic control (for example, preplanning, planning in real time, adjusting plans, and replanning).

Looking at both Hommel's and Hoc's chapters, a hierarchy in the human planning process appears. The outcome of Hoc's planning is the specification of an activity. Such an activity can consist of multiple actions that all need to be planned individually. Both kinds of planning can be compared, which will be done in the concluding chapter. Next to the differences and similarities, however, it is perhaps even more interesting how the one can become the other. As a result of learning, phase transitions can occur where a deliberate cognitive planning activity transcends into a neurocognitive stimulus–response action. An analysis of the conditions under which such a transition can occur, and the way in which our brain can decide in a split second to block the response and make a deliberation again, can be worthwhile for other kinds of planning such as in robotics and organizational planning.

3

PLANNING IN DYNAMIC SITUATIONS: SOME FINDINGS IN COMPLEX SUPERVISORY CONTROL

JEAN-MICHEL HOC

Centre National de la Recherche Scientifique et Université de Nantes, F-44321 Nantes, France

3.1. INTRODUCTION

Planning is the main feature of a number of work situations, such as computer programming, scheduling in discrete manufacturing, system designing, and so on. In these situations, plan generation is the main goal of the work activity. Separate workers can perform plan implementation. These pure planning activities have been studied in depth, either in laboratory situations (analyzing the resolution of "toy" problems like Tower of Hanoi) or in field studies. They have resulted in planning theories reviewed, for example, by Hoc (1988). The present review stresses the fact that planning, as a cognitive activity, implies not only generating action plans (action anticipation) or anticipation of changes in the environment, but also abstract representations (abstraction) capable of guiding activity during execution. Activity goes largely beyond the concrete action on the environment. It also concerns covert cognitive behaviors, such as diagnosis, prognosis, decision making, decision evaluation, and so on. For example, representational structures like syndromes (relating a variety of symptoms, as well as introducing causal structures) can guide diagnosis without being action plans, properly speaking.

Planning in Intelligent Systems: Aspects, Motivations, and Methods, Edited by Wout van Wezel, René Jorna, and Alexander Meystel

Planning does not always imply a clear-cut distinction between plan generation and plan implementation. It is especially the case in dynamic situation management, such as industrial process control, transportation, and medicine (anesthesiology), which are considered in this chapter. In such situations, the human operator does not fully control the environment and is submitted to temporal constraints. This chapter will show that well-known findings collected in static situations (fully controlled by the operator) remain valid in dynamic situations, but that the latter changes the status of planning in the activity. In fact, planning is no longer an end in itself, but rather a means to reach the supervision and control goals. For a computer programmer, planning as elaborating programs (and using old plans as well) is the main goal of the activity. For a fighter aircraft pilot, planning is a resource more than a goal, the main goal being satisfying the main constraints of the mission. Sometimes, using routinized procedures is preferable to trying to elaborate sophisticated plans, either because the time constraints are not compatible with a successful elaboration or because routines are sufficient to deal with the situation. From a psychological or sociological point of view, planning theories have been criticized by Suchman (1987). She supported "situated cognition" and did not consider these theories of great relevance to understand human cognition, which does not require planning most of the time but instead requires routines. The observer of a "natural" activity must be cautious when classifying a behavior as "planful." The plan may be more in the observer's head than in the observed individual's head.

After briefly delineating a psychological and theoretical approach to planning, based on personal work (Hoc, 1988), the main results of several studies relevant to planning within this theoretical framework will be summed up stressing the main characteristics of planning strategies in supervisory control. The principal goal of these studies, done after the elaboration of our planning framework, was not planning in itself and the issues do not cover it entirely. They stressed the relationships between planning and many other activity aspects, like adaptation, activity guidance by abstract representation, human–human and human–machine cooperation, reactive strategies, and meta-knowledge. Most of the studies referred to were conducted in close multidisciplinarity between psychologists and supervisory control researchers. Thus, implications on design will be delineated. The aim of this chapter is not a complete review of such studies, but the presentation of the main theoretical aspects of the domain relevant to planning, selecting some empirical work for illustration purpose.

Section 3.2 will introduce a general conception of planning, derived from the main literature on this question in problem solving. Two intermingled aspects of planning will be stressed: abstraction (a plan does not include all the details needed for its implementation) and anticipation (a plan always integrates a projection in the future). Since this chapter is devoted to planning in dynamic situations, as opposed to static ones, Section 3.3 will summarize the main cognitive features of this category of situations. Section 3.4 will derive implications of these cognitive properties on the development of planning in supervisory control. Section 3.5 will specify the types of occurrence of planning in the studies that will be referred to in the rest of the chapter. Sections 3.6 and 3.7 will present the main results of the studies with regard to abstraction and anticipation in planning, with some implications in terms of operator's assistance and training.

3.2. A GENERAL CONCEPTION OF PLANNING

In the present context, planning is considered from a psychological point of view (the author's) and integrates various types of "meta" activity capable of guiding concrete activity. This concept is adopted as a super-ordinate notion covering a large range of activities—for example, programming, scheduling, designing, organizing, orientating oneself in space, writing, diagnosing, and so on. Cognitive psychology of planning is supposed to pick the common psychological mechanisms brought into play within this large class of activities. However, the approach presented here has been also influenced by research in artificial intelligence. Its main source is the study of cognition in problem-solving situations—that is, those where the problem solver has a representation of a task without being able to immediately trigger an appropriate and well-known procedure to perform it (Hoc, 1988). However, one can resolve a problem without elaborating any plan— for example, making each action choice on a very local basis.

3.2.1. Sources

3.2.1.1. The Notion of Abstraction Space. Although cognitive psychological or artificial intelligence studies of planning have mainly been restricted to action plan elaboration (anticipation), the concept of abstraction space has been introduced very early (e.g., Newell and Simon, 1972; Sacerdoti, 1977). In the beginning (Newell and Simon), the top-down conception of planning was very rigid. The plan was elaborated in a planning (abstract) space and then detailed in a basic (execution) space. In case of failure, the whole work was performed anew, from scratch. Postponing the introduction of constraints on the order of execution from one abstraction space to another was a way to reduce the opportunity for planning errors (Sacerdoti). From that time, some progress has been made to introduce a bottom-up component, so that some approximation of feedback at the execution level is considered when working in abstract spaces. However, the notion of abstraction has never been abandoned later.

An action plan is never a precise description of action specifications. Instantiation is necessary and very often automatic—that is, governed by subsymbolic processes without needing attention at the symbolic level (the level of interpretation). More recently, Reason (1990) has underlined the underspecification feature of human cognition in his studies of human error. His theory considers that schemata, which are always triggered on the basis of insufficient cues, guide behavior. This underspecification at the same time explains most of the human errors, and the heuristic value of human cognition (workload regulation). These schemata may represent not only actions but also object structures (e.g., mental maps for navigation in car driving or syndromes in medicine). A variety of abstraction levels must be defined to understand human cognition, which can bear on the global analysis of a situation that can be sufficient to trigger detailed schemata.

3.2.1.2. Opportunistic Planning. After a series of planning models bearing on a strict top-down direction through the abstraction space to reach an operational plan, the notion of "opportunistic" planning was introduced by Hayes-Roth and Hayes-Roth (1979). In a study of planning shopping in a city, these authors showed that subjects made use of a mixture of top-down and bottom-up components to result in a plan. This more flexible conception of planning is also shared by the situated cognition research community (Suchman, 1987) and the naturalistic decision-making community (NDM; Klein et al., 1993).

Some authors working within the situated cognition research trend (in ethnomethodology) start from the hypothesis that humans do not plan, but respond to, affordances from their environment. The concept of affordance has been introduced by Gibson (1986) in his "ecological" theory of visual perception, which stressed the fact that stimulus features relevant to action are automatically filtered in relation to the context and action goals. For example, a stone is seen as a weapon to fight an enemy, but also as a seat to rest after the battle. Many of the supporters of situated cognition refer to Suchman's description of a native navigator who does not plan, but lets circumstances guide, the trajectory. Probably the navigator is not discovering America, but is following well-known coasts and developing a routine activity. However, this activity could be, at the same time, governed by affordances and by internal plans. The ambiguity comes from the symbolic or subsymbolic character of the plan. Symbolic representations have two facets—a signifier and a signified—and are usually accessible to verbal reports. Subsymbolic representations, within automated activities, have only one (perceptual) facet and are not accessible to verbal reports easily, but can play a major role in activity control (e.g., motor programs). However, Suchman does not deny the role of plans as something in the actor's head that governs the actor's behavior. Although a wider conception of planning—that is, integrating symbolic (explicit) and subsymbolic (implicit) plans—could be of great value, this chapter will focus on symbolic plans.

However, the approach developed in this chapter is very close to that of Klein, the leader of the "Naturalistic Decision-Making" community (Klein et al., 1993). Following this approach, expertise consists more in situation assessment (orienting toward well-known plans) than in more powerful reasoning processes (plan elaboration). Such an approach does not restrict planning processes to plan generation, but integrates situation assessment that can be produced at diverse levels of abstraction to trigger more or less abstract plans. Certainly the type of situation under study—dynamic situations governed by time constraints—is the main reason for such a stress on plan triggering and adjustment instead of plan elaboration that is more often observed in static situations like computer programming, workshop scheduling, and so on.

Excessive positions should be avoided. Obviously, every human activity is not planful in the sense of a deliberate elaboration of a symbolic plan. However, the symbolic use of a pre-built plan can play an important role in guiding activity. Plan use is part of planning activity. The notion of "opportunistic" planning stresses the fact that, in everyday life, a plan should be considered as a resource (among others) for action, and not as an end. In addition, it draws attention to the interaction between several abstraction spaces in plan elaboration and execution.

3.2.2. Planning as Abstracting and Anticipating to Guide Activity

Following Suchman (1987), the present approach to representation and planning stresses that a plan should not be considered as what is actually executed, but as what guides the activity at a certain level (Hoc, 1988). Plans can be purely declarative (such as book contents that guide writing or reading, without imposing a writing or reading order), and they can also be functional (describing an organization of functions, rather than a procedure—for example, the structure of a software menu on a computer display) or, indeed, procedural. Extending the notion of plan beyond the strict action plan [the usual conception defended by a number of authors like Jorna and van Wezel (2002) for example] enables the researcher to integrate representations that guides action organization, without being action structures. Moreover, planning integrates the use of pre-built plans stored in memory at various abstraction levels or/and elaborating new plans (often from old plans). Planning is composed of two related ingredients: abstraction and anticipation.

In industrial settings, Rasmussen [see Rasmussen, Pejtersen, and Goodstein (1994) for a recent account] has devoted some attention to abstraction by using the concept of abstraction hierarchy [means-ends hierarchy or, following Hoc (1988), implementation hierarchy], which enables the human operator (or designer) to reason on the plant or system from functions (or ends) to implementations (or means). For example, the heating function of a washing machine can be described in thermodynamic terms to solve part of a design problem and its electrical implementation in terms of electricity to solve other kinds of problems at the execution or implementation level. Orthogonal to this implementation hierarchy, Rasmussen defined a whole-part hierarchy [refinement hierarchy, following Hoc (1988)] related to the precision of the description. Figure 3.1 sums up this double abstraction space. Any level of any hierarchy (implementation or refinement hierarchy) is a planning space for the less abstract levels. The conception of abstraction referred to in this chapter is consistent with this point of view.

Indeed, planning is also anticipating [see Hoc (1988) and Jorna and van Wezel (2002)]. At the symbolic level, anticipation is elaborating a representation of the future (forecasting). At the subsymbolic level, anticipation can only correspond to the setting up of a preparatory set (implicit expectation). For example, one can be prepared to respond to an event (e.g., a storm, on the basis of a sultry weather) without forecasting explicitly this event in time, space, and strength. The abundant studies using schema theory have stressed the role of schemata in anticipation, whatever the concrete use of them: analogy, transfer, or case-based reasoning.

As shown by Cellier, Eyrolle, and Mariné (1997), expert process operators have more planning ability than beginners because they anticipate more and because they have access to a more global and functional (abstract) representation

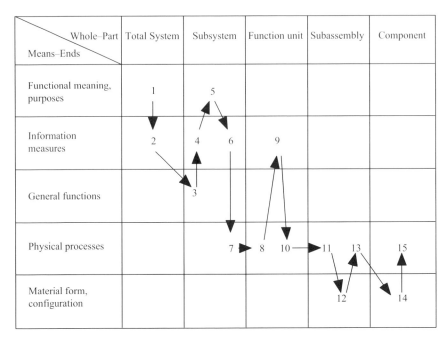

Means–Ends ╲ Whole–Part	Total System	Subsystem	Function unit	Subassembly	Component
Functional meaning, purposes	1	5			
Information measures	2	4 6	9		
General functions		3			
Physical processes		7 ▶ 8	10 ⟶ 11 13		15
Material form, configuration				12	14

Figure 3.1. Rasmussen's ends–means and part–whole hierarchies (after Rasmussen et al., 1994, p. 36). The figure illustrates the trajectory of an engineer through the workspace during computer repair.

of the system. This is consistent with research findings in the domain of physics problem solving. Experts (teachers) spend quite a long time to identify the physical principle forming the main topic of the problem, whereas beginners (students) embark themselves in calculations on the sole basis of surface features (Larkin and Reif, 1979). Although anticipation skill is very often related to abstraction skill, we will examine them successively. In dynamic situations like process control, anticipation is also tightly related to time management. This remains a difficult question that cannot be addressed here [see De Keyser (1995) for a more precise account].

This general conception of planning applies to dynamic situations. However, a more careful account of the cognitive properties of this kind of situation is needed before deriving more specific features of planning, relevant to this domain.

3.3. DYNAMIC SITUATIONS

Among dynamic situations, this chapter is restricted to the supervision and control of continuous processes as opposed to discrete processes such as assembly in manufacturing. Because most of the planning studies have been done on discrete state transformation situations, their results can be applied to manufacturing (e.g., Sanderson, 1991), although other aspects should be considered, like allocation of resources to tasks, delays, and so on (Dessouky, Moray, and Kijowski, 1995; MacCarthy and Wilson, 2001; and most of the chapters in this book). The main difference between discrete and continuous process supervision is probably the type of representation required, mainly (a) transformational for a discrete process and (b) causal or functional for a continuous process (Hoc, Amalberti, and Boreham, 1995). Obviously, topographical representations are needed in the two cases. It is interesting to evaluate the relevance of planning theories in situations where continuous transformations are observed. Although the human operator's actions are often discrete, their effects take place in a continuous way. This implies a change in type of representation from steady state to process trend. More often than not, the goal is not to change the process state, but instead to change the process spontaneous evolution. Three aspects of dynamic situations are considered here: their partial control, the role of process evolution understanding, and the integration of human operators' action plans and technical process' spontaneous evolution into overall plans (human interventions and spontaneous transformations) for controlling the process.

3.3.1. Partial Control

In dynamic situations, the human operators partly control the situation. Their actions are combined with the spontaneous process evolution to result in effects. In addition, even when operators do not act, something continues to change. Sometimes, "do not act" is the result of a deliberate decision, because the spontaneous evolution will reach a desired state by itself. Bainbridge (1978) has often stressed the difference between experts and beginners when controlling dynamic processes with time lags, on the basis of observations in the field. Experts are able to consider inertia and response delays to produce a restricted number of well-calibrated actions at the right time. On the contrary, beginners act wildly on the basis of immediate but irrelevant feedback, as if the process would be fully controlled by their actions. Other authors (Brehmer, 1995; Moray and Rotenberg, 1989) have reproduced this phenomenon in micro-world studies. Thus, partial control requires planning—or at least anticipating—the effects of one's action, the process evolution, and the combination between the two. The triggering of action on the sole basis of the present state in a reactive way is not appropriate.

3.3.2. Understanding the Situation Is Crucial

Since process operators do not fully control the situation, understanding the uncontrolled factors acting on the process and their combination with the human actions is crucial. Such an understanding aims at elaborating, reconsidering, or slightly adjusting a current representation of the situation (Hoc et al., 1995). This current representation is often referred to by the concept of situation awareness (e.g., Endsley,

1995a), which concerns the past, present, and future evolution of the situation. However, this concept is often restricted to the evolution of the technical process, whereas it should integrate the human operator as part of the situation (plans, goals, workload self-evaluation, feeling of mastering the situation, etc.). Two dynamic processes are connected to form the overall human–machine system, and the operator's understanding must integrate the two parts.

Certainly, process controllers manage technical processes (e.g., blast furnace, nuclear power plant, aircraft, etc.), but they also manage themselves, especially when they elaborate plans (e.g., mission planning in aviation). For example, pilots try to avoid situations they know they would not be able to master (Amalberti and Deblon, 1992). In fully controlled situations (static situations), at least at an expert level, human operators can easily integrate the knowledge on the technical process into the knowledge of their plans, goals, and actions. The reason is that static situations do not evolve spontaneously, without intervention from the operator. Static situations can only evolve under the operator's control, and situation states are easily translated into the human operator's plans, goals, and actions. On the contrary, in dynamic situations, these two types of knowledge are less easy to integrate since something may always happen in the process without any action from the operator (Bainbridge, 1988). In a dynamic micro-world reproducing some features of anesthesiology in the operating room, with non-expert subjects, van Daele and Carpinelli (1996) have illustrated this integration difficulty. Anticipation of the direct effects of subjects' actions has been shown to be easier than anticipation of the process evolution without action or easier than anticipation of indirect effects of the action (linked to interaction with the process dynamics).

3.3.3. Plan Integrates Operator's Plan and Process' Plan

What is going on in dynamic situations cannot be understood on the sole basis of the operator's actions. Consequently, meaningful procedural plans necessarily integrate human actions, goals, intentions, and so on, but also the spontaneous process evolution. Moreover, plans do not aim properly at transforming process steady states, but instead aim at transforming process evolution, as can be seen in some AI approaches to planning in dynamic situations (e.g., de Jong, 1994). This integrated view of planning is also true for more declarative plans such as structural or functional ones, which should take the technical process and the operator into account. For example, the trajectory of a ship is determined not only by the watch officer's helm command, but also by wind and stream current strength and direction, by the vessel inertia, and so on. The functional analysis of the system cannot be restricted to the officer's entry and must be extended to the consideration of a larger system. The plan concerns not only the human system but also the overall human–machine system.

The specific features of dynamic situations lead us to pay attention to some particular aspects of planning that will now be specified.

3.4. PLANNING IN DYNAMIC SITUATION MANAGEMENT

Conditions for planning in dynamic situation management will be made more precise, starting from a well-known theoretical framework in this domain [see Rasmussen, Pejtersen, and Goodstein (1994) for a recent account] and, then, enriching it by a more recent approach (Hoc et al., 1995). Following this approach, planning will be presented as taking place within a continuous movement of synchronization and desynchronization between the timing of the process under control and the timing of the cognitive activity. Finally, several activities related to planning will be summed up: pre-planning, planning in real time, adjusting plans, and replanning.

3.4.1. A Revised Version of Rasmussen's Step Ladder

Rasmussen's step ladder has been widely used to describe diagnosis and planning in dynamic situation management [Figure 3.2; see Rasmussen et al. (1994) for a recent account]. However, Hoc et al. (1995) consider that this model is too procedural to

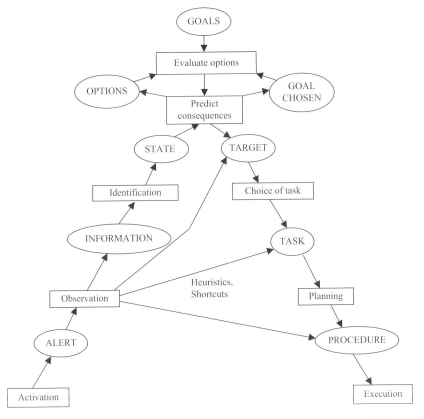

Figure 3.2. Rasmussen's step ladder. [After Rasmussen et al. (1994, p. 65).]

account for every type of dynamic situation. Rather, it should be seen as a particular model of a more general cognitive architecture,[1] only valid when the process is slow and fully understandable at the action time.

The step-ladder model is a procedural and sequential conception of diagnosis and planning cognitive mechanisms. On the left bottom, it starts from detection of an anomaly (activation) that triggers search for further information (observation), identification of the process state (or evolution), evaluation of the consequences on the system goals and integrity, and then task, procedure, and action planning. This architecture can account for activity automatization by shortcuts (e.g., direct links from observation to target, task, or procedure). Although this cognitive model has played a heuristic role in designing or evaluating systems from an ergonomic point of view (prerequisite for elementary activities, sharing of these activities between humans or between humans and machines, etc.), it suffers from several drawbacks. Three of them have been stressed (Bainbridge, 1997; Hoc et al., 1995).

1. If the aim of cognition is adaptation, it is quite surprising that feedback is not considered in Rasmussen's step ladder. Very often, action has a double status: modifying the process evolution and testing a hypothesis on the process current understanding. For example, doctors often prescribe medicines without a precise diagnosis, and the reactions of the patient to them can be a way to reach a more accurate diagnosis. More often than not, there is uncertainty, and hypothesis acceptance is not a straightforward mechanism. Thus, there is a loop between identification of the process evolution (hypotheses) and search for information (observation to test the hypotheses). Moreover, the human is basically an anticipative cognitive system. Some anticipation is explicit (e.g., identification of the process evolution), but to a large extent anticipation can be implicit. When an identification is made or an action is executed, at the same time the human operator is prepared or tuned to a certain course of events without anticipating them explicitly. For example, when entering a motorway, large trailers are automatically identified as trucks with a medium speed and not as agricultural tractor trailers with a slow speed, because of implicit expectation about the type of vehicle running on a motorway. Such an implicit expectation is triggered by the action of entering the motorway without elaborating an explicit and symbolic representation. Thus there should be feedback arrows from the right part of the step ladder to the left part, representing expectations.

2. In this architecture, there is also a lack of top-down or inner determination. The cognitive system is supposed to work on an almost reactive basis, from

---

[1]'Architecture' in this context is taken in a more general meaning than 'model.' A particular model enables the researcher to describe or predict the behavior in a particular situation. An architecture picks the common properties of models within a class of situations. Thus an architecture is less precise than a model, but more general. Our notion of architecture is different from that which is used in computer science.

detection to action. However, in dynamic situations, most of the decisions are made on an anticipation basis, because the objective reasons for action appear very often after the fact. Due to response delays, decisions must be made in advance and on the basis of partial and uncertain information to be efficient. Hence, the current representation of the situation ("state" in Figure 3.2) plays a major role in situation analysis (observation, but also activation).

3. Finally, dynamic situations are mainly characterized by temporal constraints. When human operators diagnose or plan, the technical process is not frozen and continues to evolve. When process speed is high (implying a high monitoring frequency to avoid the risk of losing important events), there can be an incompatibility between the time requirements of careful cognitive processes (e.g., causal and scientific diagnosis) and the time requirements for acting and maintaining the process under control. Rasmussen's step ladder does not account for this phenomenon, because the time dimension is not represented.

Our Dynamic Situation Management architecture (Figure 3.3; DSM: Hoc et al., 1995) gives a crucial role to the current representation of the situation (current representation), which determines the triggering of activity modules similar to those

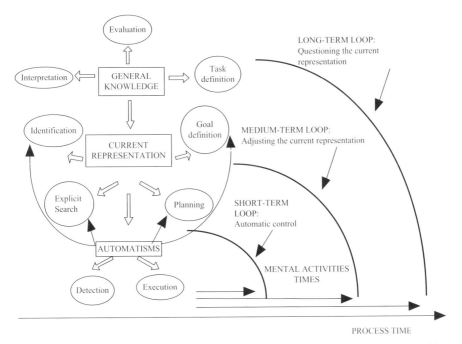

Figure 3.3. Hoc and Amalberti's Dynamic Situation Management (DSM) cognitive architecture. [After Hoc, Amalberti, and Boreham (1995).]

defined by Rasmussen. Thus, there is a shift from determination by a procedure to
control by a mental model of the situation. Such a representation is fed by general
knowledge (knowledge of the process under control and meta-knowledge on one's
own activity), by process information, and by the emergence of subsymbolic entities
into the attentional field (e.g., implicit expectations, represented in Figure 3.3 by
upward arrows). It is especially composed of plans defined at various abstraction
levels. It integrates process information and the operator's resources (such as
meta-knowledge on competency, workload, and so on), goals, and actions.

Basically, this architecture supposes at least three feedback loops.

1. Priority is given to the short-term control of the process, which is mainly controlled by automatized mechanisms, with low requirements in terms of attentional resources. Feedback is obtained within a very short term to enable the
   functioning of this kind of mechanism, which is triggered by the current plan
   at the current representation level (especially by its implicit expectations) and
   by the specific events in the process (in a reactive way). These mechanisms
   are not attentional, but can return information to the current representation on
   the basis of emergence, enabling the human operator to become aware of important but not expected events. More often than not, surprise is a way to access
   symbolic processing. For example, in car driving, trajectory following is usually
   governed by automatisms, with the help of implicit expectation on the form of
   curves. However, when a curve is atypical, the surprise triggers a symbolic control of the trajectory. This mapping of the levels of abstraction (knowledge, current representation, and automatisms) onto the temporal span of the feedback
   loops (short, medium, and long term) is a simplification. Obviously, when the
   short-term control time constraints are moderate, the abstract levels can replace
   automatisms to control the short term. For example, the control of walking can be
   either fully automatized or more symbolic (step by step).

2. At a first level of the current representation, there is a root for a medium-term
   loop of the current plan execution. Feedback for a complex plan cannot be
   attained in the short term. The automatized loop must develop, taking
   the plan for granted before its full validation. However, the current plan can
   be adjusted in the short term, by slight modifications, to adapt to some unexpected circumstances and further determine the automatized loop. Sometimes,
   several (alternative) plans are prepared, and a quick decision to replace one
   plan by another can be made on the basis of situation recognition.

3. It can happen that a third level would be brought into play when the prepared
   plans reveal themselves really inaccurate. In this case, deep replanning that
   bears on general knowledge and careful examination of the situation is necessary. This kind of mechanism takes a long time to develop, feedback will be
   realized on a very long-term basis, and the lower control loops continue to
   develop on the basis of the inaccurate plans since the technical process must
   be maintained under control, although partially satisfying. This replanning
   mechanism must also take into account the events observed in the meantime

before implementing the final plan, because the conditions that have triggered the mechanism may have changed along time. However, the intervention of general knowledge does not always mean that the processes are deliberate. It may happen that strategic knowledge related to personality or training will be brought into play automatically. For example, in anesthesia, Klemola and Norros (1997) have shown the role of this type of knowledge that has been called "habit of action" (Hukki and Norros, 1998).

3.4.2. Synchronizing/Desynchronizing Process' Time and Cognitive Activity's Time

The main feature of this architecture is an account of a possible desynchronization between problem solving (including planning), taking place at high abstraction levels and the immediate control of the process. Dynamic situation management is considered as a succession of episodes. Within some episodes, the plan stored at the level of the current representation is considered as the correct one and directly controls the action on the process. Within some other episodes, there is some misunderstanding. Priority is given to the short-term control, but some slight adjustments of the plan are being processed in parallel and will be performed and implemented in the medium term. Sometimes, in addition, the plan may reveal itself to be completely wrong, and a longer process of transforming the plan is also engaged for the long term. The complexity of the models generated by this architecture is at its maximum when the process is rapid and its predictability is low. In artificial intelligence, Bonissone, Dutta, and Wood (1994) have considered planning in dynamic situations as maintaining a dynamic balance between short-term and long-term planning.

Due to temporal constraints, a balance between time-consuming understanding (necessary to planning) and action to maintain the process under control in the short term must be managed. When planning and action execution are desynchronized, the operator is aware of the fact that the plan that guides the current action is not appropriate. However, the plan is maintained before the successful elaboration and/or retrieval of another one in parallel with the short-term control of the process.

3.4.3. Time Management: Implicit and Explicit Processes

One of the prominent features of dynamic situation management is that the process under control can show various response delays. Unfortunately, the abundant literature in psychology on time management focuses on very short periods of time (e.g., Block, 1990). However, there is an agreement on Michon's theory (1990), which considers two kinds of mental processes in time management. Implicit processes are implied when the situation is well known. Cognitive processes are tuned to the time properties of the environment. Explicit processes using symbolic representations of time are triggered when there is a problem or a communication need. Data collected on blast furnace control are compatible with this view, as will be shown further (Hoc, 1996). It is really difficult to have access to implicit time management. However, Boudes and Tremblay (1994) have shown, in air traffic control and scheduling, that time processing bears largely on pre-built temporal landmarks or Temporal Reference Systems (Javaux, Grosjean, and Van Daele, 1991) of several kinds (technical, social, etc.).

3.4.4. Pre-planning, Planning in Real Time, Adjusting Plans, or Replanning: Adapting to Temporal Constraints

As far as planning is concerned, dynamic situations brings several forms of cognitive activity into play.

1. *Pre-planning*: The elaboration or the choice of a plan before execution. This is likely to occur when the process is very rapid, letting a restricted room to planning or replanning in real time (e.g., fighter aircraft piloting), or when the process is not too slow, with some needs to prepare contingencies to avoid too costly a replanning process (e.g., anesthesia). In the two cases, the plan integrates contingencies that can be very precise to enable the operator to react very quickly.

2. *Planning in Real Time*: This enables the operators to adopt least commitment strategies, from abstract plans, highly valid but too fuzzy to result in an action decision, to precise plans, close to the implementation level, when process information is more abundant and sufficient to justify them. This can be done when the process is slow (e.g., blast furnace control) or not too rapid, but likely to result in unexpected situations (e.g., air-traffic control).

3. *Adjusting Plans*: More often than not, dynamic situations are not fully predictable. Slight modifications of plans are often required.

4. *Replanning*: When the process is slow, deep questioning of the plan resulting in the adoption of a new one can be performed. However, when the process is rapid, it is not possible to replan in real time (e.g., fighter aircraft piloting). One of the main aims of a human factors research program when designing the French fighter aircraft *Rafale* was to introduce "human-like" reasoning into an "intelligent" machine to propose new plans in real time (Amalberti and Deblon, 1992). This opens the questions of acceptability of the proposal by humans and of the well-known complacency phenomenon in aviation [see, for example, the study done by Layton, Smith, and McCoy (1994) on the use of replanning support in commercial aviation]. Human operators should be able to validate the proposal, sometimes very quickly. Thus, the rationale for the proposal should be quickly understandable when the process is rapid. The access to justification or explanation can be longer when the process is slow (e.g., Karsenty, 2000). The complacency phenomenon is related to the operators' workload that can lead them not only to accept a machine's proposal without questioning it, but also to divide the supervision field into two parts: one where the operators act, and the other one where the machine acts.

These diverse forms of planning, at the same time reveal the importance of planning in dynamic situations, and the possible ways to adapt to unexpected circumstances and to temporal constraints. In the Section 3.6, we will stress the need for abstract representations to plan accurately. This implies the acquisition of expertise and the availability of some external support. In Section 3.7, we will argue in favor of the need to establish an appropriate trade-off between reactive and anticipative strategies to cope with the constraints of dynamic situations. With the human operator being integrated into the process to be controlled, we will show that meta-knowledge is as necessary as knowledge on the technical process to anticipate situation evolution. Finally, we will discuss the need for expertise and support to anticipation. To illustrate these points, some research findings collected in experiments or case studies will be presented. At first (Section 3.5), we will summarize the main features (with regard to planning) of the technical processes that will be referred to and the way of access to cognitive activities.

3.5. SITUATIONS UNDER STUDY

This section is devoted to short technical presentations of the dynamic situations from where some properties of planning have been extracted, adopting two viewpoints: abstraction and anticipation. Blast furnace supervision is typical of a very slow process where planning in real time is feasible, except for implementing least commitment strategies in order to deal with uncertainty. Air traffic control is a medium-speed process where precise action planning is more salient and where action plans and problem structures develop in parallel. Fighter aircraft piloting is typical of a very speedy process where planning is done beforehand (mission preparation) and where plans clearly play the role of guides and resources for action. In anesthesiology, plans play the same role as in fighter aircraft piloting, but the activity takes the form of plan retrieval and selection rather than plan elaboration. Crisis management is typical of an open process as opposed to the closed processes in industrial settings where action repertories are prepared beforehand. In crisis management, planning is above all preparing resources (an action repertory). Finally, with the micro-world NEWFIRE, we have been able to control the process speed and to study the adaptation of planning strategies to the time constraints of the process.

3.5.1. Blast Furnace

Blast furnaces are used in the steel industry to produce iron (with carbon) from ore (with oxygen and diverse minerals) and coke (carbon). A blast furnace is a kind of reactor that uses carbon monoxide to take away oxygen from ore at an appropriate temperature. It looks like a high (20 m) cylinder permanently fed on the top by alternate layers of ore and coke, with hot (1200°C) air being blown and coal powder (fuel) being injected on the bottom. Cast iron and slag (minerals) are regularly emptied on the bottom. Two main phenomena are developing in parallel with very different speeds: the rapid ascent of gas (especially carbon monoxide) that takes a few seconds and the very slow charge descent that takes several hours (Figure 3.4).

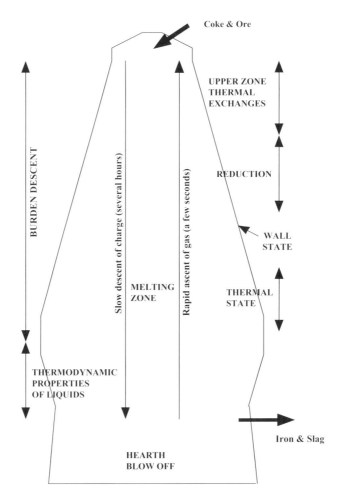

Figure 3.4. Functional and structural representation of a blast furnace.

With regard to the main phenomenon (transformation of ore into iron), the process is very slow (several hours). However, some subphenomena can be quicker (from some minutes to one hour). Planning in real time is possible, including least commitment strategies. Control is indirect: Few actions are available on peripheral parameters such as air blast flow, composition of the charge, casting frequency, and so on. The process is not directly accessible. For example, the quality of the reduction process is evaluated by the means of a mathematical model based on the analysis of gas. Accessible parameters are peripheral, such as temperatures and pressures near the walls of the cylinder, analysis of the cast iron, and so on. Cast iron temperature is a crucial parameter, but the process control feedback loop cannot be only based on this parameter, which reflects past phenomena inside the blast furnace and not the current phenomena. Hence, anticipative strategies are absolutely necessary.

The variety of possible actions on the process is very limited. The action plans can be more or less abstract (e.g., increase the thermal state or add 5 kg of coke per ore tons). They are not very complex, although most of the time they integrate short-term symptom correction (e.g., increase the air blown temperature) and long-term syndrome remediation (e.g., increase the coke proportion into the charge). The complexity of the situation is related to the inference of the process evolution on the basis of the combination of several functions such as thermal exchange in the upper zone, ore reduction, thermal evolution, and so on. The process evolution will be represented at a diverse level of abstraction under the form of a process plan to which the operator's plan will be connected in a timely way to transform it. In this context, planning is not restricted to the management of action plans, but also concerns process evolution plans.

3.5.2. Air Traffic Control

Air traffic control is more accessible to understanding than blast furnace control. Thus, we will comment on the main tools available to the "En Route" controller (managing the traffic crossing a geographical sector as opposed to the scheduling of take-off, approach, and landing close to an airport). Currently, controllers mainly use some kind of "intelligent" radar display (Figure 3.5; each series of

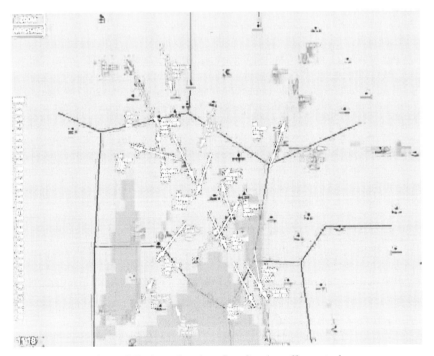

Figure 3.5. A modern interface for air traffic control.

plots followed by a line represents an aircraft, with a graphical representation of its speed and heading; clicking on it gives access to other kinds of information and tools). In parallel, they use a table of "strips," each one giving details on properties of aircraft (especially their routes and their estimated time of crossing beacons). In France, there are two controllers on a workstation: a tactical controller in communication with the aircraft and a strategic controller, assisting the first one and managing coordination with the adjacent sectors.

The controllers organize the strip table as an external memory for the traffic problems (e.g., putting together strips of conflicting aircrafts). The main task is enabling the traffic to meet crossing time, fuel consumption, and safety criteria. Many studies have been devoted to the safety task of resolving conflicts between aircraft—maintaining separation safe when aircraft cross each other. The process is quite slow: The sector crossing time represents several tens of minutes. However, conflict detection and resolution must only take a few minutes. Planning in real time is possible when the workload (e.g., number of conflicting aircraft) is not too high. Control is quite direct since, theoretically, aircraft cannot modify their planned trajectories without controller's instructions (but some factors can be difficult to control, such as wind). Access to process information is direct, especially via radar.

Strips represent flight plans expressed by a succession of beacons with crossing times. Controller's actions consist in changing these plans for a certain aircraft. However, this conception of planning is more relevant to the aircraft than to the controller. The controller's main task is frequently updating a current representation of the traffic organized as a set of almost independent problems, on the basis of aircraft entrance and exit. A problem is composed of conflicting aircrafts (i.e., several aircrafts that will cross under the acceptable separation criterion) and contextual aircrafts (i.e., several aircrafts interfering with possible resolutions). For the controller, an action plan is a succession of instructions (heading, flight level, etc.) to send to (possibly several) aircrafts having problems to resolve it and to reroute the aircrafts toward their destinations. These plans can be represented in an abstract way [e.g., resolution at the same flight level (heading change) or using several levels, turn an aircraft to the left, etc.] or in a very precise way (precise aircraft, heading, level, and time). The updating of the problem space representation is tightly related to planning. For example, a nonconflicting aircraft cannot be considered as belonging to a problem as a contextual aircraft, if the controller has no idea of the plan to be implemented. If the controller wants to turn an aircraft to the left, the contextual aircraft will be on the left side. Conversely, if the plan is to turn to the right, the contextual aircraft will be on the right. In relation to the plan, the problem can be different, and in relation to the problem, the plan can be different. Within this context, plans are not only action plans, but also plans of the traffic (problem spaces) that guide action elaboration and execution, like a blueprint for a builder.

3.5.3. Fighter Aircraft Piloting

Fighter aircraft piloting is typical of a rapid and risky process with large uncertainty. We will focus on a particular mission, namely, destroying (or taking a picture of) a target in enemy territory. The mission takes several tens of minutes at a very high speed (about 1000 kmph) and a very low altitude (about 100 m) needing a close following of the field relief. Entry to and exit from the enemy territory correspond to very thin temporal and geographical windows (a few seconds, due to preventive jamming and the risk to be wrongly destroyed by friends). Mission preparation can take a long time—for example, collecting information on threats. It results in a very precise plan specifying a series of legs between goals defined in time, location, fuel amount, and so on. (Figure 3.6).

Such a plan is not an action plan, properly speaking, since it is not always followed strictly due to threats that force the pilot to leave the plan. However, the plan is precise enough to enable the pilot to return to the plan as soon as possible. In other words, the plan is more than an action plan. It is a succession of acceptable states (navigation goals), defined within tolerance margins, each state ensuring the capability to reach the next one. If the pilot can return to one of these states, there is a high chance to be able to continue the mission from this state. Clearly the plan is a guide (and a resource) for action, but also a tool to evaluate the current state of the mission and its future.

3.5.4. Anesthesia

Anesthesia in the operating room is a good example of quite rapid and risky process control, sharing some similarities with aircraft piloting. In France, there are clearly two steps: (1) a preoperative step where the most efficient plan with regard to the patient is elaborated and (2) a peroperative step, during the operation,

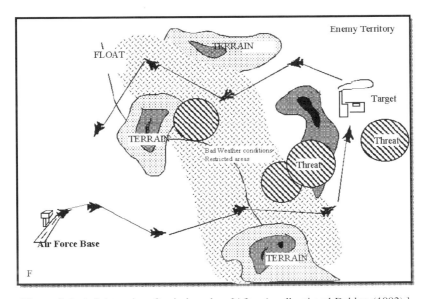

Figure 3.6. A fighter aircraft mission plan. [After Amalberti and Deblon (1992).]

where the plan is implemented and adapted to unexpected circumstances (e.g., the lengthening of the operation). Possible plans are not very numerous, but contingencies and implementation features specific to the patient must be prepared. Plan elaboration is much less frequent than plan retrieval. Plans orient toward the choice of appropriate chemical substances to reduce the pain and maintain the patient in acceptable condition. The plan specifies the doses and the time and condition of administration, in close relationship with the temporal features of the surgeon's plan.

3.5.5. Crisis Management

The main difference between crisis management and the previous dynamic situations is the openness of the process. In the previous situations, the human as well as the machine have predefined responses at their disposal. Facing a catastrophe is, by definition, a situation where predefined responses are not available or, at least, inefficient (e.g., a serious storm or flooding). In these circumstances in France, the administrative authority creates headquarters to design and implement an ORSEC plan (plan of rescue organization). It is impossible to act on the cause of the catastrophe (e.g., one cannot stop a snowstorm or rainstorm). But consequences must be reduced, at the same time for the events (e.g., reduce the consequences of a roof crushing under the snow weight) and for the intervention means (e.g., providing firemen with tracked vehicles to run on the snow). Hence, planning requirement is clear since reactive strategies cannot avoid undesirable events and can be impracticable due to the absence of appropriate resources in time.

Within this context, plans are not strictly action plans, but they mainly specify the resources needed, as well as the time and location where they are needed. For example, in the simple situation of fighting a forest fire, a plan specifies the location and the time where a certain amount of firefighting units must be available to succeed. Before a certain time, it is impossible to have the resources available (transit time) and the fire cannot be extinguished. After the time, the fire extension is too large to be contained by the conceivable resources. The situation is similar to the blast furnace in that the action plan is tightly linked to the possible evolution of the disaster (the possible plan of the disaster).

3.5.6. Micro-world (NEWFIRE)

The micro-world methodology is necessary when one wants to manipulate factors that change the dynamic characteristics of a process, each independently from the others, to enable the researcher to validate hypotheses. In particular, we have utilized a micro-world using the cover story of firefighting [developed by Løvborg and Brehmer (1991)] to manipulate process speed that is likely to play a prominent role in synchronizing/desynchronizing the dynamics of the cognitive activities and of the technical process under control (Figure 3.7).

The cover story of this micro-world is the management of firefighting units (FFUs) in a forest from a basis by a superior officer. This person is supposed to

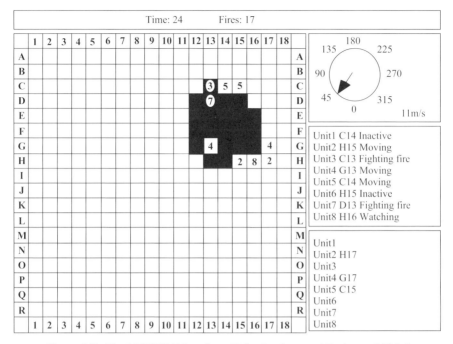

Figure 3.7. The NEWFIRE interface. [After Løvborg and Brehmer (1991).]

receive information from a helicopter about the forest fire extension, as well as about the activity and location of the FFUs (large numbers in Figure 3.7). Information is presented on an interface similar to an array composed of elementary cells representing forest areas. The officer can send instructions to FFUs in terms of target cells to reach (small numbers in Figure 3.7). Then, the FFUs are autonomous [e.g., if a FFU detects a fire in the cell (in black in Figure 3.7), it autonomously decides to fight it and it becomes available to execute a new order of reaching another location when the fire is entirely fought]. The main feature of this "toy" problem is the consideration of the time constraints of this process—time taken by an FFU to reach the target cell and to become operational, time taken by the fire to develop, and so on. The crucial rule to apply is protection instead of extinction. Thus, the best strategy is sending a FFU next to a burning cell instead of inside a burning cell. In the first case, the time to fight the fire just entering the cell will be shorter than the time to fight a cell already burning for a long time. In addition, in the second case, there is a risk to have the burning cell transmitting the fire around while it is being fought. Clearly, this situation is likely to trigger planning strategies by subjects sufficiently trained to acquire a mental model of fire development (under diverse conditions of wind speed and direction) and a model of FFUs moving.

Above all, the software enables the researcher to vary process speed without modifying the models—that is, the other process features. It is easy to find technical processes with large differences in terms of process speed (e.g., blast furnace versus

fighter aircraft). However, comparisons between strategies can be difficult to interpret because of other major differences—for example, in terms of risks (e.g., the risk
of damage on a blast furnace is much less stressing than the risk to be killed in a
fighter aircraft).

In this situation, plans are clearly action plans, specified at diverse levels of
abstraction, from the description of an overall strategy (e.g., stop the fire front in
the wind direction, stop the retro-propagation against the wind) to precise specifications of actions (set of target locations for FFUs). As is the case with blast
furnace or crisis management, the action plan must be synchronized with the fire
evolution plan.

The two last sections of this chapter present the main results of the studies,
relevant to planning, at first with regard to abstraction and then to anticipation,
the two aspects of planning as they have been stressed above. Before entering
these sections, Table 3.1 sums up the more salient features of the situations
referred to. Empty cells do not mean that the feature is absent, but that the
studies cited did not focus on it. Process speed is specified because it is an
important determinant of the planning strategies. Action plan concerns the operator's action planning. In dynamic situations, another aspect of planning must be
considered because the technical process itself is evolving: process plan understanding from both the abstraction and the anticipation viewpoints. Some situations are typical of the need for a conception of the plan as a resource for
action. All the situations introduce time constraints or lead us to deal with time
constants.

3.6. ABSTRACTION

3.6.1. Guiding Situation Understanding by Abstract Representations
(Blast Furnace and Air Traffic Control)

A series of observational and experimental studies have been done on blast furnace
supervision using diverse methods—in any case the analysis of concurrent verbal
reports (simultaneously to task execution), sometimes during the observation of
real work and sometimes in some kind of simulation (reproduction of real period
of functioning, selected on the basis of events of interest to be presented to several
operators). The verbal reports have shown that expert and efficient operators made
use of overall representations of the blast furnace operation, capable of guiding
information gathering and decision making, therefore playing the role of plans. In
other words, observable or calculated parameters, accessible in the control room
on computer displays or paper presentations of a topographical kind (in relation to
the sensors' geographical location), were organized by abstract representations
of covert physical and chemical phenomena, such as upper zone thermal exchanges,
reduction, burden descent, and so on (Figure 3.8). Such descriptors also guided
process controllers to decompose the operation into elementary components
(Hoc and Samurçay, 1992).

TABLE 3.1. Main Features of the Processes

Technical Processes	Process Speed	Action Plan	Process Plan	Plan as a Resource for Action	Time Constraints or Constants
Blast furnace	Very low	Short and abstract, high anticipation, planning in real time	Process plan understanding, abstraction, anticipation		Response lag constant
Air traffic control	Medium	Short, abstract and precise, medium anticipation, planning in real time	Process plan understanding parallel to action plan elaboration, abstraction, anticipation		Aircraft separation time constraint
Fighter aircraft	Very high	Pre-planning, anticipation		Guide for action and for evaluation, abstraction	Very high constraint
Anesthesia	High	Plan retrieval, Plan adaptation		Reference for evaluating the patient specificity, anticipation of routine failures	Synchronization with the surgeon task
Crisis management	Low	Mainly resources preparation	Process plan understanding, abstraction, anticipation		Resources availability in the right time
NEWFIRE	Various	Pre-planning or planning in real time	Process plan understanding, anticipation		Adaptation to time constraints

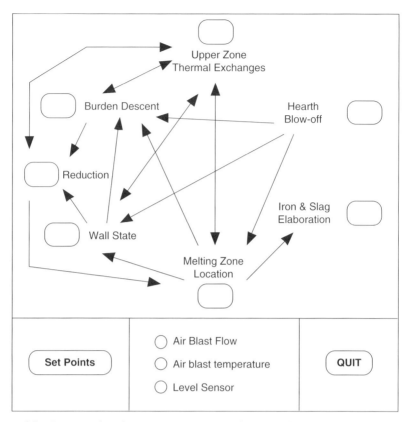

Figure 3.8. Computer interface to access to blast furnace information by the means of descriptors. Some information is directly accessible on the bottom. Circuits in causality are related to the double development of the burden descent and of the ascent of gas. [After Samurçay and Hoc (1996).]

Each descriptor was capable of guiding inductive inference (on the causes), deductive inference (on the consequences), and decision making (Figure 3.9). In addition, the same parameter, in accordance with specific points of view guided by one descriptor or another, could change its status—for example, from a causal determinant to an indicator or an effect. The importance of the descriptors was especially shown by a study of verbal reports by operators on the relations between observable parameters and confirmed by further studies (e.g., Hoc, 1991, 1996). Half of these relations were not expressed directly, but by the means of descriptors. In addition, some parameters were reported as indicators of covert phenomena referred to by these descriptors. For example, there is a causal relation between a sudden increase in wall temperature and a sudden decrease in iron temperature, but the relation is not direct. The wall temperature behavior indicates an unscaffolding [drop in of (cold) material stuck to the wall into the iron] that causes the iron temperature modification.

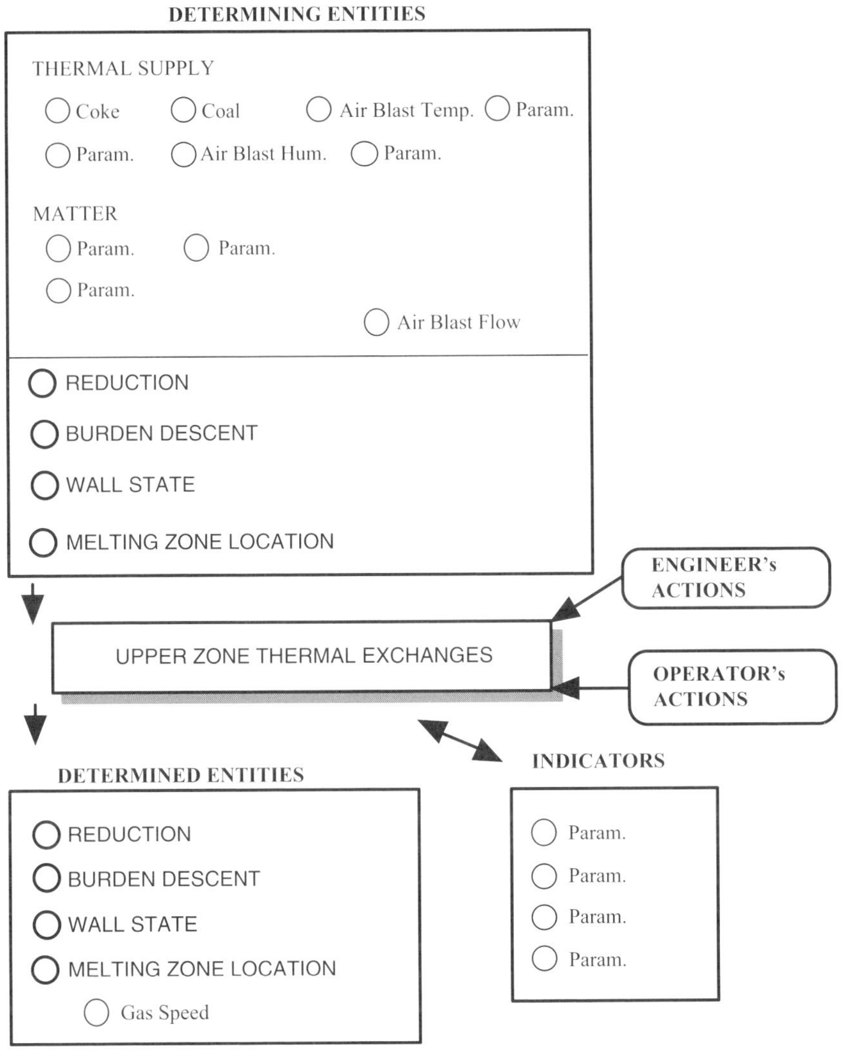

DETERMINING ENTITIES

THERMAL SUPPLY

◯ Coke   ◯ Coal   ◯ Air Blast Temp. ◯ Param.

◯ Param. ◯ Air Blast Hum. ◯ Param.

MATTER

◯ Param.   ◯ Param.

◯ Param.

◯ Air Blast Flow

◯ REDUCTION

◯ BURDEN DESCENT

◯ WALL STATE

◯ MELTING ZONE LOCATION

ENGINEER's ACTIONS

UPPER ZONE THERMAL EXCHANGES

OPERATOR's ACTIONS

DETERMINED ENTITIES

INDICATORS

◯ REDUCTION

◯ BURDEN DESCENT

◯ WALL STATE

◯ MELTING ZONE LOCATION

◯ Gas Speed

◯ Param.

◯ Param.

◯ Param.

◯ Param.

Figure 3.9. Computer interface to access to blast furnace information: a descriptor view. Parameters are accessible in accordance to their status with regard to the descriptor. For reasons of confidentiality, some parameter names are not given. [After Samurçay and Hoc (1996).]

These overall representations of phenomena appeared to be more powerful than knowledge on the relations between observable and individual parameters. The most efficient and the most experienced operators used descriptors in their reasoning processes much more than beginners (Hoc, 1989, 1996). This kind of difference due to expertise is similar to that observed between experts and beginners in physics (Larkin and Reif, 1979), the former being more likely to consider deep physical phenomena instead of shallow variables than the latter. Due to its abstraction level, a descriptor was more efficient to understand or predict a process evolution pattern (a process plan) than individual or groups of parameters.

An access to process information through this kind of logic (by means of descriptors), during a shift-handling period, has revealed itself to be more efficient than the current interface of a topographical kind (Samurçay and Hoc, 1996; Figures 3.8 and 3.9). In this experimental situation, the access to individual parameters was only possible through descriptor displays like that presented in Figure 3.9, with the help of the display of Figure 3.8 showing the causal relations between descriptors. The analysis of the situation was more structured and exhaustive with this kind of interface than with the topographical one. This principle was adopted in the interface of an expert system assisting operators in diagnosis and decision making (SACHEM).

However, the descriptors' assessment by the operators seemed to play the role of constructing a general context within which decisions were taken on the basis of individual parameters. The new interface did not improve anticipation. At least these abstract representations appeared to play a major role in situation understanding, as plans to guide diagnosis. Nevertheless, the efficiency of an interface based on a decomposition of a complex system into abstract entities is a concrete contribution to design, although these entities should be specifically defined for each system, sometimes after knowledge elicitation. In these studies on blast furnace supervision, the entities were defined by knowledge elicitation from process operators and by further research done by blast furnace engineers. Both had only part of the solution, and an integration of the two types of knowledge was needed.

In air-traffic control, we have been engaged into a series of experiments to assess a paradigm of dynamic task allocation between a radar controller and an automatic aircraft conflict resolution device (Debernard, Vanderhaegen and Millot, 1992; Hoc and Lemoine, 1998). We have also analyzed spontaneous verbal reports (among other kind of behaviors) between controllers, using scenarios of interest on a full-scale simulator. The first version of the system just enabled it to manage simple conflicts between two aircraft. The main restriction to its use appeared to be that the main problem for the controllers was not the computation of the optimal solutions. Rather, their crucial activity was the elaboration and maintenance along time of an appropriate problem space—that is, a decomposition of the overall traffic into almost independent subproblems [as shown by a recent simulator study (Morineau, Hoc, and Denecker, 2003)]. Namely, two-aircraft structures were not appropriate, since problems for controllers can imply more than two aircrafts. For example, three aircrafts may be conflicting at the same time, or the choice of a solution for a conflict between two aircrafts must consider another aircraft that is not conflicting but that can constrain the solution. Certainly, a device capable of finding a solution to a two-aircraft conflict, of implementing it, and of rerouting the aircraft can alleviate the workload. However, it would not be of great use if it goes against the controllers' abstract representation of the traffic. In a recent experiment implying two controllers (one playing the role of the machine on a simulator), most of the communications concerned the sharing of a same problem space—that is, a common decomposition of the air space into aircraft conflict patterns and action intentions (Hoc and Carlier, 2002).

In other words, finding a solution to a conflict is straightforward when the conflict is identified as belonging to an abstract class, playing the role of a plan for conflict identification (e.g., converging or following aircraft), linked to an action plan. Only the computation of the optimal and precise deviation and the recall of the right time to re-route the aircraft contribute to the workload. On conflict identification a schematic (action) plan can be formulated and transferred to a machine for implementation, with a possibility of negotiation and veto before applying the final procedure. The main difficulty is the elaboration and updating of the problem space—that is, the list of independent subproblems with their priority levels. On the basis of an analysis of the controllers' temporal tuning to the traffic, the development of a new tool is in progress (Hoc and Debernard, 2002). For example, we have identified the main priority criterion used by the controllers to prioritize problems—the time to collision (Morineau et al., 2003). We have also evaluated the delay needed between the availability of data and the identification of a problem, and between the identification and the formulation of a plan. These delays show that controllers seem to wait for some certainty of the independence of the problem before committing themselves in a resolution plan. In addition, the plan is formulated sufficiently in time for an automated system to process it. The new tool will be able to receive schematic plans for individual aircrafts to implement them. However, a list of problems (the abstract representation of the traffic) will be updated by the controllers and by the automated system (e.g., when the implementation of a plan reveals the presence of an interfering aircraft). At first conceived as a tool for plan implementation, the automated system is now integrated in the controller's activity of elaborating and updating the problem space, with graphical support consistent with the radar representation. In the current work situation, controllers update their representation of the problem space by tidying the strip table (e.g., putting together conflicting aircraft), when they have sufficient time. This external support to representation can ensure that each individual intervention is consistent with an overall traffic management plan.

This principle consists in a shift from dynamic task allocation to plan implementation delegation (Hoc and Debernard, 2002). The first paradigm assumes that the definition of independent tasks is easy to solve. In air-traffic control, tasks are not only conflicts, but also intentions on conflicts. Two conflicts are independent only if the agents have no intention on one of them that can interfere with the other. Within the delegation principle, the human defines tasks and intentions. In addition, plan implementation delegation would be more efficient than precise procedure delegation, in terms of workload alleviation. The use of the abstraction aspect of planning in this situation is supposed to solve the two problems; namely, the maintenance of a problem space at an abstract level and the use of the machine as soon as a schematic plan is elaborated.

3.6.2. Reasoning on Goals Before Means (Crisis Management)

When analyzing training situations (spontaneous verbal reports) implying fireman headquarters field officers, Samurçay and Rogalski (1988) have shown that the main difficulty to get over was processing possible goals before envisioning the means to use. The operators were likely to consider what they could do with the available means at first (e.g., classical firefighting units), closing themselves into easily attainable goals. In fact, when an appropriate goal needs to ask for exceptional means, like tracked vehicles in this particular case of snowstorm, there is a long response delay to get them actually. If the goal becomes more and more salient, there is no time remaining to get the means and the goal is abandoned. This abstraction ability (from the means to the goals) appeared to be also related to the anticipation ability—that is, the ability to anticipate the possible alternatives in the situation evolution.

For example, in a simulation exercise, reproducing the main events of a real snowstorm near Paris, the passengers of a train were (virtually) closed into the train without heating, for a lack of anticipation of the possible goal to access to the train despite the snow and to lodge them. This abstract ability (and its performance outcome) was shown to be more available to a well-designed hierarchical headquarters than to a more "anarchic" one where role allocation was more fuzzy (especially the leader role). In the same vein, a recent study of incidents in commercial aircraft cockpits (loss of situation awareness) has shown that they are more frequent when the captain is flying than when the first officer is flying and has tried to find the reasons (Jentsch et al., 1999). Among these reasons, the authors suggest that, when the captain is flying, the strategic and the tactical roles bear on the same person, so that the strategic role is badly assumed. Abstraction from the means (tactical details), is necessary to process goals (strategic thinking), and the work organization or the workload can affect this abstraction activity.

3.6.3. Guiding Actions by Plans, but Adapting to Circumstances (Anesthesia and Fighter Aircraft Piloting)

In an interesting study of anesthesia in the operating room, Gaba (1994) has described the anesthetist's activity as performing two parallel tasks: following a plan to induce, maintain, and finish the anesthesia, and at the same time detecting and correcting disturbances. His description is completely in line with our cognitive architecture for dynamic situation management, supposing a parallelism between several feedback loops (Hoc et al., 1995). However, a study done by Xiao, Milgram, and Doyle (1997) showed that contingencies are already prepared before the operation. Thus, part of the adaptation in real time is solved beforehand.

Studies on fighter aircraft piloting have shown that pre-planning is an important step to guide the activity, but the pilot is perfectly aware of the fact that the plan will not be fully satisfied, due to unpredictable events (Amalberti and Deblon, 1992). However, the plan is very precise (in terms of the series of points to cross, of flying over times, and of fuel amount on each points) to enable the pilot to return to it in case of deviation. When it is impossible to return to the plan, the pilot must abandon the mission and reach the exit of the enemy territory in time and safely. Plan adjustment is possible because the original plan implicitly integrates goals to be reached, which ensures the return to a safe airfield in case of deviation.

A reasonable hypothesis is that the speedier the process is, the more detailed the plan should be. However, this does not imply that the plan has no hierarchical structure. The mission plan is able to guide the generation of several alternative plans, because it integrates several contingencies at an abstract level.

These two examples show that the plan is not necessarily what is really executed, but what can guide the activity (at an abstract level) and can enable it to adapt to circumstances. Guidance and adaptation are the two conditions to be met by a plan in uncertain and risky situations. As far as design is concerned, the consideration of several levels of abstraction in displaying a plan is crucial. One of the main problems of replanning is identifying the relevant abstraction level to adopt to modify the plan.

Table 3.2 sums up the main results of the studies referred to in this section dealing with the abstraction point of view on planning.

3.7. ANTICIPATION

3.7.1. Anticipative Versus Reactive Strategies (Air Traffic Control and NEWFIRE)

An experiment was designed to assess two kinds of dynamic task allocation modes between air traffic controllers and an automatic conflict resolution device (ACRD). (Hoc and Lemoine, 1998). The allocation was done on the basis of the identification and resolution of binary conflicts in a context where more than two aircrafts could be implied in individual conflicts. These two modes were compared to a situation without any assistance. A previous experiment implying single controllers on night traffic (Debernard et al., 1992) had shown that a purely automatic (implicit) allocation of conflicts between controllers and ACRD, on the basis of a real-time workload evaluation, was not acceptable by controllers who preferred to decide the allocation by themselves (in an explicit way). However, a question had been raised on the possible decrease in performance related to the execution of a strategic activity (task allocation) concurrently to a tactical activity (traffic control) by the same person. In the second experiment the two allocation modes were explicit in a certain sense, but they used the usual control workstation with two controllers

TABLE 3.2. Main Results on Abstraction

Guiding situation understanding by abstract representations
- Blast furnace: descriptors of inner phenomena
- Air traffic control: decomposition of the overall traffic into conflicts and plans

Reasoning on goals before means
- Crisis management: avoiding a closure into predefined means

Guiding actions by plans, but adapting them to circumstances
- Anesthesia: following a plan, but managing disturbances
- Fighter aircraft: plans as resources for action, not designed to be strictly followed

(strategic and tactical controllers). The allocation duty was mainly entrusted to the strategic controller.

Two conditions were compared to a nonassisted condition. In the first one (explicit condition), the two operators were able to control the allocation (to the radar controller or to the machine). In the second one (assisted explicit condition), only the planning controller controlled the allocation, but with a proposal received from the machine (on the basis of an anticipation of the radar controller's future workload). The analysis mainly concerned the radar controller's behavior. As the assistance was increasing, at the same time, we observed that the performance was improving (especially in terms of near misses frequency), but that the mental workload (subjective evaluation by controllers in real time) remained constant. However, the strategies were very different. With little assistance, the strategies were reactive and the solutions were not optimal. With more assistance, the strategies were becoming anticipative (with a better maintenance of the current representation of the problem space) and the solutions were optimal. This experiment showed some kind of workload homeostasis reflecting the management of a compromise between anticipative and reactive strategies in relation to time constraints.

Within the air-traffic control context, anticipative strategies were identified in contrast to reactive strategies by three main features. Information gathering and decision making were performed more frequently within monitoring episodes (internally determined by a plan) as opposed to response to salient information (e.g., alarm—that is, an external prompt, processed in a reactive way). This was correlated with fewer interventions on aircraft trajectories; that is, interventions were done earlier and quite definitively instead of returning to them frequently to correct the previous interventions in a reactive way. In this situation, the declarative aspect of planning was identified by the frequency of tidying the strip table (e.g., putting together conflicting aircraft), interpreted as updating the abstract representation of the problem space. Although this frequency is more related to abstraction than to anticipation, it was also utilized to identify anticipative strategies, because this planning behavior is a means to increase anticipation.

Although this dynamic task allocation paradigm seemed to present some drawbacks in terms of complacency, we have interpreted the increase in anticipation positively. A next experiment on anticipation in air-traffic controllers (Morineau et al., 2003), with a SAGAT-like method (Endsley, 1995b), presented a more complex picture. The traffic was regularly frozen and controllers were invited to report the more important things they had in mind to the experimenter, with the help of a map of the air sector (without any aircraft, but with airways and beacons). The situation was similar to a shift-handling period when a controller tells the successor the current problems. All the aircraft verbally reported were spontaneously drawn on the maps. We have confirmed the well-known phenomenon of distortion consistent with anticipation (Boudes and Cellier, 1998). Aircraft were drawn in advance with regard to their actual position. Conflicting aircraft were represented closer to their crossing point than in reality. However, during the periods of control (between the freezing periods), the verbal report of a problem (conflicting aircraft) appeared to be well-synchronized to the availability of the entire data concerning the problem, although the problem could be identified earlier on the basis of some of the data. It was the same for the verbal report of a solution (sometimes a schematic plan), which took place when all the aircraft of the conflict were accessible to control (in radio-contact), although the control of one of the aircraft could be available earlier.

This contrast between anticipation ability and synchronization to the traffic is compatible with a least commitment strategy. Although anticipation is possible, operators wait for certainty and for affordances from the environment before committing themselves. Anticipation could only create a context, regularly revised, within which problem identification and plan formation take place, but commitment is postponed until reaching an acceptable certainty level and an inescapable deadline. In the design of the new assistance tool (plan implementation delegation), we are trying to support anticipation, but at the same time we are doing our best to avoid suppressing the conditions for this synchronization to be performed. Too strong a focus on anticipation when designing assistance could lead the designer to forget that reactive processes are also necessary to reach a correct performance.

Following the framework of our cognitive architecture, process speed seems an important factor that determines synchronization and desynchronization between process' time and cognitive activity's time. This was studied using the micro-world NEWFIRE, presented as an interface to command firefighting units in a forest (Hoc, Amalberti, and Plee, 2000). Engineering students were taken as subjects in the experiment, after an appropriate training. The training included (a) tests of acquisition of the way of operating the interface, (b) tests of the ability to anticipate the fire spread and (c) tests of the ability to adopt the best firefighting strategy in relation to the type of fire spread (in relation to wind strength and direction).

The process was decelerated from high speed (7 sec between state changes) to medium speed (15 sec) and then to low speed (20 sec). Time-sharing between two tasks was also studied in three conditions. A second fire could appear, either almost simultaneously (concurrence at the planning step), after a short delay (concurrence between the supervision of the first plan implementation and the elaboration of the second plan), or after a long delay (successive tasks).

In the case of attentional concurrence, performance was improving continuously as the speed was slowing down (Figure 3.10). This was interpreted as a major effect of the release of concurrence between the two planning steps (for each fire). However, with two successive tasks, the speed effect presented an optimum. When slowing down the speed, at first there was an improvement and then a worsening. In this condition of two successive tasks, the optimum was interpreted as a shift from reactive strategies to anticipative ones when slowing down the speed. At first, this had a positive effect on performance, but with a very slow process, plans appeared to be too detailed in comparison with the subjects' anticipation competency. Subjects spent too much time to refine plans that revealed themselves to be false. When the speed was very fast, subjects could only adopt reactive strategies, but with quite immediate feedback enabling them to adapt their behavior to the

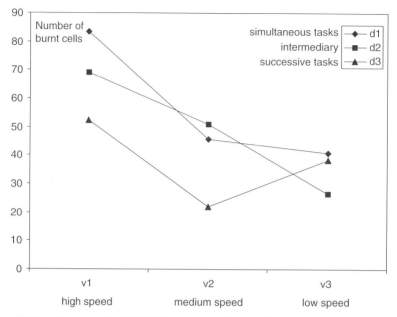

Figure 3.10. Performance in NEWFIRE (number of burnt cells when the fire is extinguished) in relation to process speed and time-sharing. [After Hoc et al. (2000).]

circumstances, reaching an acceptable performance level. Speeding down the process opened the way to anticipative strategies, but with not too delayed a feedback so that reactive adaptation could take place. Finally, when the speed was very slow, feedback was too delayed to operate on a reactive basis.

This shows that some balance must be established between anticipative and reactive strategies, in relation to competency. Computer support to anticipation is not sufficient. Training must also be considered carefully to enable operators to reach relevant anticipation. And, as was said above, in uncertain situations like air-traffic control, anticipation is not sufficient. The availability of precise information also plays a major role.

3.7.2. The Use of Meta-knowledge During Pre-planning: Fighter Aircraft Piloting and Anesthesia

In rapid and risky situations, replanning is almost impossible. In such cases, like fighter aircraft piloting or anesthesia, pre-planning is a crucial activity.

Studying the mission preparation step of fighter aircraft pilots, Amalberti and Deblon (1992) have shown the importance of meta-knowledge in relation to risk management. Namely, they have observed a large difference between experts and beginners. Beginners generated plans that were much more precise than those of experts, because beginners knew that they would not been able to manage certain situations in real time. They tended to envision much more alternatives and possible situations than experts did. On the contrary, experts elaborated very sketchy plans, because they were confident in their ability to process some possible situations in real time. This does not mean that they could process such situations without plan, in a reactive way, but that they could implement well-known and pre-built plans in real time.

The importance of meta-cognition in planning has been very well illustrated by the study done by Xiao, Milgram, and Doyle (1997) in anesthesia. They have described pre-planning as a process of preparing resources for acting. Attention is more likely to be devoted to discrepancies from usual plans—for example, expected difficulties in implementing the procedures, tasks that are specific to the case, unusual operating procedures, and so on. Some time was allocated to preparing memory support, posting papers on instruments to remember nonstandard steps during operation. Thus, knowledge of one's way of reacting and of committing errors is utilized to design one's own support.

In laparoscopic surgery (operation without opening and with the help of optical fibers), Dominguez (1997) has shown the importance of meta-knowledge in plan implementation. From the pre-operation consultation and until the last time, opening remains a possible issue if the surgeons consider that they will not be able to operate safely with the laparoscopic technique. Large differences were observed in relation to expertise during this long decision-making process.

In artificial intelligence, Boddy and Dean (1994) have acknowledged the fact that meta-knowledge is necessary to plan in time-constrained environments.

This question of meta-knowledge should be considered when designing planning support in situations where operators' self-confidence is a major concern. Within other contexts than assistance to planning, there are several examples of automation rejection on this basis. The machine can be rejected or shortcut when the operators think it leads them in situations they guess they could not manage (Hoc, 2000).

3.7.3. Computer Support to Anticipation: Blast Furnace

Although the blast furnace process is submitted to various response latencies (from ten minutes to several hours, sometimes more), operators' verbal reports of time are not frequent (about 40% of the grammatical propositions), and among them very few express anticipation (less than 10%) (Hoc, 1996). However, experts more frequently express anticipation than beginners (Hoc, 1991).

For several years, computer support for anticipation (IRMA) has been available in a blast furnace control room. From data automatically collected on the process and possible actions entered by the operators, IRMA is able to forecast the iron temperature evolution (a crucial parameter in controlling this process). (Figure 3.11).

During this period the use of IRMA was not mandatory. Some operators have been using it on a regular basis and are identified as "regular users." They said to use it in a mutual control way to compare their own anticipation to IRMA's one and conversely. The others used it seldom and were qualified as "casual users." They said that they were able to anticipate without IRMA and that, when they were willing to use it, the situation was not normal and that IRMA's forecasting was not valid.

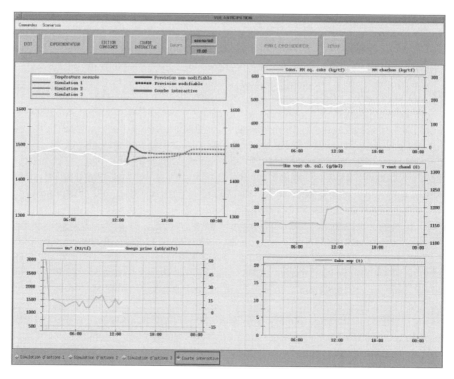

Figure 3.11. Computer support for anticipation in blast furnace control. Comparison between operator's and SIAA's forecast is displayed on the top right. The current instant is approximately 12:20. Before it, the curve displays the actual evolution of the iron temperature. After it, the top curve corresponds to the model forecast, and the bottom curve the prevision drawn beforehand by the operator. The other curves show the actions on the entry parameters. [After Denecker (2000).]

Two groups of operators (regular and casual users), at a homogenous level of expertise (seniority and status), were submitted to a simulated shift-handling period with the necessary data and some curves supposed to be drawn by the software (certain curves were wrong). (Denecker and Hoc, 1997). As compared to casual users, regular users showed a higher ability to criticize their own forecasts and those of IRMA, a better quality and speed of situation analysis, and a better risk management strategy. They maintained a better balance between the short-term control (urgent measures to maintain the process between acceptable limits to prevent a serious breakdown) and the long-term control (waiting the right time and a low uncertainty before deciding decisive measures). Apparently, the use of the software in a mutual control way could be one of the main sources of improvement.

A second experiment was performed with an improved version of the software (SIAA). The previous factor (regular versus casual users) was crossed with two conditions of SIAA use (active versus passive) during a simulation of several

TABLE 3.3. Main Results on Anticipation

Anticipative versus reactive strategies
- Air traffic control: parallelism between anticipative and reactive strategies
- NEWFIRE: limits of the anticipation competency

Meta-knowledge in pre-planning
- Fighter aircraft: role of expertise in the anticipation level of precision
- Anesthesia: anticipation of routines' lack of reliability faced to nonstandard case

Computer support to anticipation
- Blast furnace: role of the assistance experience and of the operator's active role

scenarios (Denecker, 2000). In the active mode, operators were forced to produce their forecasts (with some tools on the display) before accessing to those of SIAA (Figure 3.11). In the passive mode, they could directly access SIAA's forecast. The results showed a benefit of the active mode (mutual control) in comparison with the passive mode, but rather among regular users than casual users. The access to a mutual control opportunity appeared to be an important factor for the improvement of anticipation and performance, but probably the elaboration of a model of the other agent is needed beforehand. This kind of result completed the findings published by Smith and Crabtree (1975) on the way human schedulers utilized simulation tools (on a mutual control basis) or on the benefits of an active strategy in expert system use (Roth, Bennett, and Woods, 1988).

In design terms, this kind of result reinforces the argument presented above on the necessity to consider training needs when designing a support to anticipation. In addition, it suggests devoting more attention to the cooperative properties of human–machine interaction (Hoc, 2001). Table 3.3 sums up the main results presented in this section on anticipation.

3.8. CONCLUSION

In conclusion, we will sum up the main results presented in this chapter and sketch some future research directions—on desynchronization between cognitive processes and technical processes, on abstraction, and on anticipation. The implications in terms of assistance and training design will be recalled.

3.8.1. Desynchronization

In dynamic situations, planning is concurrent to the immediate control of the situation. Pre-planning at least implies plan adjustment; sometimes replanning and some research effort should be devoted to computer assistance with regard to replanning in time-constrained situations. The workload introduced by parallelism or time-sharing between long-term replanning and short-term control of the situation should be alleviated. In some situations the problem is solved by allocating the strategic and the tactical duty to different operators (e.g., captain and watch officer in a ship, captain and first officer in an aircraft). However, the relation between the two control levels must be insured by efficient communication to enable adaptation. In some other situations, the same operator manages the two levels (e.g., single-seated fighter aircraft) and computer assistance can be envisioned, such as an electronic copilot capable of proposing new plans. In any case, the priority to short-term control should be considered, so that replanning assistance should not be designed in such a way that communication with the assistance jeopardizes the mastering of the short-term situation.

3.8.2. Abstraction

Planning includes abstraction—that is, the use of overall representations of situations and actions stressing the crucial properties (e.g., ends, structures, etc.). The question is finding the right abstraction level to guide the individual or the collective activity reducing the complexity of the data, allowing some degrees of freedom and providing resources for adaptation to circumstances.

In the blast furnace example, the abstract representations of the process were used to reduce the complexity of the data, but also as a basis for least commitment strategies. In air traffic control the common representation of the problem space is defined at the right abstraction level to minimize the interference between the two controllers and the cost of its communication.

A major ingredient of planning is the availability of a mental model of the process under control composed of several abstraction levels. Rasmussen's approach is too sketchy to apply to every situation without ambiguity. For all, a general scheme should be elaborated, without exploding into a myriad of techniques specific to each work domain. However, in many real cases, there is no accurate model of the process available, at least not for malfunctions. It must be elaborated not only from knowledge in the domain, but also from operators' knowledge. The blast furnace studies illustrate this mutual enrichment. Studies on "ecological" interface design (e.g., Vicente and Rasmussen, 1990) trying to make "visible" the abstraction hierarchy are promising to provide operators with external supports compatible with several levels of processing.

Abstraction as the movement going from means toward goals and means has been shown to require training (firemen officers in charge of crisis management). Thus an "ecological" interface cannot be usable by operators who are not well-trained. Making abstract representations visible is not sufficient. The ability to interpret them is crucial.

3.8.3. Anticipation

Anticipation is costly and limited by time constraints. It can be a handicap when it goes beyond actual competency, so that reactive strategies are necessary. The focus on planning strategies should not let us forget the adaptive power of reactive strategies, especially when time constraints are high or process knowledge is weak.

The main problem to solve is finding an efficient compromise between anticipative and reactive strategies to reach a satisfying performance level.

Anticipation also needs meta-knowledge (competency on one's own competency). In dynamic situations, the operators must anticipate not only the process evolution but also their own activity, especially in terms of resources. In fact, the main risk they must manage is the loss of control of the situation. For that, meta-knowledge is needed.

Computer assistance to anticipation could be efficient when utilized as a mutual control tool, but with some relevant model of the computer (or model) functioning.

However, most of the studies done in complex situations are devoted to a limited part of anticipation mechanisms, those that are explicit and reported verbally. Symbolic anticipation is certainly important to consider, but some anticipation mechanisms are implicit and do not result in explicit forecasts. Implicit anticipation would result in preparation states of which the operators are not aware, but which could play a prominent role. Adaptation to a situation can be very successful without forecasting it explicitly. A large part of the cognitive activity is regulated at a subsymbolic level without emerging within the attention field. Subsymbolic activity does not necessarily mean that plans are not used, but these plans can be represented in the organism without needing attention. This is a line for future studies, but we are confronted with very difficult methodological problems to access to this kind of plans. Symbolic assistance should be developed with caution, because there is a risk to close the operators into a symbolic mode of processing, losing their subsymbolic skills.

INTRODUCTION TO CHAPTER 4

Jorna continues the line of reasoning that we started with Hommel Hoc. The topic of research is again the human planner, not where he is planning for himself but where he is a planner in an organization. Jorna uses classical theories of cognitive science to exemplify what planners cognitively do. Cognitive science has, of course, mainly studied cognition of individuals doing, for example, errands and other simple tasks. In our earlier terminology, this means planning for yourself. In this chapter, planning for oneself is nested within planning for others. However, where Hommel is looking at planning at the less-than-one-second time horizon, Hoc and Jorna are studying planning at the more-than-five-second time horizon. Whereas Hoc is mainly studying planners as operators of dynamic processes in organizations, Jorna is investigating what planners who plan or schedule lorries, staff, or machine operators are actually doing. In all three cases, they are studying planners as cognitive and mental systems.

Jorna's chapter addresses four main issues. The first theme concerns approaches in planning support design. The second is about the special characteristics of planning as a human problem-solving activity. The third theme deals with the relevance of the characteristics of the domain in which planning takes place. The fourth theme is a methodological one and regards the empirical or quasi-experimental study of planners' behavior. We will discuss the four themes in greater detail.

Bottom-Up Task Support Planners are ever more supported by computers and software. Making plans and schedules by hand or on small or large pieces of

Planning in Intelligent Systems: Aspects, Motivations, and Methods, Edited by Wout van Wezel, René Jorna, and Alexander Meystel
Copyright © 2006 John Wiley & Sons, Inc.

paper is nearly impossible for planners. Usually, the software that supports them is developed by nonplanners. Software engineers and information specialists are, by definition, nonplanners and are often focused on (models of) optimization possibilities. The developed planning and scheduling software support often forces planners to follow routes and to use planning solutions that are in contrast with their own planning intuitions and practices. In terms of planning for yourself and planning for others, this so-called top-down approach to planning is like planning for others where the nested planning for yourself is replaced by nested planning by others. In this chapter, Jorna defends and discusses another approach, namely, a bottom-up approach to develop planning support.

Planning and Problem Solving The advance of considering planning as a kind of problem solving is the possibility of reuse of the conceptual apparatus of problem solving: state space, initial and goal states, search and operators, and methods. If planners solve problems, the conceptual problem then is how anticipation and overview, as elementary aspects of planning, can be incorporated. From a cognitive perspective, the issue boils down to the representations of planners. If planning is a kind of problem solving, production rule representations are the standard. If anticipation, overview, and schemes are relevant, representations can better be seen as scripts and frames.

Domain Relevance Planning is a cognitive task, and tasks consist of more or less fixed sequences of reasoning steps. In general, planning tasks can be discerned from diagnostic and other kinds of tasks. Therefore, planning can be seen as a generic task. The question is whether the domains that planners are planning have an effect on the reasoning steps of the planners. If a generic task perspective holds, characteristics of domains should be of minor relevance.

Empirical Study Jorna reports about an empirical study where 34 planners from two countries and three domains solved similar manipulated planning problems. Gathered data consist of protocols, solution times, and information about used representations, memory statements, and the use of external visual aids. As was hypothesized, domain knowledge is important, but does not deeply effect the reasoning steps of planners. In the empirical study, planners are planning for others, in an organizational setting, but without taking into account aspects of organizational forms and coordination mechanisms. This topic is discussed in the chapter by Gazendam (Chapter 5).

4

COGNITION, PLANNING, AND DOMAINS: AN EMPIRICAL STUDY INTO THE PLANNING PROCESSES OF PLANNERS[1]

RENÉ JORNA

Faculty of Management and Organization, University of Groningen, Groningen, NL-9700-AV Groningen, the Netherlands

4.1. INTRODUCTION AND FORMULATING THE PROBLEM: A COGNITIVE APPROACH TOWARD PLANNING

In this chapter we will present an empirical study. In this study the influence of domains on cognitive process of planners is investigated. Here *domains* refers to the areas in which planning takes place: transportation, staff, or production. In the study I will try to corroborate the claim formulated by the generic task approach that cognitive processes in planning are dominated by the task structure and its cognitive processing and not, or to a minor extent, by domain characteristics. In this chapter the empirical study is preceded by an extensive literature survey regarding cognitive aspects of planning, problem solving, and decision making. The goal of the empirical research and the literature study, is to go through the arguments in favor of planning support developed from a descriptive planner's (and cognitive) perspective and not primarily from a prescriptive modeling perspective. At the end of this

[1] I would like to thank Endah Premashwari (Indonesia) and Jelle Pentinga (Netherlands) for their efforts in conducting the empirical research in the Netherlands and Indonesia. Especially with regard to the operational aspects of this research, they were indispensable.

chapter we will discuss the consequences of the descriptive perspective, also called the bottom-up approach, for software support.

Planning and scheduling are mostly studied from the perspective of optimization or maximization. Especially in designing and implementing support systems, complicated models of planning and scheduling are constructed. Often, information from planners, operators, and managers is gathered and discussed to realize the planning model. However, this information is usually not very detailed and is certainly not related to (a) how planners do the actual planning, (b) what cognitive processes are involved, and (c) what interactions between planners take place.

Our perspective in analyzing planning situations and implementing planning support is to look at what planners in which context and for what reasons actually do. We call this the bottom-up approach toward planning and planning support. It is in contrast with the earlier described modeling approach, which principally has a top-down perspective. Within the modeling approach domains, processes and departments or units are analyzed and support is implemented, accordingly. In this (prescriptive) approach, tasks and humans as executers of tasks in which they use knowledge are the underrated final pieces in realizing planning support.

The bottom-up approach can also be called the cognitive task analysis approach. Three important themes can be discerned in this approach. The first concerns the characteristics of the planner as a human information processing system supported by theory from cognitive science. We discuss this in detail in Section 4.2.1.

The second theme concerns (cognitive) task analyses in which planning and scheduling are treated as tasks or, to be more precise, as *generic* tasks. In the generic task perspective we follow and expand common-KADS (Breuker and van de Velde, 1994). We believe that the analysis of task performance of planners is the initial stage in realizing task support. The assumption is that a software support system that results from this analysis is more dedicated to actual planning activities of planners. There is, however, also a drawback to this approach. Because support realized in this way enables a planner to improve his planning tasks and subtasks, the initially adequate support will, over time, become less adequate. This requires a continuous update of task analysis and support performance. The positive side of this continuous change is that updating and adjusting are activities build into the process of software support. This is not common practice in the top-down approach in planning support (Davis and Olson, 1985). We will discuss this in Section 4.2.2.

The third theme concerns the importance of the domain in which planning or scheduling is executed. It is generally stated that characteristics of a domain are very important factors in plan execution and planning support—for example, in production planning and operations management (Smith, 1992; Stadtler and Kilger, 2002; Bertrand and Fransoo, 2002). The question is, How important are the domain characteristics? Especially in production planning and operation management, the dominant perspective, for good reasons, is to model the domain and its characteristics and to design algorithms to solve the planning problems. The human factor and human processing is suppositious. That is logical, considering the fact that machines and devices do most of the work and have to be used as efficiently as possible. This seems to imply that humans in operations management do not plan. This is not true. Planners are also active in these environments, but characteristics of the domain seem dominant. For that reason, one could argue that production planning is completely different from, for example, transportation planning or staff planning. To put it bluntly, it could be argued that the domains of staff, production, and transportation planning have nothing in common and that planning task and planning support for domains are therefore incompatible. This is not our view. We believe that a consequence of the generic task approach is that domains are less relevant than cognitive processes of planners. The empirical study presented in Section 4.3 is performed to gain more insight into this issue.

The three themes of cognition, task, and domain are, of course, interconnected and especially the relation between task and domain is very tight, meaning that if the domains of staff, transportation, and production are almost independent in the planning discussion, dealing with planning as a generic task becomes very difficult. If domain specifications determine execution and support of planning and scheduling, generic task support almost becomes an illusion. Clearly, the generic task perspective denies this strong domain determination.

To study and analyze better the themes, we will start with an extended section about theory. Because the individual planner is central in our bottom-up approach, we start with theory from cognition and human information processing in Section 4.2.1. In Section 4.2.2 I continue with a detailed description of the literature on planning and scheduling from a cognitive perspective. In Section 4.2.3 we will go into the details of the discussion about the relevance of the domain, the bottom-up approach, and its elaboration in the (quasi)-experiment. This theoretical part is necessary to design the quasi-experiment that will be discussed in Section 4.3. In Section 4.3.1 we describe the subjects, material, and procedure, whereas in Section 4.3.2 the data and results are presented. In Section 4.4 we will return to software support of planning and scheduling, and in Section 4.5 we give conclusions.

4.2. THEORETICAL BACKGROUND CONCERNING COGNITION, PLANNING, DOMAIN, AND SUPPORT

4.2.1. The Planner as a Human Information Processing System

4.2.1.1. Cognition and Levels of Description. In research on planning, usually processes and structures of organizations are studied. We already argued that we want to start with the planner, his task, and his knowledge: the so-called bottom-up approach. The distinction between bottom-up and top-down not only can be formulated into prescriptive and descriptive, but also can be formulated as different levels of investigation. Top-down starts and uses the organizational level, whereas bottom-up starts with the individual level. However, the choice for the individual level itself is not self-explanatory. Studying reasoning and thinking of planners involves invisible mental processes. In our planning research I study the intangible phenomenon of the human mind (cognition). Concerning the study of cognition, various perspectives can be applied, simultaneously. The perspectives depend on various levels of aggregation, also called levels of description for cognitive phenomena, or as Newell (1990, p. 118) puts it: "Levels are clearly abstractions, being alternative ways of describing the same system, each level ignoring some of what is specified at the level beneath it."

The idea of levels of description or explanation for a (cognitive) system has been worked out most elegantly by Dennett (1978, 1987, 1991). He distinguishes three independent levels: (a) the physical stance, (b) the design (or functional) stance, and (c) the intentional stance. Other authors (Newell, 1982, 1990; Pylyshyn, 1984) gave similar accounts in which, however, the number of levels varies. We will follow Dennett.

The physical stance explains behavior in terms of physical properties of states and behavior of the system under concern. For its proper functioning the human organism requires a complex interaction of its parts and with the external world. The central nervous system and the endocrine system transmit information that reveals the state of one part of the system to other parts. We can also mention the transmission of currents in the synaptive system of neurons. Within the study of cognition, this stance is the endpoint of ontological reduction.

The second level concerns the functional design of a system. In a functional description, knowing the components of a system, how they are defined, and how components and subcomponents of the cognitive system are connected are important. Stated differently, if input and output of each component are known, then with a certain input at the beginning of the system, resulting behavior can be predicted on the basis of characteristics of components. Behavior of a system is conceived of as the result of interaction between many functional components and processes. The physical structure of the system is not explicitly taken into account, although it may impose constraints on the behavior of the system. Capacity limitations of human memory, for instance, will impose a boundary on the complexity of decision making or on what a planner can remember.

In the third place, Dennett distinguishes the intentional stance. Complex behavior adapted to prevailing circumstances, according to some criterion of optimization, is said to be rational or intelligent. A behaving system to which we can successfully attribute rationality or intelligence, qualifies as an intentional system. Possessing rationality or intelligence is not necessary for a behaving system, as long as the assumption allows us to predict the behavior of the system on the basis of our knowledge of circumstances in which the system is operating correctly.

The chapters by Hommel and Hoc (Chapters 2 and 3) can be combined with the perspective in this chapter. Hommel partly discusses the physiological properties of cognitive processes, whereas Hoc focuses on the functional and even the intentional stance, comparable to the stance we take in this chapter.

The discussion about various levels is closely connected to the relation between levels. This is a recurring debate (Nagel, 1961). Some cognitive scientists (Churchland, 1984) argue that the level's distinction will ultimately show that intentional levels will be reduced to functional ones, and these will be reduced to physical levels. In the philosophy of science, this debate is called reductionism. In more simple terms, reductionism states that higher levels are in one way or another reducible to lower levels. Just as psychology should be reduced to biology, and from there to chemistry and physics, so in cognitive science intentional statements should be reducible to physiological or neurological ones. This so-called vertical reductionism presupposes the existence of bridging laws, which can completely explain concepts of one level in terms of another, lower level.

Many cognitive scientists have an ambivalent relation with reductionism. On the one hand, the study of physiological or neurological structures is important, because they determine the constraints on reasoning. On the other hand, reasoning, thinking, and problem solving can be studied at their own (functional) level of description. Components and their properties at a higher level are more than just compositions of properties and components at a lower level. Higher levels can never completely be understood in terms of properties at a lower level. Stated differently, lower levels "underdetermine" higher levels. Newell and Simon's (1976) physical symbol system hypothesis is an example of this position. After the 1990s there was a strong tendency in cognitive science to favor the more reductionist position in which, if neurology is able to explain cognitive phenomena, higher levels of description are superfluous.

In our opinion, the discussion about the levels of description very well shows that cognitive science and therefore the study of problem solving, decision making, and planning cannot be reformulated merely as a technological discipline, in which more powerful and more sophisticated computations (and computers) will explain the proper functioning of the human mind or can replace problem solving or planning as performed by human cognition. Nor will better neurological research unveil the ultimate characteristic of human reasoning or planning. Better knowledge of computations and neurons is necessary, but this knowledge only gives a better understanding of the boundary conditions for thinking, reasoning, and planning, not for these activities themselves. Not only rational behavior, but especially behavior at the social band—as Newell (1990) called it—requires the existence of independent (higher) levels of description.

From the above it can be deduced that we clearly argue in favor of the study of problem solving and planning at a functional level of description. We are looking at what planners are actually doing. In the empirical study in Section 4.3 we will look at aspects of memory, representation, and processing steps, but before we can go into the empirical details we have to explain better what it means to say that a planner uses his cognition and is a human information processing system.

4.2.1.2. Cognitive Architecture and Representations. Research into the nature and functioning of mind and brain has a long and rich conceptual tradition (Gregory, 1987; Posner, 1989). Over the centuries, various terms have been coined to describe and explain mental or cognitive phenomena. Examples of these are ideas, images, symbols, representations, knowledge, neurons, consciousness, association, homunculus, intelligence, memory, reasoning, and thought. The enumeration of these terms is not at random. Two large categories can be distinguished. One of them focuses on the basic elements or entities involved in or forming the basis of cognitive or mental phenomena, such as ideas, images, symbols, neurons, or representations. The other expresses the structure, wholeness, or togetherness of cognition with terms such as association, intelligence, memory, knowledge, or reasoning.

This fundamental distinction remains present in the conceptual framework of cognitive science until today. The two categories are now called (a) representations and (b) cognitive architecture, respectively. To this framework a third category is added: (c) computations or operations on representations. Within this framework, Newell and Simon (1972, 1976) have formulated their earlier mentioned hypothesis of the physical symbol system. It states that human thinking and reasoning consist of the manipulation of (internal) symbols. Symbols or representations are the basic constituents of our thoughts, and manipulations are operations such as to create, copy, delete, move, and integrate symbols. The symbols or representations are treated as functional entities, but they have a material carrier. Therefore, the attribute "physical" is used. In human information processing systems, the material carrier is the brain. In computers it is the physical processor. The functional stance, related to the brain as the neurological tissue in our head, describes our cognitive architecture.

An architecture without content is empty. In cognitive science, representations (or symbol structures) form the content. As basic constituents of our thinking, they concern images, propositions, semantic nets, scripts, and other expressions of mental content (Jorna, 1990). For example, if a person is doing errands, it means that this person builds up a mental model of the shops he has to visit. Operations on these representations are called activities of symbol manipulation. Within cognitive science the conceptual framework to deal with representations can be found in the approaches of classical symbol systems, of connectionism, and of situated cognition (Posner, 1989; Newell, 1990, Dölling, 1998; Smolensky, 1988; Jorna, 1990). The basic idea is that humans as information processing systems have and use knowledge consisting of representations and that reasoning, problem solving, and planning consist of manipulations of these representations at a functional level of description. A system that internally symbolizes the environment is said to have (mental) representations at its disposal. A representational system learns by means of chunking mechanisms and symbol transformations (Newell, 1990).

A cognitive architecture, consisting of memory components, perceptual and motor systems, and various kinds of central processors (Posner, 1989), implements the design and organization of the human mind. It is meant to present the various functions and properties of the mind and their interrelations. An architecture imposes all kinds of constraints on functioning. The most widely known cognitive architecture is a production system. A production system describes the human mind as consisting of a working memory, a collection of production rules, and a set of priority rules that determine the order of firing of production rules. A production rule itself is a condition–action combination. Production systems started with the General Problem Solver (GPS; Newell, Shaw, and Simon, 1958). SOAR (Laird, Rosenbloom, and Newell, 1986) is an implementation of the production system architecture, consisting of mechanisms to learn other production rules and to make decisions. Another more extended implementation of this cognitive architecture is ACT-R (Anderson and Lebiere, 1998).

If we use this cognitive approach to look at planning, we can also formulate this as the bottom-up approach. It starts with planners, their task execution, and their knowledge. The basic assumption in this approach is that planners make plans by using their cognitive system. They reason, memorize, judge, and solve planning problems with which they are confronted. Planners are human information processing systems, and these systems consist of the components that we discussed in this section. Now that we have formulated various characteristics, we can turn to the planning task itself. After reviewing the state of affairs in the planning literature from a cognitive perspective (Section 4.2.2), we will continue with the research questions studied in the empirical research (Section 4.2.3).

4.2.2. Planning and Scheduling: Characteristics of the Problem-Solving Processes

4.2.2.1. Planning in Different Scientific Fields. Planning is a thoroughly investigated research topic in many domains—for example, in economy—in organization and (operations) management science, in computer science and in cognitive science (Zweben and Fox, 1994). Therefore, finding one definition that is common to all fields is impossible. In organizational and economical perspectives, mainly formulated in economic or financial terms, a distinction is made in planning and scheduling. Planning is often called the determination of levels of production or resource quantities, whereas in this perspective scheduling is the allocation of resources to production process on a (ratio) time scale (Baker, 1974; Mintzberg, 1994; Jorna et al., 1996).

Within cognitive science and psychology the study of planning contains the study of human (intelligent) activities (tasks). In our framework for planning discussed in Chapter 1, we here have a mixture of entities (in this case human actors) that plan for themselves and entities that plan for another. Within a planning task that has to arrange lorries, shifts, or machines, a planner uses his cognitive system to solve planning problems. Our main orientation in this chapter is the planner that plans for others. However, performing this task implies that the planner uses his own mental planning strategies. We can describe it as a nesting of planning for yourself within planning for others. In both cases this means sequencing a set of one's own and of others' actions. By investigating how planners use their cognitive strategies, it is possible to gain insight into how planners solve the planning problems in the various domains we mentioned earlier. Outcomes of these studies can be used in the bottom-up approach to planning support. We start, however, with a detailed description of what a planner as a cognitive system does (for himself).

Within a cognitive perspective, we start with an old definition of planning that says that a plan is a hierarchical process within an organism that controls series of operations (Miller, Pribram, and Galanter, 1960). Hoc (1988) extends this definition and says that planning always involves anticipation and schematization. What he means is that planning consists of two parallel processes, in which a future state is taken into account (anticipation) and in which a (stored) mental scheme can be applied if a planning problem arises. Therefore, Hoc talks about (cognitive) bottom-up and top-down processes that are always involved in making a plan.

Because of the terminology Hoc uses, he is implicitly taking a position in the complex debate about planning and scheduling. Among others, this debate involves two questions. The first is whether planning is a form of problem solving (Newell and Simon, 1972) or whether planning and problem solving only overlap (Das, Kar, and Parrila, 1996). The second is about the question of whether human planners work hierarchically (Newell and Simon, 1972), opportunistically (Hayes-Roth and Hayes-Roth, 1979), or with the help of scripts (Schank and Abelson, 1977). We will discuss the issues in greater detail, first planning and problem solving, then hierarchical and opportunistic planning.

4.2.2.2. Planning, Problem Solving and Decision Making. Simon and Newell (1958) described a planning method as part of a general problem-solving technique. It consisted of a reformulation of a problem in more abstract and restricted terms, its solution in a simplified problem space, its retranslation into the original problem situation, and subsequently its solution. In later articles, Newell and Simon (1972) renamed the planning method as "problem abstraction." This was useful if a problem was not solvable within its original state space. Because planning and also problem solving mean searching for routes (i.e., sequences of actions) that lead to a solution or a goal state, the explicit distinction between planning and problem solving disappeared in the later work of Newell and Simon. Planning is just one (very interesting) example of the general problem-solving approach.

Das et al. (1996) argue against this "planning is a subset of problem solving" approach in saying that differences exist in problems to prove and problems to find. According to Das et al. (1996, p. 40), "Planning is a more pervasive, general regulating process than problem solving, with problem solving being a part of a planning process." Planning includes anticipation and overview and refers to future actions, whereas these components seem absent in problem solving.

In our opinion, this almost seems to be a game with words, because one could state that searching and trying to reach a goal and constructing a problem space with states and operators imply future actions and anticipation. Das et al., however, have a point with respect to one important point in the debate. An enigmatic element in the problem-solving approach of Newell and Simon is the starting point of the problem-solving process. How does a problem solver construct a problem space? Where does the choice for a particular problem space come from? Why does a problem solver construct this special problem space and not another? In terms of Newell and Simon, we are talking about the step where a task environment gets its representation in a state-space description. Saying that one has a new problem here is easy, which requires a second-order state-space description. Although this might be true in the strict sense of the word, it does not solve the issue. Perhaps something like what Das et al. (1996) called "overview" or "having a higher perspective" is necessary. The difficult point is that these processes are not absent from the "planning is a kind of problem solving" perspective that Newell and Simon defended. For example, in the later developments of artificial intelligence, the SOAR-architecture, they use a complicated mixture of planning, decision making, and problem solving. This position has also been formulated by Anderson with ACT-R (Anderson and

Lebiere, 1998). An intelligent architecture solves problems, by planning various steps that have to be executed in so-called decision cycles.

The discussion of how planning differs from problem solving and also from decision making is until now not settled. Even a look at lemmas for these concepts in the *Encyclopedia of Cognitive Science* does not solve the conceptual problems. In that encyclopedia, "planning is the process of generating (possibly partial) representations of future behavior prior to the use of such plans to constrain or control that behavior" (Wilson and Keil, 1999, p. 652). Except for the action aspect, this generally fits the definition of planning we gave in Chapter 1, namely, "planning is the attunement or assignment of multiple object types taking into account constraints and goal functions." Many have argued that if setting a course of actions equals planning, then decision making and problem solving consist of many very small planning activities. For example, if I want to strike a key on the keyboard, I have to plan that action mentally, although it takes between 200 and 500 milliseconds. In this chapter we do not mean planning in this sense. The time horizon in the planning area we are studying is between 5 and 30 seconds. Issues concerning tasks executed within hundreds of milliseconds are discussed in Chapter 2.

In the *Encyclopedia of Cognitive Science* a problem is defined as "transforming a given situation into a desired situation or goal" (Wilson and Keil, 1999, p. 674). Problem solving is the recognition of a discrepancy between an existing and desired situation for which no automated series of actions exist to resolve that discrepancy. Otherwise, it is an algorithm. Problem solving requires setting up a problem space, using legitimated operations (may be combined in a method) and search. Problem solving in a cognitive sense always requires representations.

And if we conclude with the definition of decision making in the encyclopedia, we find that "decision making is the process of choosing a preferred option or course of action from among a set of alternatives" (Wilson and Keil, 1999, p. 221). Critical aspects in calling an activity decision making are as follows: discrepancy between existing and desired situation, having the motivation and the means to act, putting an irreversible investment in a course of actions, and completely or partly uncertain outcome of the decision (Vlek and Wagenaar, 1976). We leave out of the discussion the notion of decision cycles, such as formulated by Newell in SOAR (1990). A decision cycle there is a very small step to fulfill an action. Striking a key on a keyboard involves a decision cycle of an actor, but has nothing to do with deliberate decision making. In this sense of the notion of decision cycle, planning and problem solving consist of many decision cycles.

Because we believe that it is not possible to give definitions of planning, problem solving, and decision making that clearly separate one from the other, we suggest that we look at the three activities in a different way. In the following we describe various aspects that may be applied for problem solving, decision making, and planning. For planning we make a distinction in planning for oneself and planning for others. We first describe aspects that can be used for differentiation:

- *Working with (Mental) Representations*: An abstraction from reality; discrepancy between initial and end or desired state.

- *Uncertainty*: This can be partial or complete; without uncertainty we have automatization.
- *Irreversible Investment*: If no investment is made, we speak about scenarios.
- *Problem Space*: It is necessary to formulate a problem space and search within that space.
- *Certain Object Types Must Be Present*: For planning in this book, we at least talk about time.
- *Process or Outcome Orientation*: We here mean the emphasis on process or outcome. Of course a plan or a solution as outcome are important, but we believe in contrast to making a decision, which one does momentarily, that in planning and problem solving the (extended) process is more important.
- *Specific Methods*: In planning, for example, no general applicable method is available.
- *Choose Ourselves*: We here mean the importance of an acting person, an actor, or subject.
- *Real Life*: For example, a decision is made and the world changes, whereas in planning and problem solving, the activity not necessarily leads to an action or a change in the world.
- *Actor for Actor or Actor for Organization*: This refers to a distinction we made in Chapter 1.

Table 4.1 contains our interpretations of the various aspects for planning, decision making, and problem solving. It is not our intention to settle the discussion between planning and problem solving; we only want to analyze the confusing discussion.

There are several ways to integrate planning, problem solving, and decision making. Depending on definitions of planning, decision making, and problem solving, they can all be expressed into one another. We will give some examples. If Simon (1960) says that the decision-making process involves the phases of intelligence, design, and choice and if the intelligence phase and partly the design phase require setting up a problem space, then problem solving is a part of decision making. If planning is solving a problem for the allocation of resources with the special requirement of time, then planning is a kind of problem solving. If planning is related to various time horizons, ranging from making a meal to deciding what jobs will be available for me the next five years, problem solving is a part of planning. The common sense idea is that planning, problem solving, and decision making are overlapping. They are not the same, but they have various activities, starting points, and aspects in common. This may relate to the individual or group, to the processes, to search activities, to the outcomes and the results, to single or multistep activities, and to the phases that can be discerned in planning, decision making, and problem solving.

From the various and extended literature in all three fields, it cannot be decided what is the real definition of planning, decision making, and problem solving. In this

TABLE 4.1. Comparison of Planning for Oneself and for Others, Problem Solving, and Decision Making

Various Aspects	Planning for Oneself	Planning for Others	Problem Solving	Decision Making
Working with representations?	Yes	Yes	Yes	Yes
Discrepancy between desired and existing situation?	Yes	Yes	Yes	Yes
(partly) Uncertain?	Yes	Yes	Yes	Yes
Irreversible investment in time, energy, and intelligence?	Yes	No	No	Yes
Must generate a representation or problem space?	No	Yes	Yes	No
Certain object types must be present?	Time	Time (place)	No	No
More process or outcome oriented?	Outcome	Process	Process	Outcome
Use of specific methods?	No	No	Yes (e.g., means/ends)	Yes (e.g., smart)
Choose ourselves (in contrast with confronted with)?	Yes	No	No	Yes
Will be effectuated in real life?	Yes	Maybe	Maybe	Yes
(1) Actor for actor or (2) actor for others (organization)?	1	1 and 2	1	1

book the various chapters exemplify the close connection between planning, problem solving, and even decision making. Our perspective is planning (and scheduling), and because this means going from an existing not well-defined situation with resources and constraints to a (sub)optimal or even satisfying situation, it necessarily overlaps with issues in decision making and problem solving.

In our view, planning is a kind of problem solving (in terms of process, generating and exploiting a problem space and search) with the important difference that if time, in terms of sooner or later or in terms of seconds and hours, is involved in the generation of the problem space, it is (a) planning (problem). After this generation the normal processes of solving the problem or planning are mostly similar. If the time factor (or object type) is taken out, we have a sequence of problem-solving activities. This means that opening a door that is surprisingly locked up can involve a problem-solving activity, whereas composing and preparing a meal and buying ingredients mostly is a planning problem and not a problem-solving activity. The trivial part of decision making is involved everywhere, because I decide to open the door and I decide to prepare a meal, and so on.

Because we think that the issue of "planning or problem solving" is relevant in the practice of planners, we operationalized this issue in the experiment in Section 4.3 by defining the (planning) problem in our study in such a way that an overall check can be made at the beginning of the problem-solving situation. This overall check of the problem shows the fact that planners realize that they have to solve a problem (in state space terms) and at the same time it may give insight in the kind of helicopter view the planners have in dealing with a planning problem. The expectation we have is that at least some planners in the production domain try to construct such an overview, which is called a capacity check, because this is the normal procedure in production planning. The question is, What do planners in the staff scheduling and transportation planning do?

4.2.2.3. Hierarchical, Opportunistic, and Script-Based Planning.

The planning/problem-solving discussion is closely connected to the second issue, whether the way the plan execution or the problem-solving procedure is carried out is hierarchical or opportunistic. First, the suggestion may be that solving a problem with or without an overview is done straightforward. One just has to follow a couple of rules from top to bottom and one ends up with a solution. Second, the issue of the overlap between planning and problem solving very much depends on the format of representations in the information processing system of the human planner. Do planners use production rules? How are these rules controlled? Or do planners use scripts, schemata, and frames? Both issues come together in the discussion started by Hayes-Roth and Hayes-Roth (1979) about hierarchical and opportunistic planning.

Hierarchical planning means that there is a nested number of goal and subgoal structures or a hierarchy of representations of a plan. The highest level in the hierarchy may be a simplification or an abstraction, whereas the lowest level is a concrete sequence of actions to solve (a part of) the planning problem. One solves a planning problem by starting at the highest level, and then one continues by realizing subgoals until one reaches the final solution. Hayes-Roth and Hayes-Roth relate this to a distinction in the overview aspect and in the action aspect of plans that they successively call plan formation and plan execution.

Unjustly, but quite understandably, the hierarchical approach is attributed to Newell and Simon. They started to talk about problem solving in terms of problem spaces, goal hierarchies, and universal subgoaling, but never advocated a strict hierarchical approach; one only has to recall Simon's notions of "bounded rationality" or 'satisfying" concept (Jorna, 1990; Augier and March, 2004).

In contrast to the hierarchical view on plan execution, Hayes-Roth and Hayes-Roth propose an opportunistic process of performing a planning. This nonhierarchical planning assumes that a plan is executed with the help of some kind of mental blackboard where pieces of information, relevant cues, and possible subgoals are stored. They claimed and showed that planning happens asynchronously and is determined by the momentary aspects of a problem. No fixed order of operations exists; the plan execution and the steps to be taken grow out of the problem stage at hand. When planners solve a planning problem, they start with the top goal, but very soon lose track of the goal structure and then continue to fulfill the goals that are reachable within reasonable time. The hierarchy very soon vanishes, and what remains is some sort of heterarchy. For that reason, this planning behavior is called opportunistic. This is not to say that the planners behave irrationally; on the contrary, there are often very good reasons that an intended course of action is not continued. Planners do not have an in-depth and complete overview, but act according to changing states of affairs.

Although the contrast with the hierarchical approach may be large, a strong similarity also exists between the hierarchical and opportunistic way of proceeding. In the hierarchical as well as in the opportunistic approach, the fundamental assumption is that planning is problem solving that can best be described in terms of problem spaces, production rules, and goals. That is, the basic descriptive structure is the same for both, but real behavior within the problem space is executed differently.

With regard to the problem space description, hierarchical as well as opportunistic planning differ from the perspective defended by Schank and Abelson (1977) and Riesbeck and Schank (1989). There, the representation of planning problems is described in terms of scripts and frames consisting of objects, slots, and relations. The basic structure is what they called a knowledge structure (Schank and Abelson, 1977). It gives form to the organization of a pattern of actions by means of scripts, plans, goals, and themes. In this respect the most important ones are scripts and plans.

Concerning scripts, take the following example. If someone states that they are going to a restaurant, one can assume, given some general knowledge of the human biological system, that the event has something to do with food. Beyond this, the fact that the human memory system also contains specific knowledge means that humans can assess certain characteristics of situations and can quickly make all sorts of inferences. If someone goes to a bakery and returns with a loaf of bread, the specific knowledge that people have at their disposal enables them to infer that the bread has been bought and that certain actions had to be carried out in order to accomplish this. People have standard knowledge concerning standard situations at their disposal (Schank and Abelson, 1977, p. 39). Some of these chains always appear in a certain order, and this means that some bits of knowledge are organized in (larger) conceptual units; that is, there are groups of causal chains. In a memory system, such a structure only functions if at least two sorts of mechanisms are present. The first consists of a mechanism that makes it possible to retrieve events from the memory system in an outline form. In the most extreme case, this mechanism must be able to retrieve a global event on the basis of one part of the causal chain. The second mechanism that is necessary is one that enables us to fill in detailed elements, after the global event has been retrieved. Detailed elements may be necessary in order to understand the total event.

Schank and Abelson call this structure, in which the mechanisms as well as the mutual connections between parts of an event are represented correctly and at an adequate level, a script. "A script is a structure that describes appropriate sequences of events in a particular context. A script is made up of slots and requirements about what can fill those slots. The structure is an interconnected whole, and what is in one slot affects what can be in another" (Schank and Abelson, 1977, p. 41). A script is therefore a pattern of actions with a stereotyped sequence.

Human memory consists of many scripts—that is, scripts for buying things, for going to parties, for traveling by train, and so on. Schank and Abelson are very well known for their elaboration of the "restaurant" script. The central element here is the following story. "John goes to the restaurant. He orders a steak from the waitress. He gives a large tip and leaves the restaurant." Someone who hears this story will readily understand its meaning. The whole "restaurant" script is actually one large causal chain which Schank and Abelson elaborate in great detail.

Not all scripts are of the same type. There are situational scripts, personal scripts, and instrumental scripts. Situational scripts and personal scripts are closely connected. The difference is that situational scripts define the social interactions between people rather accurately (Schank and Abelson, 1977, p. 61), whereas in personal scripts individual persons have more "degrees of freedom" in their behavior. The instrumental script is a sort of procedure and looks very similar to recipes provided in cookery books or followed by a chemist. They look like situational scripts in the sense that they also represent sequences of actions, but the instrumental scripts are much more constraining in the pattern they use (Schank and Abelson, 1977, p. 65). Examples are: starting a car, baking an egg, making coffee, or starting a computer program.

If we combine the knowledge structure scripts with plans, it can be said that scripts are realizations of plans. A plan can be defined as a series of intended actions in order to realize a goal (Schank and Abelson, 1977, p. 71). In contrast to a script, a plan is more concerned with general information. "A plan is intended to be the repository for general information that will connect events that cannot be connected by use of an available script or standard causal chain expansion" (Schank and Abelson, 1977, p. 70). A plan is the result of an operation. Something happens and someone performs an action in which the intermediate mental state can be viewed as a plan (Schank and Abelson, 1977, p. 72). In the category of plans we find named plans and plan boxes. A named plan is a plan that contains a fixed sequence of instrumental goals that are necessary in order to reach a certain goal. Such a named plan is retrieved from memory and is automatically executed (Schank and Abelson, 1977, p. 79).

The most important aspect of scripts or plans in the perspective of Schank and Abelson is that some kind of representational skeleton or framework is retrieved from (long-term) memory. Stored plans contain guidelines for resolution of sorts of problems. In this process, two stages exist. First a skeleton plan is found, and second the abstract steps in a plan are filled with concrete operations. Although general cognitive processing is involved in making a plan, the emphasis in this approach is on the memory system. Plans at different levels of abstraction and in different formats are stored in and retrieved from memory. There are strong similarities with the approach to planning that Hoc (1988) proposed.

The described approaches of hierarchical, opportunistic, and script-based planning are all about cognitive processing within a human information processing system. In hierarchical and opportunistic planning, the emphasis is state spaces and search within. The script-based planning focuses more on the role of memory and its structures. Furthermore, script-based planning argues that fixed structures are used in planning, whereas hierarchical and opportunistic planning work with production rules that can be combined and recombined.

4.2.3. Planning Domain, Planning Support, and the Empirical Study

In discussions about cognition (Section 4.2.1) and generic tasks (Section 4.2.2) similarities in planning situations are emphasized. Planners as cognitive systems are, of course, different in terms of what they know about contexts and organizations, but their processing of information, their memory system, and their attention system are mostly similar. The same assumption of similarity is inherent in the notion of *generic* task. In terms of (mental) processing, a planning task is a planning task whether it concerns staff, machines, transportation, or products. The question is whether and to what degree this general similarity is influenced by the domain factor.

As we earlier argued, the dominance of machines, product specifications, and production lines in production planning may very easily lead to a view that undervalues the role of cognitive processes and human reasoning [see van Wezel (2001) for a description of production planning]. This fixed and complicated domain specification makes this planning incomparable with, for example, planning or scheduling of nurses and shifts in hospitals. The claim is that the specificity and therefore the differences of domains exceed the similarities from the perspective of cognition and generic tasks. The question is in what sense the domain in which the planners are working effects their problem-solving behavior. This is one of the main research questions in the empirical study to be discussed in Section 4.3.

In the empirical study we used a planning problem for three different domains. From a mathematical point of view the problems are identical. We will explain the details in Section 4.3. Although our study is about planning behavior, our main intention is, besides acquiring more knowledge of reasoning of planners in planning problems, to use the outcomes for design and development of knowledge-based decision support systems, what we earlier called the bottom-up approach in software support [see also Klein and Methlie (1990)].

As far as we know now, the special software systems that we built in the past, such as the ZKR system for nurse scheduling, proved to be successful in concrete task support. However, we developed these systems for isolated domains, such as nurse scheduling, planning bank employees, or certain kinds of transportation planning. It is also important to develop a general perspective on plan execution (planning behavior) as well as on plan formation. Of course we want to know what planners do in practice in order to design and implement dedicated support systems. Nevertheless, we also wanted to generalize from this specialized support to a more general framework on plan execution and plan formation that can be used in a wider sense and is suitable for reuse (van Wezel, Jorna, and Mietus, 1996, and Chapter 7 of this book). This was the conclusion we drew from the design and development of ZKR and other programs. It was a success, but we also draw a lesson from it (Mietus, 1994; Jorna, 1994; van Wezel et al., 1996). The realization of ZKR itself did not show our shortcomings. What did show our shortcomings, however, was the transfer of knowledge to other planning applications. To make our position concerning user-oriented planning support and domain-independence problem solving strategies more clear, we will shortly go into the basic assumptions that were behind the development of the nurse scheduling support system ZKR.

ZKR stands for "ZieKenhuisRoostersysteem" (scheduling nurses in hospitals) and was designed to support nurse scheduling in hospital units (Mietus, 1994). For the development of this system a planner (user)-oriented perspective was used. More than 20 nurses were extensively studied in their planning practice during several phases of system development. The nurses solved assignments with increasing levels of difficulty. Their scheduling procedures were monitored before and after finishing the scheduling support system. Three more general conclusions came out of the research.

First, we found that different schedulers solving the same scheduling problem strongly differed in their problem-solving strategies and also in their outcomes. One overall cognitive strategy to solve nurse scheduling problems did not seem to exist. However, there are fixed as well as floating patterns within the various strategies. Second place, we found that schedulers wanted to control the planning session until the very end. They even wanted to understand the intermediate outcomes of the program. In the third place it turned out that many decision points in the problem-solving strategy can be grouped together in such a way that different planners with different strategies can be effectively supported by one modular program (Mietus, 1994).

The ZKR system can be conceived of as a knowledge-based decision support system (KB-DSS). The basis of this approach consists in the elicitation of the knowledge of individuals to solve complex problems. Computational or mathematical elegance is not emphasized, but instead human information processing. To elicit knowledge, several strategies can be followed. In the ZKR case, we used pre-test and post-test comparisons and extensive protocol analyses. In the empirical study discussed in Section 4.3, we designed a planning problem of which the protocols were collected and analyzed. One can also use prototyping of ready-made support systems to find out about cognitive strategies of problem solvers (Jorna and Simons, 1992). The essential starting point is that an individual user has to solve a complex task.

Cognitive task analysis, which in our opinion is the core in the realization of knowledge-based decision support, is disputed within the information sciences. Although we practiced and supported this approach, there are three good reasons to be a bit reluctant to consider this analysis as a panacea for all problems in task support. First, some problems have a clear (mathematical) formula that solves a problem. Why bother yourself with asking people how they think the problem should be solved, if an algorithm does it also and often better. That is, in such a case a normative approach is preferred to a descriptive approach. Second, a cognitive task analysis means much work and requires special skills of software designers or knowledge engineers. It always remains the question whether the extensive analysis was deep enough. Knowledge engineers never know this for sure. Third, the problem is that the analysis of a large number of users brings about a very diverse repertoire of solutions. As a consequence, a knowledge engineer may end up with as many supporting systems as there are users. If this is the ultimate outcome of the dedicated user-orientation approach, it is a threatening phantom for software designers.

The empirical study for three different domains discussed in Section 4.3 is meant to partly deal with these drawbacks. First, we would like to argue that many planning problems cannot be solved by using algorithms only. From a mathematical perspective, planning problems are NP-complete, and the ZKR research showed that making calculations and using algorithms is only a part of the overall planning task (Mietus, 1994).

Second, we would like to resist overindividualism. On the interface level there may be as many views as there are users. One level below, however, a common orientation is necessary. The question, of course, is whether this should go as far as to incorporate not only different forms of, for example, staff planning, but also other planning domains. The present study is one step in the direction of a search for possibilities of similarity in planning behavior regardless of domains. Moreover, the more similarity—and, as a consequence, the more reuse—is possible, the more the time spent on cognitive task analysis may be shortened.

The last point we want to make with respect to software support for planning is related to the astonishing fact that most of the software that has been developed for several forms and domains of planning is still rarely used. Surveys in the past (Berenschot and Logiplan, 1994; van Wezel, 1994) showed that the purchase of planning software is limited. That has not changed with SAP and ERP systems. The least used modules in these information systems are the planning and scheduling modules. Despite elegant algorithms in these systems, real practical planning— that is, fine tuning, overviews, and myopic firefighting—is done by human planners, often by hand and with paper and pencil. We believe that this practice is encouraged by the top-down approach used in these information systems. The planner is supposed to adjust to the systems model. Real, actual planning behavior of planners is often not taken into account. The empirical study discussed below is carried out to know more about practical plan execution—that is, planning behavior of individual planners in various domains.

The literature on cognition, planning, and support is rich, ambiguous, and not integrated. Our empirical study will not change this situation. However, what we aim at in the study is not common practice in this area of research. We study real planning behavior, of real planners, with domain differentiation and applying findings and theories of cognitive science. One of the methods we use is protocol analysis. Before we continue with the details of the empirical study, we conclude this section with some expectations.

Revealing different mental representations that planners use in solving planning problems is very difficult. Asking them whether they use production rules or scripts is not reliable and might also give them cues. However, we still want to know whether the protocols could give us hints concerning the kind of representation the planners use. This was one of the reasons that we formulated the same planning problem in three different domains. We used a staff scheduling domain with shifts and nurses and opening hours of a clinic. We also used a production planning domain with products, machines, and processing times and we used a transportation domain with lorries, distances, and products to be transported. If the domain is important, the protocols should contain remarks referring to the planners' normal way of handling the problem and should also have all kinds of expressions of memory retrieval. This implies explicit memory usage. If the domain is not important, the protocols should contain remarks that explicitly refer to production rules "if I do so ... then so and so will follow." The assumption here is that production rules are more abstract than memory expressions like "this looks like a problem I have been solving last time." Varying the domain, therefore, sheds light on the questions, What kind of representation is favored by the individual planners?

With respect to the hierarchical and opportunistic way of planning, we do not expect the hierarchical way of problem solving to be the standard way. Opportunistic behavior is the standard, and opportunism may go as far as that it results in chaotic behavior, meaning that the planner does not have a specific (sub)goal available anymore after some time.

We also expect planners to prefer a bottom-up procedure to a top-down approach. Here, bottom-up means that a planner starts with detailed and concrete information, whereas top-down means that an empty structure is the starting point that will be filled during the problem-solving process.

Mietus (1994) showed that planning as an integrated task consists of various subtasks such as counting, negotiating, evaluating, and problem solving itself. She found that in some cases simple counting takes more than 15% of the time to solve the planning problem. Even for the scheduling of 20 staff members, this sometimes results in more than 300 simple addition and subtraction problems. Mistakes can easily be made in these simple addition activities, especially when they are done by hand. Very simple additions or subtractions in large quantities lead to many mistakes that will interact with the overall problem-solving process. We expect the same kind of outcomes regardless of the domain for which the planning problems were formulated—that is, much counting will occur and mistakes will be made.

In the discussion on whether planners explicitly use so-called rules, indicating (complex) condition–action pairs or so-called memory tags, expressed in remarks like "this situation looks similar to the one I solved last week," we analyzed the protocols in terms of "if–then relations" and "memory expressions." The first is an indication of the production rule perspective that Newell and Simon have on problem solving, the second is in line with the scripts and frame-oriented work by Schank and Abelson.

In relation to software support of planning, the question is what kind of visual aid the planners will use. Therefore we analyzed the protocols and collected the white papers on which notes and diagrams were made. Our expectation (Mietus, 1994; Numan, 1998) is that planners will use simple schemes without much quantification. This is in line with many remarks from practice saying that planners normally make their plans and schedules on the back of an envelope.

Our most important expectations concern similarities and differences in domain. Although it is often argued that planning is determined by the domain in which the planners are working, we do not expect differences to be spectacular in terms of problem-solving strategies. Whether one has to plan cars and locations in the domain of transportation or nurses and shifts in the domain of personnel, the cognitive processes in solving the planning problem should, to a large degree, be similar. We extended this expectation by conducting the experiment in two countries. However, because it may be the case that the domain in which the planners regularly work does effect the plan execution, we used a questionnaire to get information about aspects of the regular planning in their own organizations, such as who is responsible for the plan, whether fixed or variable time horizon planning is used, whether they have one plan (planner) or several plans (planners), and whether they work informal or bureaucratic. Although we think that there are differences, we have no explicit expectations concerning these variables.

From the above discussions, the following expectations can be summarized:

1. A capacity check is not standard, but, if present, it is more often found in the production domain.
2. Opportunistic planning behavior is more common than hierarchical planning behavior.
3. Planners prefer bottom-up (starting detailed) planning strategies to top-down (starting rough) planning strategies.
4. Making plans implies many simple calculations enlarging the risk of small mistakes.
5. If visual aids are used, they concern diagrams and pictures, not numbers and figures.
6. The differences in planning behavior are larger within domains than between domains.

4.3. THE EMPIRICAL STUDY: PLANNING IN DIFFERENT DOMAINS

4.3.1. Material, Procedure and Subjects (Planners)

Hayes-Roth and Hayes-Roth (1979) and other cognitive psychologists analyzed cognitive strategies in controlled environments with small problems, sometimes related to doing errands. Unfortunately, however, real planning problems always take place in uncontrolled environments. Errand problems are simple problems compared to planning tasks in organizations. The planning problems that are common in factories and plants take much time to solve and cannot clearly be separated and controlled. Therefore, we decided to take the best of two and to use a "real" planning problem that can be "solved" in restricted time in a real practice environment.

The planning or scheduling problem we used for the empirical research came from a hospital somewhere in the Netherlands and was slightly adjusted to serve our purposes. We even decided to keep the problem unsolvable, as it originally was. Unsolvable, of course, is relative, because every planning problem is solvable, provided that one adjusts the constraints or goal functions. We had two reasons for doing this. In practice, it is usually the case that a planner has to deal with problems that are not well-defined. A planning problem is hardly ever solvable in its first presentation. One has to adjust or release constraints or has to forget about certain goal functions. The second reason has to do with different planning domains. We wanted to know what types of constraints planners will evaluate if a planning problem is not solvable in its original formulation. We again realized the best of two—that is, dealing with real scheduling problems and in semicontrolled settings to find out about the cognitive strategies of planners in different domains.

The study was conducted in the Netherlands and in Indonesia with the same problem, the same procedure, and organizations from similar branches. Therefore, we were also able to compare results of different countries with one another. The choice of countries is coincidental. The instruction, formulation, and requested solutions of the staff scheduling problem were as follows; in Appendix I the same problem is formulated for the production and transportation domain.

The Staff Scheduling/Planning Problem

Instruction: We ask you to read this problem and answer the question. Please do this step by step while telling us what you are thinking of.

Problem: In a clinic that will be opened next week, the staff will work on morning and afternoon shifts. One morning or one afternoon is one shift. Until now, there are three qualified nurses A, B, and C. They work respectively 8, 8, and 3 shifts in the week. The doctor (specialist) of the clinic works 3.5 days a week: Monday, Tuesday morning, Wednesday, and Thursday. On these days the doctor needs three nurses for assistance. When the doctor is not working, only paperwork has to be done and only one nurse is needed. The clinic is open 4.5 days a week. Friday afternoon the clinic is closed. One more nurse, D, is recruited for 4 shifts. This new employee can only work on Mondays and Tuesdays.

Question: Make a schedule for the next week. If you think the problem is unsolvable, give us your proposed solution.

The problem in the staff scheduling domain is graphically represented in Figure 4.1. Whatever combination a planner tries, a solution cannot be found within the constraints that have to do with opening hours, staff quantities, doctor–nurse

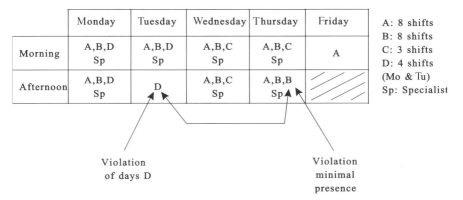

Figure 4.1. A diagram of the planning problem for the personnel domain.

ratio, and preferences of the nurses. The only solution lies in relaxing one of the constraints.

The staff scheduling problem was reformulated such that it suited a production and a transportation domain. This was verified in production and transportation firms. Although these firms did not really have the same problem in reality, it was confirmed that organizations might structure their production or transport in the way it was formulated in the problem.

The staff scheduling problem has the following organizational characteristics. It is realized by one planner. Once a week a plan is made. A fixed planning horizon is used, and in principle the planning may be different every week. As already mentioned, from a linear programming perspective the problems in the various domains are interchangeable. That is, mathematically and in terms of used quantities the problem is the same (see Appendix I). The overall comparison in terms of quantities and constraints is depicted in Table 4.2. The columns represent the various domains,

TABLE 4.2. Three Problem Domains and the Similarity of the Characteristics

	Staff Problem	Production Problem	Transport Problem
General layout (opening, machine, lorry)	Open: morning and afternoon (2)	Machine I and II (2)	Lorry I and II (2)
Elements (A, B, C, and D)	Persons (4)	Products (4)	Products (4)
Quantities (8, 8, 3, and 4)	Shifts per person	Operations per product	Containers per product
General occupation (3 and 1)	Doctor/three nurses, one nurse	Machine I + II, machine II	Lorry I + II, lorry II
Particular occupation (7 and 9)	Doctor on clinic, only clinic	Machine I + II, machine II	Lorry I + II, lorry II
Properties of the elements	A, B, C, no D: first four time periods	A, B, C, no D: first four time periods	A, B, C, no D: first four time periods

whereas the rows are about the aspects in quantitative terms that are similar in different domains. Initially, 34 subjects participated in the research. It was our intention to have equal proportions in both countries; but due to unforeseen problems in Indonesia, we ended with 18 planners in the Netherlands and 16 in Indonesia. The amount and distribution of planners are shown in Table 4.3. The companies in the Netherlands and Indonesia were matched as best as possible. The problems and the questionnaires were formulated in Dutch and Bahasa Indonesia. The procedure in the empirical research was as follows. After informing the planners by telephone and asking them for participation, an appointment was made in the organization to do the research. We asked the planners to solve the problems in their office, not in the factory, so disturbances were as minimal as possible. However, in some cases the planners were needed in the factory. This was taken into account in scoring, solution times, and protocols. The same order of things took place for every planner in both countries. After some words of welcome the planners were informed about the aim of the research. Then they were instructed about the questionnaire and the questionnaire was filled in. This was the first part of the research.

After that we presented the planning problem and we asked them to solve the problem by thinking aloud. Thinking aloud was also demonstrated and practiced with examples before presenting the problem. There was no time pressure in solving the problem. During the process of problem solving the planners were sometimes reminded to think aloud as much as possible. Staff planners got the staff scheduling problem, production planners got the production planning problem, and transportation planners got the transportation problem. During the sessions the think-aloud protocols were audio-taped. If the planners made computational mistakes during the session that gave them the wrong impression that the problem was solved, they were corrected if they persisted in their mistakes. The corrections only consisted in telling that something went wrong, not in providing a solution. The starting time and ending time of the problem solution were registered in minutes. During the problem-solving process the planners were informed that they could use visual aids—that is, paper was provided on which diagrams and annotations could be made. Afterwards the paper material was collected for analysis.

Four kinds of data were collected: (1) answers to the questionnaire that provided us with information about regular planning practices in organizations; (2) answers that were given as a solution to the problem; (3) solution times (response latencies) of the problem in minutes; (4) "think-aloud" verbal protocols that resulted from

TABLE 4.3. Amount of Cooperating Planners in the Netherlands and Indonesia

	Number of Planners in the Netherlands	Number of Planners in Indonesia
Staff scheduling	6	5
Production planning	6	5
Transportation planning	6	6

recording the problem-solving processes were analyzed and categorized. The verbal protocols were all transcribed and purified from statements like "let's see" or "hum hum." The transcriptions were used for analysis.

4.3.2. The Results: Questionnaire, Solutions, Times, and Protocols

The questionnaire about the organization provided information about organizational settings in the countries. A note of warning has to be made, here. Our analyses were done with small groups of planners. We were not able to control all possible disturbing variables. This is one of the consequences of doing research outside the laboratory. It is therefore not possible to easily generalize to larger populations. The organizational differences gave some impression about the domain the planners are normally working in, but they do not explain the differences and similarities in planning behavior. In the remainder the following results will be discussed: the organizational questionnaire (Section 3.2.1), the outcomes of the planning task and the time it took the planners to "solve" the problems (Section 3.2.2), and the differences in planning behavior (Section 3.2.3). As explained in Table 4.3, 18 planners from the Netherlands and 16 planners from Indonesia participated. In the protocol analysis, 3 Indonesian planners sometimes refused to explain their reasoning (think aloud in some parts of the problem solving). Therefore, N was usually 34, but in some situations it was 31. This is indicated in the tables.

4.3.2.1. Results: The Organizational Questionnaire. Big differences occurred in the way the planners perceived their own organization (Table 4.4). The difference is significant ($\chi^2 = 7.38$; $df = 3$; $p < 0.025$), meaning that even in this small sample the Dutch consider their organizational structure to be more informal, whereas the Indonesians view it as hierarchical. Concerning the number of plans that were made in different kinds of organizations in different countries, the results were less clear (Table 4.5). Although we selected organizations such that they matched in size, type and branch, we had no detailed knowledge of the usual planning practices in the organizations. The results show that the differences are large if we compare the two countries for each domain, separately. If we look at the total for the two countries, in the Netherlands one overall plan occurs as often as several plans, whereas in Indonesia often several plans are used in one organization ($\chi^2 = 3.69$; $df = 1$; $p < 0.05$). This situation may be due to the organization of the planning. However, it can also be because of differences in the number of

TABLE 4.4. Organizational Structure in Two Countries ($N = 34$)

Organizational Structure	Netherlands	Indonesia
Hierarchical	4	8
Bureaucratic	0	2
Informal	14	5
Other	0	1

TABLE 4.5. Number of Plans in Staff, Production, and Transportation Domains in Two Countries ($N = 34$)

Number of Plans	Netherlands				Indonesia			
	Staff	Production	Transportation	Total	Staff	Production	Transportation	Total
One overall plan	4	2	3	9	2	1	0	3
Several plans	1	4	3	8	2	4	6	12
No response	1	0	0	1	1	0	0	1

people that worked in organizations. Labor in Indonesia is extremely cheap compared with that in the Netherlands, which means that much more people "walk around" and more people often means that more planning(s) has to be done.

We also asked the planners to indicate the planning in their organization, with which they were familiar, as fixed or incremental horizon planning (Table 4.6). "Fixed" means that a plan has to be made for the next week or month and that within this horizon all resources or elements (object type and tokens) have to be attuned. "Incremental" means that at any time something can be added to the plan. The plan grows. The planning horizon is rolling on. This is important because the problem we presented the planners is a fixed horizon planning. The results showed that there are no big differences between staff, production, and transportation planning domains in the countries. Fixed and incremental horizon planning occur almost equally often. The only interesting phenomenon consists in a small nonsignificant difference in the overall situation for the Netherlands and Indonesia ($\chi^2 = 2.58$; $df = 1$; $p < 0.18$). In the Netherlands there is a tendency to work with fixed horizon planning, indicating perhaps a more rigid planning perspective compared with Indonesia. In Indonesia, planning is more realized in an incremental way.

4.3.2.2. Results from the Planning Problems: Solutions.
The problems were not solved by all planners (Table 4.7). In this case, "solved" means that they recognized that the problem was not solvable and came up with a suggestion for a constraint violation. Three Indonesian planners refused to solve the problem. We can only guess about the reasons. In the statistics only the solved and nonsolved problems

TABLE 4.6. Fixed and Incremental Time Horizon Planning for Three Domains in Two Countries ($N = 34$)

Time Horizon	Netherlands				Indonesia			
	Staff	Production	Transportation	Total	Staff	Production	Transportation	Total
Fixed time horizon	4	4	3	11	3	2	2	7
Incremental time horizon	0	2	3	5	2	3	4	9
Other	2	0	0	2	0	0	0	0

TABLE 4.7. Solutions of the Planning Problems for Dutch and Indonesian Planners ($N = 34$)

	Netherlands				Indonesia			
	Staff	Production	Transportation	Total	Staff	Production	Transportation	Total
Solved	6	6	4	16	3	2	5	10
Not solved	0	0	2	2	1	1	1	3
No answer	0	0	0	0	1	2	0	3

were included. There was no significant difference between Indonesia and the Netherlands ($\chi^2 = 0.79$; $p < 0.37$; $df = 1$). Differences between various domains were not significant as well. It took the planners much time to accomplish the assignment. The average solution was 18.61 minutes (Table 4.8).

A strong country effect occurred for the planning problem ($F = 5.85$; $p < 0.02$; $df = 1$). This means that all the planners in the Netherlands solved the problem faster than the Indonesian planners. Interesting was the absence of effects related to domains. There was a tendency, but no significance, for the domain in the problem ($F = 2.89$; $p < 0.12$; $df = 2$). In Table 4.8 it can be seen that the transportation problem took a shorter amount of time for the Dutch planners compared with the staff and production problem, whereas it took longer for the Indonesian planners to accomplish this problem. We can only speculate about the reasons. There was no interaction effect of domain and country ($F = 0.55$; $p < 0.31$; $df = 3$).

4.3.2.3. Results of Planning Behavior: Strategies, Subtasks, Constraints and Memory.
The analysis of protocols provided results of the cognitive strategies (Section 4.3.2.3.1), explicit capacity checks (Section 4.3.2.3.2), counting procedures (Section 4.3.2.3.3), mistakes (Section 4.3.2.3.4), constraints that were adjusted (Section 4.3.2.3.5) and representation in memory and use of visual aids (Section 4.3.2.3.6). Scoring of the protocols was independently done by two researchers.

4.3.2.3.1. Cognitive Strategies. Two kinds of cognitive strategies were investigated in the protocols. The first concerned hierarchical and opportunistic or chaotic planning procedures in the solution process (Table 4.9). The results showed no differences for the countries ($\chi^2 = 0.90$; $p < 0.63$; $df = 2$) or for the domains ($\chi^2 = 4.01$; $p < 0.40$; $df = 4$). This means that there were no differences between

TABLE 4.8. Results in Solution Times for Problem (in Minutes) ($N = 31$)

Problem	Netherlands	Indonesia	Domain Overall
Staff problem	16.67 min	18.67 min	17.33 min
Production problem	19.00 min	22.50 min	19.88 min
Transportation problem	14.00 min	24.40 min	18.73 min
Country overall	16.56 min	22.30 min	18.61 min

TABLE 4.9. Cognitive Strategies of Planners in Countries and Domains ($N = 31$)

Cognitive Strategy I	Country		Domain		
	Netherlands	Indonesia	Staff	Production	Transportation
Hierarchical	7	3	2	4	4
Opportunistic	6	5	3	2	6
Chaotic	5	5	5	3	2

countries or domains to prefer a hierarchical to an opportunistic or chaotic procedure. Interesting in the results is the presence of variety, indicating that in contrast to the remarks by Hayes-Roth and Hayes-Roth, some people prefer to plan hierarchically, whereas others do it opportunistically. Still some others work chaotically, meaning that they are completely confused and proceed without any guiding principle.

The second cognitive strategy was related to a bottom-up or a top-down procedure (Table 4.10). There was a striking difference in this case, showing that the Dutch preferred a top-down strategy, whereas the Indonesians mainly used a bottom-up strategy ($\chi^2 = 5.14$; $p < 0.06$; $df = 2$). Although we had some expectations concerning the same kind of effect for the domains with especially the production planners doing it more top-down, no differences were found ($\chi^2 = 1.66$; $p < 0.67$; $df = 4$). We will discuss the outcomes of the cognitive strategies in Section 4.4.

4.3.2.3.2. Capacity Check. In planning literature it is often claimed that a capacity check must be performed at the beginning of a planning (Smith, Lasilla, and Becker, 1996). The results showed the differences (Table 4.11). Dutch planners used the capacity check, whereas Indonesian planners completely neglected a capacity check ($\chi^2 = 8.24$; $p < 0.02$; $df = 2$). Concerning the domains, a tendency exists that a capacity check is more usual in the production domain than in other domains. However, the difference was not significant ($\chi^2 = 5.93$; $p < 0.20$; $df = 4$). The difference can be completely attributed to the Dutch planners. We expected a stronger effect for both countries, but it was absent.

4.3.2.3.3. Amount of Counting. The protocols also indicated whether the planners were explicitly counting (Table 4.12). We categorized the evidence that if they counted only once it was scored as little, two or three times as moderate and four

TABLE 4.10. Cognitive Strategies of Planners in Countries and Domains ($N = 31$)

Cognitive Strategy II	Country		Domain		
	Netherlands	Indonesia	Staff	Production	Transportation
No answer	0	2	1	1	0
Top-down	12	4	5	5	6
Bottom-up	6	7	4	3	6

TABLE 4.11. Capacity Check for Countries and Domains ($N = 31$)

	Country		Domain		
Capacity Check	Netherlands	Indonesia	Staff	Production	Transportation
No answer	0	1	0	1	0
Present	10	1	2	5	4
Absent	8	11	8	3	8

times or more as much. Indonesian planners counted more than Dutch, but the difference was not significant ($\chi^2 = 4.71$; $p < 0.19$; $df = 3$). No difference between domains was found ($\chi^2 = 2.85$; $p < 0.82$; $df = 6$).

4.3.2.3.4. Amount of Mistakes. The amount of mistakes indicates that we had to correct the planners if they unjustly thought they were finished; that is, they solved the planning problem (Table 4.13). The kind of categorization (in little, medium, and much) used for counting was also used for mistakes. If they corrected the mistakes themselves, it was not scored. There was an overall tendency of making only a few mistakes, showing no differences between countries ($\chi^2 = 4.95$; $p < 0.17$; $df = 3$) or domains ($\chi^2 = 6.79$; $p < 0.30$; $df = 6$).

4.3.2.3.5. Constraint Relaxation. Although the domains were different, the mathematics behind the problem was the same. The reason we manipulated the planning problem in this way was that we wanted to have information on the problem representation of the planners. We argued earlier that we wanted to find out whether the domain determines the way planners solve a planning problem. We hypothesized that planners from whatever domain use a general (cognitive) planning strategy. The planning problem was created such that the planner was not able to solve the problem within the constraints. The constraints could be relieved in several ways. Table 4.14 enumerates the constraints mentioned by the planners. It reads as follows. In the staff scheduling problem, for example, the ratio of nurses and doctors could be changed from 3:1 into 2:1 for some days. In the production planning problem the service of one of the machines could be postponed, and in the transportation planning problem the properties of the containers with the products could be changed.

TABLE 4.12. Counting During Problem Solving in Countries and Domains ($N = 31$)

	Country		Domain		
Amount of Counting	Netherlands	Indonesia	Staff	Production	Transportation
No answer	0	2	0	1	1
Little (<2)	7	3	3	3	4
Medium (2–3)	4	1	1	1	3
Much (>4)	7	7	6	4	4

TABLE 4.13. Mistakes During the Problem-Solving Process in Countries and Domains ($N = 31$)

Amount of Mistakes	Country		Domain		
	Netherlands	Indonesia	Staff	Production	Transportation
No answer	0	2	0	1	1
Little (<2)	12	9	7	4	10
Medium (2–3)	3	0	2	1	0
Much (>4)	3	2	1	3	1

As we showed in Section 3.1, the constraints were formulated in terms appropriate for the specific domain. The results showed a strong difference between Dutch and Indonesian planners ($\chi^2 = 19.13; p < 0.00; df = 5$). Many Dutch planners changed the properties of the elements A, B, C, or D, whether it be staff members, products in the orders, or products in the containers. None of the Indonesian planners did so. They opted for service delay or for a higher occupation rate, or they did not want to give an answer. Remember that planners were considered to have solved the problem, if they indicated it was unsolvable. Some planners hesitated in making a choice for a particular constraint. In contradistinction with the country result, it was interesting to find no differences between domains ($\chi^2 = 8.57; p < 0.57; df = 10$). This means that different planners in different domains to a certain degree relieve the same types of constraints. This might be an artifact of the problem presentation, but it might also point to a similar representation.

4.3.2.3.6. Representation in Memory and Visual Aids. It is always difficult to see what people really think when they solve difficult problems (Newell and Simon, 1972). In Section 4.2.2.3 we discussed the controversy regarding the issue whether problem solving consists in following a set of (production) rules or whether it consists in applying schemata and frames (from memory). An indication for the latter are remarks such as "this looks like something I did then and then" or "I remember such a problem and then I did so and so." We analyzed the protocols for this kind of remarks and we saw a difference between the Dutch and Indonesian planners

TABLE 4.14. The Relaxation of Constraints in Countries and Domains ($N = 31$)

Constraints Relaxation for Problem I	Country		Domain		
	Netherlands	Indonesia	Staff	Production	Transportation
No answer	0	5	2	1	2
More elements than 4	0	1	1	0	0
Higher occupation	4	5	1	3	5
Change ratio (1:3)	2	0	1	0	1
Change prop. A, B, etc.	11	0	5	3	3
Service delay	1	2	0	2	1

TABLE 4.15. Usage of Memory Retrieval During Solution in Countries and Domains ($N = 31$)

	Country		Domain		
Retrieval from Memory	Netherlands	Indonesia	Staff	Production	Transportation
No answer	0	2	0	1	1
Yes	8	1	2	5	4
No	10	10	8	3	8

(Table 4.15). The situation for the Dutch was almost equal regarding the presence and absence of memory remarks, but the Indonesian planners hardly made memory remarks ($\chi^2 = 6.81$; $p < 0.03$; $df = 2$). Regarding the domains the results showed no significant differences ($\chi^2 = 2.46$; $p < 0.65$; $df = 4$). Only the production environment showed a little bit more use of memory remarks, but this can only be attributed to the Dutch planners.

Finally we wanted to have some information about the kind of visual aids the planners used in solving the problems. Because they were allowed to make drawings and notes on paper, we analyzed this information in terms of the categories: matrix with figures, matrix without figures and no matrix at all. No significant effect for the countries was found ($\chi^2 = 0.80$; $p < 0.66$; $df = 2$). It can be seen (Table 4.16) that a matrix without numbers was drawn by many planners regardless of the domain. Only for staff planning matrices with numbers were used. This may be an indication of the fact that a schedule or plan always includes at least two axes and that planners are familiar with this. From the point of view of software support, the interesting question is how planners who do not use a matrix solve planning problems. We do not know. In the next section the results will be discussed in the light of the various aspects and expectations concerning planning behavior.

4.4. CONCLUSIONS FOR THE PLANNING PRACTICE

From a methodological point of view, it is questionable whether generalizations of the results of a cognitive task analysis in general are possible. It is often argued that cognitive task analysis in relation to KB-DSS can only be performed

TABLE 4.16. Usage of Visual Aid During the Solution Process in Countries and Domains ($N = 31$)

	Country		Domain		
Usage of Visual Aid	Netherlands	Indonesia	Staff	Production	Transportation
Matrix and numbers	3	2	4	0	1
Matrix, no numbers	13	8	6	7	8
No matrix at all	2	3	0	2	3

in an individualistic way. We think we demonstrated that it can also be done in a more extensive and, more important, in a more controlled and systematic way, using a quasi-experimental design. We are aware of the fact that in this way dedicated task performance may be lost.

It was not our purpose to contribute to theories of cognitive architecture or performance. We wanted to investigate some basic cognitive issues in solving realistic planning situations. Therefore, we used real problems that were nonsolvable. We also found out that using protocol analysis in countries where the separation of person and task is not as strong as in most European countries is very difficult.

The expectations formulated at the end of Section 4.3 concerned a capacity check, a hierarchical versus an opportunistic planning strategy, bottom-up and top-down strategy, small calculations and mistakes, and memory representation and visual aids. Furthermore, it was argued that the differences within domains were larger than between domains. Concerning the differences within and between countries, no explicit expectations were formulated. We will discuss the outcomes concerning the expectations, successively.

Concerning the capacity check, it was clear that Dutch planners are more used to calculate the difference between present and required capacity. This was not the case for the Indonesian planners. It also turned out that planners in the production domain are more used to work with capacity checks than planners in the staff and transportation domain. One may speculate that materials and products are more easy to quantify and calculate than persons in staff scheduling or locations in transportation planning. Looking at the protocols, we found that present and required capacity are calculated more or less precisely by every planner, but for most of them during the problem-solving activity, not at the beginning of the planning problem. From a support point of view, a help function in planning software may overcome this "mistake."

Concerning cognitive aspects of planning behavior, such as opportunistic versus hierarchic behavior and bottom-up versus top-down problem-solving behavior, the results of planners' performance in domains and countries showed that although opportunistic planning may be the main orientation, many planners work hierarchically, whereas still others do it completely chaotically. This means that the conclusions of Hayes-Roth and Hayes-Roth are too strong. The opportunistic planning strategy is not default. There are many different ways of making a plan. The same is the case for the top-down or bottom-up strategy. There is no clear way of working. Some do it top-down, others bottom-up. One can argue that top-down is better, because this goes from the overview to the detailed filling in of gaps, but various individual planners do it differently. The interesting group, of course, is the one that plans chaotically. They react ad hoc. Opportunities are not caught and an "overview" is missing. This behavior is not as foolish as it may seem. If you cannot solve a problem, you look around for things you might have missed. If this does not give you clues, you will do whatever comes up and try and fail and try again and so on. The problem is not only the presence of this behavior, but particularly the support of this kind of behavior. Real planning does not consist of clear-cut, well-defined and neatly represented problems. Some molding or selfish modeling always has to be done. The important lesson is that solving a planning problem consists of two stages, creating a problem space and solving the problem within that space. Chaotic behavior is a result of the lack of both.

We did not find systematic differences between domains and countries. This implies that planning strategies are not determined by domain or country. Only the top-down versus the bottom-up strategy showed a difference for countries. Dutch planners work more top-down, which is in line with the organizational result of one overall plan for the Dutch organizations, but it is in contradistinction with the less hierarchical organizational structure the Dutch planners indicated.

In contrast with earlier work by Mietus (1994), this study showed that little counting in the domains and countries took place and that most planners made little mistakes. This might be an effect of the kind of problem we presented, although it seemed to be difficult enough. The planners worked with very small numbers. This is a characteristic of the planning problem in the empirical study. However, as a subtask of the overall planning task, counting very often occurs.

For us it was no surprise to see that concerning visual aids, 26 out of the 31 planners used some kind of matrix. This is in line with what we expected. However, 21 of the 26 used matrices or diagrams without numbers. And perhaps, even more important, 5 planners did not use external visual aids. The question for us is, How do these planners solve planning problems if not by figures, drawings, or matrices? This outcome needs further investigation.

We conducted the study to find out about the influence of domains. What kind of constraints in which domains are alleviated? To what extent are production, transportation, and staff planning completely different? Or, to put it stronger, every planning situation is different. If this is the case, different ways of planning result in different adjustments of constraints. This is not what we found. We found a difference in preference of constraint to alleviate between Indonesia and the Netherlands, but not between the domains. Regardless of the domain, most Dutch planners changed the same constraint. This can only be explained if we accept the presence of a (partly) common planning representation. The question of course is what this representation is. In terms of the form of the representation, we did not get a clear answer. A third of the planners, all from the Netherlands, made remarks about remembering a similar problem and tried to remember what it looked like. There was no difference between domains.

The study showed that there are differences between countries in solving real live planning problems. We did not expect this in the strong sense as we found it. We think it might be related to organizational factors in the countries. In Indonesia, organizational structures are much more formal, leaving little space for people's own initiative. Furthermore, the labor resources in Indonesia seem to be inexhaustible. Also the perspective on time as a resource is different in Indonesia compared with the Netherlands. To put it in methodological terms, in Indonesia time is perceived at an ordinal level of measurement, whereas the Dutch planners in this experiment viewed it at a ratio level. For a high-level planning perspective there is no problem in working with the ordinal level, whereas concrete attuning (scheduling) requires an interval or ratio level.

Although we carefully selected the companies in both countries to match as much as possible, we found that comparable organizations had large differences in the number of plans they make. The Dutch try to minimize the number of plans, whereas the Indonesians are satisfied with many plans, connected in one way or another. According to us, this also explains the preference of the Indonesians to work bottom-up, compared with the Dutch of doing it top-down. The Dutch organizations also had a strong orientation toward planning with a fixed horizon, whereas Indonesian organizations rather work with a variable (moving) horizon. This very well fits the differential perspective on the capacity check, the bottom-up procedures, and the number of plans. The Indonesian way of planning includes, if one might say so, much more improvisation, whereas the Dutch way is to integrate as much as possible. For both perspectives the bottom line is the human cognitive architecture and cognitive system. For the former, optimal improvisation requires almost unlimited monitoring facilities, whereas for the latter, optimal integration mostly goes beyond computational capacities.

The second overall conclusion is that differences expected in relation to production, transportation, and staff planning did not show up. As we earlier indicated, it is often argued that strong and important differences exist between various planning domains. This might be true in many respects, although we argued against this view (Jorna et al., 1996); it is certainly not true in this empirical study. Taking a cognitive perspective, production planners are not different from staff planners. Consequences of plans may be different in different domains, but that is because machines or lorries do not have facilities to adapt themselves to small changes in conditions, whereas individuals (staff members) in staff planning are able to do so. It is also possible to state that the presented problem is only the same from a mathematical perspective and that most planners do not look at planning or scheduling this way. We think we put a step in pulling down the overestimated differences in the execution of production, transportation, and staff planning. However, as a result, a much bigger problem comes up. It is the question, Is there a basic planning representation through all the apparent differences and what does it look like? At the moment we do not know. What we do know, however, is that there are many ways of making a plan. Planning procedures in plan execution are diverse, but the variety is limited. This gives hope for reuse in the design and development of planning support systems.

4.5. DISCUSSION: IMPLICATIONS FOR THE IMPLEMENTATION OF PLANNING SUPPORT SYSTEMS

This empirical study was conducted with real planners, no software support, and manipulated planning problems. We used protocol analyses, among others, as an instrument to gain better insight in planning strategies of planners. This way of working is the starting point in what we in Section 4.1 called software development from bottom-up. There is a good reason for doing this. Planners and schedulers, whether they are doing staff, production, or transport planning, are not very satisfied with most present-day software support for these tasks. Instead of looking for the "things" that are wrong in software programs or in organizations, we took a different perspective by looking at the task performance of individual planners. We think that "real" software support should start here, and we have three good arguments for our position. First, computers will become more integrated in normal task performance. This already happened for all kinds of low-end tasks. Tasks requiring more complexity and uncertainty will follow in the near future. These tasks in which intelligence is combined with dedicated computer support require detailed cognitive task analysis that starts with carefully looking at what users, or planners, really do.

Second, computers are becoming ever more powerful and "intelligent," asking from users behavior that is up to the computer standard. For that reason, computer performance and outcomes presented by software should be transparent to the user, and this can only be accomplished if the user's knowledge is (partly) integrated in the program.

Third, the skills and performances of highly professional users will change as a result of the interaction of user and computer. In order to adapt new (releases of) software to changing wishes of users (planner), detailed pre- and post-program interaction should be recorded, analyzed, and implemented. We consider the empirical study that we described here as a step on this road toward planner-oriented software support.

We did not talk in detail about programs to support planning and scheduling; this can be found elsewhere (van Wezel et al., 1996; Jorna et al., 1996; van Wezel, 2001), but from the above empirical study several conclusions can be drawn for the development of dedicated planning support.

The first conclusion is that the use of cognitive task analysis, necessary for the development of knowledge systems, has limitations. More than with Dutch planners, Indonesian planners have real difficulties in providing us with information. According to them, knowledge is not neutral, but is instead combined with a person's place among peers and super- and subordinates. An error is a humiliation, not something that can be corrected. This might cause problems for knowledge acquisition and knowledge elicitation, if planner-tailored dedicated task support programs are being developed in non-European countries. The future will tell.

As a second conclusion we found many differences between individuals, countries, and domains, implying that a uniform kind of task support does not exist. We saw that planners used bottom-up, top-down, hierarchical, opportunistic, and sometimes capacity check procedures. However, finding common patterns in the protocols is very difficult. Production planners do not do it top-down, and nor do Indonesian planners do it hierarchically. As a consequence, we think that structured uniform software packages for intelligent task support will not work. Does this mean that a software phantom is real, namely that in intelligent task support every user needs an individual program? To a certain extent the answer to this question is affirmative. However, the story is a little bit more complicated. Conceptual and software modularity provide a solution to this phantom. Small modules can be fitted together in such a way that reuse and uniqueness both are realized. This requires, however, a general consistent conceptual framework not only for the planning task, but also for all kinds of other tasks, from diagnosis, monitoring, and decision making to advice tasks (Clancey, 1985; Breuker and van de Velde, 1994). We worked in this perspective with regard to the domain and organization of planning and scheduling (Jorna et al., 1996), but having a better look at the variety of planning behavior now, we know that we still have a long way to go in relation to scheduling and planning.

The third conclusion is that our empirical study showed that production planning is not completely different from staff scheduling, which is different from transportation planning and so on. Of course, it goes without saying that (the properties of) lorries are different from those of staff members, but that is not interesting. What we think we have challenged is that the cognitive procedures in plan formation and plan execution are domain-dependent. They are different, but not along the well-known demarcation lines of domains. We think this is good news for software support. A common ground for plan execution can be determined regardless of the domain. This, however, remains to be done. We have only made some first steps, in an empirical research with real tasks surpassing the simple errand planning of Hayes-Roth and Hayes-Roth. The next step has to be, for example, the construction of a dictionary of cognitive procedures, cognitive mechanisms, and representations in relation to planning and scheduling. After its realization, the development of software for scheduling and planning support can continue in combination with cognitive task analysis. However, we know that we are not talking about the near future (van Wezel and Jorna, 1999).

The fourth conclusion in relation to software support is a continuation of an inventory of the domain, the organization, but especially the execution of planning, the so-called planning behavior. This inventory will contribute to the realization of a help function in planning and scheduling support systems. This might even take shape in the form of a general course. In this course a planner can be taught that in making a plan regardless of what domain, several necessary steps have to be made. In this way the gap between the prescriptive way of planning, familiar in mathematics and Operations Research (and partly in management science), and the descriptive way, familiar in cognitive science, can be bridged. Then it might be possible that software not only supports planners, but, to a certain degree, also guides planners.

And finally, what does this empirical study mean for the distinction in planning for yourself and planning for others? Although we did not study planning for yourself in this empirical research, the question is, In what way do planners that plan for themselves differ from making a plan for others? As far as it concerns the cognitive functional level with a time horizon of more than 5–10 seconds, we claim that there is no difference between planning for yourself and planning for others. However, planning for yourself is nested within planning for others. As far as it concerns planning at the borderline between the functional and the neurological or physiological level with a time horizon less than 1–5 seconds, there is a big difference. Planning for yourself at this level is what Hommel discussed in Chapter 2. Planning for others is not relevant in that respect. Here we see an example of what we try to accomplish in this book. As soon as one goes into the details of planning issues, a general notion of planning does not apply anymore. A more detailed view with aspects like time horizon and functional and other levels of description makes clear that planning for yourself and planning for others are different and similar at the same time.

APPENDIX I

Planning Problem for the Production Domain

Problem: There are two machines: I and II. When machine I is running, two products have to be processed at the same time on that machine. This is because of high operating costs and the ability to work on two products at the same time. Machine II is more simple and processes only one product at a time. Orders are received for three different products A, B, and C that have to be produced within the next 9 time periods. The products need respectively 8, 8, and 3 "treatments" to be produced. Each treatment costs one time period. The orders are accepted. Only one treatment on a product can be done at the same time. The treatments on one product do not necessarily have to be done in one production run. After every time period it is allowed to wait a couple of time periods before starting with the next treatment. Tool and product changing times may be neglected. Machine I is not functioning on time periods 4 and 9 because of service. Machine II is running all the 9 time periods. Because of the high operating costs of the machine, they have to be fully used when they are available. An order is received for a new product, D, which has the same constraints as the products A, B, and C. This product needs four treatments and has to be delivered right after the fourth time period. This order is accepted.

Question 1:   Make a schedule for the next 9 time periods and use the whole machine capacity. If you think that the problem is unsolvable, give your proposed solution.

Planning Problem for the Transportation Domain

Problem: For the next 9 days a company wants a number of containers with different kinds of products to be transported from their production unit to their distribution center. The company uses two trucks for this job. The trucks need a whole day for one round-trip. Truck I is a "combi". Truck II is smaller. The following containers have to be transported: 8 containers with product A, 8 containers with product B and 3 containers with product C. Because of production and storage constraints, there is only one container of every product each day ready for transportation to the distribution center. Every day only one container with a certain product can be transported. Truck I always takes two containers at the same time to drive economically. This is also its maximum capacity. Truck II can only transport one container at a time. For service reasons the combi is not available on days 4 and 9. On other days the truck is operational. Truck II drives every day. Because of the high operating costs the trucks always have to drive fully loaded. Unfortunately, the return from the distribution center is always empty. Because of a sudden rise of a new product, D, an order is accepted with four containers of this new product that have to be transported the first four days to the distribution center.

Question 1:   Make a schedule for the next 9 days using all the truck capacity. If you think that the problem is unsolvable, please give us your proposed solution.

INTRODUCTION TO CHAPTER 5

With Gazendam we are leaving the perspective of the human planner that we saw in the chapters of Hommel, Hoc, and Jorna. Gazendam starts with the notion of a multi-actor system, because he wants to refer to actors of various kinds within an organization, but more important because he wants to analyze what is going on between actors. "Actor" is a primitive term in Gazendam's chapter. Of course the most realistic situation is that where cognitive plausible actors cooperate in an organization to reach certain goals, what we call the "real world" situation. Actors can also be empty actors—that is, noncognitive actors, as is usual in economy, or actors can be departments or organizations. In the latter case a multi-actor system is a group of collaborating individuals. Important in Gazendam's chapter is the assumption that as soon as workload or primary processes in an organization are too intensive or too complex for one person to handle, an activity of subdivision takes place, which by necessity requires an activity of coordination. Planning is then one of the many possibilities to realize coordination. Others are, for example, standardization, commanding, or controlling.

Gazendam does not believe in superstructures or idealized structures within or above organizations. Gazendam argues that every coordinating activity is in the end principally done by human actors. Gazendam takes the received view of (cognitive) psychology regarding human actors for granted. This implies that concepts of coordination ultimately reside in the information processing systems of human actors. Gazendam calls these concepts social constructs. Actors in organizations have norms and representations of property rights, responsibilities, and obligations,

Planning in Intelligent Systems: Aspects, Motivations, and Methods, Edited by Wout van Wezel, René Jorna, and Alexander Meystel

to name but a few, at their disposal. These are the social constructs organizations live by. Planning and all its consequences and presuppositions is also a (complicated) social construct. The interesting thing with social constructs is that not every actor has the same detailed knowledge of this construct—for example, planning. That is also the reason that thoroughly discussed (ex ante) plannings do not result in similar plans (ex post) in reality.

For Gazendam the notions of multi-actor system and social construct are deeply rooted in semiotics. Semiotics, the study of sign structures and sign understanding, is also used to describe organizations. Actors in organizations, says Gazendam, deal with a semiotic Umwelt. This is an environment consisting of models, documents, communication, and representations. All these "objects" basically are sign structures. Cooperation between actors therefore always consists of communication in the form of sign structures. This also applies to planning, whether it is between human actors or between organizations consisting themselves of human actors. This approach makes it possible to analyze the consequences of innovative organizational forms of planning—for example, production scheduling in and by focused factories (see Chapter 6) or self-scheduling by a team of nurses (Teahan, 1998).

At the end of his chapter, Gazendam elaborates something that is very rarely done in planning areas. He proposes a cost–benefit analysis—not in classical financial terms, but in terms of costs and benefits of primary processes and secondary processes, such as planning. For example, if a planning activity in an organization consists in making a plan and if a performance indicator is the number of activities or units that were not planned (categorized to some criterion), then this number should stay below 1%. Or, to give another example, if the planning activity of accepting the plan and if as a performance indicator the number of improvised activities deviating from the plan is used, then the number should stay below 2%. This kind of careful quantification and explicitness of plans is relevant if one wants to start a discussion about the quality of planning, not only with respect to the plans as outcomes, but also in relation to the processes of planning. Every planning is (necessarily) loaded upon the performance of primary processes in organizations.

Planning for others within organizations is therefore different from planning for oneself. The coordination costs in the former case can be measured, quantified and, therefore, valued. It is not a usual procedure to make these (coordination) costs in one way or another visible.

5

COORDINATION MECHANISMS IN MULTI-ACTOR SYSTEMS

HENK W. M. GAZENDAM

Faculty of Public Administration, Twente University, NL-7500-AE, Enschede,
the Netherlands; and Faculty of Management and Organization,
University of Groningen, NI-9700-AV Groningen, the Netherlands

5.1. INTRODUCTION

Organizations that have to function in a real world and in real time have to cope with risk, uncertainty, imperfect knowledge, bounded rationality, and limited communication. In such situations, organizational forms based on centralized planning and control suffer from brittleness, rigidity, complexity, large planning overhead for small tasks, limits to information processing in the central decision-making function, and limited learning capabilities. There is a need for interpretation, negotiation, and discussion. For instance, if a goal is not for 100% attainable, will 90% do? And at what costs?

Therefore, it is necessary to look for organizational forms based on decentralized planning and control by relatively autonomous actors. Such a multi-actor system is characterized by the autonomy, independence, dialogue, negotiation, and cooperation of actors (Wooldridge, 2002). Multi-actor systems do not differ from centrally controlled systems with respect to the necessity to find solutions for problems while doing their tasks. However, multi-actor systems find these solutions by the cooperation of individual actors. These processes can take the form of organizing, planning, and improvisation. The organizational efficiency of central planning and

Planning in Intelligent Systems: Aspects, Motivations, and Methods, Edited by Wout van Wezel,
René Jorna, and Alexander Meystel

139

control on the one hand, and mutual adjustment on the other hand, can be compared by estimating the costs and benefits of coordination (Jorna et al., 1996).

In our investigation of decentralized planning and control we have to use an adequate theoretical viewpoint. For instance, multi-actor planning (as opposed to planning in general) requires specific attention for the representations used by the theorists studying planning, the representations used by the actors in the organization, and the processes that are important in forming and using plans. Therefore, we explain multi-actor planning in this chapter by focusing on the following questions:

1. What type of representation does multi-actor theory use for investigating organizations and planning?
2. What representation types do actors need for communication and reasoning in the context of multi-actor cooperation?
3. What role do social constructs (for instance, plans) play in achieving coordinated action by actors?
4. How can individual actor plans be made compatible by mutual adjustment and resolving inter-actor conflicts resulting in a coordinating plan?
5. How can actors set boundaries to the time and resources they spend on cooperation and planning?

Multi-actor theory aims at gaining insight in the cooperation of actors in a multi-actor system. An actor is an autonomous and intelligent being that is able to perceive and act. A multi-actor system is a collection of cooperating actors, together with the work processes, sign structures, and objects that these actors see as belonging to the organization. *What type of representation does multi-actor theory use for investigating organizations and planning?* We have to go beyond the notion of an organization as a system that can be described adequately by state-space functions. Because of the use of sign structures by actors, a state-space representation with the associated operators, functions, and equations becomes insufficient. It is necessary to go to representations based on computational mathematics, where the interactions of many simulated actors generate complex behavior (Holland, 1995, 1998; Wolfram, 2002) (Section 5.2).

Planning in for instance robotics (based on direct representations) typically uses representation structures like multiresolutional hierarchies of state spaces. But a hierarchy of direct representations in the form of a multiresolutional hierarchy of state spaces is not sufficient for an actor functioning in a multi-actor system. Because in multi-actor systems there is no longer one actor in whose mind all planning happens, there is a need for communication and negotiation. One could say that an actor does not live in the physical world only, but in the semiotic world (a semiotic Umwelt) as well, and adequate representations are thus necessary in the actor's cognitive system. *What representation types do actors need for communication and reasoning in the context of multi-actor cooperation?* Language representations are necessary for communication. More abstract, conceptual, representations are required to be able to handle concepts in the field of cooperation and coordination—for instance, organization, contract, plan, task, responsibility, initiative, and commitment. Semiotics gives us a useful categorization of representation types: direct representations, language representations, and conceptual representations. The knowledge of an actor consists of these three types of representation. The use of language representations and conceptual representations also means that resolution (of direct representations like images) is not the only mechanism for handling representations, but that narration (for language representations) and especially abstraction (for conceptual representations) become important. Abstraction enables us to understand how individual actor plans can coexist with a minimized common plan (Section 5.3).

Coordinated action is characterized by task fulfillment where actions are synchronized to reach augmentative effects, where tasks are allocated in order to profit optimally from the specialized knowledge of actors, where a system of checks and balances provides for robustness of results, and where conflicts are avoided. According to classical management theory, coordination is achieved by processes of organizing, planning, coordinating, commanding, and controlling. In the light of organizational semiotics, these processes must be seen as creating social constructs that guide individual actor behavior. *What role do social constructs (for instance, plans) play in achieving coordinated action by actors?* A social construct is a relatively persistent socially shared unit of knowledge, reinforced in its existence by its daily use. A plan is a social construct. Social constructs enable us to understand how plans, agreements, task specifications, and so on, can be used as explicit instruments for coordinating actor behavior. A social construct is a conceptual representation, and abstraction is an important mechanism in handling social constructs. If we analyze organizations from the viewpoint of social constructs, we see that an organization can be seen as a shared idea that a specific organization exists (this shared idea is called the organizational root) to which a work organization, a formal organization, and an organization culture are attached (Section 5.4).

In a multi-actor system the entity that makes the plan generally is a multi-actor system. The entity that performs the plan is also a multi-actor system. Plans in a multi-actor system are often distributed. This means that we have to investigate processes for forming and using plans other than the problem-solving, command, and control mechanisms of centralized planning. In a multi-actor system, planning is a process in which negotiation and problem-solving are intertwined. In many cases the aspect of negotiation in order to reach an agreement, a consensus ad idem, turns out to be more difficult than the problem-solving aspect. *How can individual actor plans be made compatible by mutual adjustment and resolving inter-actor conflicts resulting in a coordinating plan?* Mutual adjustment and resolving conflicts are only done when necessary. Therefore, detecting potential conflicts is important. Solutions to potential conflicts are constructed in negotiation processes. The solutions the actors agree upon can be seen as social constructs that emerge as a result of these negotiation processes. The multi-actor planning process generally consists of several stages (Section 5.5).

Cooperation must give results that are not possible when working alone. In other words, the cooperation must create a surplus compared to working alone.

Furthermore, the distribution of that surplus must give each participant benefits compared to the situation of noncooperating. *How can actors set boundaries to the time and resources they spend on cooperation and planning?* An estimation of their share in the costs and benefits of cooperation and planning enables each actor to set boundaries to the time and resources spent on cooperation and planning (Section 5.6).

5.2. MULTI-ACTOR SYSTEMS

5.2.1. Multi-actor Theory

Multi-actor theory aims at gaining insight in the cooperation of autonomous entities (actors) and the resulting forms of organization. The multi-actor theory explained in this chapter is especially interested in actors that are human beings or computer actors that simulate human beings using the findings of cognitive psychology, and it investigates the patterns that emerge at the organizational level resulting from the interaction of such actors.

5.2.2. Actors

An actor is an *autonomous* and *intelligent* being that is able to perceive and act. *Autonomous* implies being independent of guidance through an external source. *Intelligent* implies being able to interpret, determine goals, reason, and decide. Human beings, animals, robots, and the more or less autonomous and intelligent entities realized by software on a computer can be seen as actors. The more or less autonomous and intelligent entities realized by software on a computer are called computer agents or virtual actors. They are part of information systems. Human beings, animals, robots, and computer agents are functionally equivalent according to Newell and Simon's (1972; Newell, 1990) physical symbol system hypothesis. These individual actors have to be distinguished from corporate actors. Organizations are such corporate actors. Corporate actors are not functionally equivalent to individual actors. However, because organizations can only do something through the actions of individual actors belonging to that organization and because the interactions of organizations are in many cases computationally equivalent to the interactions of individual actors, it is sometimes useful to see organizations as actors as well.

   Autonomy can be defined in several complementary ways (Meystel, 1998). Autonomy is being independent of guidance through an external source because of

1. The ability to develop a world model by interaction with the environment
2. The ability to develop goals and norms
3. The ability to control a considerable part of the environment

An actor can only be autonomous based on having a world model, a representation of the world it is living in. Cooperation with other actors requires representations of those other actors. For cooperation, it is also necessary to communicate. Communication presupposes the ability to utter and perceive signs, an ability that is dependent on the biological or technological species of the actor.

5.2.3. Characteristics of Multi-actor Systems

A *multi-actor system* is a collection of cooperating actors, together with the work processes, sign structures, and objects that these actors see as belonging to the organization.

Based on the types of actors we have distinguished, we can define some subtypes of the multi-actor system. Multi-actor systems can consist of human beings, computer agents (virtual actors), or multi-actor systems. A multi-actor system consisting of human beings only is a human organization, or just an *organization*. A multi-actor system consisting of virtual actors only is an *information system* or a multi-agent system. A multi-actor system consisting of human beings and virtual actors is a *virtual organization*. A multi-actor system consisting of multi-actors systems is an *organization network*.

There are two special types of organization networks that are interesting from the point of view of multi-actor planning: the multi-site organization network and the multi-company organization network. In a multi-site organization network, actors that belong to different multi-actor systems differ in their characteristics and capabilities because of a difference in location and perhaps resources and knowledge bound to these locations. However, they generally do not have potential conflicting interests stemming from legal or formal relationships, although their interests may differ, being complementary or parallel (like production sites and financial officers have different, but complementary interests). In a multi-company organization network, actors that belong to different multi-actor systems have potentially conflicting interests stemming from legal or formal relationships. This means that multi-site planning and multi-company planning are only gradually different from a multi-actor point of view, and they differ mainly with respect to the role potentially conflicting interests play.

Multi-actor systems belong to the physical world as well as to the semiotic world. The actors and the activities they perform belong to the physical world, while the sign structures they use (for instance, their knowledge and their communication utterances) belong to the semiotic world. To be more precise, we have to distinguish programs, tasks, triggers, activities, and processes. A coherent description of a quantity of work that is executable by an actor can be seen as a *program*. This description includes a collection of action descriptions, and possibly the associated goals, norms, boundary conditions, procedures that must be followed, and behavior rules that have to be applied. If the actor is a computer, then the program is a computer program. A plan is a kind of program. A *task* is a program of which the responsibility to execute it has been assigned to a specific actor. To let an actor perform a task, an event is necessary: a *trigger*. The performance of a task is an *activity* that happens in real time (see Figure 5.1). A *process* is a collection of coherent activities. In Figure 5.1, the objects and processes belonging to the physical world are drawn as rectangles, while the sign structures belonging to the semiotic world are drawn as rounded rectangles. This figure also shows that activities are performed as a result of task performance of an actor. A plan may be one of the programs that are relevant for the task performance. Because plans generally underspecify what must be done, the actor has to use additional programs resulting from his personal knowledge.

5.2.4. Multi-actor Simulation Models

Multi-actor theory is based on the idea that a system that shows complex behavior has to generate this behavior by performing computations. We see the behavior of such a system—for instance, an organization or society—as complex because that behavior cannot be described by traditional mathematical tools—for instance, mathematical equations (Wolfram, 2002, p. 3). The shortcut taken by traditional mathematics will only work when the behavior of the system is simple. In the case of complex behavior, this behavior can more often than not be simulated by computations that use the interaction of computer agents following simple rules. This is the basic idea behind *computational mathematics* (Holland, 1995, 1998; Wolfram, 2002). The complex behavior at the system level of description can be seen as *emergent* relative to the simple rules represented at the agent level of description (Holland, 1998). This discovery has led to a new form of theory development based on the principle of computational equivalence. *Computational equivalence* means "that whenever one sees behavior that is not obviously simple ... it can be thought of as corresponding to a computation of equivalent sophistication" (Wolfram, 2002, p. 5). Because of the

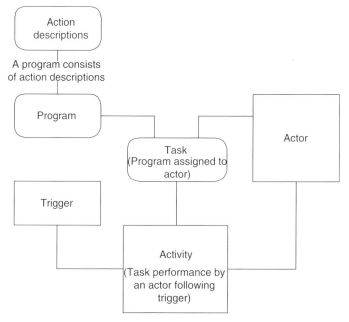

Figure 5.1. Program, task, and activity.

idea of computational equivalence, we can study human organizations based on simulation models consisting of computer agents.

Multi-actor simulation models realized as multi-agent systems (Carley and Gasser, 2001; Wooldridge, 2002) have been very important in developing the theoretical apparatus of multi-actor theory. Multi-actor simulation models have started with systems of few complex actors with poor communication abilities (e.g., multi-actor SOAR). Nowadays, we see more systems of many simple actors with standardized interaction and communication abilities (Holland, 1995, 1998; Wolfram, 2002).[1] There is a trade-off between actor complexity, communication capabilities, and the number of actors.

In the simulation of interacting individual actors within an organization, individual actors cooperate and try to coordinate activities. Important issues are (a) the interaction with, and representation of, the environment (space, objects, itself, other actors), (b) communication using signals, symbols, and language actions, and (c) the handling of (networks of) decision situations using social constructs. Actors reason about their environment (including space, objects, and actors) and try to synchronize their actions by communication processes (van den Broek, 1997). They are concerned with making and breaking cooperative relations based on estimations of cooperation benefits and costs (Klos, 2000). In the estimation of cooperation benefits and costs, an economic as well as a political dimension can play a role (Homburg, 1999; Gazendam and Homburg, 1999).

5.3. SEMIOTICS OF MULTI-ACTOR SYSTEMS

5.3.1. The Physical World and the Semiotic World

Planning in, for instance, robotics (based on direct representations like images) typically uses representation structures like multiresolutional hierarchies of state spaces. But a hierarchy of direct representations in the form of a multiresolutional hierarchy of state spaces is not sufficient for an actor functioning in a multi-actor system. Because in multi-actor systems there is no longer one actor in whose mind all planning happens, there is a need for communication and negotiation. One could say that an actor does not live in the physical world only, but in the semiotic world (a semiotic Umwelt) as well. The environment that humans and animals live in can be seen as a physical world and as a semiotic world. When we see the environment as a *physical world*, we describe it as a system maintaining physical laws. Recurrent structures of events and regularities in measured properties can be described as physical laws, and we try to see physical laws as being based on an underlying structure that can be described by theories. When we see the environment as a *semiotic world* (a semiotic Umwelt), we are interested in the sign properties of objects and

---

[1]Active research groups can be found at:
- the MIT software agents group: agents.www.media.mit.edu/groups/agents
- the Santa Fé Institute (SWARM, ALIFE): www.santafe.edu
- www.cs.wpi.edu/Research/airg/Agents-hotlist.html

structures, the use of signs by animals, humans, and artificial agents. We try to describe the use of signs in terms of systems (social systems or evolutionary systems), or in terms of patterns in communicative behavior, or in terms of sign structures that describe the content of communication. These three directions roughly correspond to the systems-theoretical, behavior-oriented, and knowledge-oriented approaches in organizational semiotics (Gazendam, Jorna, and Cijsouw, 2003, p. 1). The physical world and the semiotic world are levels of description that differ because they focus on different types of patterns and use other types of theory. The semiotic world can be seen as based on the physical world because everything that happens in the semiotic world has to be based on the mechanisms of the physical world.

This means that it is no longer sufficient to pay attention to the physical world only, but that we also need to focus on the world of cognition and the semiotic world. The distinction between the physical world and the semiotic world goes back to Locke (1690/1993, pp. 414–415):

> All that can fall within the compass of human understanding [...] may be divided properly into *three sorts*:
>
> *First*, The knowledge of things as they are in their own proper beings, their constitutions, properties and operations [...] This, in a little more enlarged sense of the word, I call [Physics], or *natural philosophy*. [...] *Secondly*, [Practice], the skill of right applying our own powers and actions. The most considerable under this head is *ethics*. [...] The third branch may be called [Semeiotics], or the doctrine of signs [...], it is aptly enough termed also [*Logic*].

In an article written in 1861, Peirce distinguishes the categories of (1) matter, (2) mind, and (3) idea (Murphey, 1967, p. 71; Brent, 1993, pp. 54–58). A similar distinction has been made by Karl Popper (1974, p. 183):

> If we call the world of "things"—of physical objects—the *first world*, and the world of subjective experiences (such as thought processes) the *second world*, we may call the world of statements in themselves the *third world*. (I now prefer to call these three worlds "world 1," "world 2," and "world 3" ....)

According to Rastier (1998, p. 305) Popper's World 1 can be seen as the physical world, World 2 as the world of human cognition, and World 3 as the semiotic world. Human cognition acts as the mediator between the physical world and the world of representations, the semiotic world.

In the study of human behavior from the viewpoint of cognitive psychology, we use the concept of *task environment*. The task environment is that part of the physical world and semiotic world that is relevant for doing a task by an actor.

Theories of the semiotic world are: the semiotic Umwelt theory, the information field theory, and the regionalization theory.

Actors live in a semiotic Umwelt (von Uexküll and Kriszat, 1936/1970). The *semiotic Umwelt* is an environment around a human being or animal based on the signs and symbols that it creates and perceives. The types of signs and symbols that can be created and perceived depend on the biological species. The basic structure of the semiotic Umwelt, its space and time, depends on the sign processing capabilities of the living being. Time is dependent on its biological rhythms. Space is structured in a way that the signs an organism can perceive are localized in a meaningful way.

> Während wir bisher sagten, ohne Zeit kann es kein lebendes Subjekt geben, werden wir jetzt sagen müssen, ohne lebendes Subjekt kann es keine Zeit geben ... das gleiche gilt für den Raum .... Ohne ein lebendes Subjekt kann es weder Raum noch Zeit geben. (von Uexküll and Kriszat, 1936/1970, p. 14; von Uexküll, 1998, p. 2189)

The semiotic Umwelt supports the survival of human and animal actors, and it affords certain species-specific behavioral patterns (Gibson, 1969; von Uexküll, 1998). Based on the development of these species-specific behavioral patterns, an actor has access to a task environment that is structured in terms of space, time, objects, resources, other actors, and signs. The actor's development of a world model is connected with its development and exploration of its semiotic Umwelt. What would a scientist be without his Umwelt of books, pencil and paper (and, nowadays, computers), and other scientists? The development of a world model is an interactive learning process in which the internal world model and the external semiotic Umwelt are strongly connected. During this interactive learning process, world model and semiotic Umwelt are reorganized. This interpretation of learning contrasts with more traditional opinions in symbolic artificial intelligence, in which learning is some kind of internal stacking and adaptation of knowledge units (rules, productions). Interactive learning, other than memorizing and rote learning (speeding up based on experience), presupposes (van den Broek and Gazendam, 1997) no unlimited mental powers, a need for optimizing and reorganizing knowledge, sufficient but not unlimited memory, capabilities for abstraction, deduction, induction, and abduction, and variation in experience. The sign perception capabilities of a living being are connected with its action capabilities in a semiotic function cycle. The structure of its action capabilities is very important for concept formation and the organization of its world model. For instance, a being that can only go forward, backward, left, and right will develop a world model based on two spatial dimensions ("horizontal" and "vertical") (van den Broek and Gazendam, 1997). A shared semiotic Umwelt can be formed when actors are able to produce signs in a way that other actors can perceive and understand based on their species-specific communication and interpretation abilities.

In the semiotic study of organizations and social systems, the *information field* is an important concept. The information field is the structure of socially shared physical or social affordances and norms in a subculture that enables people to behave in an organized fashion (Stamper, 2001, p. 153). The semiotic Umwelt of a person can be seen to consist of a species-specific biological layer and of a social layer consisting of the information fields corresponding to the subcultures in which he or she participates. Processes of coordination can be understood as the creation of a shared information field leading to shared actor knowledge about what to do when. Other semiotic requirements for coordination have to do with the development of a language that the cooperating actors understand, hand in hand with a structuring of the shared information field in objects, properties, actions, and so on. The latter structuring can be described in a theoretical way as an ontology. The characteristics of the language can be theoretically described based on its syntactics, semantics, and pragmatics. With respect to syntactics, multi-actor systems need a language that is structured with the help of syntactical rules and a lexicon. Specialized actor languages (Wooldridge, 2002, p. 168) have been developed for multi-agent systems. In the field of semantics, multi-actor systems need a common ontology (Wooldridge, 2002, p. 180). In the domain of pragmatics, multi-actor systems need protocols for defining and assigning tasks and standard protocols of interaction (Dietz, 1992, 1996). Information systems need protocols for the handling and routing of events, queries, and messages (pragmatics) (Gazendam, 1997). Recurrent patterns of language interaction can be studied as genres or work practices (Clarke, 2001) or iterators (Bøgh Andersen, Nielsen, and Land, 1999).

The *regionalization theory* says that trajectories in time and space of the daily, weekly, monthly, and overall life paths of individuals in interaction with each other create a space and time structure in the shared semiotic Umwelt (Hägerstrand, 1975; Giddens, 1984, p. 112):

> Interactions of individuals moving in time-space compose bundles ... meeting at stations or definite space-time locations within bounded regions (e.g., homes, streets, cities). (Giddens, 1984, p. 112)

This zoning of time-space in relation to routinized social practices is called regionalization by Giddens (1984, p. 199). Space and time in the shared semiotic Umwelt are also structured using signs that help in communication and cooperation. For instance, meeting places or marketplaces are often recognizable based on signs. Another example is that, in the nineteenth-century clock, time was synchronized in cities connected by railroads (in order to be able to make timetables). Based on that, people were able to make appointments based on this new clock time. Planning encompasses a form of (temporal) regionalization of time and space.

5.3.2. Representation Types

Actors need adequate representations in order to cooperate in multi-actor systems. *What representation types do actors need for communication and reasoning in the context of multi-actor cooperation?* Direct representations (for instance, images and sound patterns) are needed to process information stemming from the physical environment. Language representations are necessary for communication. More abstract, conceptual, representations are required to be able to handle concepts in the field of cooperation and coordination—for instance, organization, contract, plan, task, responsibility, initiative, and commitment. All three types of representation are necessary for actors that function in a multi-actor system.

Direct representations are more or less direct mappings of perceived objects and situations in time and space. *Language representations* are based on symbols and the information transfer-oriented organization of language. *Conceptual representations* are based on abstract concepts and the patterns used in reasoning. Direct representations, language representations, and conceptual representations are connected.

In the mapping from a direct representation to a language representation, there is an *information loss* and a *gain of structure*. The same holds for the mapping from a language representation to a conceptual representation. A gain in structure generally results in a shift to a lower rate of change and a coarser time scale. Because of this, the representation types distinguished differ in their rate of change (time scale). Peirce (Hausman 1993, p. 96) says:

> ... the function of conceptions is to reduce the manifold of sensuous impressions to unity.

The gain in structure is based on the use of reusable, standardized elements in the form of signs based on sign types, and on conventions for composing these elements. For instance, in the mapping from the music you hear (a direct representation) to a language representation, you need to decompose the music into (1) standard waveforms for the various instruments, (2) a musical score which is a text based on a musical notation, and (3) some information about dynamics (volume and speed). In this decomposition, there will be information loss. Furthermore, if you consider the musical score only, without the additional information about instrument waveforms and dynamics, there is an extra information loss. However, the musical score in its more abstract text form is more easily discussed, modified, and analyzed than the original direct representation. It needs less information to transmit from a sender to a receiver. Maybe it is less easily understood because of the need to know the conventions of the language used and to have a degree of versatility in using its language expressions. Language expressions are in fact a special type of direct representations (see Figure 5.2). They have to be direct representations

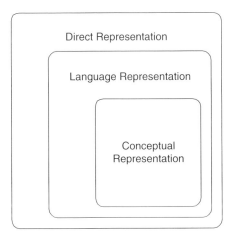

Figure 5.2. Representation types.

because they must be perceivable. A copier can reproduce a printed text, which is a language representation, without knowing anything about language because it works based on direct representations.

Conceptual representations are, in the same way, a specialized type of language representations that represent the network-like conceptual structure behind reasoning (see Figure 5.2). For depicting conceptual structures, graphs are often used. But also other language types can be used like hypertext, programming languages, and logic. The structure of language expressions is a linear narrative; the structure of conceptual expressions is graph-like or hypertext-like. In the mapping from language expressions to conceptual expressions, there is information loss. For instance, the translation into a form of logic with compositional semantics that has no special provisions for handling situations, processes, or worlds, all information that is not based on that compositionality, and information that is bound to a specific situation, process, or world will be lost. Also, the special color of language use stemming from choice of words, choice of narrative structure, and so on, will be lost. This information loss goes hand in hand with a gain in structure that makes deduction and other reasoning forms possible.

The distinction between direct representations, language representations, and conceptual representations is important because planning generally uses conceptual representations. Compared to what happens in the world, or what is projected to happen in the world, the representations used in planning are characterized by less information content and more structure. The step from the world as perceived and described in language toward plans representations is done by abstraction, and the step back from plans to the world in which actions must be taken is done by decomposition, combination, and application.

Processes of *knowledge creation* like induction and abduction require cooperation between the three representation types. For instance, in abduction, you have a surprising fact (a direct representation), about which there is a discussion (in a language representation), while you try to use and combine knowledge (a conceptual representation) with creative jumps (often based on a direct representation or randomized language representation) to find a hypothesis. You can also connect the use of the elements and structures of language representations and conceptual representations with a "feeling" for using these elements and structures. You can see this "feeling" as a *wave function* (Bøgh Andersen, 1999), which is of course a direct representation. The processes of self-organization of this "feeling" wave function can create creative jumps and new language use.

Resolution organizes spatial–temporal direct representations. Resolution is the mechanism of distinction of features of a perceived object, based on the granularity of the spatial–temporal grid used and of the feature grid used. By using multiple layers of granularity of the grids used, a hierarchy of direct representations can be obtained (Simon, 1962; Meystel, 1995c, 1998b; Meystel and Mironov, 1998). General systems theory people often use the state-space representation, which is a kind of direct representation, as their basic view on a system. The problem, however, is that language representations lead to a state space where the dimensions are changing after each time step. There is a combinatorial explosion not within the state space, but on the dimensions of the state space. This has as a consequence that there is no easy translation between state-space representations and dynamic language representations. Because intelligent systems use language representations and conceptual representations, this means that the direct representation, along with the connected type of theorizing in general systems theory, is not sufficient for the description of intelligent systems.

Narration organizes language representations according to levels of semiotic granularity. Narration is necessary for knowledge transfer. Narration presupposes a system of conventions ordered according to levels of semiotic granularity, the use of common object identification and naming, and the use of common predicates, classifications, and thesauri or lexicons based on categories. Using language representations presupposes the existence of a (at least partially) common ontology (a set of conceptual representations) for reaching common understanding of language expressions. *Interpretation* is the reverse of narration.

Abstraction organizes conceptual representations. Because planning uses conceptual representations, abstraction is very important in planning. According to Hoc (1988, p. 144), plan abstraction is one of the bottom-up strategies for constructing a plan. Abstraction enables us to understand how individual actor plans can coexist with a minimized common plan. Because plans are conceptual representations, they underspecify the processes that they give rise to. Because of this, there is room for individual actor plans to specify part of the "gaps" in the common plan. The common plan has as most important tasks to solve potential problems stemming from conflicting actor plans.

Abstraction leads to modularization of knowledge (knowledge packages). According to Peirce, abstraction is separation of elements, sorting out elements and aspects (Hausman, 1993: 101). Three *levels of abstraction* (Gazendam, 1993, p. 93) can be distinguished: (1) individuals, (2) concepts, and (3) categories, along with programs that write programs. There are three basic types of abstraction: individual/individual abstraction, concept/concept abstraction and concept/individual abstraction.

In *individual/individual abstraction*, wholes are distinguished from individuals. An example of individual/individual abstraction is structure abstraction. In *structure abstraction*, a structure (whole or system) is distinguished from its constituent parts: for instance, a process as a whole is distinguished from subsequent situations. Another example is the distinction between a collection and its members. We can see this as the application of a structure-forming operator. The reciprocal of the individual/individual abstraction is the *decomposition* of structures. *Structure–decomposition operators* decompose a structure (a whole or system) into its constituent parts. Goal decomposition is mentioned by Hoc (1988, p. 153) as a top-down strategy in plan construction.

In *concept/concept abstraction*, a concept (predicate, type, category, method, program, operator, or habit) is seen as derived from several more primitive concepts. This corresponds to Peirce's idea of *prescision* (Hausman, 1993, p. 101). Examples of concept/concept abstraction are predicate abstraction, commitment abstraction, and modal abstraction. In *predicate abstraction*, a complex predicate is seen as a combination of more basic predicates, and types are seen as derived from more basic types. In *commitment abstraction*, a commitment about an action program is seen as a combination of a commitment type and a program. In *modal abstraction*, a proposition is seen as a combination of a more basic proposition and a modal proposition that says something about that basic proposition. The reciprocal of concept/concept abstraction is the *combination* using combination operators. Common combination operators are commitment-forming operators and modal operators. *Predicate-forming operators* construct (1) a predicate based on more basic predicates and (2) a subtype based on supertypes. *Commitment-forming operators* combine a program and a commitment type into a commitment with respect to performing that action program. *Modal operators* combine a proposition and a modal proposition into a combined proposition.

In *concept/individual abstraction*, a concept (type, function, method) is distinguished from individuals. Plato already distinguished ideas or forms (concepts) from souls or beings (individuals). Examples of concept/individual abstraction are type abstraction and method abstraction (Gazendam and Simons, 1999). *Type abstraction* takes a set of propositions and abstracts from it an object or a situation. This leads to a type. Devlin (1991) has described this operation as restriction. It requires the distinction between object or situation and (composite) predicate. *Program abstraction* takes a process or activity that occurs or has occurred in time, and it abstracts the situations (characterized by location and time), actors, and objects (in other words, all individuals) from it, giving a program (or method, or pattern) (see Figure 5.3). A program or method is some way of doing, while a pattern is a more specialized program that encompasses some kind of solution to a problem. A variant of program abstraction is the function abstraction defined in lambda calculus. It requires the distinction of operator from operand.

The reciprocal of concept/individual abstraction is the *application* of a concept to individuals. There are two types of application: type application and method application. In *type application*, it is stated that an object is of a certain type, giving a proposition. In *program application*, a program (or method, or pattern) is applied to a set of situations, actors, and objects, giving an activity or process. If we return to Figure 5.1, we see that this is an example of program application. The program in Figure 5.1 becomes a task by combining an actor commitment with it and its application to an actor. The task becomes an activity by its application to a trigger consisting of a situation (time and location) and a collection of objects.

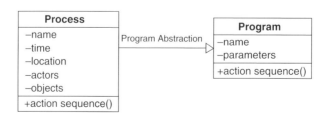

Figure 5.3. Program abstraction.

The goal instantiation strategy for constructing plans distinguished by Hoc (1988, p. 153) is a kind of application of an abstract program to a set of individual situations, actors, and objects.

Abstraction as well as its reciprocals (decomposition, combination, or application) can be seen as semiotic operators. Now we have explained these semiotic operators that are relevant in handling conceptual representations, and we can compare our operators to the *plan construction strategies* distinguished by Hoc (1988). Hoc (1988, p. 144) distinguishes three bottom-up strategies for constructing a plan: plan abstraction, retrieving a suitable plan from the actor's memory, and revision of an existing plan. Plan abstraction is a form of abstraction. Plan revision is done in a multi-actor system during negotiations as soon as potential conflicts are detected (see Section 5.5). Hoc (1988, p. 153) also mentions three top-down strategies in planning: goal decomposition, goal instantiation, and interaction analysis of multiple goals. Goal decomposition is a kind of decomposition. Goal instantiation is a kind of application. Interaction analysis is done in multi-actor planning by a pairwise interaction analysis of actor plans (see Section 5.5).

We see that semiotics gives us a useful categorization of representation types: direct representations, language representations, and conceptual representations. The knowledge of an actor consists of these three types of representation. The use of language representations and conceptual representations also means that resolution (of direct representations like images) is not the only mechanism for handling representations: Narration (for language representations) and especially abstraction plus application (for conceptual representations) also become important. Abstraction enables us to understand how individual actor plans can coexist with a minimized common plan.

5.4. COOPERATION BETWEEN ACTORS

5.4.1. Motives for Cooperation

Schmidt (1991) distinguishes three motives for cooperation: augmentative cooperation, integrative cooperation, and debative cooperation (Figure 5.4). Gazendam and Homburg (1996) add conflict handling. *Augmentative cooperation* is based on the fact that single actors are limited by mechanical and physiological capacities, and cooperation can be useful to overcome these limitations. *Integrative cooperation* brings in the specialized knowledge of the participants necessary for performing a common task. *Debative cooperation* brings in a variety of values and interests and aims at acceptable conclusions. Knowledge-based work processes are fragile and contestable. The function of debative cooperation is to alleviate this deficiency. Debative cooperation can be found in scientific communities and, for example, in the organization of governments in clearly independent executive, legislative and judiciary bodies that realize a system of checks and balances (the separation of powers). Conflict handling avoids destructive conflicts and deadlocks by, for instance, the use of authority, regulated dialogue and negotiation, and regulated competition between contestants.

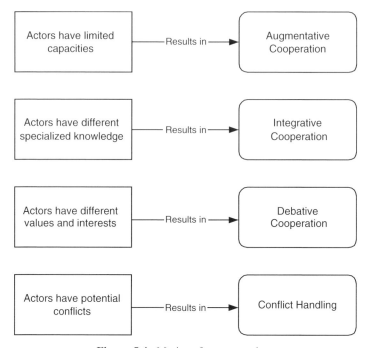

Figure 5.4. Motives for cooperation.

We see that augmentative and integrative cooperation are motivated by capabilities, namely capacities for augmentative cooperation and knowledge for integrative cooperation. Debative cooperation and conflict handling are motivated by interests, namely parallel or complementary interests for debative cooperation and potentially conflicting interests for conflict handling. Based on our distinction of multi-site organization networks and multi-company organization networks in Section 5.2.3, we can now say that multi-site planning will have the handling of different capabilities (capacities and knowledge) as a main topic, while in multi-company planning the focus will also be on the handling of interests (parallel, complementary or potentially conflicting). The handling of interests by actors based on cost–benefit considerations is explained in Section 5.6.

5.4.2. Coordinated Action

Coordinated action is characterized by task fulfillment where actions are synchronized to reach augmentative effects, where tasks are allocated in order to profit optimally from the specialized knowledge of actors, where a system of checks and balances provides for robustness of results, and where conflicts are avoided. By coordinated action, a multi-actor system can perform tasks that are beyond the capacity of a single actor. Moreover, capacities of actors and means can be utilized optimally, and some tasks can be done at lower costs. In economic theory, these effects are known as *economies of scale*. However, economies of scale can only be reached by making *coordination costs*. Planning costs are part of those coordination costs.

Coordination is the activity aimed at achieving coordinated action. Coordination has to address the problem of how to reach a state in which the desired results of coordinated action are attained, but also the problem of how to distribute the advantages resulting from that cooperation over the participating actors.

The classical managerial function gives us a picture of coordination as a management process that consists of five subactivities: to plan, to organize, to coordinate, to command, and to control. These subactivities are defined as follows (Fayol, 1916/ 1984, p. 13):

1. To plan: ... lay out the actions to be taken.
2. To organize: lay out the lines of authority and responsibility, build up the dual structure, material and human, of the organization.
3. To coordinate: lay out the timing and sequencing of activities
4. To command: put the plan into action; set the work in operation.
5. To control: monitor and correct; see that everything occurs in conformity with established rules and expressed command.[2]

Based on this analysis of the management process, we can conclude that the formal organizational structure is created by acts of planning, organization, and coordination, while work is done based on commands and obedience to commands. Obedience to commands and adherence to rules is stimulated by control activities.

In order to use this Fayolian theory in the context of multi-actor systems, we have to add some extra explanations relating the management subactivities to the concepts used in multi-actor theory (as defined in Section 5.2.3). To *organize* can be seen as the design of tasks, namely to lay out the lines of authority and responsibility as well as the organization structure in terms of places for actors, and as the design of programs, namely the business process structure. It also encompasses the establishment of standards. To *plan* can be seen as the allocation of means (including actors) to the organization structure and the process structure. To *coordinate* can be seen as a synchronization or time–space regionalization task, namely to

---

[2]"Administrer, c'est prévoir, organiser, commander, coordonner, et contrôler;

Prévoir, c'est-à-dire scruter l'avenir et dresser le programme d'action;

Organiser, c'est-à-dire constituer le double organisme, matériel et social, de l'entreprise;

Commander, c'est-à-dire faire fonctionner le personnel;

Coordonner, c'est-à-dire relier, unir, harmoniser tous les actes et tous les efforts;

Contrôler, c'est-à-dire veiller à ce que tout se passe conformément aux règles établies et aux ordres donnés."

(Fayol, 1916/1999, p. 8)

Note how in the English translation of Irwin Gray the role of the coordinating activity has shifted from an information processing and adjusting activity, logically following the command activity, to a scheduling activity that logically precedes the commanding activity.

lay out the timing of the activities in terms of a coherent system of triggers (a schedule). To *command* can be seen as a combination of to *negotiate* and to *improvise*. To *negotiate* means that actors discuss the activities to be performed and decide about an acceptable way to perform them. To *improvise* means to choose the relevant activity dependent upon the situation and to set the work in operation. The command subactivity is followed by the performance of activities, to execute. To *execute* means to carry out the activities—that is, in the case of coordinated action, to cooperate. To *control* means to see that everything occurs in conformity with established rules and expressed command, to correct where necessary, and to give feedback to earlier phases. This results in the management subactivities depicted in Figure 5.5, all contributing to coordinated action.

Planning in a wider sense can be seen as a combination of "to plan," "to coordinate," and elements of "to organize." It encompasses defining activities in terms of programs, allocation of means and synchronization of activities. In practice, a mix of the coordination mechanisms has to be used. In this mix, planning can have a

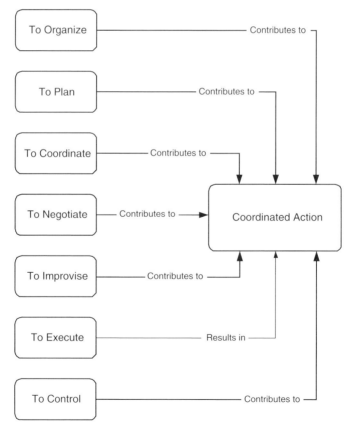

Figure 5.5. Management subactivities.

prominent role, a less prominent role, or even no role at all. For instance, negotiation and improvisation based on behavior rules and a market mechanism with brokers can be an alternative for planning.[3] Coordination can also be mainly based on organizing.[4]

One could argue that plans can never fully specify what is going to happen and that actors always have to decide, based on the circumstances at hand, how the plan has to be executed. Such a position is taken by Suchman (1987). She says that plans often are used as a rationalization afterwards for actions that in reality have been chosen in a decentralized and adhoc manner, based on the situation at hand and some general rules of behavior. She calls this form of action choice *situated action*. Suchman's observation highlights the importance of choosing the adequate coordination mechanisms and of avoiding resource-consuming forms of ineffective ritualized planning. In using an adequate mix of the coordination mechanisms, a balance can be struck between autonomous action and concerted action in order to gain an optimal performance of the multi-actor system.

5.4.3. Social Constructs

In the light of organizational semiotics, the management subactivities explained in Section 5.4.2 must be seen as processes creating social constructs that guide

---

[3]An example of coordination using a market mechanism and behavior rules is the following one. For the operation of a sugar factory during the beet campaign in autumn, sugar beetroots have to be collected from the farmers. For this transport, one-man businesses made up of a driver and a truck, often so-called free riders, register. The procedure is as follows. At four o'clock in the morning, the drivers report at the factory. There, they line up at the work distributor's office. This work distributor has a prepared a stack of notes with the addresses of the farmers where the beetroots have to be collected. The driver that is in front of the line takes the topmost note of the stack. If he does not like the address of the farmer, he puts the note back and queues up at the end of the line. The work distributor takes care that a driver does not refuse an address too often, because he thinks that every driver should do some unpopular addresses during the campaign. When the driver is ready with his route, he goes again to the work distributor's office, except when he thinks that he has done enough for that day. The drivers get paid per route. In such a situation, the planning and scheduling of routes is not necessary. The necessary coordination is done by the market mechanism and the behavior rules. In his preparation, however, the work distributor does some planning by deciding about the order in which farmers will be visited.

[4]The following situation is an example of coordination by organizational task allocation. There are seven bridges along a canal. In the past, there used to be a house next to each bridge where the bridge man lived. When a vessel approached during daytime, the bridge man opened and closed the bridge on the spot. At nighttime, the bridges were not operated. When the bridge man took a holiday, he had to find a replacement himself. In the case that a bridge man was called away suddenly, he provided for a colleague that took over temporarily. In such a situation there is no need for a common year plan or schedule. Each bridge man made his individual plans for holidays and similar occasions.

Nowadays, we have six bridge men that work 36 hours a week and have four holiday weeks a year, instead of the seven bridge men that were available permanently. In the holiday periods, one works with extra temporary personnel. There are three shifts (early shift, late shift, and night shift). In every shift, one bridge man operates all seven bridges using modern equipment, and one other bridge man is standby. This situation needs a year plan and a weekly schedule. This because of less personnel capacity, more service hours, and the combination of seven autonomous organization units into one larger one.

individual actor behavior. *What role do social constructs (for instance, plans)*
play in achieving coordinated action by actors? A *social construct* is a relatively
persistent socially shared unit of knowledge, reinforced in its existence by its
daily use. Social constructs persist through years, decennia, and even centuries
(take, for instance, the social construct of property/ownership). They have a
key position in communication, learning, and developing social behavior by
human beings. Social constructs can be seen as knowledge units that are
shared in groups or even social systems, reinforcing themselves by communication and their daily use. These shared knowledge units can influence individual
behavior by forming habits, thus creating a cycle of selection and reinforcement,
where some knowledge units are reinforced and others disappear. Social
constructs are negotiated, with conceptual representations belonging to the
semiotic world that have to be distinguished from natural entities like persons
or robots.

In organizations, social constructs take the form of, for instance, shared stories,
shared institutions (behavior rule systems), shared designs, shared plans, and
shared artifacts. These social constructs support habits of action aimed at
cooperation and coordinated behavior. Each habit of action consists of a commitment to act in a certain way, along with a more or less flexible action program
that governs the actual acting. If we look at people in organizations, they do not
necessarily require similar representations of the organization they are participating
in. However, people participating in organizations need a certain minimum of shared
social constructs, and perhaps other shared knowledge, in order to be able to
cooperate and coordinate their actions.

Commitments to act in a certain way and norms can be seen as being attached
to social constructs. For instance, there are norms attached to the general social
construct of "property" that are inherited by the specific instance of that social
construct in the form of the social construct "ownership of my bicycle." An example
of these norms is the rule that no one can use my bicycle without first asking my
permission to do so.

We have to explain what we mean when we say that a social construct is a unit of
socially shared knowledge. Not all knowledge and all norms attached to a social
construct will be shared by all the people that see themselves as committed to
that social construct. What is shared is the knowledge of, and commitment to, the
social construct as a "root concept" with some norms or default behavior patterns
connected. The root concept enables us to find out more about the social construct,
if necessary. For instance, if I fill out my income tax form, I feel committed to the
social construct of paying taxes, I recognize the social construct of authority of the
tax service, and I have a very limited knowledge of all laws and regulations concerning taxes. Whatever I need to know about filling out certain fields in my tax form, I
can look up in a tax compendium, which is only a short abstract of all tax laws and
regulations.

According to the Stamper school of organizational semiotics (Stamper, 1973),
there are main social constructs called *social affordances*, to which norms are
attached. Norms can be specified by if–then rules that comprise deontic operators

(Liu, 2000). Furthermore, each social construct starts and finishes by an actor having an adequate authority for this. Each social construct may presuppose other social constructs; for instance, to establish a marriage there must be a law or regulation saying how to establish this and what behavior rules are attached to marriage. According to the language action school, there is a more or less standardized process (scenario) for establishing a social construct between two actors. So we arrive at the following architecture of social constructs. A main social construct ("social affordance") is the root, to which are attached (1) norms, (2) the authority under which it starts, (3) the time of start, (4) the authority under which it finishes, (5) the time of finish, (6) prerequisite social constructs from which norms can be inherited and that define the authorities (2) and (4), (7) the authority that is created and allocated as part of the social construct, and (8) a scenario for establishing the social construct (see Figure 5.6).

Important types of social constructs are models and plans, contracts, organizations, and behavior rule systems. *Models and plans* are social constructs that contain action programs to the implementation of which individuals or groups can be committed. These social constructs help to determine the actions to be taken. Roles and tasks can be seen as belonging to this type of social construct. *Contracts* are social constructs that form a relation between two actors. The actors create obligations and a certain dependency between themselves. An *organization* can be seen as a shared idea that a specific organization exists, to which a work organization, a formal organization, and an organization culture are attached. *Behavior rule systems* or institutions are social constructs consisting of behavior rules and norms that are shared in an organization, community, or social system. An important part of these rule systems is the description of punishments in case of misbehavior. In these behavior rule systems, the responsibility, authority, and power relations between actors can be described. Sometimes these behavior rule systems are established and modified by authoritative rituals, or take an authoritative form as formal laws or regulations. Behavior rule systems express general values and norms—for example, Kant's categorical imperative and Asimov's laws (Gazendam, 1997). Kant's categorical imperative reads in

Social Construct
Name
1. Norms
2. Starting authorities
3. Starting time
4. Finishing authorities
5. Finishing time
6. Prerequisite social constructs
7. Defined authorities
+Scenario for creation()

Figure 5.6. Social construct architecture.

normal English: "Do unto others as you would they should do unto you."
Asimov's laws (1953) hold for robots and virtual actors:[5]

> *First Law*: A robot may not injure a human being, or, through inaction, allow a human being to come to harm.
> *Second Law*: A robot must obey orders given it by human beings, except where such orders would conflict with the First Law.
> *Third Law*: A robot must protect its own existence as long as such protection does not conflict with the First or Second Law.

5.4.4. Organization

If we analyze organizations from the viewpoint of social constructs, we see that an *organization* can be seen as a shared idea that a specific organization exists (this shared idea is called the organizational root) to which a work organization, a formal organization, and an organization culture are attached (see Figure 5.7). We see that "organization" is a complex concept because it can be defined in comp-lementary ways, each of which refers to observable reality in a specific way (Jorna et al., 1996). The *organizational root* or organizational actor is a social con-struct that is used for defining a group to which actors belong based on agreements or contracts. The *work organization* is a group of cooperating actors and their work activities (Fayol's corps social) and the material resources they use (Fayol's corps matériel). The work organization can be identified and demarcated based on stable patterns of coordinated action. It is a physical system acting in real time. The action programs in an organization can be seen as knowledge that is the basis of the work organization. This knowledge may be implicit, embedded in the minds of actors, or explicit—that is, expressed in documents and other sign struc-tures. The *formal organization* or institution is a collection of contracts, roles, tasks, rule systems, plans, models, and other formal social constructs. These formal social constructs are generally expressed in documents. They reflect an agreement between actors about behavior patterns. The formal organization can be observed based on documents, especially legal and financial documents. A special place is reserved for the formal properties of the organization as a whole (the organizational root)—for instance the name, its legal status (for instance, a pri-vate limited company), ownership, its logo, and so on. An organization generally will have its own system of rules and norms, while other rules and norms may be inherited from legislation. The *organization culture* is a collection of shared ideas, metaphors, stories, and artifacts that guide cooperative behavior of actors. It is a collection of nonformal social constructs. As a nonformal social construct, some of the slots in the general architecture of social constructs, like the authority slots, may remain unfilled. The organization culture generally will be implicit and partially explicit. The organizational root, the formal organization, and the

---

[5]See for an interesting overview and comments: http://online.anu.edu.au/people/Roger.Clarke/SOS/Asimov.html.

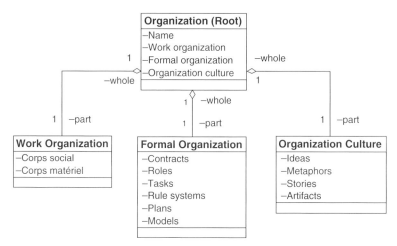

Figure 5.7. The organizational system.

organization culture belong to the semiotic world. The work organization belongs to the physical world and to the world of human cognition. From a semiotic point of view, one can say that the actors in a multi-actor system have created a semiotic Umwelt consisting of documents and other sign structures that helps them in creating, storing, and learning knowledge, agreements, and so on.

The distinction between work organization and formal organization has been proposed by Schmidt (1991). According to Schmidt, formal organization is a (not always congruent) layer on top of the work organization safeguarding the interests of the owner and regulatory bodies (Schmidt, 1991, p. 103). In a similar way, the organization culture adds a collection of ideas that stimulates cooperative actor behavior to the work organization and the formal organization.

People can flow into and out of an organization, and yet the characteristics of that organization often stay more or less the same. This can be explained based on the relative stability of the task performance activities, of the semiotic Umwelt, and of the actor knowledge in the organization. In other words, an organization belongs to the physical world, the world of human cognition, and the semiotic world, and the semiotic part of the organization seems to be the most stable. The latter is accomplished by the processes of learning and adaptation that newcomers in the organization have to go through. Therefore, a multi-actor system can be observed not only as a collection of cooperating actors, but also as (a) the activities that make up their task performance and (b) the documents and other sign structures that make up their semiotic Umwelt.

Organizing uses social constructs to reach agreements between actors and to define actor responsibilities, thus creating guidelines for actor behavior. Some social constructs that are often used are the role, the task, and the contract. The *role* (or position, or function) is a social construct that can be attached a single actor within the organization. It is a vehicle for attaching authority descriptions and responsibilities in the form of tasks. The *task* is a social construct defining an action program for which a single actor may be held responsible. A *contract* defines a formal relation between two actors. Norms—for instance, the conditions under which an actor will work for an organization, its remuneration, and its role—can be attached to it.

Social constructs can be seen to form a structure based on prerequisite relations, called *ontological dependency* by Stamper and Liu (Liu, 2002, pp. 65 and 78). The existence of an organization is a prerequisite for defining a role within that organization and for creating a contract between that organization and an actor. Roles can also be seen within the context of a contract; in that case, the existence of a contract is a prerequisite for the existence of a role within that contract. The existence of a role can be seen as a prerequisite for defining tasks within that role.

According to Fayol, the stability of an organization depends on striking a balance between (Fayol, 1916/1999; Gazendam, 1998; Gazendam and Simons, 1999) (i) legitimate authority and mechanisms of enforcing responsibility (a formal organization dimension), (ii) individual interest and general interest (a formal organization dimension), (iii) initiative and central planning and control (an work organization dimension), and (iv) exploration/learning and exploitation (a work organization dimension).

5.5. MULTI-ACTOR PLANNING

5.5.1. Characteristics of Planning in a Multi-actor System

In a multi-actor system the entity that makes the plan generally is a multi-actor system. The planned entity, the entity that performs the plan, is also a multi-actor system, possibly different from the planning entity. In a multi-actor system, planning is characterized by four aspects:

1. Multi-actor plans are distributed, which means that they generally are represented at many places: in the minds of actors and in the documents that actors use (see this section).
2. The planning process aims at creating or maintaining coordinated behavior or social order by creating social constructs in the forms of plans (see this section).
3. The planning process is characterized by problem solving intertwined with negotiation. In this process, social constructs (plan elements) emerge out of resolving potential conflicts (see Section 5.5.2).
4. In the planning process, actors determine the acceptability of a proposed course of action by estimating their share in the costs and benefits of the resulting cooperative activity. Much in the same way the actors set boundaries to the planning activity itself by an estimation of its costs and benefits (see Section 5.6).

In a multi-actor system, a plan can be centralized, distributed, or shared based on where it is represented (Durfee, 2001, p. 139; Wooldridge, 2002, p. 218). Furthermore, we can distinguish actor plans from coordinating plans. A *centralized plan* is represented in its entirety in one authoritative place. Actors may have copies of this centralized plan that are represented in their minds, or they may use documents containing a copy of the plan. A *distributed plan* is nowhere represented in its entirety, but exists as a distributed collection of plans represented in the minds of actors or in documents that these actors use. A *shared plan* is a plan that is known by all actors, and therefore represented in the minds of actors. An *actor plan* is the plan that an actor has made for its own actions. A *coordinating plan* is a plan that has been made to coordinate the individual actor plans. This coordinating plan will often be centralized or shared. Two special cases of multi-actor planning are multi-site planning and multi-company planning. Actors differ because they belong to different sites or different companies. The location at different sites results in differences in actor capabilities in the field of capacities, resources, and knowledge, see also Chapter 9 by Sauer. The employment at different companies results in different interests of actors; these may be parallel, complementary, or potentially conflicting. In multi-site planning the handling of different capabilities is a main topic, while in multi-company planning the focus is also on the handling of interests.

From a semiotic point of view, a plan is a *social construct*. Plans, as social constructs, will therefore have an architecture of norms, connected and defined authorities, prerequisite other social constructs, and a scenario for establishing the plan, this all built around a core of actor programs. Looking at the effects of planning, we can see planning as an effort to create or continue coordinated behavior or order in the planned domain by using social constructs that regulate actor behavior. *Social order* is a situation where actors act coordinated. Looking at the activity of creating plans, we can see planning as problem solving, but also as reaching an agreement, a consensus ad idem, between actors about what to do.

A *program* is a description of a collection of actions to be performed by an individual actor, and possibly of the associated goals, requirements, boundary conditions, procedures that must be followed, and behavior rules that have to be applied. The actions in an actor program can be specified using deontic operators, distinguishing actions that have to be performed in all circumstances from (a) actions that are forbidden and (b) actions that have to be performed when certain conditions are fulfilled. Planning is finding a set of actions that will lead from an initial state to a state that satisfies a given set of goals as good as possible. These goals can relate to both (a) the actions themselves and (b) the process of finding the actions. This means that *planning* has to encompass the activity of making programs (programming). In order to realize the activities that enable the reaching or maintaining of a goal state, planning must also include the allocation of responsibilities for executing programs to actors (thereby defining tasks), the allocation of means, and the definition of a coherent collection of triggers (a schedule) to set the task performance in motion. A *plan* generally will consist of a coherent collection of programs to act, the means and actors allocated for executing those programs, and a collection of triggers defining the synchronization of the resulting activities. A plan generally is aimed at reaching or maintaining a desired situation.

5.5.2. The Planning Process: Problem Solving Intertwined with Reaching Agreements

In a multi-actor system, planning is a process in which negotiation and problem solving are intertwined. In many cases the aspect of negotiation in order to reach an agreement, a consensus ad idem, turns out to be more difficult than the problem-solving aspect. Traditionally, the planning literature has emphasized the problem-solving aspect of planning and formulated idealized forms of planning, the so-called rational-comprehensive planning. A well-known and widely used elaboration of this idealized form of planning has been given by Anthony (1965), who distinguishes strategic planning, management control, and operational control, forms of planning that cohere in a planning hierarchy. Rational-comprehensive planning has been criticized in the planning literature since the work of Lindblom (1965), who states that rational-comprehensive planning is not possible and not desirable either. Rational-comprehensive planning is not possible because of the limits to human cognition, and it is not desirable because of incompatibility with democratic principles. In a democratic way of decision making, reaching consensus ad idem is important. Decision-making proceeds in small steps corresponding to the actions or social constructs that the participants can agree upon.

How can individual actor plans be made compatible by mutual adjustment and resolving inter-actor conflicts resulting in a coordinating plan? Mutual adjustment and resolving conflicts are only done when necessary. Therefore, detecting potential conflicts is important. Solutions to potential conflicts are constructed in negotiation processes. In the multi-actor planning process, there generally are five stages (adapted from Durfee, 2001, pp. 124 and 140): (1) The task is decomposed into subtasks that can be performed by individual actors, (2) these subtasks are assigned to actors in the most optimal way—for instance, based on their experience, expertise, and authority status, (3) the actors each make a plan for their subtask, and (4) the actors discuss potential problems with respect to actions that need to be synchronized (for instance, in the case that actors have to lift a heavy stone together) or that might lead to conflicts (for instance, when two actors want to use a resource at the same time), and they adjust their individual plans based on that discussion, and (5) a coordinating plan is constructed in which all solutions for potential problems about which the actors have reached agreement are represented (see Figure 5.8). In all phases there is problem solving, and in phases 1, 2, 4, and 5 there is deliberation and negotiation in order to reach agreement.

For the decomposition of the task into subtasks (phase 1) and the assignment of subtasks to actors (phase 2) there are two approaches: the contract net protocol and partial global planning. In the *contract net protocol* (Davis and Smith, 1983; Wooldridge, 2002, p. 194), the decomposition of the task into subtasks (phase 1) is done by a single actor—for instance, by the actor responsible for doing that type of task, or by an actor that has the role of president. The resulting subtasks are then farmed out over the actors by a process of bidding, where the actor that offers to do the subtask for the lowest cost and that has records of sufficient

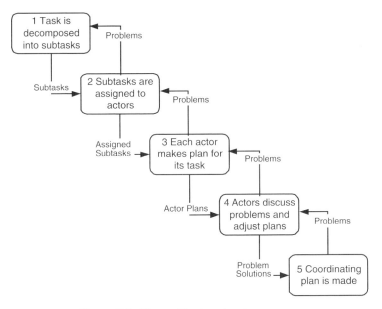

Figure 5.8. The multi-actor planning process.

expertise gets that subtask (phase 2). In the *partial global planning* approach (Durfee, 1988; 2001, p. 153) it is assumed that the total task is inherently decomposed (for instance, because there has been an organizational allocation of responsibilities beforehand) and that no actor might be aware of the global task or state. The rewards that actors get when reaching the overall goal must be sufficiently attractive for actors in order to get a positive stimulus to coordinate their actions. In the partial global planning approach, the way to decompose into subtasks (phase 1) and to assign subtasks to actors (phase 2) is to let every actor propose its own task. After that, each actor makes a plan for its subtask (phase 3). The positive effects of coordinated action are especially achieved in the phases of discussing problems (phase 4) and making a coordinating plan (phase 5), and they are dependent on the agreement that the actors can achieve in these phases. In order to identify potential problems (in phase 4), the actors may do a pairwise interaction analysis of their plan with another agent, where all actions in each plan are screened on their possible effects on the execution of the other plan (Durfee, 2001, p. 142; Wooldridge, 2002, p. 219). The results of the planning process are only where necessary included in the coordinating plan (in phase 5), which means that most planning results stay local in the minds or documents of the individual actors.

The discussion of potential problems and what to do about them (in phase 4) is characterized by trying to *reach agreement*, a consensus ad idem about what to do. This discussion may happen in a way that is centrally coordinated—for instance, a blackboard structure—or may happen in subgroups. In the former case, one of the actors acts as the president of the blackboard session. In the latter case, a subgroup is

formed by the actor who sees a potential problem by inviting the actors that are connected to this problem. In both cases, the deliberations may consist of a limited
number of rounds following a basic protocol like the following protocol [adapted
from Dietz (1992, 1996)]: (a) The group president states the problem and asks the
other participants for proposals to solve it, (b) the participants that want to make
a proposal say so and deliver their proposal, (c) all participants vote about acceptability and preference of the proposals, and finally (d) the president chooses a proposal and closes the deliberation, decides for a new round with an adapted problem
statement, or closes the deliberation without having found an acceptable proposal.
After the deliberations, the participating actors have to adjust their individual
plans, and they announce their plan changes. When certain actors (the "dissidents")
fail in their plan adjustment, this can be a new problem that has to be addressed. Like
in the Soar architecture (Laird, Rosenbloom, and Newell, 1986; Newell, 1990), the
multi-actor system learns from solving conflicts or impasses by recording the results
of deliberations and storing them as social constructs (plan elements) in the minds of
actors that have participated in the deliberation, and possibly in a coordinating plan
document. In other words, the conflict solutions that actors agree upon are stored as
new socially oriented knowledge, as social constructs.

The construction of the coordinating plan (in phase 5) can be done based on the
results of the problem solving activities in phase 4. When problems arise during this
construction, these problems have to be solved using the phase 4 procedures.

One of the topics that should be decided upon by the agents before starting the
planning process is the limits that have to be set for the process of deliberation—
for instance, in time and resources, or in terms of a maximum number of subgroups
discussing potential problems and in terms of a maximum number of deliberation
rounds per subgroup. Setting limits may be based on an analysis of the costs and
benefits of planning, where each agent has to estimate under which conditions its
cooperation in the multi-actor system is still worthwhile. Setting such limits causes
a trade-off where the most urgent problems are discussed and decided upon, and
less urgent problems sometimes remain unsolved. When these problems arise, they
have to be solved by improvisation, which can have the form of making a decision
by the most authoritative actor, or perhaps a small-scale replanning activity.

Many problems and conflicts in multi-actor planning can be avoided by the
formation of a more permanent organization structure beforehand, in which each
actor is assigned authority areas and task responsibility areas, and where there are general behavior rules and norms. In this case, part of the coordination is achieved before
the actual planning occurs by the social constructs of authority and responsibility in
connection with a system of behavior rules and norms (Wooldridge, 2002, p. 213).

5.6. COSTS AND BENEFITS OF PLANNING

5.6.1. Benefits and Costs of Actor Work

An actor's work must pay in order to let him continue this work. In other words,
there must be an actor surplus equal to or greater than zero. The following example

explains this. Let us suppose we have an actor Abrahamson that works alone. In order to earn his costs of living CA (costs of actor), he starts a flower shop in the city of Appletown. Twice a week, on Monday morning and Thursday morning, he goes to the flower auction to buy plants and flowers, and during the rest of the week except Sundays he sells plants and flowers in his shop from 8.00 AM to 8.00 PM. His costs of purchasing plants and flowers, his transport costs, and his other costs for running the shop are CB1 (costs of basic operation 1). Although Abrahamson works alone, he is dependent on the community of Appletown he lives in, not at least because they have to buy his products. This community demands that he pays taxes, his bank demands interests on the money they have lent him, and his shareholder aunt Charlotte expects some payments now and then too. Let us call these costs stemming from the community he is dependent on *stakeholders costs CS1* (costs of shareholders 1). To make a decent living, Abrahamson has to sell for at least CA + CB1 + CS1. Let us suppose his turnaround is VP1 (value of products 1), then there may be a surplus SA1 (surplus for the actor 1):

$$SA1 = VP1 - (CA + CB1 + CS1)$$

If this surplus SA1 remains negative after a necessary period of startup and settlement, Abrahamson will be forced to close his shop.

5.6.2. Benefits and Costs of Cooperation

Planning is a form of coordination, Coordinated action leads to *benefits* because of (Schmidt, 1991; Gazendam and Homburg, 1996) (a) a better utilization of the capacities of actors, means of production, and raw materials, leading to a higher quantity of delivered products, (b) a better utilization of the specialization of actors and means of production, leading to a better quality of the products, (c) a better balance of the interests of the participating actors, leading to more highly motivated actors and, by that, to a better quality of the production process, and (d) the avoidance of destructive deadlocks and conflicts. A better quality of the production process generally leads to (a) an optimal quality and timeliness of services and products and (b) flexibility in delivering services and products to customers. Planning aims at realizing these benefits of coordinated action. These benefits can only be attained by making coordination costs, especially planning costs. The benefits of planning are parts of the total value of the coordinated activity VP that is measured in terms of the value of the services and products delivered.

Coordination costs originate from coordinating activities like organizing, planning, and improvisation. Besides that, the slack capacity of actors, means of production, along with materials in stock, have to be included in the coordination costs. Planning aims at minimizing these costs of slack capacity, while coordination by organization and by improvisation use a certain amount of slack capacity. This leads to the following sources of coordination cost CC (Jorna et al. 1996, p. 29): (a) organization, including establishing contracts with organizations that perform work that is contracted out, (b) improvisation, (c) slack capacity of actors, means of production and materials in stock, (d) making plans, (e) replanning and adjusting plans, (f) storing and communication of plans, including the costs of maintaining an information and communication system, and (g) accepting plans by the actors that have to perform the plans as well as by other stakeholders. The planning costs CP consist of (d), (e), (f), and (g).

Cooperation will only take place if two conditions are met (Gazendam and Homburg, 1999). These conditions are a subject of negotiation between actors. First, the cooperation must give results that are not possible when working alone. In other words, the cooperation must create a surplus compared to working alone. Second, the distribution of that surplus must give each participant benefits compared to the situation of noncooperating. Therefore, we have to distinguish between the aspect of producing the desired results (the production side) and the side of distributing the advantages resulting from that cooperation (the surplus allocation side).

Let us explain the benefits and costs of cooperation based on the example of Abrahamson. Abrahamson's cousin, Brandson, also has a flower shop, but in the city of Peartown lying at about an hour's journey from Appletown. The two cousins decide to cooperate in the field of buying at the flower auction, the field of advertisements, and the case of special assignments like work for weddings and funerals. This means that there must be a better planning of the stocks they want to hold, the plants and flowers they want to buy, and occasionally the special assignments. They reserve Wednesday mornings for doing this planning work and invest in a computerized planning system. Due to this cooperation, Abrahamson can now open his shop also on Thursday morning because Brandson then goes to the auction, and he sees his turnaround rise with VP2 (value of products 2), especially due to extra special assignments. However, Abrahamson's basic costs of operation have risen with CB2, while his stakeholder's costs have risen with CS2. The costs of planning and other coordinating activities that Abrahamson must make are CC (coordination costs). In order to be worthwhile, the cooperation must have a positive coordination surplus SA2 (surplus for the actor 2) for each participating actor. For Abrahamson, this surplus is

$$SA2 = VP2 - (CC + CB2 + CS2)$$

In other words, actors determine the acceptability of a proposed course of action by estimating their share in the costs and benefits of the resulting cooperative activity. It might be that for Abrahamson, a positive coordination surplus SA2 compensates a negative surplus SA1; in this case Abrahamson cannot end the cooperation because then he would have to close his shop.

5.6.3. Setting Limits to Coordination Efforts

It turns out that coordination can have a positive effect. However, it is clear that if actors spend a disproportional amount of time and resources on planning activities, this will not pay. This raises the question, *How can actors set boundaries on the time and resources they spend on coordination amongst which planning?* Can more coordination lead to an even better result in the case of the cooperating cousins Abrahamson and Brandson? Let us suppose Brandson proposes a more extensive planning based on advertisement campaigns in connection with a quantity rebate the cousins can get on plant-related articles like pots, baskets, and candles. However, it turns out that the gain in turnaround ΔVP minus the extra costs of operation ΔCB and minus the rise in cost of stakeholder's ΔCS is not greater than the extra coordination costs ΔCC. This means that there is no extra surplus for Abrahamson due to this extra planning, and this extra coordination activity is not worthwhile. In other words, an extra coordination effort is only worthwhile if

$$\frac{\Delta SA}{\Delta CC} > 0, \qquad \text{where } \Delta SA = \Delta VP - (\Delta CC + \Delta CB + \Delta CS)$$

This means that an estimation of their share in the costs and benefits of coordination enables each actor to set boundaries to the time and resources spent on coordination. Much in the same way it can be said that an extra planning effort costing ΔCP is only worthwhile if

$$\frac{\Delta SA}{\Delta CP} > 0$$

Other interesting measures are the overall efficiency of coordination (Jorna et al., 1996, p. 30)

$$\frac{VP}{CC}$$

and the overall efficiency of planning

$$\frac{VP}{CP}$$

All these measures are actor-specific when used by actors in a multi-actor system to determine their course of action, but can also be used for a multi-actor system as a whole. These measures also allow actors to compare the organizational efficiency of different forms of planning and coordination.[6]

5.6.4. A Generalized View on Cooperation Costs and Stakeholder Costs

A more general picture of coordination costs can be given based on agency theory, property rights theory, and resource dependency theory. *Transaction cost economy* (Coase, 1937/1993; Williamson, 1975, 1985; Eggertson, 1990, p. 3; Homburg,

---

[6]In the example of the bridge men there is a lot of slack human capacity, and there are hardly any costs of coordination and planning. As long as the personnel costs per time unit remain low, this can be an acceptable situation. As soon as the personnel costs per time unit start to rise, a level of personnel costs can be reached at which planning can deliver such savings in the field of slack capacity that planning becomes sensible.

1999, p. 88) sees transaction costs as an important factor in the explanation of the choice of a coordination structure between organizations (hierarchical organization, market, or something in-between).

> In general terms, transaction costs are the costs that arise when individuals exchange ownership rights to economic assets and enforce their exclusive rights. (Eggertson, 1990, p. 14)

These transaction costs CT include (Eggertson, 1990, p. 15) costs for searching potential buyers and sellers and information about them, costs of bargaining, costs of the making of contracts, costs of monitoring the contract partners, costs of enforcement of the contract, and costs of protection of property rights. Transaction costs can be seen as a special type of coordination costs, namely the external coordination costs for building and maintaining an organization network. Companies must strike a balance between intra-organizational coordination (explained in Sections 5.6.2 and 5.6.3) with costs CC and inter-organizational coordination with costs CT.

Stakeholder costs CS are elaborated by the property rights theory, the agency theory, and the resource dependence theory. Stakeholder costs are often expressed as the right of a stakeholder to get funds or other advantages from an organization. *Property rights theory* (Alchian, 1961/1965; Furobotn and Pejovich, 1972, Eggertson, 1990, p. 33; Homburg, 1999, p. 94) discusses the rights that result from ownership of an organization. Full ownership rights entitle the appropriation of the full surplus while attenuated ownership rights only entitle part of the surplus. Full ownership rights are seen as an important incentive for rational action by the owners. When ownership power is low because of unclear or attenuated ownership rights, managers can let the costs for coordination rise until the resulting surplus that is available for the owners is almost nonexistent, even if there is a potential high surplus because of a monopolistic position of the organization. This seems to be the situation in many quasi-autonomous governmental, semi-governmental, and nongovernmental organizations—for instance, those created by processes of privatization or contracting out. Such situations can put planning in a bad light as unnecessary management luxury, and they can emphasize the necessity of an examination of the organizational efficiency of planning on a regular basis. An estimation of the costs and benefits of planning enables the setting of boundaries to the time and resources spent on planning.

Agency theory (Jensen and Meckling, 1976; Jensen, 1983; Eggertson, 1990, p. 40; Homburg, 1999, p. 86) discusses, amongst others, the relationship between owner and managers, and it distinguishes between costs of monitoring of managers by owners and costs of hiding sensitive data for the eyes of owners by managers. *Resource dependency theory* (Pfeffer and Salancik, 1978; Homburg, 1999, p. 106) sees the dependency of an organization on resources owned by another organization as a situation where the resource-owning organization can exploit the dependent organization, thereby in fact attenuating ownership rights. In order to avoid this, an organization will strive after autonomy. An example of exploitation is, for instance, the dependence of an organization on the government of the community or country in which it resides, leading to the right of that government on raising taxes. Another example is that the surplus of an organization can be lowered in situations of nonideal markets where suppliers and/or buyers have excessive power. This can modify the price of the services or goods delivered and thus can modify the surplus gained. This can be seen as belonging to the costs of being exploited by actors having power over resources.

The resulting picture seems to be that the distribution of costs and surplus is dependent on the relative power of the actors in and around an organization. Owners and organizations with resource power will maximize their share of the surplus, while managers have interest in sufficient funds for coordination (including planning costs, costs of organization, costs of improvisation, costs of slack capacity, and transaction costs) (see Figure 5.9).

In situations where there are no alternatives for an actor with respect to participating in an organization and the benefits he receives from the organization are insufficient, political motives—that is, influencing the form of coordination (including planning) and the pattern of distribution of the surplus—become dominant. From a political point of view, actors will strive after obtaining sufficient political

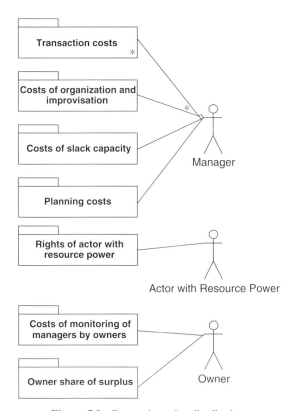

Figure 5.9. Cost and surplus distribution.

resources in order to realize a political program, and in such a way that a minimum of political risk is taken (Puviani, 1903/1960; Pierson, 1994).

5.6.5. The Quality of Planning

The quality of planning depends on the ability to perform all stages in the planning process successfully, from the making and adjusting of plans to the communication and acceptation of plans. The quality of the planning process is as good as the weakest link in this process admits. Therefore, it is important to monitor the quality of the products that each step in the planning process delivers. This can be part of a quality control system for planning. For each step in the planning process, performance indicators can be observed based on the products that are delivered. As soon as the products that are delivered do not fulfill certain minimal requirements, a procedure should start to handle the situation (this might be a repair or redo activity, but

TABLE 5.2. Performance Indicators for Planning

Planning Activity	Performance Indicator	Must Stay Below
Making the plan	Number of activities or units that were not planned (to be categorized according to dimensions or objects)	1%
Making the plan	Number of participating actors and main stakeholders that is not satisfied with the plan	10%
Making the plan	Exceeding the completion time t1 with tx; time of coming into operation is t2	tx is 10% of (t2 − t1)
Adjusting the plan, replanning	Speed of plan adaptation	1% of (t2 − t1) (see above)
Adjusting the plan, replanning	Number of activities or units that were not planned (to be categorized according to dimensions or objects)	1%
Adjusting the plan, replanning	Number of participating actors and main stakeholders that is not satisfied with the plan	10%
Communicating the plan	Number of activities that were not performed due to the unfamiliarity with the plan	1%
Accepting the plan	Number of improvised activities deviating from plan	2%

also the decision to go on and to analyze what went wrong later on). An example of possible performance indicators is given in Table 5.2 (Jorna et al., 1996, p. 31). It must be stressed that the numbers given in this table are, although based on some practical experience, only examples. Each organization must set its own standards for the planning performance indicators.

For the quality of the plan, the quality of plan adjustment and replanning is as important as the initial planning. Until the moment that the plan has been performed successfully, adaptations of the plan may be necessary. Events may happen that necessitate an immediate adaptation of the plan. The planning process must be organized in such a way that adaptation of the plan can be efficiently done. Simple adjustment must be possible and complete replanning (when not done automatically) must be avoided. According to Simon (1962), this means that a plan has to consist of a hierarchy of nearly decomposable (this means more or less independent) subplans. The benefit of such a structure is that necessary adaptations generally can be localized in only one subplan.

5.7. DISCUSSION

The negotiated order in multi-actor systems can be seen as an alternative for centralized planning. Although multi-actor systems will have to solve problems like centrally controlled systems do, multi-actor systems use different methods for finding solutions based on a diversity of representations, social constructs, finding potential conflicts, mutual adjustment of actor plans, and deliberation about costs and benefits of a proposed form of cooperation. Semiotics, especially organizational semiotics, multi-actor simulation theory, and organization theory, contribute to the development of a coherent theory.

INTRODUCTION TO CHAPTER 6

In the previous chapter, Gazendam described planning as a way to realize coordination between tasks in an organization. He provides us with a number of abstract building blocks that can be used to describe organizational planning. From Gazendam's chapter, we know what elements are available to design the planning functions and tasks in an organization. What we do not know, however, is how we can combine the various elements to make planning successful; organizational theory does not provide design rules specifically for planning. Although we can of course apply generic organizational theories to planning, we then do not use the many specific things we know about planning—for example, the problem-solving strategies that are specific to planning (Chapter 4), the relation between planning and other forms of coordination (Chapter 5), the kinds of planning support that are available (Chapter 7), and the kinds of mathematical planning and scheduling algorithms that are available (Chapters 8 and 11).

In the next chapter, McKay and Wiers essentially arrive at the same conclusion from a different starting point. Looking at traditional literature that is meant to contribute to planning problems in organizations, they note that "there has been little similarity between the highly abstracted concepts used in research papers and planning and scheduling in practice." According to McKay and Wiers, traditional scheduling and planning literature often overlooks the cognitive processes of human planners and ignores the organizational context of the planning problems that are solved.

Planning in Intelligent Systems: Aspects, Motivations, and Methods, Edited by Wout van Wezel, René Jorna, and Alexander Meystel

At this point of the book, a major shift of focus happens. Chapter 2 to Chapter 5 are mostly based on paradigms from psychology, sociology, and semiotics, thereby representing a behavioral, descriptive approach to planning. Chapter 7 to Chapter 11 are design-oriented; that is, constructs are created to perform or support planning. A strict line between descriptive versus design cannot be drawn and most chapters contain both. For several reasons, however, it can be argued that the shift of focus is in this chapter of McKay and Wiers.

In their chapter, McKay and Wiers propose a framework in which the organizational context of factory planning and scheduling can be described. In their framework, they discern structural and functional interconnections. The structural interconnections relate the decomposition of the planning problem to the characteristics of the decisions that are the result of this decomposition. For example, when there is uncertainty in the environment, and the planning tasks are ordered hierarchically, there is the question at what planning level the uncertainty should be handled. The functional interconnections depict the characteristics of the information that flows between the planning department and other departments. The planning context and planning task division determine the complexity of the relationships between the planner and the other departments such as production, sales, and accounting.

This chapter contains both descriptive and design aspects of planning. It is descriptive because the framework is based on empirical research of the authors and because it is primarily meant as a framework for describing and understanding specific planning situations. However, the aspiration of the framework is not describing per se, but to be able to improve the embedding of planning in organizations. For example, on the basis of an analysis in a company, it could be concluded that the horizon of their planning decisions does not really fit the uncertainty in the environment. Changing the planning practice in such a situation would improve the quality of the planning and therefore the performance of the company.

6

THE ORGANIZATIONAL INTERCONNECTIVITY OF PLANNING AND SCHEDULING

KENNETH N. MCKAY

Department of Management Sciences, University of Waterloo, Waterloo, Ontario, Canada, N2L 3G1

VINCENT C. S. WIERS

Institute for Business Engineering and Technology Application (BETA), Eindhoven University of Technology, Eindhoven 5600-MB, the Netherlands

6.1. INTRODUCTION

Planning is a basic cognitive ability that humans use to organize their life and to achieve objectives. While we plan at the individual level, organizations such as manufacturing firms also have formal or institutional level planning and this planning is often linked to the value chain. Any value chain consists of resources that must perform some kind of task, and the aggregation of the tasks address the main purpose or objective of the chain. In such value chains, decisions are made continuously and must be carried out if the objectives are to be met. In theory, in a rational process, the planning and scheduling problem starts with the organization formulating objectives about how value will be generated. These objectives are then used to identify what should be done when, and with what resources. The resources then execute effectively and efficiently to achieve the objectives.

In research, planning and scheduling are often looked at in isolation, independent of organizations and with a focus on optimal sequencing, batch sizing, late jobs, lead

Planning in Intelligent Systems: Aspects, Motivations, and Methods, Edited by Wout van Wezel, René Jorna, and Alexander Meystel

times, and inventory levels. This has been the traditional world of academic research on the topic. Unfortunately, there has been little similarity between the highly abstracted concepts used in research papers and planning and scheduling in practice (e.g., Buxey, 1989; Dudek et al., 1992; Graves, 1981; MacCarthy and Liu, 1993; Pinedo, 1995; Rodammer and White, 1988; Wiers, 1997a). In the traditional research papers, scheduling is usually defined as "allocating tasks to resources in time," whereas planning is defined as "ordering actions." Using these definitions, the planning and scheduling problem has been defined in a highly transparent way, and thousands of papers have been written on these stylized problem definitions. However, there are at least two key areas traditional research has generally overlooked when considering real factories and real planners and schedulers:

- The cognitive processes of the actual planner and scheduler
- The organizational environment within which planning and scheduling is undertaken.

Fortunately, there has been renewed research on these gaps. The individual's contribution in real settings is being addressed by a number of chapters in this book and by some prior research (e.g., Crawford, 2000; Wiers, 1997b; Higgins, 1999; McKay, 1987, 1992). There has been less research on the organizational context, and that is the focus of this chapter.

When planning and scheduling are placed in an organizational context, decision making rapidly get messy and very complex. Anybody who attempts to study planning and scheduling in practice is confronted with questions such as: "What is scheduling?" or "What is the difference between planning and scheduling?" There might not even be someone specifically called a scheduler! For example, when approaching a logistics staff member with the question "Are you allocating tasks to resources in time?" they may not know what you mean, but there will be many answers and there will be little information to identify a scheduler or distinguish a scheduler from a planner. In other words, when looking at human planners and schedulers in practice, it can be challenging to match the abstract problem with what the human is actually doing. This is the start of the complexity and difficulty—understanding the real-world context and putting planning and scheduling in that context.

Figure 6.1 illustrates the context of the planning and scheduling problem. A planning or scheduling *problem* is often assigned to an employee: a planner or scheduler, respectively, who executes the planning or scheduling *process* and hence carries out a planning or scheduling *task*. The human is part of an *organization* that provides the inputs for, and requires the results from, the planning and scheduling processes. Depending on the factory, the tasks might be done by machine operators, line supervisors, area foremen, production control staff (possibly someone called a planner, scheduler or dispatcher), someone in materials, a manager, or even someone in sales and marketing. These people will be part of formal and informal organizational structures, and these structures will influence the tasks and how the problem is solved.

Figure 6.1. Planning and scheduling context.

This chapter will focus on the relationship between the planning and scheduling process or task and the organization. The objective of the chapter is to propose a framework that describes the interconnections between production planning and scheduling within the organization where these tasks are carried out. The purpose of the framework is to help decompose, align, and structure various characteristics of the planning and scheduling task such that better field studies can be performed, various phenomena observed in a field study can be systematically categorized, and field studies can be compared and contrasted in a consistent way.

This chapter has six main sections. Following the introduction, Section 6.2 briefly reviews production control research results or concepts that have an organizational element to them. Section 6.3 presents the proposed framework composed of structural and functional elements. Sections 6.4 and 6.5 then discuss each set of elements in turn. Section 6.6 concludes with a discussion of issues and opportunities for future research.

6.2. SCHEDULING IN PRACTICE

6.2.1. Literature Review

There have been a number of studies of planners and schedulers in laboratory settings or in limited simulations (e.g., Sanderson, 1989, 1991; Dutton, 1962, 1964; Dutton and Starbuck, 1971; Fox and Kriebel, 1967; Hurst and McNamara, 1967; Thurley and Hamblin, 1962; Tabe et al., 1988) and while these have probed the phenomena of sequencing, they have ignored the task structure and complexity of the real world—both organizationally and individually. There have also been some studies that have looked at the individual in real settings. Some of the studies have been primarily focused on the individual (e.g., Higgins 1999; van Wezel and Jorna, 2001) while several others have had either a major or minor organizational focus.

The number of extensive studies on real schedulers in real settings which have addressed organizational aspects is relatively few. The Crawford (2000) and McKay (1987) studies have some individual aspects, but also a large organizational component. McKay's (1992) subsequent research was focused on the individual's cognitive skill in planning and scheduling, but also included aspects of organizational interaction with regard to constraints and information sources. Wiers (1997b) was focused on the individual for the most part, but also included observations and issues that were of an organizational nature.

McKay (1987) studied real-life job-shop scheduling and identified many factors that schedulers need to take into account during their task, such as operational and physical constraints, routings, workforce, and administration. To be able to take the extensive list of factors into account, McKay describes a variety of information inputs, far beyond what most theoretical scheduling models prescribe, which need to be gathered from various points in the organization.

Crawford (2000) conducted an extensive study in practice on the roles and tasks of the human scheduler and its interrelationships with the business environment. Her research process was of a grounded and qualitative nature. The environmental factors identified by Crawford are: organizational, manufacturing, planning and scheduling information systems, people, and performance measures. However, the type of information exchanged between the scheduler and the various environmental factors is not researched in detail.

In McKay (1992) the studies focused on the task specifics associated with what the schedulers have been charged to do. The particular decisions associated with detailed, direct, restrictive, and sustained control were analyzed. Two extensive field studies on the scheduling task are reported in the context of research on the effectiveness of the hierarchical production planning (HPP) paradigm in dealing with uncertainty. In one of the studies, a task analysis at a printed circuit board (PCB) factory was used to identify the decisions made in response to uncertainties in the manufacturing system. The field study in the PCB factory is reported in McKay et al. (1995a). In this paper, the formal and informal scheduling practices are compared in the context of managing uncertainty. Several interesting aspects of the scheduling practices are mentioned in this study. The scheduler did not take the current situation for granted; instead, he endeavored to influence the amount and allocation of short-term capacity, the immediate shipping patterns, and the technical characteristics of machines (e.g., a machine's tooling and fixtures). The scheduler employed a large number of heuristics (more than 100) to anticipate possible problems and take precautionary measures. Hence, the scheduler's task and role turned out to be a problem anticipator and solver, instead of a simple sequencer or dispatcher. This task analysis provides a clear view of what is meant by control—what is being controlled, when it is controlled, and what feedback is used to execute and sustain control. The study also captured where control existed and how the scheduler had to interact with different parts of the organization. In essence, the organizational perspective delegates control to a certain level, and the task view details what that control is. In the production control situations studied, the control was centered around uncertainty.

It may be interesting to note that the situation noted by McKay (1992) is similar to an early definition of what a scheduler was expected to do:

> The schedule man must necessarily be thorough, because inaccurate and misleading information is much worse than useless. It seems trite to make that statement but experience makes it seem wise to restate it. He must have imaginative powers to

enable him to interpret his charts and foresee trouble. He must have aggressiveness and initiative and perseverance, so that he will get the reasons underlying conditions which point to future difficulties and bring the matter to the attention of the Department Head or Heads involved and keep after them until they take the necessary action. He is in effect required to see to it that future troubles are discounted (Coburn, circa 1918, p. 172).

In summary, while there has been some research on the organizational elements and environment within which planning and scheduling executes, it can be at best described as very preliminary and exploratory. There has not been any results presented in the literature that has explicitly and extensively discussed the organizational aspect of planning and scheduling. In the following sections, we will take an initial step toward formalizing a framework or set of constructs with which to view the organizational context.

6.2.2. Scheduling Objectives

In highly abstracted terms, scheduling is the problem of allocating jobs to resources in time—basically sequencing tasks. This simplistic definition has been disputed by McKay and Wiers (1999), who emphasize the problem-solving nature of the scheduling task, the tasks associated with scheduling, and the situation within which scheduling occurs. In our view, the task of the scheduler is to anticipate future problems and to discount them, operationally and tactically. This objective is performed in the context of an organizational structure.

6.2.2.1. Scheduler Traits. An ideal scheduler has many desired characteristics (McKay and Wiers, 2004). They have to be able to maintain a cognitive map of the present situation and what the situation might look like in the near and distant future. They need good numeric skills and must be able to think quantitatively. These and other skills assist in the basic mechanics of sequence generation, tracking, and reconciliation. In an organizational situation, we consider these types of skills necessary but not sufficient for anticipating the future and discounting them. Anticipating, planning for the future, and addressing problems in advance of their occurrence is not easy and does not happen without effort and work. Why would a scheduler expend extra effort in coordination and planning? One reason we have observed is laziness. Let us illustrate this by describing three extremes. First, there is the scheduler who loves to solve problems when they occur. When a "fire" is detected, he tries to put it out, and he derives his job satisfaction from having saved the factory from yet another disaster. Second, there is the ignorant scheduler, who has told the world the truth over and over again, but the world would not listen. So now, he or she has put up a mental white flag, does a minimal job, and blames other people when things go wrong. Officially, such a scheduler cannot be blamed, but we believe that the work ethics of any scheduler should be like the next stereotype. These first two types of schedulers do not put any extra effort into the planning and coordination task. There is little or no anticipation of future problems.

The third type of scheduler understands that whereas putting out fires is heroic, it is not as effective as installing fire-preventive measures. They recognize that it takes less effort in advance of a problem to minimize or avoid the impact than it does to deal with it later. We have observed this laziness driving anticipatory control and risk minimization. This practice calls for knowing and manipulating many aspects of the factory, to prevent problems from happening, and forces the scheduler to be very active in the organizational network. The scheduler gathers information from any available source, and he tries to influence as many factors as possible that are important for meeting the schedule. His goal is to minimize the total effort equation on his part.

Such a scheduler might appear to be relaxed and not having much scheduling to do (McKay, 1992). However, schedulers that focus on anticipating and discounting problems when they occur, are constantly looking for bits and pieces of information. They may wish to be lazy and not do anything, but when you study them, you discover that they are working quite hard at trying to get the plant to run smoothly. Furthermore, they will make sure that there are key players in the factory that they can rely on to supply information and to implement actions. These schedulers are communicating constantly, and they step over the boundaries of the formal organization without second thought. The central question to them is not "Am I allowed or supposed to do this?" but instead "Is this useful, can it be done, and can I get away with it?" They do not care much for what they perceive as arbitrary policies and decisions dictated by higher-ups. However, they care about quality and the customer and we have not observed those aspects compromised when the schedulers got creative.

In studying such schedulers, it is possible to observe how they manipulate the organizational context, how they use informal and formal knowledge, and how problems are anticipated and mitigated. It is possible to observe how they manipulate the system in their quest to satisfy their objective of having the plant run smoothly. A key aspect for how well the scheduler will be able to achieve the smoothly running objective is where the scheduler is situated within the organization.

6.2.2.2. Scheduler Position Within the Organization. A scheduler's creativeness in getting information and implementing actions across the organization depends on two factors: (1) the structure of the scheduling problem and (2) the structure of the formal organization. For example, if the scheduler is part of the production department, it might be easier to have the schedule executed as it is, without local changes. However, if the scheduler is in a logistical department situated between production and sales, and the production department focuses on efficiency, and sales focuses on service, then the situation might be different.

When removed from the immediate department, the scheduler might have a hard job in convincing production to reduce the quantity on one job to help a job in next week's schedule, or to use an alternative process, or to use different material. Production might claim that it is technically infeasible to shorten the runs, to use an alternative machine, or to use material which has already been produced but which is slightly off-spec. For a scheduler, it might be difficult to convince them to sacrifice an immediate objective for a future one.

If the scheduler exists in an isolated situation with any reasonable amount of uncertainty in forecasts or production output and simply receives orders from sales, the future production will also be uncertain. The scheduler will create batches, sequence them, and pass them to production. It will likely become a question of factors such as politics and chance which orders will be produced when and what efficiency will be reached. If the scheduler is isolated, the effort to anticipate and control the future might not be considered worthwhile. It is also possible that in an isolated case, the scheduler might not be involved in the recovery process and the production unit must perform any schedule corrections locally without the benefit of a larger picture.

Regardless of a scheduler's official position within an organizational structure (isolated or integrated), it is a challenge for the scheduler to understand the requirements from both sales and production very clearly, to strike a compromise, and to convince everyone that the recommended solution is indeed the best thinkable one. This requires not only a great amount of knowledge and persuasiveness, but also a good relationship with key players in all relevant parts of the organization. The following section describes an initial idea for a framework that attempts to capture the organizational context within which the scheduler functions.

6.3. FRAMEWORK FOR ORGANIZATIONAL CONTEXT

In this chapter, structural and functional interconnections associated with the planning and scheduling tasks will be discussed. The purpose is to create a view of planning and scheduling as being a rather complex and broadly defined task, and to show that planners and schedulers have a dynamic and adaptive role to play in the industrial setting. The various case studies and empirical research from which the chapter has been derived can be distilled into potentially key factors: structural and functional interconnections.

6.3.1. Structural Interconnections

The structural aspects of the planning and scheduling decision-making tasks can be looked at as decisions regarding risk and uncertainty. This follows directly from what has been observed in field studies (e.g., McKay 1992) and is the main theme of what planning and scheduling is all about—the main objective. Elliott (1998) reviews the literature on decision making under risk and uncertainty and discusses the experimental structures used in the research. The role of information is highlighted in this review and discusses how additional information has been shown to reduce variability in results and lower uncertainty. While it is relatively easy to say that the appropriate information should be provided and that if used, it will benefit the decision-making process, there are no specific theories or concepts for what type of information is actually necessary for planning and scheduling. One source from which inspiration can be drawn is the famous Beer Game (Sterman, 1989). In this simulation activity involving a multi-stage supply chain, the information visibility and feedback issues are focused upon. The decision makers at each stage have limited visibility about the horizon and about what is going on around them—upstream and downstream. The insights from the simulated Beer Game support the field observations (e.g., McKay, 1992) and suggest that three dimensions of the decision task might be important for decomposing and analyzing the problem. These are:

- *Information Visibility.* The portion of the horizon being considered, which can be very near term measured in hours to the distant planning horizon of years.
- *Depth of the Decisions.* The portion of the product portfolio, which can be from a very limited portion of the portfolio (e.g,. one product) to all of the products being shipped from the plant (e.g., 100% of the portfolio).
- *Breadth of Decisions.* The portion of the supply chain being considered by a task can range from dispatching at a cell or machine, to scheduling or planning a department, to the factory, and beyond the factory to consider upstream and downstream supply chain dynamics—microlevel or macrolevel decision making.

6.3.2. Functional Interconnections

Staudenmayer (1997) surveys and reviews various theories relating to functional dependency between organizational groups. A subset of the theories can be considered information-based, and the proposed framework in this chapter can be grouped into this category. The information processing category of interdependency research focuses on the tight coupling between the groups. Table 1 in Staudenmayer summarizes the characteristics of the information processing theories. Several of the characteristics are as follows: The units of analysis are the tasks performed by work units, departments; antecedents of interdependency are inherent in the information requirements of internal or external tasks; the consequences of interdependency are uncertainty and information processing; implicit assumptions in the theories are that the tasks are pre-identifiable and stable, clearly visible, and recognizable and that the basic results of the information theory approaches are that tight couplings are the most difficult to coordinate. While the general information oriented theories address high-level issues such as serial or parallel dependencies, the theories lack the lower-level granularity to address the context sensitivity of specific task-oriented activities, such as the planning and scheduling relationships. The high-level theories suggest that the planning and scheduling relationships in unstable manufacturing plants with other departments will be tightly coupled and will be difficult to coordinate. To probe further, we propose a framework that looks at the characteristics of the information situation between the departments. The three dimensions in the proposed framework are as follows:

- *Information Flow.* The amount and quality of the raw data to be acquired and disseminated to be used for scheduling and planning; this can be very limited and very clean (e.g., matching data found in the ERP system), or it can be very extensive and include many tacit elements found in the organizational knowledge pool.

- *Scope and Formalism.* The number of players involved; this can be limited (e.g., only a few parties involved on a regular basis) or can be wide-ranging within the organization and include almost everyone.
- *Solution Space.* The density and elasticity of constraints and options represented by the information; this can be very small and have few choices, or the solution space can be quite large with many options and situations to consider when determining the sequence and related decisions.

6.3.3. Discussion on Structural and Functional Interconnections

The structural and functional dimensions are summarized in Figure 6.2.

For different planning and scheduling functions in a company, the values of some of the dimensions in Figure 6.2 might differ and often do. This is especially true for the structural interconnections, as different planning levels are positioned differently within the production control structure. For example, a planner in a particular firm might have a decision depth involving all products, whereas there is a scheduler that only needs to consider a few products.

In our experience, the functional interconnections at different levels will often share certain characteristics. This is because policies and procedures can be company-wide and affect various levels to the same degree. For example, if the firm has relatively strict policies at the planning level that constrain what might be considered planning and what tasks must be performed as part of planning, it is likely that the scheduling level will be similarly defined with relatively strict policies. If the firm likes to have small or large meetings of people working on planning (e.g., the scope and formalism), the same degree of scope is also likely at the scheduling level. The functional interconnections appear to be culturally and organizationally driven and are not dependent upon the planning or scheduling task requirements.

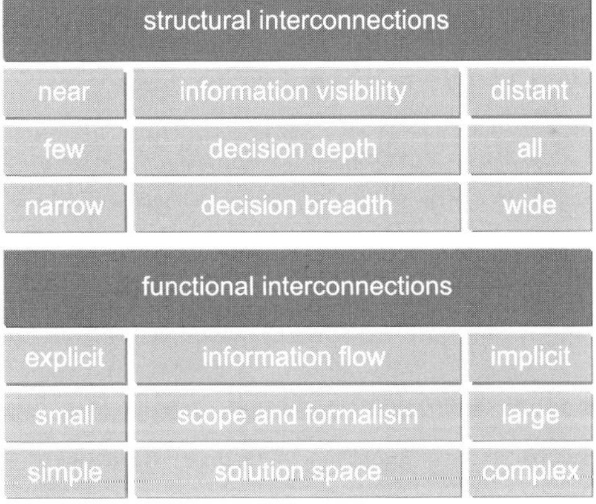

Figure 6.2. Overview of interconnections.

When the two dimensions are combined and the three elements of each are probed, it is our preliminary claim that the organizational context of scheduling is revealed and the situation can be better understood. As stated in the introduction, "the purpose of the framework is to help decompose, align, and structure various characteristics of the planning and scheduling task such that better field studies can be performed, various phenomena observed in a field study can be systematically categorized, and field studies can be compared and contrasted in a consistent way." For example, differences in scheduling behavior and output might be able to be classified as to the information that is visible, how much of the problem is being scheduled in terms of breadth and depth, how the functional task is structured in terms of the explicitness and formality of the information flow, and how complex the solution space is. It is not claimed that this is the only taxonomy, nor the best, for such analysis purposes. However, we are not aware of any similar concept in the literature, and it is suggested that the proposed framework might serve as a starting point for structuring the planning and scheduling problem in the factory setting. This research has been driven from factory and plant situations, and it is not suggested that the framework can be directly applied to other types of planning and logistics. However, it is suggested that similar frameworks, if proven reliable and valid, would assist with analyses in other domains. As an initial proposal, the framework described in this chapter is at the plant level and interdepartmental. Within a department, there are also many interconnections and structures that guide, constrain, and facilitate the decision processes. The intradepartmental linkages within a production control department (if centralized) or within an operational unit (if decentralized scheduling is performed) have not been explored per se. The goal of the framework is to provide the larger structures which can then in turn be explored at smaller levels of granularity. Future research planned by the authors is intended to explore the intradepartmental linkages.

The next section, which discusses structural interconnections, explores the relationship between the structural dimensions and the concepts of hierarchical production planning, autonomy of decision making, and focused factories. It illustrates how the proposed structural elements can be applied to existing situations.

6.4. STRUCTURAL INTERCONNECTIONS

In a real factory, the structural interconnections can be isolated and documented. In this section, we will discuss how the concepts map onto several common manufacturing structures: hierarchical production planning, autonomy of decision making, and focused factories.

6.4.1. Hierarchical Production Planning

Within a plant, hierarchical organization structures have long been used and were formalized by Anthony's seminal work (1965). Most companies use the hierarchical model and production control models, and concepts have been developed to map onto the hierarchical structure.

In essence, hierarchical production control is a way to decompose the problem into manageable pieces. For any reasonably sized factory, it is almost impossible for any single individual to construct plans or schedules for the whole production system. Therefore, the production problem is decomposed along hierarchical lines, creating various levels of control. Higher levels of control usually have a wider scope in terms of the supply chain, greater visibility of the horizon, and a reduced or aggregated view of what is made in the plant. The lowest control level typically corresponds to a part of the production system and has a restricted view of the supply chain, limited visibility of the horizon, and a detailed view of components, subcomponents, and purchased parts which go into the final, shipped products.

There are many books and research results targeting the HPP paradigm and its various aspects (e.g., a review of HPP and its appropriateness is presented in McKay et al., 1995b). A variety of models and concepts for how to view HPP have been developed. For example, Bertrand et al. (1990) distinguish between goods flow control, which concerns planning and control decisions on the factory level, and production unit control, which concerns planning and control decisions on the production unit level. The goods flow control level also coordinates the various underlying production units. A production unit is an outlined part of the production process of a company that produces a specific set of products from a specific set of materials or components, with a specific set of capacity resources. This is depicted in Figure 6.3.

Hierarchical control and the decision-making process is independent of the physical layout of the plant, which can be either functional or flow. It is also independent of how work is controlled in an operational sense, be it just-in-time pull triggers or (MRP-generated) work orders. The goods flow control in Figure 6.3 corresponds to the breadth and visibility aspects of the proposed structural framework. The decoupling points in Figure 6.3 highlights the logical boundaries that relate to the differences in the depth dimensions—the areas of concern faced by the decision maker.

In terms of the structural dimensions of the framework, the hierarchical position of the decision maker restricts the visibility, depth, and breadth. Someone planning (called a planner or not) sees a larger horizon than someone dispatching or scheduling. A high-level planner might plan all of the product families for the factory and

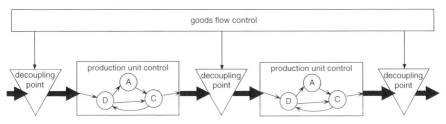

Figure 6.3. Goodsflow control and production unit control. [Adapted from Bertrand et al. (1990).]

might consider the situation of major suppliers and customers. Compromises might be made in the raw materials area or finished goods stock to deal with perceived problems. Someone scheduling would have a shorter horizon, would perhaps be restricted to a functional or process area of the plant, and would be concerned with the internal resources of the facility. If the HPP approach is not suitable, the visibility, depth, and breadth aspects of the real situation can be considered at odds with what is required. Perhaps the scheduler requires greater visibility, greater depth, and less breadth in order to carefully orchestrate the resources.

6.4.2. Autonomy

Each level or area within a factory has some kind of autonomy—what they can decide to do without seeking explicit authority from a higher power. Some form of task list or requirement is input, and objectives are stated. The more detailed and constrained the instructions and guidelines, the less autonomy exists. The general concept of autonomy and its relationship to uncertainty and control was explored by Wiers (1997a, b).

When dealing with uncertainty, the question of how much autonomy to allocate to the shop floor becomes important. On the one hand, it can be argued that operators and teams on the shop floor are better equipped to deal with disturbances than a scheduler sitting in an office. The operators might have more detailed manufacturing knowledge, and they will receive information earlier. In the sociotechnical paradigm, it is often advocated that shop floor workers can and should be able to make detailed scheduling decisions (Bauer et al., 1991). On the other hand, the people on the shop floor might miss the overall view, or other pieces of information. For example, operators might not know about customer priorities, or the situation at downstream operations. Wiers (1997a, b) identifies four situations based on uncertainty and operators' ability to take corrective actions, and he links these situations to a proposed amount of autonomy for the shop floor. These are depicted in Table 6.1. As depicted in the table, the names of the stereotypical production units imply a certain division of autonomy between the scheduler and the production unit. The amount of autonomy in a firm can depend upon a number of factors. For example, quality can be a constraint on autonomy: Operators in the animal feed industry might not be allowed to change the sequence of batches because a risk of contamination might be introduced. A choice to allocate autonomy to the shop floor is in many cases not only dependent on the four types identified by Wiers

TABLE 6.1. Production Unit Types

	No Uncertainty	Uncertainty
No human recovery	**Smooth shop:** optimize	**Stress shop:** support reactive scheduling
Human recovery	**Social shop:** schedule as advice	**Sociotechnical shop:** schedule as framework

(1997a, b), because the culture in an organization is also an important factor. To talk in extremes, are workers seen as production capacity that should carry out orders, or are they seen as knowledge workers who are able to make control decisions?

The concepts of visibility, depth, and breadth relate to the theme of autonomy. What an area will have autonomy over, will depend on the breadth and depth assigned to it. The horizon or zone within which autonomy can execute will depend on the visibility it is handed. If the situation warrants a certain visibility, depth, and breadth in terms of structural interconnections and is not so structured, it is possible to speculate about the quality of decision making and what the situation will be like. The greater the mismatch between structural requirements and structural existence, the greater the control problem.

6.4.3. Focused Factories

In focused factories, large manufacturing processes are still decomposed, but, in contrast to the hierarchical production planning paradigm, not along hierarchical or functional lines. The characteristics associated with focused factories were first described by Robb (1910) and later brought to the modern production control context by the seminal work of Skinner (1974). In this approach, the problem is decomposed along so-called deliverable or mission lines. That is, if the factory makes four major product lines, the factory is organized so that each product line has its own factory-within-the-factory. The focused factory approach is therefore not applicable to job shop or functional physical layouts, as explained in Figure 6.4. The factory must be product flow-oriented, and it should be possible to physically separate the product flows to make a decomposition along these lines.

A focused factory implies that there is dedicated support personnel and very little is shared between the areas, with the exception of some basic facilities such as the physical building. The idea is to dedicate resources so that they can specialize, focus, and concentrate on something—a focus on depth, not breadth. Not only is it a personnel and physical restructuring, it is a logical and control restructuring as well.

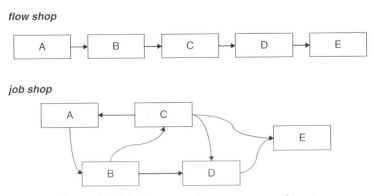

Figure 6.4. Job-shop versus flow-shop process layout.

For the planning and control tasks, this means that instead of having people do the planning for all four products, having other personnel do the scheduling for each of the four areas, and having others make dispatch decisions for each of the four, the attempt is made to have one person do the planning, scheduling, and dispatching for a complete product line. This has the benefit of closing the feedback loops on decisions, actions, and results. It also has the benefit of increased knowledge and information for any decision.

The type of knowledge and information in focused factories is organized differently than in a hierarchical factory. The knowledge is concentrated on the product being produced and is not normally diluted by noise about other products and issues in the factory. The people can remain focused on the task at hand without being interrupted by other tasks relating to other products. The ability to learn and adapt is theoretically higher in a focused factory since loops are closed and individuals from all functional areas are more likely to participate in the process from start to finish. From an organizational perspective, production planners in a focused factory are more likely to interact with fewer people, have fewer stages for information to flow through, and have fewer communication failures than their counterpart in a hierarchical situation. In addition to the improvement in product flow and efficiency, this can result in stronger relationships with counterparts in the other departments, creating trust, understanding, and willingness to help each other (Bauer et al., 1991).

This means that in a focused factory, the scheduler/planner/dispatcher is a central pivotal point in orchestrating the use of resources. The reduced product variety, the clarity of the planner's role, and better development of knowledge makes the situation less complex to control. This means that the planner will need less creativity in the sense of breaking official organizational boundaries, and coordinating actions with functional groups will be easier as they all focus on the same product line.

In comparing the focused factory approach to HPP, the three dimensions of the framework are fundamentally different. For their portion of the final product catalog, the decision maker in a focused factory will have visibility to the horizon, will be concerned with the broad linkages of the supply chain, and will be aware of the various levels of production necessary for success.

6.5. FUNCTIONAL INTERCONNECTIONS

Planners or schedulers in either a hierarchical or focused setting do not live on an island, isolated from all others and totally self-sufficient. They rely on information, formal and informal, from others in other departments. They also rely on others to help prepare the situation for execution, to perform the actual execution, and to deal with the results of the execution. For each of these stages, there are direct and indirect activities ranging from operators loading material and flipping switches to the material handlers, the industrial engineers, the electricians, the cleaners, and so on. In this subsection, two key interdependent organizational elements will be discussed in light of the three functional interconnection dimensions: information flow, scope and formalism, and solution space. First, the impact of hierarchical versus focused factory styles of organizational structure will be discussed in the context of functional interconnections. Second, the variety of functional interconnections and interdependencies with various disciplines found within a manufacturing concern will be briefly highlighted.

6.5.1. Interconnection Space

The complexity of the interrelationships between the scheduler and functional staff such as purchasing, sales, quality, and product development is strongly affected by the structural interconnections. In a hierarchical production planning situation, there are several planners and schedulers responsible for a part of the production process of the complete product assortment of the company. On the other hand, the functional staff is responsible for all products and for all steps. This means that the knowledge and information flow is much more fragmented than in a focused factory, where one scheduler/planner/dispatcher is responsible for all the steps of one product line and for the functional staff too. In an HPP approach, there is a mismatch between the information flow requirements of production control and the supporting groups unless there are dedicated one-to-one resources. In an HPP approach, the scope and formalism is also potentially increased because of this same mismatch.

In the HPP situation, large demands are placed on the knowledge ability of the scheduler, and this affects the information flow and scope. As the complete picture about the production situation might not exist within a single individual in a functional department, such as a general purchasing group, the scheduler needs to create it by gathering knowledge from different sources. For example, there might be purchasers who deal with all of the metal components and another who purchases the plastic components. If the scheduler needs to know whether a job can be produced early, information is needed from both purchasers. Similarly, the two purchasers might be visited by multiple schedulers asking similar types of questions, each competing for attention and answers.

In the focused factory mode, the type of information flow and scope are altered. For example, it is possible that one purchaser deals with all of the material acquisition orders associated with one product. With one source, it is possible that the information flow is cleaner, contains less noise, is subject to fewer errors, and can be performed in a timely manner. These are characteristics of dedicated flows. If a flow has multiple sources and many decoupling points, the possibility for errors and inefficiency increases.

While an HPP or focused factory situation should not affect the theoretical solution space, it does. It affects how the space is created and the quality of the space. With a greater number of sources involved, the latent and inherent uncertainty, and hence more unknowns, increases. With each unknown or source of uncertainty, additional constraints and issues must be considered. A situation in a factory can be claimed to be focused or HPP. If the situation is studied and the predicted functional dimensions for focused or HPP are not observed, then a mismatch might exist and further investigation is warranted.

6.5.2. Disciplines

The product characteristics largely determine the intensity and complexity of the scheduler's interrelations with functional departments—the types of information, the number of interconnections, and the complexity of solutions. A stable production process implies that there are probably few new product introductions (or that product changes and introductions are tightly controlled), demand is relatively stable and predictable, and the manufacturing process itself is repeatable and predictable. In these stable situations, the scheduler needs little more than the job order and shift/manning information to construct a feasible schedule. Examples of this could be a latex or a tobacco plant. In a stable situation, the day-to-day information flows, informal information updates, and numbers of people involved can probably be expected to be low. There would not be the need for constant interaction with other departments such as sales, purchasing, industrial engineering, or product engineering. On the other hand, when new products are often introduced, or the technology is not mature, or the process is not in control, there can be high variance in execution—both in time and in quality. Demand might also be difficult to forecast, and the scheduler will need information from all relevant departments, including sales, product development, and manufacturing, to construct a feasible schedule. Examples of this could be an automotive supplier to an unpredictable assembly plant, or a high-tech component manufacturer. In these cases, the degree of functional interconnectivity can be expected to be high with informal and formal mechanisms in place (or if not in place, required).

In this subsection, a number of possible interconnections will be briefly described as the richness and variety illustrates the application of the functional interconnection dimensions to the organizational structures within which planning and scheduling exist. The nine interconnections described in the subsections are not all of the possible connections. In fact, some of the nine are multi-dimensional in and of themselves. In the various field studies and projects done by the authors over the past two decades, we have observed frequent—and in some cases almost constant—communication and constraint relaxation interactions between the disciplines listed and production control. If the situation is highly unstable, a great deal of each day and each week is spent cultivating and maintaining the formal and informal relationships.

The following sections describe the relationships with the following functional departments: purchasing, sales, production, quality, finance, human resources, support groups, industrial engineering, and information technology.

6.5.2.1. Purchasing. In purchasing, the tasks performed in planning and scheduling play an important role in determining the time-phased requirements of raw materials. Purchasing may have long-term contracts that enable the planner to call-off or order material based on the plan. The purchasing contracts result in constraints that may force or hinder scheduling decisions. The contracts might also provide degrees of freedom that the scheduler can exploit in periods of difficulty. In any event, the scheduler is usually not able to change the purchasing plan, and he will with some degree of likelihood experience problems when material does not arrive in time. When there is a problem, the role of the scheduler can be to contact suppliers directly or to go through the purchasing department to chase the timely delivery of materials.

In a dynamic situation, the information flow, scope, and solution space relationship between production control and purchasing should be explicitly analyzed. For example, the planners and schedulers might require frequent and open contact with purchasing—when contracts are initiated and during execution of the contract. It is not a question of authority between the two organizations, but the purchasing decisions need to recognize that the production control decision makers are key stake holders. Once the contract is authorized, the planners and schedulers are required to anticipate risks, establish inventory levels, and deal with the day-to-day material flow. The production control individuals do not have direct influence on the purchasing personnel, and this indirect influence relationship needs to be identified in a framework. If uncertainty decreases, the demands based on the functional interconnection will also decrease.

6.5.2.2. Sales. The sales department makes sure that new orders flow into the planners' and schedulers' systems. The sales department has a large influence on creating a feasible or infeasible puzzle for the planner and scheduler. One aspect of this is the setting of due dates. In many companies, the due date that is set for an order follows strict procedures to ensure a feasible capacity load for the planner and scheduler.

The perspective of sales on the scheduling process is usually not very concise. Salespersons might expect every order to be delivered in time, even if it was entered a week ago and changed five times since. The sales force might be purposefully pushing their individual goals, or it might be a form of negotiation. In any event, a scheduler might have several salespersons to communicate with, all competing for the same capacity and all insisting that their order has the highest priority. In these cases, the role of the scheduler becomes one of a negotiator. Systems that incorporate concepts such as availability-to-promise try to establish better due dates for salespersons to use, but it does not prevent dates that are politically or artificially influenced.

If the decision maker's structural situation implies a longer horizon and a broader scope, the functional interconnection with sales can reasonably be expected to be high. The scheduler or planner will need better and more frequent information about the problem space.

6.5.2.3. Production. The production department plays two roles for the planner and scheduler. First, production is a "customer" of the planner and scheduler, because they should ensure that production is able to operate efficiently. This means that orders should be planned and scheduled in such a way that issues are avoided, such as excessive setups, material shortages, and personnel unavailability. Second, the production department is a constant focus of attention and is monitored closely by the scheduler to make sure the schedule is executed. In many organizations, if the schedule is not followed, the scheduler is blamed for creating a substandard schedule, and not production—thus creating a situation similar to a parent and a young toddler. The parent is ultimately blamed for the child's actions.

As noted by Nauta and Sanders (2001), it is not uncommon for departments within an manufacturing organization to have different perspectives on goals. In our own field studies we have observed production managers often driven by resource efficiency, which means that they will strive to get long runs, minimal setups, large batches, and possibly high work-in-process. The schedulers we have observed are not normally driven by efficiency alone; instead, a balance is usually struck between resource utilization and order lateness (and a number of other factors including perceived fairness). Others such as van Wezel et al. (2004) have also documented trade-offs between production efficiency and performance flexibility. The proposed structural and functional framework suggests that how the compromise is made, depends partially on where the scheduler is structurally located and the structural dimensions. In cases where the scheduler is part of the production department, there will be more emphasis on efficiency, and when the scheduler belongs to a logistics department, it is a more balanced compromise. There are also cases where scheduling is directly controlled by sales, which does not always improve the nervousness or stability of the plan, nor the efficiency of the production unit.

A good relationship with the operators actually carrying out production is essential for any scheduler; similarly, the planner must have a good relationship with the scheduler. The planner deals with a bucketed plan, whereas the scheduler introduces more detail by specifying a start and end time for every operation of an order (McKay and Wiers, 2003b). In both cases, there is a dependency on the willingness of the lower organizational level to execute the schedule and the plan, respectively. This relates to the issues of autonomy, depth, and breadth of decision making. Although there is a formal obligation to do so, it is rarely enforced in an authoritative fashion, because the reasons to deviate from the schedule or the plan might be quite valid. The extent to which a lower control level will not obey guidelines from the higher control level is strongly affected by culture and the lower level's perception of autonomy. For example, in our own experiences in different cultural settings, we have seen cultures where formal authority is in day-to-day reality far removed from real authority. "Subordinates" will question any decision if they do not understand its feasibility or value. In other cultural situations, we have seen that it is more normal to simply carry out orders. In yet other cultures, the situation will vary widely depending on the type of firm, industry, union situation, and company. The degree of compliance can vary from healthy debate and discussion to blind following of the numbers regardless of common sense or anticipated result.

These relationships are examples of functional interconnections. Each relationship with operators and supervisors represents an information flow that has a scope and has potential contribution to the solution space. In a rapidly changing situation, it can be argued that a greater number of such functional interconnections is desired when compared to a steady and stable process.

Since the structural dimensions of HPP may imply a split or decentralized decision process for the planners and schedulers, with planners in one department and schedulers in another, it is necessary to discuss the interconnection between planners and schedulers. For the scheduler and the planner, it is only partly possible to know all the details of the next lower level. There might be a breakdown on the shop floor, and one batch might be swapped immediately for another to prevent further damage to the tooling. Such decisions that are taken locally, play an important role in solving local problems. In many companies, these local decisions are even formalized by giving autonomy to the shop floor, as discussed in the previous section. However, there is a point where the "local" decision making has an impact beyond the local level, and this is where the scheduler should be involved. For example, the job being moved ahead in time might have thermal or other physical characteristics that will create problems with inventory storage or subsequent processes once the job is done. In any factory situation where there are tight constraints (either in time or physical reality), the scheduler has to make sure that he is actually involved (and not confronted with the results afterwards), by having a good relationship with the shop floor and by taking a cooperative attitude in solving problems. The same goes for the planner's relationship to the scheduler. If this relationship does not exist, the classic results of local, myopic optimization at the cost of global suboptimization will be seen.

6.5.2.4. Quality. The level of involvement of the quality department in constructing and executing a schedule is strongly dependent on the type of product manufactured. If a product is mature and is produced in large amounts, there will be little day-to-day impact of the quality department on scheduling. The information flow will be reduced and the quality sources will not be used in day-to-day adjustments and solutions. There might be occasional problems that might delay production, but these are likely to be infrequent. However, there are also production processes with a very variable yield. The quality assessment determines if a product meets the quality standards, and this in turn determines if re-work has to be done or not, and the decision to perform re-work can have a very significant impact on the normal schedule (if re-work can be done at all). In some cases it is possible to structurally plan for re-work, but in other cases not. When there is a large product variety, and the quality defect is detected after machines have already been changed over to another setting, executing re-work can be a real problem. Thus, the interconnection between quality and production control can be very important and must be supported to the necessary level in terms of information flow, people involved, and knowledge of solutions or redress.

There are also cases where quality dictates part of the schedule—for example, in cases where products contaminate each other or where special tests are required at various processing points, such as in the food processing or pharmaceutical industries. Such special processing and tight controls on sequencing might be a problem when the scheduler is only present during the daytime and production continues throughout the evening and night. For example, if a problem occurs, the expertise to change the sequence is not present. In one factory, the scheduler had a pager and was able to be beeped at all hours of the day and night because the evening and night shifts did not have knowledge (or perhaps the skill) to decide what to do next in the event of a problem. When interdepartmental knowledge is required for schedule recovery, conscious attention to interconnections and information flows might be warranted.

6.5.2.5 Finance. Usually there is not a very formal relationship between the scheduler and the finance department. However, there are a number of interesting interconnections that can be observed.

First, it is possible that the finance department must be involved in the actual problem solving in a real-time process of decision making. For example, when penalties have to be paid when activities are carried out late (e.g., at a bulk transshipment company), the scheduler might discuss the problem with a financial expert and evaluate what the cheapest (least expensive) solution is to the problem. These types of interconnections are reasonably visible and direct.

Second, there are subtle interconnections that might not be obvious. For example, there might be less than optimal tools put in place for the organization driven for finance requirements that must be accepted in production control. Many ERP implementations are examples of this. As soon as an ERP system is being implemented at a plant, there often is a change in perspective between the planners and schedulers on the one hand and the finance department on the other hand. An ERP system covers both domains, but the ERP tool is not necessarily equally proficient in these domains. Many ERP implementations are driven from the financial perspective, leaving logistics with nonideal solutions (see also Markus and Tanis, 2000). Moreover, the finance department often demands in such an implementation that many cost centers are defined so that the value of goods can be measured precisely. However, this means that orders are generated for every step between the cost centers, leading to a very fragmented planning and scheduling problem (Wiers, 2002).

Third, there are interesting interconnections that relate to the plans and the execution of the plans. This interconnection with finance is seen in the plan tracking that may be performed daily, weekly, monthly, quarterly, or yearly. The physical production plan of what is intended to be produced is translated into financial projections by the finance department, and this is then used for cash flow analysis and for profit and loss analysis. The projections will likely include inventory, processing costs, resource efficiency, indirect support, and personnel—all implied by the plan. The planners and schedulers might be responsible for providing part of this planning and tracking information so that the finance department knows where the plant is and where it is going.

Fourth, there is another connection point during the major planning processes that might occur in the factory. During planning activities at the plant level, plans and schedules might iterate between finance (and other departments) and the production control department as one part of the firm strengthens or relaxes various constraints for inventory levels, overtime, personnel hiring, and so forth. The plans might go back and forth several times, and up to seven planning iterations have been observed in one day. The actual planning activities consume much of the planners' time (schedulers are not usually involved in such activities except in a focused factory situation). Each plan might take hours or even days to create, and the firm might do a major planning activity for each month, update quarterly plans, establish a fiscal year plan, create a three-year forecast, and perhaps even a five-year projection. During the major planning exercises, the finance department may or may not also act as the long-range sales expert—either using or modifying sales expectations or customer projections. Second guessing and altering other people's forecasts and estimates seems to be a major part of the planning process.

6.5.2.6. Human Resources. There are other linkages similar to linkages to finance in a factory setting. For example, one such linkage is that from human resources to production control when it comes to the planning and long range schemes. Personnel in human resources know who is retiring, who might be fired, the absenteeism, the training plans, and other issues relating to personnel planning. Hence, during the planning exercises, the iterations will most likely involve human resources, finance, and production control. In some cases, industrial engineering might also be involved if there are ramp-ups, learning curves, changes in efficiency planned, and so on. The information flows and interconnections between departments such as finance and human resources might not be observed or noted at other times, and this confounds any short-term or point-in-time study of the planning and control task.

There is another aspect of the human resource interconnection that might be hidden to normal view. Good scheduling decisions must match the organizational structure and reality, and this includes the human resource element. For example, a good scheduler will make sure that the skills of the operators or teams are known. He or she will not plan difficult and critical jobs on shifts that have a bad reputation for quality or substandard knowledge of quality guidelines. The scheduler might also track and understand what crews or teams paid attention during training and which ones did not.

The scheduler will also respect the position of supervisors and understands that adhering to the schedule is only one of the many criteria that need to be taken into account by these "sergeants" of the shop floor. The scheduler will also know which operators to approach for specific objectives—that is, who are the talkers, who are the problem solvers, who are the influencers, and who are mere figureheads.

6.5.2.7. Support Groups. As in any military operation or theatrical production, there are the direct players and the supporting teams. This situation is the same for manufacturing, and in some cases the supporting teams can be as important (if not more so) as the direct functions. Is there a forklift truck driver available when needed? Where are the electricians working when they are needed to help get a work center working again? Are the tools and dies ready when needed? Each of the groups has its own budget and resource problems. Each has their priorities and their management-generated objectives.

This collection of interconnections will be somewhat informal and will be one of indirect influence. The schedulers cannot order the toolmaker to work on a die or mold. The scheduler has to work with the tool room scheduler to determine what can be done and when it can be done. With reductions in budgets, the supporting groups are possibly working on a fire department model where everything might be a number one priority: You want two things done immediately; we can do one, which one do you want?

Certain departments might be flexible and be reasonably responsive. For example, electricians can easily move from work center to work center. But, once you have a work center torn apart for preventative maintenance, it might be impossible to put the center back together again at a moment's notice. When flexible, the interconnection with production control can be reduced and not be too intensive. When the supporting department is tightly constrained and there are relatively large costs or elapsed times involved, tight coordination and knowledge is important between the groups. Each group will try to negotiate and influence the other to ensure best use of resources. For example, the tooling area might try to get higher build counts for certain parts to create a window for work to be done on a die or fixture.

6.5.2.8. Product, Process, Manufacturing, and Industrial Engineering. There are three possible engineering groups that the production control department might have functional interconnections to. The actual linkages will depend on physical location corporate structures and company processes. For example, product engineering might be in a different country or supplied by the customer, and industrial engineering merges the product and process information and provides a single contact point. In many cases, engineering owns the product and process information; data management, integrity, and communication are especially crucial when new products are produced, when engineering changes are introduced to the product or process or material, and when products are phased out. In these various cases, engineering needs to make sure that (a) product information is in the information systems, (b) the actual information is available on the shop floor in time, and (c) tools and machines have been tested. These are the obvious duties and responsibilities of the various engineering organizations.

There are also other special aspects of the engineering to production control interface. There are the estimates which are used in planning for times, efficiencies, waste, and so on. There is the necessary communication about how these might change based on context and what is planned. The timing of changes and introductions is also important so that the various manufacturing resources are used wisely. For example, while it is common sense to introduce changes on Tuesday, Wednesday, and Thursday day shift and avoid evenings, weekends, and fiscal pressure points (e.g., last week of the fiscal month), we have observed many cases where the operational implications of changes is not consciously considered. The planner and scheduler might be able to influence the change and timing of change, or even request or suggest a change, but the least they can do is to maintain close communication with the engineering groups. By having timely intelligence about what might happen in the future, perceived and anticipated risks can be minimized or avoided.

6.5.2.9. Information Technology. The scheduler can either have a very intense relationship with the Information Technology (IT) group or have hardly a relationship at all. Usually, the scheduler uses some kind of transaction processing system to retrieve order data and possibly to release schedules. It is hard to think of a company entering the twenty-first century without ERP or some kind of MRP software base. Such systems are usually quite mature and do not cause much "normal" communication between the scheduler and the Information Technology department. The communication will increase when new versions are installed or when problems occur with such aspects as shop floor tracking tools, personnel recording, and production accuracy.

The introduction of an Advanced Planning and Scheduling tool may change the dynamics and interconnections with the Information Technology group. There might be file interface processes that run overnight or at 5 AM in the morning—to create a snapshot of what is where for planning and tracking purposes. The technology group might also be charged with the task of supplying help-desk functions. When things do not work at 5 AM, the reliance and interconnections become very obvious. When production records and tracking are not updated for a half day, a day, or several days, the interconnection becomes even more obvious. Information Technology for production control is not bug-free, and it is sensitive and reliant on many other aspects. When the tool, such as an APS, is used operationally or at critical points, it must be functional and operational when needed. The IT group might be required to know what the data are, where they come from, what else uses the data, how the data are derived, and so forth. The IT group might also be required to make minor changes to the configurations and options used in the ERP and APS software.

If the IT group is not tasked to work the same hours as the plant, or does not have the same skill sets on all shifts, the IT can become one of the weak links in production control. Without timely and accurate information, production control cannot function. We have often seen personal relationships used to get priority help or to have constraints relaxed—between the production control people and the IT people. These are the informal interconnections which are very important to encourage and create.

6.6. DISCUSSION

It is suggested that an existing or proposed organizational context can be mapped onto the three structural and three functional dimensions. The structural elements are relatively straightforward to explore and describe. The functional elements are multidimensional because it is possible that many functional departments are involved. The possibly many functional interconnections can be aggregated by their nature, and a general dimension state can be determined. For example, in general does the scheduler have many information flows each day, and in general does each information flow involve many people? It is not the intent of the framework to micro-analyze the interconnections, but to do a rough decomposition.

At this preliminary stage of research, the framework is largely for decomposition and descriptive purposes. Once decomposed and analyzed using the dimensions, a situation can be reviewed. For example, it might be possible to consider the reality of the situation to determine if the appropriate interconnections exist, if the wrong ones exist, or if the interconnections are functioning in a helpful or harmful fashion.

An obvious point is that there are 64 combinations implied by this framework. While some will dominate and while some may be exclusive to others in a prescribed situation, there are still a relatively large number to consider. It is not a simple 2×2 matrix. It is our opinion that overly simple models of the manufacturing context have led to overly simple solutions that rarely work in practice. Perhaps the logic that led to the six dimensions helps to explain the gap between production control theory and practice. We have casually observed in various studies (McKay and Wiers, 2003b) that different planners and schedulers in different factories focus on different horizons and are responsible for different groupings of products or processes. In all cases, they are called schedulers and there is no further distinction. We have noticed that in some factories the schedulers are constantly networking and spend almost all of their time on the functional interconnections, while other schedulers sit in a room without much external communication and simply issue a schedule to follow. The six aspects relate to some of the characteristics we try to observe and understand about a new scheduling situation we encounter. Does it walk on four legs, fly with wings, or crawl on its belly? These types of aspects help us categorize and think about the context within which the scheduling and planning tasks are done.

We have also used these six aspects informally in studies when either assessing a current situation or designing a target solution. If the situation warrants effective communication between certain groups and there are organizational or technical barriers preventing it from happening, it is a possible area to improve. A stress shop in the Wiers (1997b) taxonomy would be such a situation. In a smooth shop as described by Wiers, you would not expect much time spent on the functional interconnections; and if a major portion of each day is spent on them, it should be further investigated. If a factory is trying to do a focused factory from the physical level and is still using a hierarchical model for decision making, problems are likely to arise. If someone who is supposed to plan the factory level is restricted in the knowledge and information about upstream and downstream dynamics, there is also a possible mismatch.

The placement of a situation within the six aspects has also been used in the design of decision support systems (McKay and Wiers, 2003a). For example, what horizon does the tool have to deal with? What types of sequencing or planning decisions need to be supported? Does the tool have the necessary links to the other co-dependent groups (e.g., tool and die)? For example, consider a modern assembly plant at the end of the supply chain using dedicated assembly lines with a substantial level of automation making a relatively limited variety of products. For this factory, hierarchical planning would probably suffice, little environmental noise will affect the automated assembly lines, the plant is new enough that machines and resources still perform to specification, dynamic problem solving between multiple groups would be rare (few options to consider), and the information flow is reasonably low and is clean. For contrast, consider an upstream supplier with an older facility, aging equipment, a job shop process, and a high variety of shipped items. For this factory, the day-to-day life of the scheduler would be full of surprises in terms of demand and processes. The older environment creates instability, and more information sharing is necessary to keep on top of the situation. Some solutions might be easily crafted, while others might require negotiations between multiple groups. For the two example factories, the same decision support tool will not work. One factory has a certain profile, and a different set of operational requirements are exhibited by the other.

6.7. CONCLUSION

In this chapter, we have tried to achieve two goals. First, we have tried to describe the organizational richness of the scheduling situation as it is found in real settings. From this base, it is possible to speculate about new ways to better describe or understand the organizational context of planning situations in a more generic fashion using a common set of dimensions or factors. There are possibly many such ways to describe or capture the essence of the problem. Second, we have presented a preliminary and exploratory set of dimensions which might serve as one starting point for future research and discussion.

In a sense, the six dimensions describe the six organizational characteristics that define a scheduling situation. We believe that these are necessary to know when assessing the quality of production control decisions or prescribing a change to an existing situation. If these six elements are understood, it is not claimed that everything about the scheduling situation will be understood or that a precise match may be found for all factories. However, it is possible that the six dimensions can give a first-level decomposition to the problem. This should help in understanding what the problem is and what possible solutions make sense.

In this chapter we have focused on production planning and scheduling tasks. There will be other planning and scheduling tasks within companies, such as people scheduling or transportation scheduling. We expect that the production planning and scheduling domain has the most elaborate interconnections, because it touches upon the complete primary process of the firm. If transportation planning is done in a company with a production process, we expect the interconnections to be simpler for the transportation planning task, because it only involves a small part of the primary process. However, if the company involved has a primary process that revolves around transportation (or people), then the same interconnections can be applied to these planning and scheduling tasks.

We further suggest that the six dimensions or factors help clarify why industrial situations appear so varied and why it has been so hard to categorize, generalize, and create mathematical and decision support tools that are easy to install and use. It is also possible that by better understanding what the dimensions imply, better expectations can be created for what production can and cannot do.

ACKNOWLEDGMENT

This research has been supported in part by NSERC grant OGP0121274 on Adaptive Production Control.

INTRODUCTION TO CHAPTER 7

The chapters by Jorna (4), Gazendam (5), and McKay and Wiers (6) show that theories on planning in organizations are not unified in one single perspective. In Chapter 7, van Wezel elaborates on this in the field of computer support for planners in organizations. Although virtually all human planners use some kind of computer support, there are different approaches to design support, and there is a large gap between advances in theory and application in practice. Van Wezel describes three causes for this gap.

First, there is not much empirical research into organizational planning. A literature review shows that not much researchers look at actual planning processes. The organization of planning tasks and the individual's task performance are often neglected in planning support research; as a consequence, the relationships between organization, task, and support are difficult to make both in theory and in practice. This lack of empirical research is the main reason for the other two causes.

The second cause is the lack of an overall framework for the organizational, human, and support aspects of organizational planning. A literature review of support approaches shows that existing approaches focus on a specific problem area (mostly manufacturing), or they focus on a specific phase of the development process (mostly system design). As a consequence, research efforts are fragmented and difficult to integrate.

The third cause is in the paradigm of algorithm development. Algorithms (or heuristics) are models (or computer programs) that can generate plans and schedules. There is much research into scheduling algorithms, but most planners

Planning in Intelligent Systems: Aspects, Motivations, and Methods, Edited by Wout van Wezel, René Jorna, and Alexander Meystel

do not use such algorithms in practice. Mostly, algorithms are created by looking at the things that must be scheduled (or the domain)—for example, machines, jobs, and operators. Van Wezel discusses that looking at the domain alone results in algorithms that do not incorporate aspects that the human planner finds important, which results in negligence by the human planner that should use the algorithm.

In line with the analysis of the gap between theory and practice, van Wezel first describes a comprehensive framework for modeling organizational planning and scheduling, after which he describes a paradigm for developing algorithms that are focused more on using the algorithms and less on optimality than current approaches. Referring back to the first gap and in line with the chapters by Jorna and by McKay and Wiers, both the modeling framework and the algorithm development approach are grounded in practice; further emprical research is needed to enrich the developed concepts, and application in practice is based on analyzing the organizational as well as human aspects of the case where application will take place.

7

INTERACTIVE SCHEDULING SYSTEMS

Wout van Wezel

Faculty of Management and Organization, University of Groningen,
NL-9700-AV Groningen, the Netherlands

7.1. INTRODUCTION: THE GAP BETWEEN THE PROMISE AND THE PRACTICE OF INTERACTIVE SCHEDULING SYSTEMS

In the early days of interactive scheduling, Godin (1978) was able to make a probably almost exhaustive survey of the available systems at that time. His conclusion is that "interactive scheduling systems are sound ideas," among others, because "subjects using CRT displays perform better than subjects using teletypes" (op cit., p. 335). The advantages that he attributes to interactive scheduling support are still fully endorsed in literature. Interestingly, whereas the analysis of Godin was more than 25 years ago, even then his worries were the same as they are now: "why, then, has the utilization of interactive systems in real situations been so meager in scheduling, while being much broader in other areas?" (op cit., p. 355). Godin poses eight hypotheses why, in 1978, there is a gap between "the promise and the practice of interactive scheduling systems:

1. Scheduling problems are often huge combinatorial situations. In the past, in order to make the problems solvable, assumptions had to be made to reduce their breadth. These assumptions were frequently unrealistic and unacceptable to the operations managers responsible. The cost and time to develop and run scheduling systems which would not require such assumptions was

Planning in Intelligent Systems: Aspects, Motivations, and Methods, Edited by Wout van Wezel, René Jorna, and Alexander Meystel
Copyright © 2006 John Wiley & Sons, Inc.

prohibitive. Although great strides have been made in mathematical programming techniques over the last few years, little of this work has seen application
in interactive scheduling environments.

2. Scheduling problems change so rapidly that the systems are not flexible or
sophisticated enough to keep up with them.

3. Computers are common today, but interactive systems for solving real
scheduling problems are still rare. Few people appreciate the difference
between solution techniques utilizing interaction versus solution techniques
in a batch processing mode.

4. Operations managers frequently lack any real understanding of computer-
based systems. Thus, they display a reluctance to use such systems (interactive
or otherwise).

5. The software and hardware to support flexible interaction were not available
(at reasonable cost) until the last few years.

6. Job shop scheduling systems have not been attractive areas for commercial
ventures. A number of reasons account for this: (a) it is hard to prove cost
savings and/or other benefits; (b) each installation requires a high degree of
tailoring—almost a custom design; (c) education of the users of such systems
as well as the higher-level executives who must approve the purchase of the
system is extremely difficult.

7. Schedulers don't really have a good grasp of the implications of many of
their decisions. Since the situation is so unstructured, they build in large
slacks to allow themselves to flounder around (see Nicholson and Pullen,
1972).

8. Schedulers are, in general, buffered from outside pressures. They don't see
themselves as having much of a problem (see Pounds, 1963). Hence, motivation to design and use scheduling systems is lacking."

Reading this list, we can only conclude that not much changed in the 27 years
that have passed since Godin's survey. In the next section (7.2), we will attest
this statement by exploring the gap between theory and practice of interactive scheduling systems. This problem exploration will focus respectively on the lack of
empirical research in planning and scheduling, the lack of a comprehensive framework for design of scheduling support, and the domain-oriented approach that is
often taken in designing scheduling algorithms. In Sections 7.3 and 7.4 we propose
how the development of interactive scheduling systems can be improved. In
Section 7.3 we use hierarchies in planning to link domain models to models of
the task division and task execution. Furthermore, we propose a framework for
scheduling system development in which the domain and task models are linked
to a reusable library of scheduling specific components. In Section 7.4 we
extend the use of hierarchical models to the design of algorithms. By providing
a structure with which algorithms can be designed for subtasks rather than for scheduling problems, we expect the chances that algorithms will actually be used in
practice to rise.

7.2. PROBLEM EXPLORATION

In the previous section, we have stated that not much has changed with respect to the basic problems in applying interactive scheduling systems. In this section, we will investigate the causes of these problems in detail in two parts. First, we will provide an overview of functionality that is commonly found in interactive scheduling systems. Second, three related causes of the gap between theory and practice will be discussed.

7.2.1. Basic Components of Interactive Scheduling Systems

The amount of information that is involved in planning problems makes it necessary to use external tools for information storage or manipulation. Pen and paper ("the backside of a cigar box") or a planning board are still no exception, but computerized support is common nowadays. In practice, word processors and spreadsheets are still frequently used to support planning and scheduling, although several authors note that such general programs do not suffice for even slightly complex planning situations (Green, 1996; Kondili et al., 1993; Jakeman, 1994). Literature shows variety in functionality that is applied for scheduling systems. The following scheduling system characteristics can be distinguished:

1. *Components.* Interactive scheduling systems are basically like any other kind of decision support systems consisting of a database, a user interface, a model base with algorithms, and links to external systems. The database stores all information, the user–interface shows the stored information and provides possibilities to update and manipulate the information, and the model base contains generation algorithms. Scheduling specific functionalities are a constraint checker, a goal evaluator, and a blackboard where multiple solutions and partial solutions can be stored for later retrieval. Figure 7.1 shows a

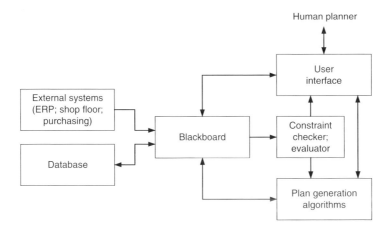

Figure 7.1. Scheduling system architecture.

typical architecture using these components. Literature contains many descriptions from different perspectives (e.g., empirical approaches, system engineering approaches, cognitive approaches) for the various components.

2. *Level of Customization.* Because situations differ, scheduling systems must also differ. The level of customization is different for each system. Two extremes on the continuum are (a) custom-made systems that are designed and programmed from scratch and (b) standard systems that cannot be customized at all. Custom-made systems are expensive but applicable to all situations, whereas standard systems are cheap but often will only support a part of the planning task. Most systems are somewhere in between. A very rough categorization is as follows:

   a. *Custom made.* No scheduling-specific components are used; they are created from scratch. Applicable to unique planning situations. For example, a system created in C++ for planning incoming flights at the airport.

   b. *Components in 3GL.* Reusable components are created in the development environment. The components can be changed and new components can be added. This is used for planning situations with specific GUI or algorithm requirements. An example is using CPLEX from ILOG in a system for routing trains on a shunting platform.

   c. *4GL.* Components and development environment are integrated. The development environment contains a workbench with a large number of scheduling components. The actual behavior of the system must be programmed, but the components cannot be changed so the application scope is limited. Suitable for planning situations that fit or can be adapted to fit the system. An example is the system Quintiq.

   d. *Setting parameters.* The system can be configured by setting parameters. Like with a 4GL system, this is useful for planning situations that fit or can be adapted to fit the system. An example of such as system is the APO scheduling add-on for SAP.

   e. *Standard systems requiring no or minimal configuration.* Such systems have a fixed planning model and user interface. This can only be used in standard environments—for example, small factories or small truck companies.

3. *System Integration.* Scheduling systems can be stand-alone, sharing information batchwise, or can be integrated real time in other systems. Typically, in a dynamic or uncertain environment, real-time data exchange between the shop floor, the warehouse, sales, and the planning is needed.

4. *Supply Chain Scope.* Suppliers and customers (both inter-organizational and intra-organizational) provide information to or get information from the planners. Information sharing can be included in the system so the data are always up to date—for example, retailers that automatically send their aggregated sales data to main suppliers who use the information to make accurate forecasts. Examples are Advanced Planning Systems (Stadtler and Kilger,

2002) and industry standards for exchange of business data (for example, PSLX and ISA-95/B2MML).

5. *Collaborative Planning.* Often, multiple planners work simultaneously. If they are planning the same resources (machines, vehicles, staff, etc.), the system should support this.

6. *Algorithms.* An important task of scheduling systems is generating schedules or parts of schedules. When the risk of suboptimal planning is high, custom-made algorithms could be worthwhile. Otherwise, general algorithm toolboxes such as CPLEX are used, or even simple priority rules.

The gap between theory and practice is most notable when one realizes that there is not much knowledge about the relations between the kind of planning problem, the way in which the planning problem is solved in an organization by human planners, and the kind of functionality that is needed in the supporting systems. In the remainder of this section, we will discuss three underlying related problems: a lack of adequate empirical research, the fragmentation in research and literature on scheduling systems, and the approach that is often taken to design algorithms.

7.2.2. The Gap Between Theory and Practice—I: Lack of Theory Due to Poor Empirical Embedding

The gap between theory and practice is frequently addressed in literature—for example, McKay et al. (2002), Halsall et al. (1994), Dessouky et al. (1995), and Buxey (1989). The basic reason for this gap is the lack of theory. In the previous chapters, many characteristics of planning have been discussed, both from an organizational perspective and from the perspective of the individual human planner. In essence, a theory for interactive scheduling systems should have design rules to link these characteristics to the design of the system. Although many descriptions of scheduling systems can be found in the literature, the theoretical relation between the organizational context, the individual task characteristics, and the planning problem characteristics, on the one hand, and the kind of support, on the other hand, is insufficient.

The main cause of the lack of theory is the lack of systematic empirical research on the relation between organization, task, and support. Sanderson (1989), Crawford et al. (1999), and Crawford and Wiers (2001) provide extensive overviews of empirical studies in planning and scheduling. Crawford et al. (1999) categorize these studies in different methodological approaches—that is, laboratory studies and theoretical models of human schedulers, reviews of human scheduling behavior, surveys, and field studies. Crawford and Wiers (2001) discuss three generations of research in planning and scheduling. First, there are studies that are motivated by intrinsic interest in human factors of planning. Second, industrial relevance has come up as a driving force for much research. Third, there are studies that try to integrate the human factors with industrial application.

In order to study human aspects of planning, one needs planners. There are two main approaches with respect to subjects: using students and using real planners.

Since students are often readily available to participate in academic studies, they are a popular category of subjects for experiments. Mostly, graduate and undergraduate students of production and operations management or industrial engineering are used for these kinds of experiments. Such students at least have some feeling with the planning domain of the experiments. There are several examples of such studies. Moray et al. (1991) investigate the effect of workload on the performance of a planning task. Nakamura and Salvendy (1988) study six students that must control an FMS. Bi and Salvendy (1994) relate human workload to the task arrival rate, task complexity, task uncertainty, and task performance requirements with 12 senior undergraduate and graduate students of the School of Industrial Engineering. Kuo and Hwang (1999) show that 16 industrial engineering students using a scheduling system with algorithms perform better than priority rules. Koubek and Clarkston (1994) show that, for letting inexperienced humans perform a control task, it is better to train abstract relationships first and only then the details than the other way around. Although planning experiments with students can yield interesting results, the use of non-experienced planners is debatable since novice and experienced planners show differences in their task performance (Bainbridge, 1974; Mietus, 1994; Bi and Salvendy, 1994).

The methodological problems that are caused by using students for empirical research can be alleviated by using real human planners. Although operations management literature clearly separates planning, sequencing, scheduling, control, and rescheduling, practice is more diffusing. There appear to be two kinds of occupations that are used for empirical research in planning tasks: planners and operators. Planners usually perform planning, sequencing, scheduling, and rescheduling tasks. Operators perform sequencing, scheduling, and control tasks. The sequencing and scheduling tasks are performed by both, but usually on a different scale of detail. Studies with planners and operators usually have the goal to formulate and implement rule-based systems or heuristics with human-based rules of thumb. Empirical studies of planners are done as case studies (Crawford, 2001; van Wezel, 2001; Wiers, 1996), longitudinal studies (McKay et al., 1995c; Hurst and McNamara, 1967), or field studies (Crawford et al., 1999; McKay and Buzacott, 2000). Examples of planning tasks of operators are described by, for example, Norman and Naveed (1990), Beishon (1974), Bainbridge (1974), Dutton (1964), and Fox and Kriebel (1967). Despite the many similarities, research results on the control task of operators need careful consideration before they are applied to the task of planners, since operators plan their own task whereas planners typically plan tasks of others (van Wezel and Jorna, 2001; Wäfler, 2001).

Our conclusion is that much empirical research is limited in scope, using the wrong subjects, and is not constructive in the sense that research projects do not build on previous research in planning and scheduling. Looking at planning and scheduling in organizations as a domain of research, it is still in its infancy. In the next two subsections, we discuss the consequences of this gap for the scheduling systems that are developed.

7.2.3. The Gap Between Theory and Practice—II: The Lack of Comprehensiveness in Scheduling System Development Approaches

The lack of empirical research in the planning and scheduling domain shows in the literature about development of scheduling systems. A "complete theory" would unequivocally link characteristics of the context, the organization of the planning tasks, the tasks themselves, cognitive aspects of human planners, and characteristics of the domain to the required functionality of the scheduling system. Development of scheduling systems would be straightforward then. Unfortunately, as will be clear from the previous gap, such a theory does not exist. This is not to say, however, that successful systems have not been made, but the lack of a unifying theory results in fragmentation of such efforts. Table 7.1 shows some examples of systems that are explicitly meant to be used in multiple cases, and thus somehow must implement a theory, hypotheses, or assumptions about what elements are reusable (van Wezel and Jorna, 1999). We will shortly discuss the systems and the approaches that are applied.

In Section 7.2.1 we discussed a categorization of ways to implement customization. The underlying system development approach used for customization can be classified in two forms of reuse: (a) generation and (b) composition (Biggerstaff and Perlis, 1989). Generation-based reuse is a *finalized domain approach*; it means that an exhaustive assessment of a domain has taken place. A system can always be generated on the basis of the characteristics of the target case that falls in the domain because everything that is needed to know about the domain is already known and implemented. Systems that are configured using parameters apply generation-based reuse. Contrary to generation-based reuse, composition based reuse is an *evolving domain approach*. It relies on application over time to collect content. The 3GL and 4GL approaches mentioned in Section 7.2.1 can use composition-based reuse if the systems (or components) that are developed can be used again for subsequent implementations.

The approaches in Table 7.1 can be categorized in the two kinds of reuse that we discussed (see Table 7.2). The generation-based scheduling support approaches tend to be domain-dependent or only applicable for a specific aspect of the development process. This is due to the fact that the diversity in the different domains is too large to put them in one generating system (see also Smith, Lassila, and Becker, 1996). The choice of domain-dependent modeling primitives, however, can preclude application to other domains. Woerlee (1991) and Ehlers and van Rensburg (1996) limit themselves to generation-based approaches for manufacturing scheduling problems. Henke (1994) and Fukunaga et al. (1997) discuss applications for spacecraft missions. They both claim, however, that their approaches are applicable or adaptable to any scheduling problem. Smith, Parra, and Westfold (1996) describe a transformation-based reuse approach to scheduling software in the transportation domain. Thus their focus is on constraint-based schedule computation.

Wolf (1994) describes a combination of a generation-based approach and a composition-based approach. He provides a basic general model for resource-constrained,

TABLE 7.1. Planning Support Approaches

References	Short Description	Domain	Problem Representation
Tate (1993) and Beck and Tate (1996)	Framework for open planning and scheduling systems, based on O-Plan and TOSCA. Mainly oriented toward constraint processing.	Domain-independent	State space
Ehlers and van Rensburg (1996)	A model with eight layers. Scheduling problems classify in one of these layers based on products, resources, processes, timeframe, and constraints.	Manufacturing	Complexity layers
Fukunaga et al. (1997)	A framework of automated planning and scheduling (ASPEN) in the spacecraft operations and control domain. Includes an object-oriented system with reusable software components, which can also be applied outside the spacecraft domain.	Spacecraft operations	Activities
Henke (1994)	An object oriented approach for scheduling space shuttle missions. Can also be applied in other domains.	Space shuttle missions	Objects
Pillutla and Nag (1996)	An object oriented framework with objects that occur in manufacturing scheduling problems.	Manufacturing	Objects

Reference	Description	Domain	Model
Smith, Lassila, and Becker (1996) and Smith and Becker (1997)	OZONE, a planning and scheduling toolkit that can generate constraint-based scheduling systems.	Domain-independent	Scheduling and planning ontology
Sundin (1994)	Problem-solving methods for assignment and scheduling problems for the CommonKads library.	Domain-independent	Kads domain model with resources and components
Woerlee (1991)	A scheduling system shell in which a production scheduling model can be specified.	Manufacturing	Tables
Wolf (1994)	A framework in which scheduling problems and constraints can be modeled and a description of a DSS for scheduling with a separation in domain-independent and domain-specific information.	Manufacturing	State space
Dorn (1993)	Task modeling with Kads in two steel-making factories.	Manufacturing	Kads models
Dorn et al. (1996)	A library with reusable and extendible classes for the construction of production scheduling systems.	Manufacturing	Objects
Smith, Parra, and Westfold (1996)	Transformational development of transportation scheduling systems.	Transportation	Domain theory
Pinedo and Yen (1997)	Architecture of an object-oriented scheduling system.	Manufacturing	Objects
Moutarlier, Geneste, and Grabot (2000)	Architecture of an object-oriented scheduling system.	Manufacturing	Objects

TABLE 7.2. Reuse Aspects of Planning Support Approaches

References	Reuse Approach	Mechanism	System Aspects
Tate (1993) and Beck and Tate (1996)	Composition	Decomposition and modularity of components.	Standard components aimed at constraint processing; constraint specification is problem instance.
Ehlers and van Rensburg (1996)	Generation	Classification of scheduling problem in one of eight layers.	Generic object-oriented components.
Fukunaga et al. (1997)	Generation	Modeling language to define scheduling problems.	System can be configured to a specific problem with the modeling language.
Henke (1994)	Generation	Object hierarchy.	Object oriented components and rule based approach.
Pillutla and Nag (1996)	Composition	Object hierarchy and class templates.	None.
Smith, Lassila, and Becker (1996) and Smith and Becker (1997)	Composition	Object-oriented framework based on a common ontology with demands, resources, operations, and products.	Generic modules are implemented and can be specialized with domain specific features when needed.
Sundin (1994)	Composition	Abstract concepts and generic problem-solving methods.	None.
Van Putten et al. (1993)	Generation	Predefined graphical representation and separation of model from representation.	System that creates an interface based on the defined axis and representation form.
Wennink and Savelsbergh (1996)	Generation	Scheduling-specific modeling primitives.	A system that can create a scheduling system based on a model is proposed but not implemented.

Reference	Approach	Description
Woerlee (1991)	Generation	Scheduling-specific modeling primitives.	Generic system that can be configured with a production system model.
Wolf (1994)	Generation and composition	Separate description of generic scheduling objects and domain-specific objects.	Generic modules are implemented and systems can be made by implementing additional domain specific modules.
Dorn (1993)	Composition	Object hierarchy and separation of domain, inferences, tasks, and strategies.	Implementation not described.
Dorn et al. (1996)	Composition	Extendable objects.	Objects are implemented in C++ classes.
Smith, Parra, and Westfold (1996)	Generation	Transformation of problem specification into executable scheduler.	The results of three scheduling systems are discussed.
Pinedo and Yen (1997)	Composition	Design is modular due to object modeling and therefore extendible and reconfigurable.	An implementation is mentioned.
Moutarlier, Geneste, and Grabot (2000)	Composition	Object-oriented framework.	Generic modules are implemented and the authors mention extensions.

time-dependent planning problems that can be represented as Gantt charts. This generic layer, however, must be supplemented with domain-specific components.

The composition-based reuse approaches are also often limited to a specific domain or a specific aspect of the development process. Pillutla and Nag (1996, p. 359) propose a composition-based approach for manufacturing scheduling problems. They hypothesize that "a store of instantiated models is inadequate in response to variations caused by new problems. What is necessary here is the build-up of a new model from segments of existing models." They indicate how the existing models can be extended by newly acquired knowledge about the domain. Their domain modeling technique is suitable to model a wide variety of planning problems. Their approach, however, does not cover organizational modeling, task modeling, or system design aspects.

Smith, Lassila, and Becker (1996) present OZONE as an object-oriented, configurable planning and scheduling framework, with its roots in the opportunistic, constraint-based scheduling approach OPIS (Smith, 1994). This framework is based on a planning and scheduling ontology that consists of demands, resources, operations, and products (Smith and Becker, 1997). They claim general applicability and have applied it for crisis-action deployment scheduling and medical evacuation planning. Like Pillutla and Nag (1996), Smith and Becker (1997) do not propose how to model the organization, planning task, or support system.

Tate (1993) and Beck and Tate (1996) describe the open planning and scheduling systems O-Plan and TOSCA. As with OZONE, these systems draw heavily on constraint processing. Decomposition and modularity of system components should enable reuse by distinguishing the architecture level from the plan or schedule representation. Planning situations are modeled from the perspective of solution generation, and organizational modeling and task modeling do not get much attention.

The DÉJÀ VU framework that is described by Dorn et al. (1996) is oriented toward the implementation side. As the aim of the framework is to support the construction of scheduling systems for specific applications, it is a component-based reuse approach. It consists of a set of C++ classes that implement elements of machine scheduling theory, and it is therefore particularly applicable in the manufacturing domain. A similar framework in the same domain is proposed by Moutarlier, Geneste, and Grabot (2000). Pinedo and Yen (1997) provide an architecture of an object-oriented scheduling system that has a more conceptual nature. Again, the domain modeling is oriented toward manufacturing scheduling problems.

The approaches that were discussed show that there are limitations in the scope of the systems. This means that there is no approach covering all aspects of system development processes. There are three main limitations. First, most approaches are domain-specific; many concentrate on manufacturing. This is not a problem in itself, but it means that such systems cannot be used for staff scheduling or transport planning. Furthermore, the manufacturing models have limitations as well—for example, because many do not contain concepts for continuous flow manufacturing, alternative recipes, uncertainty in processing time that requires rescheduling, and so on. Second, approaches only focus on a part of the development process. Most approaches focus on modeling the domain to create a part of the system—for example, a class structure, a user interface, or a constraint satisfaction model. We found no reference to a working system that could reuse task analyses.

Both in research and in practice, there are successful efforts to create scheduling systems that can be easily adapted to fit specific situations. However, the state of empirical research results in fragmentation. In Section 7.3, we will propose a framework that is more conceptual than technical, but which can be used to integrate models of the domain, the planning organization, and the planning tasks, thereby facilitating reuse for analyses of the situation next to the design of systems.

In Table 7.1 and 7.2, a number of scheduling systems are described. These systems are not meant to function in complete isolation; they will be used by human planners and schedulers. This necessitates interaction. The era of teletypes as mentioned by Godin is long gone. All scheduling systems allow interaction with a graphical user interface. Unfortunately, such interaction is usually kind of superficial. As we will discuss in the next subsection, interaction with algorithms, which could be considered as the core of many scheduling systems, is not possible with the currently used paradigms in research on algorithms.

7.2.4. The Gap Between Theory and Practice—III: A Top-Down Approach to Algorithm Design

Most research in the area of planning and scheduling is in algorithms. Algorithms can create a part of the schedule or even the whole schedule. Many scheduling problems are NP-hard. This means that there are no algorithms known that would solve these problems in polynomial time. In other words, even small scheduling problems are transcomputational (see Chapter 1). Because of the complexity of scheduling problems, a better algorithm often yields better results than more computational power, which makes research in improving algorithms both interesting and potentially lucrative. Still, the use of algorithms in the practice of interactive scheduling systems is only a pale reflection of the advances that have been made in research. This is the third gap that we will discuss.

We start by discussing the three main philosophies of schedule generation. The first two categories focus on mere generation. The first category of techniques only looks at characteristics of the domain. The second category only looks at the way the problem is solved by humans. Techniques in the third category base themselves on support requirements that stem from decision support theory. Techniques in this last category try to find a balance between efficiency that can be reached by using the computer and the fact that the solution must be understood by the human planner. The three categories will be discussed respectively.

Domain-Oriented Generation Techniques. First, there are approaches that focus mainly on the domain without analyzing the way in which the problems are solved by the human planner. The possibilities of the computer are then not restricted by the human planner. In such approaches, characteristics of domain entities and their relations are analyzed (e.g., capacity of machines, shift requirements, historical data of working hours, etc.) and an algorithm is formulated that can efficiently find a schedule which does not violate constraints. There are several research approaches that deal with this kind of schedule generation. Operations Research techniques are available for all domains of plan generation such as job shop, flow shop, routing, and so on (Baker, 1974). Such techniques, however, operate under strict restrictions and limitations of the number of variables, making them often unsuitable to optimize real-world problems. Another critique on these approaches is that they are not understandable by human planners and therefore are an often neglected part of a scheduling support system. Artificial Intelligence and Computational Intelligence techniques are proposed to solve this problem (Brown et al., 1995). The so-called intelligent scheduling or knowledge-based scheduling approaches are presumed to cohere more to the problem-solving steps of the human planner, and the techniques appear more easily adaptable to changed circumstances. Examples of knowledge-based schedule generation are constraint-based search, simulation of heuristics, activity-based scheduling, and fuzzy scheduling (Smith, 1992).

The domain-oriented approaches can yield powerful algorithmic support, but the coherence with the cognitive processes of the human planner is probably small, even with the knowledge-based techniques. Note that this is not necessarily a hindrance for application in practice. Rather, it depends on the task environment characteristics whether such an approach is worthwhile or not. If much can be gained by optimization, then this approach can be beneficiary. Limiting factors are that the constraints must be clear and exhaustive, and the optimization goal must be clear. In addition, the situation must be rather stable, since changes in the domain induce changes in the algorithms, and fine-tuning algorithms is time-consuming.

Problem-Solving-Oriented Generation Techniques. Second, approaches can focus on imitating the human problem-solving processes with rule bases or expert systems. This approach is also called the transfer view because the knowledge is extracted from a human and transferred into a computer program (Schreiber et al., 1993). For this approach, the problem-solving approach of the human scheduler must be analyzed. In terms of the human problem solver (Newell and Simon, 1972), this means that the problem space and operators must be traced and implemented. As with the domain-oriented approach, the distribution of tasks between the computer and the user is mainly toward the computer, but the available computational capacity is not used since the computer is used as a symbolic processor. It is, however, understandable for the human planner why a generated plan looks as it looks, because he would have processed the symbols in more or less the same way. The main disadvantage of this approach is that the system inherits not only the capacity of abstract reasoning that is so typical of humans, but also the myopic firefighting tactics that human schedulers practice (Smith, 1992). In addition, the resulting algorithms are highly specific for the individual human planner.

Task-Oriented Generation Techniques. Third, the task-oriented or mixed-initiative approach combines the first two approaches. Domain-oriented and expert system approaches both focus on computerized schedule generation. In the mixed initiative approach, the support approach focuses on improvement of the solution by establishing a coalition between the computer and the user. Hence, neither the domain- nor the problem-solving process is the main focal point, but instead the task of the human planner. This implements the common DSS view that both human and computer should do the tasks they are best at. This is called knowledge-based decision support (KB-DSS). KB-DSS approaches are equipped to analyze the task- and problem-solving behavior of human decision makers. In this paradigm, decision support is based on the decision processes of the human decision maker. Thus, the aim is not to accurately mimic the human problem-solving process, but to provide support for the problem-solving process. In addition, by focusing on the knowledge level, it is not necessary to use techniques that come from Artificial Intelligence to provide knowledge-based support (Newell, 1982). The focus in a KB-DSS is on the level at which the system and the user communicate.

Scheduling systems often use heuristics that compromise optimality for performance reasons. Hofstede (1992) gives some prerequisites to which heuristics must comply if they are to be used in interactive support at the knowledge level. First, the user must be able to interact during operation. Second, the problem representation must consist of objects that are meaningful for the planner, and it must be possible to show the progress of the heuristic to the user. Third, the operators or transitions in the heuristic must refer to actions in the real world. Fourth, the control mechanism must allow the user to alter the current state during execution of the heuristic, and it must provide a way for the user to make a trade-off between the quality of the solution and the time spent in generating it.

Prietula et al. (1994) describe how they applied the concept of "coincident problem spaces" in the scheduling system McMerl, with the following proposition: "To configure effectively a support system that can exploit the knowledge of the scheduling expert, it is important to direct the behavior of the system to function in a manner that is consistent with the key problem spaces of the scheduler; that is, the system and the scheduler should be problem solving in *coincident problem spaces*" (p. 660). They acknowledged the restricted computational abilities of human planners, and they designed a system that could augment the search of the human with search by the computer. In addition, they used a mixed-initiative approach for the system because "the system could not anticipate the entire set of parameters that define acceptable solutions" (p. 657). In such an approach, both the human planner and the computer can take initiative in the proposition of schedule decisions. The human planner, though, always has the last word. To overcome the problem that the problem space of a human planner can change after the introduction of scheduling support, Prietula et al. (1994) apply the Soar architecture. This architecture allows (symbol-based) learning, so changes in the task that occur after the introduction of the scheduling support system can be depicted in the reasoning mechanism of the system.

Discussion. The main advantage of domain-oriented techniques is that the solutions are of a high quality. The main advantage of the problem-solving-oriented approaches is that the process of scheduling generation better suits human planners. These two advantages are presumed to be combined in task-oriented techniques.

Mixed initiative scheduling systems, however, usually use problem-solving-oriented scheduling techniques because it is easier to find points of interaction when a technique mimics a human planner. Looking at literature on domain oriented algorithms, we see the following kinds of interactions:

- The planner can choose from a number of alternative solutions that are generated by algorithms (Lauer et al., 1994; Ulusoy and Özdamar, 1996).
- The planner may specify weights on goal functions (Smed et al., 2000; Gabrel and Vanderpooten, 2002), after which the algorithm generates a schedule.
- The planner can steer the backtracking process of the algorithm (Bernardo and Lin, 1994).
- The planner can specify parameters for the algorithm (Ulusoy and Özdamar, 1996; Dockx et al., 1997; Oddi and Cesta, 2000; Myers et al., 2002).

In these kinds of interaction, human and system are not problem solving in coincident problem spaces. Rather, the algorithms are still based on domain analyses, and the human is supposed to play a secondary role. In other words, when creating an algorithm, the developer looks at the characteristics of the "objects" that must be attuned such as machines, jobs, staff, shifts, vehicles, and so on, and not at the problem solving processes of the human planners. In general, there are three phases in using such algorithms:

1. *Translation of the Domain into the Model.* This means a formalization of the objects that must be attuned, including their characteristics, constraints, and goals. Some examples of types of models are Linear Programming (LP) models, Traveling Salesman Problem (TSP) models, Assignment models, and Constraint Satisfaction Programming (CSP) models.
2. *Solving the Model.* A model contains a number of variables, constraints, and goal functions. The variables must be assigned values such that the constraints are not violated and the goal functions get the highest possible values. Often, the kind of model that is chosen goes hand in hand with the solution technique. For example, in order to use the Simplex method, the model must be formulated as a LP model.
3. *Translation of the Solution to the Domain.* Once a solution has been found, the values of the variables must be translated back to the domain.

The paradigm in algorithm development is that algorithms can solve scheduling and planning problems better than humans. This is true, but only when we look within step 2. When a model has been formulated, the computer is better and faster at finding the best conflict-free solution or a solution that violates as few constraints as possible. However, we must take into account that (a) information might be lost during the translation, and (b) the solution must be interpreted and understood by the human planner in the context of the actual situation. In other words, the algorithm is only a part of the planning process that is for the rest driven by human decision making. This is the core of the problem. Most or all of the research in scheduling algorithms is in improving the translations and improving the solution techniques. Although developers of algorithms acknowledge that humans will make the decisions and that algorithms are designed to assist the human planners, they lack tools and techniques to incorporate human factors in the development of algorithms. Algorithms are developed in isolation of human problem solving, but they are presumed to be incorporated in the actual planning processes as if they are an integrated part of it. From a Cognitive Science perspective, it is apparent, however, that cooperation between a human planner and an algorithm will only be successful if they have a model of each other (Waern 1989; Rasmussen, 1986; Vicente, 1999; Schraagen et al., 2000). As a consequence, there is a misfit between the human planners in their working practice and the conditions in which algorithms can be applied best.

7.2.5. Conclusion

In Section 7.1, we cited Godin (1978), who gave eight hypotheses regarding the gap between theory and practice of interactive scheduling systems. Using the exploration in this section, we can only conclude that the major issues are still a challenge. The main change has been that hardware and software is available abundantly for over a decade now. Still, commercial issues are a large bottleneck because investments are high and cost savings are hard to predict. Due to too little empirical research, the meaning of "interactive" in interactive scheduling systems has still no sound theoretical basis. Even with contemporary scheduling systems, the implications of a decision are still hard to predict. The way in which a system should represent constraints, goals, complexity of the scheduling problem, and worst- and best-case simulations cannot be found in literature. And despite continuing improvements in mathematics and operations research, algorithms are still seldom used in practice. This might be because algorithms require stability whereas paradigms in production still change fast. For example, in the past few years schedulers are suddenly supposed to be part of a supply chain, which means that they are not buffered from outside pressures anymore. Algorithms that focus on optimization within an organization could perform badly if the are used in supply chain scheduling problems. Furthermore, the meaning of "interaction" in algorithms is not based on collaboration between a human planner and the algorithm. As a consequence, operations managers and planners still lack real understanding of the way in which algorithms determine their solution.

Many scheduling systems are available now that can support planners; an exhaustive survey like Godin's would be impossible. The question, though, is whether the availability of scheduling systems makes the gap between the promise and the practice of interactive scheduling systems any smaller. Our analysis indicates that the gap has changed rather than having become smaller. In Table 7.3, we have categorized the causes, and the focus of planning research in these issues.

In the following two sections, we describe the approach we have taken to improve two issues. In Section 7.3, we will describe a framework including a reusable code base that we used for developing several scheduling systems. In Section 7.4 we provide a concept to include interactivity between human planner and algorithm during the problem-solving phase.

TABLE 7.3. Causes of Gap Between Theory and Practice

Challenge	Explanation	Focus of the Planning Community
Modeling argument	The problem that is solved by algorithms is not the problem in practice.	Find the balance between striving for the optimal solution and practical usability.
Intricacy of the problem structure	Effects of decisions are hard to track and understand.	What-if analyses; real-time constraint checking.
Benefits of support	Return on investment is hard to predict.	Standardization of planning processes and using APS's.
Internal dynamics	Supporting systems depend on a stable situation.	Configurable systems.
Exposure to the outside world	The scheduling task is not isolated.	Shorten the control loop.
Definition of interactive scheduling system	A concept for interactivity during problem solving is missing.	Expert systems; knowledge-based decision support.
Costs	Specific solutions for specific problems are expensive.	Reuse.

7.3. A COMPREHENSIVE MODEL FOR DEVELOPING SCHEDULING SYSTEMS

From the discussion about reuse and customization in Section 7.2, we concluded that what is missing is a comprehensive framework to model and design planning and scheduling support in organizations. The approaches that we discussed in the previous section all contain planning and scheduling specific elements. In other words, they are domain specific modeling languages (DSL). In general the process of using a DSL would be as follows. Domain modeling is facilitated by a preconfigured set of classes. In some cases, the base classes are fixed which means the application scope is predetermined (e.g., machines and jobs in a manufacturing scheduling problem). Most approaches allow extension of existing classes. The idea of most object-oriented approaches is that software components are available for the different classes in the domain models. Specifying the domain therefore means putting together a number of software components. In some approaches these components together are a system, whereas in other approaches the components provide a starting point and require further programming. France and Rumpe (2005, p. 1) describe the following advantages of domain-specific modeling languages compared to generic modeling languages such as UML that have no domain-specific content in their structure:

- "Domain-specific constructs are better suited for communication with users in the domain. The users can better understand the models if they are presented in domain-specific terms. This leads to the claim that domain-specific models are better suited for requirements engineering than UML.

- DSLs have restricted semantic scope (i.e., the number of semantic variations they have to deal with is small compared with general-purpose languages), thus developing a semantic framework is less challenging.
- Restricting semantic scope can lead to better support for generating implementations from models. Given an appropriate component-framework that implements individual constructs of the DSL, the composition of these components can lead to powerful implementations.
- DSLs increase domain-specific reuse of components, which can lead to improved quality of systems and order-of-magnitude improvements in time-to-market and developer productivity. Examples from the telecommunications sector indicate that a speedup factor of ten is possible."

The question is not whether to apply a DSL to planning and scheduling since such an approach has much advantages. The issue is how the "domain" of a planning and scheduling DSL is defined. As we discussed in the previous section, existing frameworks are either limited in the kinds of models they use (organization, domain, task, support) or in the environment that the models can be applied (manufacturing, staff scheduling, large scale military missions, etc.). In other words, we state that it is possible to make a DSL that covers more aspects of planning and scheduling and a broader application scope than the existing approaches. In this section, we will describe such a DSL (van Wezel and Jorna, 1999; van Wezel, 2001).

7.3.1. Foundations

In Chapter 1, we argued that planning is always performed hierarchically. In this section, we extend on this notion by stating that hierarchic modeling is the only way to establish comprehensiveness in a planning and scheduling DSL. This means that only if the necessary models are hierarchical we can realize a comprehensive applicability scope for all kinds of models that are needed. The approaches that were discussed in Tables 7.1 and 7.2 are a good indication that this is already being applied in existing approaches. Almost all authors describe hierarchical object-oriented frameworks or other hierarchical concepts.

Since the planning in many organizations is too large or complicated to be handled by one person, it is split up. The individual parts are then worked on by different persons; their subplans have to be coordinated and combined, which takes place at a higher hierarchical level. In Chapter 1 we have stated that the same reasoning holds for the task as performed by an individual. Exhaustive search by enumerating all possible solutions is impossible, so a human planner working on a subplan will split the problem again in smaller and more manageable parts. This substantiates the need for a hierarchical modeling language for the planning task division and the planning task itself. From this, it can be deduced that domain models need hierarchies as well; at each level (level of coordination of subplans, task level, subtask level) it must be clear what exactly the subproblem constitutes. And as the subtasks together make up the larger task, the same has to hold for the models of the subproblems; the models at the distinct hierarchical levels must be congruent. The same reasoning applies to support. Each subtask should be supported, which also means that support for a subtask should be able to manipulate the subproblem under consideration. This gives the following requirements for our planning and scheduling domain-specific modeling language:

- We need models for organization, task, domain, and support.
- All models must allow hierarchical decomposition. At each hierarchical level, processing the encompassing hierarchically lower models should solve the problem.
- The models must be inherently linked; each model should have a counterpart in the other models. A domain model must be attached to a task model, a task model should be linked to the supporting system, and so on.

In the remainder of this section, we will propose object-oriented models that conform to these requirements. The separation between organization, task, domain, and support is much influenced by the KADS method (Breuker and van de Velde, 1994), although scheduling and planning specific characteristics have been used to change the types of models accordingly.

7.3.2. Models of Domain Entities

Planning always somehow deals with arranging scarce resources. Examples of resources are products, machines, vehicles, staff, and so on. More precisely, scheduling always concerns multiple tokens of different object types. Production schedules, for example, arrange products, machines, and time intervals. In Chapter 1, we proposed the following definition: *A planning problem consists of groups of entities, whereby the entities from different groups must be assigned to each other. The assignments are subject to constraints, and alternatives can be compared on their level of goal realization.* For our purpose, we use object-oriented techniques. This adds (a) the distinction between classes or types and objects or tokens and (b) hierarchic modeling of classes to the proposed definition. The object-oriented modeling language itself is structurally empty with respect to domain knowledge, but allows for description of a domain at multiple layers of abstraction, thereby facilitating both comparison of problems at a high level and description of problems at a detailed level. The central concept of a domain model is the *object*. An object is a discernable entity in the planning process. An object can be "real world" entity (something that we can touch—for example, a machine), but it can also be a construct that the scheduler uses as a way to order his complexity. The hierarchical structure in objects is depicted by the arrangement or attunement of the objects. Two types of subplans can be distinguished in a planning object hierarchy: *aggregation* and *decomposition*. In aggregation, the dimensions that exist in the planning problem stay the same, but individual entities of a dimension are grouped. For example, a planning that contains the assignment of individual orders to production lines for a certain week can be aggregated to a planning that contains the assignment of orders per product type to production lines in that week. In this kind of subplan, the problem is looked at from multiple levels of resolution (see also Chapter 11 by Meystel). Aggregation can be used to establish boundaries or constraints for individual assignments of entities that fall within an aggregated group. For example, it is first decided how much caramel custard will be made next week. Then individual orders that fall in this product family can be assigned to a specific production time. In this way, several stages of aggregation can be sequentially followed whereby each stage creates boundaries for the next stage.

In the second type of subplan, decomposition, a subset of the entities that must be planned, is considered as a separate planning problem. Decomposition can deal with all entities of a subset of the dimensions, all dimensions with a subset of the entities, or a combination of subsets of dimensions and entities. For example, if we must attune orders, machines, and operators, we could first assign orders to machines and then operators to the chosen order/machine combinations. Or we can first assign all customer orders, after which we assign all stock orders.

Models of objects at different hierarchical levels are linked to each other by *constraints*. Constraints restrict the solution space of a decision. In an object model, constraints depict illegal combinations of object instances. Often, there are also rules that express preferences rather than illegal combinations. Such preferences are called *goal functions*. Both constraints and goal functions always belong to an object type at a certain hierarchical level. The actual values of the restrictions or preferences can be different for different object instances, but they can also be uniform across all object instances. In the former case, the constraint or goal function refers to the attribute of an object; for example, the constraint that the production date must precede the due date (both the production date and due date are attributes of an object). In the latter case, the constraint contains an explicit value. An example is the constraint that the production duration on a day may not exceed 8 hours.

An example of a nurse schedule is depicted in Figure 7.2. Objects are either *singular* (nurse, starting time, and ending time) or composed of other objects, that is, *combination* objects (shift, scheduled shift, and schedule). The nurse schedule example consists of a number of scheduled shifts. A scheduled shift links a particular shift to a nurse. Shifts themselves are composed of a starting time and an ending time. Assignments in the schedule are depicted by instances of objects. A constraint in the model in Figure 7.2 could be that student nurses may not work in the night shift. This is a constraint at the level of the scheduled shift because it can be checked only when nurses are assigned to shifts. A goal could be the minimization of the deviation of worked hours and the number of hours in the contract of the nurse. This goal is at the level of the "schedule" object because it is about collections of scheduled shifts. Of course, a domain model can contain several constraints and goals.

The following types of constraints are distinguished:

1. Constraints that are inherently part of the model. Aggregate object instances can only be created by linking other object instances. For example, a scheduled shift can only be created from existing shifts and nurses.

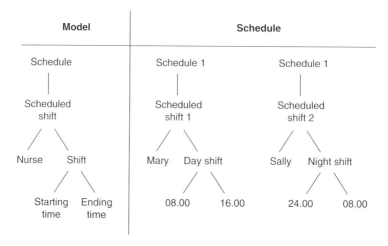

Figure 7.2. Example of object model.

2. Constraints on the number of instances that can be created. For example, time can only be used once, there is a limited amount of production lines, the total amount of orders may not exceed a specified tonnage, and so on.

3. Constraints that directly limit linkage of object instances. For example, certain products cannot be made on certain production lines people that may not work in the night shift, and so on.

4. Constraints that indirectly limit linkage of object instances. For example product A may not precede product B on the same production line or someone may not work in the night shift if he already worked in the night shift in the week before.

Generalization of object models for reuse is performed in two ways. First, singular objects are abstracted by inheritance. Properties that are common to two object types are described at a higher ancestor object type. For example, the object-type employee is an ancestor of both the object-type nurse and the object-type mechanic. These three object types show the differences and similarities between nurses and mechanics. The inheritance mechanism should not be static. The object tree must be dynamically created when searching for similar objects. If, for example, we need for some reason the distinction between men and women in the tree and not between nurses and mechanics, single inheritance would result in four object types (male nurses, female nurses, male mechanics, female mechanics) instead of the desired two (men and women). A static inheritance tree is only suitable for a domain that is analyzed exhaustively, since new knowledge could change the criteria for classification.

Our abstraction does not have an underlying ontology in which basic entities have predefined relations. Instead, we have tried to categorize the objects with terms that are used by human planners. Still, our analyses indicate that planning situations appear to always use a combination of two or more of the following seven abstract object types: person, time, task, location, product, machine, and vehicle (van Wezel, 1994; Bakker, 1995). In other words, the occurring objects in the scheduling domain seem to have one of these object types as the ultimate ancestor. This classification is confirmed by a survey of scheduling situations in more than 50 companies (Bakker, 1995) including different forms of scheduling—for example, staff scheduling, transportation scheduling, and production scheduling. We emphasize that this classification is not fixed. Other classifications are possible, since the classification scheme should remain in accordance with new scheduling and planning "realities." Note that the object orientation paradigm allows for extension of this classification without altering the structure of the modeling language. Hence, we avoid domain dependency.

The second way of generalization of object models is clustering of singular objects. We expect that in practice only a limited set of models will occur (van Wezel, 1994; Jorna and van Wezel, 1997). Staff scheduling, for example, often deals with (a) persons, tasks, and time or (b) persons, locations, and time, whereas production scheduling deals with machines, products, and time, alternatively supplemented with, for example, persons or tasks.

Objects must be assigned to each other. How this is done is modeled with task models, which will be discussed in the next section.

7.3.3. Models of Task Performance

Task models depict how the planner actually plans. The reuse and transition requirements imply that these task models must (a) refer to the domain models, (b) allow reference by models of the scheduling system, and (c) allow abstraction and comparison. The approaches that we described in Section 7.2.3 provide little reference to task performance.

As we have seen, a planning decision is either about setting constraints or making assignments. Next to the actual decision-making activities, other activities must take place, such as information collection and administration. A task model is a representation of the activities that take place with assumptions and principles about (a) the objects, properties of the objects, and the relations involved, (b) the cognitive strategies and procedures for execution of the task by the actor, and (c) the organizational context of the task (Waern, 1989; Breuker and van de Velde, 1994).

We represent the scheduling task with two model types. First, *task decomposition* denotes the subtasks that comprise the scheduling task. To meet the transformation requirements, subtasks are described as operations on objects in the domain model. This will be discussed in the next section. The highest level of task decomposition shows subtasks such as administration (collecting data, etc.), negotiation, communication, attuning or plan generation, and adaptation or replanning. The attuning and adaptation tasks deal with the actual assignment of object instances. These subtasks can be decomposed further in subtasks such as selecting, ranking, assigning, and manipulation of constraints and goals (Mietus, 1994).

Second, the *task strategy* depicts the order in which the subtasks are performed. The order of execution of the scheduling subtasks is, for example, administrate, attune, negotiate, adapt. The order within the attune subtask could be rank, select, assign, and manipulate constraints. Of course, the strategy does not have to be solely linear. Iterative sequences of subtasks are more likely to occur, as was found by Mietus (1994).

With generalization of task models, specific tasks are abstracted to task models that can be applied to multiple domain models. We follow two perspectives. First, due to their reference to objects, subtasks can be abstracted by referring to abstract object types. If, for example, a task model of nurse scheduling uses a subset of the available attributes that corresponds to the abstract object-type "employee," the task model can be used for, for example, mechanics scheduling. Second, the task strategy can be used to provide abstract descriptions of a scheduling tasks. The strategy can be described with features such as periodically or continuously, batch or one by one, top-down or bottom-up, and so on (van Wezel and van Donk, 1996; Jorna et al., 1996).

Figure 7.3 shows a simple example of the relation between subtasks and objects. Suppose a third shift from 16.00 to 24.00 must be added to the schedule in Figure 7.2. First the planner looks at all objects of the type nurse. The nurses are ranked according to some criterion; for example, nurses that have been working in the past 16 hours are getting a low rank. Subsequently, the planner selects a nurse and then assigns the nurse to the shift.

7.3.4. Task Allocation at the Organizational Level

In the same way as a human planner divides task into subtasks, a planning problem is divided into several pieces to be assigned to different planners. As discussed in

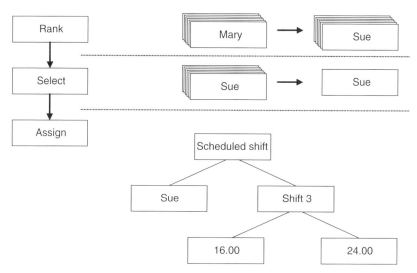

Figure 7.3. Example of model for the subtask "schedule nurse".

Chapter 1, planning is a recursive process of setting constraints and goals for lower, more detailed planning levels. Figure 7.4 contains examples of task allocation at both the individual level and the organizational level. The open circles on the left side denote problem solvers, and the closed circles on the right side are subplans. Vertical lines between circles stand for a hierarchical relation, and the horizontal dotted lines mean that a problem solver is involved in making a subplan. Figure 7.4a depicts the situation where a person aggregates a plan for himself. The planning is first made on an aggregate level before it is made at the detailed level. This could for example be done to reduce complexity, or because some preparations must be taken before all needed information is known. Figure 7.4b represents the situation where a person makes a plan by decomposing it into two subplans. In Figure 7.4c, multiple problem solvers are involved. A boss is responsible for a plan, and two subordinates each make a part of this plan. The task of the boss is to coordinate and to solve coordination disputes. Figure 7.4d shows the situation where two decision makers must make a subplan together.

For each subproblem at each planning level, basically three issues arise. First, the structure of decomposition must be determined. Second, it might prove impossible at a certain level to find a solution within the given constraints. Then coordination with the higher level is needed to determine what to do. Third, there might be a need for coordination with other subproblems at the same level of detail because the subproblems share common constraints. At the levels of organizational task division, these issues are handled differently than at the level of a human that creates subtasks for himself for the following reasons:

- The person who decides on the organizational division of tasks does not execute the tasks himself.
- At the organizational level, the task division level is not easy to change because multiple actors are involved. At the individual level, such changes are much easier to make.
- Coordination between multiple actors requires communication.
- It is easier for a human to change or violate goals and constraints that he has specified himself.

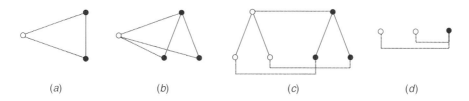

(a)   (b)   (c)   (d)

○ Problem solver
● Subplan

Figure 7.4. Basic types of hierarchical planning.

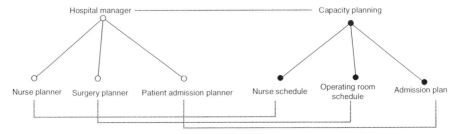

Figure 7.5. Task allocation.

We now have three modeling layers: task division at the organizational level, task division for each individual human planner, and the domain objects that are manipulated. Figure 7.5 shows a rather straightforward example of a planning task division. The hospital manager must decide on capacity—for example, how many nurses should be employed, how much surgeries can take place, and how many patients may be admissioned. Within these constraints, various planners must make more detailed decisions. These planners share constraints and must therefore coordinate their decisions. For example, the planning of surgeries depends on the exact number of nurses available and their competences. These dependencies would show if the accompanying domain models would be drawn; they would use the same objects, and the exact coordination problem would be formalized by the constraints.

In the next section, we will extend the hierarchical, object oriented modeling paradigm to modeling of scheduling systems.

7.3.5. Reusable Library for Scheduling Models

In Section 7.3.1 we have argued that hierarchical decomposition will enable linking the various models of a scheduling situation. We have now discussed how domain models, organizational models, and task models are related: (1) A task operates on a subproblem, (2) the link between tasks can be deduced from the overlap in objects that must be assigned by the tasks, and (3) this overlap and the way in which coordination issues should be solved is specified by the organizational level. These models can be complemented by extending the same line of reasoning to the design of scheduling systems.

The overview of scheduling system design approaches in Section 7.2.3 showed that most approaches use hierarchical concepts to realize reuse. In this section, we propose a similar concept, but in addition to the approaches in Section 7.2.3, we show that the models of the scheduling system can be integrated with the hierarchical models of the domain and of the task, which not only enables reuse of system components, but reuse of analysis and design efforts as well. The basis for this is in the domain models, and a strong analogy in another problem domain comes to mind.

In the database world, the introduction of relational databases, a standardized language (SQL), and standardized communication protocols (for example, ODBC and ADO) have almost eradicated the efforts that software developers must put in storing and retrieving data. As a result, developers can focus on the mapping of business model to data model and on the front end of systems rather than on the back end. Systems can easily be extended because data are separated from function. Additionally, systems can easily use each others data by using the same tables in the database.

Unfortunately, the relational structure is not well equipped to store planning models for several reasons. First, the mapping that must be made from a hierarchical planning model to a relational table structure increases the complexity of queries that are used to manipulate the data. Second, queries for storage and retrieval of data are hardly reusable, because of this complex mapping problem. Third, some characteristics that are common to all planning situations (e.g., constraint checking, goal evaluation, reasoning at multiple levels of resolution) are neither embedded in the data query language nor embedded in the relational structure. This complicates reuse of developed systems.

Analogous to the separation between data, data structure, and functionality in systems that access data using a database management system, we have designed and implemented a generic structure that can be used to specify the hierarchical planning object model and object characteristics. This provides developers with a "domain model management system," which reduces the efforts that are needed to create code for manipulation of planning models.

The system architecture that is depicted in Figure 7.1 contains components that relate to *the use of the system*. In this section, we will elaborate on the system architecture with components that relate to *reuse aspects of building the system*. The first step toward reuse is to separate code that is stable across applications from code that is specific for an application. We distinguish three layers: a generic layer for all planning systems, a domain layer for systems in a domain, and a case-specific layer (Table 7.4).

Figure 7.6 shows the components of the system when we take reuse into account. In comparison to Figure 7.1, two components are added: the domain model specification and class and object administration. Note that the functionality of these components is of course also available in systems that are based on the architecture

TABLE 7.4. Layers of Specificity

Layer	Used by	Functionality at the Layer
Generic	All planning support systems	Functionality to specify the object model and constraints
Domain	All planning support systems in a domain (for example: the food processing industries or nurse scheduling)	The structure of the object model (e.g., orders, runs, machines, etc); assignment representation (Gantt chart, dispatch list, order information interface)
Case	Planning support system for a specific case	Attributes of objects; calculations of attributes; retrieval of data from external systems; constraints; algorithms

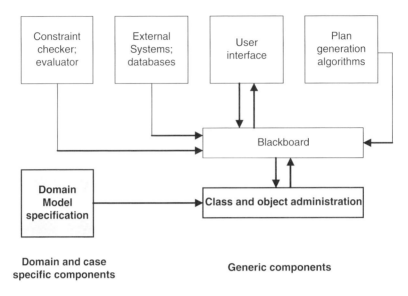

Figure 7.6. Scheduling system architecture.

in Figure 7.1. But in such systems, this functionality can be spread across the system and can be hard to change, which impairs reuse.

The purpose of the domain model specification is to make the transfer of the model of a planning subproblem to the system transparent. The functioning can be compared to making a database model: When the developer provides a conceptual data model he gets functionality to manipulate the data. Currently, the classes listed in Table 7.5 are implemented in an object-oriented programming language.

Table 7.6 shows how these classes are used in the programming environment using the example of Figure 7.2. Because of the object oriented nature of the framework, it is very easy to manipulate the underlying data of the scheduling model and to extend functionality. The three steps A, B, and C in Table 7.6 should be interpreted as follows. In step A, the domain model is specified which is not likely to change often. Step A will usually take place only during the design of the system. Step B is twofold. First, it is used to create more or less stationary data during the administration phase, for example, specifying what nurses will work, what their qualifications are, etc. Second, the constructs in step B are used to make the scheduling decisions, in this case assigning nurses to shifts. From a structural perspective, there is no difference between stationary data and scheduling decisions, because they both deal with creating and linking objects. Step C is used for deriving information from the objects and relations that are determined in step B. This information is typically used to determine constraint violations or scores on goals, or to show the schedule to the user.

The Context object contains functionality to load and save domain models; it functions as the blackboard. Currently, the framework is being extended to

TABLE 7.5. Classes of the Data Model

	Concept	Function of Class	Analog in Relational Database	Examples
1	Class	Specifies a scheduling class	Table	Order, machine
2	Characteristic	Specifies a characteristic of a scheduling class	Field	Due date, capacity
3	Object	Specifies a scheduling object instance	Record	Order 1, production line 1
4	Characteristic value	Specifies a value of a characteristic of an object	Data value	1-2-2001, 100 kilo/h
5	Relation type	Relates two classes	Relation	Orders run on machines
6	Relation	Relates two objects	Two data values in a linking fiield have the same value	Order 1 runs on production line 1
7	Schedule	A container for the six classes above	Database	
8	Context	Contains a list with schedules; it functions as the blackboard	Database management system	

implement a constraint and goal parser, aggregate functions to replace traversal such as shown in Table 7.6, and a TCP/IP-based transport layer for client/server systems. Referring to the analogue of relational database management systems, the framework can be used for the following purposes:

- Create a domain model builder much like a graphical tool to specify a database structure. Such a model builder should take into account generalization of objects as described in Section 7.3.2.
- Build generic components for scheduling systems for example, a report generator.
- Build customizable components—for example, a Gantt chart of which the axes can be assigned to object types.
- Make specific components—for example, a planning board for shunting scheduling (see Chapter 17).
- Make multiple systems that share the same domain model, and use event-based triggers to show the dependency between systems.

The taxonomy decreases the dependency on a complex data structure, since the domain models are implemented directly without a complex mapping. As a

TABLE 7.6. Example of Using the Domain Model Specification Module

A. Specifying the Structure of the Domain Model

Create a Schedule (Concept 7/8)
```
nurseSchedule:=context.addSchedule('nurse schedule');
```

Create the Object Types/Classes (Concept 1)
```
schedule:=nurseSchedule.newClass('schedule');
scheduledShift:= nurseSchedule.newClass('scheduled shift');
nurse:=nurseSchedule.newClass('nurse');
shift:=nurseSchedule.newClass('shift');
```

Adding Characteristics (Concept 2)
```
nurse.addCharacteristic('name');
nurse.addCharacteristic('qualifications');
nurse.addCharacteristic('preferences');
shift.addCharacteristic('starting time');
shift.addCharacteristic('ending time');
```

Adding Relation Types (Concept 5)
```
nurseSchedule.addRelationType('schedule','scheduled shift');
nurseSchedule.addRelationType('scheduled shift','nurse');
nurseSchedule.addRelationType('scheduled shift','shift');
```

B. Adding Objects and Relations

Creating Objects (Concept 3/4)
```
aScheduledShift:=nurseSchedule.newObject('scheduled shift');
aNurse:=nurseSchedule.newObject('nurse');
aNurse.setCharacteristicValue('name','mary');
aShift:=nurseSchedule.newObject('shift');
aShift.setCharacteristicValue('starting time','08.00');
aShift.setCharacteristicValue('ending time','16.00');
```

Relating Objects (Concept 6)
```
nurseSchedule.newRelation(aScheduledShift,aNurse);
nurseSchedule.newRelation(aScheduledShift,aShift);
```

C. Using the Built Model

```
//example: calculate the total length of the
  shifts that nurse Mary is assigned to
//Step 1: find the nurse
aNurse:=nurseSchedule.getObjectbyCharacteristicValue
  ('name','mary');
//Step 2: get all shifts that mary is assigned to
shifts:=aNurse.getObjectsbyRelationName('scheduled shift');
```

(continued)

TABLE 7.6. *Continued*

```
//Step 3: traverse the shifts
totalTime:=0;
For i:=0 to shifts.Count-1 do
Begin
 aShift:=shifts[i];
 startingTime:=aShift.getCharacteristicValue('starting time');
 endingTime:=aShift.getCharacteristicValue('ending time');
 totalTime:=totalTime+endingTime-startingTime;
End;
```

consequence, components can be made more independent, which means that changes are made easier. Furthermore, the link between tasks and subproblems remains transparent throughout the system.

In Chapter 17, we describe a scheduling system for shunting at the Netherlands Railways where we use the implemented class and object administration modules.

7.3.6. Conclusions

In Section 7.2.3, we have concluded that there is no comprehensive framework with which the elements that are part of the task of human planners can be described or designed. But we also discussed various approaches that design such elements individually. In this section, we proposed an integrated set of models to depict the organization of the planning, the entities that are planned, the task performance of human planners, and planning support systems. The basis of the concept is that planning takes place hierarchically. In this view, the following elements constitute the concept of planning as a decision hierarchy (or in short: hierarchical planning):

- Planning is a decision hierarchy or an ordered collection of decisions.
- The reasons to plan hierarchically are uncertainty and the limitation of the available information processing capacity to make decisions.
- The two types of partition criteria that are used are aggregation and decomposition.
- The possible allocations of subsystems are allocation to different people, allocation to different tasks of one person, and stages in the problem solving process of a person.

The organization, domain, and task models are mainly oriented toward the description of a situation (as opposed to design), since we have not described norms or design guidelines. For scheduling support systems, literature provides more to go on. The kind of functionality that can be embedded is fairly well known. There are, of course, gaps. In particular, it is not clear yet when and how generation techniques should be applied. This will be explored in the next section.

7.4. HIERARCHICAL MIXED INITIATIVE PLANNING SUPPORT

7.4.1. Hierarchical Schedule Generation

In Section 7.2, we argued that scheduling systems usually do not allow interaction between the human planner and the algorithm during schedule generation. In this section, we will discuss an approach that can be used to design systems that allow such interaction. It can be seen as an extension to the framework discussed in the previous section, since it builds on the planning hierarchy that is found in a task analysis. Task analyses show that a planning task consists of subtasks and that each subtask itself consists of subtasks. If we analyze *the planning problem* without looking at the planner's task performance, we come up with solutions that do not support the subtasks that the planner recognizes as important elements of his problem. He will be inclined not to use generative support that is designed in this way. If we analyze *the planner's task* without looking analytically at the elements in the planning problem, we will surely inherit planning habits that are based on the planner's limited information processing capacity. Probably not much will be gained in terms of quality of the plan. The idea is to apply algorithms to subtasks of planners rather than design algorithms for planning problems. In other words: *An algorithm should not be created for a planning problem, but instead for a planner's subtask.* Hence, we overcome both problems: The subtask division of the planner is used to a certain extent, but we do not necessarily adopt all his bad habits. We will elaborate on this argument by looking at how algorithms are used instead of how they internally work.

From the perspective of the division of tasks between the human and the computer and the resulting requirements of communication, there are three levels:

- Level of human decision making: tasks that are done solely by the human planner
- Level of solitary search: tasks that are done solely by the computer
- Level of mixed initiative: tasks that are done by both the human and the computer in cooperation

For the first two categories, only the end results of the tasks have to be communicated from human to system and vice versa. For the latter category, however, intermediate results should also be transferred because both the computer and the human planner need to understand the reasoning process that lies behind a decision. Now we presume that tasks by a computer are performed by algorithms. These might be very simple algorithms (e.g., filtering or sorting), but they might also be very complex (e.g., optimizing a large planning problem. As can be seen in our three levels, for any given (sub)task, there are two kinds of algorithms. The *first kind* is a closed-world blackbox algorithm that does not reckon with the planner's division of the task in subtasks. The *second kind* of algorithm uses the same division of the task in subtasks as the human planner. The advantage of the first type of algorithm is that there is more chance to find a globally optimal plan (under the presumption that the optimum can be defined). The advantage of the second kind of algorithm is that the semantic distance between the planner and the algorithm is reduced. The planner can understand more of the reasoning process (and, hence, more the outcome), and he can interrupt the algorithm and continue himself from there. At this point, the complexity of our argument increases. An algorithm of the second kind consists of (a) subalgorithms for each of the subtasks and (b) a management strategy to execute the subalgorithms. Each subalgorithm, however, is used to simulate or imitate a subtask. And as we saw, subtasks that are performed by a human planner consist of subtasks themselves. Therefore, *each of the subalgorithms can be of the first kind or second kind itself*, and we have the conceptual means to decide about "traditional" (mathematical or AI) algorithmic support at each hierarchical level of task execution. This relieves us from the alleged obligation to search for global optima or to decide about algorithms on the basis of an overall quantitative analysis. We can decide per subtask whether a planner needs to be able to interfere with the search process or not, as well as what kind of algorithm is needed, and create mixed-initiative planning support in which both the computer and the human planner have a role in making decisions.

Although the prerequisites of Hofstede which were mentioned in Section 7.2 provide some guidance, it is not yet clear how this can be translated in generic analysis and design rules for scheduling support. Benbasat and Todd (1996) state that a decision maker implicitly makes a trade-off between the cost of applying a decision aid (efforts to understand and employ the model and process the information) and the expected benefits (increased quality and speed of obtaining a solution). They provide a three-step procedure to improve the use of decision aids (op cit., p. 244):

1. Decompose the planning problem into subproblems and obtain estimates for the efforts (costs) to manually find solutions to these sub problems.
2. Identify the subproblems with a high potential of effort (cost) reduction for the decision maker and identify a decision aid that reduces the total effort to find and use a solution for such a subproblem.
3. Incorporate specific features for automating storage, retrieval, and computational tasks in the decision aids to manipulate the cognitive effort associated with using these decision aids.

Since a decision support system will change the current problem space of the human planner, it is not straightforward which decisions should be taken by the user, which decisions should be taken by the computer, and for which decisions the user and the computer should cooperate. Benbasat and Todd (1996) have shown that the decision strategy that is chosen by a human problem solver is contingent upon environmental demands and decision aids. They pose that human problem solvers weigh the effort that a strategy will cost against the accuracy of the expected solution. By introducing decision aids, the effort can be reduced or the accuracy (or quality) of the solution can be increased. Normative decision models can be applied if they will reduce the effort of existing strategies that the human problem solver can apply. This implies that decision support does not have to focus solely on an individual user. If a system provides enough benefits, the user will be inclined to change his own decision behavior. Benbasat and Todd (following Newell and Simon, 1972) use elementary information processes (EIP's) as the smallest task elements. Decision aids should substitute such information processes so that other EIP's (either performed by man or machine) can use the output of these small elements. In this way, intermediate results are understandable by the decision maker. What is elementary is not defined and contingent upon the goal of the analysis and the characteristics of the domain. Note that this approach focuses firstly on the decision maker and only then on the problem structure. Decomposing the problem in subproblems will probably mean that the optimal solution (or a very good solution) from a mathematical perspective will not be found. Whether this is acceptable or not is part of the trade-off between the efforts of the human planner to understand a solution and the quality of that solution.

The ideas of Benbasat and Todd (1996) can of course be applied to the domain of scheduling support. Task-oriented scheduling support focuses on both (a) the domain characteristics and computational advances that have been made to solve scheduling problems in the domain and (b) the problem-solving processes of the human planner. Changes in the task that are forced by the introduction of scheduling support do not pose a problem as long as the planner feels that either the task strain is reduced or the quality of the outcome is increased. This approach can be applied if the quality of the outcome is important, but the task environment is unstable and requires human judgment.

Consequential generation techniques can be understandable and acceptable to the user even if they are not based on symbolic information processing. Therefore, domain-based techniques seem to be at an advantage because they can compute better solutions in most cases. But such techniques should only be used for subtasks of which the human planner does not need intermediate results. Generation algorithms can also be applied for subtasks on the level of mixed initiative. Preferably, algorithms at the level of mixed initiative need to be able to communicate about the search process to the planner in a meaningful way. This can be reached if an algorithm to perform a subtask at the level of mixed initiative uses algorithms that are made for subtasks of the subtask under consideration. Then, the algorithm uses the same partitioning of the task as the planner and intermediate solutions are always understandable by the human user. For this, however, the task structure of the human planner must be extracted. This links the analysis of Benbasat and Todd to the task analyses that are used in the problem-solving-oriented generation techniques as discussed in Section 7.2.4 and in Chapter 3 (Hoc) and Chapter 4 (Jorna). In other words, making algorithms for subtasks combines the strengths of domain-oriented approaches and problem-solving-oriented approaches in the mixed initiative approach.

The concept is depicted in Figure 7.7. Each given subtask can be decomposed into smaller subtasks. For each of these subtasks, it must be decided how it will be performed: by the computer, by the human planner, or by both in interaction with each other. Each of the subtasks that will be executed in interaction can be decomposed itself. For each of the sub-subtasks, the same analysis can be made.

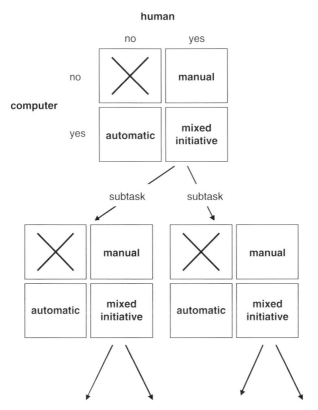

Figure 7.7. The Recursive Human/Computer Task Division Matrix.

So, in a way, generation tasks that are performed by both human and computer are decomposed until only subtasks remain that either can function as a blackbox for the human or are performed without the help of the computer. In this way, we comply with the prerequisites of Hofstede (1992). To sum up, applying algorithms to subtasks has the following advantages and possibilities (van Wezel and Barten, 2002):

1. The chance that the human planner will accept algorithms and their outcomes is increased.
2. Existing divisions of planning problems in subproblems (which a human planner learns to do by experience) can be reused.
3. Algorithms for subtasks can be used *automatically* in a sequence. If an algorithm is available for each subtask in a task, then they can be executed in one step (the 'push the button and get a plan'-approach).
4. Algorithms for subtasks can be used *interactively* in a sequence. Instead of automatically executing all subalgorithms for a task, they can be executed semi-automatically by providing the planner with a way to (manually) interfere after the execution of each subalgorithm.

5. Algorithms can be applied when the planner chooses. For example, a production planner might want to let the computer plan production orders automatically, except when the capacity usage exceeds 90%.

6. Algorithms for subtasks are not as complex to make as algorithms for whole tasks.

7. Different planners use different task strategies, i.e., they perform subtasks in another order (Mietus, 1994). Subalgorithms can be executed in different sequences and therefore they can be used for different tasks strategies.

7.4.2. Conclusions

The essence of the approach we propose can be summarized as follows (the terminology is borrowed from de Sitter et al., 1997): We propose to make the move from complex algorithms in simple human task structures to simple algorithms in complex human task structures. The main question to use this approach is, when will we let the computer perform a subtask, when will we let the human perform a subtask, and when will we let the computer and human interact? The cost/benefit criterion proposed by Benbasat and Todd (1996) needs to be explicated for the planning and scheduling domain. This question needs further research, both theoretical and empirical.

7.5. CONCLUSIONS

In 1978 Godin stated eight hypotheses why there was a gap between the promise and the practice of interactive scheduling systems. Almost 30 years of research on scheduling and planning later, nothing much has changed because the basic problems are still the same. We do not want to criticize the quality of planning and scheduling research in itself. However, from the perspective of the gap it is apparent that the requirements in many practical circumstances are not fully met by what currently is being offered in theory. Because there has been much research in the past decades, the issue with the gap is not so much a lack of basic knowledge, but a lack of knowledge about how to apply the many theoretical advances in practice and, related to this, a general lack of direction for future research on closing the gap.

The position we take is that closing the gap should start with empirical research. This should not be limited to the domain (the actual planning problem), but should include organizational task division and human task performance as well. We do not say that this means that the planning organization or planning tasks cannot be designed. On the contrary, but to design means that the characteristics of the system under consideration must be known. And planning in organizations is more than a computer program with advanced algorithms. The task performance and organizational task division is important as well, and this is where most approaches are lacking. We have proposed a framework that conceptually integrates interactive systems, algorithms, task performance, task division, and the structure of the underlying planning problems. Because the models of domain, task, and support are linked, it is not possible to design a system without thinking about the task structure and task division. The planning process is not presumed to follow the implementation of a system automatically; it is necessary to think about the human and organizational aspects of the planning tasks during the development process of interactive scheduling systems.

There has been much research on planning *problems* in organizations. Research on planning *processes* in organizations, however, is relatively scarce. In the previous chapters, Hoc, Jorna, Gazendam, and McKay and Wiers discussed their research in this area. On the one hand, these examples of planning research can be seen as state of the art. On the other hand, it also shows that much remains to be done. We hope that the concepts we have discussed and proposed will contribute to a convergence of research efforts.

INTRODUCTION TO CHAPTER 8

In Chapter 7, van Wezel discussed the kinds of algorithms in planning support from the perspective of the interaction between the human planner and the algorithm. He proposes to include human task characteristics in the cost/benefit analyses when determining the kinds of algorithms to design and implement. How such algorithms can be developed was not discussed. In the following two chapters, examples of such algorithms are described. In Chapter 8, Kroon and Zuidwijk describe how mathematical models can be used for this. In Chapter 9, Sauer will discuss how fuzzy rules rather than mathematical models can be used to support planners in their task.

Kroon and Zuidwijk start by showing how a simple planning problem can be formalized in such a way that it can be solved by a solution technique. Formalization includes converting the concepts from the scheduling problem to decision variables, constraints, and goals. The simple problem they use to demonstrate these steps gives a good basis to discuss the process of making mathematical models of more complex scheduling problems that actually occur in practice. Kroon and Zuidwijk illustrate the difficulties of such a process with the example of the circulation of trains in The Netherlands, where many constraints must be satisfied (for example, incoming trains must be balanced with outgoing trains, and trains frequently need maintenance), and goals must be weighed (the number of passengers that can be transported, the total train kilometers, the number of shunting movements, etc.).

With his concept of the recursive human/computer task division matrix, van Wezel argues that a decision about algorithmic support can be made for each

Planning in Intelligent Systems: Aspects, Motivations, and Methods, Edited by Wout van Wezel, René Jorna, and Alexander Meystel

subproblem that a human planner faces. Kroon and Zuidwijk provide us with a number of criteria on which such a decision can be based—for example, the part of the problem that cannot be handled by the algorithm and has to be done manually, the throughput time to make a schedule, and the quality of the translation of reality into the mathematical model, to name but a few.

8

MATHEMATICAL MODELS FOR PLANNING SUPPORT

Leo G. Kroon

Rotterdam School of Management, Erasmus University Rotterdam, NL-3000-DR Rotterdam, the Netherlands; and Department of Logistics, NS Reizigers, NL-3500-HA Utrecht, the Netherlands

Rob A. Zuidwijk

Rotterdam School of Management, Erasmus University Rotterdam, NL-3000-DR Rotterdam, the Netherlands

8.1. INTRODUCTION

In this chapter we describe how computer systems can provide planners with *active* planning support, when these planners are carrying out their daily planning activities. This means that computer systems actively participate in the planning process by *automatically* generating plans or partial plans. Later on, these plans can be completed and fine-tuned by the planners. Automatically generating plans by a computer system requires the application of mathematical *models* and mathematical *solution techniques*, as will be described in this chapter. Here a mathematical model is an abstract representation of the practical planning problem in mathematical terms. Solving the model leads to a solution of the planning problem, which is an abstract representation of the required plan. The currently available hardware and software allows for the generation of appropriate solutions for several practical planning problems, both in a proactive and in a reactive way.

The advantages of the automatic generation of plans are obvious: Planning support based on mathematical models may lead to *better* plans, but it may also lead to a

Planning in Intelligent Systems: Aspects, Motivations, and Methods, Edited by Wout van Wezel, René Jorna, and Alexander Meystel

reduction of the *throughput time* of the planning process. The value of better plans comes almost by definition: A better plan may lead to cost reductions, improved service performance, or other advantages. And a shorter throughput time is important because of the flexibility of the planned system: The shorter the throughput time of the planning process, the quicker the planned system can accommodate to changes in the environment. Furthermore, it may reduce the need for reactive planning. Another advantage of planning support based on mathematical models is the fact that it allows for the generation of several plans at the same time based on different scenarios, instead of the generation of just one single plan.

Mathematical models and solution techniques may be used in a variety of application areas to support both long-term and short-term practical planning processes. For example, there are applications in the financial world, in transportation planning, in production planning, in marketing, in manpower planning, and so on. Here a planning process is interpreted as a decision-making process aiming at the selection of appropriate actions that are to be carried out in practice such that the planned system will achieve certain objectives (Ackoff, 1962). The planned system may be large, such as a company that wants to minimize its costs or to maximize its service performance, or small, such as a truck driver who wants to reach his destination along the shortest or the fastest route possible.

The remainder of this chapter is structured as follows. In Section 8.2, we start with an example of a simple planning problem, and we develop a mathematical model that can be used to solve this problem. This example is used to explain certain concepts, and it serves as a reference in the remainder of this chapter. In Section 8.3, we generalize the description of Section 8.2 by presenting the planning process based on mathematical models in more general terms. Section 8.4 lists a couple of modeling techniques as well as a couple of solution techniques. This section also presents some background information on the theory of computational complexity, which is highly relevant in a planning context. In Section 8.5, we describe several methods that can be used to deal with multiple objectives. Section 8.6 describes how mathematical models can be used to support both *proactive* and *reactive* planning processes. Section 8.7 discusses modeling systems, which are quite useful tools in a modeling context, especially during the development phase of a mathematical model. In Section 8.8, we describe some issues that are relevant when applying mathematical models in practice. Section 8.9 presents a real-life example related to the planning process of the rolling stock circulation of a railway operator. The chapter is finished in Section 8.10 with some conclusions and final remarks.

8.2. A SIMPLE PLANNING PROBLEM

We start this chapter with the description of a simple planning problem, and we discuss several modeling issues based on this example. The example is used to explain certain concepts and as a reference in the remainder of the chapter. The example problem deals with a number of "jobs" that need to be processed on a number of "machines." Each of the jobs requires a certain amount of processing time on either of the machines. The problem that needs to be solved is: "Use the machine capacity in an efficient way while processing the jobs." More specific descriptions of "efficient use" are: "Process all jobs in as little time as possible, given the number of available machines" (the required amount of time is called the *Makespan*), or "use as little machines as possible, given a certain amount of time in which all jobs need to be processed." Later on, we shall discuss decision making on the assignment of jobs to machines where these two objectives are combined.

We shall first present a tiny example of an instance of such a problem. In this example, there are two machines and there are six jobs to be processed on either of the machines. The processing time of job j (here j is an integer value running through the values $1, \ldots, 6$) is denoted in an abstract way as p_j. Table 8.1 provides the processing times for the six jobs (in hours). One remark should be made about these processing times. Obviously, it is assumed that the processing times are all known in advance. In practice, such data are typically obtained through experience in the past. One can use average processing times for each job type. More advanced models than the one presented here may take into account variability of processing times by introducing stochastic processing times and by using stochastic optimization techniques. However, this strongly complicates the situation and falls outside the scope of this introductory example. Observe further that we implicitly assume that the processing times of the jobs are independent of the machines. In other words, the machines are assumed to be identical. After the model formulation of this simple planning problem, we shall discuss other variants of this problem, which is usually referred to as a "job scheduling problem" (Baker, 1974).

Although the problem formulation may seem quite concrete, it is rather abstract in fact. This is due to the fact that the notions "machine," "job," and "processing time" refer to the structure of the problem more than to actual objects in reality. Indeed, this model can be applied to situations where "machines" are teams of people working on a project, a clerk working on a document, a straddle carrier moving a maritime container on a container terminal, and so on. Of course, in each of these cases, the problem formulation may require further specification in one direction or the other.

This chapter focuses on mathematical models, so let's *make* a mathematical model that can be used to tackle the job scheduling problem! The aim of the model should be to generate good decisions about how to allocate the jobs to the machines. Therefore, we need "decision variables" that are used to represent the decisions to be taken. Furthermore, in order to specify what is meant by "good" decisions, we need an "objective function" that expresses what we are aiming at. Moreover, there are certain "constraints" that we want our decisions to respect, such as the fact that each job is to be carried out on one of the machines

TABLE 8.1. Processing Times of the Jobs

Job number j:	1	2	3	4	5	6
Processing time p_j:	8	7	4	3	3	3

and not on both. We are only interested in decisions that respect all the specified constraints—that is, the ones that are "feasible."

In order to "model" this job scheduling problem, we introduce decision variables that are to describe which jobs are processed on which machines. If we want to express that job j is processed on machine m, we state that the value of the decision variable $A_{j,m}$ equals one. Otherwise, the value of this decision variable equals zero. Formally, $A_{j,m}$ is a binary decision variable (only assuming the values 0 or 1) satisfying the following:

$$A_{j,m} = 1 \text{ if and only if job } j \text{ is processed on machine } m \qquad (8.1)$$

Note that the indicated decision variables are indeed *variable*, in the sense that values for these variables are not known in advance (i.e., before the model has been solved). Another decision variable that we need is the *Makespan* denoting the makespan corresponding to a certain assignment of jobs to machines. The latter is equal to the total time required to process all jobs. In this example, we state as objective that the *Makespan* is to be minimized. In the remainder of this chapter, we shall identify decision variables by using capitals as opposed to input parameters such as the processing times p_j.

In order to get a feasible plan, the decision variables $A_{j,m}$ need to satisfy several constraints. First, each job is to be processed on exactly one machine. This is expressed by the following constraints:

$$A_{j,1} + A_{j,2} = 1 \qquad \text{for } j = 1, \ldots, 6 \qquad (8.2)$$

Since $A_{j,m}$ only assumes the values 0 or 1, these constraints state that either $A_{j,1} = 1$ or $A_{j,2} = 1$. This is equivalent to stating that each job j is to be processed either on machine 1 or on machine 2.

Furthermore, the *Makespan* cannot be less than the total processing times on each of the machines. This can be expressed by the following constraints:

$$\sum_j p_j A_{j,m} \leq Makespan \qquad \text{for } m = 1, 2 \qquad (8.3)$$

For $m = 1$, this constraint states that the total processing time on machine 1 equals the sum of the processing times of the jobs that have been assigned to machine 1. Indeed, the processing time p_j of job j is added to the left-hand side of this constraint only if the decision variable $A_{j,1}$ has the value 1, and otherwise it is not added. For $m = 2$, a similar explanation holds. Now the constraints state further that the *Makespan* is not less than the total processing times on both machines.

Figure 8.1 recapitulates the complete mathematical model, whose solution provides an assignment of jobs to machines resulting in a minimum *Makespan*, in a more general form. Here the number of jobs is denoted by J and the number of machines is denoted by M.

The model can be solved by using an appropriate mathematical solution technique. Here "solving" the model refers to the process of computing appropriate

Minimize *Makespan*

by changing the binary variables
$A_{j,m}$ $\qquad\qquad\qquad\qquad$ $j = 1,\dots,J, m = 1,\dots,M$

under the constraints

$\sum_{m} A_{j,m} = 1$ $\qquad\qquad\qquad$ for $j = 1,\dots,J$

$\sum_{j} p_j A_{j,m} \le Makespan$ $\qquad\qquad$ for $m = 1,\dots,M$

$A_{j,m} \in \{0,1\}$ $\qquad\qquad\qquad$ for $j = 1,\dots,J, m = 1,\dots,M$

Figure 8.1. A mathematical model for solving the simple job scheduling problem.

values for the decision variables, such that all constraints are satisfied and such that the objective function has an optimal value. The latter means that none of the feasible assignments of jobs to machines has a strictly lower *Makespan*.

The model described here is an Integer Programming model. For solving such a model, one may use a so-called Branch and Bound solution technique as is provided by general-purpose solvers such as CPLEX or LINDO. An optimal solution for the instance described in Table 8.1 is shown in Figure 8.2. Since this instance is very small, the computation time for finding an optimal solution is negligible.

The tabular representation of the solution shown in Figure 8.2 is listed in Table 8.2. Obviously, the solution is not unique. For example, one of the jobs 4 or 5 can be exchanged with job 6. Furthermore, since the machines are identical, they can be interchanged as well. In other words, replacing $A_{j,m}$ by $1 - A_{j,m}$ for all jobs and both machines gives another feasible schedule with the same makespan.

In the case that the number of machines is variable (as opposed to the example described so far), the makespan of the optimal solution clearly depends on the number of machines involved. Calculation shows a relation between the *Makespan* of the optimal solution and the *Number of Machines* in Figure 8.3. Indeed, the ideal *Makespan* would follow the relation

$$Makespan \times Number\ of\ Machines = 28$$

which would mean a full utilization of the available machines during the processing of the jobs. Figure 8.3 shows the relation between the minimum *Makespan* and the available number of machines. The lower "curve" in this figure indicates full machine utilization, assuming that jobs can be cut into subjobs of any size. The latter is also known as *preemptive* processing of the jobs.

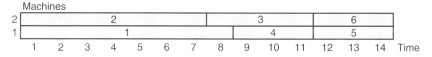

Figure 8.2. Optimal solution for the simple job scheduling problem.

TABLE 8.2. Optimal Solution in Terms of the Decision Variables

Makespan = 14		
$A(1,1) = 1$	$A(2,1) = 0$	$A(3,1) = 0$
$A(1,2) = 0$	$A(2,2) = 1$	$A(3,2) = 1$
$A(4,1) = 1$	$A(5,1) = 1$	$A(6,1) = 0$
$A(4,2) = 0$	$A(5,2) = 0$	$A(6,2) = 1$

There are several variants of the scheduling problem and hence of the mathematical model that are worth mentioning. First of all, one may consider the situation that the machines are not identical and that the jobs need to be processed first on machine 1 and then on machine 2. In such cases, a job often refers to a (physical) object that requires consecutive processing on the two machines. For example, machine 1 adds a circuit board to a computer assembly, while machine 2 adds the cover and seals the product. Both processes related to each job (in this case a computer assembly) take a certain amount of time on each of the machines and in a fixed order (first the process on machine 1, and then the process on machine 2). The preceding model did not take into account such precedence relations. This variant of the planning problem is also known as the Two-Machine Flow Shop Problem.

Other job scheduling problems are described in Baker (1974). For example, a more complex variant of the Two-Machine Flow Shop Problem is the Two-Machine Job Shop Problem. In this variant there are again jobs that need to be processed on two machines, but in this case the order in which the jobs are to be processed on the machines is not the same for all jobs: Each job may have its own routing along the machines. Further obvious variants are the general Flow Shop Problem and the general Job Shop Problem with more than two machines.

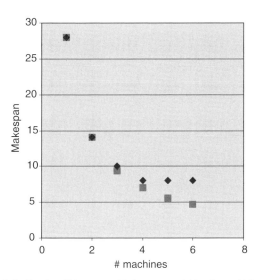

Figure 8.3. Trade-off between *Makespan* and *Number of Machines*.

Another issue that may be relevant in practice has to do with the dynamic character of practical scheduling problems. This dynamic character may be modeled to some extent by introducing so-called *release* dates and *due* dates for the jobs: The processing of a job on a machine cannot start before the job's release date and is to be completed before the job's due date.

Although at first sight these variants of the initial scheduling problem may seem to be rather similar, there are strong differences between them. Especially from the point of view of mathematical models, solution techniques, and computational complexity, there are differences, as will be explained later.

An important representative of a *routing* problem with many important applications in practice is the so-called Traveling Salesman Problem (Lawler et al., 1985). Here the problem is to find the shortest route along a number of locations that returns in the end to the same place where the route started initially. The Traveling Salesman Problem has many important applications.

8.3. THE MATHEMATICAL MODELING PROCESS

As we have seen in the preceding discussion, mathematical models and solution techniques can be used to support decision-making processes in practice. First, one needs to model certain parts of reality. Here one can choose between a large variety of model types, and it requires some skills (besides mathematical ones) to choose the appropriate type of model, next to choosing, for example, the appropriate level of detail of the model. Pidd (1999) describes the modeling process as "Just Modeling Through." This puts emphasis on the development of the model as a process (the modeling process) instead of on the end product (the model). Mathematical models can be seen as entities on their own, which can be used to solve planning problems. However, this approach underexposes important aspects of problem solving by means of models. Indeed, let's consider the modeling process in somewhat more detail. This process has been represented schematically in Figure 8.4. Generating a proper *Problem Formulation* (see Figure 8.4) is difficult

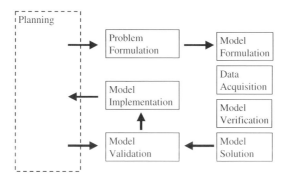

Figure 8.4. The mathematical modeling cycle.

and not without ambiguities. For example, a planner may consider the legacy approach as satisfying or even as irreplaceable, while at a management level, one agrees on extended automatic support of the planning process. The scope of the problem may also depend on the viewpoint of the problem owner, and it requires thorough investigation. Indeed, if one chooses the scope of the problem too small, then a solution to the posed problem will not solve the actual problem, and if one chooses the scope of the problem too large, then one will probably be forced to oversimplify. The problem owner, who states the problem and sponsors the development of the model, and the planners, who are supposed to use the model in practice, need not be the same persons nor share the same viewpoints, which may complicate their communication with the model builder. The model builder should provide a *Model Formulation* (see Figure 8.4) that rephrases the problem in terms of a mathematical model.

One of the advantages of the modeling process is the fact that alternatives, constraints, and objectives have to be described explicitly during this process. In practice, the discussions that should lead to this explicit description of alternatives, constraints, and objectives are sometimes already as valuable as the final solutions generated by the model, since they generate a lot of insight into the planning process itself and into the hierarchy of preferences that is used by the planners.

In practice, it may be necessary to adapt the original problem formulation to the modeling possibilities. Indeed, one may need to restrict oneself to a tractable subproblem, or to reformulate it in such a way that both the required input and the required output are quantities that are measurable and that make sense. For example, it may be necessary to state the "quality of resources" in more specific terms (e.g., productivity or flexibility) or to state that a "good" schedule is a schedule that respects the due dates and costs less than a certain amount of money.

The formulation of the model itself starts with the choice for a specific model type. Some examples of these are presented in Section 8.4. Important decisions in formulating the model further are the model size (e.g., the level of detail), the scope of the model (what should be included and what not?), the decision variables (as opposed to fixed parameters), the decision objective(s), and the constraints.

Mathematical models need data, therefore *Data Acquisition* is required (see Figure 8.4). In the modeling process, this certainly is an issue. It does not make sense to make a large model that requires a lot of data, if such data are not available. Furthermore, the phrase "Garbage In, Garbage Out" expresses the need for high-quality input data. On the other hand, one should not focus on the available data too much, because it may blur the requirements to solve the problem at hand ("Don't fall in love with data," as Pidd says). Figure 8.5 represents the general situation, where data (input parameters) are fed into the model and where the model provides decisions and an objective value as outcome.

The decisions are represented by the values of the decision variables of the model, which are determined by applying an appropriate solver to the model. This process is described in Section 8.4.

Because mathematical models may be rather complicated, they need to be tested: Does the model actually compute what the model builder expects it to compute? If

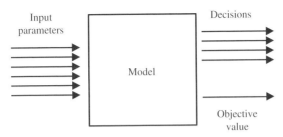

Figure 8.5. Input (data) and output (decisions, objective value) of a model.

the model provides "optimal solutions" that do not satisfy the posed constraints, something is obviously wrong. It can be concluded that thorough *Model Verification* (see Figure 8.4) is required—that is, verifying that the model and the applied solution techniques are correct. Nevertheless, even if the model works all right technically, the *Model Solution* need not be valid in practice. Nonrealistic parameter values or other fatal deviations from reality may result in model outcomes that are not usable in practice. Since a model always describes only certain parts of reality; in an abstract way, this so-called *Model Validation* (see Figure 8.4) can be a serious hurdle. In this stage, feedback from the planners is indispensable, since the solutions generated by the model should be acceptable to the planners. Usually a first evaluation of the obtained solutions by the planners leads to new alternatives or to new constraints that are to be taken into account. After several iterations, this process may lead to a model and solutions that are indeed acceptable.

After one has obtained an initial solution that seems to be acceptable in practice, a next useful step is to carry out an extensive *sensitivity analysis*. This is especially the case if parts of the input data are uncertain or only approximately known, or if several scenarios with different input values need to be discerned. To that end, one may study the response of the model outcomes to (small) changes in the data (see also Figure 8.5). Somewhat related to sensitivity analysis is the notion of a *robust* solution to an optimization problem. An optimal solution is called *robust* when it is optimal or nearly optimal for a wide range of values for the input parameters. One may also require that the objective value of the solution is not too sensitive to changes within this input parameter range.

If one agrees that the model provides valid output, then one can start with *Model Implementation* (see Figure 8.4). This final step usually comes down to establishing a computerized tool based on the model that can actually be used by the planners. For that reason, the model has to be implemented into a user-friendly decision support system, since only experts in Operations Research or Mathematics know how to work with a mathematical model in its basic form. However, a model becomes much more effective in practice if it can be used by the planners themselves, who are the real domain experts. A decision support system should allow the planners to specify the scenarios to be studied in a user-friendly way based on the available data, and it should provide appropriate solutions for these scenarios within an acceptable amount of time, preferably in cooperation with the planners.

Obviously, there are many more requirements for a decision support system, but in this chapter we will not elaborate on these. For further specifications we refer to the relevant other chapters of this book. We only want to note here that the specifications of such a decision support system may lead to a loop back to the formulation of the underlying mathematical models. Therefore, the step-by-step description in Figure 8.4 should be enriched with feedback loops that result in a process referred to as "prototyping." Finally, it is not uncommon that, once a decision support system is operational in practice, it leads to new questions that the users of the system want to answer with it. The implementation of such functionalities into the system may require the adaptation or the extension of the underlying mathematical models. It can be concluded that the modeling cycle depicted in Figure 8.4 hardly ever ends in practice.

8.4. MATHEMATICAL MODELS, ALGORITHMS, AND COMPLEXITY

As indicated already in Section 8.3, mathematical models exist in a large variety. Relevant classes that can be distinguished are the class of *optimization* models and the class of *simulation* models. Optimization models are used to determine a set of decisions satisfying certain restrictions that are "optimal" in a certain sense. Therefore, such models are also called "how-to" models—for example, how to assign jobs to machines or how to minimize the operational costs of the production process.

On the other hand, a simulation model provides an abstract description of a real-life system, and it allows one to study the behavior of this system by simulating the system under varying conditions. Therefore, simulation models are also called "what-if" models. For example, what happens with the customer waiting time if we double the number of counters? Simulation models may be used to evaluate a system along several dimensions. Improvements of the system can be studied by varying the operating conditions of the system in the simulation model.

Other classes of models that can be distinguished are the classes of *deterministic* and *stochastic* models. Within a deterministic model, all input data are assumed to be deterministic and given, whereas in a stochastic model some of the input data have a stochastic character.

Within an *operational* planning context, it seems that *deterministic optimization models* are more relevant than other types of models. First, in a planning context, one wants to know how certain processes are to be carried out. Hence for providing active support in the planning process, optimization models seem to be more appropriate than simulation models. Second, if the planning process has an operational nature with a relatively short planning horizon, then it is usually defendable to assume that the input data are deterministic. The latter holds in particular because stochastic optimization models are usually much more complex than deterministic ones. Nevertheless, it is obvious that also in operational planning processes, stochasticity may play an important role. However, this may also be handled by applying an adequate sensitivity analysis afterwards.

Usually, models that are used for supporting *tactical* or *strategic* planning process are of a different nature than models for supporting operational planning process. The former have to take into account a longer time horizon, which may lead to a higher level of uncertainty. In this case, an extensive analysis of several scenarios may be even more important than in an operational planning context. Furthermore, in such models usually a lower level of detail is taken into account.

8.4.1. Deterministic Optimization Models

Within the class of deterministic optimization models for supporting operational planning processes, at least the following modeling techniques can be distinguished:

- Linear Programming
- (Mixed) Integer Programming
- Network Modeling
- Nonlinear Programming
- Goal Programming
- Dynamic Programming
- Constraint Programming

In this chapter, we do not go into the details of the mentioned modeling techniques, since we consider the details of these techniques to lie outside the scope of this chapter. Such details can be found in any Operations Research textbook (e.g., Hillier and Liebermann, 1995; Wagner, 1970). Anyway, the common elements of all techniques are (i) a representation of a set of potential decisions in terms of decision variables, (ii) a set of restrictions to be satisfied, represented by a set of mathematical constraints, and (iii) one or more objective functions that describe the objective(s) to be pursued in the planning process. The model for solving the simple job scheduling problem described in Section 8.2 is an Integer Programming model. In practice, the most widely used modeling technique is Linear Programming, probably due to the fact that it is a relatively simple technique for which many powerful solvers and other tools are commercially available.

The techniques for solving a mathematical model are usually related to the applied modeling technique. For example, for solving a Linear Programming model, one may apply the Simplex Method (Dantzig, 1948). For solving Mixed Integer Programming models, one may apply Branch and Bound or Branch and Cut methods (Gomory, 1958). Column generation methods are also popular nowadays (Barnhart et al., 1998). And for solving Network Models, one may apply techniques for finding Shortest Paths, Minimum Spanning Trees, Matchings, or Single Commodity Flows, such as Maximum Flows or Minimum Cost Flows (Gondran and Minoux, 1984).

Solutions for a certain problem instance of a deterministic optimization problem may also be generated by applying general-purpose approximation techniques such as Simulated Annealing (Aarts and van Laarhoven, 1987) or Tabu Search (Glover and Laguna, 1997) or by applying heuristics. Again, the details of the mentioned techniques fall outside the scope of this chapter, but the following section presents some relevant considerations.

The choice for using a certain modeling technique may be guided by several aspects. First, in a certain application, one technique may be more appropriate than another. For example, if a certain problem is known to be *NP-hard*, then Linear Programming and Network techniques will not be sufficiently powerful for solving it, as will be explained in the next section. Similarly, if the involved problem has certain structural nonlinear elements that are so dominant that linearization will lead to unacceptable results, then one will have to use nonlinear optimization techniques. Hence, knowledge of the fundamental characteristics of a certain problem may be a useful guide in selecting an appropriate modeling technique. The available software may also be useful here. Software for Linear Programming and (Mixed) Integer Programming is usually more easily accessible than software for other techniques. Therefore, they are more often used than other techniques. Besides these aspects, each modeler usually has a preference of his own for certain techniques based on personal experience.

8.4.2. Computational Complexity

In practice, it turns out that some problems are much harder to solve than others. Whereas Linear Programming or Network models with hundreds of thousands of decision variables or constraints can typically be solved to optimality using the currently available hardware and software, Mixed Integer or Nonlinear models with several hundreds of variables may be too complex already to be solved. On the other hand, also with Mixed Integer or Nonlinear models one may be lucky and be able to solve quite large instances within a reasonable amount of time. Anyway, the progress in computational power that was achieved over the last decades, both by improvements in the available hardware and by algorithmic improvements, is tremendous, as is witnessed by Bixby (2002).

The foregoing has to do with the intrinsic computational complexity of the underlying problems. The study of this subject started around 1970 by Cook (1971). The theory of computational complexity usually relates the computational effort for solving a certain problem instance to the size of the instance. For example, in a job scheduling problem, a larger number of jobs J usually leads to a longer computing time. Then the way this computing time depends on the number of jobs is an indication of the complexity of the problem: A problem for which the computing time is bounded by J^3 is preferable over a problem for which the computing time is bounded by 2^J.

Details on the theory of computational complexity can be found in Garey and Johnson (1979). This theory is basically related to the complexity of decision problems: problems that can be answered either by "yes" or by "no." This is not a loss of generality, since it is easy to transform an *optimization* problem into a series of *decision* problems. The theory of computational complexity distinguishes on one hand the class of decision problems whose instances can be solved in a polynomial amount of time. The latter means that there exists an exponent m such that, if the number N is a measure for the size of an instance of the problem, then the time required for solving the instance is bounded by N^m. This class is called the class of polynomially solvable problems, or the class P. Problems in P are usually considered as well solved, since for most problems in P even large instances can be solved in a reasonable amount of time, especially if the exponent m is low. Examples of problems in P are problems that can be described by Linear Programming models and by several Network models, such as Shortest Path problems, Matching problems, and Single Commodity Flow problems.

A second class of problems that is distinguished in the theory of computational complexity is called the class of Nondeterministic Polynomially solvable problems, or the class NP. This class contains the problems with the property that a proposed solution for an instance of the problem can be *verified* to be feasible or not in an amount of time that is polynomial in the size of the instance. Obviously, problems in P also belong to NP, since *generating* a solution is more difficult than just *checking* the feasibility of a proposed solution. However, the class NP also contains a large set of problems for which, as of today (2005), no algorithm has been found that can generate feasible solutions in a polynomial amount of time. An example of such a problem is the earlier mentioned Traveling Salesman Problem. It was recognized by Cook (1971) that many of these *hard* problems in NP are equivalent in computational complexity in the following sense: There exists a subset of hard problems in NP with the property that the existence of a polynomial time algorithm for solving one of these problems would imply the existence of a polynomial time algorithm for all others in this subset. Therefore this subset of these hard *decision* problems in NP was called NP-complete. The subset of hard *optimization* problems was called the set of NP-hard problems.

The class of NP-hard problems contains problems of many different kinds for which polynomial time algorithms are lacking despite enormous research efforts over many years. Therefore many researchers consider it as highly unlikely that a polynomial algorithm for one of these NP-hard problems will ever be found. However, a positive result of these research efforts is that it has given a better insight into the boundary between the problems in P and the NP-hard problems. For example, the well-known Two-Machine Flow Shop problem can be solved easily in polynomial time by applying Johnson's rule (Johnson, 1954), but the Three Machine Flow Shop Problem is already NP-hard (Baker, 1975). This research has also revealed several special variants of the NP-hard Traveling Salesman Problem that belong to the set P (Lawler et al., 1985).

However, most practical optimization problems are known to be NP-hard, due to the many complicating issues that are to be taken into account. Therefore, searching for an algorithm that provides optimal solutions for all instances of these problems is probably not successful. Nevertheless, it may happen that large instances of these problems can be solved to optimality, since, if a problem is known to be NP-hard,

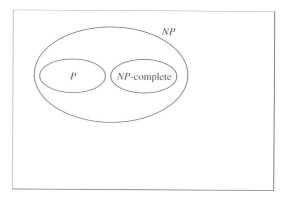

Figure 8.6. The problem classes *P*, *NP*, and *NP*-complete.

then this is only a statement about the worst-case instances of the problem. It may happen that practical instances of an *NP*-hard problem can be solved much more easily than the sometimes pathological worst-case instances that are responsible for the problem's *NP*-hardness. Figure 8.6 represents the problem classes *P*, *NP*, and *NP*-complete in a schematic way (based on the assumption that the classes *P* and *NP*-complete are disjoint). Note that the given classification of problems is just a rough one. Currently, also more subtle classifications exist. For example, within the class *NP*, one may distinguish between the problems that are *NP*-complete in the *weak* sense and those that are *NP*-complete in the *strong* sense. Furthermore, many problems do not belong to the class *NP*. For example, in the simple job scheduling problem described in Section 8.2, the problem of finding *all* schedules that meet a certain *Makespan* does not belong to the class *NP*, simply because the number of such schedules is not polynomial in the number of jobs and thus not in the size of the input.

8.4.3. Algorithms and Heuristics

For solving a mathematical optimization model, one may use a *general-purpose* solver, which basically can be applied for all problems within a certain class, or by a *special purpose* solver, which has been developed especially for solving instances of a specific problem.

The commercially available solvers CPLEX and LINDO are examples of general-purpose solvers, which can be used for solving problems that have been modeled as Linear or Mixed Integer programs. An advantage of such a general-purpose solver is the fact that it provides a lot of flexibility: As soon as one has an appropriate description of a problem in terms of a mathematical model and one also has the required data for an instance, one can use the solver to find solutions for the instance. However, a disadvantage of a general-purpose solver is the fact that it may not be able to solve instances of problems of a certain practical size, due to its general-purpose character. This may be a consequence of the fact that the problem at hand belongs to the class of *NP*-hard problems.

If this is indeed the case, then one will be forced to develop a special purpose solver, which may better take advantage of the special structure of the involved problem. Unfortunately, developing a special-purpose solver usually takes a lot of creativity and time, and, as a consequence, also a lot of money. An additional problem is that a special-purpose solver may be less flexible than a general-purpose solver: As soon as the characteristics of the problem change over time, which happens quite often in practice, then the special-purpose solver may not be able to handle the modified problem adequately, whereas the general-purpose solver is still appropriate after modification of the model.

An alternative to a solver that determines solutions for which it is guaranteed that they are optimal, given the involved objective function, is a *heuristic*. Heuristics are solution methods that are usually based on approximation techniques, rules of thumb, or on a decomposition of the problem into less complex subproblems. The solutions provided by a heuristic may not be optimal, given the involved objective function, but they may be "acceptable" or "good." The latter means that the solutions are at least as good as the solutions that have been obtained manually. Furthermore, an appropriate heuristic determines such acceptable or good solutions in a fraction of the time that is required by an optimal solver. However, it should be noted that a really simple heuristic that is developed for solving a very complex problem may not lead to acceptable solutions in practice. In fact, planners usually have so much planning experience that they easily outperform a heuristic if the latter is too simple.

A heuristic can be classified as a *generating* heuristic or as an *improvement* heuristic. A generating heuristic *generates* an initial solution for a certain problem instance, and an improvement heuristic tries to *improve* an initial solution. For example, a simple generating heuristic for the earlier mentioned Traveling Salesman Problem is the well-known Nearest-Neighbor rule. A class of simple heuristics, parameterized by the parameter δ, for solving instances of the simple job scheduling problem described in Section 8.2 could be the following:

1. Sort the jobs in order of decreasing processing time.
2. Compute the average processing time per machine T:

$$T = \frac{1}{2}\left(\sum_j p_j\right)$$

3. Set $T_1 = T_2 = 0$.
4. For $j := 1$ to J do
    If $T_1 + p_j \leq T + \delta$
        Then   assign job j to machine 1, and set $T_1 := T_1 + p_j$
        Else   assign job j to machine 2, and set $T_2 := T_2 + p_j$

In other words, "long" jobs are assigned to machine 1 as long as the total processing time on machine 1 does not exceed the value $T + \delta$. In this heuristic, the processing time of the sorting step 1 is proportional to $J \log(J)$. The processing

Figure 8.7. The schedule produced by the generating heuristic with $\delta = 0$.

time of the assignment step 4 is obviously linear in J. Since the running time of such a heuristic is obviously extremely low, one may try this heuristic for several values of the parameter δ and retain the best result. If this very simple generating heuristic is applied to the instance of the simple job scheduling problem described in Section 8.2 with the parameter $\delta = 0$, then it produces the schedule with *Makespan* 16 which is represented in Figure 8.7.

If this heuristic is applied to this instance with the parameter $\delta = 1$, then the result is a schedule with *Makespan* 15. A simple improvement heuristic inspired by the schedule in Figure 8.7 is the rule: "Assign the last job to the machine with the lowest workload." This rule would also result in a schedule with *Makespan* 15. Improvement heuristics usually try to exchange certain parts of an obtained solution, as in the well-known 2-Opt and 3-Opt heuristics for the Traveling Salesman Problem. A more sophisticated improvement heuristic in this area is the Variable-Opt method developed by Lin and Kernighan (1973). An improvement heuristic in the same vein for improving a solution of the job scheduling problem described in Section 8.2 could be the following:

1. For each job j_1 assigned to machine 1 do
2. For each job j_2 assigned to machine 2 do
   - If   switching the assignments of jobs j_1 and j_2 reduces the *Makespan*
   - Then   switch the assignments of jobs j_1 and j_2
3. Repeat step 1 until there are no further improvements.

If this improvement heuristic is applied to the schedule that was produced by the generating heuristic described above with the parameter $\delta = 0$ (see Figure 8.7), then it indeed provides an improvement: The assignments of jobs 2 and 3 are interchanged. However, the resulting schedule, represented in Figure 8.8, is still not optimal, since its *Makespan* equals 15.

In this improvement heuristic, the processing time for step 1 is obviously proportional to J^2. The number of times that step 1 can be executed is bounded

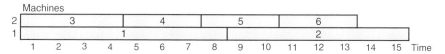

Figure 8.8. The schedule produced by the improvement heuristic.

by J. Therefore, the total processing time of this improvement heuristic is certainly proportional to J^3.

When dealing with approximation methods or with heuristic methods, it may be useful to develop lower bounds or upper bounds. Such bounds give an indication of the gap between an obtained solution and the optimal solution. For example, if one has a solution with objective function value V, and one can prove by applying lower bounding techniques that the minimum value of the objective function cannot be less than $0.95V$, then one knows that the optimal value of the objective function does not differ from the obtained value by more than 5%.

If the problem at hand is a minimization problem, then a *lower* bound can be generated by a relaxation of some of the constraints: The optimal solution of the relaxed problem gives a lower bound to the optimal solution of the original problem. This is useful if the relaxed problem can be solved more easily than the original problem. For example, if the problem at hand is an Integer Program, then a straightforward relaxation is its Linear Programming relaxation. This means that, instead of requiring the decision variables to be integer-valued, they are just required to be real-valued. This simple relaxation often leads to useful lower bounds. A lower bound for the *Makespan* of an instance of the simple job scheduling problem described in Section 8.2 is obviously

$$T = \frac{1}{2}\left(\sum_j p_j\right)$$

If the problem at hand is a minimization problem, then each feasible solution provides an *upper* bound to the minimum value of the objective function. Indeed, the solution is feasible, but it may be nonoptimal. Therefore, the minimum value of the objective function will be less than or equal to the objective function value of the obtained feasible solution. In other words, the latter is an upper bound.

There exist many situations in which it is very difficult to develop an appropriate heuristic. This may be the case if finding a feasible solution for a problem is already difficult, let alone finding an acceptable or a good solution. In particular, in situations with very limited resources, a straightforward heuristic may not be capable of generating solutions effectively. In such situations, an approach that may work for finding an initial solution may be to use a general-purpose solver and let it run until an acceptable solution has been found. This may work, since such solvers sometimes find a good solution quickly and then spend a lot of time on proving that this solution is optimal or nearly optimal.

8.5. EVALUATION OF A SOLUTION

In Section 8.2, we introduced a simple job scheduling problem, where the *Makespan* was to be minimized for a given set of jobs and a given number of machines. However, in practical planning situations it is very rare that only one single objective function is used to evaluate the obtained solutions: In most practical situations, at least two objective functions are to be considered. Usually these objective functions are conflicting, which means that optimizing the first objective function leads to a different solution than optimizing the second objective function.

For example, one may want to minimize the *production costs* and at the same time to maximize the *quality of the services* to the customers. Another important example of multiple objectives, mainly related to the application of mathematical models, is to use the objective of minimizing the infeasibility of a solution next to the "real" objective of the planning problem at hand. Indeed, in practice there may be so many constraints to be taken into account that a solution satisfying all constraints simply does not exists: The problem is *overconstrained*. In such a case one may look for a solution that violates the constraints as few as possible.

In order to deal with optimization problems with multiple objectives, an extensive Multi-Criteria optimization theory has evolved over the last decades (e.g., Keeney and Raiffa, 1976). Examples of well-known Multi-Criteria optimization techniques are Goal Programming and Analytical Hierarchy Processing. Again, we do not go into the details, but we provide some general remarks.

If multiple objective functions are to be considered, then an important issue is the fact that one cannot really speak about *the* optimal solution of an instance of a planning problem, which can be determined in an *objective* way. The obtained solution depends on the way the multiple objectives are combined or weighted with each other. The user of the Multi-Criteria optimization technique is required to provide external information about his or her preferences. The foregoing also implies that optimality in practical terms may be quite different from optimality in mathematical terms.

For example, Figure 8.3 illustrates for the simple job scheduling problem, described in Section 8.2, how the minimum *Makespan* and the *Number of Machines* are related there. Assume we were to minimize the total operational costs, where the *Makespan* incurs costs per hour w_1 and where resource costs per machine are equal to w_2. For each schedule involving a given *Makespan* and a given *Number of Machines*, the following total costs occur:

$$Total\ Costs = w_1 \times Makespan + w_2 \times Number\ of\ Machines$$

Not every combination of *Makespan* and *Number of Machines* is feasible: Only the points in the plane above the curve in Figure 8.3 indicate feasible combinations. Observe that we have reduced the two objective functions into one single objective function by expressing both objectives in terms of costs. This may not always be possible, in particular if the objectives are very different.

More generally, consider the situation shown in Figure 8.9. This figure corresponds to an instance of a planning problem to be solved, thereby taking into account two objective functions F_1 and F_2. Both objective functions are to be minimized. The shaded area in Figure 8.9 represents the set of feasible combinations of values of these objective functions for the instance of the planning problem at hand. This set of feasible combinations of objective function values is also called the *function space*. Note the similarity of this figure with Figure 8.3. Obviously,

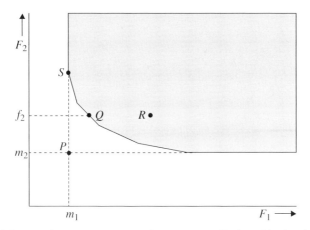

Figure 8.9. Function space corresponding to two conflicting objective functions.

in Figure 8.9 the objective functions are conflicting, since the minimum value for F_1 (denoted by m_1) cannot be reached at the same time as the minimum value for F_2 (denoted by m_2). The point P in Figure 8.9 corresponding to the minimum value for F_1 *and* the minimum value for F_2 is called the *ideal* point or the *Utopic* point.

Point Q is an example of a *Pareto-optimal* or *efficient* point in the function space: Both objective functions can be improved with respect to their values in Q, but *not* at the same time. In other words, for all points Q' in the function space with $F_1(Q') < F_1(Q)$ it holds that $F_2(Q') \geq F_2(Q)$ and for all points Q' with $F_2(Q') < F_2(Q)$ it holds that $F_1(Q') \geq F_1(Q)$. Obviously, point R in Figure 8.9 is not Pareto-optimal, since both objective functions F_1 and F_2 can be improved there.

It is well known that optimizing the combined objective function $F = w_1 \times F_1 + w_2 \times F_2$ (where w_1 and w_2 are non-negative weights) over all feasible solutions of an instance of a planning problem leads to a Pareto-optimal point in the function space. Indeed, the obtained point in the function space is the point where a so-called *iso-cost* line with the equation $F = w_1 \times F_1 + w_2 \times F_2$ just touches the function space. This geometric interpretation implies that a higher weight for one of the objectives will lead to a lower value for this objective. Studying the set of Pareto-optimal points of a planning problem may provide insight into the relative importance of the different objective functions. It may also help in determining a trade-off between these objectives, since it shows how much of some of the objectives is to be sacrificed in order to get a certain improvement in the others.

Instead of combining several objective functions into one weighted objective function, one may also treat the objective functions in a so-called *lexicographic* way. That is, one first looks for a solution by minimizing the first objective function. Then, given the minimum value for the first objective function, one minimizes the second objective function. This is repeated until all objective functions have been taken into account. If this lexicographic method is applied to the instance represented in Figure 8.9 (first F_1 and then F_2), then this leads to the Pareto-optimal point S in the figure.

A somewhat more subtle method than the lexicographic one uses some of the objective functions as a constraint, and then it optimizes over the others. For example, if in the example shown in Figure 8.9 one minimizes F_1 under the additional constraint that $F_2 \leq f_2$, then one obtains the Pareto-optimal point Q in the function space.

8.6. PROACTIVE AND REACTIVE PLANNING

In this section we explain the differences between proactive planning and reactive planning, and we show that both planning processes can be supported by applying mathematical models.

So far, we assumed that the planning process starts completely from scratch. That is, before starting the planning process, no plans or partial plans are available yet. Also the models that we described so far aimed at generating plans completely from scratch, not taking into account earlier generated plans. In this case, we talk about a *proactive* planning process. In this case, the planning process may be triggered by the fact that the plans are to be updated with a certain fixed frequency. For example, a public transport company usually updates his basic logistic plans at least once per year.

However, there is necessarily a certain time interval between the start of the proactive planning process and the execution of the plan in practice. In complex planning processes, it is even usual that there is a certain *planned* time interval between the *end* of the proactive planning process and the execution of the plan. The latter is meant as a buffer in order to be able to cope with uncertainties in the duration of the proactive planning process. The initial plan that is generated in the proactive planning process is based on the information that is available at the moment that this plan is generated. However, as time goes by, it may happen that, during the generation of the initial plan or after the initial plan has been generated, new information becomes available and has to be taken into account in the plan as well. An example of this is a rush order that has to be planned and carried out as soon as possible. Another example may be that, on second thought, the processing time of a certain job is longer than it was estimated earlier. A final example concerns the resource availability: After the proactive plan has been generated, it may turn out that one of the machines is temporarily not available due to maintenance. Of course, if the machine maintenance department had communicated the maintenance plan of the machines earlier, then this would not have happened.

Note that the execution of a plan in practice usually needs to be monitored continuously. This may lead to updates of the plan in *real time*. Indeed, due to external disruptions during the execution of the plan, the plan may become infeasible and therefore it has to be updated. For example, the operational traffic control center of a public transport company has to deal with external disruptions quickly and adequately in order to have as few as possible delays in the operational transport processes.

In all these cases, the initial plan has to be updated in order to be able to take into account the additional information, thereby changing the initial plan as few as possible. Furthermore, during the execution of the plan, one usually wants to be able to return to the initial plan as soon as possible, since the plan is considered as an important guideline for managing the operational processes. Requirements for the latter are that the initial plan is sufficiently *robust* and *stable*, so that it can be picked up easily after certain external disruptions have taken place.

Generating an updated plan based on an initial plan and on additional information that was not available during the proactive planning process is called *reactive* planning. Usually, the objectives pursued in a reactive planning process are different from those pursued in a proactive planning process. This may be due to the fact that a reactive planning process is carried out closer to or during the execution of the plan in practice. The latter implies that a reactive planning process is carried out under a certain time pressure. As a consequence, the main objective in a reactive planning process is to find a *feasible* plan that takes into account the additional information and that *differs* from the initial plan *as little as possible*. Here the underlying idea is that in the proactive planning process more time has been available to optimize the quality of the initial plan. Therefore, if the modified plan differs as little as possible from the initial plan, it cannot be too far from optimality. Although in the reactive planning process one usually focuses on restoring the feasibility of the plan by modifying the initial plan as little as possible, also other objectives may be pursued then. This is particularly the case if a simple update of the initial plan turns out to be insufficient and a more rigorous modification of the plan is required.

8.6.1. An Example of Reactive Planning

In the following, we illustrate how a mathematical model can be applied usefully also in a reactive planning process in order to take into account some new information. This illustration is based again on the simple job scheduling problem described in Section 8.2. Again, we consider the instance of this job scheduling problem shown in Table 8.1. We also assume that in the proactive planning process the initial plan shown in Figure 8.2 was generated. This initial plan is now considered as part of the input of the reactive planning process, and it is represented by the parameters $a_{j,m}$ for $j = 1, \ldots, J$ and $m = 1, \ldots, M$. That is, $a_{j,m} = 1$ if and only if in the original plan job j is to be processed by machine m.

Next suppose that, after this initial plan has been generated, one realizes that the processing time of job 6 has been estimated too optimistically. A better estimate seems to be 4 hours instead of 3 hours. Furthermore, also a rush order with job number 7 and a processing time of 3 hours is to be taken into account. One way to incorporate this additional information into the model is represented in Figure 8.10. This model is basically the same as the model described in Section 8.2. The only difference is found in the objective function. Due to this modified objective function, the model focuses on staying as close as possible to the original plan. Indeed, if $a_{j,m} = 1$, then a value 1 for the decision variable $A_{j,m}$ is preferred

Minimize *Objective*
by changing the binary variables
$$A_{j,m} \qquad\qquad\qquad j = 1,\ldots,J,\ m = 1,\ldots,M$$

under the constraints

$$Objective = \sum_{j,m:a_{j,m}=1}(1 - A_{j,m}) + \sum_{j,m:a_{j,m}=0} A_{j,m} + w \times Makespan$$

$$\sum_{m} A_{j,m} = 1 \qquad\qquad \text{for } j = 1,\ldots,J$$

$$\sum_{j} p_j A_{j,m} \le Makespan \qquad\qquad \text{for } m = 1,\ldots,M$$

$$A_{j,m} \in \{0,1\} \qquad\qquad \text{for } j = 1,\ldots,J,\ m = 1,\ldots,M$$

Figure 8.10. Mathematical model for reactive planning support.

over a value 0, due to the fact that the *Objective* is to be minimized. Similarly, if $a_{j,m} = 0$, then a value of 0 for the decision variable $A_{j,m}$ is preferred over a value 1.

Note that all assignments have the same weight, but, obviously, the assignments might have been given different weights as well. Note further that the *Makespan* has also been included in the *Objective* with a certain weight w, which describes the relative importance of the *Makespan*. If the *Makespan* would not have been included in the *Objective*, then the optimal solution to the model would obviously be the solution $A_{j,m} = a_{j,m}$ for $j = 1,\ldots,J$ and $m = 1, 2$. On the other hand, if the weight w is chosen too large, then the objective of minimizing the differences between the modified and the original plans will be dominated by the objective of minimizing the *Makespan*, which may lead to a modification of many of the initial assignments. Therefore, selecting the weight w is highly important in such cases. Note that also the other Multi-Criteria optimization techniques that were described in Section 8.5 may be applied in this case, where two objectives play a role. An optimal solution to the modified model is shown in Figure 8.11. This solution is obtained with the value 3 for the weight w, so that each unit of increase of the *Makespan* is considered as costly as 3 changes of a job assignment. Note that for the original jobs only the assignments of the jobs 1 and 2 have changed. The other assignments are the same as in the initial plan (see Figure 8.2). Furthermore, job 7 has been assigned to machine 1. From the foregoing, it also follows that, if the weight w of the *Makespan* in the objective function has a value less than 2, then the assignment of the original jobs in the optimal solution will be the same as in Figure 8.2 and job 7 will be assigned to machine 1, which results in a *Makespan* 17.

Figure 8.11. Optimal solution taking into account the additional information.

One may want to fix certain parts of the initial plan when generating a modified plan, particularly if one is satisfied with these parts of the initial plan and if these parts of the initial plan do not have a direct relation with the additional information responsible for the need to generate the modified plan. If the modified plan is to be generated by a mathematical model, then such a fixation of certain parts of the initial plan can be accomplished by adding additional constraints to the model. For example, in the model described in Figure 8.10, one may select a certain subset S of jobs and then add a corresponding set of constraints of the following form:

$$A_{j,m} = a_{j,m} \qquad \text{for all } j \text{ in } S \text{ and for } m = 1, 2 \qquad (8.4)$$

8.6.2. Conclusion

The foregoing illustrates the fact that it is important that the length of the time interval between the start of the proactive planning process and the execution of the plan in practice is as short as possible. The shorter the length of this time interval, the less time there will be for outside requests to modify the initial plan. Therefore, there will be fewer reasons for a reactive planning process. However, the length of this time interval cannot be less than the throughput time of the proactive planning process, which obviously cannot be reduced to zero. Therefore, there will always be a reason for a reactive planning process before the operational execution of the plan. Based on these observations, it can be concluded that it is important to reduce the throughput times of both the proactive and the reactive planning process as much as possible. Mathematical models may be useful here.

Note that reactive planning in real time during the operational execution of the plan usually cannot be avoided as well, since external disruptions during the execution of the plan will happen. In real-time reactive planning, one should take into account the stochastic nature of the system explicitly. For example, if, in case of disruptions in a public transport system, the traffic control center suggests certain travelers to take an alternative route, then they should first have made a well-founded estimate of the probability that this alternative route will indeed bring these travelers to their destinations. Thus, forecasting the future states of the planned system is particularly important during the operations. In order to be able to do so, the continuous availability of up-to-date information on the current state of the planned system is required.

8.7. MODELING SYSTEMS

Modeling systems are extremely useful tools, especially during the development phase of a mathematical model. These systems enable one to translate a conceptual mathematical model into comparable terms that can be understood by a solver. Most of these systems are devoted to Linear Programming and Mixed Integer Programming models. Usually, these systems provide links to spreadsheet or database systems for getting the data into the model. They also provide links to one or more standard solvers such as CPLEX or LINDO as well. Some modeling systems have their own presentation system or they provide links to external presentation systems for presenting the data or the results of the model in a graphical way. Currently, several modeling systems are commercially available. Well-known examples of such systems are OPL Studio, GAMS, AMPL, and AIMMS.

As an example, Figure 8.12 shows the representation of the model for the simple job scheduling problem described in Section 8.2 in the modeling system OPL Studio. Note the similarity between the conceptual mathematical model and its representation in OPL Studio. Hence, once one has developed the conceptual mathematical model, its implementation in OPL Studio is usually a straightforward process. Furthermore, it should be noted that, apart from some syntactical details, the modeling languages of the other mentioned modeling systems are very similar to the one of OPL Studio. An advantage of the use of a modeling system is the fact that such systems provide a lot of flexibility in the development phase of a model. Within such a modeling system, adapting a model is relatively easy. Thus, these systems provide the flexibility to experiment with several formulations of a model to add or delete decision variables or constraints, and so on. This is especially useful in discussions with the problem owner or the planners, when there is still a lot of uncertainty about the specifications and the structure of the model. The flexibility provided by a modeling system may enable the model builder to modify the model within a few minutes and to present the results to the problem owner or the planners immediately thereafter. Furthermore, modeling systems usually also provide a lot of support in the sensitivity analysis of the results obtained by the solver.

Since the currently available modeling systems usually provide links to several *standard* solvers only, it may happen that these solvers are not powerful enough for solving real-life instances of a certain problem. In that case, it will be required to develop a special-purpose solver or a heuristic, as described in Section 8.4 of

```
var float+ Makespan;
var int    A[Job,Machine] in 0..1;

minimize Makespan,
subject to
{  // each job is to be processed exactly once
   forall (j in Job)
       sum(m in Machine) A(j,m) = 1;

   // the makespan is not less than the workload of each machine
   forall (m in Machine)
       sum(j in Job) p(j)*A(j,m) ≤ Makespan;
};
```

Figure 8.12. Representation of the simple job scheduling problem in OPL Studio.

this chapter. But also in the latter case, the added value of the modeling system is mainly lying in the support provided during the development phase of the model. This is usually one of the hardest parts of the solution process based on mathematical models.

8.8. APPLICATION OF MATHEMATICAL MODELS IN PRACTICE

As was mentioned earlier, practical planning problems usually belong to the class of *NP-hard* problems, since many complicating practical issues are to be taken into account. The foregoing implies that the computation times for solving instances of these problems usually increase quickly with the sizes of the instances. On the other hand, in practice one may be inclined to take the instances to be solved as large as possible, since decomposition of an instance into smaller subinstances usually leads to suboptimality. In cases where large instances lead to unacceptable running times, one will have to deal with this adequately. One of the following options may be chosen:

- One may apply a heuristic or an approximation algorithm in order to compute an approximate solution for the problem instances. Drawbacks of this approach are that (i) the development of such methods may require a lot of time and money, (ii) the resulting method may be not quite robust with respect to changes in the problem specification, and (iii) the planners may not be satisfied with the results if the approximation method is not powerful or detailed enough.
- One may decompose an instance into subinstances that can be solved to optimality in an acceptable running time. By choosing the subinstances in a clever way, thereby also taking into account decompositions that are relevant in practice, and by considering the interdependencies between the subinstances and the results of previous subinstances in the analysis of the next ones, the implied suboptimality may be kept within acceptable limits.

Although mathematical models and solution techniques are intended to actively *support* the planners in their daily planning activities, they will never be able to *replace* these planners. First, planners are usually much more *creative* than mathematical models. If planners really cannot find a solution that satisfies all practical constraints, then they may still find a "feasible solution" by relaxing some of the constraints in a creative way. However, "solutions" that do not fit within the constraints of the model are considered as infeasible by the model. They are not generated by the corresponding solution technique therefore. If, nevertheless, a "feasible solution" needs to be generated by the model, then one or more of the constraints of the model have to be relaxed explicitly. Note that, in such a case, the model may provide support in finding a "feasible solution" that violates the constraints in some *minimal* way, thereby also taking into account the *hardness* of the constraints. However, incorporating too many of such exceptions may complicate the solution process of the model substantially.

Second, planners will be required in the planning process to specify the relative importance of the different conflicting objectives. This may lead to a large number of scenarios, each of which possibly leading to a different solution. These scenarios may be run on different computer systems in parallel, so that the throughput time of this process may be the same as the throughput time for running just a single scenario. Thereafter the expertise of the planners is required for selecting a preferred solution from the generated ones. The latter is in contrast with the situation where the planning process is carried out completely manually. In that case, one is usually already satisfied as soon as one has found exactly one acceptable solution that satisfies all or almost all practical restrictions.

Finally, mathematical solution techniques usually have more *computational power* than human planners, and this computational power is increasing with each new hardware generation and with each further improvement of the applied solution technique. Moreover, these techniques are not bored by doing the same computations over and over again, and their error rate is usually much lower than the human error rate. Therefore, a planning support system that facilitates a certain synergy between the planners' creativity and flexibility and the computational power and endurance of the currently available hardware and optimization techniques may lead to "optimal" results in practice.

8.9. A PRACTICAL APPLICATION

In this section, we describe a practical application of mathematical models for supporting the solution of real-life planning problems. We focus on the planning of the rolling stock circulation of an operator of passenger trains. It should be noted that mathematical models may provide useful support in other railway planning processes as well—for example, long-term planning processes related to demand forecasting, capacity planning of the infrastructure, the rolling stock and the train crews, and relatively short-term planning processes related to the structure of the timetable, crew scheduling, maintenance routing, and shunting. Many of theses issues are relevant in public transport planning in general as well.

For an operator of passenger trains, the rolling stock circulation is of paramount importance, since it influences both the service to the passengers, the operational costs for the railway operator, and the logistic robustness of the system. The rolling stock circulation gives rise to huge planning problems that have to be solved as quickly and effectively as possible. These planning problems are complex, because usually many complicated rules are to be taken into account, and multiple objectives are to be pursued. Examples of important objectives are (i) to maximize the effective capacity, (ii) to minimize the number of train unit kilometers, and (iii) to minimize the implied number of shunting movements.

The first objective is especially important during the rush hours, since most railway traffic takes place in these periods. Therefore it is important to schedule the rolling stock in such a way that as many passengers as possible can be transported according to the usual service standards. The second objective is obvious, since train unit kilometers are major cost drivers in a railway system. The last objective stems from the desire to have a robust railway system: Many additional shunting movements in and around railway stations may disturb the regular railway traffic. Note that the three mentioned objectives are conflicting, so a well-founded trade-off between them has to be made.

Mathematical models may be quite helpful in carrying out such a trade-off between such conflicting objectives. Therefore, quite some research has been carried out in this area recently (e.g., Ben-Khedher et al., 1998; Cordeau et al., 2001; Lingaya et al., 2002; Schrijver, 1993).

8.9.1. Background Information

In the Netherlands, most trains are operated with train units. An example of a train unit of the so-called type *Mat'64* with two carriages is shown in Figure 8.13. Train units of type *Mat'64* also exist with four carriages. Train units are indivisible units that can move individually in both directions without a locomotive. Train units of the same train type can be combined with each other into longer trains.

The way the train units can be put together into longer trains is shown in Figure 8.14. This figure shows a time-space diagram for part of the trains of the 8800 regional train line between Leiden (Ledn) and Utrecht (Ut). Trains of the 8800 line run twice per hour. The numbers at the top of the figure indicate the time axis. The dashed diagonal lines indicate the timetabled trains and the adjacent numbers are the train numbers. Each line represents one train unit of type *Mat'64* with two carriages. Train 8820, for instance, is run with three train units. Upon arrival in Leiden, two train units return to Utrecht on train 8833, and the third train unit remains in Leiden. This train unit is stored on the local shunting yard, and is used only in the afternoon rush hours on train 8865, as is indicated in the figure. Something similar happens with one train unit of train 8822 upon arrival in Leiden as well as with one of the train units of the trains 8829 and 8831 upon arrival in Utrecht.

The rolling stock circulation problem has to be solved not only for each single day, but also in such a way that the consecutive days fit after another: The number of train units ending in the late evening in a certain station should match with the number of train units that are required there the next morning. Nevertheless, in the planning process, usually a decomposition per day is applied. Initially, the ending night balances for day d may be used then as boundary conditions for the

Figure 8.13. A train unit of type *Mat'64* with 2 carriages.

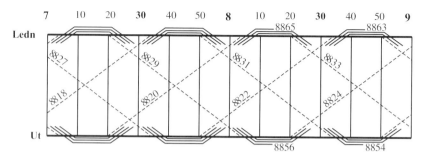

Figure 8.14. Part of the rolling stock circulation of the 8800 regional trains.

rolling stock circulation on day $d + 1$. The final night balances are fixed in a second planning step.

Another complicating factor is the fact that each train unit needs maintenance check-ups regularly, which also have to be planned. However, the latter very short-term planning is close before the actual operations, because otherwise the probability that the maintenance schedules will have to be replanned continuously is high.

8.9.2. Model Description

In this section we briefly describe an optimization model that can be used to solve the rolling stock circulation problem for a single type of rolling stock on a single day. In this model, the timetable is assumed to be represented by a set of trips, where each trip t has an origin o_t, a destination d_t, a start time s_t, and an end time e_t. The parameters $d_{t,c}$ represent the expected numbers of passengers on trip t in class c, k_c represents the number of seats in class c per train unit, and v denotes the total number of available train units. Apart from these parameters, the model also needs as input several weights w_t^N, w_t^C, w_t^U, $w_{t,c}^S$ for making a trade-off between the different objectives.

The main decision variables in the model are the variables N_t describing the number of train units to be allocated to trip t. Furthermore, the decision variables $S_{t,c}$ describe the number of shortages of seats on trip t in class c, and the decision variables C_t and U_t describe the number of train units that are coupled/uncoupled to/from a train just before this train starts to carry out trip t. Finally, V_s denotes the number of train units that are available in the early morning in station s before the first train arrives or leaves there. Then the model reads as follows:

$$\text{Min} \sum_{t \in T} \left(w_t^N N_t + w_t^C C_t + w_t^U U_t + \sum_{c \in C} w_{t,c}^S S_{t,c} \right) \qquad (8.5)$$

Subject to

$$S_{t,c} = \max\{0, d_{t,c} - k_c N_t\} \qquad \text{for all trips } t \text{ and classes } c \qquad (8.6)$$

$$\sum_{t':o_{t'}=s \wedge s_{t'} \leq s_t} N_{t'} \leq V_s + \sum_{t':d_{t'}=s \wedge e_{t'} < s_t} N_{t'} \qquad \begin{array}{l} \text{for all stations } s \text{ and} \\ \text{all trips } t \text{ with } o_t = s \end{array} \qquad (8.7)$$

$$N_t = N_{t'} + C_t - U_t \qquad \begin{array}{l} \text{for all pairs of consecutive trips} \\ t' \text{ and } t \end{array} \qquad (8.8)$$

$$\sum_{t:o_t=s} N_t = \sum_{t:d_t=s} N_t \qquad \text{for all stations } s \qquad (8.9)$$

$$\sum_{s \in S} V_s = v \qquad (8.10)$$

In the above model, the objective function (8.5) expresses the fact that one wants to minimize a weighted combination of carriage kilometers, shunting movements, and shortages of seats. Note that such a combination of multiple objectives may also be handled differently, as explained earlier in Section 8.5. Constraints (8.6) link the shortages of seats per trip and per class to the expected numbers of passengers per trip and per class and to the allocated length of the train. Note that these constraints are not really linear. However, they can be linearized easily. Constraints (8.7) are the balancing constraints per station: For each station and for each departing train from that station, the number of departing train units before and including the train's departure should not exceed the initial stock of train units at that station plus the number of train units that arrived there earlier. Constraints (8.8) link the number of shunting movements to the numbers of train units in consecutive trips. Constraints (8.9) require that in each station the number of train units by the end of the day equals the number of train units by the start of the day, so that the circulation can be repeated on the next day. Note that this is a simplification, since the rolling stock circulations on consecutive days need not be identical. According to constraints (8.10), all train units are stored in one of the stations during the night. Finally, constraints (8.11) declare all decision variables as integer-valued.

Figure 8.15 shows the representation of the above model in terms of the modeling system OPL Studio. Note that only the decision variables N_t are required to be integer valued. In any optimal solution, *all* decision variables are integer-valued as soon as the variables N_t are integer-valued.

8.9.3. Model Extensions

Basically, the model as described above is a relatively simple extension of a Single Commodity Flow problem on a network that is very similar to the graph in Figure 8.3. As was noted earlier, Single Commodity Flow problems can be solved efficiently, since they belong to the class P. As a consequence, large instances of

```
var float Objective;
var int   N[Trip]       in 0..5;
var float C[Trip]       in 0..5;
var float U[Trip]       in 0..5;
var float S[Trip,Class] in 0..1000;
var float V[Station]    in 0..100;

minimize   Objective
   subject to
   {  // minimize carriage kilometers, shunting movements, and shortages
         Objective = sum (t in Trip)  ( wn[t]*N[t] +  wc[t]*C[t] + wu[t]*U[t] +
                                       sum (c in Classes) ws{t,c}*S[t,c] );

      // link between passenger demand, train units and shortages
         forall (t in Trip, c in Class)  S[t,c] >= d[t,c] - k[c]*N[t];

      // balance constraint after each departure from a station
         forall (s in Station, t in Trip: o[t]=s)
                sum (t1 in Trip: (o[t1]=s)&(s[t1]<=s[t])) N[t1] <=
                sum (t1 in Trip: (d[t1]=s)&(e[t1]< s[t])) N[t1] + V[s];

      // link between shunting movements and incoming and outgoing train units
         forall (t, t1 in Trip: t = Next[t1])  N[t] = N[t1] + C[t] - U[t];

      // final stock per station equals the initial stock there
         forall (s in Station)
                sum(t in Trip: o[t]=s) N[t] = sum(t in Trip: d[t]=s) N[t];

      // all train units are stored somewhere during the night
         sum (s in Station)  V[s] = v;
   };
```

Figure 8.15. Representation of a rolling stock circulation model in OPL Studio.

this problem can be solved to optimality by standard optimization software such as
CPLEX or by applying special-purpose Single Commodity Flow techniques.

Straightforward extensions of the above model may deal with, for example,
(i) certain minimum or maximum lengths of trains on certain trips, (ii) the fact
that shunting movements require time, or (iii) prescribed night balances per station.
However, dealing with train units of different subtypes requires a far more complex
model. In that case, a train with composition *Mat'64-2/Mat'64-2/Mat'64-4*
is different from a train with composition *Mat'64-2/Mat'64-4/Mat'64-2*:
Although they have the same capacities for transporting passengers, they have
different transition possibilities. Therefore, one has to take into account the positions
of the train units within the trains then. As a result, the mathematical model is a
Multi-Commodity Flow problem, and it even is an *Ordered* Multi-Commodity
Flow problem. Such problems are usually hard to solve to optimality. Another

highly complicating issue for modeling the rolling stock circulation is the fact that trains are sometimes split or combined in certain locations or the fact that certain trains are operated with locomotive hauled carriages. Nevertheless, a lot of progress in modeling such complicated issues has been achieved recently (Fioole et al., 2004).

8.9.4. Practical Experiences

The Logistics department of NS Reizigers is responsible for the planning of the timetable, the rolling stock circulation, and the crew schedules of NS Reizigers. Here the models described in this section as well as several extensions have been implemented as prototypes within the modeling system OPL Studio, and they have been solved by the standard solver CPLEX. These models have proved to be very useful within the planning process of the rolling stock circulation of NS Reizigers. In almost all cases, the results of the models are at least as good as the results obtained manually by the planners, sometimes even in all three objectives. Moreover, the results are usually obtained in just a fraction of the manually required amount of time. This comparison of the model results with the manually obtained results can be considered as a validation of the models, as described in Section 8.3.

The availability of the models allows one to study the set of Pareto-optimal solutions of an instance of the rolling stock circulation problem, as described in Section 8.5. The latter is useful in determining a trade-off between the different objective functions. For example, one may find out that the shortages of seats can be further reduced, but only at the expense of a very high number of additional train unit kilometers. In that case one will probably be satisfied with the available solution. Also the fact that the models enable one to quickly evaluate the consequences of different scenarios—for example, related to changing passenger demands, changing availabilities of rolling stock or different rolling stock types—is appreciated both by the planners and by the management of the Logistics department.

Nevertheless, the application of these models usually does not lead to rolling stock schedules that can be applied in practice immediately. The latter is due to the fact that, in practice, the complete rolling stock circulation planning problem is really a huge and complex problem: It has to be solved for all rolling stock types, for all lines, and for a whole week. Indeed the initial rolling stock circulation is usually cyclic with a cycle length of one week. However, the models described so far deal with a limited number of rolling stock types, on a subset of the lines, and for a single day only. But, as was mentioned earlier, the planners in practice usually also start to solve the rolling stock circulation problem on a line-by-line basis and for a single day, in order to reduce the complexity of the problem. Hence the mathematical models provide the planners with useful initial solutions, but these initial solutions have to be fine-tuned and fit together manually in a second step. The latter may involve, for example, the fixing of the night balances. Note that, in principle, the fixing of the night balances could also be supported by mathematical models, but such models have not been developed yet. Furthermore, since a rolling stock circulation that is completely line-based may lead to a suboptimal utilization of the rolling stock, several interconnections between the rolling stock circulations of the single lines are made manually. In other words, the inefficiencies that are due to the decomposition of the rolling stock circulation problem on a line-by-line basis are reduced afterwards as much as possible.

The available models have not yet been embedded in user-friendly decision support systems. However, a prototype interface between the databases that can deliver the input data for the models and that can restore the solutions of the models into these databases has been developed. Moreover, a simple graphical interface for representing the solutions of the models as in Figure 8.14 has been developed as well. A more sophisticated integration of the models into the regular planning processes of NS Reizigers is currently (2005) under construction.

8.10. FINAL REMARKS

In this chapter we described how mathematical models and solution techniques can provide planners with *active* support in their daily planning activities. Mathematical models and solution techniques can be used to generate solutions or partial solutions for complex planning problems. These solutions may be used directly in practice, or the planners may further refine them manually if they consider this as necessary. In this final section, we summarize some of the raised issues.

In this chapter, we pointed out that most practical planning problems belong to the class of *NP*-hard problems. Therefore, the probability that solution methods exist that solve all instances of such a planning problem efficiently is considered as small. For solving practical instances of such a planning problem, one will therefore have to be satisfied with *approximate* solutions. Nevertheless, the time required to generate an acceptable solution is usually shorter than if the solution had to be generated manually. The latter may lead to a reduction of the throughput time of the planning process. This will allow the organization to react faster to changing external circumstances, which may have a positive effect on the flexibility of the organization.

A consequence of the foregoing is that developing a mathematical model requires one to balance the required *level of detail* of the model carefully with the implied *complexity*. However, in practice there is often a tendency to incorporate as many details as possible into a model. The latter may have a detrimental effect on the model's complexity. Creating mathematical models and corresponding solution techniques that are really useful in practice is therefore more an art than a science.

A further important point is that optimality in *practical* terms need not be the same as optimality in *mathematical* terms. In practice, usually several conflicting objectives play a role. Therefore it is impossible to talk about *the* optimal solution, since the quality of a solution depends on the relative importance that is given to the different objectives. However, a mathematical model allows one to compute a trade-off between the different objectives: How much of a certain objective is to be sacrificed in order to get a certain improvement in another one?

From the foregoing, we may conclude that, if designed and developed appropriately and applied sensibly, then mathematical models and solution techniques may have a positive influence on the obtained solutions and plans, the planning process itself, and the work contents of the planners.

INTRODUCTION TO CHAPTER 9

In the following chapter, Sauer extends on the previous chapters in two ways. First he discusses multisite scheduling, and then he applies Artifical Intelligence (AI) scheduling algorithms. This is a logical step in the organizational planning line in this book. This line started in Chapter 4, where Jorna discusses individual aspects of the planning task. Following that, Gazendam (Chapter 5) and McKay and Wiers (Chapter 6) look at the organization of planning tasks. In Chapter 7, van Wezel discusses the link between the organization of the planning and the individual planning tasks on the one hand and computer support on the other. In Chapter 8, Kroon and Zuidwijk discussed in detail how an organizational planning problem can be supported with mathematical algorithms. Looking at the coordination of plans between organizational units is a logical next step, but it places specific requirements on the algorithms that are used.

Often, production processes of a manufacturing company are distributed over several manufacturing sites. The output of one site can be the input for another site, which means that their activities must be coordinated. Sauer distinguishes two levels in multisite scheduling problems: the global and the local level. On the global level the requirements for the individual sites are determined. On the local level, these requirements are translated into detailed production schedules. Both levels have predictive, reactive, and interactive phases. Sauer proposes techniques for the global level as well as for the coordination between the local and global level. He argues that for the global level, optimization is not possible because detailed information of all machines and jobs in each site would be needed. This

Planning in Intelligent Systems: Aspects, Motivations, and Methods, Edited by Wout van Wezel, René Jorna, and Alexander Meystel

information is not available on the global level, and it would create a much too complex scheduling problem anyway. Therefore, at this level heuristics and fuzzy techniques are appropriate. On the local level, techniques such as Operations Research and constraint-based scheduling algorithms (described in Chapter 8 and Chapters 14–17 in this book) can be used. For communication between the local and the global level, Sauer proposes to use a blackboard approach. All sites and the global level use the blackboard to put on relevant tasks and events, and a controller is used to check for conflicts.

Chapter 9 is the last theoretical chapter that deals with organizational planning. However, we come back to organizational planning in the practical part of the book (Chapters 12–17), where different approaches are applied to the same planning problem.

9

MODELING AND SOLVING MULTISITE SCHEDULING PROBLEMS

JÜRGEN SAUER

Department of Computer Science, University of Oldenburg, D-26121 Oldenburg, Germany

9.1. INTRODUCTION

Planning and scheduling are areas that have some subjects in common but also differ in some ways. Both rely on activities that have to be performed in order to achieve some goals stated. All the activities need resources, and a set of constraints has to be observed in order to get valid solutions. Sometimes even a definition of optimality for the solution to be found is given. The result of both planning and scheduling is often called a plan, but we will differentiate between plan and schedule. One of the main differences between planning and scheduling is the use of temporal issues. Scheduling in nearly all cases has to deal with concrete temporal assignments of activities to resources, whereas planning mainly deals with the order in which the activities have to be performed; that is, planning focuses on "what has to be done," whereas scheduling focuses on "when this has to be done." Often planning and scheduling are interconnected in the way that planning produces a plan of activities to be performed and scheduling finds the best-suited temporal assignment of the activities from the plan to the available resources.

Scheduling problems can be found in several different application areas—for example, the scheduling of production operations in manufacturing industry, computer processes in operating systems, truck movements in transportation, aircraft crews, and so on. One of the most important application areas is the scheduling

Planning in Intelligent Systems: Aspects, Motivations, and Methods, Edited by Wout van Wezel, René Jorna, and Alexander Meystel

281

of production processes, often called production planning and scheduling. Here we often find a hierarchical multistage scheduling process where in a first step the master schedule is computed. It is a rough cut capacity planning and shows the mid or long-term production figures of a company—for example, how many cars have to be produced within every month of a year. Here often linear programming techniques are used. The master schedule is then transformed to a detailed schedule showing on a short-term basis the activities and when they should be performed— for example, what parts of a car have to be produced, transported, and assembled within every hour or day of a week. Here data of the material management regarding items in stock and items to be purchased, as well as detailed production plans showing the order in which parts have to be produced and machines that have to be used, are a necessary input. To solve these problems, most often heuristic planning and scheduling approaches are used. The division of the planning and scheduling process into subproblems which are solved individually has historical validity, because this was the only way to solve the complex scheduling problems within production planning and scheduling. New approaches try to integrate some of the formerly single problems to regard all the constraints in one system. Most of the approaches mentioned here and especially the multisite scheduling approach, belong to this category of systems.

As mentioned above, the main task of scheduling is the temporal assignment of activities to resources where a number of goals and constraints have to be regarded. Scheduling covers the creation of a schedule of the activities over a longer period (predictive scheduling) and the adaptation of an existing schedule due to actual events in the scheduling environment (reactive scheduling) (Kerr and Szelke, 1995; Sauer, 1999; Smith, 1992). But scheduling has also a very important inter-active dimension because we always find humans within the scheduling process, who have to decide, interact, or control. Several decisions have to be taken by the human scheduler (the user of the scheduling system)—for example, introducing new orders, canceling orders, changing priorities, setting operations on specific schedule positions—and these decisions have to be regarded within the scheduling process (Hsu et al., 1993).

The complexity of real-world scheduling is mainly determined by

- The requirements imposed by numerous details of the particular application domain (e.g., alternative machines, cleaning times, setup costs, etc.)
- The dynamic and uncertain nature of the manufacturing environment (e.g., unpredictable setup times, machine breakdowns, etc.)
- Conflicting organizational goals (e.g., minimize work-in-process time, maximize resource utilization)
- The need of interaction with a human scheduler

To deal with these problems, an appropriate problem representation and a sophisticated problem-solving techniques are necessary.

For the description of scheduling problems, constraint-centered representations have succeeded (Beck and Fox, 1998). According to Sauer (1993a,b), scheduling problems can be described by the following components (in parentheses there are examples for a local scheduling scenario):

R: a set of required resources (the machines used to perform the manufacturing tasks)

P: a set of producible products (products that can be manufactured)

O: a set of actual orders (orders for an amount of products to be finished within a time period)

The set of constraints can be divided into

HC: a set of hard constraints that have to be fulfilled (technical restrictions on machines)

SC: a set of soft constraints that may be relaxed (e.g., due dates)

E: a set of possible events that can occur and change the scheduling environment (breakdown or maintenance of machines, changes of orders)

G: a set of goal functions used to evaluate the schedules created (e.g., time-based functions like lateness or tardiness)

The result of scheduling is a (production) schedule showing the temporal assignment of operations of the production process of a product to the resources to be used—that is, *which* resources should be used *when* for the manufacturing of a particular product for which an order exists. We distinguish valid solutions, which are solutions where all hard constraints are met, and consistent solutions, which are valid and where all soft constraints are met.

As we will see later, this general description can be used to describe scheduling problems on different levels—that is, both local and global scheduling problems.

Because traditionally scheduling has been regarded as a combinatorial optimization problem (i.e., the problem of optimizing an evaluation function with respect to a given scheduling problem), most algorithmic solutions presented belong to the class of optimization algorithms (e.g., linear programming). In order to determine an optimal solution, different restrictions have been imposed on the problem domain (e.g., a static problem environment), which makes the application of the results to real-world scheduling problems very difficult or even impossible because most of the constraints of the scheduling environment are not regarded.

Therefore the objective in real-world scheduling tasks is the determination of a "good" and feasible solution regarding all the objectives and preferences of the scheduling environment. Very important for this task is the (heuristic) knowledge of the human domain expert who is able to solve distinct scheduling problems and to judge the feasibility of schedules by virtue of his/her gained experience. Several knowledge-based approaches have been developed, mainly influenced by artificial intelligence (AI) and operations research (OR). AI provides not only new paradigms for problem solving but also new representation formalisms which allow the explicit representation and use of the knowledge of the domain, mainly by rule-based and constraint-based representations of scheduling knowledge. The investigated techniques are as follows (Dorn and Froeschl, 1993; Kempf, 1989; Sauer, 2000; Smith, 1992; Tate, 1996; Zweben and Fox, 1994):

Heuristics. Heuristic scheduling is based on heuristic search techniques and general heuristics such as problem decomposition together with problem specific knowledge adopted from scheduling experts in order to guide the search process. Often, constraints are used to guide the search. Knowledge representation is rule- or frame-based (object-oriented). Important strategies are order-based, resource-based, or operation-based decompositions together with additional heuristic rules for solving the subproblems (e.g., selecting the "right" resource out of alternatives).

Constraints. In constraint-based scheduling, the scheduling problem is defined as a constraint satisfaction problem, that is, the problem is described by a set of variables of certain domains and a set of constraints restricting these domains (Kumar, 1992). For the solution of problems presented as constraint nets, efficient systems have been developed implementing fast constraint handling algorithms—for example, ECLIPSE, CHIP, or ILOG (Baptiste et al., 1995; Dincbas et al., 1989). Problems exist with the handling of hard and soft constraints as well as with reactive scheduling tasks.

Iterative Improvement Strategies. In contrast to the other techniques which mainly construct a solution (schedule), iterative improvement techniques are working on complete solutions. The improvement techniques look at scheduling as a combinatorial optimization problem, start with any solution, and try to find an optimal or near-optimal solution by iterative improvements (Dorn, 1995). This means they generate new solutions and check whether the objective value has improved. Genetic algorithms, simulated annealing, taboo search, threshold acception, grand deluge algorithms, and iterative deepening belong to this class of strategies.

Fuzzy Techniques. Fuzzy scheduling provides the possibility to deal with the inherent dynamic and incompleteness of the scheduling area. It allows the representation (by fuzzy sets and linguistic variables) and the inference (by fuzzy rules) from vaguely formulated knowledge (Slany, 1996; Türksen, 1991). The main types of imprecise scheduling information addressed by fuzzy sets are vaguely defined dates or durations (e.g., due dates), vague definitions of preferences (e.g., preferences between alternatives), uncertainty about the value of scheduling parameters (e.g., process times), and aggregated knowledge (e.g., machine groups instead of individual machines). Fuzzy controllers are used to implement the handling of the fuzzy rules and fuzzy sets. Thus fuzzy scheduling may be interpreted as a special form of heuristic rule-based system.

Neural Networks. Neural networks too have been investigated for solving scheduling problems. Neural networks solve complex functions represented by a set of connected neurons and are mainly used for pattern recognition, fore-casting, classification, and data mining but are also useful in other application domains. In scheduling up to now, only a few problems have been investigated for the use of specific neural networks allowing optimization (Biethahn et al., 1998). One main disadvantage is the inflexibility of the networks, that is, for slightly changed situations, new networks have to be established.

Distributed Problem Solving (Multi-agents). Here the cooperative character of problem solving is emphasized. The systems developed are based on the idea of cooperating intelligent agents, each of them responsible for solving a specific task of the whole scheduling problem (Jennings et al., 1998). Often, an active control-oriented approach is preferred, where the control of the actual shop floor is highlighted and predictive scheduling is only of secondary importance. The main questions in the design of agent-based sys-tems are how to divide the system into agents, what are the responsibilities and facilities of an agent, and how the agents communicate. A major point is the kind of scheduling knowledge that is incorporated in an agent. All the approaches mentioned before may be useful here. Therefore, a lot of research is actually done in this area.

Table 9.2 will show the appropriateness of the problem-solving strategies for the scheduling tasks mentioned above.

In spite of a large number of developed scheduling methods, only a few practical applications have entered into everyday use in industrial reality. Most of them have been created for scheduling tasks of local production sites (Sauer and Bruns, 1997; Zweben and Fox, 1994), all using the experience of human experts and problem-specific knowledge of the application domain. Experience, especially obtained in projects addressing real-world scheduling problems, has shown that not only the applied scheduling methods, but also several other features play a significant role for the acceptance of scheduling systems (Kempf et al., 1991). Hence, some of the important features of a scheduling system should be:

- *Information Presentation.* The information necessary for the scheduling task has to be presented in an appropriate manner, showing specific information at a glance (e.g., capacities or alternative process plans).
- *Interaction.* Interaction shall allow for full manual control of the scheduling process.
- *Incorporation of Scheduling Expertise.* Most knowledge-based approaches focus merely on predictive scheduling. Reactive scheduling is the more significant problem in many applications and has to be supported algorithmically as well.

Systems developed in the research group of the author are as follows (Henseler, 1995; Sauer, 1995; Sauer and Bruns, 1997):

- *PROTOS.* Scheduling system for the chemical industry with a lot of alternative routings and resources.

- *PSY.* Scheduling system for discrete manufacturing including long- and short-term scheduling.
- *REAKTION.* Scheduling system especially designed for reactive scheduling tasks.
- *MEDICUS.* Scheduling system for scheduling the heart surgery in a hospital.
- *METAPLAN.* Meta-scheduling system for the selection and the test of appropriate scheduling strategies.

9.2. THE MULTISITE SCHEDULING PROBLEM

Scheduling problems are usually treated in a single plant environment where a set of orders for products has to be scheduled on a set of machines (Dorn and Froeschl, 1993; Sauer and Bruns, 1997; Zweben and Fox, 1994). However, within many industrial enterprises the production processes are distributed over several manufacturing sites, which are responsible for the production of various parts of a set of final products. Usually, there is no immediate feedback from the local plants to the logistics department, and communication between the local schedulers takes place without any computer-based support.

Figure 9.1 illustrates a hierarchical two-level structure of multisite scheduling reflecting the organizational structure often found in business. On the global

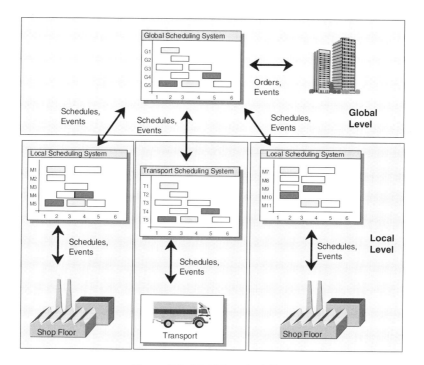

Figure 9.1. Multisite scheduling.

level, requirements are generated for intermediate products manufactured in individual locations. Local scheduling (at individual locations) deals with the transformation into concrete production schedules which represent the assignment of operations to machines. On both levels, predictive, reactive, and interactive problems are addressed, not only to generate schedules but also to adapt them to the actual situation in the production process. This scenario can easily be extended to multilayer hierarchies and adapted to other application areas (e.g., distributed software development or other projects).

Due to the distribution of production processes to different plants, some specific problems arise:

- Complex interdependencies between production processes that are performed in different plants have to be regarded. For example:
  - Temporal relations between intermediate and final products (e.g., if an intermediate product that is manufactured in plant A is needed in plant B).
  - The same item can be manufactured in different plants (possibly at different costs).
  - The transport of parts between different plants needs transportation capacities and is time- and cost-intensive.
- In global scheduling, generalized data are used instead of precise data; these are, for example:
  - Capacity information referring to machine groups instead of single machines.
  - Information on the duration of manufacturing processes for intermediate or final products that are often estimated values.
- Existing (local) scheduling systems for individual plants that accomplish the local realization of global requirements should be integrated.
- The coordination of decentralized scheduling activities for all plants within one enterprise is necessary since several levels of scheduling with their specific scheduling systems have to work cooperatively in a dynamic distributed manufacturing environment.
- The uncertainty about the actual "situation" in individual plants has to be regarded.
- Different goals have to be regarded on the different levels:
  - The goals of the global scheduling activities such as meeting due dates of final products, minimizing transportation costs and work-in-process times. Furthermore, the solution of the global scheduling problem should be as robust as possible; that is, it should give enough flexibility for a local scheduler to react to local disturbances without affecting the other sites. This can be achieved amongst others by using buffer times in the time windows for local production and by trying to optimize the load balancing on the machine groups.
  - The goals of the local scheduling level such as optimizing machine utilization, setup times and meeting due dates of intermediates, which are often in contrast to each other.

• Additional goals, especially for the effectiveness of a multisite scheduling system, are the early detection of capacity problems; in case of reactive scheduling, one of the main goals is to preserve as much as possible of the existing global schedule in order to minimize the subsequent effort on the local level.

Therefore, the multisite scheduling problem can be divided into global and local scheduling tasks together with communication tasks. On the global level, products must be distributed to plants where the intermediates have to be produced. On the local level the intermediates have to be scheduled within the local production sites. On both levels, predictive and reactive scheduling is necessary to create respectively maintain the global or local schedules. Additionally, the coordination between these tasks has to be supported in order to provide all components with actual and consistent information.

On the basis of the description above, we therefore can identify as typical tasks of multisite scheduling:

   I. On the Global Level

     1. *Global Predictive Scheduling.* A global-level schedule with an initial distribution of internal orders to local production sites has to be generated.

     2. *Global Reactive Scheduling.* If problems cannot be solved on the local level or the modified local schedule influences other local schedules (inter-plant dependencies), global reactive scheduling can then cause a redistribution of internal orders to local plants and adapt the global schedule.

  II. On the Local Level

     1. *Local Predictive Scheduling.* Based on the global schedule, the local plants draw up their detailed local production schedules.

     2. *Local Reactive Scheduling.* In case of local disturbances, the local reactive scheduler first tries to remedy them locally by interactive repair.

 III. Between the Levels

     1. *Communication and Coordination.* Both levels shall be provided with data as actual and consistent as possible. At least the following items of information have to be sent.

       a. From the global to the local level:

         i. The global schedule consisting of information on internal orders, affiliated intermediate products, machine groups to use, time windows that should (possibly) be met, and required quantities of intermediate products.

        ii. Unexpected events that affect the local level (e.g., the cancellation of an order).

    b. From the Local to the Global Level:

        i. The local realization of the global requirements with information on internal orders, affiliated intermediate products, start and end time of all locally scheduled activities, and used machine groups.

        ii. Appearance of failure events, suggestions for possible local rescheduling.

The goals and events for the *reactive tasks* are quite similar on both levels. For example:

- As goals
  - Conserve as much as possible of the former schedule.
  - React almost immediately.
- As events
  - Breakdowns of resources.
  - New or canceled orders.

Only a few approaches have been presented for multisite scheduling (Bel and Thierry, 1993; Liu and Sycara, 1993; Wauschkuhn, 1992). Most of them try to solve the multisite scheduling problem by generating a better initial distribution of orders to the different production sites; that is, they are restricted to global predictive scheduling. In classical production planning and control systems there is only a simple distribution when machine groups are used instead of machines in the materials requirement and capacity planning. But here the actual situation at the local plants is not taken into account, and feedback is not integrated.

For the problem at hand we now have to investigate if some of the approaches presented so far can be used also for the multisite scheduling problem. This means especially, if it is possible to use the constraint-based modeling technique and selected problem-solving strategies for the tasks in multisite scheduling. This is possible as the following sections will show.

9.3. THE MULTISITE SCHEDULING APPROACH

We have developed a model for solving the multisite scheduling problem that is based on the following ideas:

- Use the general modeling approach of the local area for all levels of multisite scheduling.
- Check the appropriateness of the local scheduling strategies for the scheduling tasks of the global level.
- Find an appropriate communication and coordination mechanism to support the coordination tasks.

This will also allow for the reuse of system components of earlier developed scheduling systems. The resulting model will be described in this section.

9.3.1. Modeling the Global and Local Scheduling Problems

First we have to look at the modeling task. As described earlier, the problem of multisite scheduling can be divided into some subproblems that have to be solved in connection. The local scheduling problem description corresponds to the 7-tuple introduced in Section 9.1. The global scheduling problems can be described quite similar so that we can use the same approach for representing it.

Table 9.1 comprises the models of the different levels together with the generic scheduling problem representation. Thus, the new task of modeling the global scheduling problem can be easily done using the formalization of Chapter 1 with:

R:	Resources are now machine groups or other cumulated resources of the local levels.
P:	Products are the finished products, which the customer can order. These finished products consist of a set of intermediate products that are manufactured in the plants of the local level.

TABLE 9.1. Modeling Global and Local Scheduling

Generic Model	Local Scheduling	Global Scheduling
Resources	Machines	Groups of machines
Products	Intermediate products consisting of several production steps (operations)	Final products consisting of several intermediate products
Orders	Internal orders for intermediates	External orders for final products
Hard constraints	Schedule all orders, regard production requirements (one variant, precedence constraints)	Schedule all external orders, regard production requirements (one variant, precedence constraints, capacity)
Soft constraints	"Optimal" machine utilization, meet due dates, minimize work-in-process costs.	Meet due date, minimize transportation times/ costs, use production equally, reduce inventory costs.
Events	Breakdown of machines, changes in internal orders	Breakdown of machine groups, changes in external orders
Goal functions	Minimal work in progress, optimal utilization of machines, meet due dates	Meet due dates

O: Orders are orders for finished products which are given by customers or the logistics department.

HC: Hard constraints are the constraints of the global area that cannot be violated—for example, precedence constraints.

SC: Soft constraints may be relaxed—for example, due dates of the ordered end products.

E: Events of the global level are external events initiated by customers or the logistics department—for example, new, changed, or canceled orders, or internal events from the local scheduling systems representing the local realization of the global orders or events like breakdowns that are important for the global or other local schedulers.

G: The objective functions are also quite similar to those of the local schedulers—for example, meeting the due dates or minimizing costs.

9.3.2. Scheduling Techniques for the Global and Local Problems

For the solution of the predictive and reactive scheduling tasks, several problem-solving approaches are useful. Within the local area (i.e., for the local predictive and local reactive scheduling tasks), all the approaches presented above may be used. To solve the tasks of the global level (i.e., the global predictive and global reactive scheduling as well as the coordination), the strategies of the local level can be evaluated whether they are appropriate.

Because the global scheduling level uses mainly cumulated and imprecise data, the algorithms focusing on optimization seem not appropriate. On the other hand, it will be too difficult and complex to build an optimization problem for the global predictive problem using all information from the external order down to the machine level. Therefore heuristics, fuzzy techniques, and partly constraints remain as candidates for the global scheduling tasks. Table 9.2 gives an overview of the tasks and some of the appropriate methods from which several are investigated in the MUST project. Schultz and Mertens (2000) present similar results on the appropriateness of techniques. The techniques written in bold will be described in more detail in the following section.

9.3.1.1. Strategies for Global Predictive Scheduling. The global predictive scheduling problem is characterized by the use of highly imprecise and cumulative data; for example, machine groups or plants represent a huge set of single machines. In order to find a realistic and good schedule that distributes the external orders to the local facilities and deals with the vague data, heuristics and fuzzy techniques seem to be most appropriate. Both approaches have been evaluated for the MUST system (see below).

Heuristics for Global Predictive Scheduling. The heuristic approach is based on an order-based strategy and aims at creating a global schedule with a "balanced" use of

TABLE 9.2. Scheduling Tasks and Methods

Scheduling Area	Techniques
Global predictive scheduling	**Heuristics** (constraints), **Fuzzy-Logic**
Global reactive scheduling	Interaction, Heuristics (constraints)
Local predictive scheduling	Constraints
	Heuristics
	Genetic algorithms
	Neural networks
	OR-systems
Local reactive scheduling	Interaction
	Heuristics
	Constraints
	Multi-agents

machine groups and time intervals trying to avoid bottlenecks and to provide as much latitude as possible for rescheduling activities of the local schedulers. The heuristic knowledge used in this strategy is represented by heuristic rules or procedures and uses a dynamically updated worst-case analysis of the capacity needed by the external orders. If a conflict has to be solved, alternative machine groups are checked. If there is no feasible alternative, then new start times for the intermediates or alternative routings are tried. At last the given time interval for the final product is expanded in order to find a solution. The overall strategy is shown in Table 9.3.

Within the select statements, heuristic knowledge for selection of appropriate objects is represented. For example:

- Select *orders* (`select_most_critical_order`). Try critical orders first; that is, avoid bottlenecks. The criticality is calculated dynamically for every scheduling step.

TABLE 9.3. Heuristic for Global Predictive Scheduling

```
calculate_static_criticalities
WHILE orders_to_plan DO
     capacity_analysis;
     select_most_critical_order;
     select_interval_of_order;
     select_least_critical_variant;
     WHILE intermediates_to_plan DO
            select_most_critical_intermediate;
            select_start_time;
            select_machine_group;
            IF ok THEN plan_intermediate ELSE solve_conflict
     END WHILE
END WHILE
```

- Select *time windows* for orders (`select_interval_of_order`). Try the given interval first, else shift to the future.
- Select *variants* (`select_least_critical_variant`). Try the least critical variant first—that is, the one that uses less bottleneck resources. Again this avoids bottlenecks.
- Select *intermediates* (`select_most_critical_intermediate`). Try the most critical intermediate first—that is, the intermediate that will most likely lead to a bottleneck.
- Select *start of operation* (`select_start_time`). Try the earliest possible start time first to avoid lateness.
- Select *machine group* (`select_machine_group`). Try the machine group that is less occupied, again to avoid bottlenecks.

The dynamic calculation of the critical orders, steps, and machine groups is done by a worst-case analysis based on the already scheduled orders and the orders to be scheduled. If a conflict has to be solved (`solve_conflict`), the following strategy is used:

```
(1) first try all alternative machine groups;
(2) then try new start time;
(3) if given time window is exceeded then try next variant if
    available;
(4) if there is no variant, then extend the given time window.
```

The strategy chosen leads to good results, although it is much slower than strategies using simple heuristic rules (see below).

Fuzzy Techniques for Global Predictive Scheduling. Fuzzy techniques are widely used to represent and handle imprecise knowledge. Therefore it seems especially suited for the problems of global predictive scheduling. The system is realized by a so-called fuzzy controller. For this the characteristic data of the problem domain have to be described by linguistic variables and fuzzy values, and fuzzy rules are used to infer new information (the schedule) (Sauer, Appelrath, and Suelmann, 1997).

In a first step the scheduling knowledge has to be classified and described by linguistic variables; for example, the needed capacity is characterized by (`very small`, `small`, `medium`, `high`, `very high`). For each of these linguistic representations membership functions have to be provided to transform the crisp input values to the linguistic representation (fuzzyfication).

In the global scheduling domain, we describe the scheduling objects by the following features:

- *Resources.* By capacity of machine groups, machine utilization, fuzzy transportation costs and times, consumption of materials, and wear and tear of tools.
- *Products.* Product capacity and time consumption for a product.
- *External Orders.* Time demand and priority.

To allow for further modeling of distinctions between individual orders, dates and priority of an external order are represented by linguistic variables as well as by hard and soft constraints. All other features are characterized by crisp values.

The next step is to find the rules that infer new knowledge (i.e., the schedule or part of it or input data for further processing steps), from the given and fuzzificated input data. To deal with the complexity of the problem, we use an overall strategy based on a heuristic problem decomposition in three subproblems that are then solved by rule bases.

Depending on the objectives (e.g., preferring valuable products, optimizing machine utilization, and meeting all due dates), several different rule bases can be created for the three steps. So it is easily possible to create strategies for changing objectives. The steps are as follows:

1. Generate a sequence of orders in which they will be scheduled. This is done by rules that characterize the orders with regard to their importance. The more important an order is, the earlier it is scheduled. Within this step, all orders are rated by all rules of the belonging rule base and then sorted by the resulting importance. Rules of the rule base for the first step looks like:

```
/* rule base to determine the importance of orders*/
IF       Time_demand(complete) FUZZY_OR Date(complete)
 THEN Importance(important);
IF       Product(EP05) FUZZY_OR Product(EP01) FUZZY_OR Date
            (complete)
  THEN Importance(very important);
```

2. Now the orders are scheduled according to their position in the sequence by rules reflecting hard and soft constraints as well as other heuristics. For every order a set of possible temporal assignments to machine groups is calculated and rated by the rules of this rule base. The position-rated maximum denotes the favorable machine group and is scheduled. Here the rules look like (soft constraint 8 checks the possibility of scheduling as early as possible, and soft constraint 3 tries to optimize load balancing):

```
/* rules to determine the best scheduling position */
IF       Machine_Group(MG03) FUZZY_OR Soft_Constraint_8
            (very good)
   THEN Importance(very important);
IF       Machine_Group(MG03) FUZZY_OR Soft_Constraint_8
            (good)
   THEN Importance(important);
IF        Soft_Constraint_8(medium)
   THEN Importance(normal);
IF        Soft_Constraint_8(bad)
   THEN Importance(unimportant);
IF        Soft_Constraint_8(very bad)
    THEN Importance(very unimportant);
```

```
IF     Soft_Constraint_3(met) FUZZY_OR Soft_Constraint_8
          (met)
   THEN Importance(very important);
```

3. At last the demand for material is computed by summation of all products in the form of the given values of the linguistic variables.

This concept permits a segregation of the knowledge bases for each action and with that a directed and independent update of (sub-)strategies or rules by the user. The distributed knowledge management can also be used to enhance the performance of the fuzzy controller, a feature that is important for quick decision making.

The fuzzy logic approach leads to good results and especially provides a good representation and handling of imprecise knowledge. Thus, it will be part of the scheduling systems of the future.

Table 9.4 shows the result of a comparison between the approaches mentioned and an algorithm using a priority rule for the selection of the orders to schedule. The orders are then scheduled to their earliest possible position. DynH represents the heuristic approach with dynamic heuristics, and RB1–RB4 denote four different rulebases created for different objectives. The evaluation is based on a set of 5 products with 3 variants per product and 1–5 steps per variant. For these set 20 orders are created. The number of possible solutions exceeds 10^{79} (Sauer, 1993b). Although the heuristic as well as the fuzzy-based approach involve more than only meeting the due date, they perform well even in this case. In particular, the fuzzy approach uses buffers to provide more flexibility for the local schedulers.

9.3.1.2. Global Reactive Scheduling. The global reactive component of the MUST system has been designed as a (global) scheduling system supporting interactive repair by means of a sophisticated graphical user interface as well as a heuristic

TABLE 9.4. Comparison of the Global Scheduling Approaches

Strategy	Runtime (seconds)	Lateness	Tardiness
EDD	3	−74	421
FIFO	3	1132	1578
PRIO	3	1132	1578
SPT	3	1224	1487
LPT	3	1187	1664
LIFO	3	761	1118
JIT	3	1048	1555
dynH	114	−136	324
RB1	11	241	474
RB2	11	1052	1330
RB3	11	1506	1923
RB4	11	644	948

reactive scheduling algorithm (Lemmermann, 1995; Sauer, 1998). It uses several repair strategies based on the conflicts that evolve from the events (e.g., capacity overflow of a machine group).

9.3.1.3. Local Scheduling Tasks. For local scheduling, existing scheduling systems from previous projects and approaches from the literature have been evaluated and can be integrated into the system. Table 9.3 gives an overview of the possible combinations.

For the local predictive scheduling tasks, several approaches have been implemented—for example, heuristics (Sauer, 1993a), genetic algorithms (Bruns, 1993), neural networks (Märtens and Sauer, 1998), and iterative repair (Stegman, 1996).

The local reactive scheduling is based on a similar approach as the global reactive part. A local scheduling system has been realized including interactive as well as heuristically guided reactive repair possibilities (Henseler, 1995).

9.3.1.4. Coordination and Communication. One of the important tasks within a multisite scheduling approach is the coordination of scheduling activities on different levels. Most of the work has to be done on the global level—that is, distribution of the internal orders and reaction to events from the local schedulers as well as to external events. Additionally, both levels have to be provided with data as actual and consistent as possible. Therefore, information has to be sent between the levels—for example, the global schedule consisting of information on internal orders, affiliated intermediate products, machine groups to use, time windows that should (possibly) be met, required quantities of intermediate products, and unexpected events that effect the local, respectively, global levels (e.g., the cancellation of an order or breakdowns of machine groups).

This communication is done using the blackboard approach. The blackboard approach (Sadeh et al., 1998) is widely used for distributed problem solving and is based on a common data structure called blackboard, which all participating systems can read from or write to. A controller is used to avoid conflicts and to order the tasks on the blackboard. In the MUST approach every scheduling system (the global system and the local systems) has its own blackboard on which the tasks and events important for the system are noted. Figure 9.2 shows the blackboard of the global scheduling system and the blackboard of one local system to illustrate the flow of information. The control of the blackboard is integrated in the corresponding scheduling system.

9.4. THE MUST SYSTEM: PROTOTYPICAL IMPLEMENTATION

Within the project, the MUST System (Multisite Scheduling System) has been implemented prototypically in PROLOG, reflecting the ideas presented above. It consists of a global scheduling level (logistics level) and a local scheduling level (single plant level) with predictive, reactive, and interactive scheduling components on both levels. Figure 9.3 shows the architecture of the MUST system.

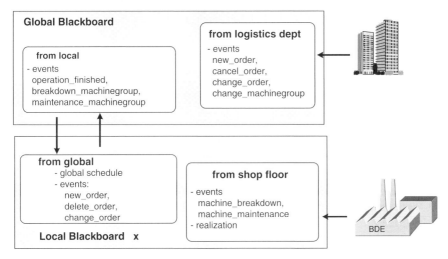

Figure 9.2. The MUST blackboard system.

The architecture shows the system consisting of one global scheduling subsystem and several local subsystems, one for each individual production site. Common features of all subsystems of the multisite approach are as follows:

- All components are based on knowledge-based techniques; that is, problem-specific knowledge is identified, represented, and applied for the solution of the addressed problem.

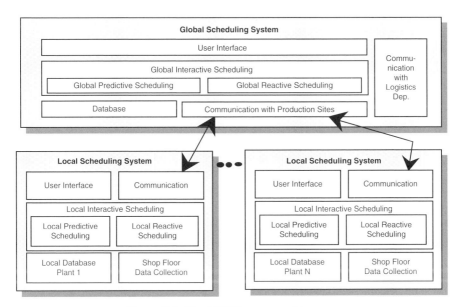

Figure 9.3. The MUST system architecture.

- Several problem-solving techniques have been used in the scheduling components:
  - Global predictive scheduling: heuristic approach like that presented above.
  - Global reactive scheduling: interaction and heuristics as described in Lemmermann (1995).
  - Local predictive scheduling: heuristic approach adopted from Sauer (1993a).
  - Local reactive scheduling: interaction and heuristics adopted from Henseler (1995).
- The reactive scheduling components on both scheduling levels are realized as a scheduling system with a sophisticated graphical user interface, where the schedule is repaired interactively using knowledge-based reactive search algorithms, which make use of heuristic knowledge to solve the constraints violated.
- The user interfaces are window-oriented, and most functions are mouse-sensitive, thus providing a comprehensive presentation of and easy access to relevant information (e.g., graphical Gantt-chart representation of the current schedule). Figure 9.4 shows a screenshot of the global user interface.
- The database components provide access to global, respectively, local databases containing global or local scheduling information (e.g., the master schedule, information about products, resources, orders, inventory, etc.).
- Communication is performed using a blackboard. Each of the systems maintains a blackboard where the tasks and events relevant for the system are monitored. Local systems write to the global blackboard, the global system as well as the shop floor data collection writes to the local blackboards involved.

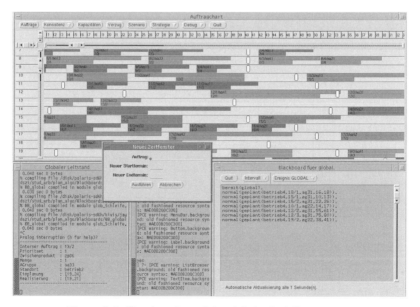

Figure 9.4. User interface of the global scheduling system.

9.5. CONCLUSION

The problem of multisite scheduling together with an approach for modeling and solving the scheduling problems within the multisite scheduling area have been presented. It is based on research done in the area of local scheduling and tries to reuse as much as possible of the modeling and problem-solving techniques of this area. The prototypical multisite scheduling system (MUST system) supports all the scheduling and coordination tasks of a distributed production environment. Within the system several existing methods of solving scheduling problems as well as new problem-solving techniques have been evaluated. All scheduling subsystems of the two-level multisite approach consist of a user interface allowing interactive as well as predictive and reactive scheduling and of communication facilities for data exchange between the systems and the environment.

Actual research is done on further scheduling approaches, on other communication possibilities (e.g., based on protocols like contract nets), on a multi-agent realization of the system (Sauer, Freese, and Teschke, 2000), on object-oriented techniques for realization of scheduling systems, and on a design support system which integrates our experience to support the creation of knowledge-based scheduling systems (Sauer and Appelrath, 1997). It will combine knowledge about the design of scheduling systems with the necessary components to build a system that fits the user's needs.

INTRODUCTION TO CHAPTER 10

The chapter by Bowling et al. differs from the foregoing chapters by Hommel, Hoc, and Jorna in one way and from the chapters by Gazendam, McKay and Wiers, van Wezel, and Sauer in another way. Bowling et al. study multi-agent planning. Agents can be software programs or robots as acting software programs. "Multi" in this context means that the agent can cooperate or can combat. When Bowling et al. talk about planners, they do not mean human planners or software programs that support, for example, planning in organizations. Planners are artificial entities that plan for themselves. The contrast with Hommel, Hoc, and Jorna is that they talk about natural planners that plan for themselves (and others). According to Bowling et al., planners are not software systems that support the planning in organizations. This differs from Gazendam, McKay and Wiers, van Wezel, and Sauer, who discuss activities in real organizations.

Because Bowling et al. talk about planners as software agents, they have to carefully design the environment where these planners operate. Therefore, they work with simple domain models. The planners are also truncated, because they are not real-world planners. All activities of the planners are also carefully designed. The simplicity of the domain and the planners do not alter the fact that the complexity of the designs is enormous. Suppose two situations—one where two robots play soccer against each other, and the other where two robots form a team. It will be clear that in both situations the robots plan and that they primarily plan for themselves. Suppose also that the soccer field is a large matrix with many cells. Which assumptions have to be formulated to mimic something like real soccer?

Planning in Intelligent Systems: Aspects, Motivations, and Methods, Edited by Wout van Wezel, René Jorna, and Alexander Meystel
Copyright © 2006 John Wiley & Sons, Inc.

In both situations the planners use state-space descriptions, as Bowling et al. explain. In the first situation the planners have to consider three important slightly connected aspects. First, the planner must have knowledge of his own goals and of the availability of possible actions—for example, scoring a goal and to make a move to the right or the left to pass the opponent. We leave out of the discussion the fact that some actions are prohibited—for example, kicking the opponent on the "artificial" head. Normally these actions are not part of the larger program. Second, the planner must have knowledge of the environment where he "lives" in. Finally the planner must have knowledge of what the opponent might do. To a certain extent, this knowledge can be called meta-knowledge. Bowling et al. do not go deep into the details of this kind of knowledge (see, for example, van den Broek, 2001). It is something like "What should I do when I go to the left and my opponent also goes to the left?" "In that case I better go the right, but then ...." It will be clear that the opponent has the same knowledge at his disposal but in a reverse way, as in a mirror.

The second situation is also very interesting, because here two planners work together. The planners as a team have to accomplish certain actions or goals. The same aspects are relevant as in the first situation, but there is one important difference. The team situation exemplifies a multiplanning situation. In this multiplanning it is important to search for equilibria, because a planner plans not only for himself but also for others. Bowling et al. describe the above situations as three planning problems. Planner A has goals that are opposed to the goals of planner B, the opposing soccer players. Planner A has the same goals as planner B, in which case we have a multiplanning situation. Together the soccer players try to score a goal, for example. The third situation is explained in detail in the subsequent chapter—that is, where the goals of B are a subset of the goals of A. It will be clear that the explicit search for optima and equilibria is very important in this kind of planning research. This is different for the situation with natural planners, because they naturally have the procedures and structures in their cognitive system.

10

MULTI-AGENT PLANNING IN THE PRESENCE OF MULTIPLE GOALS

Michael H. Bowling, Rune M. Jensen, Manuela M. Veloso

Computer Science Department, Carnegie Mellon University,
Pittsburgh, PA 15213-3891

10.1. INTRODUCTION

Traditionally, planning involves a single agent for which a planner needs to find a sequence of actions that can transform some initial state into some state where a given goal statement is satisfied. A good example of such a problem is how to solve Rubik's cube. The initial state is some configuration of the cube, and we need to find a sequence of rotations such that every tile on each side has the same color. Even though this problem is hard, the planning agent has full control over the situation. The outcome of a rotation action is completely known.

Real-world planning problems, however, seldom conform to this simple domain model. There may be uncontrollable actions of other agents in the domain interfering with the actions applied by the planning agent. Such uncertainty can be modeled by nondeterminism where actions may have several possible outcomes. One approach is to assume that transition probabilities are known and produce plans with a high likelihood to succeed (e.g., Kushmerick, Hanks, and Weld, 1995; Haddawy and Suwandi, 1994). The scalability of such planners, however, is limited due to the overhead of reasoning about probabilities. In addition, it may be hard to gather enough statistical data to estimate the transition probabilities. In this chapter, we consider a simpler model of nondeterminism without transition probabilities. The effect of a nondeterministic action is given as a set of possible next states.

Planning in Intelligent Systems: Aspects, Motivations, and Methods, Edited by Wout van Wezel, René Jorna, and Alexander Meystel

Recently, efficient planners have been developed for this class of nondeterministic domains (e.g., Cimatti et al. 2003; Jensen, Veloso, and Bryant, 2003). These planners represent states and perform search implicitly in a space of Boolean functions represented efficiently with reduced Ordered Binary Decision Diagrams (OBDDs) (Bryant, 1986). The plans produced by these planners are encoded compactly with OBDDs and correspond to *universal plans* (Schoppers, 1987) or policies in Reinforcement Learning (Littman, 1994). Hence, a *nondeterministic plan* is a state-action table mapping from states to actions relevant to execute in the state in order to reach a set of goal states. A plan is executed by iteratively observing the current state and applying one of the actions associated with that state.

In this chapter, we specifically examine nondeterministic planning in domains where nondeterminism is caused by uncontrollable agents with specific goals of their own. Such problems have been considered in the AI literature on multi-agent systems—in particular, concerning cooperation and negotiation (e.g., Carbonell, 1981; Zlotkin and Rosenschein, 1985; Kreifelts and Martial, 1990; Georgeff, 1983; Durfee, 1988; Jennings, 1995). They have also been studied in game theory and formal verification under various forms (e.g., Osborne and Rubinstein, 1994; De Alfaro, Henzinger, and Kupferman, 1998).

The novelty of our work is twofold. First, we introduce *adversarial planning problems* and a class of adversarial plans called *strong cyclic adversarial plans*. An adversarial planning domain has a single system agent that is controllable and a single environment agent that is uncontrollable and may be an opponent to the system agent. The task is to synthesize plans for the system agent that is robust to any plan of the environment agent. We go beyond theoretical work and present an OBDD-based planning algorithm that efficiently can generate strong cyclic adversarial plans. This algorithm has been fully implemented in the OBDD-Based Informed Planning and Controller Synthesis Tool (BIFROST) 0.7 (Jensen, 2003). Second, we formally define our concept of *multi-agent planning equilibria* for multi-agent domains inspired by the game theoretic notion of equilibria (Owen, 1995).

In Section 10.2, we begin by presenting the foundations of our research on multi-agent planning equilibria. First, we demonstrate intuitively through simple examples that plan solutions depend on the goals of all the agents. We also present the formal notion of a planning domain that we use throughout the chapter. In Section 10.3, we introduce adversarial planning. We present an algorithm for synthesizing adversarial plans and demonstrate theoretically and experimentally that the generated plans are robust to any strategy of the environment. In Section 10.6, we generalize the notion of accounting for an adversary with the solution concept of multi-agent planning equilibria. We formalize this notion for planning environments where all the agents' goals are explicitly specified. We also analyze this notion of equilibria in a variety of domains.

10.2. FOUNDATIONS FOR MULTI-AGENT PLANNING

Plans are contingent upon the agent's goals. Plans are usually evaluated as to whether they achieve the goals—sometimes considering how quickly, with what probability, or from what initial states. In addition, goals are often the driving mechanism for finding good plans through heuristics and Means-Ends Analysis (Newell and Simon, 1963; Pearl, 1984). In multi-agent domains, plans are of course still contingent on goals. There is an additional dependence, though. Good plans also depend on the plans of the other agents, which, as we have stated, depends heavily on their goals.

We assume that agents are synchronized and defined by a set of actions. The world consists of a finite set of states. In each time step, each agent applies exactly one action. The resulting action is called a *joint action*. Thus, a domain is a finite graph where vertices are states and edges are joint actions. A plan of an agent is a state-action table mapping states to actions relevant to execute in order to achieve the goals of the agent. We will illustrate our concept of multi-agent planning through a small two-agent soccer domain.

10.2.1. The Soccer Domain

Consider the simple soccer-like grid domain simplified from Littman's two-player grid game (Littman, 1994), which is diagrammed in Figure 10.1. There are two agents A and B, each of which solely occupies one of the four unshaded squares on the field. Agent A begins in possession of the ball. The shaded squares are out-of-bounds for our simplification of the domain. The agents have operators or actions associated with each of the compass directions (N, S, E, and W) or can wait, holding its position (H). The two agents in this domain select their actions simultaneously, but in execution there is an undetermined delay before these actions are carried out. So, the execution is serial, but it is nondeterministic as to which agent's action is carried out first. The effect of an action is to simply move the agent in the specified direction as long as the target square is unoccupied. If the target is occupied, then the agent does not move, but if the agent was carrying the ball it loses the ball. For agent A, losing the ball terminates execution as a failure. The goal for agent A is to move into either of the two labeled goal squares, which also terminates execution.

Figure 10.2 shows two examples of how the agents operators affect the state. From the initial state, if both agents choose their south operator (S, S) they will both simply move south. But if agent A selects south and agent B selects east (S, E), then there are two possible outcomes depending on their order of execution: (i) Agent A moves south first, and then agent B moves east into the now unoccupied

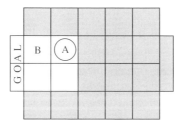

Figure 10.1. A soccer-like grid domain.

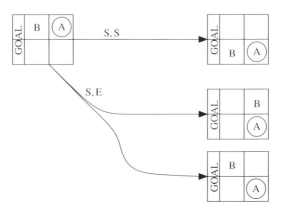

Figure 10.2. Two example effects of joint actions in the grid-soccer domain. The ordered pairs of actions represent the actions of agents A and B, respectively.

square; or (ii) agent B bumps into agent A first causing no position change, and then agent A moves south.

10.2.2. Possible Plans

There are a number of different possible plans for agent A to achieve its goals in this domain. The various plans depend on what actions we expect agent B to perform. We describe these plans without rigorous definitions or proofs, appealing to the reader's intuition as to what constitutes a "good" plan. The concept of a "good" plan will be formalized later in the chapter.

Nondeterministic. One very simple case is if we believe agent B has no goals in particular and will select its actions nondeterministically, that is, randomly. A sensible plan would be to hold position until the other agent's actions carry it into the bottom right state. From this position, regardless of the action of the other agent, a plan of two consecutive west actions is guaranteed to reach the goal. Since agent B selects actions nondeterministically, it will eventually enter the bottom right state and so this plan is guaranteed to reach the goal. Other plans risk agent B's random actions causing it to move in the way, resulting in the loss of the ball and failure. Although this plan guarantees reaching the goal, it does not necessarily guarantee achievement in a finite time, because it requires waiting a possibly infinite number of cycles before agent B moves to the bottom right square.

Teammate. Because we assume that most agents have goals, and often these goals are known, we go beyond the assumption that the other agent selects actions randomly. Their actions therefore are not likely to be nondeterministic but rather planned carefully to reach their own goals. Consider the case that agent B is actually agent A's teammate and therefore they have an identical set of goal states. Then there is a much more efficient plan. Agent A should simply hold at the initial state while its teammate moves south out of its way. Then move west into the goal, without fear that the other agent will move in front of it. As a teammate it can be sure that the agent will comply with these assumptions since its goals are identical.[1] This plan is guaranteed to reach the goal in a finite number of steps, as opposed to the plan for the nondeterministic agent.

Adversary. Neither of these plans though have any guarantees if agent B is in fact planning to stop agent A from succeeding. If agent B simply holds its ground, then neither the nondeterministic nor teammate plan for agent A would ever reach its goal. In this situation an adversarial plan, as described in Section 10.3, that can provide worst-case guarantees is more appropriate. One such plan is to nondeterministically select between holding and moving north or south until the other agent is not in front of it. Then, move west into the goal hoping its action gets executed first. This plan has no guarantee of success because the opponent may still move in front of it while it advances toward the goal, causing the ball to be lost. It does, though, have some possibility of success. In fact, against a good plan by the opponent this is all that can be guaranteed.

Overlapping Goals. A whole new situation arises if we believe that agent B is not quite an opponent but not quite a teammate. Suppose its goal is to have agent A score, but only across the south square. In this case, moving south from the initial state and then west would reach the goal without its interference. This plan, like the teammate plan, is guaranteed to succeed in a finite number of steps. Notice that the teammate-based plan and the nondeterministic-based plan would both fail in this case because both agents would hold indefinitely.

These four plans are all completely different, despite the fact that the conditions that generated the plans, the domain rules, and the agent's goal did not change from situation to situation. This demonstrates that multi-agent planning solutions need to take into account the goals of the other agents.

10.2.3. A Formalization

We first begin by formalizing the notion of planning domain and agent behavior, which we will use throughout the chapter. The definitions parallel closely with Cimatti and colleagues' single-agent formalization (Cimatti et al., 2003).

Definition 10.1 (Multi-agent Planning Domain). A multi-agent planning domain D is a tuple $\langle \mathcal{S}, n, \mathcal{A}_{i=1...n}, \mathcal{R} \rangle$ where

- $\mathcal{S}$ is the set of states,
- n is the number of agents,

---

[1]This admittedly does not address crucial issues of how this team compliance can be achieved, and it may require planned communication and coordination strategies for distributed execution.

- A_i is agent i's finite set of actions, and
- $\mathcal{R} \subseteq \mathcal{S} \times \mathcal{A} \times \mathcal{S}$ is a nondeterministic transition relation where $\mathcal{A} = \mathcal{A}_1 \times \ldots \times \mathcal{A}_n$ and must satisfy the following condition. If $\langle s, a, s' \rangle \in \mathcal{R}$ and $\langle s, b, s'' \rangle \in \mathcal{R}$ then, $\forall_i$ there exists $s''' \in \mathcal{S}$,

$$\langle s, \langle a_1, \ldots, a_{i-1}, b_i, a_{i+1}, \ldots, a_n \rangle, s''' \rangle \in \mathcal{R}$$

That is, each agent's set of actions that can be executed from a state are independent.

In addition, let $\text{ACT}_i(s) \subseteq \mathcal{A}_i$ be the set of applicable or executable actions in state s. Formally,

$$\text{ACT}_i(s) = \{a_i \in \mathcal{A}_i \mid \exists \langle s, \langle \ldots, a_i, \ldots \rangle, \cdot \rangle \in \mathcal{R}\}$$

The additional condition in the planning domain definition on $\mathcal{R}$ requires that each agent be capable of selecting actions independently. Formally this amounts to the following. For all states s and executable actions for the agents $a_i \in Act_i(s)$ there exists some transition $\langle s, \langle a_{i=1\ldots n} \rangle, s' \rangle$ that is in $\mathcal{R}$.

A Simple Example—The Narrow Doorway. Consider a two-agent robot domain where both agents are in a hallway and want to move into the same room through a single doorway. The agents have an operator to go through the door (G) that only succeeds if the other agent is not also trying to go through the door. They also have the choice of waiting (W).

This domain can be defined using the formalization of a multi-agent planning domain above. There are four states in the domain $\mathcal{S} = \{0, 1, 2, 3\}$ corresponding to the four possible configurations of the two agents in the room. n is two and $\mathcal{A}_{A,B}$ is the set of actions $\{G, W\}$. The transition relation $\mathcal{R}$ is defined by the rules described above. The complete enumeration of states and transitions is shown in Figure 10.3. Note that the domain satisfies the independent action condition on $\mathcal{R}$.

The behavior of agents is assumed to be governed by a *state-action table*. In each execution step, each agent chooses randomly between the actions associated with the current state in its state-action table. Thus, the agents have no memory of previously visited states.

Definition 10.2 (State-Action Table). A state-action table π_i *for agent* i in domain $\mathcal{D}$ is a set of pairs $\{\langle s, a_i \rangle | s \in \mathcal{S}, a_i \in \text{ACT}_i(s)\}$. A joint state-action table π constructed from state-action tables for each agent $\pi_{i=1\ldots n}$ is the set of pairs

$$\{\langle s, \langle a_1, \ldots, a_n \rangle \rangle | s \in \mathcal{S}, \langle s, a_i \rangle \in \pi_i\}$$

A (joint) state-action table is complete if and only if for any $s \in \mathcal{S}$ there exists some pair $\langle s, \cdot \rangle$ in the state-action table.

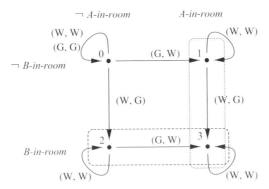

Figure 10.3. Doorway domain ⬚ and ⬚ represent A's and B's goal states and will be discussed further in Section 10.6.

For the doorway domain, a state-action table (or plan) for each agent might be

$$\pi_A = \{\langle 0, G\rangle, \langle 1, W\rangle, \langle 2, G\rangle, \langle 2, W\rangle, \langle 3, W\rangle\}$$
$$\pi_B = \{\langle 0, G\rangle, \langle 0, W\rangle, \langle 1, G\rangle, \langle 2, W\rangle, \langle 3, W\rangle\}$$

These are also *complete* state-action tables since they specify at least one action for each state. We can combine these tables into a complete *joint* state-action table. In general, a joint state-action table together with a multiagent planning domain determines the entire execution of the system. In order to define what it means for a plan to be a solution to a planning problem we need to formalize the notion of reachability and paths of execution. We will do this by first defining the execution structure of the multi-agent system.

Definition 10.3 (Induced Execution Structure). Let π be a joint state-action table of a multi-agent planning domain $\mathcal{D} = \mathcal{P}, \mathcal{S}, n, \mathcal{A}_i, \mathcal{R}$. The execution structure induced by π from the set of initial states $\mathcal{I} \subseteq \mathcal{S}$ is a tuple $K = \langle Q, T\rangle$ with $Q \subseteq \mathcal{S}$ and $T \subseteq \mathcal{S} \times \mathcal{S}$ inductively defined as follows:

- If $s \in \mathcal{I}$, then $s \in Q$.
- If $s \in Q$ and there exists a state-action pair $\langle s, a\rangle \in \pi$ and transition $\langle s, a, s'\rangle \in \mathcal{R}$ then $s' \in Q$ and $\langle s, s'\rangle \in T$.

A state $s \in Q$ is a terminal state of K if and only if there is no $s' \in Q$ such that $\langle s, s'\rangle \in T$.

Intuitively, Q is the set of states that the system could reach during execution of the plan π, and T is the set of transitions that the system could cross during execution. For our doorway domain the execution structure induced by our example joint state-action table is

$$Q = \{0, 1, 3\}$$
$$T = \{\langle 0, 1 \rangle, \langle 0, 0 \rangle, \langle 1, 3 \rangle, \langle 1, 1 \rangle, \langle 3, 3 \rangle\}$$

We can now formalize an execution path.

Definition 10.4 (Execution Path). Let $K = \langle Q, T \rangle$ be the execution structure induced by a state-action table π from $\mathcal{I}$. An execution path of K from $s_0 \in \mathcal{I}$ is a possibly infinite sequence $s_0, s_1, s_2, \ldots$ of states in Q such that, for all states s_i in the sequence:

- either s_i is the last state of the sequence, in which case s_i is a terminal state of K, or
- $\langle s_i, s_{i+1} \rangle \in T$.

A state s' is reachable from a state s if and only if there is an execution path with $s_0 = s$ and $s_i = s'$.

For our doorway domain and example joint state-action table one execution path from the initial state is

$$0, 0, 0, 0, 1, 1, \ldots$$

Let EXEC(s, π) denote the execution paths starting at s. Let the length of a path $p = s_0 s_1 \cdots$ with respect to a set of states C be defined by

$$|p|_C = \begin{cases} i & \text{if } s_i \in C \text{ and } s_j \notin C \text{ for } 0 \leq j < i \\ \infty & \text{otherwise.} \end{cases} \tag{10.1}$$

We will say that an execution path p *reaches* a state s iff $|q|_{\{s\}} \neq \infty$. The definition of execution paths serves to formalize solution concepts in the remainder of the chapter.

In the next section we present a definition of the adversarial planning problem. We also present and analyze an algorithm for finding plans with strong guarantees in adversarial domains. In Section 10.6 we generalize adversarial planning problems to a more general multiagent planning problem where all agents' goals are made explicit. We then introduce the general solution concept of multiagent planning equilibria and analyze it in a variety of domains.

10.3. ADVERSARIAL PLANNING

An adversarial planning problem is a multiagent planning problem with two agents called the *system agent* and the *environment agent*. The system agent is controllable and its goal is to reach a state in a set of goal states. The environment agent is uncontrollable. It might be an adversary to the system agent trying to prevent it from reaching its goals.

Definition 10.5 (Adversarial Planning Problem). Let $\mathcal{D} = \langle S, 2, \mathcal{A}_s, \mathcal{A}_e, \mathcal{R}_i \rangle$ be a multi-agent planning domain with a system and environment agent and a deterministic transition relation. An adversarial planning problem P for $\mathcal{D}$ is a tuple $\langle \mathcal{D}, \mathcal{I}, \mathcal{G} \rangle$, where $\mathcal{I} \subseteq S$ is the set of possible initial states and $\mathcal{G} \subseteq S$ is the set of goal states for the system agent.

An *adversarial plan* for an adversarial planning problem P is a state-action table π_s for the system agent such that all execution paths starting in an initial state eventually will reach a goal state. Thus, an adversarial plan cannot reach dead ends or loop indefinitely.

As an example, consider the adversarial planning problem shown in Figure 10.4. The actions of the system and environment agents are $\mathcal{A}_s = \{+s, -s\}$ and $\mathcal{A}_e = \{+e, -e\}$, respectively. Transitions are labeled with the corresponding joint action. There are 5 states, namely I, F, D, U, and G. I and G are initial and goal states. D is a dead end, since the goal is unreachable from D. This introduces an important difference between F and U that captures a main aspect of the adversarial planning problem. We can view the two states F and U as states in which the system and environment agent have different opportunities. Observe that the system agent "wins"—that is, reaches the goal—only if the sign of the two actions in the joint action are different. Otherwise it "loses" since there is no transition to the goal with a joint action where the actions have the same sign. The goal is reachable from both state F and U. However, the result of a "losing" joint action is different for F and U. In F, the system agent remains in F. Thus, the goal is still reachable. In U, however, the agent may transition to the dead end D, which makes it impossible to reach the goal in subsequent steps.

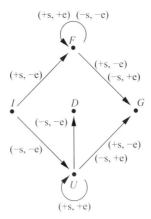

Figure 10.4. An example of an adversarial planning problem.

Now consider how an adversarial environment agent can take advantage of the possibility for the system agent to reach a dead end from U. Since the system agent may end in D, when executing $-s$ in U, it is reasonable for the environment agent to assume that the system agent will always execute $+s$ in U. But now the environment agent can prevent the system agent from ever reaching the goal by always choosing action $+e$, so the system agent should completely avoid the path through U.

This example domain illustrates how an adversarial environment agent can act purposefully to obstruct the goal achievement of the system agent. We will use it in the following sections to explain our algorithm. A solution, guaranteeing that G is eventually reached, is $\pi_s = \{\langle I, +s\rangle, \langle F, +s\rangle, \langle F, -s\rangle\}$.

10.3.1. The Algorithm

We use a generic procedure $\text{PLAN}(\mathcal{I}, \mathcal{G})$ for representing nondeterministic planning algorithms that produce state-action tables as solutions. The algorithms only differ by the definition of the function computing the precomponent ($\text{PRECOMP}(C)$).

> **function** $\text{PLAN}(\mathcal{I}, \mathcal{G})$
>
> $SA \leftarrow \varnothing;\ C \leftarrow \mathcal{G}$
>
>   **while** $\mathcal{I} \not\subseteq C$
>
> $SA_p \leftarrow \text{PRECOMP}(C)$
>
>   **if** $SA_p = \varnothing$, **then return** *failure*
>
>   **else** $SA \leftarrow SA \cup SA_p$
>
> $C \leftarrow C \cup \text{STATES}(SA_p)$
>
>   **return** SA

The procedure performs a backward breadth-first search from the goal states to the initial states. In each step, the precomponent SA_p of the set of states C covered by the plan is computed. The precomponent is a state-action table forming a partition of the final plan with relevant actions for reaching C. If the precomponent is empty, a fixed point of C has been reached that does not cover the initial states. Since this means that no plan can be generated that covers the initial states, the algorithm returns *failure*. Otherwise, the precomponent is added to the plan and the states in the precomponent are added to the set of covered states.

A space and time efficient implementation of the procedure uses Ordered Binary Decision Diagrams (OBDDs) (Bryant, 1986) to represent sets and mappings. An OBDD is a compact representation of Boolean functions. Thus, states and actions are represented by bit vectors, and sets of states and actions are encoded by OBDDs representing their *characteristic function*. The set operations intersection, union, and complement translates into conjunction, disjunction, and negation on the corresponding characteristic functions.

The procedure can be used to synthesize *weak, strong cyclic*, and *strong plans* (Cimatti et al., 2003) in domains where the effect of uncontrollable actions is modeled implicitly as nondeterminism of controllable actions. An execution path of a strong plan is guaranteed to reach states covered by the plan until a goal state after a finite number of steps is reached. An execution of a strong cyclic plan is also guaranteed to reach states covered by the plan or a goal state. However, due to cycles, it may never reach a goal state. An execution of a weak plan may reach states not covered by the plan, it only guarantees that some execution exists that reaches the goal from each state covered by the plan. A limitation of these solutions when nondeterminism is caused by uncontrollable actions of an adversarial environment is that they are optimistic in the sense that they assume the environment to be friendly. For instance, a valid strong cyclic plan for the example problem is

$$\pi_s = \{\langle I, +s\rangle, \langle i, -s\rangle, \langle U, +s\rangle, \langle F, +s\rangle, \langle F, -s\rangle\}.$$

Given an adversarial opponent in our example domain, this plan may enter a livelock in state F, since the environment agent may choose only to execute action $-e$. Thus, strong cyclic plans may loop indefinitely in adversarial domains.

The Strong Cyclic Adversarial Precomponent. A valid adversarial plan ensures that the environment agent, even with complete knowledge of the domain and the plan, is unable to prevent the goal states to be reached. We formalize this idea in the definition of a *fair state*. A state s is fair with respect to a set of states C and a plan SA if, s is not already a member of C and for each applicable environment action, there exists a system action in SA such that the joint action leads into C.

Definition 10.6 (Fair State). A state $s \notin C$ is fair with respect to a set of states C and a plan SA iff $\forall a_e \in \mathrm{ACT}_e(s) . \exists \langle s, a_s \rangle \in SA, s' \in C . \langle s, \langle a_s, a_e \rangle, s' \rangle \in \mathcal{R}$.

For convenience, we define an *unfair* state to be a state that is not fair. The adversarial precomponent is a strong cyclic precomponent (Cimatti et al., 2003) pruned for unfair states. In order to use a precomponent for OBDD-based nondeterministic planning, we need to define it as a Boolean function. We first define a Boolean function representing the transition relation $T(s, a_s, a_e, s') = \langle s, \langle a_s, a_e \rangle, s' \rangle \in \mathcal{R}$. A core computation is to find all the state-action pairs where the action applied in the state can lead into a set of states C. This set of state-action pairs is called the *preimage* of C. The preimage of joint actions is

$$\mathrm{JPREIMG}(C)(s, a_s, a_e) = \exists s' . T(s, a_s, a_e, s') \wedge C(s')$$

By abstracting environment actions, we get the preimage of system actions

$$\mathrm{PREIMG}(C)(s, a_s) = \exists a_e . \mathrm{JPREIMG}(C)(s, a_s, a_e)$$

We can now define a Boolean function representing the state-action pairs of a plan *SA* for which the state is fair with respect to a set of states *C*:

$$\text{FAIR}(SA, C)(s, a_s) = SA(s, a_s) \wedge \neg C(s) \wedge$$
$$\forall a_e.[\text{ACT}_e(s, a_e) \Rightarrow \exists a_s. SA(s, a_s) \wedge \text{JPREIMG}(C)(s, a_s, a_e)]$$

where $\text{ACT}_e(s, a_e) = \exists a_s, s'. T(s, a_s, a_e, s')$. The strong cyclic adversarial precomponent (SCAP) is computed by iteratively extending a set of candidate stateaction pairs and, in turn, pruning the following:

- State actions that can reach states not covered by the current plan or the states in the candidate.
- State actions of states that are unfair with respect to the currently covered states.

The computation of the precomponent terminates either if the pruned candidate has reached a nonempty fixed point or if it is impossible to extend the candidate further. In the latter case, the returned precomponent is empty.

Definition 10.7 (SCAP). The strong cyclic adversarial precomponent of a set of states *C* is the set of state-action pairs computed by function SCAP(*C*).

function SCAP(*C*)
1 *wSA* ← ∅
2 **repeat**
3   *OldwSA* ← *wSA*
4   *wSA* ← PREIMG(*C* ∪ STATES(*wSA*))
5   *wSA* ← PRUNE(*wSA*, *C*)
6   *SCA* ← SCAPlanAux(*wSA*, *C*)
7 **until** *SCA* ≠ ∅ ∨ *wSA* = *OldwSA*
8 **return** *SCA*

function SCAPLANAUX(*startSA*,*C*)
1 *SA* ← *startSA*
2 **repeat**
3   *OldSA* ← *SA*
4   *SA* ← PTUNEOUTGOING(*SA*, *C*)
5   *SA* ← PRUNEUNFAIR(*SA*, *C*)
6 **until** *SA* = *OldSA*
7 **return** *SA*

function PRUNEOUTGOING(*SA*, *C*)
1 *NewSA* ← *SA*\PREIMG($\overline{C \cup \text{STATES}(SA)}$)
2 **return** *NewSA*

function PRUNEUNFAIR(SA, C)
1 $NewSA \leftarrow \emptyset$
2 **repeat**
3      $OldSA \leftarrow NewSA$
4      $FairStates \leftarrow C \cup$ STATES($NewSA$)
5      $NewSA \leftarrow NewSA \cup$ FAIR(SA, $FairStates$)
6 **until** $NewSA = OldSA$
7 **return** $NewSA$
PRUNE $(SA, C)(s, a_s) = SA(s, a_s) \wedge \neg C(s)$
STATES(SA)(s) = $\exists a_s \cdot SA(s, a_s)$

For an illustration, consider the first candidate of SCAP(G) shown in Figure 10.5a. Action $-s$ would have to be pruned from U since it has an outgoing transition. The pruned candidate is shown in Figure 10.5b. Now there is no action leading to G in U when the environment chooses $+e$. U has become unfair and must be pruned from the candidate. The resulting candidate is shown in Figure 10.5c. Since the remaining candidate is nonempty and no further state-action pairs need to be pruned, a non-empty strong cyclic precomponent has been found.

The generic nondeterministic planning algorithm using the SCAP precomponent returns the following strong cyclic adversarial plan for the example problem

$$\pi_s = \{\langle I, +s \rangle, \langle F, +s \rangle, \langle F, -s \rangle\}$$

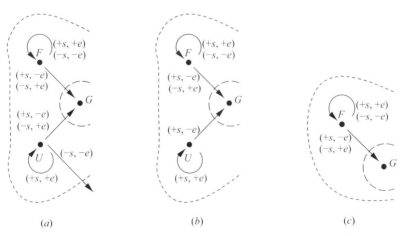

(a) (b) (c)

Figure 10.5. (a) The first candidate of SCAP(G), for the example shown in Figure 10.4. (b) The candidate pruned for actions with outgoing transitions. (c) The remaining candidate pruned for unfair states. Since no further state-action pairs are pruned, this is the strong cyclic adversarial precomponent returned by SCAP(G).

This plan corresponds to the plan that we earlier argued would guarantee goal achievement by avoiding the state U.

10.4. ACTION SELECTION STRATEGIES

A strong cyclic adversarial plan guarantees that no intelligent environment can choose a plan that forces executions to cycle forever without ever reaching a goal state. In principle, though, infinite paths never reaching a goal state can still be produced by a system that "keeps losing" to the environment. However, by assuming the system selects randomly between actions in its plan, we can show that the probability of producing such paths is zero.

Theorem 10.1 (Termination of Strong Cyclic Adversarial). By choosing actions randomly from a strong cyclic adversarial plan π for the adversarial planning problem $\mathcal{P} = \langle \mathcal{D}, \mathcal{I}, \mathcal{G} \rangle$, any execution path will eventually reach a goal state.

Proof. Since all unfair states and actions with transitions leading out of the states covered by π have been removed, all the visited states of an execution path will be fair and covered by the plan. Assume without loss of generality that n strong cyclic adversarial precomponents were computed in order to generate π. Due to the definition of precomponent functions, we can then partition the set of states covered by π into $n+1$ ordered subsets $C_n, \ldots, C_0$, where $\mathcal{I} \subseteq C_n$, $C_0 = \mathcal{G}$, and C_i for $0 < i \leq n$ contains the states covered by precomponent i. Consider an arbitrary subset C_i. Assume that there were m iterations of the repeat loop in the last call to PRUNEUNFAIR when computing precomponent i. We can then subpartition C_i into m ordered subsets $C_{i,m}, \ldots, C_{i,1}$ where $C_{i,j}$ contains the states of the state-action pairs added to *NewSA* in iteration j of PRUNEUNFAIR. Due to the definition of FAIR, we have that the states in $C_{i,j}$ are fair with respect to π and the states C given by

$$C = \bigcup_{k=1}^{j-1} C_{i,j} \cup \bigcup_{k=0}^{i-1} C_i$$

By flattening the hierarchical ordering of the partitions $C_n, \ldots, C_0$ and their subpartitions, we can assume without loss of generality that we get the ordered partitioning $L_T, \ldots, L_0$ where $L_0 = C_0$. Given that actions are selected uniformly in π, the fairness between the states in the levels guarantees that there is a nonzero probability to transition to a state in $L_{i-1}, \ldots, L_0$ from any state in L_i. Consequently, an execution path only reaching states covered by π will eventually reach a state in L_0.

10.5. EXPERIMENTAL EVALUATION

The performance of the strong cyclic adversarial planning algorithm is evaluated in two domains. The first of these is a parameterized version of the example domain shown in Figure 10.4. The second is a grid world with a hunter and prey. All experiments are carried out using the BIFROST 0.7 search engine on a Pentium III Redhat Linux 7.1 PC with 500 MHz CPU and 512 MB RAM. Total CPU time is measured in seconds and includes time spent on allocating memory in the OBDD software library and parsing the problem description.

10.5.1. Parameterized Example Domain

The parameterized example domain considers a system and environment agent with actions $\{+s, -s, l\}$ and $\{+e, -e\}$, respectively. The domain is shown in Figure 10.6. The initial state is $\mathcal{I} = \{I\}$ and the goal states are $\mathcal{G} = \{g_1, g_2\}$. Progress toward the goal states is made if the signs of the two actions in the joint action are different. At any time, the system agent can cause a switch from the lower to the upper row of states by executing l. In the upper row, the system agent can only execute $+s$. Thus, in these states an adversarial environment agent can prevent further progress by always executing $+e$. Figure 10.7 shows the total CPU time and the size of the produced plans of the strong cyclic algorithm compared with the strong cyclic adversarial algorithm. Due to the structure of the domain, the length l of a shortest path between the initial state and one of the goal states grows linearly with the number of states. Since each of the two algorithms at least must compute l preimages, their complexity is at least exponential in the number of Boolean state variables. The experimental results seem to confirm this. In this domain, there only is a small overhead of generating adversarial plans compared to nonadversarial plans. The quality of the produced plans, however, is very different. For instance, the strong cyclic adversarial plans only consider executing $-s$ and $+s$, while the strong cyclic plans consider all applicable actions. The strong cyclic adversarial plan is guaranteed to achieve the goal. In contrast, the probability of achieving the goal in the worst case for the strong cyclic plan is less than $(\frac{2}{3})^{N/2-1}$, where N is the number of states in the domain.

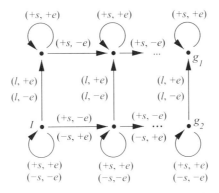

Figure 10.6. The generalized example domain shown in Figure 10.4.

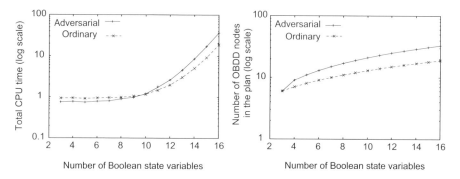

Figure 10.7. Results of the parameterized example domain.

10.5.2. Hunter and Prey Domain

The hunter and prey domain consists of a hunter and prey agent moving on a chess board. Initially, the hunter is at the lower left position of the board and the prey is at the upper right. The initial state of the game is shown in Figure 10.8. The task of the hunter is to catch the prey. This happens if the hunter and prey at some point are at the same position. The hunter and prey move simultaneously. They are not aware of each others moves before both moves are carried out. In each step, they can either stay at the spot or move like a king in chess. However, if the prey is at the lower left corner position, it may change the moves of the hunter to that of a bishop (making single step moves). This has a dramatic impact on the game, since the hunter then only can move on positions with the same color. Thus, to avoid the hunter, the prey just have to stay at positions with opposite color. A strong cyclic adversarial plan therefore only exists, if it is possible for the hunter to find a plan that guarantees that the prey never gets to the lower left corner. A strong cyclic plan, on the other hand, does not differentiate between whether the hunter moves like a king or a bishop. In both cases, a "friendly" prey can be caught.

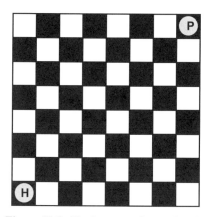

Figure 10.8. The hunter and prey domain.

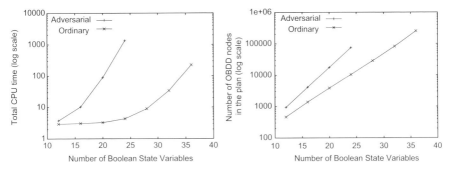

Figure 10.9. Results of the hunter and prey domain.

We consider a parameterized version of the domain with the size of the chess board ranging from 8×8 to 512×512. Figure 10.9 shows the total CPU time and the size of the plans produced by the strong cyclic algorithm compared to the strong cyclic adversarial algorithm. In this domain, strong cyclic adversarial plans are larger and take substantially longer time to generate than ordinary strong cyclic plans. The strong cyclic adversarial algorithm spends more than 4000 seconds for problems with 28 Boolean state variables or more. However, as discussed above, it is nontrivial, if there exists a strategy of the hunter that guarantees that the prey never succeeds in reaching the lower left corner. Thus, we may expect these plans to be computationally harder than strong cyclic plans.

Our experimental evaluation shows that the relative complexity difference between synthesizing adversarial and non-adversarial plans is problem dependent. For some problems, the structural difference between adversarial and non-adversarial plans is so little that there only is a small overhead of synthesizing adversarial plans. For other domains, however, this structural difference is significant and may cause adversarial plans to be hard to synthesize relative to non-adversarial plans.

10.6. EQUILIBRIA IN MULTI-AGENT PLANNING

In this section, we introduce a more general framework for multiagent planning. We explicitly specify all of the agents goals, and introduce the solution concept of multiagent planning equilibria that accounts for all of the agents goals. The definitions and concepts presented in this section are not bound to any particular planning algorithm or language. The reader may find it easier to look at some of the examples given in Section 6.2 before moving to the formalization given below.

10.6.1. The Formalization

We start by formalizing the notion of a multiagent planning problem that explicitly enumerates all of the agents' goals.

Definition 10.8 (Multi-agent Planning Problem). Let $D = \langle S, n, A_{i=1...n}, R \rangle$ be a multiagent planning domain. A multi-agent planning problem P for D is a tuple $\langle D, I, G_{i=1...n} \rangle$, where $I \subseteq S$ is the set of possible initial states and $G_i \subseteq S$ is the set of goal states for agent i.

Recall the doorway example shown in Figure 10.3. The goal states for agent A are $G_A = \{1, 3\}$ and for agent B are $G_B = \{2, 3\}$. The initial state set is the singular set $\{0\}$.

We can now formalize our notion of a plan as a state-action table. We actually define multiple concepts increasing in strength. These concepts formalize some of the intuitive discussion from the previous section about whether a plan has one or more of the following properties:

- The possibility of reaching the goal
- A guarantee of reaching the goal
- A guarantee of reaching the goal in a finite number of steps

These concepts and their formalization are inspired by and highly related to Cimatti and colleagues' single-agent solution concepts (Cimatti et al., 2003). They are also strongly related to the properties of the adversarial planning algorithm described in Section 10.3.1.

Definition 10.9 (Multi-agent Planning Solutions). Let D be a multi-agent planning domain and $P = \langle D, I, G_{i=1...n} \rangle$ be a multi-agent planning problem. Let π be a complete joint state-action table for D. Let $K = \langle Q, T \rangle$ be the execution structure induced by π from I. The following is an ordered list of solution concepts increasing in strength.

1. π is a *weak solution* for agent i if and only if for any state in I some state in G_i is reachable.
2. π is a *strong cyclic solution* for agent i if and only if from any state in Q some state in G_i is reachable.
3. π is a *strong solution* for agent i if and only if all execution paths, including infinite length paths, from a state in Q contain a state in G_i.
4. π is a *perfect solution* for agent i if and only if for all execution paths $s_0, s_1, s_2 \ldots$ from a state in Q there exists some $n \geq 0$ such that $\forall_i \geq n, s_i \in G_i$.

A state-action table's strength STRENGTH(D, P, i, π) is the largest number whose condition above applies for agent i. If no conditions apply, then STRENGTH$(D, P, i, \pi) = 0$.

For our doorway domain, the joint state-action table is a strong cyclic solution for both agents but not strong (i.e., it has a strength of 2 for both agents). This means that there is a path to the goal from any reachable state. But there are also paths that do not include either agents' goal states, and so it is not a strong solution for either agent.

The plans from the soccer domain can also be described under this solution framework. The plan that handles the nondeterministic agent B is a strong cyclic solution since a goal state is always reachable but there are infinite execution paths where agent A does not reach the goal (e.g., if agent B holds indefinitely). For the teammate case, the plan is a perfect solution since it is guaranteed to reach the goal in three steps and remain there. The same is true for the situation where agent B's goal is to have the ball scored in the southern square. In the adversarial case, the plan is only weak since some execution paths result in losing the ball and failing.

Notice that the adversarial planning algorithms also give similar guarantees. For example, a strong cyclic adversarial plan along with *any* plan by the other agent has a STRENGTH of 2. Likewise, an optimistic adversarial plan along with *any* plan by the other agent has a STRENGTH of 1.

These solutions define what it means for one agent to be successful given a joint state-action table. The goal of planning from one agent's perspective is to find a plan that has the highest strength given the plans of the other agents. But the other agents' selection of a plan is equally contingent upon the first agent's plan. This recursive dependency leads to the main contribution of this section: multi-agent planning equilibria.

Definition 10.10 (Multi-agent Planning Equilibria). Let $\mathcal{D}$ be a multi-agent planning domain and $\mathcal{P} = \langle \mathcal{D}, \mathcal{I}, \mathcal{G}_{i=1...n} \rangle$ be a multi-agent planning problem. Let π be a complete joint state-action table for $\mathcal{D}$. Let $K = \langle Q, T \rangle$ be the execution structure induced by π from $\mathcal{I}$. π is an equilibrium solution to $\mathcal{P}$ if and only if for all agents i and for any complete joint state-action table π' such that $\pi_{j \neq i} = \pi_j$,

$$\text{STRENGTH}(\mathcal{D}, \mathcal{P}, i, \pi) \geq \text{STRENGTH}(\mathcal{D}, \mathcal{P}, i, \pi')$$

That is, each agent's state-action table attains the strongest solution concept possible given the state-action tables of the other agents.

Note that our example joint state-action table for the doorway domain is *not* an equilibrium. Both agents A and B currently have strength 2, but B can achieve a strength of 4 by choosing a different state-action table. Specifically, B should select the wait (W) action from the initial state and the go (G) action in state 1.

10.6.2. Examples

To make the concept of planning equilibria clearer, we will examine it in a number of illustrative domains. We first examine the doorway domain along with a couple of variants. We then consider a domain representation of the children's game Rock–Paper–Scissors, and finally we reexamine the various plans in the soccer domain.

10.6.2.1. Doorway Domain. We gave above an example joint state-action table that is not a multiagent planning equilibria for this domain. An equilibria is the following state-action tables:

$$\pi_A = \{\langle 0, G\rangle, \langle 1, W\rangle, \langle 2, G\rangle, \langle 3, W\rangle\}$$
$$\pi_B = \{\langle 0, W\rangle, \langle 1, G\rangle, \langle 2, W\rangle, \langle 3, W\rangle\}$$

In this case, agent A goes through the door while agent B waits and then follows through the door. This is a perfect plan for both agents, and so obviously no agent can achieve a higher strength with a different state-action table. Similarly, the symmetric tables where agent B goes through the door while agent A waits is also an equilibrium. There is an additional equilibrium,

$$\pi_A = \{\langle 0, G\rangle, \langle 0, W\rangle, \langle 1, W\rangle, \langle 2, G\rangle, \langle 3, W\rangle\}$$
$$\pi_B = \{\langle 0, G\rangle, \langle 0, W\rangle, \langle 1, G\rangle, \langle 2, W\rangle, \langle 3, W\rangle\}$$

Here both agents nondeterministically decide between going through the door and waiting. This results in a strong cyclic solution for both agents; however, given this state-action table for the other agent, no strong or perfect plan exists for either agent. So this is also an equilibrium although obviously inferior to the other equilibria where both agents have higher strength plans. In game theory, such a joint strategy is called Pareto-dominated.

Collision Variation. Consider a variation on this domain where collisions (when both agents choose G) result in the robots becoming damaged and unable to move. In this case, the first two state-action tables above remain equilibria, but the third inferior table no longer is an equilibrium. This joint plan is now only a weak solution for both agents since there is a possibility of never achieving the goal. Each agent can also change to a different plan where it waits for the other agent to get through the door, thus achieving a strong cyclic plan and a higher strength.

Door Closing Variation. Finally, consider that one agent entering the room sometimes causes the door to close behind it. Once the door is closed, it cannot be opened and the doorway cannot be used. In this case, the same two joint plans are again an equilibrium but now they have different strengths for the different agents. The first joint state-action table is a strong plan for agent A, but only a weak plan for agent B, though it can do no better. The second is just a symmetry of this.

10.6.2.2. Rock–Paper–Scissors. Consider a planning domain representation of the children's game Rock–Paper–Scissors. Each agent simultaneously chooses one of rock (R), paper (P), or scissors (S). The winner is determined by a cyclic rule: Rock loses to paper, paper loses to scissors, scissors loses to rock. Figure 10.10

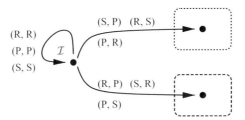

Figure 10.10. Rock–Paper–Scissors as multi-agent planning.

gives the enumeration of states, transitions, and goals for this planning problem. In this case, there is a unique planning equilibrium where each agent's state-action table contains every action. This joint plan is a weak solution (strength 1) for both agents, and neither agent can switch to a different plan and get a higher strength. This plan is analogous to the game's game-theoretic equilibrium, which randomizes evenly between all three actions (Fudenberg and Levine, 1999).

10.6.2.3. Soccer Domain. Let us reconsider the soccer-like domain. We presented three distinct planning problems where agent A's goals remained constant, but agent B's goals varied from having identical goals to A, opposing goals to A, and a subset of A's goals. The example plans described for these situations, if we add in the implied plan for agent B, are all equilibria to their respective multi-agent planning problems. In the teammate case and the overlapping goal case, the equilibrium is a perfect solution for both agents. So, obviously, no agent can switch plans to improve on this solution. In the adversarial case, it is a weak solution for both agents, and neither agent can improve on this strength. This formalization of the planning equilibrium matches well with our intuitive notions of "good" plans in multi-agent domains.

10.6.3. Discussion

Multi-agent planning equilibria is a powerful concept both to understand the multi-agent planning problem and as a viable solution that accounts for the other agents' goals. It also opens up many avenues for further research and understanding. We consider a couple important questions this work raises.

The first issue is the number of planning equilibria. The doorway domain shows that multiple equilibria may exist. Although some equilibria are obviously inferior to others, the equilibria framework need not define a single solution plan. For example, the two symmetric equilibria in the doorway domain are not equivalent, nor is one Pareto-dominant. This calls for coordination or communication mechanisms to decide between competing equilibria. In addition, some problems may have no equilibria. Figure 10.11 gives an example planning problem with no equilibrium. Each agent has three possible complete state-action tables, and a simple examination of the nine possible pairs will demonstrate that none are equilibria. Still, large

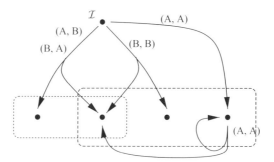

Figure 10.11. Domain without an equilibrium.

classes of domains can be proven to have equilibria (e.g., team domains and adversarial domains.) Other interesting questions are whether equilibria exist in most useful domains, or what are reasonable plans when they do not exist.

Second, this work presents a compelling framework and solution concept for multi-agent planning, and it gives the challenge of devising methods to find planning equilibria. The equilibrium definition involves universal quantification over an agent's possible plans, which is exponential in the number of states, which in turn is exponential in the number of state variables. This is intractable for anything but domains with a handful of state variables. This opens up a new realm of interesting issues relating to efficiently finding equilibria under different planning frameworks, languages, or classes of domains. Planning for agents with identical goals is essentially a single-agent planning problem. In the case of adversarial settings, the algorithm in Section 10.3 can find half of an equilibrium plan. These special-case algorithms are evidence that multi-agent planning equilibria can be both a theoretically and practically powerful concept.

One possible general technique for finding equilibria comes from game theory's alternating-move Cournot process (Fudenberg and Levine, 1999). The basic idea would be to start each agent with a complete state-action table, and then each agent alternates finding a new complete state-action table that achieves the highest strength given the other agents' tables. This process is stopped if none of the agents can improve on their current table given the others, and so the joint state-action table is an equilibrium. This technique may hold some promise. If the initial state-action tables include all available actions to the players, this process could actually find equilibria in every example presented in this chapter. Details of the technique, such as how to select among equally strong state-action tables, would be critical to an actual implementation and analysis. This does, though, give insight into how a planning equilibrium may be found in practice.

10.7. CONCLUSION

In this chapter, we explored the importance of accounting for all of the agents' goals when planning in a multi-agent environment. We examined this fact in planning for an adversary, and we also defined a more general solution concept that explicitly depends on all of the agents' goals.

We contributed a new OBDD-based nondeterministic planning algorithm, namely, strong cyclic adversarial planning. This algorithm naturally extends the previous strong cyclic algorithm to adversarial environments. We have proven and shown empirically that, in contrast to strong cyclic plans, a strong cyclic adversarial plan always eventually reaches the goal.

We also presented a formalization of multi-agent planning where all agents have individually specified goals and introduced the concept of a multi-agent planning equilibrium. This is the first known solution concept that explicitly accounts for the goals of all the agents. This provides a unifying framework for considering planning in multi-agent domains with identical, competing, or overlapping goals. It also opens up many exciting questions related to practical algorithms for finding equilibria, the existence of equilibria, and the coordination of equilibria selection.

ACKNOWLEDGMENTS

This research is sponsored in part by the Danish Research Agency and the United States Air Force under Grants F30602-00-2-0549 and F30602-98-2-0135. The views and conclusions contained in this document are those of the authors and should not be interpreted as necessarily representing the official policies or endorsements, either expressed or implied, of the Defense Advanced Research Projects Agency (DARPA), the Air Force, or the US Government.

INTRODUCTION TO CHAPTER 11

The previous nine chapters all dealt with planning. The order of these chapters is not arbitrary. In Chapters 2 and 3, Hommel and Hoc discussed theories about humans that plan their own activities. Chapter 4 (Jorna), Chapter 5 (Gazendam), and Chapter 6 (McKay and Wiers) changed focus by studying humans that plan organizational processes. As was noted several times, planning for yourself differs from planning for others. In the subsequent chapters by van Wezel (Chapter 7), Kroon and Zuidwijk (Chapter 8), and Sauer (Chapter 9), the focus again changed. Organizational processes were still the topic, but now the planning entity was not a human but an artifact (software or algorithm). And in Chapter 10, Bowling et al. discuss an example of the remaining kind of planning: an artificial entity (a robot) that plans his own activities. In Chapter 18, we will compare and analyze the differences and similarities of these kinds of planning, and the basis for much of the findings there can be found in the next chapter by Meystel.

Meystel focuses on planning as problem solving within intelligent systems. He provides us with a basic framework that is applicable to all intelligent systems, whether they be human or machine. Three basic starting points underlie the analysis of Meystel. First, each intelligent system functions according to the Elementary Loop of Functioning (ELF) consisting of sensing in the external world, making judgments, generating behavior, and implementing the behavior in the external world. Although the background of much of Meystel's observations is in autonomous robots, he claims the ELF holds for all intelligent systems. Second, each system functions hierarchically at multiple levels of resolution in order to handle

Planning in Intelligent Systems: Aspects, Motivations, and Methods, Edited by Wout van Wezel, René Jorna, and Alexander Meystel

complexity. By necessity, ELFs at different levels of resolution are congruent by means of generalization and instantiation. In other words, an intelligent system will usually solve a problem stepwise by (a) recursively searching a region in which the best solution will be found and (b) looking at that region in more detail. Third, intelligent systems are capable of simulation. This means that they can envision possible events in the external world, reason about what decisions they or other actors would make, and imagine the effects that their actions would have.

These three building blocks of intelligent reasoning provide the means to describe how planning takes place no matter who or what the planning entity and planned entity are. The simulation of effects of plans can be done by humans as well as by artificial systems. Furthermore, one's own actions can be simulated as well as the actions that others would perform. Using ELFs at multiple resolutions provides the means to describe planning at multiple hierarchical levels—for example, organization, task, and individual (see also Chapter 7). In the conclusions in Chapter 18, we will use the threesome ELF, multiresolutional problem solving, and the ability to reason about possible future events to compare and analyze the various kinds of planning.

11

MULTIRESOLUTIONAL REPRESENTATION AND BEHAVIOR GENERATION: HOW DOES IT AFFECT THE PERFORMANCE OF AND PLANNING FOR INTELLIGENT SYSTEMS

ALEXANDER MEYSTEL

Drexel University, Philadelphia, PA 19104

11.1. INTELLIGENT SYSTEMS: INVOKING THE DESIGN SPECIFICATIONS

Multiple characterizations of intelligence and intelligent systems have been collected in Meystel and Albus (2001) and Albus and Meystel (2001). The meanings of the terms are instilled by our associations with human beings, or even with living creatures in general. The desire to create similar properties in constructed systems has determined the tendency to anthropomorphize both faculties and function gadgets and systems belonging to various domains of application. This starts with categorizing objects into *actors*, or *agents* that produce changes in the state of the world by developing *actions*, and the *object of actions*—that is, the objects upon which the *actions* are applied. *Actions* are the descriptions of activities developed by *actors*.

Planning in Intelligent Systems: Aspects, Motivations, and Methods, Edited by Wout van Wezel, René Jorna, and Alexander Meystel

Yet, this does not give an opportunity to exhaustively, or even simply and adequately describe intelligent systems in the terms of design specifications. One reason for this is that specifications are never complete. They are never fully appreciated and understood either. We first give four examples.

Example 11.1. Spot Welding Robot. These are the features that are frequently claimed:

- It has basic intelligence. The meaning of this assertion does not extend beyond the simple salesman decorative phrase. Even in universities, courses on binary logic and circuits with switches are called "Introduction to Intelligent Systems." Even a wall switch can be characterized as a carrier of intelligence of making the light "on" or "off."
- Programmed for a specific task. Certainly, the number of programmed functions is very limited in a robot. Yet, probably, any number of functions being preprogrammed is evidence of intelligence (the one of the designer, the ability of the system to store information, "to memorize things." Memorization what should be done in response to a particular command is considered a certain level of animal intelligence.
- No operator is needed. When you see this statement in the list of welding robot specifications, you should raise a question what is the quality of the results of this welding compared with welding by a human operator. Even now, the feedback systems are limited in their ability to eliminate the need in a good professional welder.
- Can only perform repetitive tasks without deviation from programmed parameters. No doubt about it: One should realize that this statement is rather a disclaimer than a claim of intelligent functioning.

Example 11.2. Mars Sojourner. The word "Mars" evokes associations of machines of the future. However, no real faculties of intelligence could be listed (the welding robot was substantially "smarter").

- Remote control should not be considered a property of intelligence, because by extending the distance between the operator and the machine we do not make the machine smarter, or more sophisticated, or capable of dealing with unexpected situations, or interpret illegible commands.
- Light elements of autonomy. The specifications do not expand on this concept ("autonomy"). Probably, the ability to provide a feedback control can be (arguably) interpreted as an element of autonomy.
- Can perform a variety of maneuvers (limited). This property seems to be similar to having preprogrammed functions.
- A particular maneuver is performed independently. All available maneuvers should be discussed and evaluated separately. Indeed, the maneuver of "turning

right" and the maneuver "make a K-turn in a particular tight space" require different levels of intelligence: from zero up to the substantial degree of perception-based autonomy.

- Not capable of deciding what to do next (no planning). Absence of "planning" in most cases means no intelligence.
- Problem: There is a 10-minute communication lag between Earth and Mars (and probably, the guy does not know what to do next and does not dare to think about it!)

Example 11.3. Bomb Disposal Robot. This is another case of the device for remote performance (extension of capabilities of a human operator). These robots are called "intelligent" because of the importance of their mission and also because they should be able to reproduce human movements with absolutely no mistakes.

- Remote operation with high accuracy creates the aura of respect. If the "increase in accuracy" could be claimed, this would be a very conspicuous demonstration of (an) intelligence.
- Requires a very skilled operator. This is a claim of the intelligence of the operator. However, it is an important assertion that this remote control device cannot substantially detriment the skills of the operator.
- Incapable of acting on its own (does not have any intelligence at all). This is related to most of the remote controlled devices.

Example 11.4. Intelligent Network. An example of the communication system with intelligent systems as the nodes of the network is shown (Dawidovic, 2002). The description of the communication network containing intelligent systems demonstrates (a) the concepts of closure within the intelligent node, (b) the multi-resolutional distribution of information, and (c) that heterarchical networks are characteristic for this example. This was not observed in the Examples 11.1 through 11.3. Thus, one might assume that our dissatisfaction with Examples 11.1 through 11.3 was based upon an existing difference between classes of systems as far as the level of their intelligence is concerned.

In our further discussion, we will call all objects including *actors* and *objects of action* by the term **entity**. The *action* can be characterized and represented within the control theory as a discrete event (DE). The concrete choice of the phenomena and objects as actors, DE and objects of action are determined by a combination of temporal and spatial resolution that are characteristic for a particular level. The structure of the object at a particular level of resolution is shown in Figure 11.1. The structure of the DE for a level of resolution can be introduced in a similar way. The structure is a recursive one because each "part" can be substituted by a similar structure, and the representation of objects will evolve into the high-resolution domain. Similar evolution is possible into the low-resolution domain. Figure 11.1 should be used for representing each of the parents.

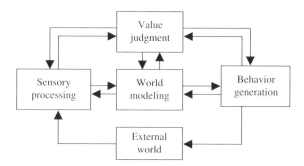

Figure 11.1. Elementary loop of functioning (ELF) for representing an intelligent control system.

Thinking about constructed intelligent systems brings the designer and/or researcher to the idea of autonomous robots that are capable of understanding incomplete assignments (commands) and can apply the general intention of a command to a particular situation at hand.

How about conveying the command by telling the robot: "Go to the window and alert me if something unexpected appears in the street." Apparently, this is the performance of an intelligent system that is justifiably expected to emerge in a market of intelligent systems soon enough.

11.2. ELF: ELEMENTARY LOOP OF FUNCTIONING

The Law of Closure. Closure is the foremost property of intelligent systems (IS) and should be satisfied at all levels of its architectures. The elementary loop of functioning (ELF) of an IS can be defined at each level of the IS and should be consistently closed in each communication link between the subsystems of ELF as described in Meystel and Albus (2001), Albus and Meystel (2001), and Messina and Meystel (2000). Otherwise, the system consists of *objects* interconnected so as to satisfy the specifications. Unlike the classical "feedback loop," ELF is not focused upon deviation from the goal: It is focused upon the goal. As soon as we can explain for a particular scene and/or for a particular situation what are the objects considered to play the roles of actors (who are the *actors*?), what *actions* do they develop, and upon which *objects of action* their actions are applied, the ELF can be found (Figure 11.1). The subsystems of this loop determine basic properties of the intelligent system. *Sensors* (S) are characterized by their ultimate resolution and their scope of the information acquisition per unit of time. In *sensory processors* (SP), the primary clustering is performed (together with organizing and bringing all available data to the total correspondence), and the resolution of the clustered entities is evaluated. The *world model* (WM, or knowledge representation repository, KRR) unifies the recently arrived and the earlier stored information within one model of representation that determines the values of resolution for its subsets. Mapping the couples (goal, world model) into the sets of output commands is performed by *behavior generation* (BG) for the multiplicity of available *actuators* (A), and it actually maps the resolutions of the *world model* into resolutions of the output trajectory.

Closure of all units $(\ldots \rightarrow W \rightarrow S \rightarrow SP \rightarrow WM \rightarrow BG \rightarrow A \rightarrow W \rightarrow \ldots)$ is determined by the design of the system and the learning process of defining the languages of the ELF subsystems. The First Fundamental Property of Intelligent Systems Architectures (the property of the existence of intelligence) can be visualized in the law of forming the loop of closure. Closure is satisfied and the consistency of ELF holds when the unity of language (vocabulary and grammar) holds for each communication link between every pair of ELF subsystems. Regardless of the nature of the intelligent system and regardless of the object-oriented domain under consideration, the structure of closure is always the same.

Statistical Closure. Functioning of the ELF cannot be impeccable because of noise and disturbances arriving from the external world and because of the errors of computations within ELF itself. Thus, as a result of mistakes, the property of closure is not satisfied impeccably and therefore we should expect that only statistical closure can be satisfied reliably. The phenomenon of the time span between "cause" and "effect" is observed for both the closure of "in-level" functioning and the closure that is demonstrated for a reduction of resolution when the information is integrated bottom-up. The following observations are important for interpreting reported information on the events in a system:

- The existence of closure at the lower (generalized) levels of resolution was considered a surprise and was even given a special term: *statistical closure* (Pattee, 1987). Every closure is a statistical closure, including closure reflected by the *in-level* functioning as well as closure obtained as a result of generalization of information to the lower level of resolution.
- Obviously, there are no cause–effect events that happen simultaneously: If absence of the time span was reported, there is no basis for considering particular events of having "cause–effect" relationships.
- The time of any event is an integration of realistic or statistical results of the potential multiple experiments. This should be realized while determining whether the events are separated by a time span.

These observations can often protect us from a misinterpretation, but not in all cases. Even consistent ELFs are capable of generating misinterpretations related to causality. For example, it is known that 80% of patients with hip fracture die within a year not because of hip fracture complications but because they had another condition that brought them to fall (they had it prior to the hip fracture). Obviously, many of these misinterpretations ascend to the formation of the languages for the subsystems of an ELF. The purpose may not always be explicitly represented, but it can always be explicated by conducting the analysis of causes. Properly organized planning activities are rooted within the well-organized etiological information base. Although etiological analysis (contemplation of possible and plausible causes) is always presumed, it is seldom performed.

11.3. LEVELS OF RESOLUTION AND INTENTIONALITY: MULTIRESOLUTIONAL ANALYSIS

We need to reduce the complexity of computations by grouping similar units (entities) into a larger formation that can satisfy the definition of an entity, too. The words "we need" are italicized, because the issue of "need" is a critical one in the very emergence of this phenomenon: multiple levels of resolution. The needed entity is a "lower-resolution" entity: The details of high resolution are unified together under a specific objective (representing the intentionality). The totality of lower-resolution entities forms a "lower-resolution world" of representation, or the "lower-resolution level." Within the "scope of the world" considered at the higher resolution, we will have a much smaller total number of entities, and for the same computational power, the scope of the world or the efficiency of computation can be substantially increased. This is why we are searching for the lower-resolution entities and producing generalizations.

There are numerous ways of representing information at the level of resolution. The most widespread method presumes performing a sequence of the following steps, also called the Algorithm of Information Organization:

Step 1 (S1). Hypothesizing the entities within particular boundaries separating them from the background and other hypothesized entities. More than one hypothesis for an entity is expected to be introduced.

Step 2. Searching for confirmation of the hypotheses {H} of Step 1 (HS1) and for evaluation of current probabilities of HS1 being the "truth."

Step 3. Hypothesizing a meaning of the hypothesized entities [$HS1_i \rightarrow M_i$]; call this couple "a meaningful entity." More than one hypothesis for the meaning is expected to be introduced. A list of hypotheses is supposed to be formed and maintained.

Step 4. For each hypothesized meaningful entity [$HS1_i \rightarrow M_i$] determine its plausible goal (objective) {[$HS1_i \rightarrow M_i$] under the goal G}. This is associated with the ability to hypothesize (and verify) the "cause–effect" couples and hypothesize a purpose of events (etiological analysis).

Step 5. For each {[$HS1_i \rightarrow M_i$] under the goal G} determine its relationships with other meaningful entities of the "scene," going back to Steps 1 and 2. Consider different hypotheses; converge to the maximum values of the probabilities evaluation.

Step 6. Constructing the entity–relation network for the scene (ERN_j).

Step 7. Search within ERN for island candidates for generalization into the entities of lower resolution. As the candidates have been determined, consider them to be hypotheses of entities with particular boundaries similar to those mentioned in Step 1 and GO to Step 2. If no new islands emerged, EXIT from the recursive search from entities and GO to Step 8.

Step 8. Submit the hierarchy of ERNs to the World Model.

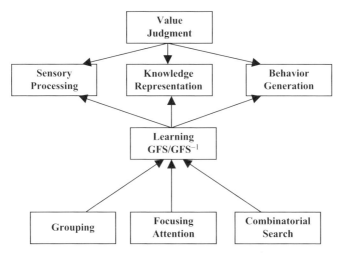

Figure 11.2. Combinatorics of GFACS/GFACS^{-1} functioning.

The multiplicity of steps allows for receiving multiple combinations of functioning as shown in Figure 11.2. This sequence of steps can be applied to any type of information representation including visual, audio, verbal, and so on. The sequence can be illustrated by using a set of multiresolutional images (see Morrisons, 1982). One can see that some logic is presumed to be introduced for dealing with the multiresolutional information at hand. Unlike the standard propositional and predicate calculi, this logic has to predicate various situations and related subsituations by their goals (purposes, objectives), being important factors in the process of inference. We believe that an *intensional logic of entities* (Objects) can be proposed to be used in the system with multiresolutional ELFs. An important role is here allocated for the concept of alternative worlds (possible situations or possible worlds). This can be considered an extension of the known notion of the "world model." This allows looking for alternatives to the actual course of events in the world. On the other hand, adding the hypothesized purposes makes all statements intentional as well.

Intentional logic with explicated intentionality should become a basis for the introductory multiresolutional analysis (MRA). The latter can be defined as constructing the representation and using it for purposes of decision making. Using computational algorithms leads to taking advantage of representing the world as a set of subworlds, each with its individual scope and level of detail.

The possibility and the need for MRA is looming as can be seen from Dennett's (1996) multiresolutional stance where the property of considering many levels of resolution is being associated with intentionality:

> To explain the intentionality of a system, we simply have to decompose the system into many, slightly less intelligent, subsystems. These subsystems can also be broken down into many more or less intelligent subsystems. We can continue to break up these larger systems until eventually we find ourselves looking at individual neurons.

11.4. GFACS AND GFACS^{-1}: GENERALIZATION AND INSTANTIATION BY USING GFACS OPERATOR

The abbreviation GFACS is deciphered as "Grouping, Focusing Attention, and Combinatorial Search." Both the direct set of GFACS (that performs *generalization*) and the inverse set of GFACS^{-1} (that performs the *instantiation*, or finds the components of previously generalized object, or process) consist of simpler procedures that perform elementary *grouping, focusing attention*, and *combinatorial search*. Most of the elementary procedures that are being applied for computer vision and other intelligent activities are, in turn, based upon the GFACS set of procedures. "Windowing," broadly applied for the selection of the representative part of the information set, is actually performing the operation of searching (combinatorially): CS. Masking irrelevant subentities actually is focusing attention, FA. On the other hand, the same "windowing" contains a substantial component of "masking" and thus can be interpreted as "focusing attention" (FA) in addition to searching combinatorially (CS). All algorithms of "clustering" can justifiably be interpreted as "grouping" (G). Algorithms of "filtering" are "focusing attention" (FA). Hypothesizing the entity in an image always includes all of the above: G, FA, CS.

Level-to-Level Transformation: Generalizing by GFACS. The Algorithm of Information Organization presented above (see Section 11.3) contains the operator of generalization explained in Step 7. It can be further decomposed into the following substeps:

- Search within ERN for island candidates for generalization into the entities of lower resolution. This search will include forming tentative combinations of high-resolution entities into subentities that allow for a consistent interpretation. Logic of this "combinatorial search" includes "focusing attention" upon the results of tentative "grouping" and determining properties of these tentative groups and their relations with each other.
- As the candidates have been determined, finalize "grouping" and label the groups.
- Consider these groups to be hypotheses of entities and analyze the corresponding ELFs.

Generalization is finished after the newly synthesized entity becomes a part of the corresponding ERNs and ELFs.

Instantiations: GFACS^{-1}. In the inverse procedure, the system is searching for the plausible decomposition of a legitimate entity (that received a status of "group" as a result of prior "generalization"). Usually, this requires performing several acts of rehypothesizing the components of entities and grouping them again to check whether they retain the meaning declared earlier. This features the following steps of instantiation: The hypotheses of instantiations are arriving from the adjacent level of lower resolution after hypothesizing (i.e., are arriving from "above") and should be verified by repeating the procedure of "grouping" at the level of higher resolution (i.e., "below"). Figure 11.3 illustrates the richness of procedural capabilities that is achieved in a single ELF as a result of GFACS/CFACS $^{-1}$ functioning. From Figure 11.3, one can see that the generalization/instantiation couple can be considered a core of unsupervised learning (Meystel and Albus, 2001). This determines the need of a special logic of inference.

Advanced Logic Induced by Generalization/Instantiation. Indeed, the standard set of the inference tools is taken from the arsenal of propositional calculus and predicate calculus of the first order. It builds inference processes that are primarily based on the undeniable conclusions that can be made from having a set of properties known for a particular class (ergo: belonging to this class), or conclusions that can be made from the fact of belonging to a particular class (ergo: having properties characteristic for this class). Forming new objects and/or new classes, growth of object and events hierarchies are new phenomena in the domain of inference.

Even more powerful are the capabilities linked with new abilities to infer the purpose, construct hierarchies of goals, and imply cause–effect relationships. In Figure 11.3, it is demonstrated that the introduction of logical capabilities and the enhancement of the ability to infer emerges as a result of the incorporation of computational capabilities based upon equipping the system gradually by the new computational tools, including rule selection, forming combinations of rules, forming new rules (as a result of learning), grouping the rules, forming combinations of the states and the context.

Unlike the symbolic logic that is supposed to be precise, free of ambiguity and clear in structure, the logic of multiresolutional system of ERN is limited in precision by the demands for associative disambiguation (see Section 11.7) that spread into the adjacent levels of resolution (no "logical atomism" is presumed).

Learning, Imagining, and Planning. The Tools and Skills of Anticipation. Since the etiology enters the discussion, it would not be an exaggeration to state that

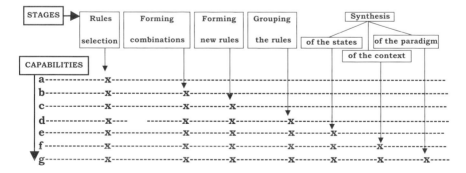

Figure 11.3. Logical properties acquired at different stages of the intelligence development.

the GFACS/CFACS^{-1} couples induce the knowledge of a future and give the intelligent system the skill of anticipation. Thus, learning invokes imagining "what if" and various alternatives are being simulated to exercise the alternatives for estimating the future and planning the future as it was described and illustrated (Meystel, 2000).

11.5. INTELLIGENT ARCHITECTURES AND THE KINDS OF INTELLIGENCE THEY EMBODY

More About Multiresolutional Combinatorial Search. Complexity in a multiscale Decision Support System depends on the number of levels of resolution. In Figure 11.4 the linkage between computational complexity and the number of levels of resolution is shown for the problem of path planning. The example with DEMO III would clarify how the levels of resolution differ in their parameters. Actually, lowering the resolution bottom up fits within the hierarchy of command, and the increase of the planning horizon and re-planning interval helps to bring the best properties of the system to a realization. The following are 4-D/real-time control system (RCS) specifications for the planning horizon, re-planning interval, and reaction latency at all seven levels (see Table 11.1).

Existing Architectures. Multiresolutional processing is one of the important features of the reference architectures promulgated by NIST (National Institute for Standards and Technology) for application in intelligent systems. It is easily recognizable that heterarchies similar to the one shown in Figure 11.5 fit within the paradigm of large complex systems including intelligent autonomous robots, unmanned power plants, smart buildings, and intelligent transportation systems including large

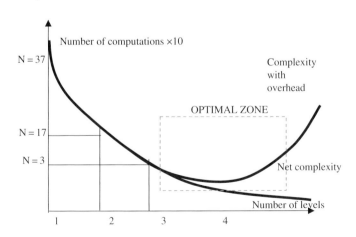

Figure 11.4. Computational complexity is reduced by introduction of additional levels of resolution.

TABLE 11.1. Specifications for Parameters of Multiresolutional Planning in DEMOIII (Meystel and Albus, 2001)

Level	Planning Horizon	Re-plan Interval	Reaction Latency
1 Servo	50 msec	50 msec	20 msec
2 Primitive	500 msec	50 msec	50 msec
3 Subsystem	5 sec	500 msec	200 msec
4 Vehicle	50 sec	5 sec	500 msec
5 Section	10 min	1 min	2 sec
6 Platoon	2 hr	10 min	5 sec
7 Battalion	24 hr	2 hr	20 sec

automated bridges. It fits perfectly also to the DOD systems of command, control, communication, and intelligence. It is characteristic of heterarchies that, while having top-down and bottom-up hierarchical components, are not hierarchies. Heterarchies are not tree architectures. However, in each heterarchy, a multiplicity of hierarchies can be discovered and employed including heterarchies of top/down-bottom/up processing, heterarchies of "in-level" processing, and others. Similar relationships and transformations are characteristic of entity–relation networks (ERN) that are obtained from semantic networks for using in knowledge representation repositories.

11.6. TESTING THE PERFORMANCE AND INTELLIGENCE

Kinds of Intelligence. Concerning general intelligence many and equally unclear definitions are known from the literature. We refer here to two definitions that seem to be both applicable and instrumental ones.

Definition 11.1 (Internal). An intelligent system has the ability to act appropriately in an uncertain environment, where an appropriate action is that which increases the probability of success, and success is the achievement of behavioral subgoals that support the system's ultimate goal" (Albus, 1991).

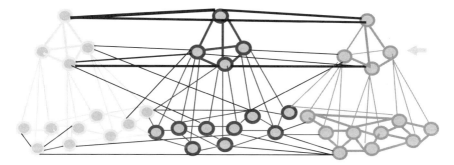

Figure 11.5. A community of interacting heterarchies.

Definition 11.2 (External). "Intelligence is a property of the system that emerges when the procedures of direct and inverse generalization (including focusing attention, combinatorial search, and grouping) transform the available information in order to produce the process of successful system functioning" (Meystel, 2000).

These definitions should be supplemented by a description of the trade-off to be achieved by any intelligent systems no matter whether they are oriented (a) toward the goal achievement (articulation of functioning), (b) toward sustaining oneself, realization of self, or (c) toward "feeling better" (avoiding paradoxes, antinomies, contradictions). The trade-off is illustrated in Figure 11.6. The general lessons of the existing experience consist in testing the performance of systems. This can be especially informative if we succeed in explicating the interrelatedness of performance and intelligence. The need to explicate this phenomenon can be formulated as follows.

Performance can be different for an IS and a non-IS. Breaches in communication that are taken care of by human operators in a non-IS are covered by automated subsystems in an IS. However, all expected cases might not be reflected in the pre-programmed menu. Thus, learning is the only way to compensate for inadequate pre-programming. Nevertheless, the failures in representation are expected to endanger the quality of operation even in the most intelligent system. Another cause of the inevitable failures is the incomplete or inadequate goal specifications.

We already discussed the fact that the main advantage of intelligence is the ability to deal with unexpected predicaments. Because of this, the main advantage power that intelligence brings to the system is unspecified (and probably not specifiable). It should not be forgotten that many things are *not* and frequently *cannot* be specified.

Testing Generic Capabilities of Intelligent Systems. The following capabilities can be checked and statistically validated via experimental testing in a functioning system on-line.

- All terms from the assignment are supposed to be supported by high-resolution, low-resolution, and associative knowledge.
- Each level must demonstrate its ELF consistency. Standard testing scenarios can be constructed and exercised.

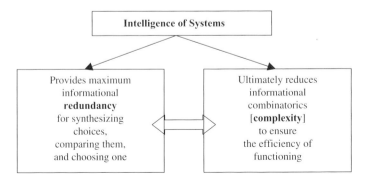

Figure 11.6. Trade-off achieved by intelligence of systems.

- Functioning presumes the ability to work under incomplete assignment (including incomplete statement of what should be minimized or maximized).
- Functioning should be possible under not totally understandable assignment.
- Functioning should be possible under not totally interpretable situations.

Skills that Can Be Checked Off-Line. Off-line testing allows for enabling better preparedness of the system for critical situations.

- Multiple channels of enabling functions (allows working under the condition that a part of the capabilities is disabled).
- The existence of the internal model of the world that is capable of planning and developing "the best" responses to the changing environment and the dynamic situation by using a simulated system.
- The ability to learn from experience of functioning: Learning can be verified prior to future situations of functioning.
- The ability to judge the richness of MR ontologies. Indeed, the vocabularies and grammars of all levels allow for shaping and refining them prior to real operation.
- The ability to re-plan and/or adjust plans is important when the original ones are no longer valid; this is another crucial aspect that must be evaluated.

Understanding Commander's Intent. One of the important functions of intelligence is restoring the intent of the node that is the source of the goal. In other words, a system with intelligence ought to have the capability to understand its higher level—that is, the lower resolution level (where the "supervisor" or "commander" is situated). The incoming "goal" is frequently presented rather as an abstract combination of terms. The system should be capable of supplementing the submitted command with additional information (sometimes, contextual) that helps to generate more specific plans internally. This is almost equivalent to creating the goals for itself: The elements of future autonomy emerge in the intelligent systems as tools of performance improvement.

11.7. CONDUCTING DISAMBIGUATION

We have addressed the need to verify the consistency of statements generated at a level by their compatibility with the adjacent levels above and below. Clearly, they should not violate generalizations creating objects and events of the level above, and the results of decomposition of the entities and events at a level of consideration should not violate consistency of the higher-resolution representation and decision making.

The following capabilities are expected from the system of disambiguation.

1. Hypotheses should be formulated of generalizations for the upper level and instantiations for the lower level. These hypotheses are obtained by GFACS

and GFACS^{-1} within the context of the situation represented by the ELFs of three adjacent levels under consideration.

2. When the hypotheses generation is completed (a ranked list of hypotheses is constructed), the consistency of the hypotheses should be verified along with the adjacent ith, $[i+1]$th, and $[i-1]$th levels. Verification can be done by checking whether the closure of each ELF still holds. This operation is an example of creating a "Tarsky's hierarchy" that should eliminate the possible contradictions that are expected because of Godel's theorem of incompleteness.

3. The other hypotheses on the lists should also be checked. We should observe what is the change in the situation when the hypothesis is changed. Are the ELFs closures violated and what is the relative compatibility of other hypotheses to the BG solutions contemplated?

In Figure 11.7, an example of an ambiguous situation is presented. The right alternatives are hypothesized, and the disambiguation is easily performed by the human viewers even not familiar with the original phenomenon (e.g., see http://www.ournet.md/~mythorm/LochNess.htm).

One can easily check that the activities for disambiguation performed in a natural way are similar to those presented in the above list. One can hypothesize the connectivity of all segments of the expected body of a living creature (H1), hypothesize the radius of the "underwater" part (H2), verify the H1 with available information of possible living creatures, verify H2 by comparing it with the visible radius of the part above the surface of "water," and so on.

11.8. MULTI-RESOLUTIONAL METRICS

The concept of value judgment introduced by Albus (2000) and expanded by Meystel and Albus (2001) and Albus and Meystel (2001) is expected to be a useful component of measuring the performance of systems—in particular, intelligent systems.

Figure 11.7. Ceramics "Loch Ness Monster" installed on a polished wooden surface.

Although this concept seems to be almost trivial, coinciding with the concepts of *cost/reward* applied in one set of research results and repeating the premises of *utility function* from another set of research results, it has more obscurities than can be allowed for applying this concept in practical cases. In this work, the issues are listed that should be clarified, properly stated, and resolved before using the concept of *value judgment* would be scientifically justified.

We have some light problem with computing and using the issues of *value* and *value judgment* (VJ). Indeed, a value judgment system can evaluate what is good and bad and what is important and trivial, and it can estimate cost, benefit, and risk of potential future actions. However, it is difficult to find objective evaluators. Indeed, scalar evaluators need a tool for assigning weights to various components of VJ. Vector evaluators intend to escape the need for dealing with the idea of relative importance of the components of the vector. Actually, neither is achieved in practical cases. This is why:

- There are many factors of preferences that cannot be easily transformed into physical values or money.
- Preference that is delivered by emotions is still a subject of discussion. It is unclear how to assign a numerical value to the degree of preference brought by one's loyalty. Why? Among others, the following factors should be taken into account:
  - Even if the problem of computing the value judgment is resolved at a particular level of resolution, one cannot present any meaningful techniques of consolidating all measures into a single numerical value.
  - The previous problem might be considered easier if at least we knew where to cut off building representations of the next level of resolution from above and from below. These are silly but "fundamental" considerations: The limit of generalization from above is achieved when we stop blurring particular details since it affects the interpretation. The limit of instantiation below is considered to be achieved when we do not know how to make a further decomposition of the representation.
  - One of the areas containing results and intuitions related to multiresolutional analysis is not sufficiently analyzed by scientists in multiresolutional representation and behavior generation: the on-standard analysis of Robinson (1974). He stops decimating space at the indifference zone level (the limit of tessellation from below).

11.9. GLOBAL SEMIOTICS OF VIRTUAL AGENTS: SIMULATING COMPLEX SYSTEMS

11.9.1. Semiotics and Agents—Our Tools of Simulation

The *Encyclopaedia Britannica* defines **simulation** in "industry, science, and education, as a research or teaching techniques that reproduce actual events and processes under test conditions." Certainly, the term "reproduce" is a stretch: Most of the simulation techniques do not aspire to achieve more than just approximate this actual event/process. The *Encyclopaedia Britannica* says: "Developing a simulation is often a highly complex mathematical process. Initially a set of rules, relationships, and operating procedures are specified, along with other variables." That's true. Simulation starts with developing a model as a combination of diversified tools. Undoubtedly, this process is not bound by just "mathematics." Anything goes—just make the system of these tools approximate well. Once the contrivance of the model is here, we can do with it much more than we intended. As the *Encyclopaedia Britannica* promises: "The interaction of these phenomena creates new situations, even new rules, which further evolve as the simulation proceeds."

The description of simulation with its goal, its tools, and its promises is amazingly similar to the description of intelligence. The latter has been developed in living creatures as a mechanism of simulation. It is intended to reproduce events and processes with maximum similarity; it requires a model, which usually employs a system of knowledge representation. Once emerged, it helps us to create images of possible worlds, simulate unexpected situations in these worlds, and derive new rules, theories, and laws. It is commonplace for it to use signs and symbols to model, and it develops possible worlds that are quicker and cheaper than the real world; thus it can help to learn the future before it happens, it allows to anticipate, and it warns, alerts, and tempts with all consequences of these unsettled verbs. Of course, this requires more than mathematics: It requires the amalgamation of **Semiotics** (including mathematics). So, it looks like semiotics (including mathematics) is the proper toolbox applied by our intelligence. More people are interested in semiotics than in mechanisms of intelligence. If you have doubts, check the cyberspace. However, only a small fraction of these people links semiotics with what semiotics really is: the science of intelligence. Before the nineteenth century, intelligence was a nonconstructive subject, it was an introspective issue. The twentieth century has demonstrated that intelligence is the core of all issues, while semiotics is a tool of understanding and constructing Intelligence. This role of semiotics generally follows from its definitions: We just should read them properly.

The ubiquitous *Encyclopaedia Britannica* says also that semiotics "is the study of signs and sign-using behavior, including the use of words, of tone of voice, tempo, or drawl, of body motions and gestures and animal communication." Although this definition appeals to and is understood by laymen, it contains the spirit of the semiotic essence: semiotics is a science of signs. Why signs? The signs transmit compressed information, or messages; the messages contain meanings concerning the events and processes; the meanings are constructed and produced by intelligence from signs and the inner knowledge; now, we are equipped for further simulating activities.

So, signs and their processing (the body of semiotics) embody intelligence (the machinery for simulation). Some would even say that they embody "Life and Intelligence," since the manifestations of these phenomena are very similar as far as signs are concerned. In Figure 11.8, the types of semiotics are shown that depend on the general strata of human activities where semiotic is used. Then the descriptive

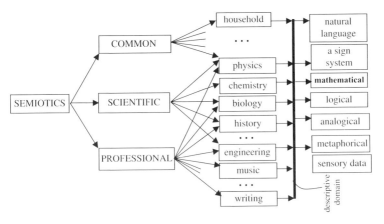

Figure 11.8. Types of semiotics.

domains within these areas are shown. Finally, it boils down to the five major groups of methodological tools employed within semiotics.

Yet, I would like to be fair to the rest of nature. Inanimate objects produce signs, too. They even can be considered signs of themselves. The process of communication between two atoms of hydrogen and one atom of oxygen leads to a formation of the molecule of water. Does this look like a stretch? I would not say so: The laws of the formation and communication of messages in this example are similar to the corresponding laws typical for living creatures.

11.9.2. The Worlds Are Multimodal

As soon as we apply semiotic methodology for simulating the world, we should be proficient in the formal techniques that semiotics employs: natural language, mathematics, logic, the skill of finding analogies, and the skill (art) of constructing metaphors. However, there is one additional important distinction between the information units and their semiotic carriers. This distinction is related to sensory modalities of communication associated with all information units represented via semiotic entities. Indeed, information units can be communicated in natural language by using various modalities: oral (the source of the message is talking, the recipient is listening), written (the source is writing, the recipient is reading), visual (the source of language moves lips, the recipient reads the lip movements; both the source and recipient use a sign system based upon natural language), tactile (natural language statements are transmitted via system of tactile signs). Obviously, the worlds are encoded by using a combination of sensory modalities. As we can see from Figure 11.9, the descriptive domain is irrelevant.

11.9.3. The Worlds Demonstrate the Property of Closure

Semiotic systems for understanding the worlds are shown on the right side of Figure 11.9. Protolanguages encode the diversity of sensory information so that

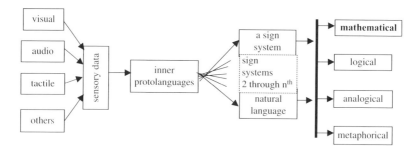

Figure 11.9. Transformation of sensory modalities into semiotic representations.

unity could be achieved in the world representation. Obviously, using only proto-languages for understanding and communicating this understanding is insufficient, and a variety of sign systems emerge: mathematical, logical, analogical and meta-phorical languages. All of them offer their tools of generalization and inference. All of them allow for representing the world's closure as the template for registering consistency of the world, as the initial source of causal explanations of the empirical reality.

Closure in a space of tasks such that this occurs is an objective property of real systems (Albus and Meystel, 2001; Meystel and Albus, 2001). This is shown in Figure 11.10. The closure emerges because the world is sensed (*sensors*), encoded and perceived (*sensory processing*), and represented and reasoned (*world model*) not only for communication, but in order to generate behavior (*behavior generation*) and enable actions (*actuators*) that eventually change the *world*. If closure would not hold, the goal-oriented activity would not be possible. The phenomenon of closure reflects the thesis of rationality underlying the very thesis of the need for simulation. The elementary loop of functioning (ELF) was already illustrated in Figure 11.1. If ELF cannot be demonstrated, then information of the system, its components, its

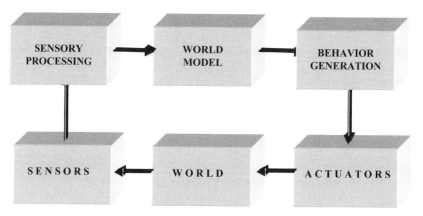

Figure 11.10. Semiotic closure.

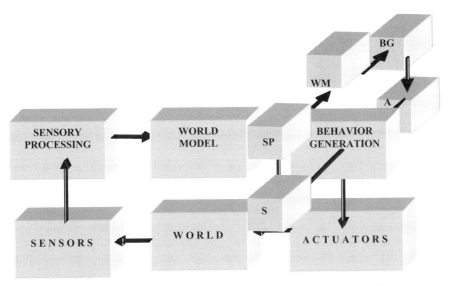

Figure 11.11. ELF for a system shown with ELF of one of its modules.

variables, and its goals must be incomplete. Semioticians call this loop the loop of semiosis. In this loop the process of learning and interpretation is run, and the convergence of it should be achieved.

Thus, as we reason about the world and its processes, the property of closure should be satisfied. Thus, as we construct a simulation system, the property of closure should also be satisfied. In Figure 11.10, a structure of closure is shown as an ELF for the case of intelligent controller simulated functioning.

The modules *actuators-world-sensors* are to be substituted by a simulation system that receives control commands from the intelligent controller and generates simulated sensor inputs for it. For a simulation system, the components of a system's functioning associated with value judgment should be explicated and made available for observation. Certainly, the functioning of ELF's modules can be described adequately only if ELFs can be constructed for its modules, too. An ELF within an ELF is shown in Figure 11.11 for the behavior generation module.

11.9.4. The World is Not Flat: It is Multi-resolutional!

Through the millenia, people used to benefit from the phenomena of larger and smaller pictures, like *bird's-eye view*, and so on. However, only recently we have arrived at the scientific awareness of the following: We see the same things and recognize different objects and phenomena depending on the spatial and temporal resolution of our interest. Mandelbrot's (1982) fractals came as a surprise, because suddenly it was realized that at different scales there is always more than the unequipped eye can see. All signs pertain to some particular scale of consideration. Semiotics offers its views also in scales: It is a multiscale, or multiresolutional phenomenon, too (Meystel, 1995c).

Therefore, no matter whether you are a follower of Frege's analysis of dual correspondence between the sign and the object, or you consider Peirce's triangles scientifically adequate, do not forget that each triangle pertains to its own resolution. Each scale encompasses a particular world with its vocabularies, grammars, goals, and pursuit of happiness pertaining to this particular scale.

Each scale has its system of signs and is related to the adjacent scales by the set of rules that represent relationships of generalization (bottom-up) and instantiation (top-down) that exist between the scales. In Figure 11.12, an example with two scales of resolution is demonstrated. It is equivalent to the simultaneous existence of two ELFs, one at a high resolution and one at a low resolution (two loops of semiosis). It is possible to demonstrate that all paradoxes emerge because of squeezing together different scales of the world—that is, putting together different levels of resolution into a unified flat crowd of things that actually do not belong to each other. Kant's double-sided table of antinomies (1794) has the scale-related interpretation deeply ingrained in it, although it might take a semiotician to recognize this. The logical inference should always appreciate the fact of multiscale character of the world: Slowly we are approaching understanding of Godel's Theorem of Incompleteness, but the phenomena emerging in self-referential systems (Smullyan, 1992) boil down to the multiscale world representations. What is logical and consistent at one level of resolution might be totally intolerable at another. The loop of semiosis can be constructed only separately at each level. It is imperative not to confuse multiple resolutions for the ELF of interest (the process to be simulated) and the set of all ELFs

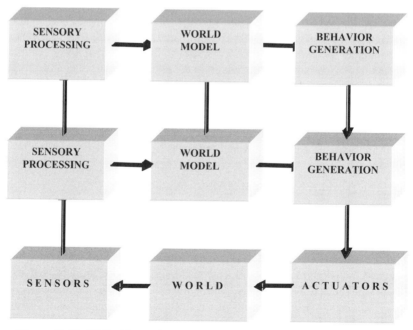

Figure 11.12. ELF with two levels of resolution (two scales of representation).

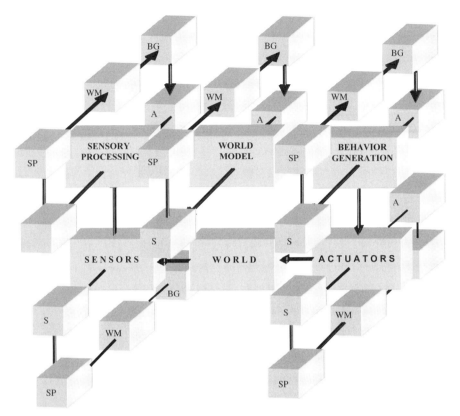

Figure 11.13. ELF of a particular level with the full set of its ELFs of the corresponding modules.

for the modules of the main ELF. In Figure 11.13, all ELFs of interest for the modules are shown: ELF_S, ELF_{SP}, ELF_{WM}, ELF_{BG}, and ELF_A.

11.9.5. Properties of Semiotic Agents

In his set of lectures, Kaufmann (1996) talks about autonomous agents in a system-theoretical way having in mind to establish the biophysical fundamental of life. His autonomous agents are living semiotic creatures as simple as cells, maybe groups of cells, and as complex as animals, maybe even as populations of animals.

Life and intelligence, science and engineering, literature and art, journalism and cinema, physics and chemistry, computers and internet, stock market and politics— these are just domains that serve as metaphor generators. They pursue the truths by the virtue of metaphors generation if no regular formal theory is in sight.

Let us concentrate on the special particular tools of metaphor generation: the metaphor of a special type of process with autocatalytic properties. The latter leads to several concepts that are either overlapping or compatible with concepts that are used in the areas of intelligent systems and semiotics (see Figure 11.14).

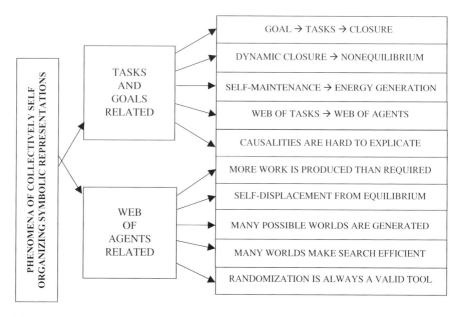

Figure 11.14. The derivative concepts of the collectively self-organizing symbolic representation.

A concept of *task space* entails the concept of *task closure* for an *autonomous agent*. Thus, the *autonomous agent* is driven by its task that allows for determining what is the goal. An *autonomous agent* achieves a new kind of "closure" in a space of "catalytic" and work tasks such that the components of the *agent* are amplified or reproduced and all the tasks are accomplished. Living cells are collectively auto-catalytic systems. The *author* and the *reader* with a new novel are an autocatalytic system generating the truth. This closure means that an *autonomous agent* is a functionally coherent self-sustaining system with a goal. In addition to the strong line of the goal-dependence, Kaufmann emphasizes the issues of consistency, self-consistency, collective self-consistency, and coherence. This means that the issue of efficiency, for example, is some measure of performance (e.g., *autonomous agents* sustainability). This coincides with our evaluation of the role of *value judgment.* Kaufmann attempts to interpret such agents as nonequilibrium Maxwell demons. This esoteric creature symbolizes the need to represent something, which is not very clear for us: the phenomenon of choice. This connection of goal-orientedness and fighting with the Second Law of Thermodynamics is looming in many multiple-agent intelligent architectures.

11.9.6. Knowledge Representation for Multiscale Communities of Agents

The need in building up the system of *world representation* is fundamental in our views (as it should be in a semiotic treatment). It also can be seen fundamental in

Kaufmann's theory, although he never talks about this explicitly. He does not call any collection of information "representation" or "knowledge base," instead he calls it propagatable records, which seems to be a more appropriate term for a biologically inclined system (coalition or a community of agents). For engineering professionals, one might prefer using the term world representation. To extract work from their environments, Maxwell demons must make records of their environments, transform these records, and pay a cost for this transformation.

Work and constraints, therefore, must jointly and self-consistently arise in *agents* and must be parts of their ongoing coherent organization, which cannot be understood otherwise than as an architecture. Records (propagatable records, or world representation) are correlated, coherent macroscopic states usable to extract work. This biological lingo can be considered for us a metaphorical and/or analogical representation which allows for confirming a part of what we are doing now, anyway.

Given a physical definition of an *autonomous agent*, the semantics succeeds in acquiring a physical meaning. Here, Kaufmann alludes to the semiotic concept of relations between the physical objects (i.e., the sign) and the way it is interpreted: "Peirce's triad of signs is present once there are agents." Its self-consistent structure and dynamical logic constitute the embodied "record" of its environment, and its reproduction and proliferation carry out linked work cycles and simultaneously, via mutation and selection, update its record.

This leads to a more general concept that "organization" is fundamentally related to the coordination of matter and energy, which enables and controls the constrained release of energy—since work is to be propagated. Such coordination is achieved, fundamentally, by doing work to create structures that alter the potential barriers involved in the release of energy from components in the system. Work is done to construct the agents that then self-organize into a membrane that is, actually, a decision-making mechanism of applying constraints for making choices.

11.10. EVOLUTION OF INTELLIGENT SYSTEMS WITH PLANNING: WHAT SHOULD BE MEASURED?

11.10.1. Intuitive Approaches to the Concept of Intelligence

An attempt is made to approach the concept of intelligence constructively and from scratch. This analysis and research are motivated by the need of using the results for constructing (primarily, engineering) intelligent systems and agents. For the author, Descartes' problem (of the mind existing separately from the body) simply doesn't exist, because the mind of the constructed machine is undoubtedly produced by its body. Nevertheless, the author doesn't adhere to the technological paradigm alone. Both the examples of intelligence and its architectures will be discussed for all domains shown in Figure 11.15. The goal to construct architectures of intelligence and analyze their evolution can be achieved if a comprehensive definition of intelligence is introduced. It seems meaningful to derive the definition from

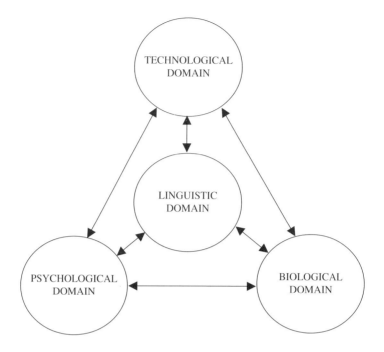

Figure 11.15. Techniques linked with and stemming from the concept of intelligence.

integrating the phenomena characteristic for intelligence. Obviously, they can be demonstrated in relevant systems belonging to all these domains. Interestingly enough, within each of these domains, there are common habits of discussing intelligence. Possibly, this is a result of the fact that all of them depend on the linguistic domain. The main habits of talking about intelligence can be listed as follows:

1. The functioning of intelligence is frequently characterized in anthropomorphic terms of mental conduct.
2. Intelligent activities are attributed to levels of generality (levels of scope).

11.10.2. Redundancy as a Characteristic for Intelligent Control

Cultivating the accepted degree of redundancy is a prerequisite of intelligence. Redundancy of systems is understood as having their resources, components, or properties in abundance, or in excess. This property of redundancy is very important and very characteristic for intelligent systems. They should always be ready to withstand uncertainty, and since the survival is at stake, the property of redundancy helps to minimize the risk of failure. Ruspini (2000) has mentioned a rule: Systems should have more intelligence than needed for solving the particular kind of a problem.[1] Obviously, the same problem can be resolved with a different level of intelligence. Then, the results of this problem-solving process could be used for evaluating the level of intelligence. This level might depend on the level of redundancy.

Although redundancy as a property is evaluated in a negative way (indeed, using more resources than we need actually can be interpreted as wasting resources), only intelligent systems do not fight redundancy, but rather explore, use, and even cultivate the redundancy. Redundancy is the tool for combining and testing new alternatives of decisions and, eventually, novel behaviors. After evolving, an intelligent system develops a mechanism of exploring things within its "virtual reality." Redundancy is becoming a tool for planning and a tool for learning without actually having physical experiences.

Different mental models exercised computationally are a kind of a physical experience when the results of implementation are explored rather than stored from prior experience. They are not taken from one's experience but are rather tentatively explored; for example, one could determine them by predicting.

Autonomous systems should acquire new information by exploring the physical (realistic) and/or the imaginary playgrounds. The following factors are being displayed and they are related to the concept of redundancy:

- Playfulness *seems to be* a property observed in living creatures or linguistic systems that are characterized by a very high level of intelligence. Playfulness of an intelligent system is to be considered a part of the exploration, which is a component of a learning process.

- Redundancy supports various manifestations of the pragmatic property called superficially "just a desire" including all known classical desires that determine foraging and reproductive activities.

- Certainly, speaking about "playful ameba" might be a stretch. However, searching activities are observed even for amoebas (Passino, 2000) and *E. coli* (Parkinson and Blair, 1993) and this allows talking about certain degrees of intelligence even in these classes of living creatures (Kolmogorov, 1956). If we look for an appropriate epithet for an *E. coli*, it would be more appropriate to say "pragmatic *E. coli*" rather than "playful *E. coli*."

11.10.3. Reduction of Complexity Is a Working Technique of Intelligence

How is it possible to cultivate redundancy and yet fight complexity? This paradoxical ability is a hallmark of real intelligence. Practically, it means that the tools of complexity reduction should not curb the combinatorial capabilities of the system. Such a tool exists, consisting of the organization of information in a multiresolutional fashion (Maximov and Meystel, 1993; Meystel, 2000).

---

[1]In an exchange during the panel on Intelligent Control at IJCNN'2000, E. Ruspini commented that probably such a creature as *E. coli* possesses all intelligence it needs for functioning. A. Meystel proposed a paradoxical definition for intelligence that further develops Ruspini's statement: "The system is intelligent if it has more intelligence than it needs."

The need to evaluate and reduce complexity was always clear in computational mathematics, and this led to the concept of ε-entropy, ε-entropy in symbolic form, and techniques of its evaluation (Kolmogorov, 1956). Many elegant mathematical techniques of complexity reduction have been developed [e.g., like in Rackovic et al. (1999)]. Specifications of application domains were also developed; see Weyuker (1998) for software complexity, Boekee et al. (1982) for syntactic complexity, Abu-Mostafa (1986) for complexity of information extraction, and Zames (1979) for information of a control system.

However, using multiresolutional organization of information for complexity reduction was not immediately considered an understandable and desirable tool, although publications (Maximov and Meystel, 1993; Meystel, 2000) helped to clarify the situation. Further explanation of relations between multiresolutional tools of complexity reduction can be found in Meystel (1995a,b).

In all systems (technological, biological, psychological, and linguistic) the formation of multiresolutional representation is a technique of complexity reduction. Even *E. coli* fights the complexity by forming at least two levels of resolution (high resolution—single *E. coli*; low resolution—swarms formed as a result of bacteria gathering in groups (Parkinson and Blair, 1993).

11.10.4. Loop of Semiotic Closure Is the Primary Architecture of Intelligence

The modules of (1) World, (2) Sensors, (3) Perception, (4) World Model, (5) Behavior Generation, and (6) Actuators (see Figure 11.1), connected in a loop of closure, are forming an elementary functioning loop, or ELF (Meystel, 1996; Maximov and Meystel, 1993). The module of World (1) is the ambient environment including a source of information from the process generated by Actuation to be observed by Sensors. This component of the World also consumes the energy submitted by the module of Actuation. If one interprets Figure 11.16 as a general structure of an intelligent vehicle, then the module of the World is the couple of Vehicle-Road [IS A COUPLE Vehicle ↔ Road].

The energy is conveyed through this couple to the body of the moving Vehicle, and the vector of speed is measured for the Vehicle relative to the unit of Road within this couple. In addition to transducing, the information from the domain of the physical reality to the information carrier is accepted by the system of computation. Sensors are a part of additional complicated activities linked with the organization and coordination of testing. These activities are a part of another loop of closure (Messina and Meystel, 2000).

The module of Sensory Processing organizes the information and submits it to the World Model that puts the units of acquired knowledge into a form appropriate for storing and utilization by the module of Behavior Generation. The latter may vary from a simple look-up table to complex devices that explore alternatives of plans by simulating them before submitting their values to the module of Actuation. The simple look-up table would contain the list of control functions $f(t)$ together with previously experienced or expected measures of achievement

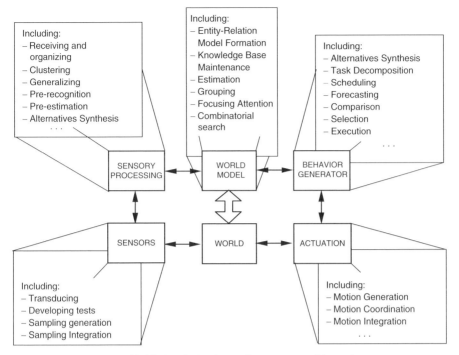

Figure 11.16. Semiotic closure for a system with motion.

$J(f, x, x^*)$ for the given goals $x^*(t)$ and present situations $x(t)$ as couples:

$$x^*(t), \qquad x(t) \to f(t), \qquad J(f, x, x^*) \qquad (11.1)$$

The concept of semiotic closure is not an obvious one. It exceeds the straightforward idea of feedback that can be formulated as follows. In a system, there exists a monitor (a human or an electronic/mechanical device) that compares what is happening at time t, $x(t)$, with some standard of what should be happening $x^*(t)$. The difference or error $\varepsilon t = x(t) - x^*(t)$ is fed to a controller for generating an action by a control function $f(t) = y(t + k)$, which can be applied only at a later time, $t + k$.

Thus, the feedback equation

$$y(t + k) = f[\varepsilon t] = f[x(t) - x^*(t)] \qquad (11.2)$$

presumes some standard value known, some variable compared with this standard, and some device that computes and applies to the system the "feedback compensation." The standard might be assigned as a goal externally, or stored in the module of the World Model. The device that computes the "feedback compensation" can be associated with the module of Behavior Generation. Often, the components of Sensors, Sensory Processing, and World are meant, but not expli-cated. Certainly, this concept should be enhanced substantially to be transformed into the concept of semiotic closure shown in Figure 11.16.

Semiotic closure was anticipated in 1967 by von Bertalanfy (Meystel, 1995c), who considered feedback to be "a special case of general systems characterized by the presence of constraints which led the process in the way of circular causality, thereby making it self-regulating." This loop of *circular causality* was dubbed *semiotic closure* by Pattee in 1973. It was introduced to the analysis of intelligent systems in Albus (1991) and Rock and Palmer (1990). Semiotic closure can be constructed for any domain and any system that exhibit elements of intelligence.

11.10.5. An Entity–Relation Network (ERN) Is a Frequent Form of Constructing the Representation at a Level of Intelligent System

It would be more prudent to say that as a general recommendation we do not know any alternative to an entity–relation network (ERN). Of course, we can approximate an ERN by a multiplicity of tables and approximate each of the tables by an analyti-cal function. We are doing this for the variety of manual activities. Thus, a problem of generalization emerges as a problem of local substitution of large accurate tables by small tables with a larger but still acceptable error. If we do this, then instead of a global gigantic ultimately accurate but practically unobservable ERN, we receive a set of local ERNs $\{ERN_i\}$, $i = 1, 2, \ldots, n$, where 1 is the index (number) of the level with highest resolution and n is the index of the level with the lowest resolution. The system does not have all these levels in its storage because the amount of infor-mation in $\{ERN_i\}$ would substantially exceed the amount of information in its level of highest resolution ERN_1.

The system remembers only levels with middle (average) resolution and selected traces at the level of higher and/or lower resolution. If it requires lower-resolution information, it generalizes the middle-level information as necessary. If it requires higher-resolution information, it instantiates (decomposes) the information top down as requested. The system $\{ERN_i\}$ is a nested system; that is, the conditions of inclusion should be satisfied for the ontologies constructed for the worlds represented at each particular level of resolution. The same conditions should be realistically satisfied for the objects and actions represented at the levels.

Such a system can exist if it is supported by the operators of grouping, focusing attention (selection), searching for combinations of interest (combinatorial search), and the operators that ungroup, defocus, and eliminate the results of search.

Each level of representation has granularity that is a result of generalizing infor-mation from the lower level of higher resolution (Meystel, 1997). Both objects and actions of the real world have their representatives at several (at least at two) levels of resolution and therefore are multiresolutional. The mechanism of obtaining lower-resolution objects and relationships out of higher-resolution objects and relationships is called generalization.

The need for a computational theory of generalization was emphasized by McCarthy (1987). One of the possible algorithms of generalization is demonstrated in Figure 11.17. One can see in that example that the algorithm consists of operators that perform Grouping (G), Focusing Attention (FA), and Combinatorial Search (CS) together (the subscript means the level it works for). We will call GFACS their joint set. Thus, the joint using the computational procedures of grouping, focusing attention, and combinatorial search (GFACS) is inevitable in intelligent systems: the level of generalized information cannot be built otherwise. GFACS generalizes information bottom-up. Decomposition top-down requires an algorithm of instantiation ($GFACS^{-1}$). There exists a vast multiplicity of algorithms belonging to the class of GFACS—for example, ARMA (auto-regressive moving average) (Politis, 1993; Combetes and Pesquet, 1998) or CMRA (convex multiresolutional analysis) (Bangham et al., 1996). $CFACS^{-1}$ has its prototypes, too, such as the Sieve Decomposition algorithm (Meystel, 1985).

Encoding of stored information is done in a multiresolutional fashion too, and this leads to a further reduction of complexity. The mechanism of storing entities is to store their code and regenerate (reconstruct) the required information as necessary. Storing information in the form of DNA is an example of storing multiresolutional system with reconstruction.

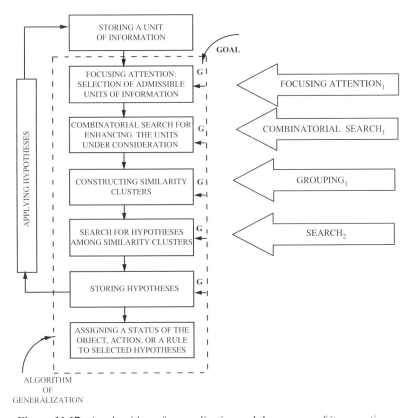

Figure 11.17. An algorithm of generalization and the essence of its operations.

11.10.6. Cost Functions

The need in a reduction of computational complexity would be easy to resolve by abandoning computation. Yet, this cannot be done because the system has a goal to fight for reducing the time and energy that are required to reach the target. This determines the conditions of the optimization process. As far as computational complexity is concerned, the results of optimization are driving the process of forming levels of resolution. The optimization for an *E. coli* sounds like working under the heuristically introduced cost function of foraging (Parkinson and Blair, 1993).

$$J = \frac{E_{\text{consumed}} \pm E_{\text{lost}}}{t_{\text{curr}} - t_0} \tag{11.3}$$

or

$$J = \frac{E_{\text{consumed}}}{E_{\text{lost}} \cdot (t_{\text{curr}} - t_0)} \tag{11.4}$$

Using (11.3) and (11.4) for performance evaluation is a not a very simple matter. The system might actually have many cost functions pertaining to different levels of resolution. This can entail mutually conflicting processes of optimization. Therefore searching for an optimum motion trajectory in the multiresolutional state space would require recursive top-down/bottom-up algorithms of searching.

11.10.7. Resolution

The term *resolution* related to the accuracy of detail in representation, and sensor output is often confused with the term *resolution* from the subsections of logic in artificial intelligence (resolution refutation). Resolution of the system's level is determined by the size of the indistinguishability (indifference) zone (tile) for the representation of goal, model, plan, and feedback law. Any control solution alludes to the idea of resolution, explicitly or implicitly.

Resolution determines the complexity of computations directly, because it determines the number of information units in a representation. In complex systems and situations, one level of resolution is not sufficient, because the total space of interest is usually large and the final accuracy is high enough. So, if the total space of interest is represented with the highest accuracy, the ε-entropy (the measure of its complexity) of the system is very high.

The total space of interest is to be initially with a much lower resolution. Only a subset of interest is considered with even higher resolution, and so on, until the highest resolution is achieved. This consecutive focusing of attention with narrowing the subsets' results in a multilevel task decomposition. The following terms are intermittently used with resolution: granulation, scale. "Granule" is another term for the distinguishability zone (pixel or voxel).

11.10.8. Multiresolutional Representation

The term *multiresolutional representation* is defined as a data (knowledge) system for representing the model of our system at several levels of resolution (or granulation, or scales). In order to construct a multiresolutional (multiscale, multi-granular) system of representation, the process of generalization is consecutively applied to the representation of the higher levels of resolution. As a result of applying the algorithm of generalization to the modules of ELF (see Figure 11.2), the new levels of Sensory Processing, World Model, and Behavior Generation emerge that are attached to the initial ELF as the next "floor" of this structure. If generalization is performed on the modules of the new level, an additional "floor" of the structure would emerge.

11.10.9. Generalization

The term *generalization* is a formation of new entities (groups, classes, assemblies) where the parts to be assembled are not prespecified, and new classes of properties can emerge: synonym (sometimes)—abstraction; antonym—instantiation. Generalization usually presumes grouping (clustering) of the subsets focused upon as a result of searching and consecutive substitution of them by entities of the higher level of abstraction. This is why instead of the term "resolution levels" we use sometimes the expression "levels of abstraction," which means the same as levels of generalization, or levels of granularity. Take the following example. In most of the cases when humans encounter new situations they face the need to create groups. They make groups or assemble together components, which are not specified as parts belonging to each other, and new classes of properties should be proposed on the flight.

It would be instructive to demonstrate how the term *generalization* differs from the terms *aggregation* and *abstraction*. Aggregation is the formation of an entity out of its parts. Each of the parts can also be obtained as a part of the aggregation: synonym—assembling; antonym—decomposition. As an example, the entity is formed out of its parts. Information of belonging is contained in the description of the objects. We will consider this process to be an example of a very simple group formation: We know what is the whole, and we know what are the parts. Assembling of parts into the whole, or formation of an aggregate, is determined by specifications.

Formation of a class of objects which is characterized by the same property, along with labeling this class with the name of this property, is called abstraction: synonyms—class formation and (sometimes) abstraction; antonym—specialization. As an example, the properties, which characterize objects, can be considered objects by themselves. We won't be surprised if one calls kindness an entity. The fact that color is a property belonging to most physical objects of the real world makes it an important scientific and technological entity of a system of knowledge. It is important to indicate that the formation of such entities is possible only by grouping together all similar properties of different objects. A red apple, red ink, red birds, and red cheeks all belong to the class of objects containing "redness."

So, generalization performs aggregation even when parts are not specified. This means that it subsumes the aggregation. It subsumes the abstraction, too. In all cases concerning abstraction the term *generalization* is applicable. Generalization is typically applied when a similarity and observations are discovered, and a general rule should be introduced. The term *abstraction* is inappropriate in this case. Conclusion: Generalization subsumes both aggregation and abstraction. This is a more general procedure of which aggregation and abstraction are particular cases.

11.10.10. Nesting

Nesting is a property of recursively applying the same procedures of multiresolutional knowledge processing by using the operator of processing at a level for consecutively processing information of all levels. The results of Sensory Processing of all levels are nested one within another, World Models are nested one within another, and the decisions generated within the module of Behavior Generation are nested one within another. Levels of a multiresolutional ELF are nested one within another, while the levels continue to function as separate independent ELFs. This separation of levels is a result of a need to reduce the complexity of computations. Thus, instead of solving in one shot the whole problem with the maximum volume of the state space and with the amount of high-resolution details, one may choose to solve several substantially simpler problems that are nested one within another.

11.10.11. Learning

The process of generalization upon the time-varying functions of a control system is called *learning*. It results in creating and constantly updating the multiresolutional system of representation and, thus, in an improvement of plans and feedback control laws. Learning is a component of this multiresolutional knowledge processing. Evolution of knowledge of the system can be demonstrated as shown in Figure 11.18. Obviously, learning is tightly linked with the property of Intelligent Systems of being equipped by the systems of knowledge representation (e.g., the module World Model in ELF). Another question is that the module of representation might not necessarily be physically lumped in one specific place: WM can be distributed over a multiplicity of agents, or otherwise over the physical medium used in the intelligent system.

Updating the World Model and the enhancement of its multiresolutional system of knowledge representation is done by the process of learning, which employs the set of GFACS operators that has been described above. Levels of resolution are selected to minimize the complexity of computations. Planning and determining the beneficial feedback control laws is also done by a joint using of generalization, focusing attention, and combinatorial search (GFACS). The operation of learning was associated with layers: Each layer learns separately. Learning experiences can be organized only by using a multiresolutional structure. Levels are not hard-wired; they are constructed from the information at hand, as is done in neural nets, for example.

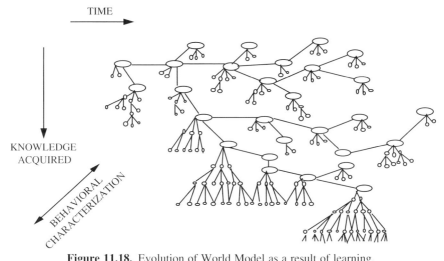

Figure 11.18. Evolution of World Model as a result of learning.

Mathematics of various operators of focusing attention, grouping, and searching usually employed by GFACS algorithms can be found in Sternberg (1982).

One can see from Figure 11.19 that learning in an intelligent system boils down to collecting experiences, applying GFACS to them, and explicating objects, actions, rules, and theories that might be used by the module of Behavior Generation.

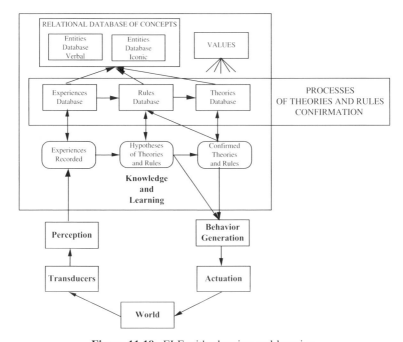

Figure 11.19. ELF with planning and learning.

Combining ELF that acquires experience with imagination gives an opportunity to learn not only from real experiences of acting within the environment but also from the imaginary experiences of simulating within the imagination of the intelligence.

11.10.12. Evolution of Intelligence

In nature, the evolution of intelligence can be demonstrated as the development of the tool of survival. This tool has emerged in order to control systems in better correspondence with changing environmental conditions and with maximum satisfaction of evolving needs. As the complexity of needs grows, in addition to creating ways of their satisfaction, the duty to fight is an equally important task of the mechanism of intelligence. The combined task "*needs satisfaction + computational complexity reduction*" can be considered the major destination of intelligence.

Increasing functionality (for needs satisfaction) together with reducing computational complexity is the performance index that can be used for judging the results of the evolution of intelligence. The evolution of intelligence can be unequivocally interpreted as a development of both the system and its controller. This development allows for increasing the functionality of the system jointly with reduction of its computational complexity. This is why the ability to generalize emerges as the ability to lump together entities of matter and/or information for more effective storing and computation. Generalization is a tool of creating new, abridged systems and their representations, creating representations in generalities, and creating new levels of lower resolution with new metrics or granulation. At the lower level of resolution, the tools of intelligence can afford a larger scope of attention and solve a problem of a larger picture with a longer horizon of planning. So, decision making on any given resolution should be preceded by the pre-planning at a lower resolution level.

The biological models allow us to observe the growth of the degree of intelligence in living forms starting with single-cell organisms, through *E. coli* (Parkinson and Blair, 1993), via substantially more complicated living forms from mollusks to mammals, and concluding with human beings (Fodor, 1987).

A similar evolution can be observed in the domain of technology and in the domain of linguistics. The processes of intelligence evolution extracted from these domains are discussed in a generalized form. One can easily see that the evolution is a "punctuated" one[2] [in the sense of Albus and Meystel (2001)], since the new blocks only occasionally emerge in the architectures of intelligent systems.

11.10.13. Mechanisms of Intelligence: The Real Basis of Planning

Analyses of the processes of structural evolution in the area of intelligence allow for discovering the following mechanisms of intelligence.

- A semiotic closure is the basic structure of intelligence (see also Figure 11.2). It differs from a simple feedback loop because each element of the closure is a source of redundancy and a generator of the adjacent resolution levels by the virtue of the GFACS operation.

- Evolution of multiple-choice pre-programmed behavior into a multiple alternative creation ends up with multiple theories development (the latter is performed in the imagination).
- Through combinatorial search, focusing attention and grouping performed in nature by the mechanism of natural selection[3] the discovery of more efficient techniques was done. It was discovered by the intelligent agents that storing information about objects of the world, actions they encounter, and rules entailed by the changes are more efficient. Indeed, it is less expensive than testing the same material (often, living) samples again and again to receive similar results.
- Generalization and learning through natural selection from the choices created by material alternatives have demonstrated to be a waste of time, energy, and matter. It is more efficient to learn by dealing with information only—that is, by theorizing (*theory → the result of generalization upon rules, rule → result of generalization upon experiences*).
- Any rule discovered by an intelligence is a statement of some generality: It cannot refer to all details of realistic test cases. The selection of the proper details for the particular state of affair is performed by the mechanism of focusing attention.
- Multiresolutional storage obtained via consecutive generalization turned out to be the most efficient method of storing information.

Finally, it would be desirable to determine what the relation between conventional control and intelligent control is. The following statements are based on the preceding materials.

1. Conventional control is about feedback. The goal formation is external to the problem. When we include the goal formation the problem becomes IC-embedded because the goal for each level of the higher resolution is created as a result of BG-module functioning at the level of lower resolution.
2. The structures of intelligent control are formed as semiotic closures, mostly the multiresolutional ones, which contain an element that can be called "feedback." But feedback is not the entire issue. The transformations within the feedback loop are more important. The classical feedback does not need to have any redundancy in it. This is why the concept of intelligent control can be associated with "recognition" in the loop.
3. We would expect that the feedback of the semiotic closure contains GFACS as a rule.
4. Optimization as a part of functioning of the conventional controller presumes searching at a level, but stops short from recognition its embedding within the multiresolutional hierarchy of top-down constraint propagation.

---

[2]Punctuated evolution demonstrate periods of changes with intervals of the absence of any development.
[3]Actually, the reader should have already anticipated the conjecture that natural selection in Nature played a role similar to the algorithmic mechanisms of generalization and learning.

PART II

PRACTICAL

INTRODUCTION TO PART II: FROM PLANNING APPROACHES TO PLANNING PRACTICE IN THE NETHERLANDS RAILWAYS

In the preceding 10 chapters that constitute the theoretical part, we illustrated the various "intelligent" approaches to planning. In every chapter, planning was realized with some kind of intelligent actor: an individual, an organization, a carefully designed program that works together with a planner, and an independent piece of software or robot. They are all intelligent to a certain degree; that is they antici- pate, they have representations or models of the future, they apply search to solve problems, and they are goal-directed. The theoretical chapters also follow various methodological traditions, from simulations and conceptual theorizing to empirical, quasi-experimental, and case study research. Although the authors of the 10 chapters each emphasize their own approach and solution methods, they are all aware of the diversity in the overall planning field.

Much research and literature in planning and scheduling is about algorithms and mathematics, but we explicitly did not want to follow that tradition or track. How- ever, it is an important tradition and therefore one chapter in the theoretical part (Kroon and Zuidwijk, Chapter 8) deals with solution techniques to planning and scheduling problems. Also only one chapter tries to (re)conceptualize planning pro- blems in terms of multiresolution methods (Meystel, Chapter 11). Discussions about algorithms and mathematical solutions for planning problems often only result in so- called optimization issues. This is not to criticize these approaches—on the contrary. Algorithms and other mathematical tools are a necessary part of any planning pro- blem, but they do not cover the complete planning problem. They often start from closed world assumptions and a model of the problem and then focus on the opti- mum, maximum, or minimum with much elegance, rigor, and sophistication. How- ever, the basic assumption in each of the algorithmic approaches is that a planning

Planning in Intelligent Systems: Aspects, Motivations, and Methods, Edited by Wout van Wezel, René Jorna, and Alexander Meystel
Copyright © 2006 John Wiley & Sons, Inc.

problem can be solved by such a particular approach or a slightly adapted version of such an approach.

We saw in the 10 preceding theoretical chapters how rich and complicated the planning field is, even if one beliefs in the omniscient algorithmic and mathematical methods and techniques. We would like to argue that planning practice is even more opaque and interconnected. Neither one method nor one approach is applicable in the complicated planning practice in organizations. This discussion could become a matter of ideology, which we do not prefer, and therefore we tried to find a way to demonstrate the complicatedness of the combination of (a) theoretical richness, (b) mathematical and algorithmic rigor and desired uniformity, and (c) practical diversity and stubbornness. We were in the unique situation that we encountered and could use research conducted in the overall planning of the Netherlands Railways.

The Netherlands Railways is a large organization where more than 300 planners daily make plans for various activities, such as timetables, rolling stock, rolling staff, and engine driver and ticket collector scheduling for the Dutch railways network. We will describe the detailed situation in Chapter 12. In the Netherlands Railways, five groups of researchers with different backgrounds and experience in various techniques and methods worked on the same planning problem. The specific problem concerns the shunting planning for a representative medium railway station and junction (a shunting yard) in the northern part of the Netherlands. The Netherlands Railways started a research project, called Rintel, where the five groups of researchers worked on the same problem. The details of the groups and approaches will also be discussed in Chapter 12. In short, the groups used the following techniques and approaches: task analyses of planners (Chapter 13), constraint satisfaction programming (Chapter 14), mixed integer programming (Chapter 15), dynamic programming (Chapter 16), and mixed initiative planning (Chapter 17). In the various chapters, domain and planners are described and techniques and methods are applied. The structure of the organizational planning unit(s) and of the Netherlands Railways were left out of the research.

This unique research setting within the Netherlands Railways showed two very interesting general conclusions. The first conclusion is that planning practice is too complicated for each approach and each technique on its own. Within each approach, constraints of the planning problem had to be left out, assumptions had to be adapted, and the characteristics of the planning domain had to be cut off. So, no one approach or technique could deal with the problem in its totality. The second conclusion is that various approaches can be applied to the same planning problem. If dynamic programming is better for some aspect B, then constraint satisfaction programming is better for another aspect C, and cognitive task analysis is better for aspect A. It seems that the various approaches are complementary. We believe that the two conclusions of partial applicability and differential usefulness should make us modest with respect to overall claims that one just has to wait for the right mathematical model and that then every planning problem in the end is "easily" solvable.

Planners are the intermediaries between management and employees. Managers often have a control perspective, whereas planners know that (control) structures and targets often require adaptation. Planning practice is and will remain an open world issue. Our point is that almost all mathematicians and planning researchers know this, but that many managers at different levels in organizations do not want to know this. They wait (and pay) for the "push-on-one-button" solution that, as all dedicated planners and researchers know, will not come. The five chapters in the practical part provide evidence against this "one-button" thinking.

12

PERSPECTIVES ON SHUNTING PLANNING: RESEARCH IN PLANNING SUPPORT AT THE NETHERLANDS RAILWAYS

WOUT VAN WEZEL

Faculty of Management and Organization, University of Groningen, NL-9700-AV Groningen, the Netherlands

DERK JAN KIEWIET

Faculty of Management and Organization, University of Groningen, NL-9700-AV Groningen, the Netherlands

12.1. INTRODUCTION

The Dutch railway network consists of approximately 3000 km of railway track and some 400 stations. This infrastructure is used on a daily basis by a total of 4500 scheduled trains on lines ranging in length between 15 and over 200 km. Approximately 1 million passengers travel more than 40 million km each workday, which makes the Dutch network one of the most heavily utilized networks in the world. In 1995 the company has been split up, and as a consequence the tracks—the network, the switches and the signals—are still managed by the Dutch government, whereas the company that owns the trains and provides the transport is independent from the government and profit-oriented. This reorganization, along with ongoing integration of the information systems including the planning systems, initiated the question what paradigm should be used for the new planning and scheduling systems. Therefore, the Netherlands Railways invited a number of researchers from, respectively, management and organization, operations research,

Planning in Intelligent Systems: Aspects, Motivations, and Methods, Edited by Wout van Wezel, René Jorna, and Alexander Meystel
Copyright © 2006 John Wiley & Sons, Inc.

and artificial intelligence to look from their perspective at shunting planning as an exemplar planning problem. The researchers all investigated the same problem, and they got the same data set that they could use to solve the planning problem. The project—called Rintel—was meant not as a competition, but rather to see the advantages and disadvantages of the respective approaches and techniques in the context of shunting planning support. In the next sections, we will describe the planning at the Netherlands Railways in general, after which the shunting planning is discussed in more detail and the various chapters will be introduced.

12.2. PLANNING AT THE NETHERLANDS RAILWAYS

It is not hard to imagine that the planning of a railway operator is very complex. There are three main dimensions that the Netherlands Railways use to partition the planning:

1. Central versus local planning. Planning departments located in the main office in the city Utrecht make plans for the rail sections that run between stations. Planning departments at a number of large stations make plans for train movements on the stations.
2. Planning phases. There are three phases in the planning process. First, a week pattern is being made by several units of "Year Plan." This plan covers the 7 days of the week. It is the input for several units of "Day Plan." In day plan, the year plan for a given date is adapted to circumstances that are specific for that day—for example, football matches or track maintenance. Changes that have to be made shortly before or during plan execution are handled by traffic control. All three phases are essentially plan adaptation because the main timetable is only slightly changed a few times a year.
3. The third distinction is rolling stock (trains) versus rolling staff (engine drivers and ticket collectors).

On the highest hierarchical level, these three partition dimensions result in eight different plans: central year plan for rolling stock, local year plan for rolling stock, central day plan for rolling stock, and so on. All these plans are tightly connected and continuously worked upon by approximately 300 full-time planners. In the Rintel research projects we have looked at shunting planning, which is a part of the local rolling stock planning. In the next section, we will describe shunting planning in more detail.

12.3. PLANNING OF TRAIN SHUNTING

Trains that arrive at a station do not necessarily leave in the same configuration. A train can be split into its individual units or coaches, and these coaches can be combined again in another train. For example, the train from Groningen to

Zwolle consists of two coaches, and the train from Leeuwarden to Zwolle consists of one coach. In Zwolle the trains are connected, after which they leave as one train to Den Haag. During the night, passenger trains stay at the station. The "storage" capacity, however, is limited. Additionally, some operations must be performed during the night such as washing, cleaning, and fuelling. Roughly speaking, the task of the planner is to plan the movements of the trains and coaches and to decide on what track trains stay during the night. Some of the characteristics and requirements for shunting are:

- There must be a train driver to drive the train at the specified time.
- There must be a route available to drive the train from the source track to the destination track. This can be difficult at peak times, because there must be a certain amount of time between two movements on a track.
- If a train must be split into units or if a train must be composed of units, one or more train shunters must be available.
- There are several types of train units. Only units of the same type can be connected. The configuration of incoming and outgoing trains is specified on unit type level, not on individual unit level.
- The train units are symmetrical and have their own locomotive. So they can drive in both directions.
- Multiple units can be put on one track. This is necessary at night because there is only a limited number of "parking" tracks. A logical consequence is that a train cannot be moved if there is a train parked in front of it.
- The time it takes to wash a train is largely independent from the size of the train. Because the track where trains can be washed is a bottleneck capacity, it is advantageous to combine units in trains before they are washed.

Planning is mostly done manually. The planning system is used to get information from and to put the schedule in, but the schedule itself is usually made on paper first. Figure 12.1 shows an example of such a plan. Approximately 150 planners from five major stations in the Netherlands plan the shunting operations for all stations. One of these stations is Zwolle, a city in the northeastern part of the Netherlands. The Rintel research projects all focused on scheduling the shunting operations of one day and one night of the Zwolle station. In this day, there were 55 arriving and 45 departing trains. Figure 12.2 shows the layout of the station. There are many constraints that must be satisfied. For example:

- Of the tracks shown, only a few can be used to park the trains on.
- Washing must be done at the cleaning track.
- Not all tracks can be used by electrically powered trains.
- For safety reasons there must at least be 5 minutes of time between two train movements on a track.

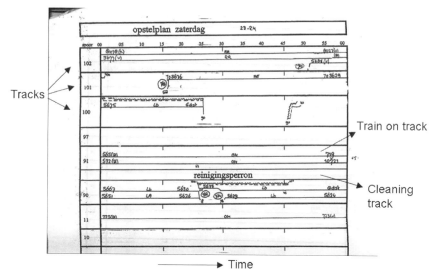

Figure 12.1. Part of shunting plan.

There are also several goals that are taken into account by the planners, for example:

- The number of train movements must be minimized.
- The walking distance of train drivers must be minimized.
- The schedule must be robust.
- The number of trains that does not depart from the originally planned track must be minimized.

In the next five chapters, the shunting planning problem will be discussed from the following perspectives:

- Chapter 13: Kiewiet et al. look at the organizational context and at the characteristics of task support.
- Chapter 14: Abbink uses a constraint-based scheduling algorithm.

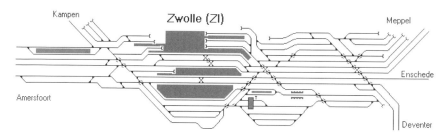

Figure 12.2. Layout of Zwolle [From Chapter 15 (Lentink et al.).]

- Chapter 15: Lentink et al. use a mathematical approach.
- Chapter 16: Haijema et al. developed an algorithm that is based on dynamic programming.
- Chapter 17: Riezebos and van Wezel combine a task analysis with mathematical models.

Each of the chapters again provides a short description of the shunting problem, thereby focusing on and extending the aspects that are relevant for the chosen solution technique.

13

TASK ANALYSIS FOR PROBLEMS OF SHUNTING PLANNING WITHIN THE NETHERLANDS RAILWAYS

DERK JAN KIEWIET, RENÉ JORNA, AND WOUT VAN WEZEL

Faculty of Management and Organization, University of Groningen,
NL-9700-AV Groningen, the Netherlands

13.1. INTRODUCTION

Planning support can, in principle, take place in two ways: (a) modeling the planning problem with mathematics and (b) studying the solution processes of human planners.

In the first approach, an empirical planning problem is translated into a mathematical model in which variables, relations between variables, goals, and constraints all together form the structure. Subsequently, by applying mathematical solution techniques, often translated into algorithms, values are found for the variables so that it becomes possible to attain goals without violating constraints. These values then form the solutions to the mathematical model of the planning problem. Next, they are translated into quantities, whereby the empirical planning problem is basically solved. We say "basically" because this depends on how well the mathematical model describes the mathematical planning problem and how well the mathematical solution can be converted into an empirical solution. In other words, the internal and external validity of the mathematical model determine how useful the mathematical solution actually is in practice.

Apart from the problem of validity, there is another reason why this kind of planning support is not always successful in practice. This is because by using mathematical models and solving techniques, a planning problem is often dealt

Planning in Intelligent Systems: Aspects, Motivations, and Methods, Edited by Wout van Wezel, René Jorna, and Alexander Meystel

with in a way that is not sufficiently comprehensible, or not comprehensible at all, to the planners. This means that whenever we literally interpret support as helping the human planner[1] in the planning process in which he is the one who takes the final decisions, the lack of transparency in the way in which a solution is found can lead to problems. This may imply that the mathematical solution does not correspond with the solution coming from the planner, which is based on his knowledge of the planning situation as well as knowledge gained by experience and education. Therefore, from a cognitive point of view, it is not an easy task for the planner to (a) renounce his own ideas about problem solving in which he believes, and (b) accept those which are obtained in an abstract way.

In addition, for several reasons a planner may decide that a solution cannot be implemented as such, because it still requires some adjustments—for example, because situations change or because the planner has the opinion that a mathematical solution cannot properly be applied in the empirical situation. If it is not clear how a mathematical solution is attained, it sometimes becomes difficult to readjust the solution in such a way that it is suitable. Or: sometimes insight into the solving technique is required to readjust a solution adequately. As a result of these problems of validity and cognition, a mathematical model is not always the best way to give support in solving a planning problem.

The second approach of supporting a planning situation is not to look at the planning problem itself in the first instance, but to study the way in which planners deal with the problem. One then has to look at the planners' behavior with respect to decision making, the use of principal rules, the search for and the use of information, and the approach to the problem. This approach is essentially different from the approach of the mathematical model. Although such a model also makes use of information from the planners, ultimately the planning problem is abstracted. In the second approach the information from the planners is considered important not only to gain more insight into the planning problem, but also to solve the problem. By pointedly including the way in which planners carry out their planning activities in the process of planning support, planners can keep a clear view of the planning. Moreover, they can better use the computer system, because the way in which the planning is supported is clear to them.

It appears, though, that both ways can be applied simultaneously, on condition that one seriously considers the manner in which mathematical model solutions play a role in solving the planning problem. Many planning problems consist of smaller subproblems that are suitable for the application of a valid mathematical model whose solutions the planners accept as optimizations but which cannot easily be realized by a human planner. However, with respect to this type of hybrid approach to a planning problem, it is important that the mathematical model techniques are only deployed in small, demarcated areas of the total planning problem, that planners can change the model parameters of these models relatively

---

[1] If this were not the case, we would be referring to planning *replacement* rather than planning *support*.

easily, and that the support of the overall solution of the planning problem is based on the approach of the planners (see also Chapters 7 and 17).

However, the second method of planning support requires more insight into how planners actually deal with a planning problem. Therefore, in developing a planning support method of this kind the first step is a task analysis that clarifies what the planning task consists of and which elements of the planning situation play a role in the planning problem.

In this chapter we will look at the planning support in a planning problem of the Netherlands Railways. We will first, in Section 13.2, briefly explain the theoretical perspective of (cognitive) task analysis and knowledge modeling. In Section 13.3 we continue with a task analysis for this particular planning problem in which first the domain of the problem will be established, then the (sub)-tasks will be determined, and finally the goals and constraints that will be dealt with within the problem area will be specified. Next, in Section 13.4, we will briefly indicate how the knowledge about the task analysis can be used in a planning support system. In Section 13.5 we give conclusions.

13.2. COGNITIVE TASKS AND KNOWLEDGE MODELING

Our approach to model task and knowledge of planners is based on the KADS methodology (Knowledge And Documentation System), also called Common-Kads (Schreiber, Wielinga, and Breuker, 1993; Schreiber et al., 2000). KADS is a methodology to model and implement knowledge systems. From our perspective the difference compared to other methodologies for software development is that KADS does not start with a model that says what a planner (user) must eventually do, but that it starts with an analysis of what a planner actually does.

KADS starts with the assumption that a planner is a human information system—that is, a cognitive system. Such a system has a cognitive architecture, uses (mental) representations, and performs manipulations on these representations (Newell and Simon, 1972; Newell, 1990). This human information perspective is the explanatory structure behind reasoning, thinking, judging, decision making, problem solving, and all the other cognitive tasks humans do.

KADS is a methodology and as such it consists of a description of activities (task decomposition, rule specification), of concepts to describe objects in the methodology (the modeling language), and of various tools and techniques to make the other two possible. In the process of acquiring knowledge from human experts—in our case the planners in the Netherlands Railway—KADS suggests the following phases: (a) knowledge identification (linguistic analysis, audio-recording), (b) knowledge conceptualization (modeling in conceptual relations), (c) epistemological analysis (structural features of conceptual knowledge; concept types and knowledge sources), (d) logical analysis (formalizing inferences and derivations), and (e) implementation analysis, machine and software requirements; matching, testing slot-filling. In our research we used knowledge identification and conceptualization and epistemological analysis. The phases of logical analysis and implementation analysis were not relevant at this stage, although at the end of this chapter we suggest an implementation—that is, a software architecture that has proven successful in other application domains (Mietus, 1994; Jorna and van Wezel, 2002).

Next to the five phases in the process of knowledge modeling, KADS works with four layers to analyze the structure of knowledge of human users in various strata. The four layers are the domain, the inference, the task, and the strategy layer. We will explain the layers in greater detail.

The domain layer is used to model concepts, relations, and complex structures. In the example of the Netherlands Railways and the shunting planning problem, concepts are, for example: time, track, train composition, train carriages, and platform, whereas relations are "a kind of" (AKO) or "is a" (ISA) and "consists of" and "depends on." The domain layer is the basis for the inference layer. Inferences are the smallest reasoning steps. They use the domain layer, but function on their own. In the research project we discerned for planning and scheduling the following inferences: counting; concluding; classifying; evaluating; making hypotheses; identifying; introducing; dissolving; selecting; sorting; joining; comparing; erasing. The 13 inferences represent the possible reasoning steps in solving a planning or scheduling problem. There are many other inferences, and each inference has a domain part as an input and, depending on the kind of reasoning step, results in an output. For example, if a planner has the arrival times of various trains (domain layer), he ranks the times in a descending order (an inference or a combination of inferences) and has an ordered list as an outcome (again the domain layer). A relative stable combination of (many) inferences results in what is called a task. Here, we enter the task layer. For example, a diagnostic task consists of different combinations of inferences compared to a planning task. According to KADS, every task has its special set of combinations of inferences. In this respect, KADS uses the term "generic task." A task itself is defined as a set of actions leading to a set of goals taking into account a set of constraints (see also Waern, 1989). A combination of tasks is guided by a strategy. A strategy is a set of meta-rules or higher-order reasoning steps to go around or solve impasses and look for repairs. For example, if a planner cannot find a solution for a planning problem, he may go to a manager to discuss new resources or relax a very important constraint. This kind of activity is not a detailed planning activity, but has to do with negotiating skills. The step to go to his superior is outside the planning as task as such and therefore a strategic move. The performance of a planner without such a strategy is often worse than the performance of a planner that has such a strategy layer. In a hierarchical perspective the strategy layer controls the task layer, which controls the inference layer, which is applied to the domain layer.

In the following section we discuss in greater detail the domain layer and the task layer. The layers of inference and strategy remain implicit in this chapter (however, see Kiewiet, Jorna, and van Wezel, 2005; Kiewiet and Jorna, 2005).

13.3. THE PLANNING OF SHUNTING ACTIVITIES WITHIN THE NR

13.3.1. What is Shunting Planning?

The planning of the train-passengers traffic in fact consists of formulating a large number of subplans that are all interrelated. For example, there is the timetable, which indicates the days and times when a train is at a station, the train planning, which lists the rolling stock of which a train consists, the service planning, indicating the services on a train, and a planning of the rolling staff, which links the services to the personnel. Here, we deal with the so-called planning of shunting activities. As far as the train-passengers traffic is concerned, a distinction can be made between two types of stations: through-stations and shunting stations. At through-stations a train comes in and stops on a particular track, passengers leave or enter the train, and a moment later it leaves again from the same track. However, at shunting stations more happens: railway carriages are coupled or uncoupled; and before leaving the station again, trains are (sometimes for a long period of time) shunted into a siding. So, at locations of this kind, there is a great deal of shunting activity: A train comes in at track A, and some time later it leaves from track B, but in the meantime it cannot stay on track A or B because these are used by other trains. In this case the train has to be shunted from track A to another track C before it can return to track B to depart from there. This process of shunting has to be planned.

In the process of planning shunting activities, the main task of the planners at a shunting yard is planning the course of shunting within that particular location. During their planning activities, this main task is divided into a number of subtasks. The division into subtasks takes place at two levels: the macro and the microlevel. At the macrolevel, some examples of subtasks are: the administration of data, the search for information, consultation with colleagues, communication with the coordination center, determining the available and required capacity, and the actual scheduling, the so-called problem solving. This problem solving is called the microlevel, and it is also divided into a number of (sub) subtasks that we prefer to call: planning steps, strategies, and inferences. As regards the subtasks at the microlevel (problem solving or puzzling), a number of so-called object types are mutually attuned. These object types form the domain of the planning.

13.3.2. Domain

Object types refer to those elements in the planning task that actually have to be planned. Object types can occur at different aggregation levels. At a high aggregation level the object types indicate the important elements of a planning task. For example, with respect to planning shunting activities, "departing train series" and "incoming train series" are object types at a high aggregation level. These object types can then be described more thoroughly with the aid of more detailed elements of planning. In this way the object type "departing train series" could be considered as a collective term for the object types "time," "track," and "train." Between these two subsequent aggregation levels, only 1:1 relations exist: One departing train series is de-aggregated into one departure time, one departure track, and one train. However, between two aggregation levels there can also exist 1:n relations. For example, at an even lower level the object type "train" could be more thoroughly described with the aid of the object type "kind of rolling stock," which in turn can be considered as consisting of the object type "type of rolling stock." It can then be claimed that there is a 1:1 relation between "train" and "kind of rolling stock," and there is a 1:n relation between "kind of rolling stock" and "type of rolling stock." In other words, one train consists of one kind of rolling stock. However, a certain kind of rolling stock can consist of several types of rolling stock. At the lowest level an object type always consists of a collection of concrete entities, the so-called instantiations. An example of an instantiation of the object type "engine driver" is the engine driver with the name "Karel Bakker."

In the process of planning shunting activities, a large number of object types play a role. In order to map out these object types, we will first look at the typical pattern of a train instantiation at a shunting yard. Starting from this pattern we will then make abstractions into the various object types. At a certain point in time, a train enters the shunting yard. This train has certain characteristics. For example, it is part of a so-called train series (a train series is a number of trains all having the same point of departure and the same destination, and all stopping at the same intermediate stations), and it is composed of a number of train carriages that all have to be of the same kind (otherwise they cannot be coupled into one train), but it can differ with respect to stock type (for instance, a type consisting of three carriages and a type consisting of four carriages). This train enters the shunting yard on a particular track.

Subsequently, it is checked from which track and at what time the train has to be ready for departure. If the arrival track and the departure track are not the same tracks, it may be necessary to shunt the train. If this is actually the case, a shunting movement will at a certain point take place replacing the train either to an intermediary siding or to the track of departure. Which one of these two shunting movements are carried out depends on the use, by other trains, of the arrival track or the departure track of the train under consideration, as well as on the time between arrival and departure. In the case that during the time between arrival and departure both the arrival track and the departure track are used by other trains, it may be necessary to put the train on a siding in the meantime. If a siding is used, shunting will have to take place again afterwards: At some point the train will have to be shunted to the departure track. It is also possible that the train is shunted from one siding to another. It goes without saying that for each of these shunting movements, an engine driver is required.

During the shunting process the train may have to be rearranged: several railway carriages (either of the same or of a different rolling stock type) could be coupled, but they could also be uncoupled. For both coupling and decoupling carriages, shunting movements are necessary: The carriages that have to be coupled have to be moved to the track where the train has been placed, and the uncoupled carriages have to be removed. Whenever there is, a coupling or decoupling of trains, there is, apart from the engine drivers involved, a shunter present who makes sure that the physical coupling between railway carriages is either carried out or terminated. If the times of arrival and departure are on the same day, one speaks of a day transition, and in this case the above-mentioned pattern is followed. However, if the times of arrival and departure are on different days so that there is a night transition, a number of other activities can be added to the earlier mentioned pattern, such as cleaning of the train or maintenance.

From the description mentioned above, we can derive object types in the domain of the planning of shunting activities. Figure 13.1 depicts the domain of the day transitions.

13.3.3. Tasks

As already stated, in the planning process the subtasks can be divided into both subtasks at macrolevel and subtasks at microlevel. Except for the actual scheduling (problem solving or puzzling), we will leave all other subtasks at the macrolevel aside and only deal with the microlevel subtasks. All these microlevel subtasks make use of one or more object types as defined above.

In the process of shunting planning, there are three important subtasks at the microlevel: "positioning," "routing," and "planning of services":

- The subtask "positioning" consists of either decoupling railway carriages from a train (splitting up the train) or coupling them (combining). When executing the subtask in the case of decoupling, attention is paid to which carriages have to be decoupled from which train, when this has to take place, and at which track the train is at that particular moment. In the case of coupling carriages, it has to be determined which ones have to be coupled, at which track(s) they are at that moment, to which train the carriages have to be coupled, at which track the coupling of carriages has to take place and when. So, in this subtask the object types "train," "railway-carriage," "track," and "time" are mutually attuned (assigned).

- The subtask "routing" consists of selecting the route along which a shunting movement takes place. This subtask starts with determining that a railway carriage, which is placed on a certain track (starting track) at a certain time, has to be on another track (ending track) at a later time. Next, it is determined when a carriage has to leave the starting track at the latest, when at the latest it has to be on the ending track, and which tracks the carriage will use in the meantime. In this subtask the starting track can be either the arrival track or the siding. The same applies to the ending track. During the execution of this subtask the object types "railway carriage," "time," and "track" are mutually attuned.

- In the subtask "planning of services" the transactions described in the previous two subtasks have to be assigned to the rolling staff. During this subtask the actual people are not scheduled, but different services are connected to the transactions that have to be carried out. In this way it is guaranteed that for each transaction an engine driver and/or shunter is available.[2]

---

[2]In the planning of rolling staff, services are connected to persons.

384

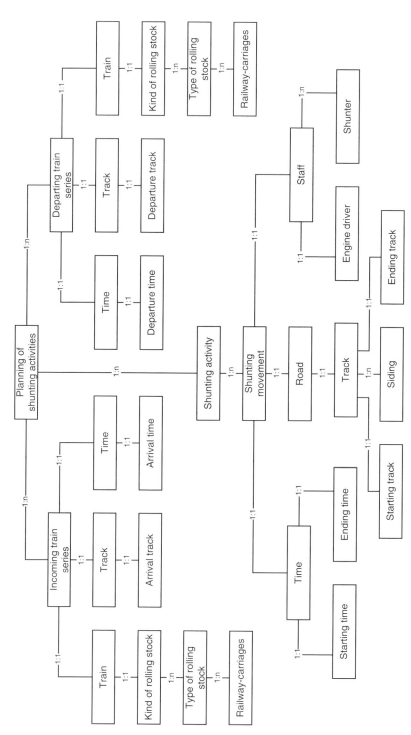

Figure 13.1. Object types (various levels of aggregation) in the domain model of planning shunting activities.

The description above shows that the three subtasks are closely connected. One could say that the output of the subtask "positioning" forms the input of the subtask "routing" and that the output of the subtask "routing" is the input of the subtask "planning of services." However, this structure is not necessarily linear. In the execution of the subtask "routing," it is possible that no suitable route can be found. This means that within the constraints of planning, there are no tracks available to take a carriage from a starting track to an ending track, or that conflicts arise because, for example, all in-between tracks are used by other carriages. In this case, the subtask "positioning" is again executed; however, based on the knowledge acquired from the subtask "routing," other possibilities are looked for to decouple or couple the railway carriages. The same applies to the subtask "planning of services"—for example, when no service appears to be available to carry out the routing task. Also in that case one will re-address the previous subtask.

In addition, the routing subtask is often carried out recurrently. In order to shunt a railway carriage from a starting track to an ending track, as a result of occurring constraints, it may be necessary to place the carriage on a siding for a certain period of time. Within the subtask "routing," another routing subtask is in fact performed twice: once to find a route from starting track to ending track, and once to find a route from siding to ending track. And within each of the two routing subtasks, another routing subtask can, in principle, again be carried out.

The tasks, subtasks, combinations of inferences, and their mutual relationship together form the task structure at the overall microlevel. In Figure 13.2 this structure is schematically depicted. Making a plan for shunting activities can be

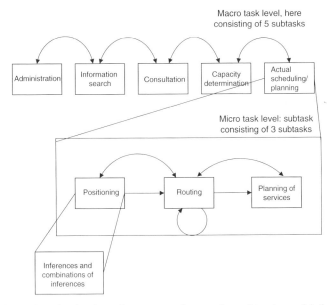

Figure 13.2. Task and subtask at the macro, micro, and combinations of inferences level (shunting planning).

considered as executing a range of coherent subtasks. As regards this range of sub-tasks, it is not true that, by carrying out one subtask, all instantiations of object types that play a role are in fact planned all at once. Often only a subset of all occurring instantiations will be manipulated. The sequences in which subtasks are performed in the planning process, together with the subset of instantiations that is actually used within a subtask, constitute the task strategy. A task strategy can be different for each planner. In the previous example, for instance, it is possible that one planner first carries out the positioning, routing, and planning of services subtasks for all night transitions, and after that for all day transitions. At the same time, another planner may start by executing the positioning and routing subtasks for all night transitions after which he deals with all day transitions. Only after he has finished these subtasks may he choose to carry out the planning of services subtasks for both night and day transitions.

This individual interpretation of the task strategy has far-reaching consequences for the support of the planning. If in the planning support the planners cannot recognize their own task strategy, there is a risk that they lose their grip on the planning task and that intermediary interventions do not have the desired effect. Therefore, in the process of planning support the individuality of task strategies has to be accounted for and has to be integrated in the software.

13.3.4. Constraints and Goals

In attuning the instantiations of object types within the subtasks, attention has to be paid to occurring constraints, while the realization of goals has to be pursued. As regards the planning of shunting activities, there is a large number of constraints, which can be divided into three classes. First, there are constraints in terms of safety. Examples of such constraints are as follows:

- A passenger train has to enter and leave a track adjoining a platform.
- Two trains cannot stand or move on the same physical piece of track at the same time.
- The length of a train has to be shorter than the length of a platform.

These are hard constraints; under no circumstances is it possible to deviate from the constraints belonging to this class. If during the execution of subtasks a constraint from this class appears to be violated, a different solution will have to be found.

The second class of constraints refers to the timetable that is used for the shunting activities in question. In this timetable for a particular location, both the times of arrival and of departure of the trains and the departure tracks are mentioned.

The third and last class of constraints has a bearing on constraints caused by the infrastructure of the shunting yard. Examples of constraints belonging to this third class are as follows:

- Through-trains should not come in at so-called terminus tracks (terminus tracks are tracks terminating at the shunting yard: at the end of the track there is a buffer).

- The standard times denoted for specific shunting movements have to be followed.
- Electric trains can only move on tracks with an overhead wire.

The constraints of the second and third class can, in principle, all be taken into consideration loosely. If the circumstances should require it, these constraints could be ignored (with the aid of a diesel locomotive, even an electric train can move on a track without an overhead wire). As a consequence, a "feasible" plan is in fact always possible: If at a certain point a plan does not appear to be attainable because constraints of the second and third class are violated, the constraints making the plan impossible will be "simply" ignored. Similar to the task strategy, ignoring constraints is also done on an individual basis. Different planners may make different choices regarding constraints that have to be ignored, and in doing so they may come up with different solutions for the same planning problem. If this is considered undesirable by the planning organization (which does not necessarily have to be the case), it is essential to formulate a clear planning policy that indicates which constraints can or cannot be ignored, under which circumstances and in which order. It may be obvious that a planning policy of this kind does not suffice in eliminating ambiguity in solutions.

Apart from constraints, also goals play a role in the process of mutually attuning instantiations of object types. Goals can be made operational in goal functions that have to be maximized or minimized. Examples of goals functions that play a role in the planning of shunting activities include the following:

- Minimizing the costs
- Minimizing the number of shunting movements
- Maximizing the number of trains leaving in time

However, as is the case with many planning problems, in the process of planning shunting activities goal functions can be competitive. For instance, optimizing one goal function could lead to suboptimizing (or even losing) another goal function. Maximizing the goal function "number of trains that leave in time" could, for example, lead to a larger number of shunting movements than is strictly necessary, with the result that the goal function "minimizing the number of shunting movements" is largely neglected. In order to work with several planners in an unambiguous way within this range of potentially competing goals functions, clear choices should be made in the planning policy with respect to establishing priorities, putting goals functions into operation, and interpreting them. Moreover, these choices have to be understood, supported, and applied by the planners.

13.4. SUPPORT OF PLANNING

In this chapter, planning support is defined as support in performing the various subtasks at the microlevel with the aid of software. Support at the macrolevel can also be defined and can easily be incorporated within existing information systems, such as databases, spreadsheets, and visualization software. How the macro- and micro-level supports are integrated is domain- and organization-dependent.

When making choices regarding planning support, the specific nature of the sub-areas of the subtask should be taken into account. For some sub-areas it is important that the planner himself can generate solutions, because otherwise he will lose his insight into and grip on the planning problem. On the other hand, with respect to other sub-areas, mathematical algorithms can be used to create solutions. The system that supports the planning process has to be able to deal with this hybrid nature: Planners should be able to adjust model parameters easily, as well as manipulate algorithm solutions. Furthermore, these solutions should be suitable for an easy integration into the activities that the planner himself carries out. Taking the aforementioned into account, we can distinguish the following kinds of support: Editor, Controller (Inspector), Evaluator, and Generator (Interactor). With Editor, Controller, and Evaluator the planner starts the initiative for making a plan and the computer aids in valuating the solutions, whereas with the Generator the computer has the initiative and the planner evaluates the outcomes. In all cases the planner is in the end in control.

A. An *Editor*. This is an electronic planning board by which planning infor-mation can be (re)presented in various forms (graphical images, scale models, text). Here it is essential that the planner himself can manipulate the object types and instantiations in an easy way and can find his own sol-ution to the planning problem. The Editor can also contain a macro-editor, enabling the planner to fix as well as retrieve the range of steps he himself has chosen during the process of solving a planning problem.

B. A *Controller*. This software checks whether certain constraints are violated because of a solution generated by a planner. Here the planner can indicate for which subset of constraints the solution has to be checked. Moreover, the planner can decide to ignore certain violations (the constraints are relaxed) and proceed with the solution that he has come up with.

C. An *Evaluator*. This device checks to what extent the goal functions are attained. The evaluator can include a weighing option for the various goal functions, so that an end assessment (in terms of goal functions) can be given with respect to the solution. However, it is also possible that for each separate goal function a score is calculated and that the planner combines these scores. In any case, the planner decides to what extent the evaluation is valid.

D. A *Generator*. The Generator contains mathematical models, translated into algorithms, enabling the planner to find optimal solutions for subproblems occurring within the entire planning problem. These solutions are presented to the planner, who can subsequently either accept or adjust them in the Editor. He can also combine them with the solutions of other subproblems.

To make the Editor, Controller, Evaluator, and Generator interact, a Blackboard is used. In this Blackboard, data required by one or several support components are

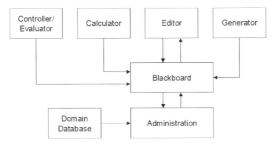

Figure 13.3. System architecture for planning support (see also chapter 7).

retrieved from a domain database, after which it can be modified. The architecture of a system of this kind is shown in Figure 13.3. In the system architecture of Figure 13.3 also Calculator and Administration are mentioned. The function of the Calculator is calculating and importing new data, while Administration keeps count of which data from the database are placed in the Blackboard. So both Calculator and Administration are used to assist the planning supporting components of the system.

A characteristic of the architecture mentioned above is that the components, used to create solutions (Editor and Generator), are separated from the information that is required to find solutions (data regarding domain, goal functions, constraints and calculations). This separation offers the following possibilities:

1. Components can be modified relatively independently. A change in the goal function has no influence on the solutions provided by the Generator, and only a very limited effect (or possibly no effect at all) on the way in which the goal function is shown in the Editor. In other words, components are robust with regard to (small) changes in other components of the system.

2. By using a Blackboard, components can simultaneously work on different solutions. In this way the planner can work on one solution by using the Editor, while at the same time the Generator is working on another solution, after which the two of them are offered to the Evaluator.

3. Because the Generator works separately from the other components, new mathematical algorithms can easily be connected to the system by means of an interface.

4. By the use of an Editor (planning board), the domain can be represented for several planners in several ways, in accordance with individual requirements, while the other components are universal. This enables planners to have a good "feel and touch" of the planning problem, while aspects of the problem that (may) generate small differences for planners occur in the system in a more generic way.

13.5. CONCLUSION

In this chapter a task analysis approach is given for the planning of shunting activities within the Netherlands Railways. On the basis of a description of the domain model, three subtasks on the microlevel are described within the macrolevel subtask "actual scheduling/planning." From this task structure, various task strategies can be derived. In addition, a number of goal functions and constraints are listed, and what also applies here is that while making use of various subsets of goal functions and constraints, within these subsets planners have different methods of weighing those goal functions and constraints. In order to have a real support system for the planning of shunting activities that corresponds with the planners' way of working, their individuality has to be accounted for. Only in this way planners will be able to recognize their own methods of planning, whereby the acceptance of a planning supporting system will be increased. In the second part of this chapter the architecture of such a system is described. By starting from four relatively independent components (Editor, Evaluator, Controller, and Generator) a modular system can be designed in which the separate components can be modified relatively easily. Furthermore, this system has the potential to actually support a whole variety of task strategies.

However, in designing such a system there is the paradox of task support (van Wezel, 2001). It has already been argued that planning a support system has to fit in with the planners' way of working. But the implementation of a system of this kind will, by definition, affect the working methods of the planners. Yet, the support system does enable planners to use other task strategies that could not be applied before. Also other domain representations, which in turn can lead to other strategies, are possible as a result of the implementation of such a system.

In addition, the system can take over certain planning activities (Calculator, Generator), providing the planner with more time, for example, to search for better solutions. But after some time, the system will no longer fit in with the approach of the planners. Both a new task analysis and a new or adapted system are then required. Unfortunately, at that point the paradox will emerge again, causing the situation to repeat itself. It would be a good thing to develop a learning theory that indicates how planners react to support in the planning process, so that changes in the cognitive execution of tasks can, to a certain degree, be anticipated.

14

INTELLIGENT SHUNTING: DEALING WITH CONSTRAINTS (SATISFACTION)

ERWIN ABBINK

Department of Logistics, NS Reizigers, NL-3500-HA, Utrecht, the Netherlands

14.1. INTRODUCTION

This chapter deals with our approach to the problem as described in Chapter 12. In this section, we will give a brief introduction on the shunting problem. In the subsequent sections we will explain the approach, the model, and the results of our research. We will finish this chapter with some conclusions.

14.1.1. Problem Description

As explained, the problem is to route rolling stock units of the arriving trains on the platform tracks to the shunting area (where the siding tracks are allocated) and to choose a track to store the units. Vice versa, the units have to be routed from the shunting area to the platform tracks of the departing trains.

A scheduling problem is usually related to assigning routes to resources. In our case, the main elements of the problem are the shunting activities and the resources consisting of rolling stock and tracks. The shunting activities have a start and an end time from which a duration period can be derived. Each activity claims a certain amount of the available resources. Each shunting activity involves the following:

- At least one rolling stock unit
- One route
- One position on a track to store the unit

Planning in Intelligent Systems: Aspects, Motivations, and Methods, Edited by Wout van Wezel, René Jorna, and Alexander Meystel
Copyright © 2006 John Wiley & Sons, Inc.

A shunting activity involves the transportation of rolling stock units (possibly of different types) to a siding track. In addition, all possible routes or elements playing a role in the planning process are given. For each shunting activity a number of routes can be mapped out and selected, starting or ending at the right track and in the right zone. The routing problem involves selecting one route for each activity. All possible tracks, including their capacity (meters), are given. For each shunting activity, one track has to be selected. We call this problem the track assignment problem.

In our case (i.e., the shunting problem for Zwolle), when interviewing the planners, we found out that the assignment problem was more complicated than the routing problem, which they solved by applying some general heuristics. Therefore, in this project we have initially focused on this complicated assignment issue.

The Track Assignment Problem. For each kind of train and platform track, planners have a set of siding tracks on which they prefer to store the units. There are (only) two tracks that are suitable for storing diesel trains because these are provided with battery recharging equipment, called depot feeding.

The planners prefer to schedule units of the same type on the same track. This is because whenever a unit needs to be moved back toward the platform, it is not important which one is moved, as long as that unit is of the right type. When multiple units of the same type are stored on the same track, the planner can simply select the first one, because units of the same kind are interchangeable. If types are mixed, there is a higher risk that the divergent types of material will block the route to the platform.

Routing Problem. Planners know the layout of the stations by heart. For each destination or departure track, they know which alternative routes can be used. They do not plan the routes in detail. They globally check for conflicts in routes. Based on the timetable, planners know when complete sets of routes (e.g., all routes crossing the right-hand side of a station) cannot be used.

14.1.2. Approach

In this section we will explain the technique we have chosen to tackle the problem we are dealing with. We will also present and explain the criteria we have chosen in our selection of this scheduling technique. The set of criteria is developed with the pragmatic goal of acquiring a proper insight into the different capabilities of the various techniques in order to select a suitable one. It is not our aim to establish a complete set of criteria.

The following criteria have been applied:

- **The Technique Should Provide (Near) Optimality**. In real-life optimization problems, such as the one we are dealing with here, complexity is often a good reason for applying heuristics that focus on finding a good solution rather than the optimal solution. A requirement for this approach is that the solution found cannot be improved "easily" by hand. If this were to be the case, the planners would not accept the solution. Therefore we suggest that, when solving a real-life problem, we should try to use an approach that will provide us with an optimal solution that cannot be improved. In addition, due to the intensive usage of the infrastructure and the high costs involved, the need for an optimal solution is clear. The technique used should provide us preferably with the best solution. In this study we will be satisfied with any solution, but in the future we want to extend the model to be able to find the best possible solution. Technical solutions (software and hardware) are still improving at a very rapid pace (ILOG closing the gap). Complex problems can increasingly be solved by proven (near) optimality.

- **It Should Be Able to Handle Large Cases**. The complexity of the case indicates that the problem can be solved integrally for one station; there is no reason to divide the problem into several subproblems. Moreover, it would be hard to find a good partitioning criterion. Partitioning very often leads to suboptimal solutions. Because we want to solve a case that is quite large, we have to select a technique that has proven itself in solving large cases.

- **It Should Involve a Heuristic Approach**. A heuristic approach would be to use the problem-solving knowledge of the planners. We think that computational power alone is not enough to solve our problem. The generic problem-solving techniques provided by a scheduling engine should be combined with domain-specific knowledge related to solving the case. The technique to be used has to support this integration of both knowledge types.

- **It Should Support Problem Formulation**. The technique should support problem formulation in a natural manner. This would have a positive effect on the development time and the maintainability of the model.

- **It Should Be Robust in Finding Good Solutions**. The technique should not be too sensitive to deviations. Each station in the Netherlands has its own particularities regarding the shunting problem. If we want to apply the technique in all cases, it should be robust.

- **It Would Have to Meet the Industrial Standards for Scheduling**. We want to use a technique commonly used for scheduling that has proven its applicability and lives up to the industrial standards.

- **It Should Enable Us to Solve the Problem Integrally**. On the basis of our experiences with other scheduling problems in the railway domain, we have concluded that we have to find a solution method that can solve the problem integrally. Methods (heuristics) that split up the problem into several subproblems that have to be solved sequentially or even iteratively undermine, in most cases, the chances of finding feasible solutions in difficult cases. In addition, we find that dividing the problem into smaller parts and subsequently integrating them again makes it harder to solve the larger puzzle. This may eventually lead to having to solve the problem manually again rather than using computer support.

We have applied these criteria to several scheduling techniques. This method of weighing was based on our own research and experiences and therefore can be considered as rather subjective. For this reason we will not include all details in this chapter. In the end, we chose to apply Constraint Satisfaction Programming and Domain Reduction to model and solve the problem. This technique is commonly abbreviated as CSP and will be further described in Section 14.2.2.

One of the reasons to choose the CSP technique is that our shunting problem appears to have a lot in common with problems that can be solved with this technique. CSP is an appropriate approach to problems with highly different variables and constraints, such as those involving integer, logical, and choice variables and/or linear and logical constraints.

The second idea behind opting for this approach is that we think it is essential to separate the problem model from the solution method. This will give us flexibility in future adaptations of the model, which will certainly be necessary. The notion of making a distinction between generic task inference and domain-specific input with respect to such a task can also be found in the theory of CommonKADS. We will give a short description of this theory in Section 14.2.1.

For the development of the prototype, we have selected a general-purpose optimization package, ILOG Solver (ILOG) based on the CSP paradigm, which enables us to focus on the domain specific issues. This software handles generic issues, such as propagation of constraints and backtracking in the search. It has a built-in mechanism to apply a CSP-guided search. One of the reasons to choose this package was that it is recommended in Fernandez and Hill (2000).

We used OPL Studio to model the problem. This tool provides functionality to formulate the domain knowledge of used objects and constraints. Moreover, it provides the possibility to formulate a strategy that guides the search for a solution. The tool interacts directly with the Solver, so no technical programming has to be performed.

Complicated scheduling problems that cannot be solved integrally have to be solved by means of heuristic approaches. A commonly used heuristic approach is to split up the problem into less complicated subproblems and solve them independently. Afterwards, the solutions to the subproblems are integrated, and in this way a solution to the larger problem is found. The advantage of this approach is that the subproblems can be solved in a relatively small amount of computation time. However, one no longer has the guarantee of optimality.

Another possibility is to apply heuristics to search for the best solution. These can be based on mathematical theory (such as column generation with for cost feedback) as well as on knowledge of human problem solvers. In a large number of MIP (Mixed Integer Programming) problems, one could use this approach in the selection of the variables and further elaborate it. Together with the constraint propagation and the domain reduction techniques, it has proven to be a very powerful approach. We used it in the attempt to solve our shunting problem. As explained earlier, we want to solve the problem integrally.

14.2. THEORY

14.2.1. CommonKADS

One of the well-known methods for implementing knowledge-based decision support systems is CommonKADS (Schreiber et al., 2000). CommonKADS provides a structured method for knowledge elicitation, knowledge modeling, and task decomposition. An important principle of the CommonKADS method is the knowledge level principle: The first focus should be on the conceptual structure of the knowledge, which should be complemented with implementation and programming details in a later stage.

Often the main focus is on the development of the system. Some real-life examples at NS Reizigers (NS-Passengers) have shown that this is not always the best approach. Besides system development, the human factor is a very important aspect in the implementation of new working processes and supporting systems.

In a real environment, knowledge and behavior reside. Experts are part of an organized context, which influences the way of executing a task. CommonKADS provides mechanisms to preserve the structure of the knowledge. It helps in finding answers to three types of essential questions:

Why? Why is a knowledge system a potential help or solution? To which problems? Which benefits, costs, and organizational impacts does it have? Understanding the organizational context and environment is the most important issue here.

What? What is the nature and structure of the knowledge involved? What is the nature and structure of the corresponding communication? The conceptual description of the knowledge applied in performing a task is the main issue here.

How? How does the knowledge have to be implemented in a computer system? How do the software architecture and the computational mechanisms look? The technical aspects of the computer realization are the main focus here.

All these questions are answered by the development of (pieces of) aspect models. CommonKADS involves a predefined set of models:

- **Organization Model**. The organizational model supports the analysis of the major characteristics of an organization in order to discover problems and opportunities to be dealt with by knowledge systems, to establish their feasibility, and to assess the impacts of intended knowledge actions on the organization.
- **Task Model**. Tasks are the relevant subparts of a business process. The task model analyzes the global task layout, its inputs and outputs, preconditions and performance criteria, as well as required resources and competences.
- **Agent Model**. Agents are executors of a task. An agent can be a human, an information system, or any other entity capable of carrying out a task. The agent model describes the characteristics of agents—in particular their competencies,

their authority to act, and their constraints in this respect. Furthermore, an agent model lists the communication links between agents when carrying out a task.

- **Knowledge Model**. The purpose of the knowledge model is to explicate in detail the types and structures of the knowledge used in performing a task. It provides an implementation-independent description of the role that different knowledge components play in problem solving in a way that is understandable to humans. This makes the knowledge model an important vehicle of communication between experts and users about the problem-solving aspects of a knowledge system, both during development and system execution.

- **Communication Model**. Since several agents may be involved in a task, it is important to model the communicative transactions between the agents involved. This is done by the communication model in a conceptual and implementation-independent way, similar to the approach of the knowledge model.

- **Design Model**. The above-mentioned CommonKADS models together can be regarded as a construct constituting the specification of requirements for the knowledge system, divided into different aspects. On the basis of these requirements, the design model provides the technical system specification in terms of architecture, implementation platform, software modules, representational constructs, and computational mechanisms, required to implement the functions laid down in the knowledge and communication models.

Together, the organization, task, and agent models analyze the organizational environment and the corresponding critical success factors of a knowledge system. The knowledge and communication models bring forth the conceptual description of problem-solving functions and data that are to be delivered and handled by a knowledge system. Due to the limited time available, we did not include all models in our research project. In further research studies, the models that have not yet been used should be integrated.

We aim at creating a system that supports the planner to solve the planning problem. In our opinion, this should be done by creating a system in which the (domain and task) knowledge of the planners is represented. This knowledge can then be used by the automated inference of the system to support the planner in a natural manner. This approach is quite suitable for the CommonKADS paradigm.

14.2.2. The CSP Technique

Domain reduction and constraint propagation are especially appropriate for problems involving integer variables and logical constraints, such as scheduling problems. The combination of domain reduction and constraint propagation with linear programming can be very effective when solving problems involving both real and integer variables and linear constraints.

This technique starts with the premise that it may be more efficient to identify the solution only after it has been quantified. Every decision has a domain of possible values; for example, a real variable can take any value in the range $[l, u]$; an integer variable can take any integer value in the range $[l, u]$, and a logical variable can take the value 0 or 1. Domain reduction systematically removes values that are no longer valid from each variable domain.

If there is a sufficient number of constraints, the domains may be dramatically reduced. If a variable has an empty domain, the problem becomes infeasible, meaning that there is no possible value for that variable, so the problem has no solution. Constraint propagation works by systematically reducing all variable domains. Each constraint is linked to an associated set of variables that are affected by that constraint. Each variable belongs to the associated set of at least one constraint; if not, it is an unconstrained variable. If the domain of that variable is altered, the associated set of variables of each of these constraints will also be affected. This change to their domains will, in turn, affect other variables via other constraints. The effect of a change in one variable is propagated via constraints throughout all the decision variables. The effectiveness of this approach increases as the network of constraints expands.

Example. Consider three variables X, Y, Z with:

$$\text{domain } X = \{1 \ldots 5\}$$
$$\text{domain } Y = \{1 \cdots 5\}$$
$$\text{domain } Z = \{1 \cdots 5\}$$
$$\text{constraint } C1: X > Y$$
$$\text{constraint } C2: X + Z = 4$$

Apply domain reduction:

$$
\begin{aligned}
C1 &\Longrightarrow \text{domain } X = \{2 \cdots 5\} \\
&\qquad\text{domain } Y = \{1 \cdots 4\} \\
C2 &\Longrightarrow \text{domain } X = \{1 \cdots 3\} \\
&\qquad\text{domain } Z = \{1 \cdots 3\} \\
C1 + C2 &\Longrightarrow \text{domain } X = \{2 \cdots 3\} \\
&\qquad\text{domain } Y = \{1 \cdots 2\} \\
&\qquad\text{domain } Z = \{1 \cdots 2\}
\end{aligned}
$$

The domain reduction technique reduces the domains of each variable from 5 to 2 possible values.

Now we assign a value to X, $X = \{2\}$.

Constraint propagation:

$$
\begin{aligned}
C1 &\Longrightarrow \text{domain } Y = \{1\} \\
C2 &\Longrightarrow \text{domain } Z = \{2\}
\end{aligned}
$$

Each variable has an unique value assigned to it: solution found.

Domain reduction and constraint propagation provide a platform for diverse problem formulations. Because these techniques incorporate many types of variables and functions, it can be applied to most problems. In most cases, they give a compact representation of the feasible solution space.

The weakness of this approach becomes apparent when trying to find a feasible region for an optimal solution. If the feasible region is large, the approach may become inefficient in finding the best solution. If both linear and nonlinear constraints are involved, the use of linear programming solvers for linear constraints and domain reduction solvers for nonlinear constraints provide efficient search engines for constraint propagation. Combining these techniques provides an approach that can be applied to a broad range of problems. Our chosen tool OPL Studio uses its built-in linear solver to guide the CSP algorithm. Through our research project we want to find out whether the shunting problem is within the range of problems that can be solved by using CSP.

The architecture of OPL Studio enables the modeling of an optimization model as an addition to the separate models proposed by CommonKADS. Domain Knowledge can be modeled as data types and constraints. Also task knowledge can be represented in the search method. This search is supported by a built-in search method based on CSP. It can be considered as elementary inference knowledge that can be applied to a generic scheduling problem.

14.3. THE MODEL

14.3.1. General

In this chapter we will present the model that was created during the project. We will also describe the simplifications we made regarding the real-life problem. These simplifications relate to the omission of aspects, such as washing, cleaning, refueling, and the scheduling of personnel. We will not only present the physical constraints formulated, but also give an outline of the way in which the search strategy was adapted to the domain-specific problem.

When constructing the initial model a number of ideas were developed for adding more detail to the model in the future. In the final part of this chapter, we will present these ideas.

14.3.2. OPL Notation

We will now describe the model as developed for and implemented in the prototype. The model has been created by using the Optimization Programming Language (OPL), supported by OPL Studio. This is a high-level modeling language that supports the creation of Linear and Integer Programming models as well as models to be used in the CSP technique. A description of this language can be found in Hentenryck (1999).

The selected tool also provides mechanisms to create models by using standard programming languages, such as Java and C++, but these models are less readable and do not provide natural representations of the actual problems. The OPL language enables us to create a readable model that is not dependent on any programming language and that is supported by the development tool.

An optimization model consists of input data, decision variables, an objective function, and constraint functions. These elements will be described in the remainder of this section.

14.3.2.1. Input Data. A number of shunting activities are given for which we have to determine or assign the siding track and find a route that leads to or from that track. Also a number of regular train activities are given. These are fixed and reduce the available tracks and routes at the station. Other input involves the description of the infrastructure, tracks and routes, and information about rolling stock, type, and length.

14.3.2.2. Decision Variables. The model contains several integer variables. In this model the integer variables are binary variables, which means that there are two possible values: 0 and 1. We have created several sets of variables. Each variable is composed of several elements. We will present the name of the set and list the elements used to construct a set of variables:

- *FromTrainTrack*
  - *TrainNumber.* A corresponding train number: the unique identification of a shunting activity. Only the activities carried out from the platform to the shunting areas are included.
  - *Track.* A siding track that can be assigned to a shunting activity. An assignment consists of positioning the units related to the activity on that track.
  - *Phase.* A phase, that side ([A, B], left or right) of the track, which is used to enter the track.
  - *RsPosition* (Rolling Stock Position). Each element represents an entry in a matrix, which is explained in the next section about scheduling elements, in particular reservoirs.
- *ToTrainTrack*
  - *TrainNumber.* A corresponding train number: the unique identification of a shunting activity. Only the activities carried out from the shunting area toward the platform are included.
  - *Track.* A siding track that can be assigned to a shunting activity. An assignment consists of removing the units related to the activity from that track.
  - *Phase.* A phase, that side ([A, B], left or right) of the track, which is used to depart from.
  - *RsPosition* (Rolling Stock Position). Each element represents an entry in a matrix that is explained in the next section about scheduling elements, in particular reservoirs.

- *FromTrainRoute*
  - *TrainNumber.* A corresponding train number: the unique identification of a shunting activity. Only the activities carried out from the platform to the shunting areas are included.
  - *Route.* The route from a platform to a siding track.
- *ToTrainRoute*
  - *TrainNumber.* A corresponding train number: the unique identification of a shunting activity. Only the activities carried out from the shunting area toward the platform are included.
  - *Route.* The route from a siding to a platform track.

Sets of variables are created containing elements that can be used in combination with each other. For instance, we will only create an element for *FromTrainRoute* for a certain combination of Activity and Route, if the route departs from the track where the shunting activity starts and ends in the zone where the activity is supposed to end.

For each set of variables we will create an array, indexed by the variables. Each element of this array can have the value 0 or 1. A value 1 for an element means that the corresponding variable is selected in the solution. A value 0 implies the opposite. When a variable is selected, it means that either the shunting activity is carried out along a certain route or, depending on the type of variable, that the corresponding unit is placed at a certain location on a siding track, or removed from it.

An alternative would be to (a) create an n-dimensional matrix including all combinations and (b) add constraints to the model to ensure that only the right combinations are chosen in the process of finding a solution. However, this would increase the number of variables and constraints, thereby in turn increasing the amount of internal memory and computational time required to find a solution.

The chosen representation, in which these constraints are checked during initialization rather than during scheduling, reduces the size of the problem drastically.[1] A large number of variables that are obviously not suitable for use in the solution process are removed.

We have included an array of dummy variables called *DummyTrack*, which is used to solve feasibility problems caused by errors in the input data. In this pilot we did not have data on the number and location of rolling stock units at the beginning of the scheduling interval. If a shunting activity starts at a moment when units of a certain kind have not yet arrived, we can use additional units to attain a feasible solution. We assume that for each kind of rolling stock and for each position on the tracks, there is an additional unit that can be used.

In reality the rolling stock roster, the input for the shunting problem, is balanced. This means that for every unit that departs, another unit arrives. Therefore, if we have the correct data, we will not have to use any additional units.

---

[1]Experiments during the development of the prototype have shown that the number of constraints were reduced from 6,000,000 to 12,000.

Scheduling Objects. OPL Studio provides a set of scheduling objects. Basically there are two kinds: Activities and Resources. In our model we use certain types of activities to represent the shunting activities and a special kind of resource called "reservoir" to represent the infrastructural capacity.

The activity has three properties: Start, End, and Duration. We use three kinds of activities:

1. **Activity *ShuntAct*.** The *ShuntAct* is an activity to represent the shunting activity. The start time of the *ShuntAct* is equal to the start time of the shunting activity, and the end is equal to the end of the scheduling interval. This implies that the activity claims the resources from the moment the activity starts until the end of the scheduling interval. Recourses will become available when the units stored during the previous activity are used again in a new activity.

2. **Activity *ShadowAct*.** The *ShadowAct* is an activity to free resources temporarily claimed by the *ShuntAct*. The start time of the *ShadowAct* is equal to the start time of the shunting activity plus 1 minute. The end is equal to the end of the scheduling interval.

3. **Activity *DummyDayAct*.** The *DummyDayAct* is an activity to represent the start time of the *DummyTrack* activities. The start and end of the *Dummy-DayAct* are equal to the start and end of the scheduling interval.

These activities determine the intervals during which reservoirs are used. The reservoir consists of the properties "maximum capacity" and "initial capacity." During the scheduling interval, capacity can be withdrawn (required) and added (supplied).

Three kinds of capacity reservoirs are implemented:

1. ***TrackCapacity***, representing the length of the track in meters. The maximum capacity is the length of the track. The initial capacity is the maximum capacity minus the sum of the lengths of the units that are stored on the track at the beginning of the scheduling interval. When a rolling stock unit is stored on a track, the length of the unit is subtracted from the available capacity, and when a unit is removed the length is added to the available capacity.

2. ***TrackPositionInd***, representing a position on the track. In the model, each track is segmented into six parts, also called positions. These parts do not have any physical boundaries and they are used to indicate that a unit is stored at the left or right side of other units. To each unit, one position on the track is assigned. In this way we can see whether one unit is blocked by another and cannot enter or leave the track at that particular moment. In the future, when we are able to store more than six units on a single track, the number of positions will be increased. The maximum capacity of the reservoir is 1. If a *TrackPositionInd* is used, the capacity becomes

zero, which implies that no other unit can be located in this position. When a unit has to be stored in a certain position, we have to ensure that there are no other units blocking the route toward it. This is represented by the constraint that all positions leading to the required position are occupied for one minute. The solver determines whether this is not feasible as a result of the fact that other units have already occupied the positions. The one-minute occupation is accomplished by using a set of shadow activities that succeed the original activities by one minute. The original activities occupy (claim) the route, and the shadow activities free the route.

3. **TrackRsPosition**, representing a Type of Rolling Stock that is placed in a certain position on the track. The predetermined scheduling objects provided by ILOG have a limitation. We can model that a reservoir is used, but we cannot express directly that a reservoir is used by a certain kind of rolling stock. Therefore, we have created a third kind of reservoir called *TrackRsPosition*. This is a three-dimensional (Track, Kind, Position) matrix of reservoirs. This third kind of reservoir is only used to ensure that the right kind of rolling stock is chosen when we remove units from a shunting position in a certain area. In this case, both a track and position can only be selected if a unit of the right kind is available at the requested moment.

Example: Positioning a Unit of Type T2 on Position P3 from the Left Side.

Initial situation:

	P1	P2	P3	P4	P5	P6
T1	0	0	0	1	0	0
T2	0	0	0	0	0	0
Position	0	0	0	1	0	0

There is one unit of type T1 stored on position 4.

Intermediate situation:

	P1	P2	P3	P4	P5	P6
T1	0	0	0	1	0	0
T2	0	0	1	0	0	0
Position	1	1	1	1	0	0

There is one unit of type T1 stored on position 4. One unit of type T2 claims capacity on positions P1, P2, and P3. P1 and P2 are claimed to move the unit to position P3.

Final situation:

	P1	P2	P3	P4	P5	P6
T1	0	0	0	1	0	0
T2	0	0	1	0	0	0
Position	0	0	1	1	0	0

There is one unit of type T1 stored at position 4, and one unit of type T2 is stored at P3. Positions P1 and P2 are available again and can be used by other units.

The initial situation shows that it is not possible to store the unit on position P3 from the right side. This is because we cannot claim position P4 twice. To remove a unit from a certain position, the opposite procedure has to be followed.

14.3.2.3. Objective Function. We define two objective functions that can be used alternately.

Objective 1:

$$OPL > Min \; Obj$$
$$OPL > Obj = 1;$$

This first objective to minimize Obj is not really an objective function. Usually the objective is dependent upon a number of decision variables. This one is merely a constant, and the objective is used to create a model that merely searches for a single feasible solution. When any solution is found, this will be the "best" solution because it has resulted in attaining the minimum objective. This is useful particularly when the model and the constraints themselves are developed. This first objective is only used to give a good indication of the technical validity of the model.

Objective 2:

$$OPL > Min \; Obj$$
$$OPL > Obj = sum \; (s \; in \; Tracks, p \; in \; RsPosition) \; DummyTrack \; [s, p];$$

The objective is equal to the sum of the value of all Dummytracks. This value can either be zero or one, which implies that the sum is equal to the number of dummy units used. Since we want to minimize the objective, we try to minimize the number of dummy units used. The second objective function is used in case no solution can be found as a result of incorrect input. If this occurs, it is acceptable to use additional (dummy) units. We want to limit the number used in order to determine the minimum number of units that need to be available in reality. This can be achieved by this objective.

The result can be used to correct the input data so that we can rerun the problem without having to use additional units. The final Rintel system will check whether the input data are correct, ensuring us that there is no need to use additional units

In this stage of our research, we did not focus too much on finding a meaningful objective function, because in our view such a function only becomes relevant in the stage when the model itself has matured some more. For instance, searching for the shortest route is only relevant if the determination of conflicting routes is also included in the model.

14.3.2.4. Constraint Functions. It is not difficult to observe that scheduling is an activity with a high degree of symmetry. Moving units to and from the siding tracks are two separate processes that share the same characteristics, but involve opposite series of actions. This is reflected in the model. For almost all constraints, a corresponding constraint can be found with an opposite activity.[2] Therefore, we will only explain the constraints relating to the activities carried out on the route toward the shunting tracks. They will be explained in the remainder of this section.

For each shunting activity we have to select precisely one track on which the rolling stock unit can be placed.

Constraint 1:

> *OPL > forall (t in FromTrains)*
>> *sum(trs in FromTrainTrack:trs.TrainNr=t) ShuntAway [trs] = 1;*

For each shunting activity (*t in FromTrains*) we have to select precisely one route to transport the rolling stock unit. The sum of all chosen routes related to this activity (trs.TrainNr = t) has to be equal to one.

Constraint 2:

> *OPL > forall (t in FromTrains)*
>> *sum(tr in FromTrainRoutes:tr.TrainNr=t) ChosenFromRoute [tr] = 1;*

For each shunting activity and selected track (OPL>ShuntAway[trs]=1) we have to select a route that ends at that track and enters it at the right phase.

---

[2]For example, for the first constraint we have an "opposite" one:

Constraint 1a:
> *OPL > forall (t in ToTrains)*
>> *sum(trs in ToTrainTrack:trs.TrainNr=t) ShuntBack[trs]=1;*

Constraint 3:

OPL > forall (trs in FromTrainTrack)
      (ShuntAway [trs] <=
      (sum(tr in FromTrainRoutes:tr.TrainNr = trs.TrainNr and
                        tr.Route.ToStation = trs.Track.Station and
                        tr.Route.ToTrack = trs.Track.Track and
                        tr.Route.DirectionEntry = trs.Phase)
    ChosenFromRoute [tr]));

Constraint 3 ensures that at least one route will be chosen, corresponding to the selected track. Please note that we can select a route for a train (right-hand side is 1) while the position on the track has not yet been selected (left-hand side is 0) for that train. The reason for this is that we only select one out of six possible positions. Whenever a position on the track is selected, we also have to select a route toward that track.

Constraint 2 limits the number of routes that can be selected per activity to one. Therefore, the combination of constraints will ensure that, for each activity, one route, corresponding to the chosen track, will be selected.

If a unit has been stored on a track (*ShuntAway*[trs]=1), the capacity of that track has to be reduced by the length of the unit. In OPL we state that an acitivity (*ShuntAct*) requires a certain amount of capacity from a resource (*TrackCapacity*), namely the length of the unit.

Constraint 4:

OPL > forall (trs in FromTrainTrack)
        ShuntAct[trs.TrainNr]
                requires(ShuntAway[trs]*Length[trs.RsPosition.RsType])
                    TrackCapacity[trs.Track];

If a certain kind of unit is placed in a position (*TrackMatPosition*) on a track, the capacity of that position has to be reduced by 1.

Constraint 5:

OPL > forall (trs in FromTrainTrack)
        ShuntAct[trs.TrainNr]
                requires(ShuntAway[trs])
                    TrackRsPosition[trs.Track,trs.RsPosition];

If a unit is placed in a position (*PositionInd*) on a track, the capacity of that position has to be reduced by 1.

Constraint 6:

OPL > forall (trs in FromTrainTrack)
          ShuntAct[trs.TrainNr]
                    requires(ShuntAway[trs])
                              TrackPositionInd[trs.Track,trs.RsPosition.Position];

If a unit is placed in a position on a track and it enters that track from phase A, the capacity of all positions (left side) smaller than the required position has to be reduced by 1.

Constraint 7:

OPL > forall (trs in FromTrainTrack, p1 in PositionInd:
          p1 < trs.RsPosition.Position)
                    ShuntAct[trs.TrainNr]
                                        requires (ShuntAway[trs]*(trs.Phase="A"))
                                                  TrackPositionInd[trs.Track,p1];

When entering a track from the other side, the opposite applies.

Constraint 8:

OPL > forall (trs in FromTrainTrack, p1 in PositionInd:
          p1 > trs.RsPosition.Position)
                    ShuntAct[trs.TrainNr]
                                        requires(ShuntAway[trs]*(trs.Phase="B"))
                                                  TrackPositionInd[trs.Track,p1];

If a unit is placed in a certain position on the track and the unit enters the track from phase A, the capacity of all positions (left side) smaller than the required position has to be increased by the shadow activity by 1. This will release (provide) the temporarily claimed capacity of the track.

Constraint 9:

OPL > forall (trs in FromTrainTrack, p1 in PositionInd:
          p1 < trs.RsPosition.Position)
                    ShadowAct [trs.TrainNr]
                                        provides (ShuntAway[trs]*(trs.Phase="A"))
                                                  TrackPositionInd[trs.Track, p1];

When entering a track from the other side, the opposite applies.

Constraint 10:

$OPL > forall$ *(trs in FromTrainTrack, p1 in PositionInd:*
$\qquad$ *p1 $>$ trs.RsPosition.Position)*
$\qquad\qquad$ *ShadowAct[trs.TrainNr]*
$\qquad\qquad\qquad$ *Provides(ShuntAway[trs]*(trs.Phase="B"))*
$\qquad\qquad\qquad\qquad$ *TrackPositionInd[trs.Track,p1];*

This constraint completes the description of the initial model. In addition to the model, we have developed a small search strategy that is presented in the next section.

14.3.2.5. Search Strategy. Although the used software has a built-in mechanism to find solutions, this does not guarantee that a particular solution will be found within a reasonable computation time. If the default strategy would be elaborated by some specific problem-solving knowledge, the performance could be improved.

The idea is to first schedule all activities moving toward and from one particular shunting area (*ShuntAreas*). This is because there is no interdependency between the assignment problem and the shunting areas. Second, we will try to combine all activities of the same rolling stock types (*RsTypes*). Finally, we will try to schedule per track and per position. The aim is to store units of the same kind on the same track. This is a heuristic approach applied by the planners as explained in Section 14.1.1.

We have developed the following search strategy:

```
OPL>search{
    tryall (z in ShuntAreas)
      tryall (m in RsTypes)
        tryall (s in Tracks:TrackZone[s]=z)
          tryall (p in RsPosition:p.RsType=m){
            tryall (trs in FromTrainTrack:trs.Track=s and trs.RsPosition=p)
              ShuntAway[trs]=1;
            tryall (trs in ToTrainTrack: trs.Track=s and trs.RsPosition=p)
              ShuntBack[trs]=1;
          };
    };
```

This strategy tries to assign the value 1 to the elements of the arrays *ShuntAway* and *ShuntBack*, representing the choice of assigning a track, a position and a track entrance side to a shunting activity. The order of assignments is defined by the *tryall* statements.

These few statements are all that we have defined in the implementation of the search strategy. The assignment of routes has not as yet been based on domain specific knowledge. The internal mechanism handles the checking and propagation of the constraints as well as backtracking and the assignment of values to variables that are not included in the domain-specific search strategy.

14.4. THE RESULTS

Unfortunately, we were not able to test a large number of cases. We will present the results of scheduling shunting activities in our first implementation. With the help of simplifying assumptions, in this case we were able to find a solution. We will evaluate the current implementation on the basis of some criteria mentioned in succeeding sections.

14.4.1. Quality of the Solution

First of all, the solution has to obey all constraints relating to the problem. After that, the quality can be measured according to a yet-to-be-defined, objective function. In this initial version we consider finding a feasible solution to be the most important aspect.

So, the first objective of the prototype is finding a feasible solution. The efficiency of the solution is not an issue. The prototype finds a solution that satisfies all conditions of the model in terms of constraints. It can therefore be stated that any solution generated is of good quality.

One experiment to deal with the number of additional dummy units was performed by applying an objective function. The system had no problems in finding a solution with a minimum number of additional dummy units.

We know that the solution obtained may not be the best solution, both in the opinion of the planners and of the company. To determine whether the system can find a solution of ultimate quality, we will have to implement a more advanced objective function. This is something that we can do after this first pilot. The OPL language will enable us to model a more advanced objective function. The biggest problem is always to model the objective in such a way that it reflects the preferences of planners. These preferences can be rather subjective and may be based on intuition or experience, which makes it hard to verbalize them. Technically, we do not foresee any problems with respect to the creation of a new objective function.

Once a new objective function has been developed, we expect the search method to be aligned to this objective. For instance, if we want to minimize the distance of the selected routes, the search mechanism should retrieve the routes tested for assignment to the shunting activities on the basis of distance. In this way we should be able to find a solution of good quality efficiently.

14.4.2. Computational Time to Find a Solution

Not only do we want to find a solution of sufficient quality, we also want to find it within a limited computational time. We want to schedule the shunting activities at the end of the scheduling process, after the planning of the timetable, the rolling stock and the train personnel. For this reason, the time to find a solution is limited. By applying this initial model, we expect to find a solution within a few minutes.

In this case, we have tried to solve two subproblems. The first problem we dealt with was a set of shunting movements (35) related to a shunting zone consisting of three tracks that could only be entered from one side. The second problem referred to a set of activities (21) related to a shunting zone containing four tracks that could be entered from both sides.

Both problems related to all shunting activities carried out in an entire day according to the schedules created by hand. We did not have the time to create a data set for all activities at once. There was no point in doing so by means of our initial prototype, because two subproblems only then become interdependent when conflicts in routes occur. Since we have not yet implemented this option in our model, there is no relation between the activity schedules in the different shunting zones.

Each problem can be solved within 1 minute. Initialization takes 30 seconds per subproblem. If we were to try to solve the complete case, we expect that the time required would still be acceptable. In our case, the most difficult part is track assignment, which we have initially investigated. In our view the tool has delivered a very good performance in our case, which will be very difficult to exceed with a custom-made algorithm programmed in a general-purpose programming language (like C++, Pascal, or Java).

14.4.3. Degree of Detail

The quality of the solution and the processing time depend on the degree of detail of the model. The initial model is not very detailed and we can therefore expect that, in practice, the solution generated will not be completely feasible. On the other hand, because not all of the details have to be taken into account, we can expect to find a solution within minutes.

The goal of this pilot was to implement an initial prototype to solve a scheduling problem. This implies that we were free to choose the level of detail to be implemented in the prototype. We focused on the part that was assumed to be the most difficult: the track assignment. Especially the "blocking-in" mechanism was expected to be difficult.

We found a way to implement this mechanism by applying a number of constraints that are relatively easy to understand and, in addition, provide a basis for the determination of conflicts in routes. There are two extensions that have to be implemented (multiple units and additional shunting activities) before the track assignment part can be completed. We think that the current model addresses the track assignment problem in a sufficiently detailed way. The missing details can additionally be incorporated relatively easily.

14.4.4. Extensibility of the Model

One further aspect entails (a) the possibility to add additional detail to the model and (b) the estimated impact this will have on the performance of the prototype.

In the next chapter, we will give some suggestions for extensions to the model. These extensions could be incorporated into the model quite naturally. To add these extensions, the model does not need to be changed drastically. This is one of the assets of the model. Although it is an initial version, the model reflects the real scheduling problem in such a way that no special tricks or techniques have to be applied in order to extend it.

14.5. RECOMMENDED EXTENSIONS

It was not the goal of this project to create a complete prototype, but to develop an initial one. However, with respect to each extension, we will try to consider whether it could be incorporated into our model and what effect it may have on the performance of the tool. This will be taken into consideration when we present our conclusions and results in the following sections.

14.5.1. Multiple Units per Shunting Activity

Currently only one rolling stock unit is assigned to a shunting activity. In practice, per activity multiple units are shunted. An extension would be to replace the single unit involved in the activity by a set of units, possibly of different kinds. This change would then have to be accompanied by a change in the usage of the reservoirs. The model would have to assure that, during each activity involving N units, N consecutive positions are occupied on one track. Also the corresponding TrackMatPositions would have to be occupied.

We expect that this implementation will not be too complicated. Occupying multiple positions can be implemented in a similar way to the implementation of the current usage of reservoirs. We do not expect that the search strategy needs to be adapted.

14.5.2. Inserting Additional Shunting Activities

Sometimes it may not be possible to find a solution by means of the current variables. It may, however, be possible that, in some of these cases, there is a solution in which units are (temporarily) removed to other tracks in order to use the units that would otherwise be blocked-in. This is done by creating additional shunting activities.

We could, for instance, create a small number of activities that could be assigned to any unit and to any start and end track for which an intermediate route exists. We could determine the start and end times dynamically. The start time would have to be later than the moment when the unit arrives at the start track. It would also have to be at a moment when the departure route is free. The end time would have to be before the time when the "blocked-in" unit is needed.

We should have to adapt the objective so that the number of additional shunting activities is minimized. We cannot determine at the start of the search process whether the minimum number of shunting activities are going to be carried out. Therefore we propose a trial-and-error process whereby the allowed number is increased each time no feasible solution can be found. If we were to use a large number by default, the complexity of the problem could increase to such an extent that it may not be possible to find a solution within reasonable time.

14.5.3. Conflicting Routes

During the development of the model, we have carried out a small trial for the implementation of a mechanism to prevent conflicts in routes. We extended the model both to occupy the selected track and to free (provide capacity at) the starting track. Since a track can only be freed if it has been occupied first, we needed to insert train activities that provide the units that need to be shunted. These activities will cause the starting track to be occupied (require capacity). This experiment was successful with a limited set of data. The idea needs to be elaborated to include both the start track of the route and the intermediate tracks as well as the intersections of a route.

All infrastructure elements that are part of a route can be modeled as reservoirs. When an activity is carried out along a particular route, the corresponding reservoirs have to be occupied or claimed. The time and duration of the occupation have to be determined. These depend on the driving time required to transport the rolling stock via the route. We suggest to apply some predetermined times per route. These times will serve as input. This approach matches with the way in which a planner determines the driving time. Planners also make use of a predetermined driving time per route.

A reservoir is either free or occupied. In this way we prevent a reservoir from being used for multiple activities. Moreover, we do not need to concern ourselves with intersecting routes or the times when they are used. The ILOG scheduler will automatically make calculations to create a correct schedule.

This extension will increase the number of variables and constraints without enlarging the combinatorial complexity. The number of routes and tracks that have to be selected remains unchanged. The additional train activities are carried out along a predetermined route, and also the number of tracks that are occupied is predetermined. Some constraints will be added to the model, but there is no need to make additional choices.

Adding additional reservoirs will also increase the number of constraints. However, again there will be no increase in the number of variables. The additional constraints imply that, with each choice, we have to compute a larger number of constraints. On the other hand, additional constraints limit the solution space that has to be searched for, which could speed up the solution time. Overall, we expect that the computation time will increase but that we will still be able to find a solution within a reasonable time.

14.5.4. Dynamic Start Times

In the current implementation, the start and end times of the activities are fixed. However, this may hinder us in finding a proper solution. The times supplied should be used as a guideline, because they are computed calculations based on a heuristic that does not guarantee that they are optimal. We can adapt the model so that the times of the shunting activity lie within an interval covering the supplied times.

As an example, we introduce the following constraint on the starting time:

$OPL > forall$ (t in Trains){
$\quad\quad\quad\quad$ ShuntAct[t].start $>=$ ShuntMovement[t].StartTime $-$ 5;
$\quad\quad\quad\quad$ ShuntAct[t].start $<=$ ShuntMovement[t].StartTime $+$ 5;
$\quad\quad\quad\quad$ };

This constraint ensures that the scheduled start time is within 5 minutes of the supplied time. Additional constraints have to be added to ensure that a unit does not depart before it has arrived. We suggest implementing this extension after implementation of the previously suggested extension to avoid conflicts in routes. Only then can the solution technique fully exploit this additional flexibility and still provide solutions that are feasible in practice.

The objective function can be adapted to support the system in finding solutions in such a way that using the same infrastructure maximizes the number of times that activities succeed each other. In this way we can create a schedule that provides a buffer to disturbances in the real time operation.

The determination of the starting times is also dependent on the personnel available to perform the activities. In order to create efficient schedules, we also may want to adapt the times of the shunting activities. This is one of the subjects that still need to be investigated.

14.5.5. Cleaning, Washing, and Refueling

One of the major simplifications of the problem is the omission of the washing, cleaning, and refueling activities. We propose to add three activities of the aforementioned types to each unit that is shunted toward the shunting area.

On the basis of a number of guidelines, we need to determine the priority of each of these activities with respect to their scheduling. For example, we do not need to refuel all units, and not all units need to be washed every night. Some of the activities are required, while for others we have to adapt the objective function to schedule them properly.

To schedule the activity, we need to determine the start and end times, the track on which the activity can be performed, and the route to and from this track. We suggest to use the mechanism that is already incorporated in the current model dealing with the assignment problem, which applies the activities and reservoirs provided by the tool. We propose to create a specific kind of reservoir for the tracks with washing facilities and model the constraint that the washing activity can only be performed at these reservoirs. Cleaning and refueling can be handled in the same fashion.

The initial problem is extended by the fact that not all activities need to be scheduled. Whether or not to schedule an activity will depend on an objective function. Opposed to the initial case, there may be an additional activity between the arrival and the departure from the platform tracks. Using these additional activities, we may be able to release blocked-in units.

The additional activities and constraints will increase the complexity of the problem. If a solution cannot be found, we will have to determine the (combination of) activities and constraints that cause the infeasibility. Experiences with the development of other scheduling systems have shown that this can be very difficult. We need to develop a mechanism to obtain this information. This is an issue that needs to be studied more thoroughly after this project.

We think that this problem cannot be avoided. Even by applying a custom-made scheduling tool, it will be very hard to obtain this information. Therefore, this problem is independent of the usage of a generic scheduling tool and does not undermine our approach.

Finding a solution for this aspect of the case entails three parts that need to be investigated: modeling the input data as well as the case-dependent and generic search strategies. We think that with respect to solving this case there will not be any reason to adapt the generic search algorithm. The usage of the generic tool supports us in focusing on the models of the input data as well as on the case-dependent search strategy. This is, in our opinion, an advantage. It supports our idea to use a generic scheduling tool to solve our case.

14.6. OVERALL CONCLUSIONS

In our opinion, the presented model is flexible and can be expanded in a straightforward way. This is because we make use of generic scheduling objects, such as activities and resources. These fit in quite naturally with the real-life problem. Problem extensions can be modeled by using the same objects.

The prototype performs very well. Of course we are dealing with a simplified case. However, the prototype shows no serious problems with respect to any of the criteria. We think that the current model implemented in the prototype provides a solid basis for further development. After this project, the next step should be that, besides focusing on the technical aspects, the organizational aspects as well as the interaction of the planners with the solution process should be studied in detail.

15

APPLYING OPERATIONS RESEARCH TECHNIQUES TO PLANNING OF TRAIN SHUNTING

RAMON M. LENTINK

Rotterdam School of Management (RSM), Erasmus University Rotterdam, NL-3000-DR Rotterdam, the Netherlands

PIETER-JAN FIOOLE

Department of Logistics, NS Reizigers, NL-3500-HA Utrecht, the Netherlands

LEO G. KROON

Rotterdam School of Management (RSM), Erasmus University Rotterdam, NL-3000-DR Rotterdam, the Netherlands; and Department of Logistics, NS Reizigers, NL-3500-HA Utrecht, the Netherlands

COR VAN'T WOUDT

Department of Logistics, NS Reizigers, NL-3500-HA Utrecht, the Netherlands

15.1. INTRODUCTION

Within the rush hours, the rolling stock of a passenger railway operator is typically operating the timetable or it is in maintenance. However, outside the rush hours, an operator usually has a surplus of rolling stock. These surplus train units can be parked at a shunt yard in order to be able to fully exploit the main railway infrastructure by other trains. Especially during the night, many passenger train units have to be parked, since usually there are just a few night trains. In the Netherlands, mainly freight trains operate at night.

Planning in Intelligent Systems: Aspects, Motivations, and Methods, Edited by Wout van Wezel, René Jorna, and Alexander Meystel

The process of parking train units at a shunt yard together with several related processes is called *shunting*. The corresponding planning problem is called the *Train Unit Shunting Problem* (TUSP). A major complicating issue is the fact that train units are strongly restricted in their movements by the railway infrastructure. In addition, time is also a restrictive resource for shunting. For example, for safety reasons it is mandatory to respect a certain minimum headway time between two train movements on the same track. Finally, arrivals and departures are typically mixed in time. It is common to solve the TUSP for a 24-hour period, as well as station by station.

During the night, the goal of shunting is to select the positions and compositions of the trains at the shunt yard in such a way that the operations in the next morning can start up as smoothly as possible. This selection is subject to certain restrictions with respect to several related processes, which are introduced below. Furthermore, the created plans should be robust for it is certain that disruptions will occur in real time. When this happens, the plans should need as little changes as possible.

The Dutch railway network consists of approximately 3000 kilometers of railway track and some 400 stations. This infrastructure is used on a daily basis by a total of 4500 scheduled trains on lines ranging in length between 15 and over 200 kilometers. Approximately 1 million passengers travel more than 40 million kilometers each workday, which makes the Dutch network one of the most heavily utilized networks in the world. During the weekend, the infrastructure is used less intensively.

In the Netherlands, most trains are operated by train units, which are classified according to types and subtypes. Train units can move bi-directionally without the need for locomotives. Only train units of the same type can be combined to form trains, which contain at most 15 carriages. Subtypes belonging to the same type are discerned from each other by their numbers of carriages per train unit. The different subtypes of train units have different characteristics such as seating capacity and length. Figure 15.1 depicts an example of a Dutch train unit with three carriages. This particular type of train unit (ICM) consists of subtypes with three or four carriages, which are typically used for intercity services.

In general, train units of the same subtype can be used interchangeably. This flexibility implies that, given a timetable with times and exact compositions of the arriving and departing trains, a planner has to determine a matching of arriving and departing units at a station. A large part of this matching is already prescribed by the timetable.

For an appropriate introduction of the shunting process, we will start with the description of some relevant terms. We define an *arriving shunt unit* as a train unit that has to be parked at a shunt yard, and, similarly, define a *departing shunt unit* as a train unit that has to be supplied from the shunt yard. Arriving shunt units are uncoupled from through trains, which continue their service after

Figure 15.1. An example of an ICM train unit with three carriages (ICM_3).

Figure 15.2. Elements of the shunting problem.

a short dwell time or come from complete ending trains. Departing shunt units are units that are coupled onto through-trains or form complete starting trains. The related shunting processes are depicted in Figure 15.2. These related processes make the train units "flow" through the shunt yard between arrival at and departure from the station.

It is mandatory that train units be checked every 48 hours for defects. This check can be done locally at the stations. Furthermore, all train units that lay over at a station with internal cleaning facilities should be cleaned internally. Finally, train units should be cleaned externally on a regular basis, which takes place at a so-called train wash, which is available at some stations.

Routing of the train units takes place from the platform to the shunt yard and back. Sometimes it is possible to leave a train unit for a certain period of time on a platform track or to park it there some time before it is actually necessary. This introduces some flexibility with respect to the timing of the routing. Additional routing could be necessary for internal or external cleaning operations. Of course, the routes of the different train units should neither conflict with each other nor conflict with the routes of the through-trains or other infrastructure reservations, such as track maintenance.

The tasks that result from the routing of train units, the coupling and decoupling of them, the cleaning, and the maintenance checks have to be assigned to shunting personnel. This personnel is local shunting personnel at the station under consideration. Since the different shunt tracks can be located quite far from each other, it is important to incorporate sufficient slack time between two tasks. In addition, there is uncertainty with respect to the exact arrival times and the process times of the activities. Finally, the schedules need to comply with union regulations as well as several laws. This particular crew scheduling problem has been analyzed by Hoekert (2001).

The parking of train units is far from trivial because space is usually scarce. In addition, the choice to park a shunt unit on a particular shunt track has several implications. First, when train units are of different subtypes, then the order of the train units on a shunt track is important. Second, the possible routes between the platforms and shunt tracks are restricted by this decision. Third, crew has to be available to carry out the resulting shunt activities within certain time intervals. Finally, planners prefer certain routes and shunt tracks over others. Here, a track is less desired if it is used frequently for other purposes—for example, for through-trains or for temporary parking, or if it is located far away from the platform tracks. A robust solution would be to park only units of the same subtype on each shunt track. This way, the planner can pick the first train unit if he desires a unit from this track. The disadvantage is that it may require additional activities in the morning for coupling units of different subtypes to form departing trains. Moreover, if the number of subtypes of train units is larger than the number of available shunt tracks at a certain point in time, mixing of subtypes is unavoidable.

Figure 15.3 shows the layout of the station Zwolle, which is a station in the northeastern part of the Netherlands. The rectangles in the figure represent the platforms, while next to the platform tracks and below those tracks several shunt tracks are located.

Station Zwolle is a challenging station since the capacity is rather scarce and it has facilities for cleaning and washing train units. A smaller station is station Enschede, which is located in the eastern part of the country, near the German border. At station Enschede, fewer train units arrive and depart, and also fewer different subtypes of train units arrive and depart, as compared to station Zwolle. The layout of station Enschede is given in Figure 15.4.

An important characteristic of a shunt track is its *approach type*. Some of the tracks have a dead-end side. We will call these *LIFO tracks* (Last In, First Out). Tracks that do not have a dead-end side are called *free tracks*. In particular, these free tracks greatly complicate the parking problem, even though planners typically have a preferred side for each track. This is caused by the fact that one needs to decide the arrival and departure side for each train unit that one wants to park on a certain shunt track, which implies a huge increase in the set of feasible solutions for the parking subproblem.

In this chapter, we will give a short literature review and we will present our solution approach for decision support for the routing and parking processes. Section 15.4 describes how our solution approach supports the planners in creating shunt plans. In Sections 15.5 to 15.8 we discuss the four parts of our solution approach in more detail. Hereafter, we will give some computational results of the steps of the solution approach before the conclusions and suggestions for further research are given in Section 15.10.

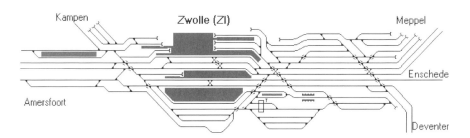

Figure 15.3. The layout of station Zwolle.

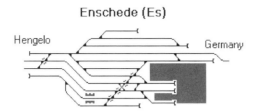

Figure 15.4. The layout of station Enschede.

15.2. A SHORT LITERATURE REVIEW

Cordeau et al. (1998) provide a recent overview of the use of Operations Research in railway systems, focusing on train routing and scheduling problems. In addition, a good introduction to the TUSP and a detailed introduction to the main part of our solution approach including computational results can be found in Freling et al. (2005).

Some special cases of the TUSP have recently been dealt with by Winter and Zimmermann (2000) and Blasum et al. (2000) for dispatching trams in a depot. Winter (1999) extends this approach with length restrictions, mixed arrivals and departures, and an application in a bus depot.

Di Stefano and Koci (2003) study theoretical properties of several variants of subproblems of the TUSP. Furthermore, they also present algorithms for solving some of these subproblems.

Furthermore, Gallo and Di Miele (2001) discuss an application for dispatching buses in a depot, with an extension of their models to take into account mixed arrivals and departures.

Tomii and Zhou (2000) and Tomii et al. (1999) propose a genetic algorithm that takes into account some of the processes of Figure 15.2. However, their problem is of a less complex nature, since in their context at most one train unit can be parked on a shunt track at the same time.

Lübbecke and Zimmermann (2003) discuss a problem similar to the TUSP that arises at an in-plant private railroad. In this problem, one assigns transportation requests to certain regions of the in-plan railroad and selects carriages of specific types from a shunt track in this region. However, the authors only discuss LIFO tracks and assume that there is no prescribed sequence of different types of carriages in a train. In addition, it is assumed that there are no limitations for this temporary parking.

In addition, the subject of the paper by He et al. (2000) is the separation of train units from arriving trains, sorting these according to their destination and finally combining them to form new departing trains, which resembles the matching of arriving and departing shunt units.

Dahlhaus et al. (2000) discuss the rearranging of carriages in one train to group them by destination, which is a similar problem. Their goal is to use a minimum number of tracks for this rearrangement and to show that this problem belongs to the class of most difficult optimization problems.

Zwaneveld (1997) also studied a routing problem for train units over railway infrastructure. In this problem, one is looking for a set of routes for trains in a 1-hour period where arrival and departure times are fixed. He develops a solution approach based on state of the art techniques from the field of Operations Research. This approach is applied to a number of railway stations in the Netherlands. Compared to the problem of Zwaneveld, our problem is complicated by the flexible start and end times, the fact that infrastructure can already be reserved for certain time intervals for (for example) through-trains, the splitting and recombining of train units, and a different planning period (typically 24 hours instead of 1 hour).

15.3. SOLUTION APPROACH

For practical instances, the TUSP becomes far too large to be solved as one integrated optimization problem. Therefore, the problem is decomposed in four parts, and we developed a four-step algorithmic solution approach that assists planners in creating parts of the shunt plan. The decomposed approach enables planners to view and possibly modify partial solutions between the steps. The four steps are:

Step 1. Matching arriving to departing train units
Step 2. Estimating routing costs of train units
Step 3. Parking of train units on shunt tracks
Step 4. Routing of train units

In the first step, we match arriving shunt units to departing shunt units. In this problem, the order of the subtypes of train units in the train, prescribed by the timetable, is considered fixed and has to be respected. Furthermore, type mismatches between the desired subtype and the supplied subtype are not allowed. This step results in a set of so-called *blocks*. A block is a set of shunt units that remain together from their arrival at the station until their departure from the station. The main objective in this step is to create a minimum number of blocks since this implies a minimum number of shunt activities.

The second step computes a lower bound on the routing costs of each block from its arrival platform to each shunt track and back to its departure platform. These lower bounds are required as input for Step 3, where we choose a shunt track for each train unit that needs parking. Here, we take the routes of through-trains and freight trains and other known infrastructure reservations into account. Elements of the routing costs of one block are costs for the traveled distance and costs for the number of reverses in direction. A reverse in direction requires the driver to walk to the other end of the train because he needs to be upfront. This takes additional time. This step is based on work by van't Woudt (2001) and Fioole (2003). Note that the costs can differ for different approach sides of free shunt tracks.

Step 3 decides for each block on which shunt track it should be parked, taking into account certain preferences of the planner. Furthermore, the capacity of the shunt tracks should never be exceeded and it is not allowed for a block to obstruct another block upon arrival or departure, which we will call a *crossing*. Note that, for free tracks, the side of arrival or departure on a shunt track also influences whether or not a crossing occurs.

The fourth step determines the final routes of shunt units, where we also incorporate the relations among the routes of the blocks. This will result in a proposal for the final routes of the blocks to the planner. Again, this step is based on work by van't Woudt (2001), with extensions from Fioole (2003).

The steps are chosen in such a way that the scope of the presented models can easily be extended. An example of such an extension is to incorporate the planning of the internal cleaning of rolling stock. Of course, the described decomposition can result in solutions of inferior quality. This effect is studied by Fodor Birtalan (2003), which provides sufficient support for the proposed decomposition.

15.4. HOW DOES THE SOLUTION APPROACH SUPPORT THE PLANNER?

We have been developing a prototype of a decision support system for the TUSP. Besides algorithms that are able to solve parts of the problem, this system also contains (a) an intuitive interface for operating these algorithms, (b) several graphical representations of the solutions, and (c) facilities for interactively changing the solutions.

In the first step, the planner is able to fix a part of the matching of arriving shunt units to departing shunt units a priori. This fixation would reflect considerations of the planner that are not taken into account in the underlying mathematical model. Moreover, the planner is also able to change the solution of the first step afterwards to some extent.

In the third step, the system supports the planner in determining the tracks where the blocks will be parked. Again, the planner has a lot of flexibility for creating a solution. He can determine a subset of the shunt tracks where a block should be parked beforehand. For example, blocks containing diesel units need to be parked on specific tracks with fueling facilities. Furthermore, he can also prohibit to park blocks on a certain track. This means that blocks containing electrical train units cannot be parked on shunt tracks without catenary. Finally, the planner also has the possibility to guide the optimization into certain directions by attaching certain weights to elements of the objective function. These elements are as follows:

1. Penalties for not parking blocks. Blocks that cannot be parked need special attention of the planner, since either he has to plan the parking himself or he needs to check if the units can remain at the arrival or departure platform.
2. Penalties for parking blocks with different subtypes of train units on a shunt track. With this element the planner can favor solutions where units of the same subtype are parked on the same shunt track.
3. A bonus for corresponding blocks that are parked on the same shunt track next to each other in the right order. This occurs when the shunt units of the blocks

leave in the same departing train but come from different arriving trains. When these blocks are parked next to each other on the same track and in the right order, they can be combined on the shunt track and considered as one block when the train units need to be routed to the departure platform, which results in less work. When these blocks are not parked next to each other on the same track or are parked in the wrong order, we call the departing train a *broken departure*.

4. Penalties for using certain shunt tracks. Sometimes, shunt tracks can be of strategic importance for related processes, such as cleaning, or they may be used for freight trains at night. With this penalty a planner can try to use such undesired tracks as little as possible. Furthermore, with this penalty the planner can also indicate that a certain track is out of service due to maintenance.

Related to the routing steps 2 and 4, the user can configure 15 different parameters in total. Six of these deal with the amount of time that in an infrastructure should be reserved for a train movement. Obviously, if these parameters are set relatively low, then more movements can be planned, but the solution will also be less robust. Moreover, the planner can specify a number of minutes he prefers a shunting movement to take place after arrival of a train (or before departure) and set a penalty for each minute the movement deviates from the specified time. Moreover, for a reverse in direction, the required time can be specified by a constant time and an additional time dependent of the length of the train. In addition, a penalty for reversing the direction of the train can be set. This way, the planner can influence the number of reverses in direction in all routes. Finally, a penalty can be set for movements that are planned simultaneously. Here, the occurrence of less simultaneous movements implies that fewer drivers are necessary at the same time.

As mentioned before, during the weekends fewer trains are in service, as a result of decreased demand for transportation. Therefore, typically on Friday several units arrive at a shunt yard, remain there for the entire weekend, and leave again on the next Monday. In order to incorporate this situation, the solution approach can handle more arriving shunt units than departing ones (e.g., on Friday at certain yards), such that the yard is not empty at the end of the planning period. Also, the solution approach can handle a nonempty shunt yard at the start of the planning period.

15.5. MATCHING OF ARRIVALS TO DEPARTURES

In the first step, we focus on efficiently matching arriving shunt units to departing ones. This means that we want to keep units together as much as possible since this implies less work. The matching should exactly respect the required subtypes; that is, it is not allowed to provide a train with a different train unit. Furthermore, if a train consists of several subtypes, the prescribed order of the subtypes of train units in the train has to be respected.

For each arriving and for each departing train we define a network, with nodes as the units of the train and a dummy node (with index 0; see figure 15.5). The nodes

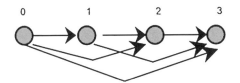

Figure 15.5. The network of a train with three units.

are places where the train can be divided into *parts*, where a part is a subset of adjacent train units of a train. The arcs represent feasible configurations of possible parts of the train. Given the parts, a block represents a combination of a part of an arriving train and an identical part of a departing train.

Figure 15.5 depicts the network for a train consisting of three units. Note that each arc corresponds to one part, and thus 6 different parts are possible in this example. Furthermore, notice that a path from the first to the last node in this network corresponds to a division of the train into parts. For example, the path $0 \rightarrow 2 \rightarrow 3$ in Figure 15.5 implies that train units 1 and 2 form one part, and train unit 3 forms another part.

Let I be the set of all possible parts for all arriving trains and let J be the set of all possible parts for all departing trains. We use I_j (J_i) as the set of arriving (departing) parts with the same matching configuration as departing part j (arriving part i) that arrive before departing part j (depart after arriving part i). Formally, we introduce a mathematical formulation with the following binary decision variables:

$$u_i = \begin{cases} 1 & \text{if part } i \in I \text{ is used} \\ 0 & \text{otherwise} \end{cases}$$

$$v_j = \begin{cases} 1 & \text{if part } j \in J \text{ is used} \\ 0 & \text{otherwise} \end{cases}$$

$$z_{ij} = \begin{cases} 1 & \text{if part } i \in I \text{ is matched to part } j \in J_i \text{ and this is feasible} \\ 0 & \text{otherwise} \end{cases}$$

A matching of an arriving part to a departing part is feasible if the units in both parts are the same, these units are in the same order, and the departing part leaves the station after the arrival of the arriving part. We define T^a (T^d) as the set of trains with arriving (departing) shunt units. The arcs in a network of train t are given in the set A^t. We additionally use A_h^{t+} (A_h^{t-}) as the set of arcs out of (into) node h for train t. Finally, the set C_t^- is the set of all intermediate nodes in the network of train t.

The model now becomes:

$$\text{minimize} \quad Q \sum_{i \in I} u_i + \sum_{i \in I} \sum_{j \in J_i} w_{ij} z_{ij} \tag{15.1}$$

$$\text{subject to} \quad \sum_{i \in A_0^{t+}} u_i = 1 \qquad \forall t \in T^a \tag{15.2}$$

$$\sum_{i \in A_h^{t+}} u_i - \sum_{i \in A_h^{t-}} u_i = 0 \qquad \forall t \in T^a, \; \forall h \in C_t^- \tag{15.3}$$

$$\sum_{j \in A_0^{t+}} v_j = 1 \qquad \forall t \in T^d \tag{15.4}$$

$$\sum_{j \in A_h^{t+}} v_j - \sum_{i \in A_h^{t-}} v_j = 0 \qquad \forall t \in T^d, \; \forall h \in C_t^- \tag{15.5}$$

$$\sum_{j \in J_i} z_{ij} = u_i \qquad \forall i \in I \tag{15.6}$$

$$\sum_{i \in I_j} z_{ij} = v_j \qquad \forall j \in J \tag{15.7}$$

$$z_{ij}, u_i, v_j \in \{0, 1\} \qquad \forall i \in I, \; \forall j \in J \tag{15.8}$$

The objective (15.1) is to minimize the weighted sum of the number of parts, with penalty Q, and the matching costs, since minimizing the number of parts results in a matching where train units are kept together as much as possible. The matching costs contain (for example) cost for the time difference between the arrival time of an arriving part and the departure time of a departing part. If these times are close, routing the unit(s) from the arrival platform to the departure platform suffices and it is not necessary to park the unit(s) at the shunt yard. Flow conservation constraints (15.2) and (15.3) ensure the covering of each arriving shunt unit by a part, while constraints (15.4) and (15.5) ensure this for each departing shunt unit. Constraints (15.6) guarantee that each arriving part is matched to a departing part if and only if the arriving part is a result of the train decomposition. Constraints (15.7) model this for the departing parts.

As mentioned before, it is possible that an arriving shunt unit is not matched to a departing shunt unit in the planning period. In this case, the unit will remain parked on a shunt track until the end of the planning period. This can be modeled easily by incorporating dummy train units, which depart after the end of the planning period. Of course, a similar argument holds for departing shunt units that are not matched to arriving shunt units.

Typically, each free track has one side that planners prefer to use, although both sides can be used. Therefore, we would like algorithms that take into account this preference. Together with the LIFO tracks, this implies that we would prefer matchings that adhere to the LIFO principle. Fodor Birtalan (2003) discusses extensions of the presented solution approach to take into account these preferences.

In Section 15.9 we will show that this formulation can be solved quite efficiently by available standard software packages from the field of Operations Research, like CPLEX.

15.6. PARKING TRAIN UNITS ON SHUNT TRACKS

As we described in the previous section, the matching of supply and demand of shunt units results in a set of blocks B. Blocks that do not need to be parked on a shunt track, because their arrival and departure times are sufficiently close, are not included in B. For each block we know the arrival and departure times and the arrival and departure platforms. In addition, in the second step we estimated the route costs between these platforms and all feasible shunt tracks for each block, which is described in the next two sections. Given this information, the third step of our solution approach consists of assigning blocks to shunt tracks at minimum costs. We call this subproblem the *Track Assignment Problem* (TAP).

We formulate the TAP as a Set Partitioning Problem with additional constraints. The Set Partitioning Problem is a well-known problem in Operations Research and is defined in Garey and Johnson (1979). We define a *track assignment*, or shortly an *assignment*, as a feasible assignment of a certain subset of blocks to a particular shunt track during the planning period. Here, an assignment is *feasible* if the following conditions hold:

1. It does not contain crossings. Recall that this occurs when a train unit is obstructing the arrival or departure of another train unit.
2. The total length of the units on the track never exceeds the length of the track.
3. All blocks of the subset are allowed to park on the track.

Let S be the set of shunt tracks, let K^s be the set of assignments on track $s \in S$, and let K_b^s be the set of assignments on track $s \in S$ containing block $b \in B$. Given these sets, we define the following decision variables:

$$x_k^s = \begin{cases} 1 & \text{if assignment } k \in K^s \text{ is used on shunt track } s \in S \\ 0 & \text{otherwise} \end{cases}$$

$$y_b = \begin{cases} 1 & \text{if block } b \in B \text{ is not parked on any shunt track} \\ 0 & \text{otherwise} \end{cases}$$

The parameter c_k^s models the costs of assignment k on track s. These costs consist of the sum of the estimated route costs of the different blocks in the assignment as well as the penalties and bonuses described in Section 15.4 regarding this assignment. In addition, the parameter d models a penalty if a block is not assigned to any track. The TAP is then formulated as follows:

$$\text{minimize} \quad \sum_{s \in S} \sum_{k \in K^s} c_k^s x_k^s + d \sum_{b \in B} y_b \tag{15.9}$$

$$\text{subject to} \quad \sum_{s \in S} \sum_{k \in K_b^s} x_k^s + y_b = 1 \qquad \forall b \in B \tag{15.10}$$

$$\sum_{k \in K^s} x_k^s \leq 1 \qquad \forall s \in S \tag{15.11}$$

$$x_k^s \in \{0, 1\} \qquad \forall s \in S, \ \forall k \in K^s \tag{15.12}$$

$$y_b \in \{0, 1\} \qquad \forall b \in B \tag{15.13}$$

We aim at minimizing the costs of a shunt plan, such that as many blocks as possible are assigned to shunt tracks, which is modeled in (15.9). Constraints (15.10) state that each block is covered by exactly one assignment for one shunt track or it is not parked at all. Constraints (15.11) model that each shunt track can have at most one assignment.

Note that the solution space, measured by the number of variables or feasible assignments of blocks to shunt tracks x_k^s, grows exponentially with the number of blocks. A way to overcome this disadvantage of exponentially many decision variables is the use of *column generation* techniques. Column generation is a state-of-the-art technique from Operations Research. It is becoming more and more one of the preferred solution approaches to deal with a huge number of variables. Although the basic theory goes back to the 1960s, the popularity of this approach started to rise only in the 1980s, stimulated by the advances in computer hardware. Lübbecke and Desrosiers (2002) provide a recent overview of applications as well as advances in theory. A standard reference on this subject is Barnhart et al. (1998), while Freling (1997) uses column generation to solve vehicle and crew scheduling problems in an integrated manner. More information on the algorithm for this application can be found in Freling et al. (2005).

15.7. MODELING THE INFRASTRUCTURE AND ITS USE FOR THE ROUTING STEPS

Before discussing Steps 2 and 4 of our solution approach related to routing problems, we will introduce a model of the infrastructure, which is suitable for solving these problems. Attention is paid to this issue because a straightforward model can be incapable of detecting all possible conflicts.

Recall that we solve routing problems in Steps 2 and 4 of our algorithmic solution approach. In Step 2 we know the configuration of the blocks. Given these blocks and the reservation of the infrastructure by the through trains, we estimate the costs of routing a block from its arrival platform to each shunt track, and from each shunt track to its departure platform. These estimated costs are part of the input of Step 3, where the actual shunt track for each block is selected. When this shunt track has been selected for each block, Step 4 tries to find routes for each block to and from it. An additional complication in this fourth step is that infrastructure reservations for the routes of the other blocks need to be respected.

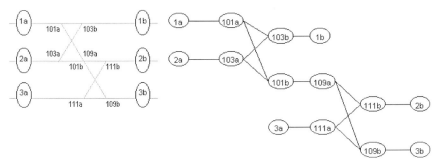

Figure 15.6. An instance of a railway infrastructure and its typical representation.

Figure 15.6 shows the standard representation of a part of a station, as used by Dutch railway organizations, and the translation of that representation into a graph. In the left part, the relevant points of the infrastructure are given, such as tracks and switches. Here, the tracks are encircled. The resulting graph is given in the right part, where all tracks and relevant points are nodes in the graph. If two nodes are directly connected in the left part, then an arc in the corresponding graph connects the nodes.

Each node has several attributes: a cost (or weight), an indicator whether or not it is possible to reverse directions at this node, at most two arcs on the left side, and at most two arcs on the right side. Suppose that in the example, reversing directions is only allowed at nodes 1b, 2b, and 3b. If, in this case, we are looking for a route from track 3a to track 2a, we need to reverse direction at either node 2b or node 3b.

Unfortunately, this model is not suitable for solving the routing problems studied in this chapter, since it does not detect all possible conflicts. Consider, for example, the routes of the trains in Figure 15.7 from track 1a to 2b and from track 2a to 1b. From a practical point of view, it is obvious that the routes in this example conflict because they simultaneously use the same switch. However, the model does not detect the conflict since the routes do not share any node in the graph.

In order to detect the conflict of Figure 15.7, we need to use a more sophisticated model. The example infrastructure results in the model of Figure 15.8. In this representation, a route from track 1a to 2b passes three nodes using switch 101 (101a, 103a, and 101b). This representation enables us to detect all conflicts on the infrastructure.

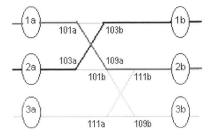

Figure 15.7. An example of conflicting routes.

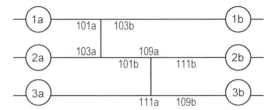

Figure 15.8. An example of the final model of the infrastructure.

We use the model of Figure 15.8 for the reservations of the infrastructure. Such a reservation by a train movement is split into reservations of route elements of this movement. This enables us to release a reservation a short period after the train has left the route element. This period of time depends on the safety system.

15.8. THE PLANNING ALGORITHM FOR FINDING ROUTES

Given the model of the infrastructure of the previous section, the reservation of the infrastructure by through-trains, and possibly other reservations of the infrastructure, we need to find routes for the shunt units. Algorithms for searching routes can be partitioned into two classes:

1. Algorithms that search routes simultaneously.
2. Algorithms that search routes sequentially.

An obvious advantage of algorithms belonging to the first class over algorithms of the second class is the possibility to compute an overall optimal solution for routing all shunt units over the infrastructure, while taking into account all restrictions and interdependencies. However, a disadvantage of such an approach is typically the amount of runtime that is needed for finding an optimal solution.

Algorithms of the second class can be partitioned further based on the characteristics *completeness* and *optimality*. A complete algorithm of the second class will find a feasible route if it exists. Optimality for such an algorithm implies that it will find the best route, given the reservations of already planned routes.

The methodology of Zwaneveld (1997) belongs to the first class of algorithms. Since practical instances typically consist of approximately 70 blocks and 20 shunt tracks, it is clear that algorithms of the first class will not be able to produce optimal solutions in reasonable computation time, typically several minutes, for the considered real-world problems. This conclusion is supported by computational results in Zwaneveld (1997). Therefore, methodology of this class is not useful for supporting planners in the TUSP. Another advantage of a sequential algorithm is that it better resembles the current practice of planners, which comforts them.

The class of *informed search* algorithms, a subset of the search algorithms, contains algorithms that are complete. Furthermore, informed search algorithms have some prior knowledge of the state space, which they are searching. This knowledge is used when extending a partial solution. For example, suppose you are interested in the shortest path from Amsterdam to Paris in a certain network and assume you have found a partial shortest path that brings you from Amsterdam to Brussels. In this case, the additional knowledge is the estimated length of the remaining shortest path from Brussels to Paris, which can be, for example, the geometric distance between Brussels and Paris.

Before discussing the general structure of informed search algorithms, we need to introduce some notation first. We define the *costs* of a partial path p, denoted with $g(p)$, as the sum of the costs of the nodes in the path plus additional costs based on the characteristics of it (e.g., penalties for reversing directions). Furthermore, the function $h(p)$ estimates the remaining costs for completing partial path p. In fact, this function models the knowledge of the state space. There is a wide range of possibilities for the functions $g(p)$ and $h(p)$. For instance, if one is interested in finding a solution as fast as possible, one can choose $g(p) \equiv 0$ for all p, and $h(p)$ as the expected number of remaining steps. Finally, we define n^* as the last node in path p and $E(n)$ as the set of edges incident to node n. The general structure of informed search algorithms is given in Figure 15.9.

A well-known and popular informed search algorithm from the field of Artificial Intelligence is A^* search, which is optimal if the function $h(p)$ is a lower bound to the actual costs of the remaining route. Typically, A^* searches for paths from a source node s to a sink node t. More information on A^* search can be found in Pearl (1984). The algorithm is suitable for solving the routing problems in this chapter, since we are able to give good lower bounds on the costs of the remaining route, which makes the algorithm fast. These lower bounds are determined by the cheapest paths on the infrastructure between all pairs of nodes, when through-trains, the other shunt movements, and track maintenance are neglected.

However, the particular characteristics of the routing problems in this chapter require special attention. In these problems, infinite routes are possible, due to the possibility of reversing directions. Furthermore, the infrastructure is well known and stable, but the nodes are not always available. This occurs, for example, when a track goes out of service due to maintenance for a certain period of time.

```
Informed Search(problem, network)

Step 1: Initialise the list of partial solutions P with an empty partial
        solution p, P = {p}
Step 2: If P is empty, P = Ø, then stop
        Else let p* = argmin_{p∈P} f(p) and remove p* from P,  P = P\{p*}.
Step 3: If p* is a feasible solution then stop
        Else for all m ∈ E(n*) do
              If q = p* ∪ {m} is a feasible partial solution then
              P = P ∪ {q} and return to Step 2
```

Figure 15.9. The general structure of informed search algorithms.

Incorporating additional stop criteria for the algorithm can easily solve the first characteristic. Due to these stop criteria, the algorithm loses optimality and completeness. However, these stop criteria exclude undesired solutions from the planners' point of view. The stop criteria we implemented are a maximum number of iterations for the overall problem, maximum costs for a route, and a maximum number of reverses in direction in a route.

The second characteristic implies that the feasibility of extending a partial path is also time-dependent. Since the route will have to take a detour when a certain node is temporarily unavailable, the function $h(\cdot)$ remains a lower bound and optimality remains guaranteed.

The routing problems in our solution approach are solved by applying the so-called Occupied Network A* search (ONA* search) algorithm. Before discussing the ONA* algorithm, we introduce some additional notation. The function $h(x, y)$ gives a lower bound on the costs of the cheapest path from node x to node y, which is computed in an empty network. In addition, $c(x)$ represents the costs of node x excluding possible penalties $C(x, p)$, for a partial path p at a node x. In addition, $d(p)$ returns the number of changes in direction in path p. Finally, N is the maximum number of iterations, M is the maximum costs of a route, and K is the maximum number of reverses in direction in one route. Given this additional notation, the ONA* search algorithm is sketched in Figure 15.10.

The ONA* search algorithm can be extended to allow for dynamic start-times of routes for shunt units. This is implemented by initializing the list P in Step 1 with a set of partial routes, one for each potential start-time. Furthermore, a variable penalty for deviations from the ideal start-time of the route will be accounted for. This feature is very helpful for planners, since it resembles their current practice: The start-times of the routes for shunt units are flexible to some extent.

As mentioned before, the sequential search approach implies that the order of selecting the routes for the blocks matters for the overall solution, since it does not necessarily find the overall optimal solution. To reduce this setback, a 2-opt improvement strategy has been implemented.

The 2-opt improvement strategy assumes that the route requests are ordered in some fashion, typically on the start-time of the request. Now, the strategy loops

```
ONA* Search(node s, node t, network)

Step 1: Initialise the list of partial solutions P with s, P = {s}, set
        g(s) = c(s) + C(s, s) and f(s) = g(s) + h(s, t). Finally, t = 0.
Step 2: If P = Ø or t = N then stop
        Else let p* = argmin_{p∈P} f(p) and remove p* from P,   P = P\{p*}.
            If f(p*) ≥ M then stop
            Else if d(p*) ≥ K then
                set t=t+1 and return to Step 2
Step 3: For all m ∈ E(n*) do
            If q = p* ∪ {m} is a feasible partial solution then
                g(q) = g(p) + c(m) + C(m, q) and f(q) = g(q) + h(m, t)
            If m = t then stop (q is the best route between s and t)
            Else P = P ∪ {q}, set t=t+1 and return to Step 2
```

Figure 15.10. The ONA* search algorithm.

over all requests. For each selected request, it performs a second loop to select a second request with a higher index and tries to swap the order of these two requests. The requests should overlap in time and should be distinct, because otherwise no improvement will occur. If this swapping results in a better overall solution, then the routes are changed. Note that for an individual route the solution might get worse but the overall solution will improve. Furthermore, note that this is a local search strategy, which does not guarantee to find an optimum solution and therefore it can be beneficial to apply the 2-opt improvement strategy more than once. This will be a subject of our computational results in Section 15.9. After introducing I as the number of requests, R as the total route costs, r_i as the costs of route request i, and b_i as the best route for request i, the framework for the 2-opt improvement strategy is described in Figure 15.11.

To illustrate the effect of the 2-opt improvement strategy, we consider a small example with only two route requests. Both requests have to end on a specific platform track t, where the order of the blocks on this track is important. Furthermore, they also originate from a track on the right side of platform t. Suppose that the route that has to end on the right side of platform track t is planned first. Finally, we assume that the timing of the reservations of the infrastructure for the first route imply that it is impossible to plan the second route before the start of the first route or after the block of the first route has left track t. Therefore the second route has to go around the first block. This situation is sketched in Figure 15.12.

However, if we change the order of planning these routes, we find an improved solution because there is no occupation for platform t for the route destined for the right side of the platform. This improved solution is depicted in Figure 15.13. Note that both routes share a major part of the infrastructure they use. This is no problem because the routes take place sequentially with enough buffer time between them.

A third extension is the focus on reducing the number of simultaneous shunt routes. Currently, personnel planning and rolling stock planning for shunting are performed consecutively. Therefore, the number of simultaneous routes is taken as a proxy for the required number of shunt personnel in a certain shunt plan. After the morning and evening rush hours, the peaks for routing shunt units occur. In order to reduce the required number of employees per time interval, and thereby to increase the possibility of a feasible solution, the algorithm can be

2-opt strategy (list of route requests, network)

```
Step 1: Set R = Σ_i g(r_i), and for all i = 1,…, I set b_i = r_i
Step 2: For all i = 1,…, I-1 do
             For all j = i+1,…, I do
                 Release the reservations for routes b_i and b_j
                 Call ONA* Search (start(b_j), end(b_j), network), save r_j'
                 Call ONA* Search (start(b_i), end(b_i), network), save r_i'
                 R' = R - g(r_i) - g(r_j) + g(r_i') + g(r_j')
                 If R' < R then set R = R', b_i = r_i', and b_j = r_j'
```

Figure 15.11. An extension of ONA* search to improve the order of route finding.

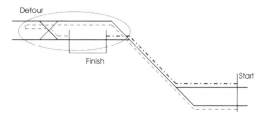

Figure 15.12. The solution to our example without the 2-opt improvement strategy.

guided toward a solution where a minimum number of concurrent routes are necessary. This is implemented by penalizing routes that are planned at the same time interval. This interval contains the actual start- and end-times of the routes as well as an additional 10 minutes before the start. These 10 minutes are a proxy for the time required to walk to the start location of a route.

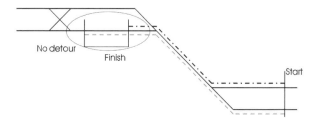

Figure 15.13. The solution to our example with the 2-opt improvement strategy.

15.9. COMPUTATIONAL RESULTS

Currently, the automated support for the planners, described in this chapter, is in a research phase. This research is conducted at stations Zwolle and Enschede, whose layouts are given in Figure 15.3 and Figure 15.4, respectively. Some more details on both stations are presented in Table 15.1.

The data set for station Enschede represents a weekend from 8:00 AM on a typical Friday until 8:00 AM on the subsequent Monday. The data set for station Zwolle represents a 24-hour period starting at 8:00 AM on a typical Wednesday. First, we will discuss the results for station Enschede, followed by the results for station Zwolle. For each data set, we discern four scenarios for Step 3 of our algorithmic solution approach:

1. Focus on parking as many blocks as possible.
2. Primary focus on parking as many blocks as possible, and secondary focus on minimizing the number of shunt tracks with more than one subtype parked on it.
3. Primary focus on parking as many blocks as possible, and secondary focus on minimizing the number of broken departures.
4. Primary focus on parking as many blocks as possible, and secondary focus on both secondary items of the previous two scenarios.

TABLE 15.1. Some Statistics on Stations Enschede and Zwolle

	Enschede	Zwolle
Number of trains (daily)	138–160	550–600
Number of train units (daily)	212–293	800–1100
Number of types of train units	4	12
Number of platforms	4	17
Number of LIFO tracks	8	4
Number of free tracks	5	15

15.9.1. Results for Station Enschede

For station Enschede, Step 1 requires a few seconds of computation time and results in 57 blocks that need to be parked at the shunt yard. The estimates for the routing costs are computed within a minute as well. With the results of the first two steps, we are able to compute the results for the different scenarios of Step 3, which are given in Table 15.2.

The results show that the algorithm is always able to park all the blocks on the shunt yard. Furthermore, we see that the secondary objectives have a desired effect on the respective performance indicators. The computation times differ substantially for the scenarios; in particular, the runtime of outlier Scenario 4 is worth mentioning here.

Given the results of these four scenarios, we can analyze Step 4 in more detail. The results for these scenarios are given in Table 15.3.

TABLE 15.2. Results for the Different Scenarios of Step 3 Applied to Station Enschede

	1	2	3	4
Number of blocks not parked	0	0	0	0
Number of adjacent different subtypes	10	0	10	1
Number of combinations of arriving blocks into one departing train	3	3	10	6
Computation time (in seconds)	34	134	22	1660

The relative gap with the minimal route costs is determined by the relative difference between the total route costs of Step 4 and the total estimated route costs from Step 2 for the selected tracks for the blocks in the third step. We see that the computations for this step are quite fast since the computation time exceeds one minute in only one case. Moreover, the 2-opt improvement strategies improve the solution by saving on secondary objectives as well as by granting more requests.

TABLE 15.3. Results for Routing Blocks in Station Enschede

	1	2	3	4
Number of route requests	545	547	540	544
No 2-opt improvement strategy				
Number of requests not found	16	20	19	35
Relative gap with minimal route costs	25.8%	29.5%	29.9%	46.7%
Computation time (in seconds)	12	14	13	17
Apply 2-opt improvement strategy once				
Number of requests not found	10	10	11	28
Relative gap with minimal route costs	17.4%	16.9%	19.4%	36.7%
Computation time (in seconds)	18	25	23	50
Apply 2-opt improvement strategy twice				
Number of requests not found	9	10	11	28
Relative gap with minimal route costs	16.8%	16.9%	19.3%	36.5%
Computation time (in seconds)	27	36	32	78

15.9.2. Results for Station Zwolle

Executing the first step for station Zwolle requires 29 seconds and results in 69 blocks that need parking. The second step estimates the costs for the potential routes of these 69 blocks in approximately 50 seconds, which is acceptable. Again, we have enough information to execute Step 3, which results in Table 15.4.

For station Zwolle, the third step is unable to park one block in one scenario. We see that the required computation time varies between 12 and over 40 minutes, thereby making this step rather intensive for station Zwolle from a computational point of view. Moreover, it is interesting to see that applying the solution approach to Scenario 4 yields very good results and requires the smallest amount of computation time.

Finally, we studied the effect of these scenarios for station Zwolle on Step 4. Our findings are summarized in Table 15.5. From this table, we can conclude that the second 2-opt improvement strategy has little added value, while the first strategy does remarkably well.

TABLE 15.4. Results for the Different Scenarios of Step 3 Applied to Station Zwolle

	1	2	3	4
Number of blocks not parked	1	0	0	0
Number of adjacent different subtypes	21	0	20	0
Number of combinations of arriving blocks into one departing train	0	4	10	10
Computation time (in seconds)	4206	738	2154	906

TABLE 15.5. Results for routing blocks in station Zwolle

	1	2	3	4
Number of route requests	740	736	734	734
No 2-opt improvement strategy				
Number of Requests not found	11	4	6	7
Relative gap with minimal route costs	34.4%	17.5%	21.4%	23.2%
Computation time (in seconds)	13	12	13	12
Apply 2-opt improvement strategy once				
Number of requests not found	4	1	1	1
Relative gap with minimal route costs	14.1%	7.4%	7.8%	6.8%
Computation time (in seconds)	25	19	22	24
Apply 2-opt improvement strategy twice				
Number of requests not found	4	1	1	1
Relative gap with minimal route costs	14.1%	7.4%	7.6%	6.7%
Computation time (in seconds)	36	27	31	36

15.10. CONCLUSIONS AND FURTHER RESEARCH

In this chapter, we introduced a model-based algorithmic solution approach for creating shunt plans in a railway station. These shunt plans prescribe what should happen with train units when they are temporarily not necessary to operate a timetable. Elements of such plans are matching of arriving and departing train units, decisions where to park blocks, and determining detailed routes of train units in a station.

Our solution approach provides support for the planners, who are creating plans for these elements as well as the shunt plans as a whole. The elements are discussed in detail in this chapter. The proposed solution approach consists of a decomposition of the problem into four subproblems, along with solving each subproblem separately. Furthermore, we provide computational results for our solution approach based on real-life data of NS Reizigers for the stations Zwolle and Enschede.

The plans generated by our approach have been validated extensively with planners at NS Reizigers. Although this led to several improvements, planners feels that this approach indeed supports them in creating shunt plans. Planners are still required to check the generated plans, make modifications, and finalize the plan. One reason for this is the fact that our proposed solution approach may not be able to find routes for all blocks in the last step.

In our future research, we will extend this solution approach with modules for internal and external cleaning and for crew planning. This will result in additional steps in our approach and maybe in minor changes in these steps. Furthermore, we will also look at other stations to apply this solution approach to.

ACKNOWLEDGMENTS

This research was partly supported by NS Reizigers, the Netherlands. The first and third authors were partly sponsored by the Human Potential Program of the European Union under contract no. HPRN-CT-1999-00104 (AMORE).

The authors want to thank several students who have implemented parts of the presented algorithms.

16

TRAIN SHUNTING: A PRACTICAL HEURISTIC INSPIRED BY *DYNAMIC PROGRAMMING*

R. Haijema, C. W. Duin, and N. M. van Dijk

Faculty of Economics and Econometrics, Universiteit van Amsterdam,
P.O. Box 19268, 100066, Amsterdam, the Netherlands

16.1. INTRODUCTION

This chapter describes a practical approach for the train-shunting problem. Solving the shunting problem is a daily difficult job for planners as will become clear in Section 16.1.1. In order to explore the possibilities to support the planners the *Dutch Railways* have formulated a research project called *Rintel*. This chapter reports on a practical train-shunting heuristic as developed in the Master's thesis of R. Haijema (2001). The heuristic shows similarities with *Dynamic Programming* (*DP*). For an outline of the chapter we refer to Section 16.1.3. First we present the shunting problem and our approach.

16.1.1. Problem Description: The Shunting Problem

The shunting problem is about moving and parking trains that arrive or depart at a railway hub. Some of the incoming trains use the hub as a transit station; soon after their arrival, they leave the hub. Other trains end their service at the hub and have to be parked somewhere at the hub. Due to the congestion of the railways, most trains cannot be parked at a main track along a platform. A substantial number of trains need to be shunted toward the marshaling yard that consists of a set of sidings. At

Planning in Intelligent Systems: Aspects, Motivations, and Methods, Edited by Wout van Wezel, René Jorna, and Alexander Meystel

some later time the material is recollected in order to compose a train that starts its service along any of the platforms of the hub.

Before we discuss some complicating factors, let us explain the parking problem at the marshaling yard. In general the marshaling yard consists of several sidings that might be spread around the main tracks of the railway hub. Figure 16.1 shows the infrastructure of railway hub Zwolle. The data set of hub Zwolle will be the test case in Section 16.4.

The marshaling yard is heavy used during the night. Due to the scarce capacity, it is sometimes really hard for planners to find a positioning of all material onto the sidings. Also challenging is setting up the morning rush, since in a short time many trains need to be shunted toward the platforms. After the morning rush, many trains are returned to the marshaling yard. Not only before and after the rushes, but also during the day a significant amount of material needs to be shunted from and toward the marshaling yard. The dynamics in the occupation of the marshaling yard is illustrated by Figure 16.15 in Section 16.4.1. The main questions to be answered by the planners are the following:

> Where should one park the incoming trains and which material should be collected to form the departures in view of a smooth traffic flow?

Each day the planners are faced with this dynamic problem of parking and matching the material of incoming and outgoing trains to realize a smooth traffic flow. This problem is complicated, since the configuration of the incoming trains and the outgoing trains is in general not the same. The latter observation requires shunters to rebuild trains by collecting train units. By parking the trains in a sophisticated

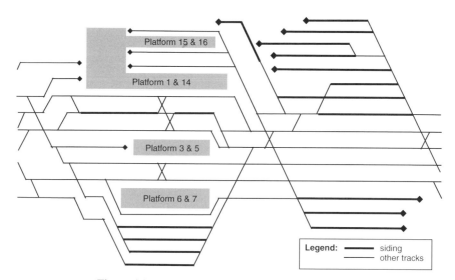

Figure 16.1. The infrastructure of railway hub Zwolle.

way, one can save on the shunting efforts. On the one hand, planners like to minimize the shunting efforts. On the other hand, planners aim at a plan that does not imply disturbances of the railway traffic. The underlying optimization problem is called the shunting problem.

The shunting problem is mainly restricted by the following factors:

- The timetable, which prescribes the order in which trains arrive and depart.
- The train properties, among which are the following:
  - The configuration: Each train has a required order of so-called train units that might vary in type.
  - The divisibility: Trains can be split only in train units of specific lengths.
  - The traction: Electric trains need overhead wires that provide traction.
- The infrastructure:
  - The location of tracks, crossroads, and so on.
  - The length of sidings.
  - The location of entrance/exit of each siding.
  - The absence or presence of an overhead wire for each track.

We discuss additional complexities of the shunting problem when presenting the algorithm in Section 16.2.

A *solution* is a plan that prescribes:

- *How* to split the trains.
- *Where* to position the train units at the sidings.
- *Which* train units to collect in order to compose each departing train.

The *quality of a solution* is the degree to which the following three objectives are achieved:

- *Minimization of the Amount of Shunting Work*: A better solution requires less movements and (de)couplings of train units.
- *Maximization of the Robustness of a Solution (Clustering)*: A solution is more robust, when one manages to group more trains of a similar type together on the same siding.
- *Minimization of the Disturbances*: In view of the congestion at the hub the planners prefer to position the material at a siding that is reachable with minimal risks of disturbing the regular railway traffic.

Since the objectives are of a conflicting nature, it is hard to define an optimal solution. Even if one could define strict optimality, there is no way of finding an optimal solution in reasonable time. In practice the planners are satisfied with a suboptimal solution.

The quality of an algorithm that solves the train-shunting problem is partly determined by the quality of the solution it generates. Other (even more) relevant factors are its speed, flexibility, and robustness.[1] Planners are interested in robust plans that imply neither much shunting work nor high risks of disturbing the railway traffic. In cases of major delays or breakdowns, planners like to quickly rerun the algorithm by inputting updated timetables, taking into account the state of the marshaling yard.

In addition, one desires that the algorithm can be adapted easily in future phases of the project. In the future the Dutch Railways wish to incorporate several other activities that impact the shunting problem. For example, the planning of shunts required for washing and cleaning trains. In developing an algorithm one should keep this in mind.

Hence it is better to develop a flexible algorithm that quickly generates robust solutions than to adopt a (slow) procedure that results in a rigid solution.

16.1.2. Approach

Even in its simplest form, the shunting problem is far too complex to find an optimal solution. Global search techniques are far too slow for problem sizes encountered in practice. With regard to solvability, problems can be categorized [see Garey and Johnson (1979)].

The shunting problem is referred to as strongly NP-hard, since it is more difficult than the bin-packing problem, which is already strongly NP-hard. Hence an approximation algorithm that searches for a good and practical solution—a so-called heuristic—is appropriate. Since the prevalent problem is parking the trains at the marshaling yard we distinguish three categories of trains based on the shunts they require. These categories are numbered I, II, and III, as illustrated in Figure 16.2.

I. Trains of category I depart along the same platform as they arrive. These trains can be treated as if they use the hub as a transit station. In the time between arrival and departure the material is parked along the platform without disturbing the rail traffic. There is no need to shunt the material of this category of trains.

II. A train of category II arrives along one platform (e.g., platform 2a as in Figure 16.2). After a while it departs along some other platform (e.g., platform 4b). In the meantime the material of the train can be parked along any platform without disturbing the rail traffic.

III. The material of trains of category III cannot be parked along any platform, since doing so would disturb the railway traffic. This category of trains need to be shunted toward the marshaling yard to be parked at a siding until the material is recollected to depart later along a platform prescribed by the timetable.

---

[1]We refer to the book by Reeves (1995) for a discussion of several criteria for selecting an algorithm.

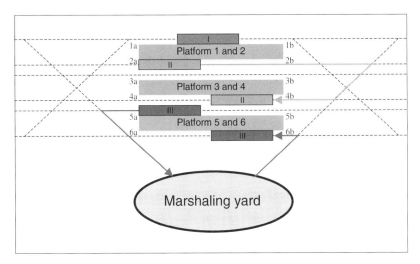

Figure 16.2. The shunting problem and three categories of trains.

As stated before, the latter category is of our main interest in this chapter; nevertheless, we provide two simple routines for the first two categories of trains.

The first routine identifies the trains belonging to the first category. For each arrival of the same configuration as the train that departs next along the platform, the routine checks whether the material might stay along the platform without blocking other rail traffic.

The second routine identifies and positions trains of category II. The process is a bit more complicated, since these trains require shunting. Nevertheless, the procedure is similar: It tries to match each arrival to a later departure and determines whether the material might be positioned along one of the platforms without blocking the railway traffic. All trains not belonging to category I and matched this way belong to category II.

All trains that end or start their service at the hub, but that are not of category I or II, belong to category III.

In contrast to the trains of the first two categories, category III trains share the capacity of the marshaling yard. Since the capacity of the marshaling yard is scarce, the shunting problem of trains belonging to category III is far more complicated. Therefore we focus on the parking problem at the marshaling yard. We take into account the shunting from the platforms toward the marshaling yard and vice versa, although in this phase of the project we have not yet implemented a route planner. The heuristic uses a (static) *"distance" matrix*, set by the planners, instead of a (dynamic) route planner. We can ignore the time required for shunting, taking the occupation time on the marshaling yard as the time from arrival up to departure.

Although we propose a heuristic, it is worth to consider an exact algorithm that provides insight in the nature of a heuristic. A widely used exact technique called *Dynamic Programming* (*DP*) inspired us to decompose the problem at a first

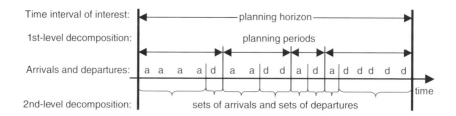

Figure 16.3. The shunting problem is decomposed at two levels.

level into stages, which we will call planning periods. A planning period is a period
of time such that after the first departure no new arrivals occur (see Figure 16.3). For
such a period a planner can simply solve the shunting problem by means of a planning board that horizontally shows the length of a track, whereas vertically all tracks
are enumerated. By placing trains or the train units onto the planning board, one
visualizes the situation at the marshaling yard. At the end of each planning
period, all departed train units are removed from the board before the arrivals and
departures of the next planning period are added.

The time interval of interest, called the planning horizon, consists of several planning periods, which can be solved successively as sketched above. The associated
subproblems are shunting problems related to the planning periods. They should
be solved in relation to each other, since the decision taken in one planning
period affects the solution space of the next planning period. The decomposition
and the backward solution process that we will propose is similar to Dynamic Programming, a powerful technique that we will discuss in Section 16.3. Figure 16.3
visualizes the decomposition of the shunting problem at two levels.

At a second level we decompose the subproblems by distinguishing a set of arrivals and a set of departures for each planning period. Planners prefer to schedule first
the positioning of departures, since this is more relevant in order to achieve a smooth
departure process. Furthermore, the uncertainty in arrival times does not allow
taking the arrivals as base of planning. Planning the departures first, apart from
the arrival, makes the algorithm and the solution more robust compared to an integral approach.

After planning the departures in a planning period, the arrivals are matched to the
positions reserved for the departures. The two processes that schedule the departures
respectively the arrivals are performed by the algorithms *Blueprint* respectively
Matching. Both algorithms are incorporated in the so-called *one-period heuristic*,
which solves the problem of one planning period.

Since the subproblems at the first level are similar to each other, they can be
solved one after another by the *one-period heuristic* in a backward fashion similar
to *DP*. How we adopt the basic ideas of *DP* becomes clear when the *one-period
heuristic* is incorporated into the so-called *multiple-periods heuristic*. The *multiple-
periods heuristic* solves the shunting problem for the whole planning horizon.
Table 16.1 summarizes the algorithms mentioned above.

TABLE 16.1. Overview of the Algorithms

Algorithm	Description	Section
Blueprint	Generates a blueprint of departures	16.2.1
Matching	Matches arrivals and departures by positioning the arriving material on the blueprint	16.2.1
One-period heuristic	Solves the shunting problem for one planning period	16.2.1
Multiple-period heuristic	Solves the shunting problem for the whole planning horizon	16.2.2

Since it is up to the planner to accept, modify, or reject a solution proposed by the heuristic, the heuristic should seek solutions acceptable to planners. Therefore we need to identify and investigate the priorities and decision rules of the planners and incorporate these in the algorithms. Adopting partly the existing planning process, the heuristic incorporates the knowledge and intelligence of the planners. In addition, the heuristic utilizes the capabilities of the computer to evaluate quickly several alternative decision rules and priorities.

16.1.3. Outline

After presenting the shunting problem in Section 16.1.1, we characterized our approach in the previous section.

The next section describes the developed heuristic in two parts. The first part (Section 16.2.1) describes the *one-period heuristic*. This heuristic serves as a building block in the *multiple-periods heuristic*, which is described in the second part (Section 16.2.2). We like to emphasize that this chapter reports on the state of the product in an early phase in the project *Rintel*. Some suggestions, though not all, for improving the heuristics during future phases of the project are embedded in the text. Note that while mentioning "the heuristic" we refer to the multiple-period heuristic, when this is not clear from the context.

Section 16.3 provides a description of the *Dynamic Programming* (*DP*) approach to the train shunting problem. One could argue to discuss *DP* before a description of the heuristic is given, but we think it would not help but disturb the reader who is not familiar with *DP*. One does not need an abstract description in *DP* terms to understand the heuristic. We emphasize that the structure of the heuristic arises from the theory of *DP* as well as from practice. Furthermore, we will briefly discuss how one can better exploit the *DP*-structure, by adopting not only the decomposition and the backward solution process, but also Bellman's principle of optimality.

In Section 16.4 the *performance of the heuristic* is discussed by showing the results based on *a test case* taken from practice.

Section 16.5 summarizes the chapter and provides an overview of the main conclusions.

In the first appendix one finds an overview of some terminology used throughout this chapter. The second appendix provides the complete solution to the test case.

16.2. DESCRIPTION OF THE HEURISTIC

Before presenting the multiple period heuristic in Section 16.2.2, we first explain in Section 16.2.1 how the *one-period heuristic* is constructed. In Section 16.2.3 the solution procedure is illustrated for a small instance of the shunting problem. We refer to Section 16.4 for results on a case taken from practice.

16.2.1. The One-Period Heuristic

A real instance of the shunting problem is rather complex to solve. Therefore we first develop a heuristic that solves a simplified instance of the problem: a shunting problem where all arrivals are prior to the first departure. For example, one could think of the shunting problem during the night such that at the end of one day all arriving trains need to be parked at the marshaling yard in order of their departure the next morning.

In mathematical terms we state that the set of arrivals (*A*) *is separated in time from* the set of departures (*D*). A period in which the set of arrivals (*A*) is separated in time from the set of departures (*D*) is called a *planning period*. In practice one often needs to identify multiple planning periods within the *planning horizon*, which is the time interval of interest. A regular *planning horizon* for the shunting problem at the Dutch Railways is from 8 AM at some day until 8 AM the next day. The *one-period heuristic* developed in this section solves problems that have only one planning period in the planning horizon. In Section 16.2.2 this heuristic is used as a *building block* in the *multiple-period heuristic* that deals with shunting problems that (might) have multiple planning periods in the planning horizon.

Figure 16.4 visualizes the *one-period heuristic* and its relation to the *multiple-period heuristic*. One clearly observes the hierarchical planning approach for each planning period: First the departures are positioned by the algorithm *Blueprint*, next the arrivals are matched to the departures by the algorithm *Matching*.

The decomposition in two algorithms as sketched in Figure 16.4 takes the departures as the base of planning. Doing so makes the planning process more robust,

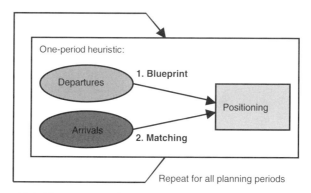

Figure 16.4. The structure of the one-period heuristic as a building block.

since departure times are more fixed than arrival times, which are uncertain due to frequent delays and breakdowns of material. Another motivation for taking the departures as base is the fact that the departures are more critical. It is common practice to minimize on (future) delays by giving priority to a smooth departure of trains. The planners follow a similar approach in claiming the departures to be more critical than the arrivals.[2]

Before we present the two algorithms that together form the *one-period heuristic*, let us simplify the discussion at this point by assuming a *balance of train units*. This means that for each type of train units the number of departing train units equals the number of arriving train units. This balance assumption is released in Section 16.2.2 when discussing the *multiple-period heuristic*.

16.2.1.1. The Algorithm Blueprint. In a hierarchical way the algorithm *Blueprint* generates a blueprint for the planning period. Train by train the blueprint prescribes from where to collect the material of the departing trains. Figure 16.5 visualizes the input–output relation of the algorithm. Given a set of four arrivals and a set of three departures within a planning period, the algorithm finds a positioning of the (11) departing train units, such that it facilitates a smooth departure. In this case, one distinguishes three types of train units of varying in length.

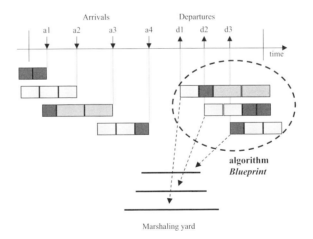

Figure 16.5. Visualization of the algorithm Blueprint.

---

[2]When solving the shunting problem, the planners apply a hierarchical approach: They plan train by train. The order in which trains are planned is not necessarily chronological. A "good" positioning of the material in order of a smooth departure is more important than a smooth direction of the arriving material toward the sidings. Clearly, planners prefer both a smooth direction and a smooth redirection of material, but these two goals can conflict. In planning train by train, so-called critical trains are planned first.

Before presenting the algorithm that generates the blueprint, consider the factors that impact the quality of a blueprint. The quality of a blueprint is the degree to which several objectives are achieved. In arbitrary order these objectives are:

- *Avoidance of exit conflicts* that occur whenever some material at a siding is blocking one or more train units at the moment of their departure.
- *Minimization of divisions*: In view of a smooth departure, planners like to minimize the number of departing trains that cannot be collected as a whole.
- *Clustering* of train units that are of the same type: Clustering makes it easier to cope with the uncertainty in the arrival times of the material. Clustering makes it possible to collect quickly material of a certain type in case of a breakdown.
- *Minimization of the shunting costs*: The *shunting costs* measure the efforts of shunting the material from the sidings toward the track from which the trains depart.

The occurrence of exit conflicts can be avoided by positioning the train units assigned to each track in order of their time of departure. However, the other three objectives might be conflicting.

The last objective needs some explanation: The shunting efforts are dependent on the routes along which the material is shunted and the congestion of that route at the time of shunting. Since we have not yet incorporated a route planner, the algorithm estimates the complexity of finding a route by using some "distance" matrix, which is set by the planner. Note that the terms "shunting costs" and "shunting efforts" are often referred to by the term "distance"; however, one should not interpret the latter term too literally.

Since the heuristic applies a hierarchical approach, the order in which the trains are planned influences the quality of the generated solution. The trains that are planned first take the best positions at the tracks and the trains that are planned at last have to accept less attractive positions. Just like the planners do, the trains are planned in a sophisticated order. The planners introduced the concept of critical trains: Trains requiring shunts along tracks that might be heavily used at the time of shunting. In addition, we associate with each train a so-called rate of flexibility, $F(d)$, that fixes the order in which the trains are planned. To reduce the risk to end up with an infeasible solution, one better plans trains that are less flexible first. Therefore the flexibility of a train is zero for a critical train. More generally, we take into account also other aspects that restrict the flexibility in shunting and parking a train; see the definition of $F(d)$ below:

$F(d)$ = the rate of flexibility in planning train d

$$= \begin{cases} 0, & \text{if train } d \text{ is } critical: \text{ it has to perform a critical shunting movement} \\ 1, & \text{if train } d \text{ is a } noncritical, electric \text{ train that departs } within \\ & \text{the planning horizon} \\ 2, & \text{if train } d \text{ is a } noncritical, electric \text{ train that does } not \text{ depart} \\ & \text{within the planning horizon} \\ 3, & \text{if train } d \text{ is a } noncritical, diesel \text{ train} \end{cases}$$

A noncritical diesel train is more flexible in shunting and parking than an electric train, since it does not require an overhead wire for traction. This definition of the function $F(d)$ is off course easy to adapt and to extend by the planners. Trains are planned in increasing order of flexibility $F(d)$. Note that $F(d)$ cannot be 2 in the one-period heuristic, since we have assumed a balance between arriving and departing train units. In the multiple-period heuristic, some trains may depart after the planning horizon.

When planning the departures the algorithm *Blueprint* has to break tie among trains that have equal rates of flexibility. Therefore another attribute of trains, not incorporated in $F(d)$, should be considered. For this purpose the length of a train suits. Since dividing a train is time-consuming and threatens a smooth departure, planners like to avoid the division of departing trains. The algorithm *Blueprint* limits the number of divisions by following a *Longest-First strategy*: the trains are planned in decreasing order of length. The length of train d is denoted by $L(d)$.

Thus the first step of the algorithm Blueprint is sorting the trains as shown in Figure 16.6. The algorithm first sorts the trains in D in ascending order of flexibility $F(d)$. Those trains that are equal in $F(d)$ are sorted in descending order of length $L(d)$. Next, the algorithm selects a "best" siding for the first train d in the ordered set D. A track t is suitable to position train d if no technical conflicts arise. This holds when the Boolean function $Suits(d,t)$ equals "true." $Suits(d,t)$ is *"false"* if, for example, d is an electric train but track t has no overhead wire. All available sidings that are suitable to position train d are candidate. These sidings are stored in set T^*. If several tracks are suitable the *track selection process* is continued. By applying the following hierarchical set of criteria, the set T^* of suitable sidings is reduced to one track, which is the "best" one. The set below resembles the priorities and rules of the planners, but is extended by theoretical observations that have proven to be effective. Though we have investigated the impact of several other rules and priorities, we do not discuss their impact in this chapter.

1. *Relaxed Distance.* Reduce T^* by selecting all tracks of T^* that are not further than *Ctol* from the platform of departure. The planner specifies the tolerance, by setting *Ctol*. In fact the distance can be seen as a cost function that quantifies how hard it is to shunt from a siding toward a platform (or vice versa). The "distance" can represent any quantity, such as the real distance in meters, in minutes but also the risk of disturbing the railway traffic. One could even choose to make the "distance" time-dependent, such that it measures the *actual shunting time* taking into account the congestion at the time of shunting. This will be easy once a *route planner* is incorporated in the heuristic. For now the "distance" is given by $C[platform(d),t]$, as a measure for the effort of shunting train d from a siding t to the platform $platform(d)$ from which it departs.

2. *Clustering.* In order to generate a robust, flexible solution, planners prefer to cluster trains. This criterion applies only to homogeneous trains. A train d is homogeneous of type u, denoted by $Hom(d) = u \neq 0$, if all of its train units are of the same type u. If $Hom(d) = 0$, then train d is composed of several

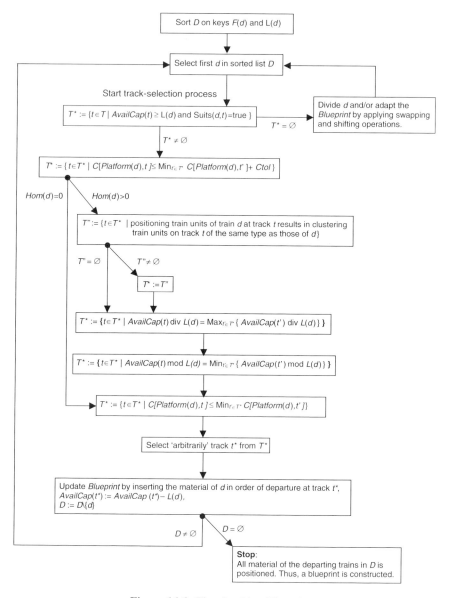

Figure 16.6. The algorithm Blueprint.

types of train units. Set T^* is reduced by selecting tracks $t \in T^*$ on which the clustering is not violated by positioning d onto track t.

3. *Remaining Capacity.* We like to position as many homogeneous trains of the same type as possible on the competing track and with the least "slack." The slack is the remaining, unoccupied meters at the track, when one decides to

position as much trains of the same type as possible on the siding. The remaining capacity of track t is abbreviated in Figure 16.6 by *AvailCap(t)*.

4. *Distance*. Select the "nearest" track(s) out of the reduced set T^*. Once again the term distance refers to the shunting costs. So, the "nearest" track is the siding from which it is easiest to shunt at the moment of departure.

5. *Arbitrary*. If necessary, the algorithm needs to reduce set T^* such that it consists of exactly one track t^*. This can be done by selecting one track arbitrary from T^* or by any other decision rule.

Finally, a best track t^* is found. The material of train d is inserted at track t^* in order of departure time, and train d is removed from D. To continue the process, a next train to position is considered until all trains are planned.

In case none of the sidings is suitable to position d, one can follow several approaches. One approach is to adapt the blueprint such that there is no need to divide train d; however, one cannot guarantee that such a blueprint exists. Another approach is the application of sophisticated techniques to divide a train.

Even if one would permit to divide trains, one cannot guarantee to find a positioning of all trains onto the blueprint. This is due to the scarce capacity of the marshaling yard and the indivisibility of train units. Alternatively, one could choose to continue the planning process and decide later about the trains that are not yet positioned. At this point we do not prescribe which approach is best, since this requires more research on division, swapping, and shifting strategies.

So due to the complexity of the problem, one cannot guarantee whether a feasible positioning of all material exists before one finds such a solution. Nevertheless, we assume that a feasible positioning exists, such that the algorithm *Blueprint* generates a feasible blueprint.

Now that we have described an algorithm that finds a good positioning of the departing train units, let us turn our attention to the algorithm that matches the arrivals and departures.

16.2.1.2. *The Algorithm* Matching.

The algorithm *Matching* matches the arriving and departing trains by finding a good positioning of the arriving material on the blueprint. Figure 16.7 visualizes the input–output relation of the algorithm. Note that the blueprint that forms the base in this example is the one generated in Figure 16.5. The algorithm *Matching* positions the arriving train units onto the blueprint. The thick lines that separate two adjacent rectangles show the distinction of subtrains.

The algorithm *Matching* applies a hierarchical planning approach. Train by train the algorithm plans the set of arriving trains A in reverse order of arrival time. The backward fashion of planning is motivated in Section 16.2.2 when discussing the *multiple-period* heuristic.

For each possible division of an arriving train the algorithm determines a promising positioning of the train units onto the blueprint. From all the *division-position combinations*, the best one is chosen.

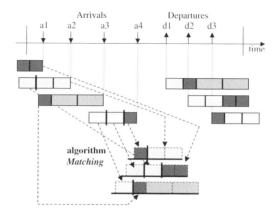

Figure 16.7. Visualization of the algorithm Matching.

For example, an arriving train a can be split in n subtrains $a_1, a_2, \ldots, a_n$. The function $Cmatch(a_1, a_2, \ldots, a_n, p_1, p_2, \ldots, p_n)$ returns the cost to shunt the n subtrains onto positions $p_1, p_2, \ldots, p_n$, where p_i corresponds to the position at the blueprint that is available and suitable for positioning subtrain a_i. In the context of the algorithm *Matching*, a "*suitable*" position on the blueprint is one at which the departing train unit and the arriving train unit are of the same type. A suitable position is "*available*" for an arriving train unit as long as no other arriving train unit is assigned to it.

The function *Cmatch* incorporates all major components that influence the amount of work to do by the shunting employees. These components are as follows:

nt is the *n*umber of *t*racks needed to position train a.

ns is the *n*umber of di*s*connections to perform on a siding in order to compose a departing train.

nc is the *n*umber of *c*onnections to make with material positioned at the same siding in order to form a departing train.

ne is the *n*umber of *e*ntrance conflicts which occur at the siding(s) in case some material blocks the entrance of the track such that an arriving train unit cannot reach its planned position without requiring additional shunts of the blocking material.

ndist is the distance[3] to travel from the main track toward the selected siding(s).

Thus we define

$$Cmatch(a_1, a_2, \ldots, a_n; p_1, p_2 \ldots, p_n) = w_t nt + w_s ns + w_c nc + w_e ne + w_{dist} ndist$$

where the values of the weight factors w_t, w_s, w_c, w_e, and w_{dist} are set by the planner.

---

[3]As in the algorithm *Blueprint*, the term "distance" should not be interpreted too literally. In the context of the algorithm *Matching*, "distance" refers to the total "shunting costs" or "shunting efforts" in shunting a train from the platform along which it arrives toward the siding(s) onto which the material is positioned.

Step 0. Preprocess: Sort the set *A* of arrivals in reverse order of arrival time,

Step 1. Select the first $a \in A$,
$$n := 1,$$

Step 2. Identify all possibilities to divide *a* into *n* subtrains $(a_1, a_2 \ldots a_n)$.

Step 3. For each division evaluate all possibilities to position the material onto the blueprint by the cost function *Cmatch* $(a_1, a_2, \ldots, a_n ; p_1, p_2, \ldots, p_n)$.

Step 4. Store the best possibility $(a_1{}^*, a_2{}^*, \ldots, a_n{}^* ; p_1{}^*, p_2{}^*, \ldots, p_n{}^*)$ to divide and position the material of train *a* that is divided into *at most n* subtrains.

Step 5. If $n < n_{max}$ and $n <$ number of train units in *a*, then $n := n+1$ and return to Step 2.
else (if *n* equals the number of train units in *a*) continue at Step 6.

Step 6. Position the material of *a* according to the best possibility found in Step 4,
$$A := A\backslash\{a\},$$
if $A \neq \varnothing$ return to Step 1,
else stop.
(all arriving trains are positioned onto the blueprint)

Figure 16.8. The pseudo code of the algorithm Matching.

Suppose planners allow any arriving train to be divided in at most n_{max} subtrains. In case no solution exists in which none of the arriving trains is divided, n_{max} should be set greater than 1 to prevent the algorithm getting stuck. To facilitate a smooth departure, planners might be forced to accept the division of some arriving trains.

The algorithm *Matching* evaluates *Cmatch* for all possible combinations of divisions $(a_1, a_2, \ldots, a_n)$ and positions $(p_1, p_2, \ldots, p_n)$, where *n* ranges from 1 to n_{max}. During this process the best possibility is stored in $(a_1^*, a_2^*, \ldots, a_n^*; p_1^*, p_2^*, \ldots, p_n^*)$.[4] According to the final best solution the algorithm *Matching* positions the material of train *a* onto the blueprint. Thus, the algorithm matches the arriving train units and the departing train units at their corresponding positions. This process is repeated for all trains $a \in A$. Figure 16.8 summarizes the process by showing the algorithm *Matching* in pseudo code.

Before we explain how the *one-period heuristic* is used in the *multiple-period heuristic*, let us summarize the heuristic so far.

After the phase of making a blueprint of the departing trains *D*, the heuristic matches the material of the arriving trains *A* onto the blueprint. Since we have assumed to this point that the number of departing train units equals the number of arriving train units, all train units are matched and positioned.

16.2.2. The *Multiple-Period Heuristic*

This section presents the heuristic that solves real shunting problems by using the *one-period heuristic* as a building block. We call the heuristic the *multiple-period heuristic*. In principal the *one-period heuristic* assumes that no train leaves the marshaling yard before the last train arrives at the marshaling yard. Within a whole planning horizon of 24 hours, many arrivals at the marshaling yard might

---

[4]If the optimal solution implies to divide train *a* in $s < n$ subtrains, then $a_i = p_i = 0$ for $i = s + 1$, $s + 2, \ldots, n$.

occur after some departures from the marshaling yard. In particular, after the morning rush some train units need to be parked temporarily at the marshaling yard in order to return in service during the evening rush and later on trains will return to the marshaling yard.

Also outside the morning and evening rushes a significant amount of material needs to be shunted from and toward the sidings. We refer to Figure 16.15 in Section 16.4.1 for a visualisation of the dynamics at the marshaling yard of the Dutch Railway hub Zwolle. In the figure, one observes the changes in the occupation rate of the marshaling yard from 8 AM until 8 AM on the next day, which is a common planning horizon for the Dutch Railways Company. The sharpest peak in shunting is typically the setup in the morning. These observations make the problem more dynamic. One has to take care of the dynamics in solving the problem. The dynamics motivates us to identify multiple planning periods within the planning horizon.

Another complication in practice is that the numbers of in- and outgoing train units are almost never in balance. For some type of train units the number of units arriving within the planning horizon might differ from the number of departures of that type. Hence the heuristic has to deal with a starting and final "inventory" of train units.

> *The multiple-period heuristic solves real shunting problems in which the planning horizon may consist of multiple planning periods for which not necessarily a balance of train units holds.*

A first pre-processing step in the heuristic solves the problem of unbalance of train units. An unbalance in train units can have several causes. Either more train units of some type will arrive during the planning horizon, or at some point during the planning horizon not enough train units have arrived to form departing trains. In the first case one ends up with a final inventory. We introduce dummy departures at the end of the planning horizon to reserve positions at the tracks for the final stock. In the latter case we assume some starting inventory (train units already parked at the tracks at the start of the planning horizon); otherwise the problem has no feasible solution. To deal with a starting inventory we introduce dummy arrivals. We do allow re-positioning of the starting stock, as if one does not have information about the current positions of the train units at the tracks; this to allow a smooth departure process in the morning.

The *dummy trains* are introduced and added to the sets A and D. So, dummy trains are train units that belong either to the starting inventory or to the final inventory. Note that even in cases where at a first glance there seems to be a *balance of train units*, there might be an unbalance due to the dynamics of the problem. For example, suppose one arrival and one departure of the same type take place within the planning horizon. In case the departure is prior to the arrival, one cannot supply the material of the departing train unless one creates a dummy arrival. Analogously, there is no departure to assign to the arrival, therefore the heuristic introduces dummy departures at the end of the planning horizon for each train

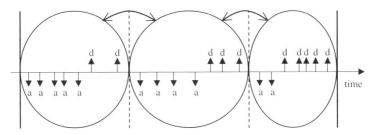

Figure 16.9. Time-decomposition by identifying planning periods.

unit of the arriving train. These dummy trains can be seen as a finishing "inventory." They are not leaving the hub within the planning horizon, but the algorithm blueprint requires them to create a feasible blueprint on which all arrivals can be positioned.

A second pre-processing step in the heuristic identifies the planning periods in the planning horizon. By their definition (see Figure 16.3), the planning periods might vary in length. Thus the heuristic decomposes the total shunting problem over the planning horizon into smaller interrelated shunting problems. Figure 16.9 visualizes the decomposition of the planning horizon into planning periods.

The subproblems are similar and related to each other, since the final state of planning period p equals the initial state of the next period, $p + 1$. This becomes clear from Figure 16.10. From Figure 16.10 we read the *DP*-structure. After making decisions about the positioning of arriving and departing trains, a transition follows from some initial state to a next state. In a *DP*-approach one also optimizes over all possible decisions to take in all possible states at a certain stage. As we will discuss in Section 16.3, this is not tractable due to the enormous amount of decisions and states one should consider.

At this point we provide a heuristic that suggests a good, reasonable set of decisions to be taken at each stage: the *one-period* heuristic. The subproblems are solved consecutively by the *one-period heuristic* described in Section 16.2.1. One has some freedom in choosing which subproblem to solve first. In terms of *DP*, one solves the subproblems in either a backward or a forward fashion. The order in which the subproblems are solved determines the expected computation time, as we discuss later in this section. In general it is good practice to solve first the problem

Initial state	Stage or Planning period p		Final state
Initial state of marshalling yard for planning period p = *Available* positions and positions that are *already reserved*	*Events:* Set of arrivals (A_p) Set of departures (D_p)	*Decisions and actions:* Positioning of arriving train units material Collection of train units forming departing trains	*Final state* of marshaling yard for planning period p = *Initial state* of marshaling yard for planning period $p + 1$

Figure 16.10. Transition from planning period p to planning period $p + 1$.

for the "bottleneck" before other related problems are considered. This is a good strategy, since the overall problem is strongly restricted by the bottleneck. The bottleneck in terms of the shunting problem is the planning period at which the problem is most tightened. Due to the scarce capacity at the marshaling yard and the setup during the morning, the last planning period is probably the tightest one.

After generating a blueprint of departing trains of the last planning period, the heuristic considers the arrivals of that period in order to match them onto the blueprint. Since the heuristic follows a backward approach, all arrivals are matched but some departing train units of the blueprint remain unmatched. These "*unmatched*" train units are matched when matching the arrivals of a planning period prior to the current planning period. The unmatched material can be seen as a *debit* that is moved to the planning period to be considered next. Thus, the generated blueprint of one planning period may restrict the problem in planning period(s) prior to the one just solved.

In finding a blueprint to another planning period, the heuristic might get stuck by the debited restrictions. This means that based on the positioning of trains planned so far, it becomes impossible to find a feasible positioning of a train that is treated later in the planning process. In practice this is not likely to occur, since the marshaling yard is not heavily used during the day. However, in case the heuristic gets stuck, we assume a procedure that slightly adapts the blueprint by swapping and shifting planned positions of train units. Of course it is best to apply these swapping and shifting operations on planned positions of material that has not yet arrived physically, and hence is not parked at the sidings; otherwise swapping implies additional shunting. By following a backward approach starting at the tightest planning period, the heuristic saves time, since there is a reduced chance of getting stuck.

Figure 16.11 illustrates the *multiple-period heuristic*. It shows how the two algorithms *Blueprint* and *Matching* of the *one-period heuristic* are incorporated. As stated before, the branch of the *Blueprint* algorithm that is entered when $T^* = \varnothing$ requires more research for good division, swapping, and shifting strategies.

The reader who is familiar with *Dynamic Programming* clearly sees similarities between the *multiple-period heuristic* and *Dynamic Programming* (*DP*). In Section 16.3 we provide the *DP*-formulation and discuss these similarities.

16.2.3. Illustration of the *Multiple-Period Heuristic*

Before relating the heuristic to *DP*, let us illustrate how the *multiple-period heuristic* works. We focus on the process of copying a blueprint from one planning period to another. Consider the following example.

16.2.3.1. Example 1. Consider a planning horizon in which a set of 19 trains need to be shunted to and collected from the marshaling yard. The marshaling yard consists of two sidings (labeled t1 and t2) of 150 meters each. Details about the timetable can be found in Table 16.2.

The letter "a" or "d" precedes the train number, meaning that the train is an arrival or a departure, respectively. For simplicity, each train is composed of only one

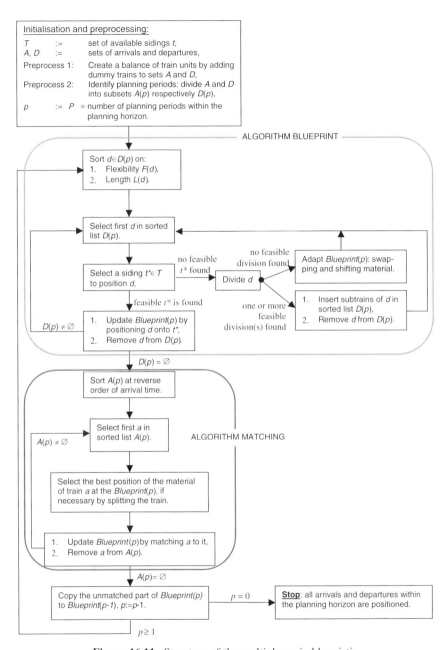

Figure 16.11. Structure of the multiple-period heuristic.

TABLE 16.2. Timetable of Example 1

Time	Train label	Type
08:15	a1	II
08:45	a2	I
09:15	a3	I
10:00	d4	I
10:15	a5	II
10:45	a6	III
12:15	a7	II
13:15	a8	III
16:45	d9	III
17:15	d10	II
23:45	a11	I
00:45	a12	III
01:15	a13	I
05:15	d14	III
05:45	d15	I
06:15	d16	III
06:45	d17	I
07:15	d18	II
07:45	d19	I

train unit. One distinguishes three types of train units: type I of length 30 meters, type II of length 40 meters and type III of length 50 meters.

16.2.3.2. Solution to Example 1. Step by step we present how the heuristic generates a solution to the underlying shunting problem of Example 1. The *multiple-period heuristic* starts with the initialization and the pre-processes:

Initialization of T, A, *and* D

$$T := \{t1, t2\}$$
$$A := \{a1, a2, a3, a5, a6, a7, a8, a11, a12, a13\}$$
$$D := \{d4, d9, d10, d14, d15, d16, d17, d18, d19\}$$

Pre-process 1: Creating a Balance of Train Units. When checking the balance, the heuristic computes that four train units of type II arrive while only three of these units depart within the planning horizon. At the end of the planning horizon, one train unit of type II stays at the sidings as final inventory. So the heuristic introduces a dummy departure d20, in order to get a correct blueprint on which all arrivals can be positioned; d20 is a (dummy) departure of a train unit of type II at 07:59h on day 2. The heuristic does not need to introduce dummy arrivals, because for each type of train unit enough units arrive prior to the departures in order to match them.

d20 is added: $D := \{d4, d9, d10, d14, d15, d17, d18, d19, d20\}$

Pre-process 2: Identify planning periods. The planning horizon from 8 AM until 8 AM on the next day is decomposed into three planning periods:

- Planning period 1:   from 08:00 h until 10:14 h
- Planning period 2:   from 10:15 h until 23:44 h
- Planning period 3:   from 23:45 h until 08:00 h

These planning periods are separated in Table 16.2 by horizontal lines. The heuristic decomposes the sets A and D into the subsets A_1, A_2, A_3 and D_1, D_2, D_3:

$A_1 = \{a1, a2, a3\}, \quad A_2 = \{a5, a6, a7, a8\}, \quad$ and $\quad A_3 = \{a11, a12, a13\}$
$D_1 = \{d4\}, \qquad\quad D_2 = \{d9, d10\}, \qquad$ and $\quad D_3 = \{d14, d16, d17, d18,$
$\qquad\qquad\qquad\qquad\qquad\qquad\qquad\qquad\qquad\qquad d19, d20\}$

The material of all trains in D_3 needs to be positioned at the sidings during the night. Since D_3 is the largest set, the last planning period is the tightest one.

Main Routine. Now that the pre-processing steps are done, the heuristic searches for a good positioning and matching of all arriving and departing trains. Starting with the subproblem of planning period 3, it solves in a backward fashion until the overall shunting problem is solved. Below we summarize the steps performed by the heuristic:

Step 1. Generating a blueprint for planning period 3 of all trains in D_3.

Step 2. Matching the arriving trains in A_3 onto the blueprint of planning period 3.

Step 3. Copying the unmatched part of the blueprint of planning period 3 to an initial blueprint of planning period 2.

Step 4. Completing the blueprint of planning period 2 by adding the trains in D_2 to it.

Step 5. Matching the arriving trains in A_2 onto the blueprint of planning period 2.

Step 6. Copying the unmatched part of the blueprint of planning period 2 to an initial blueprint of planning period 1.

Step 7. Completing the blueprint of planning period 1 by adding the trains in D_1 to it.

Step 8. Matching the arriving trains in A_1 onto the blueprint of planning period 1.

Stop: Since all arriving and departing trains are matched and positioned on the tracks.

Figure 16.12 illustrates the working of the heuristic by visualizing the results of every step. Blocks without a border are positions reserved for departing train

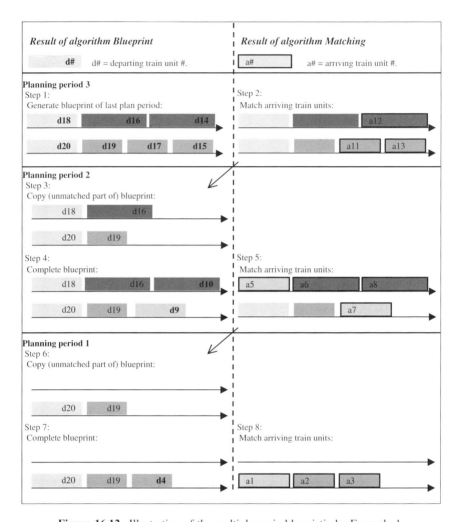

Figure 16.12. Illustration of the multiple-period heuristic by Example 1.

units. These blocks build up (the unmatched parts of) the blueprint of a planning period. The nonbordered blocks are open for arriving train units provided that these are of the same type. The arriving train units are visualized by bordered blocks. The label at the left side in the block identifies the arriving train unit. The label at the right side in the block identifies the departing train unit. Thus, the arrivals and departures are matched as shown in Table 16.3. The material of arriving train a1 is used for (dummy) departing train d20, the material of train a2 is used for train d19, and so on.

A brief comment about the names of the positions: At each track at most five ($=150$ m$/30$ m) train units can be positioned. Positions P1 to P5 are positions at track t1, and positions P6 to P10 are positions at track t2. The length of a position

TABLE 16.3. Matching of Arrivals and Departures of an Illustrative Example

Arriving Train	Departing Train	Position	Arriving Train	Departing Train	Position
a1	d20	P6	a7	d9	P8
a2	d19	P7	a8	d10	P3
a3	d4	P8	a11	d17	P8
a5	d18	P1	a12	d14	P3
a6	d16	P2	a13	d15	P9

is variable and equals zero as long as no train unit is assigned to that position. When a train unit of length L is assigned to a position, the length of that position equals L. Of course the length of a track restricts the sum of the lengths of the positions at that track. Assuming all tracks do have dead ends, positions P1 and P6 are located at the dead ends of the tracks. P5 and P10 are at the open side of track t1 and t2,[5] respectively.

Since the departing trains are positioned at the tracks in order of departure time, no exit conflict occurs. This is very important in view of a smooth departure. Due to the complexity of the shunting problem, one cannot guarantee that a solution exists that does not imply any entrance conflict. However, the procedure in Example 1 succeeds in finding such a solution. In this case no train needs to be (dis-) connected, since all trains are composed of only one train unit.

The example illustrated above shows well the processes performed by the heuristic. Nevertheless, it is hard to draw conclusions about the quality of the heuristic, since one limited example provides not enough evidence. Therefore we like to test the heuristic thoroughly on shunting problems taken from practice. Section 16.4 reports on such a test. Before taking a look at the results of this test, let us discuss the exact technique of *Dynamic Programming* (*DP*).

16.3. DYNAMIC PROGRAMMING

Although *Dynamic Programming* has inspired us, our heuristic is not a pure *DP* approach. Still it is appropriate to discuss the *DP* formulation for several reasons. First, we like to point out the similarities of the *multiple-period heuristic* and *DP*. Second, the *DP* discussion demonstrates why one better solves the shunting problem in a backward fashion. Third, the *DP* discussion illustrates why a global search technique is not applicable.

Section 16.3.1 shows the *DP* formulation for the shunting problem. In Section 16.3.2 a limited shunting problem is solved by *DP*. Section 16.3.3 discusses briefly

---

[5]Though we have implicitly discussed thus far only dead-end tracks, the heuristic treats continuous tracks as being more flexible, assuming no entrance conflict occurs on such tracks. Since in practice the sidings are of moderate length, this assumption holds. However, to improve the heuristic on this issue, more research on decision rules is necessary.

the tractability of *DP* and other exact algorithms for the shunting problem. Finally, Section 16.3.4 summarizes the comparison of *DP* and the *multiple-period heuristic*.

16.3.1. The *Dynamic Programming* Formulation

The basic idea of *Dynamic Programming* is recursion. To find an optimal solution, the problem is decomposed into a sequence of interrelated analogous subproblems, which are solved step by step. Indeed the shunting problem can be decomposed into subproblems by decomposing the planning horizon into several planning periods, according to the definition used in the *multiple-period heuristic*. In *DP*-terms a planning period is called a *stage*. So the number of stages equals the number of planning periods (P). Given the state of the marshaling yard, one needs to decide where to position all arriving and departing trains for that planning period. In the discussion below we assume the reader to be familiar with the basic principles of *Dynamic Programming*.[6]

From Figures 16.9 and 16.10 (in Section 16.2.2) the following recursive formula for the *Dynamic Programming* approach can be derived:

$$f_p^*(s_p) = \min_{x_p: feasible} \left\{ c(s_p, x_p) + f_{p+1}^*(s_{p+1}(s_p, x_p)) \right\}$$

where

- x_p is a *set of decisions* to take at stage p. For the shunting problem the set of decisions can be seen as a vector of positions for all train units that arrive or depart as part of trains in $A(p)$ or $D(p)$. The position on the marshaling yard of train unit u is stored in $pos(u)$.

- s_p is the *state* of the marshaling yard at the beginning of stage p. The state of the marshaling yard describes the positioning of the train units. For each track position on which a train unit is parked, one needs to know in which arriving train and in which departing train it takes part. Later on we show how to register a state. Recall from Figure 16.10 in Section 16.2.2 that the starting state at stage $p + 1$ equals the final state at stage p; thus s_{p+1} is a function in s_p and x_p: $s_{p+1}(s_p, x_p)$.

- $c(s_p, x_p)$ denotes the shunting cost implied by decision x_p at stage p, supposing that stage p starts in state s_p. The components of this cost function are similar to the ones used in the cost functions of the heuristic.

- $f_p^*(s_p)$ is the minimum total future shunting costs from stage p toward the end of the planning horizon as one starts stage p in state s_p.

---

[6]For those who are not familiar with *DP*, we refer to the book by Hillier and Liebermann (1995) for an introduction to the technique of *Dynamic Programming*.

$x_p^*(s_p)$ is the optimal set of decisions to make in stage p if one starts stage p at state s_p. This set of decisions minimizes the total future shunting costs over stages p, $p + 1, \ldots, P$, starting stage p at state s_p.

The recursion in $f_p^*(s_p)$ implies a stepwise backward solution procedure. One can easily transform this recursion such that a forward solution procedure can be applied; however, we prefer a backward approach.

The way in which the *DP* problem is decomposed is similar to the decomposition in the *multiple-period heuristic*. One will observe more similarities between *DP* and the *multiple-period heuristic* by considering the backward solution procedure. Later on in this section we briefly comment on a forward approach.

In solving step-by-step the *DP*-recursion, one starts solving the subproblem for the last stage, the last planning period: $p = P$. Because one has no information concerning arrivals and departures that do not fall within the planning horizon, we assume that one starts and ends up with an empty marshaling yard.[7] Hence, the unique starting state s_1 and unique final state s_{P+1} are denoted by $(0, 0, \ldots, 0)$; the zeros denote that no train unit is assigned to any position at the sidings.

As a base of the recursion we set $f_{P+1}^*(s_{P+1}) = 0$, since planning period $P + 1$ is not within the planning horizon.

Applying the recursion, one can successively compute in a backward fashion $f_P^*(s_P), f_{P-1}^*(s_{P-1}), \ldots,$ for each possible state until one finds $f_1^*(s_1)$.

Thus the overall-shunting problem is solved: $f_1^*(s_1)$ denotes the minimum total planning costs and the minimizing set of decisions to take is $(x_1^*, x_2^*, \ldots, x_P^*)$.

This way the shunting problem can (theoretically) be solved by a (backward) dynamic programming approach.

16.3.2. Illustration

The mathematical description of the *DP* approach in Section 16.3.1 is fairly technical. To clarify the solution process, we illustrate the *DP* technique by solving a small instance of the shunting problem as sketched in Example 2. We will show both a backward and a forward approach to illustrate why it is important for the *multiple-period* heuristic to start at the most restrictive planning period.

16.3.2.1. Example 2. Consider the set of trains in the timetable in Table 16.4.

For simplicity, each train consists of only one train unit. One distinguishes two types of trains units: type B and type R. Any unit of type B has length 50 m, and any unit of type R is 80 m long.

According to the timetable, three trains (labeled a1, a2, and a4) are arriving and three trains are departing (labeled d3, d5, and d6) within the planning horizon. All trains need to be positioned at two available sidings; track 1 is 70 m and track 2 is 120 m.

---

[7]The heuristic supports this assumption, since it introduces dummy arrivals and dummy departures.

TABLE 16.4. Timetable for Example 2

Time	Train Label	Configuration
09:15	a1	B (50)
11:45	a2	B (50)
17:00	d3	B (50)
19:15	a4	R (80)
22:30	d5	R (80)
00:15	d6	B (50)

In Table 16.4, two planning periods are identified within the planning horizon.

16.3.2.2. Backward Dynamic Programming. The registration of the positions on which the train units are parked is similar to the registration in the *multiple-period heuristic*. Since the smallest train unit is 50 m, it is impossible to plan more than one train at track 1; thus there is only one position on track 1. This position is labeled "position 1." Track 2 is long enough to position two train units of 50 meter, so position 2 and 3 are at track 2. Again the length of a position is variable and will be fixed by the length of the train unit that is assigned to it. For computational convenience we suppose in this example that the cost associated with planning a train unit onto a position equals the position's number. So shunting a train between a platform and position p will cost p.

The backward *DP* approach starts positioning the material of trains a4, d5, and d6. An arrival and a departure are matched in case their positions are corresponding. As one sees in Figure 16.13, in stage 2 only two decisions are feasible. In this case both decisions result in the same state: the state in which the marshaling yard is empty—except for position 1, on which d6 is planned. The theory of *DP* states that for each possible state at a stage we need to store only the best decision. In state $s_2 = [d6,0,0]$ the best decision is x_2^* (d6, 0, 0) = (2, 2, 1). This denotes that

Dynamic Programming - Backward

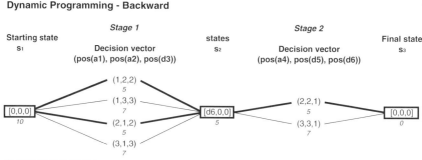

Stage p: planning period p
number of stages $P = 2$
State s_p: situation at marshaling yard at the beginning of stage p
Decision: position all train units arriving and leaving within the planning horizon
Immediate cost of decision: see numbers below the decision vectors printed in a smaller italic font

Figure 16.13. Visualization of backward DP approach.

train unit d6 is positioned at position 1 and train units a4 and d5 are matched at position 2; for a better understanding of this notation we refer to Figure 16.13. The optimal cost f_2^* ([d6,0,0]) equals 5, as shown below, the node representing the state vector [d6,0,0].

Since in planning period 2 no train unit of type B arrives, train d6 cannot be matched by an arrival in stage 2. These unmatched train units are output of stage 2 and will be matched in stage 1. The reserved positions are debited restrictions at stage 1. So one copies the unmatched part of the blueprint as a base for the state at stage 1. The process of copying a blueprint corresponds to the *multiple-period heuristic*. In fact, each of the possible states that are outputs of stage 2 are inputs to stage 1. For this limited example a backward *DP* algorithm generates only one state in stage 2. This greatly simplifies the optimization problem. Later, we will illustrate in Figure 16.14 that a forward *DP* approach would generate six different states.

The *DP* approach continues its backward solution procedure from each of the states by registering the optimal decision to take at each state. At the next stage all feasible decisions are evaluated. In case no feasible decision exists from some state at some stage, the branch in the DP graph is truncated. This means that the branch appears to be infeasible, and the time spent on generating the branch is wasted. As will be illustrated later, we state that the expected number of infeasible branches is reduced when one applies a backward solution procedure that starts at the tightest planning period.

As in the *multiple-period heuristic*, the partly copied blueprints are completed by deciding about the positioning of train units departing in planning period 1. The state transition depends on the completed blueprint and the decisions taken concerning the positioning of the arriving train units. In this case four feasible decisions with respect to the positioning of departure d3 and arrivals a1 and a2 should be evaluated in Figure 16.13. However, all four decision result in the same state, and two of these decisions are suboptimal.

Since we have imposed a *balance of train units* by creating dummy trains in the pre-process of the heuristic, the starting state of stage 1 is an empty marshaling yard. By the decisions at stage 1 and 2, all arrivals and departures are matched and all material is positioned at the sidings. Hence, an optimal solution to the shunting problem is found. In fact the problem has two optimal solutions, which incur minimum total cost (10). The two optimal solutions are indicated by the thick paths and are shown in Table 16.5.

Because this instance of the shunting problem is very limited, it is still manageable with DP. We comment later on real instances after briefly illustrating the forward *DP* approach.

16.3.2.3. Forward Dynamic Programming. Without formulating the forward recursion explicitly, we illustrate by Figure 16.14 the solution procedure of the forward *DP* approach applied to Example 2. Again we identify two optimal solutions to the shunting problem, shown by the thick paths from starting state to final state. Note that the forward approach generates many more states at stage 1 than the backward approach does. At the next stage (stage 2), most of these states

Dynamic Programming - Forward

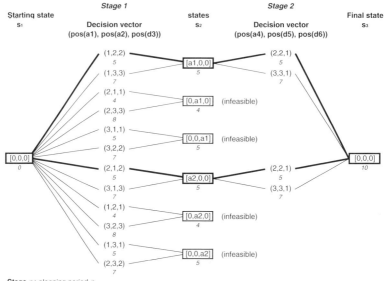

Stage p: planning period p
number of stages $P = 2$
State s_p: situation at marshaling yard at the beginning of stage p
Decision: position all train units arriving and leaving within the planning horizon
Immediate cost of decision: see numbers below the decision vectors printed in a smaller italic font

Figure 16.14. Visualization of forward DP approach.

turn out to be infeasible (sub-) solutions. The truncated branches in the DP graph represent the infeasible states.

The forward DP approach wastes relatively much computation time in generating solutions that might result into infeasible intermediate states of the main shunting problem. In general we state that an algorithm that considers the tightest planning period too late in the planning process, seems to waste much computation time by generating infeasible states. Therefore it is better to solve the shunting problem in a backward fashion as the *multiple-period heuristic* does.

TABLE 16.5. Two Optimal Solutions for Example 2 Generated by Dynamic Programming

Solution 1			Solution 2		
Train Label	Position	Matched to	Train Label	Position	Matched to
a1	1	d6	a1	2	d3
a2	2	d3	a2	1	d6
d3	2	a2	d3	2	a1
a4	2	d5	a4	2	d5
d5	2	a4	d5	2	a4
d6	1	a1	d6	1	d2

16.3.3. Tractability

In real instances of the train shunting problem the exact *DP* solution procedure would have many more states to evaluate than is computationally manageable. From all the feasible states it should evaluate all possible decisions transforming the states to other states that serve as bases in the next stage. Some of the new states coincide; however, different branches lead to that state. The *DP* optimality principle allows us to store for each state only the best branch—for example, the set of decisions that result in that state and that implies minimum costs. Thus the number of states might be strongly reduced. Nevertheless, it is highly likely that the number of states tends to grow exponentially, as discussed below.

In a *DP* graph the number of branches, corresponding to decisions, is exponential in the number of train units to consider at a stage. Figure 16.14 illustrates how explosive the number of decisions might be for even small problem instances. Below we quantify the number of decision to consider at a particular stage.

For example, consider a moderate-sized shunting problem in which one needs to position 20 train units during the night at a marshaling yard. The marshaling yard consists of 10 tracks, each with capacity for 3 train units. We need to assign 20 out of the 30 possible positions to the 20 train units, so the number of decisions is $\frac{30!}{(30-20)!} \approx 7.3 \times 10^{25}$. One can reduce this number in a heuristic way by ignoring decisions that are assumed to be suboptimal for some reason.

For example, in view of a smooth departure process, planners like to position trains in order of departure. If, in addition, planners match the arriving and departing train units in advance, one can reduce the number of decisions to evaluate. When positioning the trains in order of departure, the total number of decisions to evaluate equals $10^3 \cdot 9^3 \cdot 8^3 \cdot 7^3 \cdot 6^3 \cdot 5^3 \cdot 4^2 \approx 5.5 \times 10^{16}$. Even if a computer could evaluate the incredible number of one billion decisions per second, it would still take almost 2 years before it finds an optimal positioning!

Some additional observations, based on the structure of the shunting problem, might lead to additional optimality principles. One could incorporate these optimality principles in an exact algorithm to speed up the solution process. Nevertheless, the number of computations to perform in order to solve any real shunting problem is far too many. It is intuitively clear that in general no exact algorithm for the shunting problem is tractable. So we are at the right track by applying an approximation algorithm. In a sophisticated way, the *multiple-period heuristic* tries to find a low-cost path in the *DP* graph.

16.3.4. *DP* and the Multiple-Period Heuristic

In the discussion above, one observes some similarities between *DP* and the *multiple-period heuristic*. These similarities are:

- The decomposition of the planning horizon into planning periods.
- The backward order of solving the subproblems.
- The transition from one planning period to another by copying a blueprint.

A major difference is that *DP* solves the problem of optimality by using Bellman's principle of optimal subsolutions. The *multiple-period heuristic* solves more or less greedy. We stipulated that the complexity of the shunting problem makes it computationally infeasible to apply an exact algorithm like *DP*. Therefore one is forced to apply an approximation algorithm, like the *multiple-period heuristic*.

The *Dynamic Programming* technique inspired us to develop this heuristic in which the number of decisions and the number of states is less explosive. The *multiple-period heuristic* evaluates many decisions from which it selects the best one, but it ends up with only one state at each stage. Hence the *multiple-period heuristic* tries to find a good solution by drawing a low-cost path through the *DP* graph. In cases where the heuristic gets stuck at a state, it needs to retrace in the *DP* graph. Applying sophisticated swapping and shifting operation allows quick retracing.

The *multiple-period heuristic* follows a backward approach in order to reduce the risk of retracing. As illustrated in Section 16.3.2, a forward *DP* approach is expected to retrace more frequently in order to find a feasible solution. Also in a backward heuristic approach, one needs to be careful in choosing the decisions to evaluate. Some decisions might lead to a solution that is infeasible or far from optimal. Therefore the heuristic applies a sophisticated set of priorities and decision rules. If necessary, it applies also splitting and swapping procedures in order to find a solution. In the next section the *multiple-period heuristic* is tested by applying it to a real instance of the shunting problem.

In principle, one can extend the multiple-period heuristic by alternative decision rules in the single-period heuristic. Doing so results in evaluating more paths in the *DP* graph from which the best one is chosen. During the solution process, one can adopt Bellman's principle and reduce the computational work by leaving out nonpromising paths.

16.4. RESULTS ON TEST CASE ZWOLLE

In this section the performance of the *multiple-period heuristic* is evaluated by a test case taken from the practice of the Dutch Railway hub Zwolle. Instead of presenting the complete input, we summarize the major characteristics of the test case in Section 16.4.1. Section 16.4.2 addresses the most interesting situation at the marshaling yard: the situation during the night. Finally, in Section 16.4.3 we qualify the complete solution. The complete solution, as generated by a first implementation of the *multiple-period heuristic*, is described in the appendixes.

16.4.1. Input and Pre-processing

This section summarizes the input data and briefly comments on the results of the pre-processes. We discuss consecutively the infrastructure, the material and the timetable.

Infrastructure. As illustrated by Figure 16.1 in Section 16.1.2, the marshaling yard consists of 19 sidings, spread around the main tracks. These sidings vary in length from 114 to 415 m. The total length of the tracks equals approximately 4000 m. Some of the tracks do not provide an overhead wire and are therefore not suitable for electric train units.

Material. Each train is composed of at most four train units. Most of the trains are composed of two train units of the same type. Some trains are composed of more and different types of train units. The data set includes seven types of train units, labeled DD_AR_4, DM_90_2, ICM3, ICM4, MAT64_2, MAT64_4, and SM_90_2. The train units vary in length from 53 to 124 m. Most of the trains are electric.

Timetable. The planning horizon is from Friday 8 AM untill Saturday 8 AM. In the planning horizon the material of 55 arriving and 45 departing trains has to be shunted toward or collected from (respectively) the marshaling yard. We put the heuristic to the test by not allowing to park trains along platforms and main tracks. So all trains are fed to the heuristic for positioning at the marshaling yard. Since during weekends fewer train units are in service, one observes a relative big final inventory of train units. For the same reason, the morning rush is less heavy than during weekdays.

In Figure 16.15 we quantify the dynamics in the shunting problem by measuring the occupation rate of the marshaling yard. The occupation rate equals the total length of material at the marshaling yard divided by the total available capacity (length) of the sidings. Note that in general an occupation rate of 100% can never be achieved owing to the indivisibility of train units. The heuristic classifies 18 train units as final inventory. Furthermore, one observes a dummy arrival as starting inventory[8] at 08:00 h. By the definition of a planning period the heuristic discerns 23 planning periods in the planning horizon.

Notice the peak during the night and the sharp fall during the morning rush. As mentioned before, the later observation would be even clearer on weekdays, since the Saturday morning rush is less heavy. Nevertheless, the amount of shunting work to do in the morning is stressing.

16.4.2. Visualization of the Tightest Planning Period

Clearly the last planning period, from 00:01 h until 08:00 h on day 2, is the most interesting one: During that period the marshaling yard is heavily used, and at the end a lot of trains will depart. During the night about 87% of the capacity of the marshaling yard is used to position material of a total length of 3500 m. Because of the indivisibility of train units, the problem is even more tightened than it seems to be. For now, lets take a look at the marshaling yard during the night.

Figure 16.16 is a simplified representation of the situation at railway hub Zwolle during the night. We zoomed in at the three sections of the railway hub; together

---

[8]This dummy arrival of a train unit of type ICM4 was necessary to plan the departure at 10:44 h on day 1 of the train labeled 734. Since we have no information about arrivals prior to the planning horizon, the heuristic creates a dummy arrival to avoid the planning process getting stuck.

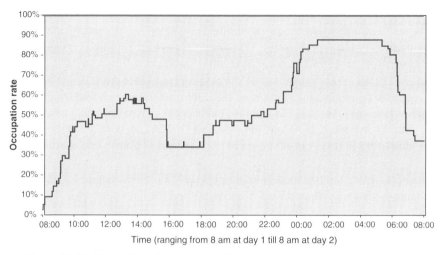

Figure 16.15. Illustration of the dynamics in capacity usage at the marshaling yard.

they form the marshaling yard. The big gray blocks are the platforms. The dashed lines visualize the main tracks, which are not available for positioning material. The other lines visualize the sidings; most of these have a dead end. The number under the lines denotes the labels of the tracks. The length of the lines is scaled on the real length of the corresponding track. The rectangles represent train units; their corresponding types are given by the legend. If two or more rectangles are attached to each other, then the corresponding train units are connected to each other in a departing train.

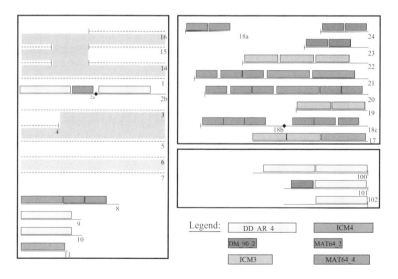

Figure 16.16. Positioning of material at Railway-hub Zwolle during the night.

However, the figure does not provide all information we need to properly evaluate the performance of the heuristic, and one may conclude that it succeeds in clustering the material by type. At track 8, 17, and 20 a violation of the clustering seems to occur, but this is because planners do prefer this violation instead of dividing a departing train. Most likely it is not possible to find a solution that positions only one type of train unit per track. Even if one could, planners would not prefer such a solution in view of a smooth departure of trains composed of different types of train units.

16.4.3. Statistics of the Complete Solution

Figure 16.16 shows how the material is clustered at the marshaling yard during the night, but planners are also interested in some other statistics of the complete solution. Below we discuss some relevant quality measures:

- None of the departing trains are divided.
- In two cases some adjacent train units, positioned at the same track, are connected when composing a departing train. This corresponds to 4% of all departures.
- When collecting the material of the departing trains, five disconnections take place. Thus disconnecting is necessary for 9% of all departures.
- Four arriving trains (7%) need to be divided in subtrains, which are positioned at different sidings.
- No entrance conflict occurs.
- By nature the heuristic avoids exit conflicts.

Because the unit of the distance matrix is in this case not meaningful, we do not discuss it. The heuristic generates the solution in half of a second on a desktop PC (Pentium III, 500 MHz). The low computation time allows for future extensions to the shunting problem.

We refer to the appendices for a description of the complete solution.

One might conclude that the heuristic shows promising results; however, it is hard to draw conclusions based on just a few test cases. We stress that the heuristic is a first product of the project. By incorporating better division, swapping, and shifting techniques, one could improve the heuristic during future phases of the project. By its construction the heuristic is easy to adapt with respect to future extensions of the shunting problem.

16.5. SUMMARY AND CONCLUSIONS

16.5.1. Summary

In this chapter we presented a solution procedure for the train-shunting problem as described in Section 16.1.1. This problem is far too complex to solve to optimality; thus planners must be satisfied with a suboptimal solution. Anyway, since the objectives are somewhat diffuse, several solutions are good in practice. The *multiple-period heuristic* constructs a good solution by applying a set of sophisticated decision rules in a hierarchical way. These decision rules were deducted from the hierarchical planning approach followed by the planners of the Dutch Railways Company. The *multiple-period heuristic* applies a method of problem decomposition. On the one hand, this is for practical reasons. On the other hand, the decomposition method is inspired by theory, in principle by *Dynamic Programming* (*DP*).

Conform the solution procedure of *DP* the *multiple-period heuristic* decomposes the shunting problem in subproblems, related to so-called planning periods. Those subproblems are solved stepwise in a backward fashion. From the discussion of a pure *DP* formulation it follows that the heuristic searches for a low-cost path in the *DP*-graph by evaluating a limited number of states and decisions.

The results of the *multiple-period heuristic* are promising for several test cases and for a real case taken from practice. To draw more definite conclusions, one should test the heuristic on more cases from practice.

By its construction the heuristic is fast and flexible and therefore easy to adapt and to extend during future phases in the project. In future implementations of the heuristic, it might be effective to generate multiple solutions from which the planner might choose. The computation time is very short (not even a second), so in future phases of the project one can evaluate more promising paths in the *DP* graph by extending the decision space with a second one-period heuristic based on an alternative set of decision rules. Another suggestion is incorporating a route planner, which schedules the required shunts at an operational level. Thus one can more accurately estimate the shunting efforts.

When developing further, one must keep in mind that delays and breakdowns of trains are likely to occur in practice. One should pay attention to the robustness of a solution as well as to a short computation time of the algorithm. In extreme cases, the Railway Company likes to rerun the heuristic quickly by inputting updated time-tables. Because of its speed, the *multiple-period heuristic* is very useful for this purpose.

16.5.2. CONCLUSIONS

Finally, we conclude with some statements about the shunting problem and its suggested solution procedure:

- The train-shunting problem is far too complex to find an optimal solution.
- The *multiple-period heuristic* searches quickly for a good, robust, and practical solution.
- The heuristic is based on time decomposition.
- The heuristic is related to *Dynamic Programming*.

Since solutions are generated quickly, planners can use the heuristic to update solutions in cases where incidences, like delays and breakdowns, take place.

APPENDICES

In the first appendix some terminology used throughout this chapter is explained. The second appendix shows the complete solution to test case Zwolle as generated by the *multiple-period heuristic*.

Appendix: Terminology

People who study the shunting problem use specific terminology to describe the planning process, the objects involved, and their motions. Here we define and explain some terminology used throughout this chapter.

(Sub-) Train, Train Unit, and Material

- train = a vehicle, consisting of one or more train units used to transport goods and/or passengers along railways.
- train unit = with regard to planning, the smallest physical unit of a train. A train unit cannot be split into smaller units. There are several types of train units, based on size and other technical characteristics.
- material of train t = the set of (loose) train units that composes train t.
- subtrain = a combination of one or more train units that together are connected to each other in a train.

We illustrate these terms in Figure 16.17, while showing the possibilities to split a train. In general, there are 2^{U-1} ways to split a train consisting of U train units into one or more subtrains. Thus a train composed of three train units can be split in four different ways.

Splitting Trains. Since the available capacity at the sidings is limited and the arriving and departing trains are seldomly of the same configuration, one needs to split some trains into subtrains. We introduce the following terminology for special cases of splitting a train:

- *Divide*. A (departing or arriving) train is divided, when the material of the train will be positioned at multiple sidings.

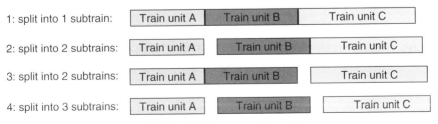

Splitting a train consisting of three train units:

1: split into 1 subtrain: | Train unit A | Train unit B | Train unit C |

2: split into 2 subtrains: | Train unit A | Train unit B | Train unit C |

3: split into 2 subtrains: | Train unit A | Train unit B | Train unit C |

4: split into 3 subtrains: | Train unit A | Train unit B | Train unit C |

Figure 16.17. Splitting a train into subtrains.

- *Connect*. Material of two (sub-) trains that are positioned next to each other at a siding, needs to be connected in order to compose a departing (sub-) train. So the departing train is split, but its train units are positioned next to each other at the same track.

- *Disconnect*. Material of one (sub-) train needs to be disconnected in order to compose two departing (sub-) trains. So the arriving train is split, but its train units are positioned next to each other at the same track.

In accordance with these definitions, we use the terms division, connection, and disconnection.

Conflicts. In positioning trains at sidings, some conflicts may occur.

Technical conflicts are conflicts like a technical mismatch in assigning a train to a track. For example, assigning an electric train to a track that does not provide overhead wires for traction is infeasible.

Another type of conflict is a *routing conflict*, which might occur when a track is used by two (or more) trains at a time. This kind of conflicts may happen at a siding or at any other track. Two special cases of routing conflicts are entrance conflicts and exit conflicts.

- An *entrance conflict* occurs at a siding when a train cannot reach the planned position at the track because some material is blocking the entrance. This requires the blocking material to be moved temporarily to another track.

- An *exit conflict* occurs when a train cannot leave a siding because some material, which is planned to depart later, blocks the exit. In order to depart, the blocking material needs to be moved.

Solving entrance and exit conflicts implies much shunting work. In general, one cannot guarantee to find a solution that implies no conflicts. Since planners prefer a smooth departure of the trains, they try to avoid exit conflicts. In exchange they are willing to accept some entrance conflicts.

Appendix: Results on Test Case Zwolle

In Table 16.6 we list a complete solution to the shunting problem of Zwolle as generated by the *multiple-period heuristic*. As stated before, this solution is generated in an early phase of the project using a simple implementation of the *multiple-period heuristic*.

The table is sorted according to departure time. In each row, one finds information about a train unit; consecutive columns give the following:

- The departure time[9] of the unit.
- The train number of the departing train that includes the unit.
- The type of the unit.

TABLE 16.6. A Complete Solution to Test Case Zwolle

Departure Time[a]	Departure Label	Type	Track Position	Arrival Label	Arrival Time[a]
10855	8023	MAT64_2	18b-3	3824	10808
10926	9125	MAT64_2	18b-2	3824	10808
10955	8027	SM_90_2	2b-1	8030	10954
10955	8027	SM_90_2	2b-2	8030	10954
11044	734	ICM4	18a-1	BV1	10759
11055	8031	SM_90_2	19-1	8024	10837
11055	8031	SM_90_2	19-2	8024	10837
11115	536	ICM3	17-1	727	10946
11121	7933	DM_90_2	2b-1	7936	11112
11155	8035	SM_90_2	17-1	8038	11154
11155	8035	SM_90_2	17-2	8038	11154
11255	8039	MAT64_2	2a-1	8034	11054
11326	9141	MAT64_2	2a-1	9128	10902
11326	9141	MAT64_2	2a-1	3844	11308
11344	746	ICM3	19-1	735	11146
11351	8543	DM_90_2	2b-1	7932	11012
11351	8543	DM_90_2	2b-2	7932	11012
11355	8043	SM_90_2	2b-1	8046	11354
11355	8043	SM_90_2	2b-2	8046	11354
11421	7945	DM_90_2	9-1	8528	10915
11421	7945	DM_90_2	9-2	8528	10915
11426	9145	MAT64_2	18b-2	3628-2	11109
11426	9145	MAT64_2	18b-3	3628-2	11109
11444	750	ICM4	2b-1	545	11415
11455	8047	SM_90_2	18a-1	8042	11254
11455	8047	SM_90_2	18a-2	8042	11254
11549	3661	MAT64_2	8-1	3622	10943
11549	3661	MAT64_2	8-2	3622	10943
11549	3661	MAT64_2	8-3	3622	10943
11549	3661	MAT64_2	8-4	3622	10943
11551	5656	DD_AR_4	100-1	5625	10940
11551	5656	DD_AR_4	100-2	5625	10940
11551	7951	DM_90_2	10-1	7926	10842
11551	7951	DM_90_2	10-2	7926	10842
11555	8051	SM_90_2	18a-1	8054	11554
11555	8051	SM_90_2	18a-2	8054	11554
11655	8055	SM_90_2	18a-1	8058	11654
11655	8055	SM_90_2	18a-2	8058	11654
11755	8059	SM_90_2	18a-1	8062	11754
11755	8059	SM_90_2	18a-2	8062	11754
11855	8063	SM_90_2	18c-1	8026	10854
11855	8063	SM_90_2	18c-2	8026	10854

(*continued*)

TABLE 16.6. *Continued*

Departure Time[a]	Departure Label	Type	Track Position	Arrival Label	Arrival Time[a]
11955	8067	SM_90_2	18a-1	8066	11854
11955	8067	SM_90_2	18a-2	8066	11854
12044	774	ICM4	19-1	743	11346
12055	8071	MAT64_2	18b-1	3824	10808
12155	8075	SM_90_2	19-1	8074	12054
12155	8075	SM_90_2	19-2	8074	12054
12251	5684	MAT64_2	2a-1	3868	11908
12359	3693	MAT64_2	19-1	3672	12209
12359	3693	MAT64_2	19-2	3672	12209
12359	3693	MAT64_2	19-3	3672	12209
20000	5688	MAT64_2	2a-2	3868	11908
20521	5614	DD_AR_4	2a-1	5683	20009
20544	8511	DM_90_2	101-1	8588	20022
20551	5616	DD_AR_4	101-1	5623-1	10909
20614	8011	MAT64_2	18b-1	3678	12343
20614	8011	MAT64_2	18b-2	3678	12343
20614	8011	MAT64_2	18b-3	3678	12343
20618	516	ICM3	17-1	1541	11315
20618	516	ICM3	17-1	766	11844
20618	516	ICM4	17-3	783	12346
20620	3623	MAT64_4	8-1	3676	12309
20620	3623	MAT64_2	8-2	5687	20117
20620	3623	MAT64_2	8-3	5687	20117
20621	5618	DD_AR_4	102-1	5623-2	10909
20627	9113	MAT64_2	18c-3	3668	12109
20649	715	ICM3	19-1	585	20015
20649	715	ICM3	19-2	585	20015
20649	3625	MAT64_4	20-4	3634	11243
20649	3625	MAT64_2	20-5	3634	11243
20649	3625	MAT64_2	20-6	3634	11243
20651	5620	DD_AR_4	100-1	5659	11809
20651	5620	DD_AR_4	100-2	5659	11809
20651	7915	DM_90_2	23-1	7982	12242
20651	7915	DM_90_2	23-2	7988	20012
20721	7917	DM_90_2	24-1	8566	11844
20721	7917	DM_90_2	24-2	8566	11844
20726	9117	MAT64_2	18a-1	9172	12002
20726	9117	MAT64_2	18a-2	9172	12002
20800	EV3	DD_AR_4	10-1	5677	12240
20800	EV7	ICM4	11-1	786-1	12348
20800	EV9	MAT64_2	18c-1	3668	12109
20800	EV8	MAT64_2	18c-2	3668	12109

(*continued*)

TABLE 16.6. *Continued*

Departure Time[a]	Departure Label	Type	Track Position	Arrival Label	Arrival Time[a]
20800	EV13	MAT64_2	20-1	9124-1	10802
20800	EV12	MAT64_2	20-2	9132	11002
20800	EV11	MAT64_2	20-3	9132	11002
20800	EV16	MAT64_2	21-1	9124-2	10802
20800	EV15	MAT64_2	21-2	3828	10908
20800	EV14	MAT64_2	21-3	3828	10908
20800	EV18	MAT64_4	21-4	3628-1	11109
20800	EV17	MAT64_4	21-5	3680	20009
20800	EV6	ICM3	22-1	778	12144
20800	EV5	ICM3	22-2	786-2	12348
20800	EV4	ICM3	22-3	787	20046
20800	EV10	MAT64_2	2a-2	9128	10902
20800	EV1	DD_AR_4	2b-1	5681	12340
20800	EV2	DD_AR_4	9-1	5679	12309

[a]See footnote 9 in this chapter.

- The position of the unit at the marshaling yard.
- The train number of the arriving train containing the unit.
- The arrival time[9] of the train unit.

The train labels, the type declarations, and the track numbering are in accordance with the notations used by the Dutch Railway Company. The track positions are preceded by the track numbers.

In the formatting of the table, all trains seem to be split into its "atomic" parts (train units), this, is however, not the case. For example, train 3661 departs at 15:49 h at day 1 composed of four train units of type Mat64_2. It is collected as a whole from siding 8, at which arriving train 3622 supplies all four train units. Neither arrival 3622 nor departure 3661 is divided.

[9]The departure and arrival times are based on the timetable and are preceded by the day number, 1 or 2; 1, in the case where the departure or arrival is at day 1; 2, in the case where the departure or arrival is at day 2.

17

PLANNER-ORIENTED DESIGN OF ALGORITHMS FOR TRAIN SHUNTING SCHEDULING

JAN RIEZEBOS AND WOUT VAN WEZEL

Faculty of Management and Organization, University of Groningen, NL-9700-AV Groningen, the Netherlands

17.1. INTRODUCTION

The field of operations research (OR) has a long-standing, reputation in supporting planning decisions. Among the planning problems studied, transportation problems, routing problems, and assignment problems are classical examples to which the OR community has been contributing. The contribution often consists of specific algorithms that can be applied to find an optimal solution to a planning problem. The task of the planner is to provide the algorithm with the correct input and specify the weights in the objective function.

Reports on the actual usage of the algorithms that are developed for planning support are scarce. In the field of transportation scheduling and railway planning, planners often prefer manual planning to the use of algorithms. A recent survey of 153 papers on train routing and scheduling problems (Cordeau, Toth, and Vigo 1998, p. 399) concludes as follows: "even though most proposed models are tested on realistic data instances, very few are actually implemented and used in railway operations."

Based on empirical research, Buxey (1989, 1995) provides insight into the applicability and usage of techniques that have been designed for production planning and scheduling. He concludes that some areas and problems are more receptive

Planning in Intelligent Systems: Aspects, Motivations, and Methods, Edited by Wout van Wezel, René Jorna, and Alexander Meystel

than others, especially if the problem size is limited and model conditions can be specified with reasonable certainty. For detailed planning and scheduling, algorithms have been of limited value. The four reasons Buxey (1989, p. 29) gives for this lack of value are: (1) inflexible models that are not able to cope with changing environments, (2) higher-level priorities that are not correctly taken into account, (3) algorithms that are not able to cope with uncertainty regarding the actual state of the system, and (4) objectives of the algorithms that are only soft constraints and that for the system as a whole are only of limited value.

These conclusions seem also valid in the related field of transportation planning and railway scheduling. Watson (2000) investigated various railway planners in the United Kingdom, and he states that the reasons for not using optimization models in railway scheduling are (1) a lack of integration with software that fits the needs of the users, (2) a lack of cooperation between software developers and model builders, (3) a lack of extendibility of the models to real-life circumstances, and finally (4) no international applicability of the models.

We suggest that the more fundamental reason for not using these models can be found in the design approach applied. Traditionally, model builders use a problem-oriented approach, focusing on the conceptualization of the planning problem as viewed by the experts. This approach ignores information on the strategies that are used by the planner in solving the problem, but focuses directly on the total problem that has to be solved by the planner. If the planner is not explicitly considered as an object of study in the design of the support system, two inherent dangers have to be faced. First, the planner may not accept the solutions generated by the support system, because he has no insight into the way these solutions are constructed. Second, the quality of the solutions may deteriorate over time due to the fact that the optimization model is not a perfect representation of the planning problem faced by the planner. Constraints that were neglected in the optimization model can at some moment in time become important for the planner to include in his solution approach. The life cycle of an optimization model is therefore often shorter than assumed by the original designer, as already noticed by Ackoff (1957, p. 27).

This chapter proposes and applies a planner-oriented focus in designing OR algorithms for a railway planning support system. This approach is compared with the traditional problem-oriented focus in OR design and a planner mimicking approach. The planner-oriented focus results in a different way of designing OR algorithms. We show that a planner-oriented focus in designing OR algorithms supports the task of the planner without encountering the inherent dangers of a problem-oriented focus.

This chapter is organized as follows. Section 17.2 describes the approach we use to analyze the task of the planner. Section 17.3 applies this approach to the problem of train-shunting scheduling and describes the solution strategies of the planner. Section 17.4 describes the design of specific algorithms that support the task of the planner. Finally, Section 17.5 presents conclusions and provides suggestions for further research.

17.2. APPROACH: BOTTOM-UP ALGORITHMIC PLANNING SUPPORT

Planning in organizations is a complex task that should be supported adequately. This notion is widely acknowledged and endorsed in both theory and practice. Furthermore, it is also generally acknowledged that planning support should be more than a bunch of algorithms with a Gantt chart. Notwithstanding the abundant research results on planning and scheduling that are published and the colorful scheduling support systems that are available, dedicated shunting planning support is not widely applied in practice (Allan, Mellitt, and Brebbia, 1996). Mostly, the use of the computer in the daily planning task in organizations is restricted to providing information (routing and processing data, order status and information). Actual support in the planning task is often limited to software for editing a plan. That software can be seen as a kind of word processor for planning. Plans can be copied, altered, printed, saved, and some basic calculations can be made. In many cases, the system that is used actually is a word processor or spreadsheet. Dedicated scheduling systems provide algorithms or heuristics that can generate solutions, but this generative support is used seldom (Watson, 2000). One of the reasons is that automated schedule generation often leaves little room for human control in the search process (Carey and Carville, 2003, p. 197). Researchers in the field of human factors argue that analytical models cannot deal adequately with uncertainty and instability of the real world (Buxey, 1989; McKay, Safayeni, and Buzacott, 1988, 1989; Sanderson, 1989).

Carey and Carville (2003) describe a human emulation approach and design algorithms that emulate the decision process of a human railway planner. They try to mimic the behavior of the human planner as much as possible. Their algorithms reduce the time necessary for performing the planning tasks. This human emulation approach is very promising. Planners tend to accept the results of the algorithms. Carey and Carville (2003, p. 198) report three reasons: (1) Algorithms embody knowledge of the planners on the problem, priorities, and data; (2) confidence of planners in solution methods is being build up by mimicking their behavior; and (3) planners can easier explain the outcomes of the planning process to other parties. However, a disadvantage of such a human emulation approach is the lack of actual support of the planner during the planning process. Algorithms replace the planner instead of providing support. The inherent danger of such an approach is a lack of adaptability of the planning process to changes in the real world.

The aim of the shunting planning support project at the Netherlands Railways is to investigate if a way in between the analytical and human emulation approaches can be found. We want both to include algorithms in the planning support and to let the human planner use them while still being in control.

The design of such algorithms requires a different model-building process. The field of cognitive science has been giving attention to the design of decision aids to support decision-making processes. Benbasat and Todd (1996, p. 251) state that a decision maker implicitly makes a trade-off between the cost of applying a decision aid (efforts to understand and employ the model and process the information) and the expected benefits (increased quality and speed of obtaining a solution). They provide a three-step procedure to improve the use of decision aids (Benbasat and Todd, 1996, p. 244):

1. Decompose the planning problem into subproblems and obtain estimates for the efforts (costs) to manually find solutions to these subproblems.
2. Identify the subproblems with a high potential of effort (cost) reduction for the decision maker and identify a decision aid that reduces the total effort to find and use a solution for such a subproblem.
3. Incorporate specific features for automating storage, retrieval, and computational tasks in the decision aids to manipulate the cognitive effort associated with using these decision aids.

In order to investigate whether this approach will also be worthwhile for scheduling and planning, we have developed a task-oriented scheduling system prototype for the shunting planners at the Netherlands Railways. This prototype implements the idea that algorithms should be created for subcomponents of the task strategy to support the problem-solving process. The focus is on the level at which the system and the user communicate (Newell, 1982). This elaborates on the research of Prietula et al. (1994, p. 660), who introduced the concept of "coincident problem spaces" in the scheduling domain with the following proposition: "To configure effectively a support system that can exploit the knowledge of the scheduling expert, it is important to direct the behavior of the system to function in a manner that is consistent with the key problem spaces of the scheduler; that is, the system and the scheduler should be problem solving in coincident problem spaces." In our research, we try to find such coincident problem spaces by looking at the subcomponents of the task strategy of human planners.

In applying a task-oriented approach, we need to analyze the way in which a human planner makes a plan. First, we apply a task analysis. A task analysis describes the activities that constitute the task and the order in which the activities are carried out (Schreiber et al., 2000). Analyses of planners have shown that planning tasks are performed in a hierarchy. Each activity, or subtask, is performed by a number of "smaller" activities itself (Wezel, 2001).

Next, we design algorithms bottom-up: First, analyze the planning subtasks; next, decide per subtask what kind of support is needed. In other words, algorithms are not created for the total planning problem, but instead created for the planner's subtasks. Because the resulting algorithms are closely related to the activities that a planner performs, we expect an increased chance in the actual usage of the system by the planner, without the risk of adopting all his nonoptimal habits.

Applying algorithms to subtasks has the following advantages and possibilities (van Wezel and Barten, 2002):

1. The chance that the human planner will accept algorithms and their outcomes increases.

2. Existing divisions of planning problems into subproblems (which a human planner has learned by experience) can be reused in algorithmic design.

3. Algorithms for subtasks can be used automatically in a sequence. If an algorithm is available for each subtask in a task, then they can be executed in one step (the "push the button and get a plan" approach).

4. Algorithms for subtasks can be used interactively in a sequence. Instead of automatically executing the algorithms for a sequence of subtasks, they can be executed semiautomatically by providing the planner with a way to (manually) interfere after the execution of each algorithm.

5. Algorithms can be applied under conditions chosen by the planner. For example, a production planner might want to let the computer plan production orders automatically, except when the capacity usage exceeds 90%.

6. Designing algorithms for subtasks is less complex than for whole tasks.

7. Different planners use different task strategies; that is, they perform subtasks in different sequences (Mietus, 1994). Algorithms can be executed in various sequences and can therefore be used in different task strategies.

There are several issues that need attention when designing task-oriented algorithmic support. First, the paradigm suffers from the paradox of task support (van Wezel, 2001). Computer support changes the tasks of the planner. Whenever tasks change, the support should also be changed. Changing the support results again in changes in the tasks, and so on. Second, evaluation of the algorithms cannot be limited to the issue of performance (solution quality versus CPU time), but needs to include the perceived support to the whole planning task as well. Third, task analyses take much time, and it is yet unknown to what extent the results of such analyses can be generalized.

At the Netherlands Railways, we were presented with a rather unique research opportunity. In most companies, only one or two planners work on the same specific planning problem. In the Netherlands Railways, about 130 shunting planners work on similar problems for different stations. This increases the probability that the results of the task analyses can be generalized to and used by many planners, and it therefore justifies the time that must be invested in task analyses and task support systems. The next section describes the problem-solving task that a shunting planner at the Netherlands Railways faces each day.

17.3. PROBLEM DESCRIPTION: TRAIN SHUNTING SCHEDULING

In the Netherlands, most passenger trains stay at a station during the night. They arrive at the end of the day and depart the next day in a possibly different configuration of carriages and probably from a different track. During the night, they must be stored on one of the shunting tracks, otherwise they would block the tracks that are needed for incoming and outgoing trains. Such "storage" capacity at a station is limited. Additionally, all trains must be cleaned both internally and externally

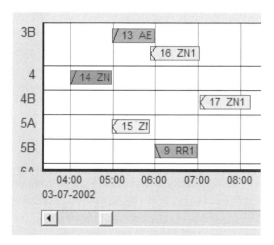

Figure 17.1. Example of a shunting plan for station Zwolle.

during the night at a track that contains the cleaning equipment. The task of the shunting planner is to plan the movements of the trains and carriages and to decide on what tracks trains stay during the night. To plan the movements, the planner must also assign train drivers, train shunters (employees that amongst other tasks connect and disconnect carriages), and routes of the trains on the station.

The complex and busy station of Zwolle, a city in the northeastern part of the Netherlands, is used to illustrate the planning problem. This station has also been studied in Zwaneveld et al. (1996) and Freling et al. (2002), where a problem-oriented focus was used in designing OR algorithms. Figure 17.1 shows an example of a shunting plan for station Zwolle. The horizontal axis denotes the time. The vertical axis contains the tracks. The bars are trains that occupy a track during a certain amount of time. For example, the train ZN1 is on track 3B from 05:52 until 07:02. At that time, it is moved to track 4B, where it stays until 08:14.

In Figure 17.1, the movement from track 3B to 4B seems instantaneous. In practice, however, the movement takes a few minutes. Figure 17.2 shows a route from track 3B to track 48. A more efficient route via track 3A is possible, but there are trains blocking that track. Sometimes it is impossible to find a feasible route between two tracks.

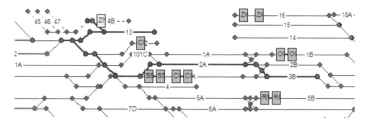

Figure 17.2. Route found from track 3B to 48 (the thicker line shows the route).

The research project studied the planning task of planners that are responsible for making short-term adjustments (one week ahead) to already created plans (stage 2 of the planning process as described by Carey and Carville (2003, p. 196). Some of their activities are as follows (unordered):

1. If one of the tracks on the station needs maintenance, all trains that are on that track during the time of the maintenance must be rescheduled to other tracks.
2. If a train will not arrive at the station due to maintenance, the plan has to be modified such that an extra train that is sent to replace the other one and arrives at another time will take the place of the original train.
3. If the time of departure of a train changes, the planner must find out the consequences and fix the plan where appropriate.
4. If a train has to be moved, the planner must find a train driver that can move the train.
5. If a train has to be moved to another track, the planner must find a feasible route.
6. If the planner detects errors in the plan, he has to correct them.
7. If the planner decides that the robustness of the plan is insufficient, he has to improve the plan.

Some of the constraints and goals that the planner takes into account are:

1. Changing the departure track of a train should be avoided as much as possible, because passengers have to be notified of such changes.
2. At least two routes should be kept free for traffic going through the station.
3. Within a three-minute time window (headway), only one movement may take place on a track.
4. Aim at efficient schedules for both drivers and shunters, resulting in minimal walking and waiting times.
5. Trains ought to be cleaned internally every day. If this is not possible at the special cleaning track, try to clean it along a noncleaning track.
6. External cleaning can be skipped one day but not for two subsequent days.
7. Check the train length with the available storage capacity at a track when allocating trains to tracks.

The planning tasks are performed manually. Some computer programs are used to collect information, but the plan itself is made on paper before it is put in the computer. From the total group of 130 planners, about 60 are involved in planning these short-term adjustments. The short-term planners are geographically special-ized, such that each planner performs these tasks for a limited number of stations.

In the research project, we have extensively analyzed the first task that is men-tioned in the list above: Some tracks need maintenance for a couple of hours during the night, and all trains that are on those tracks within that time window must be repositioned. In some aspects, this task is an easy one. The configuration of trains stays the same, so the planner only has to move trains. However, the number of shunting tracks is limited already, and when there are even less to use, it becomes a difficult puzzle. If more than two trains are put on one track, the trains in the middle can get blocked. Furthermore, fewer tracks available means also that it becomes more difficult to find free routes.

We analyzed the strategy of a planner that has a long experience in solving this task. The planner was requested to solve actual problems and to think aloud during his work. The thinking-aloud protocols were analyzed, after which we held sessions with the planner in which we actively asked for and discussed explanations of decisions.

The overall planning process is as follows. The planner receives a list of trains that occupy the tracks that need maintenance. This list is ordered on arrival time at the track. The planner starts with the first, searches for a solution, then takes the next one, and so on, until a solution has been found for all trains. For each train, he first tries to find a track that is free for the interval that is needed. If he cannot find such an interval, there are three options. First, he can try to free another track, which is explained in Figure 17.3. In that case, he must recursively follow the same procedure for each train that he moves: Search for a solution that falls within the constraints or be satisfied with a constraint violation. Second, he can try a more complicated solution—for example, changing the time of moving the train or finding a solution in which the train is moved multiple times during the interval. Again, this might include moving other trains as well. Third, he can violate a constraint—for example, skip external cleaning. The first and second options are of course preferable, but because the planner uses pencil, fixer, and paper only, backtracking is difficult and time-consuming. The depth of searching is therefore limited. The analysis shows that if a planner cannot find a solution in a few steps, he reverts to a constraint violation.

The flowchart in Figure 17.4 gives a short description of the sequence of subtasks a planner uses when making adjustments to the plan in case of maintenance of one or

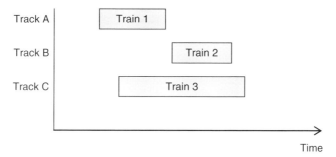

Figure 17.3. Recursive searching. For the sake of the argument, we assume that only one train can stay at a track concurrently. Suppose Track C cannot be used anymore. Train 3 cannot directly be placed at another track without violating the storage constraint. However, by moving Train 3 to Track B and recursively searching for a solution for Train 2, a feasible solution can be found: Train 2 can be placed on Track A without problems, because Train 1 will have left Track A at that time.

more tracks during a specific time window. Subtask 1 identifies trains that have to be re-planned. Subtasks 2–4 aim at finding a feasible solution to this problem. Subtasks 5–7 relax a constraint in order to find a solution for the selected train. In subtasks 8 and 9 a check is being performed whether there are a driver and shunter available and whether there is a feasible route to move the train. In subtask 10, the planner will try to find a solution for the constraint violation he caused in one of the

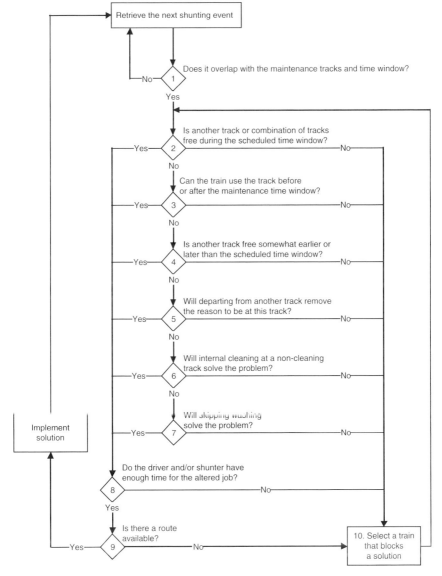

Figure 17.4. Flowchart of task structure.

subtasks 5–9. He tries to solve that violation by changing the shunting time or track of another train.

The task analysis reveals that a planner uses a large assortment of subtasks when solving a specific planning problem. The choices he makes in his solution process (i.e., the depth of search) are not necessarily identical for similar problems, because it also depends on the time available for finding a solution, the history of recent constraint violations, and the required quality of the solution. These factors are difficult to take into account in a problem-oriented focus for designing an OR algorithm that automates the solution process of a whole task. A more interactive kind of support is required. The next section details the approach we have chosen to support the planner in his task.

17.4. DESIGN OF ALGORITHMS

17.4.1. From Subtask to Algorithm

Each step or subtask can recursively be divided further into more detailed subtasks. The decision where to stop recursion and develop decision aids makes up the difference between a problem-oriented approach, a planner-oriented approach, and a mimicking approach. The ideal of a problem-oriented approach is to find the optimal solution to the integral problem. Hence, it aims at a decision aid supporting a large set of subproblems or subtasks of the planner and is focused on improving the quality of the solution. The ideal of a mimicking approach is an increased speed of finding an acceptable solution. It emulates the behavior of the planner as well as possible, resulting in the same quality as a manual solution but achieved within shorter time. Hence, a mimicking approach continues the recursion process until the process can be automated in an algorithm. Finally, the ideal of a planner-oriented approach, proposed in this chapter, is to support the planner in his task of achieving high-quality solutions within the available time. We therefore do not simply emulate the manual decision process, but stop recursion where we identify subtasks that cost a lot of effort to the planner without being very important for the acceptability of the solution. Decision aids should both be able to perform these subtasks in a shorter time than manually and include intelligence on the larger problem, resulting in a higher quality of the final solution achieved.

In a planner-oriented approach, identification of subtasks that are candidates for algorithmic support depends on the efforts associated with a specific subtask. The more frequently the subtask is repeated, the more time can be saved by using a decision aid. However, repetition is not the only factor. Subtasks that require many well-described but time-consuming administrative tasks, such as storing and retrieving information, and performing calculations, are also candidate for inclusion in decision aids. Table 17.1 shows an example of our detailed task analysis of steps 2 and 4. It provides the pseudo-codes for the activities performed manually by the planner and shows the three subtasks that we identified, two of them occurring in both steps.

We developed a prototype shunt scheduling support system with elaborate functionality for manual planning and a number of algorithms. In this chapter we will discuss the algorithms with respect to finding a free track and train routing (respectively subtasks 2.1 and 2.2). This will provide insight into the design method used and the results obtained. In the remainder of this section, we will describe the algorithms that were designed and implemented in the prototype of the planning system.

17.4.2. Design of Routing Algorithm

The repetition of the route-finding subtask 2.2 is high. Given the current plan and infrastructure information, the input for this subtask is the proposed track for a train. The originating track of this train is known as well. This is the track at which it was located before the currently scheduled move. The output of the subtask is the shortest feasible route for shunting the train to the proposed track. As distance measure, the number of times a train changes its direction is used; for example, in

TABLE 17.1. Subtask Identification for Step 2 and Step 4

Step 2. *Is there another track available for this train during the same time window?*
2.1. Find tracks where the train subsequently can be located during the time window.
    2.1.1. Select possible tracks.
    2.1.2. Seek the best track.
        2.1.2.1. Sort the tracks according to some criterion.
        2.1.2.2. Select the best track.
2.2. Propose a route for the train from the departing to the destination track.
    2.2.1. Determine the state of the network at the shunting time.
    2.2.2. Select possible routes.
        2.2.2.1. Retrieve information on train length and traction.
    2.2.3. Seek the best route.
        2.2.3.1. Sort the routes according to some criterion.
        2.2.3.2. Select the best route.
. . .

Step 4. *Is there another track available for this train during a different time window?*
4.1 Specify a different time window during which a train has to be relocated.
2.1. Find tracks where the train can be located during the time window.
    2.1.1. Select possible tracks.
    2.1.2. Seek the best track.
        2.1.2.1. Sort the tracks according to some criterion.
        2.1.2.2. Select the best track.
2.2. Propose a route for the train from the departing to the destination track.
    2.2.1. Determine the state of the network at the shunting time.
    2.2.2. Select possible routes.
        2.2.2.1. Retrieve information on train length and traction.
    2.2.3. Seek the best route.
        2.2.3.1. Sort the routes according to some criterion.
        2.2.3.2. Select the best route.

Figure 17.2 this is two times. At each change of direction, the driver must get out of the cabin and walk to the other side of the train (all trains have a cabin on both sides) to continue driving in the opposite direction. The planner may block several tracks if he wants them to be available for other purposes. A route is *feasible* if it consists of connected tracks that may be passed by this specific train within a short interval of three minutes and if the movements occur at tracks where they are allowed. If there are more solutions with the same number of direction changes, the alternatives should be ordered according to their total mileage.

This description contains several elements that point to a shortest path algorithm, which finds the shortest route from a source node to a sink node in a network of connected nodes. Several algorithms are available from operations research and computer science. Dijkstra (1959) was the first to present an algorithm that minimizes the distance from the source node to all other nodes if arc lengths are non-negative. Floyd (1962) and Dantzig (1967) generalized this algorithm to determine the shortest distance between all nodes in the network (graph). Shier (1976) found an efficient single-pass algorithm to determine the K shortest paths in an undirected graph. Eppstein (1998) gives an excellent review of different K-shortest-path algorithms for directed and undirected graphs.

The question is, Which of these shortest-path algorithms fits best with the requirements specified for the subtask, and how does this algorithm need to be tailored in order to solve the subtask? First, we note that the two objectives (the primary objective is to minimize the number of movements, and the secondary objective is to minimize the routing distance) can be transferred to a single objective by using a weight function with the weight per movement being larger than the largest distance of any route. Next, we design our network. All tracks that we might use in the route (i.e., they are neither blocked nor unavailable during the routing time window) are defined as nodes. The arc length between any pair of nodes is infinite unless the tracks of the two nodes are physically connected and reachable. Then, the arc length equals the distance between both tracks.

For this objective function and network, we modified the undirected K-shortest-path algorithm of Shier (1976) and determine the K shortest paths from the source track to the destination track. Modification of the algorithm of Shier was necessary in order to determine the occurrence of direction changes in a path. This modification will now be discussed in detail.

Direction changes are allowed at a limited number of tracks, because of the required track length and the position of signs. Figure 17.5 shows an example of

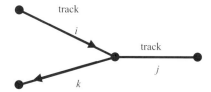

Figure 17.5. Direction change necessary at track j for path from i to k.

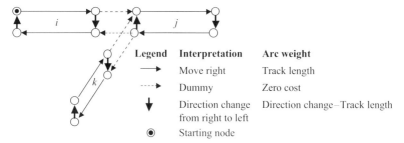

Figure 17.6. Network representation of direction change.

ALGORITHM K-Shortest-Path
Input: Nodelist   (list of nodes representing tracks available and allowed for this route)
         SourceNode
         DestinationNode
         SignNodes   (list of nodes where direction change is allowed)
         K   (number of alternative routings that have to be found)

Step 1: Initialize
     Set initial Arc Weights :
     IF (track i and track j are connected) AND (inner product track i and track j is negative)
     THEN ArcWeight[i,j] := distance between track i and track j, ELSE ArcWeight[i,j] := ∞

Step 2: Calculate K shortest paths from SourceNode to DestinationNode
     Repeat
       For k := N Downto 1 DO   //first a backward pass
        For j := N Downto k+1 DO
         Step 2A:
          IF ArcWeight[j,k]< ∞   //j and k are connected
          THEN i := Predecessor(j)
                 IF ArcWeight[i,k]<∞   //i and k are also connected
                 THEN IF j∈ SignNodes
                        THEN DistJKinPath := ArcWeight[j,k]
                        ELSE DistJKinPath := ∞   //direction change not allowed on j
               ELSE DistJKinPath := ArcWeight[j,k]   //no direction changes in path i→j→k
          ELSE DistJKinPath := ∞   //no direct arc between j and k
          DistanceToNode[k] := GenMin(GenAdd(DistanceToNode[j], DistJKinPath),
                                       DistanceToNode[k]);
          //DistanceToNode[k] is a K-dimensional array
          //GenMin contains the K smallest elements of the 2 K-dimensional input arrays
          //GenAdd contains the K smallest elements of the K^2 summations of the elements of
                                       the 2 K-dimensional input arrays
          //end step 2A
       For k := 1 TO N DO   //next a forward pass
        For j := 1 TO k-1 DO ***Step 2A;***
     Until FOR ALL k NO CHANGE IN DistanceToNode[k] //algorithm is O(K•N^3)

Output: DistanceToDestinationNode := DistanceToNode[DestinationNode]

END   **//Algorithm K-Shortest-Path**

Figure 17.7. Algorithm for subtask 2.2 (finding a route).

a direction change on the railway net. First, a node representing track i is included in the path. Next, it is not possible for the algorithm to select the node representing track k directly, because the angle between both tracks is too small. In order to include k, it first has to select the node representing track j and change direction at j. Both tracks i and j are connected, so this arc length will be finite. If the algorithm now selects the node representing track k, it will result in a direction change at track j. If it is not allowed to perform direction changes on track j, the arc length between j and k should be infinite, notwithstanding the actual distance being finite. If a direction change is possible at track j, the arc length between node j and node k should be increased with the cost of one direction change. The algorithm therefore takes the information on the preceding node into account when determining the arc length. It is possible to use an alternative directed graph that allows for a direct calculation of direction changes, as shown in Figure 17.6, but this increases the number of arcs and nodes with a factor larger than two. The final algorithm that we implemented is shown in Figure 17.7.

17.4.3. Design of Track-Finding Algorithm

Subtask 2.1 is focused on finding a track for a train that is available during a specific time window. Criteria that will affect the decision as to what track the train should be moved are amongst others: the length of the time interval it can stay at this track (robustness), the routing distance (i.e., number of direction changes and total mileage) to this track, the previous activities of driver and/or shunter, and the consequences for future actions with this train (i.e., internal cleaning, external cleaning, routing to the track from which it has to leave in the morning, etc.).

Due to the large number of criteria, we designed an algorithm for this subtask that provides several alternative solutions (tracks), accompanied by relevant information on the criteria mentioned. The planner is often not able to overview the consequences of his decision for all criteria when planning manually. The algorithm takes these criteria into account when evaluating alternatives and presents these alternatives with their consequences to the planner.

The algorithm first determines the total set of available time windows (intervals) on tracks from the moment of the actual move. These intervals are train-specific, because the length or other characteristics of the train constrain the possibility of locating it at specific tracks. An interval has the characteristics of the track to which it is associated. The problem that the algorithm has to solve is defined as finding a sequence of partially overlapping time intervals from the moment of the actual move to the moment of departure. The intervals were considered to be the nodes in the network, as illustrated in Figure 17.8. Two nodes have a finite arc length if they partially overlap in time. Node i and j partially overlap if the end time of interval i is greater than or equal to the start of interval j, while the start of interval i is smaller than or equal to the end of interval j. The length of the arc between these nodes is defined as the shortest route between the two tracks to which the intervals are associated. We assume that this route will be available somewhere during the overlapping time window. The objective of the algorithm is to find the shortest sequence of

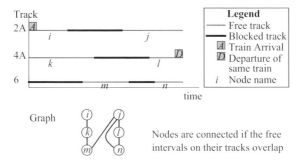

Figure 17.8. Graph construction from free intervals on railway network.

intervals from start to destination. We use a weighted criterion function that weights the total number of track changes required in order to reach the destination with the total distance of the routings between the tracks involved. In general, the planner will try to avoid track changes, so the weight of a track change will dominate the routing distance.

An additional feature of the sequence is that it has to resemble the necessity of visiting the cleaning track somewhere over time. Therefore, the algorithm will have to include the possibility of stating a set of intermittent nodes (i.e., intervals on the cleaning track) from which at least one has to be included in the final sequence before the departure track is reached. Finally, it has to be possible for the planner to block several tracks that may not be included at all in the final sequence, because they have to be reserved for other purposes.

The problem can again be solved using a K-shortest-path algorithm. We tailored the algorithm of Section 17.4.2 to solve this problem efficiently. We first determine the shortest routings between all tracks at which this train may be located. The network for this first step therefore consists of only one node per track. We repeat the Dijkstra (1959) shortest-path algorithm for each track to determine the shortest distance between tracks, resulting in an $O(1\frac{1}{2}N^3)$ complexity (with N the number of tracks). Because all arc lengths are non-negative, this is better than obtained by Floyd (1962) or Dantzig (1967). Note that this step has to be performed only once. Next, the algorithm creates a new graph, consisting of intervals as nodes (see Figure 17.8). In general, this network will contain far more nodes, depending on the utilization of the tracks over time. We apply the extended K-shortest-path algorithm of Figure 17.7 to this network, using weights for track changes and total mileage. The condition of including at least one of the intermittent nodes in the K shortest paths has been taken care of by applying a two-stage solution process. The first stage determines in a single pass of the algorithm the K shortest paths from source node to each intermittent node. The second stage applies the same algorithm for finding the K shortest paths from the destination node to each intermittent node. This approach is more efficient than applying a single-pass all-K-shortest-paths approach [based on Floyd (1962)] that determines the K shortest paths between each pair of nodes in the network. The two-stage solution approach has proven to be successful in the design of flow-shop scheduling algorithms and heuristics (Morton and Pentico, 1993, p. 306).

Finally, we present the first tracks that are proposed in the K routes found, accompanied by the information on the consequences of this choice for the moment of cleaning, the future track changes required for reaching the departure track, the total distance of the first move as well as the later moves in this sequence, and the consequences for the train drivers and shunters. The complete algorithm for this subtask is shown in Figure 17.9.

The design of this algorithm shows that it is possible to reuse the same algorithm in different subtasks, as is illustrated in Figure 17.10. It shows the relations between tasks, subtasks, and algorithms. Most of the time there is a singular relationship between subtask and algorithm. However, in some cases we can design OR algorithms such that they are able to support different subtasks.

Algorithm K-Track-Finding
Input: Nodelist   (list of nodes representing intervals available and allowed for this path)
          SourceNode
          DestinationNode
          IntermittentlNodes   (list of nodes of which at least one has to be included in path)
          K   (number of alternative paths over time that have to be found)

Step 1:   Determine distance between tracks
    Generate Tracknodelist (list of all tracks that can be used for routing in the railway network)
    Determine shortest distance between tracks:
        Repeat Dijkstra's shortest path algorithm, using each track that is related to an interval in the
        NodeList once as a SourceNode
        //a single pass of this algorithm calculates the distance to all other nodes in the network
    Output: DistanceBetweenTrack[i,j]

Step 2:   Determine distance between intervals in Nodelist
    For all i<>j ∈ Nodelist: DO
        IF interval i and interval j partially overlap,
            DistanceBetweenNode[i,j] := W+DistanceBetweenTrack[track interval i, track interval j]
            //W is the weight of a track change
    Output: DistanceBetweenNode[i,j]

Step 3:   Calculate K shortest paths from SourceNode to IntermittentNodes
    Apply step 2 of K-shortest path algorithm with SignNodes? Nodelist
    Output: For all i ∈ IntermittentNodes: DistanceFromSourceToNode[i]

Step 4:   Calculate K shortest paths from DestinationNode to IntermittentNodes:
    Apply step 2 of K-shortest path algorithm again, using DestinationNode as the new SourceNode
    Output: For all i ∈ IntermittentNodes: DistanceFromDestToNode[i]

Step 5:   Select the K shortest complete paths
    For all i ∈ IntermittentNodes DO
        DistanceViaNode[i] := GenAdd(DistanceFromSourceToNode[i], DistanceFromDestToNode[i])

Output: DistanceToDestViaIntermittentNode := GenMin(DistanceViaNode[i]; i∈ IntermittentNodes)

END   **//Algorithm K-Track-Finding**

Figure 17.9. Algorithm for subtask 2.1, which makes use of algorithm for subtask 2.2.

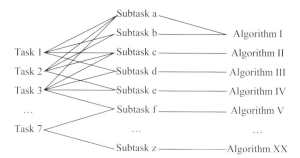

Figure 17.10. Tasks, subtasks, and algorithms.

17.4.4. Discussion

We implemented the algorithms in a prototype of a support system for the planner. The prototype is developed in the Delphi programming environment, which results in quick response times and a graphical user interface that resembles the current desktop of the planners. Figure 17.11 shows a screenshot of the system.

We applied a bottom-up approach for supporting the tasks of the planner by designing algorithms for these subtasks. This bottom-up design approach has several advantages. First, the algorithms are smaller and more robust, because they solve only a part of the whole task. Second, the same algorithms can be reused in different tasks, because identical subtasks will arise in different tasks. Third, the planner

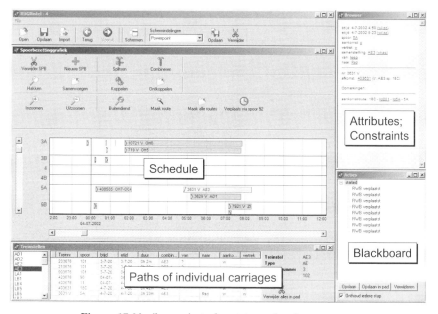

Figure 17.11. Screenshot of prototype planning system.

better understands the outcome of the algorithms, because the problem it solves is less complex. Finally, maintenance of the algorithms becomes easier because of the modular design approach applied. If circumstances change, only a small number of algorithms have to be modified.

The hierarchical view on the planning task and generation algorithms that we apply in this chapter provides stability and robustness for the design of planning support systems. For example, no matter what kind of strategy the planner uses, he will always need to perform small low-level tasks such as finding routes, selecting train drivers, matching incoming trains to departing trains, and so on.

In the design phase of the OR algorithms, we were able to evaluate the efficiency of these algorithms by comparing the complexity and CPU performance of several alternatives. However, the concept of planner-oriented design of algorithms is not easy to evaluate. Whether the algorithms effectively support the task of the planner remains an open question. We will report the results of using these algorithms in an actual planning support system in a forthcoming paper.

The current chapter compares the three design approaches. Although all approaches use operations research models, they are totally different in many characteristics. This becomes evident if we consider characteristics such as computing time of algorithms, number of alternatives presented, and so on. As an illustration, we compare three published examples of the different design approaches. As an example of an algorithm from the problem-oriented approach, we use Freling et al. (2002). They tested their algorithm on data of the same station (Zwolle, the Netherlands) as we consider in this chapter. For the mimicking approach, we use Carey and Carville (2003), who tested their algorithm on data of Leeds station in the United Kingdom. Table 17.2 compares the differences between this problem-oriented, planner-oriented, and mimicking approach. It shows that the approaches result in different algorithms and computing times, as well as a different involvement of the planner in the decision making process.

17.5. CONCLUSIONS AND FUTURE RESEARCH

This chapter sets out a planner-oriented focus of designing OR algorithms that support the task of train shunting planning. Our approach differs from the traditional problem-oriented design method in considering the planner explicitly as an object of study in the design of algorithms that are included in the support system. We propose a bottom-up task-oriented approach. First, we analyze the way a human planner makes a plan. We distinguish activities and describe the order in which they are performed. We propose to describe the tasks by using a hierarchical decomposition of each task in several subtasks. Literature on cognitive science reveals that algorithmic support should be oriented toward components of a task in order to increase the chance of actually supporting the task of planners. Therefore, we decide per subtask what kind of algorithmic support is needed. The algorithms for the selected subtasks are included in a support system with a graphical user interface and a data

TABLE 17.2. Factors in Which the Differences Between the OR Design Approaches Emerge

	Problem-Oriented	Planner-Oriented	Mimicking
Example approach	Freling et al. (2002)	Riezebos and van Wezel (2006)	Carey and Carville (2003)
Type of OR algorithms	MIP and column generation	Combinatorial optimization	Scheduling heuristics
Role planner in design process	Provides problem-related knowledge	Provides both approach- and problem-related knowledge	Provides approach-related knowledge
Role planner in solution process	Responsible for data input and weight factor setting	Responsible for solution process, decides on actual use of supporting algorithms	Planner is replaced by computer
Run time algorithm	20–40 minutes (imposed maximum)	2–5 seconds	Between seconds and a few hours, depending on the rules used
Number of solutions presented	1	5	1
Optimality gap	0–20%	0% for subtask, gap for total problem depends on planner	Heuristic, quality gap depends on planner that is mimicked
Completeness of solution	Incomplete (cleaning not considered)	Incomplete (planner supported, not replaced)	Complete

infrastructure. This presentation resembles the usual environment for planners to make a plan, and it enables them to use the algorithms in a coincident problem space.

The planner-oriented design approach has been applied to planning tasks for train shunting scheduling. During the night, trains have to be routed as well as internally and externally cleaned, and track maintenance has to be performed. The task analysis reveals that a planner uses a large assortment of subtasks when solving the specific planning problem of rerouting trains because of track maintenance. To demonstrate the design approach, we determined the pseudo-code for two subtasks, and we designed algorithms that solve these subtasks. The first subtask is to determine several alternative feasible routes for moving a train on a busy railway network. The second subtask is to determine preferable tracks to which the train can be moved during the night, considering cleaning requirements and other constraints. The algorithms for both subtasks are based on well-known combinatorial algorithms that are tailored to make them suitable for solving the subtasks. We implemented them in a prototype for planning the railway network of Zwolle, a station in the northeastern part of the Netherlands. The algorithms take into account the expected state of the system at the time of the operation that is to be scheduled. The routing decision includes the scheduling of direction changes of trains and drivers during the route. The track decision includes considerations with respect to the required visit of the cleaning track during the night. These aspects make both problems rather complex. The prototype of the support system is being developed in Delphi. Planners have been involved in the design process, during both the task analysis phase and the algorithmic design phase.

The study has shown that a planner-oriented design of algorithms requires a different methodology than usually applied when building OR-models. The planner is explicitly considered, both as object of study and as user of the algorithms. By including the planner in such a way during the design process, we achieve a higher acceptability of the outcomes of the algorithms.

Forthcoming research will give attention to the issue of evaluating the results of planner-oriented support versus problem-oriented support. Because there is a large number of planners involved and different groups of researchers have examined the situation at station Zwolle and designed OR algorithms to support the planners, there is an excellent opportunity to compare the results of the different approaches. Problems with measuring the effectiveness of algorithms in a practical setting will have to be tackled, because there are no easy ways to measure the quality of the support provided by a planning system.

ACKNOWLEDGMENTS

This study has been supported by the Netherlands Railways. We gratefully acknowledge the management and planners of this company. Specifically, we want to thank Dr. L. Kroon, Bas Barten, and the planners of the Netherlands Railways, location Zwolle, for their willingness to cooperate.

18

CONCLUSIONS FOR INTELLIGENT PLANNING: DIVERSITY AND THE QUEST FOR UNITY

RENÉ JORNA AND WOUT VAN WEZEL

Faculty of Management and Organization, University of Groningen, NL-9700-AV Groningen, the Netherlands

ALEXANDER MEYSTEL

Electrical and Computer Engineering Department, Drexel University, Philadelphia, PA 19104

18.1. INTRODUCTION: AIM OF THE BOOK, ASPECTS, AND DEFINITIONS OF PLANNING

In this concluding chapter we try to structure and (partly) integrate the various perspectives and approaches regarding planning that have been described in the preceding chapters. Although we already formulated intermezzos to interconnect the consecutive chapters in the theoretical part, we want to demonstrate in this final chapter that the various planning approaches have many similarities and, it has to be said, also various differences. It is not our intention in this chapter to delimit and strip the various approaches until their essences remain. The kernel of the essences would then resemble the core of a general planning approach. We do not believe that such an ultimate kernel exists, at least for now. The various elements in planning are so diverse that the best one can aim at are, in terms of Wittgenstein, family resemblances. Just as, in Wittgenstein's example, games have no essence, planning has no essence. However, many resemblances exist between the various kinds of planning, scheduling, and making rosters, and we will first try to point at the common elements.

Planning in Intelligent Systems: Aspects, Motivations, and Methods, Edited by Wout van Wezel, René Jorna, and Alexander Meystel

The common elements in almost all planning and scheduling concern the following: (I) the planning entity (or actor), (II) the planned entity (or actor), (III) the possible overlap between planning entity and planned entity, (IV) the planning domain, (V) the context and organization of planning, and (VI) the procedures, heuristics, and algorithms, whether it concerns problem solving, decision making, or other methods to compute, calculate, or realize a plan or schedule. The above six common elements match the five aspects described in the introduction chapter, with one difference. Because of the complicatedness of an overlap of the planning and planned entity (element III), we decided to name and treat it separately.

In the various chapters, these six elements are the natural building blocks of any planning discussion. In principle, every chapter could have dealt with each of the six common elements. However, every chapter only deals with two or three of the six elements. If one starts with element VI, the procedures, and algorithms, this implicitly involves a model of a domain (IV) and a model of an organization (V). In this situation the realization of elements I, II, and III follows the procedures/algorithms and are of minor importance or just left out. On the other hand, if one starts with the organizational and contextual elements (V), elements VI (the algorithms) and IV (domain) are less important. Because in this situation the organizational view often is an aggregate view, elements I, II, and III are supposed to be implicitly dealt with. And if one starts with the planning entity (I), the planned entity (II), and the overlap between the two (III), then depending on whether the planning and the planned entity coincide the relevance of the organization (V) and the algorithms (VI) are treated differently.

The six elements can also be seen as a tree with various branching continuations. To visualize the metaphor, planning is the tree. The branches are the various elements. The six common elements can be aligned in various ways. One may start with any element, but starting with the one makes treatment of one or more of the others unimportant or even superfluous, whereas starting with another again makes others superfluous. In principle we have 6! possibilities = 720 combinations. In practice, however, many of these 720 separate sequences are only imaginary. If a planning entity (I) and a planned entity (II) are the same (III), I plan for myself, which implies that the domain (IV) and the organization (V) are not important anymore, and so on.

We believe that the above-described analysis of the common elements and its combinations, which can be found in much more detail in the chapters, are the reason that so many seemingly incompatible planning approaches exist. They are incompatible because they start with different elements, which brings along different scientific fields. Starting a planning discussion with psychology (element I or II) implies a different route compared to starting with organizational studies (element V) or with mathematics (element VI). However, we emphasize that they are seemingly incompatible, because the incompatibility is the result of the different elements one starts with, be it I, II, III, and so on. As soon as one makes a move to a higher level of aggregation, one can see that all common elements may be relevant. That is one of the messages we have in this concluding chapter.

For a long time we expected that we could formulate an encompassing theory of planning. This belief was naive. An encompassing theory of planning implies at least four other theories, related to the individual (psychology), to the organization (sociology), to the domain (an ontology), and to heuristics and algorithms (mathematics and logic). Therefore, formulating an encompassing theory of planning seems to be too ambitious. In the old positivist perspective a theory is a coherent set of statements with regard to a topic or subject of research that enables predictions and explanations. Although an encompassing theory of planning is not reachable, this does not mean that piecemeal theories or general statements regarding the above-mentioned common elements, separately, cannot be made. As a mater of fact, we believe that the various chapters provide us with many illustrations of piecemeal theories or general statements. However, they are limited to the individual (I, II, III), the organization (I, II, III, V), the domain (IV), or the algorithms (VI).

If we look at the literature on planning and scheduling, we can bluntly and without sophistication say that there are three major traditions in planning. The first, which we did not discuss at all, is about regional planning and urban planning (Sutcliffe, 1981; Hall, 1992). In terms of objects types and domain specification, this kind of planning works with space as the always-present elementary object type. Often the elementary object type time is also involved, but not necessarily.

The second important tradition in planning concerns the mathematical and algorithmic tradition, whether it is formulated as Operations Research, Artificial Intelligence, or Mathematics and Logic. We have one chapter (Kroon and Zuidwijk, Chapter 8) in this book that explicitly deals with these matters. Much literature and many references to this tradition can easily be found, for example, also in Chapters 9, 10, and 11.

This book does not contribute to the mathematical and algorithmic tradition. We try to represent a third tradition. Or, to formulate it more accurately, many initiatives exist that deal with planning within and by individuals as well as within and by organizations, where the planning and planned entities are natural or artificial entities, taking into account domain ontologies. It is our intention to bring these initiatives together in a conceptual structure that integrates the aspects of planning and planned entity, domain, and organizational context. This book is the testimony of this enterprise.

It will be clear now that we cannot provide for an essential definition of planning. Our earlier circumscription (Chapters 1 and 4) that "planning is attuning instantiations of different object types taking into account constraints and goal functions" comes close, but leaves undefined the notions of "attuning" and "object types." We can, however, make some negative statements—that is, with regard to what planning is not or should not be. From the various chapters it will be clear that planning is not the same as reducing uncertainty or reducing flexibility. Planning is neither the fixation of the future nor the reduction of the number of alternatives. In a positive formulation the following elements—as we discussed in the beginning of this section—are important in a circumscription of planning: Planning is about making sequences of actions or activities, it assumes a planning and planned entity or actor, it is also about assigning two or more instantiations of elementary object types, it assumes an ontological structure of reality in virtual or real object types, and finally a plan or schedule always has to be made with methods and techniques within constraints or boundary conditions and has to fulfill goals.

The structure of this chapter is as follows. In Section 18.2 we will focus on the planning and planned entities and we will do this by discussing the various planning approaches and their relations with various scientific fields. In Section 18.3 we will continue with various organizational characteristics of the entity already partly discussed in Section 18.2. In Section 18.4 we will give an overview of the methodologies that we encountered in the various chapters. In Section 18.5 we go into the details of ongoing research into planning as problem solving by intelligent systems. In Section 18.6, this is extended with the concept of multiresolutional reasoning. We continue this approach in Section 18.7 where we emphasize the combination of planning and learning. Learning as a source of representation and its relation with problems of planning is discussed. Section 18.8 summarizes the essence of the planning approaches when looking from the perspective of a planning actor as a learning, problem solving entity. In Section 18.9 we give some points for a planning research agenda.

From the six common elements we described earlier, the emphasis in this chapter is on the planning entity (I), the planned entity (II), the overlap between the two (III), and the organization and the context (V). The domain (IV) and the algorithms and heuristics (VI) are implicitly dealt with, but are not the focus of our research attention and general framework. Other, much better literature is available about these topics (see also Chapters 8, 9, 10, and 11).

18.2. PLANNING APPROACHES, PLANNING ENTITIES, AND PLANNED ENTITIES

We believe that the entities that plan are essential in every discussion about planning. In the introduction we analyzed that four basic categories of entities can be discerned: natural entities (humans) that plan for themselves, artificial entities (e.g., robots) that plan for themselves, natural entities that plan for others (humans that plan in/for organizations), and artificial entities that plan for others (planning software in/for organizations).

The four basic categories are connected to various scientific domains. Natural entities that plan for themselves are studied within the cognitive and behavioral sciences, artificial entities that plan for themselves are studied in simulation studies and robotics, natural entities that plan for others are studied within a task and process perspective of organizations, and artificial entities that plan for others are studied in the domain of plan generation and software engineering for planning support. We will discuss the various categories and the related scientific fields in greater detail, respectively, after we have dealt with entities and actors and with single-actor and multi-actor systems.

Entities that plan for themselves or that plan for others can also be described in terms of actors (or agents). An actor is a special kind of entity in the sense that it is a coherent and integrated whole, it may have a bodily or physical manifestation, and it may be seen as an adaptive (intelligent) system. Every actor is an entity, but not every entity is an actor. Elsewhere (Gazendam and Jorna, 1998) we made a distinction in various kinds of actors. Actors can be individuals and, in metaphorical sense, units, groups, or organizations. Concerning actors as individuals, they can be response function systems, representational systems, or a combination. Actors are response function systems if they react to external circumstances, but do not have internal representations. Actors are representational systems if they have internal processes and mechanisms, but do not interact with the environment. Actors are both if they can react to the environment and have internal representations. An example of the first kind of actor can be found in economics: the so-called economic man. In economics, especially the human cognitive architecture and human information processing, are neglected. The actors are empty actors. An example of the second kind of actor is the AI actor or Cognitive Science actor, where an external environment is often omitted and, therefore, not modeled. Examples of the third kind of actors are humans as real information processing systems living in natural environments. The actors that we discuss in this planning book mostly concern the last kind of actors. However, developments in robotics are so fast (see Chapters 10 and 11) that one might tend to call the robots that also play soccer the *representational response function systems*. Planning research in Artificial Intelligence (AI) and Cognitive Science in the past mainly focused on representational systems. Studying planning with empty actors is not possible.

Entities that plan for themselves can also be called single planning actors, whether they are natural or artificial. If an actor or entity plans for others, we have a multi-actor system. A multi-actor system is a set of single actors together with coordination mechanisms. To make it complex, one such a coordination mechanism is planning. In this case, one or more of the actors plan for other actors, which we normally assume to be representational response function systems—that is, humans as cognitive systems.

The distinction in single-actor and multi-actor systems, in planning for yourself and planning for others and in natural or artificial entities or actors, can also be found in the various chapters of this book.

In Table 18.1, we see that concerning the distinction in single-actor and multi-actor systems, Hommel, Hoc, and Jorna only concentrate on single actors, whether it regards planning for yourself or for others. The other chapters deal with multi-actor situations in which the single actor sometimes is explicitly mentioned. With regard to the planning for yourself, Hommel, Hoc, Bowling et al., and Meystel study and discuss this kind of planning. The other chapters focus on planning for others. In discussing natural and artificial actors, only Hoc, Hommel, and Jorna explicitly deal with humans as natural actors. In the other chapters, artificial entities or constructs are discussed. A construct is a kind of entity that is not coherent or integrated and therefore is not an actor.

TABLE 18.1. Determination of Single/Multi, for Yourself/for Others and Natural/Artificial/Construct in the Chapters

	Hommel	Hoc	Jorra	Gazendam	McKay/ Wiers	Van Wezel	Kroon/ Zuidewijk	Sauer	Bowling, Jensen, and Veloso	Meystel
Single (S)/Multi (M) actor	S	S	S	M	M	S, M	S, M	M	S, M	S, M
For Yourself (Y)/ Others (O)	Y	Y	O	O	O	O	O	O	Y	Y
Natural (N), Artificial (A), Construct (C)	N	N	N	C	C	N, A	A, C	A, C	A, C	A, C

We now come back to the four approaches that can be found in the planning literature and their relation with various scientific fields. We start with the two approaches that study planning for yourself, and we later continue with the two other approaches that discuss planning for others.

18.2.1. Planning for Yourself: Cognition and Behavior

The view on planning as a system of decisions that are made by human decision makers indicates that planning can be approached as problem solving. We will come back to this issue in Sections 18.5 and 18.6. In general, human problem solving can be seen as a hierarchical structure, because heuristics and rules of thumb diminish the number of alternatives that will be considered and hence divide a system into subsystems. If these subsystems are nearly decomposable, then a problem solver at any level does not need to have detailed knowledge about the levels above, alongside, or below. Not only is the total problem decomposed in chunks that are manageable by a person, but the total number of alternatives that will be assessed is also diminished, since a decision process is organized in a number of steps that each fix a part of the decision, independent of the other parts. According to Herbert Simon, a partial result that represents recognizable progress toward the goal can be seen as a subsystem, and "problem solving requires selective trial and error" (1981, p. 205). Simon discusses two forms of such selectivity: (1) trying and finding stable subsystems from which the search can continue and (2) using a solution path that has previously led to a solution for a similar problem. Thus, a planning hierarchy requires stable sub-solutions. The second form of selectivity is equal to experience; that is, planners learn how the planning problem can be decomposed into subproblems that can be solved independently. In other words, planners find ways to decrease the number of alternatives that will be tried, and thereby they reduce their information processing load.

Cognitive models of planning take for granted that problem solving, planning, and information processing are related. Newell and Simon (1972) describe planning as a system of heuristics that is used by their General Problem Solver (GPS) "to construct a proposed solution in general terms before working out the details. This procedure acts as an antidote to the limitation of means–ends analysis in seeing only one step ahead" (op. cit., p. 428). Planning heuristics are used to guide actions when a problem is too difficult to solve by means–ends analysis. Newell and Simon assume the following steps in planning: "(1) abstracting by omitting certain details of the original objects and operators, (2) forming the corresponding problem in the abstract problem space, (3) when the abstract problem has been solved, using its solution to provide a plan for solving the original problem, (4) translating the plan back into the original problem space and executing it" (op. cit., p. 429). Complexity is reduced by leaving out details and by reasoning by analogy. In this sense, planning is a kind of problem solving.

Early models of planning within cognitive science presume that planning is always a hierarchical process that proceeds according to successive refinement. Sacerdoti (1975) implemented such an approach in his computer program NOAH.

In his view, planning is performed by recursively decomposing goals into subgoals, until a subgoal can be reached by elementary actions. As was explained in Chapters 3 and 4, this paradigm is contradicted by Hayes-Roth and Hayes-Roth (1979). In their line of reasoning, they say "that planning processes operate in a two-dimensional planning space defined on time and abstraction" (op cit., p. 312). In these terms, successive refinement would always work top-down from high to low abstraction and forward in the timeframe of the plan. Thinking aloud protocols from different subjects that perform planning tasks show that this is not always the case. Hayes-Roth and Hayes-Roth found planning actions that they call "opportunistic planning." The subjects do not work solely linear but appear to switch in levels of abstraction and move both forward and backward in time in successive reasoning steps. Behavior that can be explained by their model is called multidirectional processing in addition to top-down processing, incremental planning, and heterarchical (i.e., network) plan structures. According to Hayes-Roth and Hayes-Roth, the choice of a planning strategy depends on three variables: problem characteristics, individual differences, and expertise. Task strategies within a domain depend on individual differences and change over time if experience increases.

Riesbeck and Schank (1989) argue that planning is based on scripts. Instead of thinking up a new plan for each problem, humans try to find a plan that is used for a previously solved comparable planning problem. Then, the basic planning activity is adaptation rather than construction. In this paradigm, planning is about memory, indexing, and learning (Hammond, 1989; Veloso, 1996). Plans should be stored in such a way that it is easy to find an existing plan on the basis of a comparison of the new goal with already handled goals. There are two senses of learning in the case-based planning paradigm. First, solutions must be remembered, so they can be used for new problems. Second, a failure to execute the plan provides an indication that the knowledge the planner has of the execution world could be faulty (see also Section 18.6). Thus, script models can be seen as adding learning—but not in terms of universal subgoaling as Newell did—to the paradigms already discussed.

The discussion regarding planning for yourself describes a number of planning issues from a cognitive perspective. Although they are sometimes approached as contradictory, they are, in fact, not. More likely, the different approaches are complementary in the sense that they apply to different stages or phases of the planning process. Together, they compose a comprehensive (but not complete) model of human planning.

Script-based planning shows that planners can learn and thereby reduce their planning efforts. Obviously, when a skeleton solution cannot be found, a plan must be created from scratch, which places more emphasis on problem solving and less on memory retrieval operations. To make this more complicated, planning is one of the phases of a problem-solving cycle, and because such a planning phase can be a quite complex problem itself, it can be solved by an "inner" problem-solving cycle. For example, someone can make a plan for the whole day (go shopping, go to work, make dinner), where distinct planning problems occur that can be tackled separately (e.g., making a separate plan how to make the dinner). This partitioning of a problem also shows why the hierarchical, opportunistic, and heterarchic approaches do not preclude each other (Hayes-Roth and Hayes-Roth, 1979). It can also be dealt with from a multiresolution perspective, as we will discuss in Section 18.5.

Together, the paradigms of Newell and Simon (1972), Hayes-Roth and Hayes-Roth (1979), and Hammond (1989) provide a cognitive model for human planning. We also see this in the chapters by Hommel (Chapter 2), Hoc (Chapter 3), Jorna (Chapter 4), and Meystel (Chapter 11). In this model, planning is about how to find the actions that solve a problem or, more generally, reach a goal. The process of planning is not neatly hierarchical, but switches in level of abstraction and in the timeframe under consideration. The process itself is about formulating goals, finding similar solved goals, finding existing plans, adapting plans, learning, and storing plans in such a way that they can easily be found for future use.

Analyses of human problem solving and planning have been used as input for simulations of human problem solving, and after that as a way to direct the behavior of artificial agents such as robots (Bowling et al. in Chapter 10, but also Meystel in Chapter 11). The results of such simulations and applications are sometimes used in cognitive science to further analyze and explain behavior models. This is partly the reason that the demarcation line between models of human reasoning and models of reasoning by artificial agents is not very clear. We continue with planning by artificial agents.

18.2.2. Planning for Yourself: Simulations and Robots

The planning entities that are dealt with in AI are very much related to the entities that occur in cognitive science. This is not surprising, since the aim in AI is to mimic natural intelligence. As a result, the cognitive architecture that is commonly used to describe human reasoning is more or less simulated in AI. Artificial actors (or agents) that plan their own behavior (just as humans that plan their own task) need to be able to deal with uncertainty and incomplete information. For such agents, planning is a means to reach the goal, just as it is with human problem solving. Due to the close resemblance of human and artificial actors, planning of artificial actors is very much related to the problem-solving approaches described in Chapters 3 (Hoc), 4 (Jorna), and 11 (Meystel). Techniques from AI are used to let such actors function more or less independently in their environment and react to unforeseen events (Sacerdoti, 1975; Curry and Tate, 1991; Beetz, 2000). Much of the planning research in AI stems from the wish to let autonomous actors or agents (such as robots) perform tasks without prescribing how the task should be carried out (Fikes and Nillson, 1971). Most AI methods, whether they are called algorithms, procedures, or heuristics, are based on state-space descriptions. An agent or actor finds himself in a state, in which it can perform a limited number of actions. An action changes the state, after which it can again perform a number of actions (Meystel, 1987; see also Sections 18.5 and 18.6). The agent keeps on choosing and performing actions until the state it gets in somehow satisfies its goal. Planning is one way in which the actor can reach its goal. Other ways are, for example, trial and error or full search. To make a plan, an actor somehow anticipates the future by simulating the actions he will make. The plan is virtually executed in the model of the future (Jorna and van Wezel, 2002). This requires the existence of (internal) representations. The original link to physical entities has been relinquished somewhat, so planning actors are now often only computer programs that find a plan merely for the sake of research, and therefore not necessarily execute it. In this paradigm, planning is searching for a sequence of actions that will bring the agent from its current state to the goal state. Many examples are based on the initial General Problem Solver (GPS) of Newell and Simon, which constructs a proposed solution in general terms before working out the details, the opportunistic planning paradigm, and script-based planning. It is very clear that models of human problem solving are closely related to anticipation and planning of artificial actors.

In contradistinction to the implicit central processor perspective present in much of the GPS-based literature, Brooks (1999) argued and showed that the implicit subdivision of an intelligent system into perception, cognition, and action (motor) components does not (always) hold. The intelligent systems he developed only have perception and action parts. "It posits both that the perception and action subsystems do all the work and that it is only an external observer that has anything to do with cognition, by way of attributing cognitive abilities to a system that works well in the world, but has no explicit place where cognition is done" (Brooks, 1999, p. X). Recently this approach also emerged in cognitive science, especially from a physiological and neurological perspective. Planning in this approach is resolved into an adequate sequencing of percepts and actions. The "cognition box" is opened in such a way that this box consisted of further subdivided perception and action parts (see also Chapter 2 by Hommel, but then for humans).

18.2.3. Planning for Others: The Planning Task in Organizations

In the same way as with the cognitive and behavioral sciences (see Hommel, Hoc, Jorna, and Meystel), organization studies deal with planning at multiple time scales, differently. The big difference with planning for yourself is that we here talk about planning for others. For example, Anthony (1965) distinguishes strategic planning, management control, and operational control. Strategic planning deals with decisions on a high level of aggregation and a long time horizon (typically 5 to 10 years). Operational control deals with very detailed decisions at short notice (hours, days, months), and management control lies somewhere in between (weeks and months). The distinction of Anthony is oriented toward management decisions. Planning in organizations also occurs in the control of processes, and it is a coordinating mechanism. Although it cannot be separated from management control decisively, the emphasis is more on how, when, and where products will be made, services are delivered, and staff is present rather than on what services, products, and staff the organization chooses to deliver or use in the first place. Examples of planning and control of organizational processes are staff scheduling, production planning, project planning, workflow management, and vehicle routing (Table 18.2). A common ground for these kinds of planning problems is that they

TABLE 18.2. Examples of Organizational Planning

Kind of Planning	Contents of the Plan	Planning Activities
Staff scheduling	Who works when	Determine shifts, assign employees to shifts
Production planning	When to make what products on what machines	Determine capacity, accept orders, assign orders to machines
Project planning	Phases, due dates, project members	Determine critical path in project activities, calculate earliest and latest starting time of project phases, assign members to phases
Workflow management	Document processing	
Vehicle routing	What truck transports what products and what will be the route(s)	Weigh truck load and distance

basically concern the coordination of supply and demand, whereby (a) the supply consists of scarce capacity and (b) the way in which this capacity is put to use can make a difference with respect to the goals in the organization (Smith, 1992; Veloso, 1996; Verbraeck, 1991). Examples are producing at low costs at a production facility, having enough phone operators at a call center, or taking care that all employees work the same amount of night shifts. The way in which the coordination takes place (in other words, the planning process or the planning task) determines to a large extent the plan that eventually is executed. Not much literature or theory exists about the relations between the planning domain, the planning task, the organization of the planning, and the performance of plan execution (van Wezel, 2001; Schuitemaker, 2002). Most analyses are limited to task models—for example, McKay et al. (1995a), Mietus (1994), Dorn (1993), and Sundin (1994). Lack of a theory to explain the relation between planning complexity, planning organization, task performance, and planning support makes it difficult to pinpoint the cause of planners' dissatisfaction, to attribute the causes of poor organizational performance to planning, or to analyze and design planning practices. For example, the cause of poor factory performance can be the mere impossibility of matching the requirements (e.g., there is not enough capacity available to meet the demands), the clumsiness of the organization of the planning, the inadequacy of the human planner to solve complex problems, the absence of specialized planning support in practice, or a combination of these factors. More detailed discussion on these topics was presented in Chapters 5 (Gazendam) and 6 (McKay and Wiers).

In order to make generic statements about the planning task, it is important to know what the task performance depends upon. It should be noticed that by performance we mean execution without a qualitative connotation. According to

Hayes-Roth and Hayes-Roth (1979), the determinants of the planning task are problem characteristics, individual differences, and expertise. That the task performance depends upon individual differences and expertise is no surprise. This applies to all tasks. But the fact that the task performance also depends on problem characteristics leads to the statement that a planning problem can, at least partly, be described, independently from the planner.

Jorna et al. (1996, p. 74) describe a number of generic organizational aspects of planning that can be used to complement the description of a task as a collection of subtasks (the word "organizational" here refers to the organization of the task and therefore relates to the task strategy and not to the organization in which the planner works). A first distinction deals with the temporal relation between planning and execution. The planning horizon can be fixed or rolling (incremental), and both planning and plan execution can be organized in time buckets. A second distinction looks at the content of the plan. The planner can often use previously created (partial) plans as a starting point, and there can be patterns that the planner can use (e.g., fixed sequences of production, or fixed shift patterns in personnel planning).

Clearly, approaches to planning for yourself deal with questions other than approaches to planning for others, including organizational planning. In Section 18.3 we will analyze in greater detail what organizational characteristics are important in planning. This refers to what in Section 18.1 we called common element V—that is, the organizational and context issues of planning. First, however, we will look at computer support for organizational planning.

18.2.4. Planning for Others: Plan Generation for Organization Planning

It is widely accepted now that computer programs will not be able (in the foreseeable future) to replace human planners that plan organizational processes. Human planners are necessary. Still, much research focuses on plan generation techniques—that is, techniques that plan for others, by which we mean computerized planning support. There are two mainstream approaches in plan generation techniques.

The first is about making a quantitative model that can search for good solutions. At first glance, the same kind of reasoning is used as in cognitive science: A problem space is set up, and the aim is to find a state that satisfies all constraints and scores well on goal functions. Operators transform the states, just as in the cognitive problem-solving approaches. The difference is that states and operators comprise something else than the ones in cognitive science, namely values on variables and mathematical operations [see Chapter 9 (Sauer) for details]. Specific quantitative models exist for all kinds of processes such as routing of trucks, staff scheduling, job shop scheduling, and flow shop scheduling. Scientific fields that deal with this kind of research are Operations Research (e.g., linear programming, nonlinear programming, all kinds of heuristics) and AI (heuristics, constraint satisfaction programming, genetic algorithms). We saw the application of some of these techniques in the practical shunting problem case of the Netherlands Railways (Chapters 13, 14, 15, 16, and 17). Note that the AI approaches here differ from the ones discussed in the section about planning for yourself in AI and cognitive science, where actors make plans for themselves rather than for organizational processes. Quantitative models are usually based on an analysis of the objects (entities)—the domain—that are scheduled. For example, to make an algorithm for a planning problem in a flow shop, one has to know the capacities of machines, the setup and cleaning times, the number and sizes of orders, the processing characteristics, and so on. All these characteristics can be used to determine the best way to navigate through the problem space of possible solutions. An example of how such knowledge can be used in an algorithm is to start to plan the bottleneck first. This is often the most sensible thing to do in order to avoid problems in a later stage of the planning process. Most techniques are somehow limited in the kinds of characteristics they can handle. For example, a linear programming model cannot deal with nonlinear constraints, and temporal reasoning is difficult to implement in many mathematical techniques. Therefore, the domain analysis must somehow be translated into the quantitative model, and the solution must be translated back to the application domain.

The second mainstream approach to plan generating techniques focuses on imitating human problem-solving processes in so-called rule-based, expert, or knowledge systems, also called the transfer view (Schreiber et al., 1993, 2000), because the knowledge to solve planning problems is extracted from a human and transferred into a computer program. For this approach, the problem-solving approach of the human scheduler must be analyzed. In terms of the human problem solver (Newell and Simon, 1972), this means that the problem space and operators must be traced and implemented. In the resulting plan generators, the available computational capacity is not used since the computer is used as a symbolic processor. It is, however, understandable for the human planner why a generated plan looks as it is, because he would have processed the symbols more or less in the same way. This approach can be used if a planner is satisfied with a reduction of the efforts without much improvement of the solution—for example, if planning is a secondary task of the one who makes it. The main disadvantage of this approach is that the system inherits not only the capacity of abstract reasoning that is so typical of humans, but also the myopic firefighting tactics that human schedulers practice (Smith, 1992). In addition, the resulting algorithms are highly specific for the individual human planner.

We developed a graded architecture for planning support in which, on the one hand, support consists of doing many things by hand on the computer and, on the other hand, consists of algorithms that can be invoked to do complex computations for the planner (van Wezel and Jorna, 1999; van Wezel, 2001). The structure consists of an electronic planning board (editor), a constraints checker (inspector), a goal function evaluator (evaluator), and an algorithmic component (generator). We discussed this in Chapters 4 (Jorna), 7 (van Wezel), 13 (Kiewiet et al.), and 17 (Riezebos et al.).

18.2.5. Overview of Planning Approaches, Scientific Fields, and Planning/Planned Entities

Table 18.3 contains an overview of the scientific planning fields that were discussed in this section. In the table the common elements or the general planning characteristics discussed in this section are presented. The rows contain the common elements, and the columns contain the various approaches.

In Table 18.4 we revive the discussion we started in Chapter 1. In Chapter 1—the introductory chapter—we gave various characteristics of a planning or planned entity. Now that we have a better overview of the themes that were discussed in the various chapters combined with the scientific fields mentioned in Section 18.2, we can present in greater detail what the characteristics imply for planning for yourself and planning for others. We start with refreshing the characteristics. In Table 18.4 the characteristics are mentioned in the rows, and the scientific fields are positioned in the columns.

    a. Closed versus open world assumptions: Does the entity work within reality or a model?

    b. The information processing mechanisms: Which specifications of these mechanism are presented?

    c. Its architectural components, such as memory and attention.

    d. Representations: Does the entity work with depictions, symbol sets, or internal models?

    e. Communication, meaning and interpretation: How is this accomplished in the entity?

    f. Characteristics of coordination.

    g. Aspects of the execution of the plan.

TABLE 18.3. Overview of Characteristics of Common Elements in Various Planning Approaches

Common Element	Scientific Field			
	Cognitive and Behavioral Sciences	Organization Planning	Robotica	Computerized Plan Generation
Kind of planning entity	Natural	Natural	Artificial	Artificial
Kind of planned entity	Same as planning entity	Group of humans/ organizational processes	Same as planning entity	Group of humans/ organizational processes
Characteristics of domain	Not relevant	Very relevant	Not relevant	Very relevant
Organizational aspects	Not relevant	Relevant	Not relevant	Relevant
Algorithms	Not relevant	Not relevant	Very relevant	Very relevant

TABLE 18.4. Characteristics of Kinds of Actors Related to What They Are Planning and for Whom

Scientific Field	Cognitive and Behavioral Sciences	Organization Planning	Robotica	Computerized Plan Generation
Closed vs. open world	Fixing the reality to the solution that is found; reformulate the starting-point		Searching for a solution that fits the (modeled) reality	
Information processing mechanism	Neurological: memory structures, attention processors	Translation of internally coded information is necessary	Information processing needs not to reckon with the outside world	Translation of internally coded information is necessary. Is designed explicitly
Architectural components	Memory, attention, perception and other common cognitive building blocks	Humans and constructs like buildings, layouts, and arrangements	Electronic: memory structures, attention processors	Program components: procedures, variables
Representations	Self-representation	Representation of others	Self-representation	Representation of others
Communication, meaning, and interpretation	Internal within cognitive system	Mostly communication with sign systems or sign sets	Internal within the artificial system	Communication with sign notations
Coordination	Only with respect to anticipated actions	Coordination of actions of others	Only with respect to anticipated actions	Coordination of actions of others
Planning, execution, and control	Intertwined	Separated	Intertwined	Separated

511

18.3. CHARACTERISTICS OF ORGANIZATIONS THAT PLAN

Planning requires intelligence and learning. It requires that entities that plan are in a sense rational, have representations, process information and can anticipate. Various entities may qualify for this planning function. It may be clear that in the first place we think of humans. Furthermore, robots also qualify as being able to plan, whether they are physical as look-alikes of humans or coherent software programs. The question is, In what sense do organizations also qualify? If organizations are just collections of humans, the answer is straightforward. If humans plan, humans in organizations also plan. If organizations are more than just complicated collections of humans, the question is what it means to say that an organization plans. It is very difficult to give an indisputable answer to this question. Organizations are human-made constructs and constructs as such do not have knowledge, they also do not learn and neither do they have memory or learning abilities. For that reason, organizations in this interpretation do not plan. Of course, one can argue that organizations metaphorically plan, but this statement has a background that says, literally speaking, organizations do not plan, only the humans that make up organizations plan.

On the other hand, taking organizations as holistic units with characteristics similar to those for humans is for us a step too far to make. This is not to say that organizations as holistic entities cannot plan. A colony of ants can make plans—for example, to build and maintain their nest. Common elements of planning such as constraints, goal functions, sequencing, or attuning are also present in a colony of ants that plans. The big difference in ants that plan and humans that plan concerns the characterization of the planning and planned entities. Humans are individually capable of intelligent, purposeful, adaptive, and search behavior. This cannot be said of ants. For that reason we reserve the possibility of planning for humans. As we said earlier in the chapter, "empty" entities (actors) cannot plan.

We can also refer to the foregoing discussion in terms of ontological levels of aggregation. Moving from very low to very high on an ontological scale, the following kinds of entities can be discerned: neural nets, cognitive structures, software programs, individuals, robots, groups, organizations or firms, and communities (networks) and societies. In this enumeration we can also distinguish natural and artificial entities, as we discussed in the introductory chapter and in Section 18.2 of this chapter. The various chapters in this book deal with the various ontological levels (see Table 18.5).

As much as it is debatable whether organizations as such plan or that it only concerns the individuals in the organization that plan, it is also questionable whether neural nets and cognitive structures plan. We argue negatively; these structures do not plan themselves. One thing is sure: Neural nets and cognitive structures are the bearers of the activity of planning. With respect to individuals, planning "runs" on neural nets or cognitive structures. The same holds for the artificial entities. The electronic devices in robots and in software programs are the material on which these plannings "run."

There is also another way to look at organizations that plan. In this perspective an organization is a collection of primary and secondary processes. Planning in this

TABLE 18.5. Ontological Levels of Entities and Whether They Optimize for the Various Chapters[a]

	Hommel	Hoc	Jorma	Gazendam	McKay/ Wiers	Van Wezel	Kroon/ Zuidewijk	Sauer	Bowling, Jensen and Veloso	Meystel
Level of aggregation	I	I	I	G/N	G/N	All	G/N	G/N	I/G	I/G
Natural (N). Artificial (A). Construct (C)	N	N	N	C	C	N. A	A. C	A. C	A. C	A. C

[a]Levels of aggregation: I, individual; G, group/organization; N, network/organization; all.

513

perspective is a very important secondary process that enables an organization to have coherence and to indicate or determine directions in which an organization wants to go. Although there is always a hidden level referring to the humans and other actors to plan, planning as a secondary process can be studied on its own. We saw examples of this perspective in Chapters 5 (Gazendam) and 6 (McKay and Wiers.).

With regard to planning as a secondary process, one can even go one level deeper: the task. Any process can be split up into tasks that constitute the processes. As indicated by Schreiber et al. (2000), planning is a generic task (see Jorna, Chapter 4), in the same sense that diagnosis, repair, and monitoring are generic tasks. A generic task is characterized by a stable pattern of inferences that an actor cognitively has to go through in order to complete the task. The big advantage of working with tasks is that its analysis stays close to the executing or performing individual actor.

From the above discussions we can detect two important characteristics of an organization that plans. In the first place it should at least be an individual actor, or a structure that is reducible to an individual actor. The simple background idea is that planning requires intelligence, and this is something individual natural (and to some extent artificial) actors have. In the second place it should be possible to demarcate the (secondary) process or task. This is necessary, because if software support of the process or task is considered, it should be determined who in the interaction between human and software does what.

18.4. METHODOLOGICAL ISSUES

No evident methodology exists for research in planning and scheduling. As can be expected from a multidisciplinary, multifocal, and multi-application topic, various methodologies and empirical perspectives can be found. The analytical, conceptual, and theoretical approaches in planning have been discussed extensively in the various chapters. With regard to planning from a methodological perspective, two main contrasts can be found. The first contrast is the one in empirical studies and simulation studies, and the second is within the empirical category and contrasts surveys, case studies, and experimental studies. We will explain the relevant differences in greater detail, shortly. First, we have to discuss another issue.

The methodological contrasts should not be confused with the distinction into descriptive (realistic) and prescriptive (normative). Especially within OR, mathematics, and parts of AI, the view on planning is to design solutions or algorithms that optimize the outcomes in planning and scheduling problems. They are prescriptive in the sense that they state and can often prove what has to be done in order to reach an optimal solution. On the other hand, descriptive approaches look at what takes place in reality, whether it is the organizational, firm, human, or physiological reality. The chapters in the theoretical part of this book are a mixture of descriptive and prescriptive approaches.

The practical part of this book regarding the Netherlands Railways is of a special nature. In the practical part we had the unique possibility to treat the same shunting problem from different angles, with different theoretical backgrounds and with different techniques. Cognitive task analysis, dynamic programming, mixed integer programming, constraint satisfaction programming, and mixed initiative support were the various techniques that we applied to the same shunting problem. This five-way application showed us that no one technique is ultimately satisfactory. This outcome has a negative and a positive side. It is negative because even a well-designed and quantified problem like the shunting problem is not suitable for only one technique. On the positive side it can be stated that the multitude of techniques complete one another. It is also important to emphasize the uniqueness of the opportunity the Netherlands Railways offered the five groups of researchers (Table 18.6).

In Table 18.6 we indicated for the five applications in what sense they are different concerning the emphasis on humans (first row), the emphasis on optimization (second row), and the possibility of including organizational characteristics (third row). As can be seen, the differences are clear.

If we return to the two methodological contrasts, we want to make clear that the contrast between simulation studies and empirical studies should not be overrated. It can easily be defended that results from empirical studies are modeled and designed in simulation studies. Nice examples of these successions are discussed in the chapters by Bowling et al., Meystel, and Gazendam. Hommel, Hoc, Jorna, and McKay and Wiers represent the empirical part. The chapters by van Wezel and Sauer are examples of the design approach to planning. This can be seen in Table 18.7 (the first row). Van Wezel, Sauer, Gazendam, and Kroon and Zuidwijk are also labeled conceptual, where Kroon and Zuidwijk are especially discussing mathematical techniques.

Within the purely empirical approach, also variations can be found. Hommel is doing pure experimental work in a laboratory, whereas Hoc and Jorna—also doing (quasi-)experimental work—are studying planners in reality, in their work practice—that is, as operators, as controllers, or as planners. Bowling et al. and Meystel are also doing experimental work in a laboratory, but in this case in software laboratories. Although working with their own design and algorithmic principles, they are inspired by cooperation and adversary (Bowling et al.) or multiresolutional (Meystel) issues in human or organizational reality. This can be seen in the second row of Table 18.7.

TABLE 18.6. Different Characteristics of the Approaches/Techniques in the Netherlands Railways

	Cognitive Task Analysis	Constraint Satisfaction Programming	Mixed Integer Programming	Dynamic Programming	Mixed Initiative
Human-centered?	Yes	No	No	No	Yes
Optimization?	No	Possible	Yes	Yes	Partly
Organization included?	Possible	Possible	No	No	Possible

TABLE 18.7. Overview of Methodology: Simulation and Various Empirical Approaches in the Chapters

	Hommel	Hoc	Jorna	Gazendam	McKay/ Wiers	Van Wezel	Kroon/ Zuidewijk	Sauer	Bowling, Jensen, and Veloso	Meystel
Empirical (Emp). Conceptual (Co)	Emp	Emp	Emp	Co	Emp	Co	Co	Co	Emp	Emp
Case study (Ca). Simulation (S). Experimental (Exp)	Exp	Exp	Exp	—	Ca	—	—	S	S. Exp	S. Exp

Until now we have mainly discussed differences and similarities of the approaches that we visualized in the form of tables. In the next two sections (18.5 and 18.6) we will take a different route. We will discuss planning for yourself in greater detail. The entity we concentrate on is an artificial actor. Within this perspective the main orientation is not attuning or aligning object types (as is clear for planning for others), but is instead going through a space heading for a goal or set of goals.

18.5. PLANNING AS PROBLEM SOLVING BY INTELLIGENT SYSTEMS

We may conclude that planning is complex and multifaceted. One of the presumptions that we used throughout the book is that plans are created by intelligent systems. In Chapter 11, Meystel has provided us with an elaborate discussion about intelligent systems. He states that intelligent systems solve problems on multiple hierarchical levels, and that they are capable of planning because they are able to simulate the effects of decisions before the decisions are actually implemented. Here, "to simulate" means to anticipate and model. Scenarios are developed without actualizing them. Planning in this sense takes place in the Behavior Generation of the ELF (Elementary Loop of Functioning). In the Behavior Generation, there are many mechanisms of decision making that are realized as various techniques of planning and execution. Presently, these mechanisms and the techniques they entail cannot be considered as thoroughly known, and in a general theory of planning we must deal with overly multifaceted methodologies. One thing is common for all approaches: Planning is understood as searching for appropriate future actions leading to the goal. The differences between approaches can be expressed as the way in which the searching takes place, how the goals is established, how learning is embedded in the ELF, and so on.

Searching is performed within the system of representation. This clearly holds for entities that plan for themselves, whether they are natural (humans) or artificial (robots). However, it also holds for entities that plan for others. A planner that makes a plan for a factory determines the future actions of the organization. An organization also develops and behaves in a much richer environment, and its future directions can also be seen as trajectories through a space of possibilities. Any activity in the world can be characterized by a sequence of actions of the planned entities along which the "working point" or "present state" (PS) is traversing this space from one point (initial state, or IS) to one or many other states (goal states, GS). In the ELF of an intelligent system, this sequence of actions can be simulated in the space of the world model.

The goal states are given initially from the external source as a "goal region," or a "goal subspace" in which the goal state is not completely defined in a general case. One of the stages of planning (often the initial one) is defining where exactly is the GS within the "goal region." Here, we will focus upon planning problems in which one or many GS's remain unchanged through all period of their achievement.

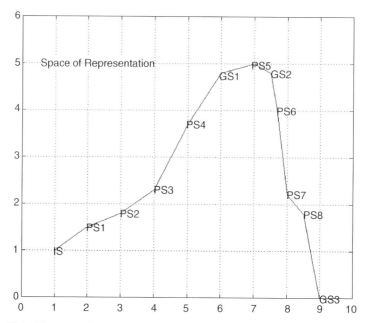

Figure 18.1. The general paradigm of planning as finding a goal state in a problem space.

Traversing from IS to GS is associated with consuming time, or another commodity (cost).

In Figure 18.1, an example of the goal region is shown. Clearly, the attendance of the goals can be ordered by coordinates of interest and/or by time. This allows considering the time sequence of goal states as a sequence of actions and arranging for reaching the goal by performing the actions in the plan (in terms of the ELF: a simulation of controlling the corresponding actuators).

All representation spaces are acquired from the external reality by processes of learning. Many types of learning are mentioned in the literature: supervised, unsupervised, reinforcement, dynamic, representational, and others. Before classifying a need in a particular method of learning and deciding how to learn, we would like to figure out what we should learn. Now, it is not clear whether the process of learning can be separated into two different learning processes:

- That of objects representation
- That of the rules of action representation

It may also be possible that these two kinds of learning are just two sides of the same core learning process.

The following knowledge should be contained in the representation space. If no GS is given, any pair of state representations should contain implicitly the rule of moving from one state to another. In this case, while learning, we inadvertently consider any second state as a provisional GS. We will call a "proper" representation any representation which is similar to the mathematical function and/or field description: At any point of the space, the derivative is available together with the value of the function; the derivative can be considered an action required to produce the change in the value of the function.

We define this as follows: *A "goal-oriented" representation is a representation in which at each point a value of the action is given, required for describing not the best way of achieving an adjacent point, but the best way of achieving the final goal.*

Both "proper" and "goal-oriented" representation can be transformed into each other. Thus, we can change the focus of attention and change the physical interpretation of the goal states: Instead of coordinates of arrival focused upon initially as a sequence of points where the goal state is, we will measure and control the movement in the problem space. Thus, instead of the goal space shown in Figure 18.1 we will study and use for control the trajectory shown in Figure 18.2. Obviously, the goal-space of Figure 18.1 was assigned by the external source at the beginning, while the new goal-space shown in Figure 18.2 should be intentionally learned. We have changed the representation space from the one that was initially assigned, to the one that was acquired by learning. In many circumstances this representation is more accurate. As was discussed in Chapter 4 by Jorna, the goals for planning cannot always be specified beforehand, nor can it be predicted with certainty whether a goal can be attained or not. This is important, because different planning entities (humans, machines) have different ways to cope with not finding the goal and subsequently reformulating it.

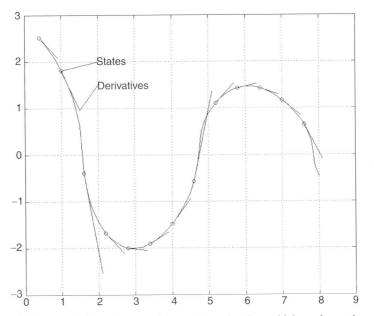

Figure 18.2. Knowledge of state, and knowledge of action, which produces changes.

A representation (that of the world) can be characterized by the following artifacts:

- The existence of states with its boundaries acquired by assignment or by learning and characterized by the resolution of the space since each state is presented as a tessellatum, or an elementary unit of representation (e.g., the lowest possible bounds of attention).
- The characteristics of the tessellatum, which is defined as the value of the indistinguishability zone showing how far the "adjacent" tessellata (the representations of the required states, or goal states, or GS) are located from the "present state" (PS).
- The lists of coordinate values of interest at a particular tessellatum in space and time.
- The lists of actions to be developed and applied to the objects of interest at a particular tessellatum in space and time order to achieve a selected adjacent tessellatum in space and time.
- By arranging the given lists, we arrive at the knowledge of the existence of strings of states intermingled with the strings of actions to receive next consecutive tessellata of these strings of states.
- A list of constraints should be obtained in addition including boundaries (the largest or the smallest possible bounds of the space) and obstacles.
- Costs of traversing from a state to a state and through strings of states.

In many cases, the available lists of states contain information, which pertains to the part of the world, which is beyond our ability to control, and this part is called "environment." Another part of the world can be controlled directly: We refer to this as "self." The makes it clear that when an entity plans the actions of other entities, there essentially is no real ability to control; the planning entity must rely on agreements that the specified actions will be performed.

From the list of artifacts it can be seen that all knowledge is represented at a particular resolution. Thus, the same reality can be represented at many resolutions and the "multiresolutional representation" is presumed. The concrete tools available in the system determine the concrete ways of representing multiple levels of resolution. This can be seen in Figure 18.3 from a low resolution to a high resolution.

Nonredundant systems contain information representing the unique trajectory of motion from one state to another state. A redundant system is defined as a system in which there is more than one trajectory of motion from one state to another. It can be demonstrated for many realistic couples "Intelligent System(IS)–Environment(E)" (Figure 18.4) that

- They have a multiplicity of traversing trajectories from an Initial State IS to the goal states (GS).
- These trajectories can have different costs, which allows for a preferable plan selection.

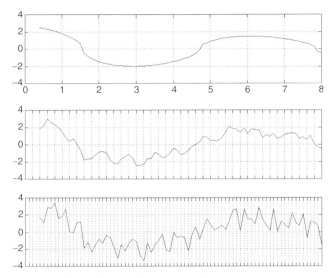

Figure 18.3. Multiresolutional representation.

Thus, these systems contain the information of a multiplicity of alternatives of problem space traversal. Redundancy grows when the system is considered to be a stochastic one. The number of available alternatives grows even higher when we consider also a multiplicity of goal tessellata of a particular level of resolution under the condition of assigning the goal at a lower-resolution level, which is the fact in multiresolutional systems. The latter issue attracts our attention to the uncertainty of the solution which emerges as a result of the stochastic component of the information amplified by the value of tessellata for a concrete resolution of the level.

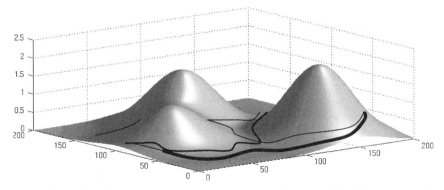

Figure 18.4. Multiplicity of plan alternatives computed for an IS within a particular environment.

In "un-redundant" (or lean) systems there may be a different kind of planning problem. Since the sequence of actions to be executed is a unique one, the problem is to find this sequence.

18.6. SEARCHING ON MULTIPLE LEVELS OF RESOLUTION

Search is performed by constructing feasible combinations of states within a subspace. Feasible means satisfying a particular set of conditions or constraints. Search is interpreted as exploring (physically, or in simulation) as many as possible alternatives of possible action sequences and comparing them afterwards.

Each alternative is created by using a particular law of producing the group of interest (cluster, string, etc.). Usually, grouping presumes exploratory construction of possible combinations of the elements of space (combinatorial search) and, as one or many of these combinations, satisfies conditions of "being an entity"—substitution of this group by a new symbol with subsequently treating it as an object (grouping).

The larger the space of search, the higher the complexity of search. This is why a special effort is allocated with and focused upon reducing the space of search. This effort is called focusing attention, and it results in determining two conditions of searching, namely, its upper and lower boundaries:

(a) The upper boundaries of the space in which the search should be performed
(b) The resolution of representation (the lower boundaries)

Formation of multiple combinations of elements (combinatorial search, CS) satisfying required conditions of transforming them into entities (grouping, G) within a bounded subspace (focusing attention, FA) is a fundamental procedure in both learning and planning. Since these three procedures work together, we will talk about them as a triplet of computational procedures (GFACS; see Chapter 11 for details). Notice that in learning it creates lower-resolution levels out of higher-resolution levels (bottom-up), while in planning it progresses from the lower-resolution levels out of higher-resolution levels (top-down).

This triplet of computational procedures is characteristic for intelligence and probably is the elementary computational unit of intelligence. Its purpose is the transformation of large volumes of information into a manageable form, which ensures the success of functioning. The way it functions in a joint learning–planning process explains the pervasive character of hierarchical architectures in all domains of activities (Figure 18.5). The need in GFACS is stimulated by the property of knowledge representations to contain a multiplicity of alternatives of space traversal (which is a property of representations to be redundant). Redundancy of representations determines the need in GFACS; otherwise the known systems would not be able to function efficiently (it is possible that redundancy of

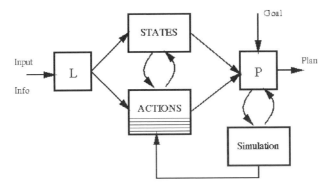

Figure 18.5. Functioning of GFACS in the joint learning–planning process.

representations is a precondition for the possibility of life and the need of intelligence).

Representations reduce the redundancy of reality. Elimination of redundancy allows for having problems that can be solved in a closed form (no combinatorics is possible and/or necessary). Sometimes, this ultimate reduction of redundancy is impossible and the combinatorial search is the only way of solving the problem. If the problem cannot be solved in a closed form, we introduce redundancy intentionally to enable functioning of GFACS. At each level of resolution, planning is done as a reaction to the changes in a situation invalidating existing plans, which invokes the need of anticipation and the active interference in order to (a) take advantage of the growing opportunities or (b) take necessary measures before the negative consequences occur. Deviations from a plan are compensated for by the compensatory mechanism also in a reactive manner. Thus, both the feed-forward control (planning) and feedback compensation are reactive activities as far as inter-action system–environment is concerned. Both can be made active in their implementation. This explains the different approaches—for example, in robotics and organizational science.

In Figure 18.6, the processes of multiresolutional planning via consecutive search in the dynamic space with focusing attention and grouping are demonstrated for the control problem of finding a minimum-time motion trajectory. The space is studied and learned in advance by multiple testing, and its representation is based upon knowing that the distance, velocity, and time are linked by a simple expression, which is sufficient for obtaining computationally the theoretically correct solution with an error accepted to be admissible. Several methods of constructing the envelopes of attention can be applied.

In Figure 18.6a the first step is shown for the process of multi resolutional planning for a dynamic system of the first order (simple inertia). The space tessellation is very sparse, and the planned trajectory found as a result of searching not surprisingly is very coarse (a broken line for acceleration, a broken line for deceleration, and "a three-point" horizontal line at the top). In Figure 18.6b we develop a new tessellation

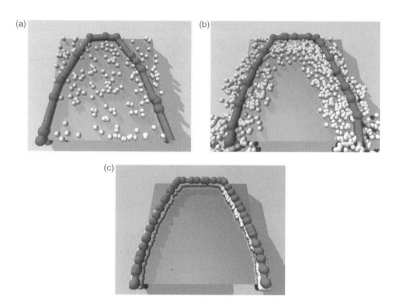

Figure 18.6. (a–c) Solving a minimum-time control problem by three-level multiresolution with grouping and consecutive focusing attention.

of higher resolution only in the vicinity of the curve obtained by the process shown in Figure 18.6a. The curves of acceleration and deceleration are definitely smoother. The area for concluding the searching activities (Figure 18.6c) is even narrower, and the results of searching are very accurate. The example of searching a path on a map is easy to envisage. However, grouping, focusing attention, and searching within the chosen boundaries are a property of searching in other kinds of problem spaces as well.

18.7. LEARNING AS A SOURCE OF REPRESENTATION AND ITS RELATION WITH PROBLEMS OF PLANNING

As we stated earlier, planning can only take place in intelligent systems and requires representation. These systems also learn. Learning is defined as knowledge acquisition from the experience of functioning. Thus, learning is the process of developing and the subsequent enhancing of the representation space. The latter (enhancing) can be produced and characterized in the following ways:

- By a set of paths (to one or more goals) previously traversed
- By a set of paths (to one or more goals) previously computed and traversed
- By a set of paths (to one or more goals) previously determined and not traversed
- By a totality of (all possible) paths
- By a set of paths executed in the space in a random way

One can see that the totality of this knowledge contains implicitly both the description of the environment and the description of the actions required to traverse a trajectory in this environment. Moreover, if some particular system is the source of knowledge, then the collected knowledge contains information about the properties of the system, which has already moved in the environment, and previous experience in planning can be considered the effort to explore the system.

All this information arrives in the form of recorded experiences that contain the information of states, actions between each couple of states, and an evaluation of the outcome. The collection of information obtained in one or several of these ways forms the knowledge of the space: KS (Knowledge Space).

If the information base contains all tessellata of the space with all costs among the adjacent tessellate, we usually call it *The Complete Representation*. Therefore, the representation is equivalent to the multiplicity of explanations and the sets of recommendations how to traverse, or how to move within the space of interest.

One may wonder what is more important: "to have the knowledge of states, or the knowledge of derivatives (actions) from a state to a state"? Apparently, each state can be characterized by some cumulative cost (*value*), while each traversal from a state to a state can be characterized by some incremental cost (*goodness of a move* or *a set of moves*). Expectantly, these two types of knowledge supplement each other, or may allow for transforming one into the other. Any problem of planning is associated with:

- The actual existence of the present state
- The actual, or potential, existence of the goal state
- The knowledge of the values for all or part of the states as far as some particular goal is concerned

From this knowledge the cumulative costs of trajectories to a particular goal (or goals) can be deduced (and computed). On the other hand, the knowledge of costs for the many trajectories traversed in the past can be obtained, which is equivalent to knowing cumulative costs from the initial state (PS) to the goal state (GS) (from which the values of the states can be deduced).

In other words, any problem of planning contains two supplementary components: The first one allows refining the goal (bring it to the higher resolution, see Figure 18.7a). The second one allows determining the path to this refined goal (see Figure 18.7b). These two parts can be performed together or separately. Frequently we are dealing with them separately. In the latter case they are formulated as follows:

(a) Given PS, GS, and KS (all paths), find the subset of KS with a minimum cost, or with a prearranged cost, or with a cost in a particular interval.
(b) Given PS, GS from the lower-resolution level, and KS (all paths), find the GS with a particular value.

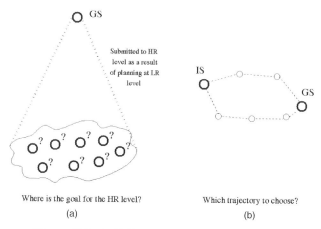

Figure 18.7. (a, b) Two parts of a planning problem.

Finding solutions for these problems is done by a process that we will call *planning*. In other words, planning is the construction of the goal states and/or strings of states connecting the present state with the goal states. As we analyze the desirable processes of planning, we notice a striking similarity between *planning* and *learning*, actually their inseparability. Indeed, the first component of the planning algorithm is the translation of the goal state description from the language of low resolution to the language of high resolution. We must learn where the goal is located, and this is done by the consecutive refinement of the initial coarse information. Frequently, it is associated with increasing the total number of the state variables. In all cases it is associated with a reduction of the indistinguishability zone, or the size of the tessellatum associated with a particular variable. We plan and learn by testing: either for planning (in the domain of modeled representation), which is equivalent to acting within the domain of "imagination," or for learning from experience (in the domain of recorded reality), which is equivalent to dealing with actual reality, for experiential learning.

The second component is the simulation of all available alternatives of the motion from the initial state, IS, to one or several goal states, GS, and the selection of the "best" trajectory. Procedurally, this simulation is performed as a search—that is, via combinatorial construction of all possible strings (groups). To make this combinatorial search for a desirable group more efficient, we reduce the space of searching by focusing attention. The need in planning is determined by the multi-alternative character of the reality. The process of planning can be made more efficient by using appropriate heuristics. In principle, planning is performed by searching within a limited subspace for:

- a state with a particular value (designing the goal);
- a string (a group) of states connecting SP and GP satisfying some conditions on the cumulative cost (planning of the course of actions).

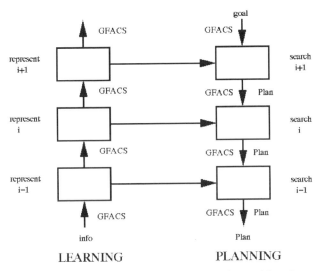

Figure 18.8. On the relations between planning and learning.

The process of searching is associated with either (a) the collection of additional information about experiences or (b) extracting from the KS the implicit information about the state and moving from state to state, or learning. In other words, *planning is inseparable from and complementary to learning* (see Figure 18.8).

This unified planning/learning process is always oriented toward the improvement of functioning—for example, in engineering systems (improvement of accuracy in an adaptive controller) and/or toward increasing probability of survival (emergence of the advanced viruses for the known diseases that can resist various medications, e.g., antibiotics). Thus, this joint process can be related to a system as well as to populations of systems and determines their evolution.

In the foregoing we discussed in detail planning as searching for appropriate future action sequences leading to a goal. We saw that planning is problem solving, that the entities that plan have to be intelligent, and that representations and learning abilities are required. An essential element also is the multiresolutional perspective.

18.8. STARTING POINTS OF PLANNING METHODS IN INTELLIGENT SYSTEMS

From the foregoing sections, we can conclude the following generic characteristics of planning in intelligent systems (see also Chapter 1). An intelligent system functions in its environment. It receives input from this environment, and it changes its environment by acting in it. One of the ways to make sure that the actions will have the desired effects is to simulate actions before they are performed—that is, imagining what effects the actions will have. Here, "simulation" means the consideration of

TABLE 18.8. Overview of Characteristics of Common Elements in Various Planning Approaches

	Cognitive and Behavioral Sciences	Organization Planning	Robotica	Computerized Plan Generation
Trigger	Change in the environment	Fixed time lapse or deviation from the earlier created plan	Change in the environment	Fixed time lapse or deviation from the earlier created plan
Simulation model	Mental activity; problem solving	Organizational structure for the lower levels of resolution/ subtasks for the higher levels of resolution	Programmed real-time behavior; simultaneous sensing, simulating, and acting. AI planning techniques	Task division between human planner and algorithm. AI scheduling and Operations Research techniques.
Multiple resolutions	Division in multiple levels is learned by experience; flexible for adaptation	Dividing the plan among multiple persons and planning work procedures for individual planners; levels are designed; inflexible with respect to adaptation of the levels; multiple levels of resolution are dealt with consecutively	Division in levels is programmed; difficult to change	Dependent upon the technique chosen; inflexible

possible scenarios without actually performing or executing them. We deliberate and devise. This is the core of planning. We simulate actions, compare the outcome of the simulation with the desired outcome, revise the planned actions, simulate and compare again, and so on, until finally the planned actions will be performed. In this book, much has been written about the way in which the simulations take place, what is being simulated, how it is determined when to stop simulating and start acting, and so on. We will not repeat all the relevant content here, but we want to make a general comparison. Almost always it is impossible to simulate all possible actions in order to choose the set of actions that closest match the desired outcome. The main task of an intelligent system is to intelligently determine what options will be looked at. In the previous sections we discussed that the building blocks for this are grouping, focusing attention, and searching (GFACS) on multiple levels of resolution. Table 18.8 provides an overview of the various planning approaches and their planning essence. "Trigger" concerns the motivation to plan, "simulation model" concerns the anticipated future, and "multiple resolutions" concerns the levels of aggregation.

We end this chapter with a few remarks about the question with which we started this book: the similarities and differences between planning for yourself and planning for others.

18.9. CONCLUSION: PLANNING FOR YOURSELF COMPARED TO PLANNING FOR OTHERS

Planning for yourself is considered to be problem solving as we saw in Sections 18.5 and 18.6, in which planning is defined as search for a trajectory through space. This space may be considered literally or metaphorically. A robot finding its way through an unknown environment is an example of the former. However, looking for a solution in a chess game may also be conceptualized as searching through a problem or conceptual space. We also saw that in planning for yourself, learning, representations, and a multiresolutional perspective are essential. The question is, What do the aspects and interpretation of planning for yourself mean for planning for others with in the back of our mind the interpretation of planning as attuning object types? What can we learn from the planning for yourself for planning for others? We will look at representations, communication, learning, and multiresolution.

From a high-level perspective it is possible to use the definition of planning as running through a (problem) space not only in the case of planning for yourself, but also for planning for others. We can see an organization as an aggregated actor that moves through a space. Planners in this organization can be conceived of as steering and directing lower-level actors that determine parts of the organization. The problem with this higher-level conceptualization is that it is too abstract. However, we do not gain much clarity in conceiving an organization as a space ship moving through a real-world–space–time continuum. It still leaves the planning issue internal in the organization a question to be answered.

The big difference with planning for others is that an organization literally does not learn, has no representations, is not able to formulate goals and does not have architectural components of its own, except for the human actors and human planners. On first sight this difference seems to have many consequences. Planning for others seems to be completely different from planning for yourself. However, if we take a closer look at planning for others and its various aspects, many seemingly disappearing aspects re-emerge.

In planning for others, planning is also a kind of problem solving. The planners try to reach goals taking constraints into account. Domain knowledge—that is, knowledge of the properties of object types—is essential. The same conceptual apparatus of problem solving that was used in the case of planning for yourself applies here, too. The planners also learn, although the organization as such literally does not learn. But planners learn themselves and from others, making things more complex. The planners in the organization also use representations of future states (simulations). Also the multiresolutional perspective that is necessary in the case of planning for yourself is applied in planning for others. It is usual in planning in organizations to determine capacities, constraints, and properties at high, intermediate, and low levels. Also in this case one goes from low resolution to high resolution.

Three important things, however, are different between planning for yourself and planning for others: the kind of actor, communication, and coordination complexity. An organizational actor is essentially different from a human actor. Communication within a human actor goes on smoothly; nothing has to be formulated and represented explicitly. Concerning planning for yourself, this is of course different in the case of natural actors (humans) compared to artificial actors (robots). In Sections 18.5 and 18.6 we discussed this. In the case of human actors and planners in an organization, communication has to be explicitly formulated or coded. And because formulations without ambiguity and model restrictions do not exist, many possibilities for misunderstanding emerge. As such, planning for others is again more complex than planning for yourself. The last difference concerns the role of coordination. In planning for others, coordination has to be explicit. The various human actors that constitute organizations need coordination to keep attuned, to stay cohesive, or to keep the organization going. This is another kind of extra complexity compared to planning for yourself.

A general theory of planning does not exist and will not emerge as a result of our efforts to assess the various planning approaches. However, we strongly believe that there are more similarities than differences. Or at least we tried to emphasize the similarities. Anyway, planning requires intelligence, representations, and a multiresolutional perspective. Perhaps it is even possible to see planning for yourself and planning for others in a multiresolutional line. Planning for yourself is high resolution and planning for others is low resolution with often a change in domain. The former is nested within the latter. Or is it the other way around?

REFERENCES

Numbers in square brackets following each reference indicate the chapters where the references are cited.

Aarts, E. H. L., and Laarhoven, P. J. van (1987). *Simulated Annealing: Theory and Applications*. Dordrecht: Kluwer Academic Publishers. [8]

Abeles, M. (1991). *Corticonics: Neural Circuits of the Cerebral Cortex*. Cambridge, England: Cambridge University Press. [2]

Abu-Mostafa, Y. (1986). The complexity of information extraction. *IEEE Transactions on Information Theory*, **IT-32**(4), 513–531. [11]

Ach, N. (1910). *Über den Willensakt und das Temperament*. Leipzig: Quelle & Meyer. [2]

Ackoff, R. (1962). *The Scientific Method*. New York: John Wiley & Sons. [8]

Ackoff, R. L. (1957). The concept and exercise of control in operations research. In: *Proceedings of the First International Conference on Operations Research*. Oxford: The English Universities Press, Ltd., pp. 26–43. [17]

Adams, J. A. (1971). A closed-loop theory of motor learning. *Journal of Motor Behavior*, **3**, 111–150. [2]

Albus, J. (1991). Outline for a theory of intelligence. *IEEE Transactions on Systems, Man, and Cybernetics*, **21**(3), 473–509. [11]

Albus, J., and Meystel, A. (2001). *Engineering of Mind: An Introduction to the Science of Intelligent Systems*. New York: John Wiley & Sons. [11]

Alchian, A. A. (1965). Some economics of property rights. *Il Politico*, **30**(4), 816–829. (Original work published 1961.) [5]

Planning in Intelligent Systems: Aspects, Motivations, and Methods, Edited by Wout van Wezel, René Jorna, and Alexander Meystel
Copyright © 2006 John Wiley & Sons, Inc.

Alexander, G. E., and Crutcher, M. D. (1990). Preparation for movement: Neural representations of intended direction in three motor areas of the monkey. *Journal of Neurophysiology*, **64**, 133–150. [2]

Allan, J. J., Mellitt, B., and Brebbia, C. A. (1996). *Computers in Railways V, Railway Systems and Management.* Southampton: Computational Mechanics Publications. [17]

Allport, D. A. (1980). Patterns and actions: Cognitive mechanisms are content-specific. In G. Claxton (ed.), *Cognitive Psychology*, pp. 26–63. London: Routledge. [2]

Altmann, E. M. (2002). Functional decay of memory for tasks. *Psychological Research*, **66**, 287–297. [2]

Amalberti, R., and Deblon, F. (1992). Cognitive modelling of fighter aircraft's process control: A step towards an intelligent onboard assistance system. *International Journal of Man–Machine Studies*, **36**, 639–671. [3]

Andersen, P., Bøgh, Nielsen, M., and Land, M. *The Present Past.* Paper presented at 2nd Workshop on Organisational Semiotics, 12–14 October 1999, Almelo. [5]

Andersen, P. Bøgh. (1999). Personal communication, 1999. [5]

Anderson, J. R. (1982). Acquisition of cognitive skill. *Psychological Review*, **89**, 369–406. [2]

Anderson, J. R., and Lebiere, C. (1998). *The Atomic Components of Thought.* Mahwah, New Jersey: London, Lawrence Erlbaum Associates. [4]

Anthony, R. N. (1965). *Planning and Control Systems. A Framework for Analysis.* Boston: Harvard. [5, 6, 18]

Aschersleben, G., Stenneken, P., Cole, J., and Prinz, W. (2002). In W. Prinz and B. Hommel (eds.), *Common Mechanisms in Perception and Action: Attention & Performance XIX*, pp. 227–244. Oxford: Oxford University Press. [2]

Asimov, I. (1993). *The Caves of Steel.* Galaxy Science Fiction. Harper Collins: New York. [5]

Augier, M., and March, J. L. (2004). *Models of a Man: Essays in Memory of Herbert A. Simon.* Cambridge, MA: The MIT Press. [4]

Bach-y-Rita, P. (1990). Brain plasticity as a basis for recovery of function in humans. *Neuropsychologia*, **18**, 547–554. [2]

Bainbridge, L. (1974). Analysis of verbal protocols from a process control task. In E. Edwards and F. P. Lees (eds.), *The Human Operator in Process Control.* London: Taylor and Francis. [7]

Bainbridge, L. (1978). The process controller. In W. T. Singleton (ed.), *The Study of Real Skills, The Analysis of Practical Skills*, Vol. 1, pp. 236–263. St Leonardgate, UK: MTP. [3]

Bainbridge, L. (1988). Types of representation. In L. P. Goodstein, H. B. Anderson, and S. E. Olsen (eds.), *Tasks, Errors, and Mental Models*, pp. 70–91. London: Taylor & Francis. [3]

Bainbridge, L. (1997). The change in concepts needed to account for human behavior in complex dynamic tasks. *IEEE Transactions on Systems, Man, and Cybernetics—Part A: Systems and Humans*, **27**, 351–359. [3]

Baker, K. R. (1974). *Introduction to Sequencing and Scheduling.* New York: John Wiley & Sons. [4, 7, 8]

Bakker, J. (1995). *Classificatie en diagnose voor scheduling situaties.* Groningen: Internal report, University of Groningen (Classification and diagnosis for scheduling situations). [4, 7]

Bangham, J. A., Chardaire, P., Pye, C. J., and Ling, P. D. (1996). Multiscale nonlinear decomposition: The sieve decomposition theorem. *IEEE Transactions on Pattern Analysis and Machine Intelligence*, **18**(5), 529–539. [11]

Baptiste, P., Le Pape, C., and Nuijten, W. (1995). Incorporating Efficient Operations Research Algorithms in Constraint-Based Scheduling, *First International Joint Workshop on Artificial Intelligence and Operations Research*, Timberline Lodge, Oregon. [9]

Bargh, J. A., and Gollwitzer, P. M. (1994). Environmental control over goal-directed action. *Nebraska Symposium on Motivation*, **41**, 71–124. [2]

Barker, F. G., II, (1995). Phineas among the phrenologists: the American crowbar case and nineteenth-century theories of cerebral localization. *J. Neurosurg.* **82**, 672–682. [3]

Barnhart, C., Johnson, E. L., Nemhauser, G. L., Savelsbergh, M. W. P., and Vance, P. H. (1998). Branch-and-price: Column generation for solving huge integer programs. *Operations Research*, **46**(3), 316–329. [8, 15]

Bauer, A., Rowden, R., Browne, J., Duggan, J., and Lyons, G. (1991). *Shop Floor Control Systems: From Design to Implementation*. London: Chapman & Hall. [6]

Bechara, A., Damasio, A. R., Damasio, H., and Anderson, S. W. (1994). Insensitivity to future consequences following damage to human prefrontal cortex. *Cognition*, **50**, 7–15. [2]

Bechara, A., Tranel, D., Damasio. H., and Damasio, A. R. (1996). Failure to respond autonomically to anticipated future outcomes following damage to prefrontal cortex. *Cerebral Cortex*, **6**, 215–225. [2]

Beck, H., and Tate, A. (1996). Open planning, scheduling and constraint management architectures. *British Telecommunication's Technical Journal, Special Issue on Resource Management*, 1995. [7]

Beck, J. C., and Fox, M. S. (1998). A generic framework for constraint-directed search and scheduling. *AI Magazine*, 101–130. [9]

Beckers, T., Houwer, J. de, and Eelen, P. (2002). Automatic integration of non-perceptual action effect features: The case of the associative affective Simon effect. *Psychological Research*, **66**, 166–173. [2]

Beetz, M. (2000). Concurrent reactive plans. *Lecture Notes in Artificial Intelligence*. Berlin: Springer-Verlag. [18]

Beishon, R. J. (1974). An analysis and simulation of an operator's behaviour in controlling continuous baking ovens. In E. Edwards and F.P. Lees (eds.), *The Human Operator in Process Control*. London: Taylor and Francis. [7]

Bekkering, H., and Wohlschläger, A. (2002). Action perception and imitation: A tutorial. In W. Prinz and B. Hommel (eds.), *Common Mechanisms in Perception and Action: Attention & Performance XIX*, pp. 294–314. Oxford: Oxford University Press. [2]

Bel, G., and Thierry, C. (1993). A constraint-based system for multi-site coordination and scheduling. *IJCAI-93 Workshop on Knowledge-Based Production Planning, Scheduling and Control*, Chambery. IJCAI 93. [9]

Bell, J. A., and Livesey, P. J. (1985). Cue significance and response regulation in 3- to 6-year-old children's learning of multiple choice discrimination tasks. *Developmental Psychobiology*, **18**, 229–245. [2]

Benbasat, I., and Todd, P. (1996). The effects of decision support and task contingencies on model formulation: A cognitive perspective. *Decision Support Systems*, **17**, 241–252. [7, 17]

Ben-Khedher, N., Kintanar, J., Queille, C., and Stripling, W. (1998). Schedule optimization at SNCF: From conception to day of departure. *Interfaces*, **28**, 6–23. [8]

Berenschot and Logiplan (1994). *Softwarepakketten voor produktiebesturing en elektronische planborden*. Amsterdam, Berenschot Netherlands (Software packages for production control and electronic planboards). [4]

Bernardo J. J., and Lin, K. S. (1994). An interactive procedure for bi-criteria production scheduling. *Computers & Operations Research*, **21**(6), 677–688. [7]

Bertrand, J. W. M., and Fransoo, J. C., (2002). Operations Management Research Methodologies Using Quantitative Modeling, *International Journal of Operations and Production Management*, **22**(2), 241–264. [4]

Bertrand, J. W. M., Wortmann, J. C., and Wijngaard, J. (1990). *Production Control—A Structural and Design Oriented Approach*. Amsterdam: Elsevier. [6]

Bi, S., and Salvendy, G. (1994). Analytical modeling and experimental study of human workload in scheduling of advanced manufacturing systems. *The International Journal of Human Factors in Manufacturing*, **4**(2), 205–234. [7]

Biethahn, J., Höhnerloh, A., Kuhl, J., Leisewitz, M.-C., Nissen, V., and Tietze, M. (1998). *Betriebswirtschaftliche Anwendungen des Softcomputing*. Wiesbaden: Vieweg. [9]

Biggerstaff, T. J., and Perlis, A. J. (1989). *Software Reusability*. Reading, MA: ACM Press. [7]

Bixby, R. E. (2002). Solving real-world linear programs: A decade and more of progress. *Operations Research*, **50**, 3–15. [8]

Blasum, U., Bussieck, M. R., Hochstättler, W., Moll, C., Scheel, H. H., and Winter, T. (2000). Scheduling trams in the morning. *Mathematical Methods of Operations Research*, **49**(1), 137–148. [15]

Block, R. A. (ed.). (1990). *Cognitive Models of Psychological Time*. Hillsdale, NJ: Lawrence Erlbaum Associates. [3]

Boddy, M., and Dean, T. L. (1994). Deliberation scheduling for problem-solving in time-constrained environments. *Artificial Intelligence*, Vol. 67, pp. 245–285. [3]

Boekee, D., Kraak, R., and Backer, E. (1982). On complexity and syntactic information. *IEEE Transactions on Systems, Man, and Cybernetics*, Vol. SMC-12, No. 1, pp. 71–79. [11]

Bonissone, P. P., Dutta, S., and Wood, N. C. (1994). Merging strategic and tactical planning in dynamic and uncertain environments. *IEEE Transactions on Systems, Man, and Cybernetics*, Vol. 24, pp. 841–863. [3]

Bonnet, M., and MacKay, W. A. (1989). Changes in contingent-negative variation and reaction time related to precueing of direction and force of a forearm movement. *Brain, Behavior and Evolution*, Vol. 33, pp. 147–152. [2]

Boudes, N., and Cellier, J. M. (1998). Étude du champ d'anticipation dans le contrôle du trafic aérien. *Le Travail Humain*, Vol. 61, pp. 29–50. [3]

Boudes, N., and Tremblay, E. (1994). Temporal landmarks in dynamic situations. Paper presented at the workshop *Time and the Dynamic Control of Behavior*. Liège, Nov. [3]

Brehmer, B. (1995). Feedback delays in complex dynamic decision tasks. In P. Frensch and J. Funke (eds.), *Complex Problem-Solving: The European Perspective*, pp. 103–130. Hillsdale, NJ: Lawrence Erlbaum Associates. [3]

Brent, J. (1993). *Charles Sanders Peirce: A Life* (revised edition). Bloomington, IN: Indiana University Press. [5]

Breuker, J., and Velde, W. van de (eds.) (1994). *CommonKADS Library for Expertise Modelling: Reusable Problem Solving Components.* Amsterdam: IOS Press. [4, 7]

Bridgeman, B., Lewis, S., Heit, G., and Nagle, M. (1979). Relation between cognitive and motor-oriented systems of visual position perception. *Journal of Experimental Psychology: Human Perception and Performance*, **5**, 692–700. [2]

Broadbent, D. E., and Gregory, M. (1962). Donder's B- and C-reactions and S-R compatibility. *Journal of Experimental Psychology*, **63**, 575–578. [2]

Broek, H. van den (2001). *On Agent Cooperation: The Relevance of Cognitive Plausibility for Multi-agent Simulation Models of Organization.* Capelle a/d IJssel: Labyrint Publishing. [10]

Broek, H. van den, and Gazendam, H. W. M. (1997). Organizational actors and the need for a flexible world representation. In R. Conte (ed.), *Simulating Social Phenomena*, pp. 303–309. Berlin: Springer. [5]

Brooks, R. A. (1999). *Cambrian Intelligence: The Early History of the New AI.* Cambridge: The MIT Press. [18]

Brown, D. E., Marin, J. A., and Scherer, W. T. (1995). A Survey of Intelligent Scheduling Systems. In D. E. Brown and W. T. Scherer (eds.), *Intelligent Scheduling Systems.* Boston: Kluwer Academic Publishers. [7]

Bruno, N. (2001). When does action resist visual illusions? *Trends in Cognitive Sciences*, **5**, 379–382. [2]

Bruns, R. (1993). Direct chromosome representation and advanced genetic operators for production scheduling. In: *Proceedings of the Fifth International Conference on Genetic Algorithms*, 1993. [9]

Bryant, R. E. (1986). Graph-based algorithms for boolean function manipulation. *IEEE Transactions on Computers*, **8**, 677–691. [10]

Butler, J., and Rovee-Collier, C. (1989). Contextual gating of memory retrieval. *Developmental Psychobiology*, **22**, 533–552. [2]

Buxey, G. (1989). Production scheduling: Practice and theory. *European Journal of Operational Research*, **39**, 17–31. [6, 7, 17]

Buxey, G. (1995). A managerial perspective on aggregate planning. *International Journal of Production Economics*, **41**(1–3), 127–133. [17]

Carbonell, J. G. (1981). Counterplanning: A strategy-based model of adversary planning in real-world situations. *Artificial Intelligence*, **16**(3), 257–294. [10]

Carey, M., and Carville, S. (2003). Scheduling and platforming trains at busy complex stations. *Transportation Research Part A*, **37**, 195–224. [17]

Carley, K. M., and Gassser, L. (2001). Computational organization theory. In G. Weiss (ed.), *Multiagent Systems*, pp. 299–330. Cambridge, MA: The MIT Press. [5]

Cellier, J. M., Eyrolle, H., and Mariné, C. (1997). Expertise in dynamic environments. *Ergonomics*, **40**, 28–50. [3]

Chugani, H. T. (1994). Development of regional brain glucose metabolism in relation to behavior and plasticity. In G. Dawson and K. Fischer (eds.), *Human Behavior and the Developing Brain*, pp. 153–175. New York: Guilford Press. [2]

Chugani, H. T., and Phelps, M. E. (1986). Maturational changes in cerebral functions in infants determined by [18] FDG positron emission tomography. *Science*, **231**, 840–843. [2]

Churchland, P. M. (1984). *Matter and Consciousness.* Cambridge, MA: MIT Press. [4]

Cimatti, A., Pistore, M., Roveri, M., and Traverso, P. (2003). Weak, strong, and strong cyclic planning via symbolic model checking. *Artificial Intelligence*, **147**(1–2), 35–84. [10]

Clancey, W. J. (1985). Heuristic classification. *Artificial Intelligence*, **27**, 289–350. [1, 4]

Clarke, R. J. (2001). Towards a systemic semiotic approach to multimedia interface design. In K. Liu, R. J. Clarke, P. Bøgh Andersen, and R. K. Stamper (eds.), *Information, Organisation and Technology: Studies in Organisational Semiotics*, pp. 247–270. Boston: Kluwer. [5]

Coase, R. H. (1993). The nature of the firm. In O. E. Williamson and S. G. Winter (eds.), *The Nature of the Firm: Origins, Evolution, and Development*, pp. 18–33. New York: Oxford University Press. (Original work published 1937.) [5]

Coburn, F. G. (circa 1918). Scheduling: The Coordination of Effort. In I. Mayer (ed.), *Organizing for Production and Other Papers on Management 1912–1924*. Easton: Hive Publishing, 1981, pp. 149–172. [6]

Combettes, P., and Pesquet, J.-C. (1998). Convex multiresolution analysis. *IEEE Transactions on Pattern Analysis and Machine Intelligence*, **20**(12), pp. 1308–1318. [11]

Cook, S. A. (1971), The complexity of theorem-proving procedures. *Proceedings of the 3rd Annual ACM Symposium on the Theory of Computing*. New York: Association for Computing Machinery. [8]

Cordeau, J. F., Soumis, F., and Desrosiers, J. (2001). Simultaneous assignment of locomotives and cars to passenger trains. *Operations Research*, **49**, 531–548. [8]

Cordeau, J. F., Toth, P., and Vigo, D. (1998). A survey of optimisation models for train routing and scheduling. *Transportation Science*, **32**(4), 380–404. [15, 17]

Craighero, L., Fadiga, L., Rizzolatti, G., and Umiltá, C. (1999). Action for perception: A motor-visual attentional effect. *Journal of Experimental Psychology: Human Perception and Performance*, **25**, 1673–1692. [2]

Crane, J. L. (1936). Planning organization and the planners. *The Planners' Journal*, **2**(3), 61–69. [1]

Crawford, S. (2000). *A Field Study of Schedulers in Industry: Understanding Their Work, Practices and Performance*. Ph.D. thesis, University of Nottingham. [6]

Crawford, S. (2001). Making sense of scheduling: The realities of scheduling practice in an engineering firm. In B. MacCarthy and J. Wilson (eds.), *Human Performance in Planning and Scheduling*. London: Taylor & Francis. [7]

Crawford, S., MacCarthy, B. L., Wilson, J. R., and Vernon, C. (1999). Investigating the work of industrial schedulers through field study. *Cognition, Technology & Work*, **1**, 63–77. [7]

Crawford, S., and Wiers, V. C. S. (2001). From anecdotes to theory: A review of existing knowledge on human factors of planning and scheduling. In MacCarthy, B. and Wilson, J. (eds.), *Human Performance in Planning and Scheduling*. London: Taylor & Francis. [7]

Curry, K.W., and Tate, A. (1991). O-plan: The open planning architecture. *Artificial Intelligence*, **51**, 1. [1, 18]

Daele, A. van, and Carpinelli, F. (1996). Anticipation de l'action et anticipation du processus: l'influence de la situation [Action anticipation and process anticipation: The influence of situation]. In J. M. Cellier, V. De Keyser, and C. Valot (eds.), *La gestion du temps dans les environnements dynamiques* [Time management in dynamic situations], pp. 200–220. Paris: Presses Universitaires de France. [3]

Dahlhaus, E., Horak, P., Miller, M., and Ryan, J. F. (2000). The train marshalling problem. *Discrete Applied Mathematics*, **103**, 41–54. [15]

Damasio, A. (1994). *Descartes' Error*. New York: G. P. Putnam's Sons. [2]

Damasio, A. R., Tranel, D., and Damasio, H.C. (1991). Somatic markers and the guidance of behaviour. In H. S. Levin et al. (eds.), *Frontal Lobe Function and Dysfunction*, pp. 217–229. New York: Oxford University Press. [2]

Dantzig, G. B. (1948). Programming in a linear structure. *U.S. Air Force Comptroller*, USAF: Washington D.C. [8]

Dantzig, G. B. (1967). All shortest routes in a graph. In *Theory of Graphs, International Symposium, Rome, 1966*. New York: Gordon and Breach, pp. 91–92. [17]

Daprati, E., Franck, N., Georgieff, N., Proust, J., Pacherie, E., Dalery, J., and Jeannerod, M. (1997). Looking for the agent: An investigation into consciousness of action and self-conciousness in schizophrenic patients. *Cognition*, **65**, 71–86. [2]

Das, J. P., Karr, B. C., and Parrila, R. K. (1996). *Cognitive Planning*. New Delhi: Sage. [4]

Davis, G. B., and Olson, M. H. (1985). *Management Information Systems*, 2nd edition. New York: McGraw-Hill. [4]

Davis, R., and Smith, R. G. (1983). Negotiation as a metaphor for distributed problem solving. *Artificial Intelligence*, **20**(1), 63–101. [5]

Dawidowicz, E. (2002). Performance evaluation of network centric warfare oriented intelligent systems. *Proceedings of PERMIS'2001*, Gaithersburg, MD. [11]

De Alfaro, L., Henzinger, T. A., and Kupferman, O. (1998). Concurrent reachability games. In *IEEE Symposium on Foundations of Computer Science*, pp. 564–575. [10]

De Keyser, V. (1995). Time in ergonomics research. *Ergonomics*, **38**, 1639–1660. [3]

Debernard, S., Vanderhaegen, F., and Millot, P. (1992). An experimental investigation of dynamic allocation of tasks between air traffic controller and A.I. system. Paper presented at the *5th IFAC/IFIP/IFORS/IEA MMS*, Amsterdam, July. [3]

Décary, A., and Richer, F. (1995). Response selection deficits in frontal excisions. *Neuropsychologia*, **33**, 1243–1253. [2]

Decety, J., Grèzes, J., Costes, N., Perani, D., Jeannerod, M., Procyk, E., Grassi, F., and Fazio, F. (1997). Brain activity during observation of actions. Influence of action content and subject's strategy. *Brain*, **120**, 1763–1777. [2]

Decety, J., Perani, D., Jeannerod, M., Bettinardi, V., Tadary, B., Woods, R., Mazziotta, J. C., and Fazio, F. (1994). Mapping motor representations with positron emission tomography. *Nature*, **371**, 600–602. [2]

Deecke, L., Grozinger, B., and Kornhuber, H. H. (1976). Voluntary finger movement in man: Cerebral potentials and theory. *Biological Cybernetics*, **23**, 99–119. [2]

Denecker, P. (2000). *Analyse cognitive des effets de l'utilisation d'un système interactif d'aide à l'anticipation (SIAA) sur les stratégies de conduite d'un processus à longs délais de réponse: le cas du haut fourneau* [Cognitive analysis of the effects of the use of an interactive system assisting anticipation on long time lag process supervision strategies: blast furnace] (Research report NEB/SOLLAC). Valenciennes: Université de Valenciennes, LAMIH. [3]

Denecker, P., and Hoc, J. M. (1997). Analysis of the effects of a support to anticipation in the supervision of a long time-lag process: The blast furnace. In S. Bagnara, E. Hollnagel, M. Mariani, and L. Norros (eds.), *Time and Space in Process Control—6th European*

Conference on Cognitive Science Approach to Process Control, pp. 165–170. Roma: CNR, Istituto di Psicologia. [3]

Dennett, D. C. (1978). *Brainstorms. Philosophical Essays on Mind and Psychology*. Hassocks, Sussex: Harvester Press. [4]

Dennett, D. C. (1987). *The Intentional Stance*. Cambridge (Mass): The MIT Press. [4]

Dennett, D. C. (1991). *Consciousness Explained*. London: Allan Lane, The Penguin Press. [4]

Dennett, D. C. (1996). *Kinds of Minds: Toward an Understanding of Consciousness*. New York: Basic Books. [11]

Dessouky, M. I., Moray, N., and Kijowski, B. (1995). Taxonomy of scheduling systems as a basis for the study of strategic behavior. *Human Factors*, **37**, 443–472. [3, 7]

Devlin, K. (1991). *Logic and Information*. Cambridge: Cambridge University Press. [5]

Di Pellegrino, G., Fadiga, L., Fogassi, V., Gallese, V., and Rizzolatti, G. (1992). Understanding motor events: A neurophysiological study. *Experimental Brain Research*, **91**, 176–180. [2]

Di Stefano, G., and Koci, M. L. (2003). A graph theoretical approach to the shunting problem. *Electronic Notes in Theoretical Computer Science*, **92**(1), 16–33. [15]

Diamond, A. (1985). Development of the ability to use recall to guide action, as indicated by infants' performance on AB. *Child Development*, **56**, 868–883. [2]

Diamond, A. (1990). Developmental time course in human infants and infant monkeys, and the neural bases of inhibitory control of reaching. *Annals of the New York Academy of Sciences*, **608**, 637–676. [2]

Diamond, A., and Gilbert, J. (1989). Development as progressive inhibitory control of action: Retrieval of a contiguous object. *Cognitive Development*, **4**, 223–249. [2]

Diamond, A., and Goldman-Rakic, P. S. (1986). Comparative development in human infants and infant rhesus monkeys of cognitive functions that depend on prefrontal cortex. *Society for Neuroscience Abstracts*, **12**, 742. [2]

Diamond, A., and Taylor, C. (1996). Development of an aspect of executive control: Development of the abilities to remember what I said and to "do as I say, not as I do." *Developmental Psychobiology*, **29**, 315–334. [2]

Dietz, J. L. G. (1992). *Leerboek Informatiekundige Analyse*. Deventer: Kluwer Bedrijfswetenschappen. [5]

Dietz, J. L. G. (1996). *Introductie tot DEMO: Van informatietechnologie naar organisatietechnologie*. Alphen a/d Rijn: Samsom. [5]

Dijkstra, E. W. (1959). A note on two problems in connection with graphs. *Numer. Math.*, **1**, 269–271. [17]

Dincbas, M., Simonis, H., and Van Hentenryck, P. (1990). Solving large combinatorial problems in logic programming. *Journal of Logic Programming*. **8**(1–2), 75–93. [9]

Dockx, K., Boeck, Y. de, and Meert, K. (1997). Interactive scheduling in the chemical process industry. Computers and chemical engineering. *An International Journal*, **21**(9), 925–946. [7]

Dölling, E. (1998). Semiotik und Kognitionswissenschaft. *Zeitschrift für Semiotik*, **20**(1–2), 133–159.

Dominguez, C. O. (1997). *First, Do No Harm: Expertise and Metacognition in Laparoscopic Surgery*. Doctoral dissertation, Wright State University. [3]

Dorn, J. (1993). Task-oriented design of scheduling applications. In J. Dorn and K. A. Froeschl (eds.), *Scheduling of Production Processes*. Chichester, England: Ellis Horwood. [7, 18]

Dorn, J. (1995). Iterative improvement methods for knowledge-based scheduling. *AICOM*, **8**(1), 20–34. [9]

Dorn, J., and Froeschl, K. A. (1993). *Scheduling of Production Processes*. Chichester: Ellis Horwood. [9]

Dorn, J., Girsch, M., and Vidakis, N. (1996). DÉJÀ VU – A Reusable Framework for the Construction of Intelligent Interactive Schedulers. *Proceedings of the International Conference on Advances in Production Management Systems (APMS November '96)*. [7]

Drewe, E. A. (1975). An experimental investigation of Luria's theory on the effects of frontal lobe lesions in man. *Neuropsychologia*, **13**, 421–429. [2]

Dudek, R. A., Panwalkar, S. S., and Smith, M. L. (1992). The lesson of flowshop scheduling research. *Operations Research*, **40**, 7–13. [6]

Duncan, J., Emslie, H., Williams, P., Johnson, R., and Freer, C. (1996). Intelligence and the frontal lobe: The organization of goal-directed behavior. *Cognitive Psychology*, **30**, 257–303. [2]

Durfee, E. H. (1988). *Coordination of Distributed Problem Solvers*. Boston: Kluwer Academic Publishers. [5, 10]

Durfee, E. H. (2001). Distributed problem solving and planning. In G. Weiss (ed.), *Multiagent Systems*, pp. 121–164. Cambridge, MA: MIT Press. [5]

Dutton, J. M. (1962). Simulation of an actual production scheduling and workflow control system. *International Journal of Production Research*, **4**, 421–441. [6]

Dutton, J. M. (1964). Production scheduling: A behavior model. *International Journal of Production Research*, **3**(1), 3–27 [6, 7]

Dutton, J. M., and Starbuck, W. (1971). Finding Charlie's run-time estimator. In J. M. Dutton and W. Starbuck, (eds.), *Computer Simulation of Human Behaviour*. New York: John Wiley & Sons, pp. 218–242. [6]

Eggertson, T. (1990). *Economic Behavior and Institutions*. Cambridge, England: Cambridge University Press. [5]

Ehlers, E. M., and Rensburg, E. van (1996). An object-oriented manufacturing scheduling approach. *IEEE Transactions on Systems, Man, and Cybernetics—part A: Systems and Humans*, **26**(1), 17–25. [7]

Eimer, M., and Schlaghecken, F. (1998). Effects of masked stimuli on motor activation: Behavioral and electrophysiological evidence. *Journal of Experimental Psychology: Human Perception and Performance*, **24**, 1737–1747. [2]

Elliott, S. R. (1998). Experiments in decision-making under risk and uncertainty: Thinking outside the box. *Managerial and Decision Economics*, **19**, 239–257. [6]

Elsner, B., and Hommel, B. (2001). Effect anticipation and action control. *Journal of Experimental Psychology: Human Perception and Performance*, **27**, 229–240. [2]

Elsner, B., Hommel, B., Mentschel, C., Drzezga, A., Prinz, W., Conrad, B., and Siebner, H. (2002). Linking actions and their perceivable consequences in the human brain. *NeuroImage*, **17**, 364–372. [2]

Endsley, M. (1995a). Toward a theory of situation awareness in dynamic systems. *Human Factors*, **37**, 32–64. [3]

Endsley, M. (1995b). Measurement of situation awareness in dynamic systems. *Human Factors*, **37**, 65–84. [3]

Eppstein, D. (1998). Finding the *k* shortest paths. *SIAM J. Computing*, **28**(2), 652–673. [17]

Evarts, E. V. (1980). Brain control of movement: Possible mechanisms of function. In P. Bach-y-Rita (ed.), *Recovery of Function: Theoretical Considerations for Brain Injury Rehabilitation*, pp. 173–186. Bern: Huber. [2]

Exner, S. (1879). Physiologie der Grosshirnrinde. In L. Hermann (ed.), *Handbuch der Physiologie*, Band 2, Teil 2, pp. 189–350. Leipzig: Vogel. [2]

Fadiga, L., Fogassi, L., Pavesi, G., and Rizzolatti, G. (1995). Motor facilitation during action observation: A magnetic stimulation study. *Journal of Neurophysiology*, **73**, 2608–2611. [2]

Fagen, J. W., and Rovee, C. K. (1976). Effects of quantitative shifts in a visual reinforcer on the instrumental re-sponse of infants. *Journal of Experimental Child Psychology*, **21**, 349–360. [2]

Fagen, J. W., Rovee-Collier, C. K., and Kaplan, M. G. (1976). Psychophysical scaling of stimulus similarity in 3-month-old infants and adults. *Journal of Experimental Child Psychology*, **22**, 272–281. [2]

Fayol, H. (1984). General and industrial management [revised by I. Gray]. New York: IEEE Press. (Original work published in Extrait du *Bulletin de la Société de l'Industie Minérale*, 3e livraison de 1916.) [5]

Fayol, H. (1999). Administration, industrielle et générale. Paris: Dunod. (Original work published in Extrait du *Bulletin de la Société de l'Industie Minérale*, 3e livraison de 1916.) [5]

Fernandez, A. J., and Hill, P. M. (2000). *A Comparative Study of Eight Constraint Programming Languages Over the Boolean and Finite Domains*, Constraints 5, pp. 275–301. Boston: Kluwer Academic Publishers. [14]

Fikes, R. E., and Nillson, N. J. (1971). STRIPS: A new approach to the application of theorem proving to problem solving. *Artificial Intelligence*, **2**, 189–208. [18]

Fioole, P. J. (2003). *Rintel, het automatisch genereren en verbeteren van een rangeerplanning* (in Dutch). Master's thesis, Erasmus University Rotterdam. [15]

Fioole, P. J., Kroon, L. G., Maróti, G., and A. Schrijver, A. (2004). A rolling stock circulation model for combining and splitting of passenger trains, CWI Report PNA-E0420 (to appear in *European Journal of Operational Research*). [8]

Floyd, R. W. (1962). Algorithm 47, shortest path, communication. *ACM*, **5**, 345. [17]

Fodor, J. A. (1987). Why There Still Has to Be a Language of Thought. In J. A. Fodor, (ed.), *Psychosemantics*, pp. 135–167. Cambridge, MA: MIT Press. [11]

Fodor Birtalan, I. (2003). *Matching Arrivals to Departures in the Train Unit Shunting Problem*. Master's thesis, Erasmus University Rotterdam. [15]

Fox, N., Kagan, J., and Weiskopf, S. (1979). The growth of memory during infancy. *Genetic Psychology Monographs*, **99**, 91–130. [2]

Fox, P. D., and Kriebel, C. H. (1967). An empirical study of scheduling decision behavior. *The Journal of Industrial Engineering*, **18**(6), 354–360. [6, 7]

France, R., and Rumpe, B. (2005). Domain specific modeling. *Software & Systems Modeling*, **4**, 1–3. [7]

Franz, V. H. (2001). Action does not resist visual illusions. *Trends in Cognitive Sciences*, **5**, 457–459. [2]

Freling, R. (1997). *Models and Techniques for Integrating Vehicle and Crew Scheduling*. Ph.D. thesis, Erasmus University Rotterdam. [15]

Freling, R., Lentink, R. M., Kroon, L. G., and Huisman, D. (2002). *Shunting of Passenger Train Units in a Railway Station*. Econometric Institute Report Erasmus University Rotterdam no. EI2002-26. [17]

Freling, R., Lentink, R. M., Kroon, L. G., and Huisman, D. (2005). Shunting of passenger train units in a railway station (accepted for publication in *Transportation Science*). **39**(2), 261–272. [15]

Fudenberg, D., and Levine, D. K. (1999). *The Theory of Learning in Games*. Cambridge, MA: The MIT Press. [10]

Fukunaga, A., Rabideau, G., Chien, S., and Yan, D. (1997). Towards an Application Framework for Automated Planning and Scheduling. In *Proceedings of IEEE Aerospace Conference*, Snowmass, CO, 1997. [7]

Furobotn, E. G., and Pejovich, S. (1972). Property rights and economic theory: A survey of recent literature. *Journal of Economic Literature*, **10**(December), 1137–1162. [5]

Fuster, J. M. (1989). *The Prefrontal Cortex*. New York: Raven Press. [2]

Gaba, D. M. (1994). Human error in dynamic medical domains. In M. S. Bogner (ed.), *Human Error in Medicine*, pp. 197–224. Hillsdale, NJ: Lawrence Erlbaum Associates. [3]

Gabrel, V., and Vanderpooten, D. (2002). Enumeration and interactive selection of efficient paths in a multiple criteria graph for scheduling an earth observing satellite. *European Journal of Operational Research*, **139**(3), pp. 533–542. [7]

Gallese, V., Fadiga, L., Fogassi, L., and Rizzolatti, G. (1996). Action recognition in the premotor cortex. *Brain*, **119**, 593–609. [2]

Gallo, G., and Di Miele, F. (2001). Dispatching buses in parking depots. *Transportation Science*, **35**(3), 322–330. [15]

Garey, M. R., and Johnson, D. S. (1979). *Computers & Intractability, a Guide to the Theory of NP-Completeness*. Bell Telephone Laboratories: W. H. Freeman. [8, 15, 16]

Gazendam, H. W. M. (1993). *Variety Controls Variety: On the Use of Organizational Theories in Information Management*. Groningen: Wolters-Noordhoff. [1, 5]

Gazendam, H. W. M. (1997). *Voorbij de dwang van de techniek: Naar een pluriforme bestuurlijke informatiekunde*. Rede uitgesproken bij de aanvaarding van het ambt van hoogleraar Bestuurlijke Informatiekunde voor de Publieke Sector, in het bijzonder Financiële Informatiesystemen, 16 Oktober 1997. Enschede: Universiteit Twente, 44 pp. [5]

Gazendam, H. W. M. (1998). The concept of equilibrium in organization theory. *The Journal of Management and Economics*, **2**(2), *November 1998*, 16 pp. Buenos Aires, Argentina: University of Buenos Aires, http://www.econ.uba.ar/www/servicios/publicaciones/[5]

Gazendam, H. W. M., and Homburg, V. M. F. (1996). Emergence of multi-actor systems: Aspects of coordination, legitimacy and information management. In *Proceedings of the COST A3 Conference 'Management and New Technologies', Madrid, June 12–14, 1996*, pp. 323–327. Luxembourg: Office for Official Publications of the European Communities. [5]

Gazendam, H. W. M., and Homburg, V. M. F. (1999). Efficiëntie en verzelfstandiging: Economische en politieke efficiëntie als verklaring voor verzelfstandigingen. *Bestuurskunde*, **8**(1), 19–27. [5]

Gazendam, H. W. M., and Jorna, R. J. (1998). *Theories about Architecture and Performance of Multi-agent Systems.* University of Groningen: SOM Research Report 98 A02. [18]

Gazendam, H. W. M., and Simons, J. L. (1999). How to preserve the richness of interpretation frames and reasoning mechanisms in formalizing organization theory? In *Computational and Mathematical Organization Theory Workshop, Cincinnati, OH, May 1st and 2nd, 1999*, pp. 45–47. [5]

Gazendam, H. W. M., Jorna, R. J., and Cijsouw, R. S. (2003). Introduction. In H. W. M. Gazendam, R. J. Jorna, and R. S. Cijsouw (eds.), *Dynamics and Change in Organizations: Studies in Organizational Semiotics*, pp. 1–11. Dordrecht: Kluwer Academic Publishers. [5]

Georgeff, M. P. (1983). Communication and interaction in multiagent planning. In *Proceedings of the 3rd National Conference on Artificial Intelligence (AAAI'83)*, pp. 125–129. [10]

Georgopoulos, A. P. (1990). Neurophysiology of reaching. In M. Jeannerod (ed.), *Attention and Performance XIII: Motor Representation and Control*, pp. 227–263. Hillsdale, NJ: Lawrence Erlbaum Associates. [2]

Gerstadt, C.L., Hong, Y.J., and Diamond, A. (1994). The relationship between cognition and action: Performance of children $3\frac{1}{2}$–7 years old on a Stroop-like day–night test. *Cognition*, **53**, 129–153. [2]

Gibson, J. J. (1986). *The Ecological Approach to Visual Perception* (originally published 1979). Hillsdale, NJ: Lawrence Erlbaum Associates. [3]

Giddens, A. (1984). *The Constitution of Society.* Berkeley, CA: University of California Press. [5]

Gigerenzer, G., and Goldstein, D. G. (1996). Reasoning the fast and frugal way: Models of bounded rationality. *Psychological Review*, **103**, 650–669. [2]

Glover, F., and Laguna, M., (1997). *Tabu Search.* Kluwer Academic Publishers. [8]

Godin, V. B. (1978). Interactive scheduling: Historical survey and state of the art. *AIIE Transactions*, **10**(3), 331–337. [7]

Goldstein, D. G., and Gigerenzer, G. (1999). The recognition heuristic: How ignorance makes us smart. In G. Gigerenzer, P. M. Todd, and the ABC Research Group. *Simple Heuristics that Make Us Smart*, pp. 37–58. New York: Oxford University Press. [2]

Gomory, R. E. (1958). Outline of an algorithm for integer solutions to linear programs. *Bulletin of the American Mathematical Society*, **64**, 275–278. [8]

Gondran, M., and Minoux, M. (1984). *Graphs and Algorithms.* New York: John Wiley & Sons. [8]

Goodale, M. A., Pélisson, D., and Prablanc, C. (1986). Large adjustments in visually guided reaching do not depend on vision of the hand or perception of target displacement. *Nature*, **320**, 748–750. [2]

Goodale, M. A., Milner, A. D., Jakobson, L. S., and Carey, D. P. (1991). A neurological dissociation between perceiving objects and grasping them. *Nature*, **349**, 154–156. [2]

Goodman, N. (1968). *Languages of Arts.* Brighton, Sussex: The Harvester Press. [1]

Goschke, T., and Kuhl, J. (1993). The representation of intentions: Persisting activation in memory. *Journal of Experimental Psychology: Learning, Memory, and Cognition*, **19**, 1211–1226. [2]

Goten, K. van der, Lammertyn, J., Caessens, B., Vooght, G. de, and Hommel, B. (submitted). The functional basis of backward-compatibility effects: Selecting emotional actions primes the perception of emotional words. [2]

Grafton, S. T., Arbib, M.A., Fadiga, L., and Rizzolatti, G. (1996). Localization of grasp representations in humans by positrone emission tomography. 2. Observation compared with imagination. *Experimental Brain Research*, **112**, 103–111. [2]

Graves, S. C. (1981). A review of production scheduling. *Operations Research*, **29**(4), 646–675. [6]

Green, J. (1996). Manufacturers meet global market demands with FCS software. *IIE Solutions*, **28**(8), pp. 26–31. [7]

Greenwald, A. (1970). Sensory feedback mechanisms in performance control: With special reference to the ideomotor mechanism. *Psychological Review*, **77**, 73–99. [2]

Gregory, R. L. (Ed.) (1987). *The Oxford Companion to The Mind*. Oxford: Oxford University Press. [4]

Gretch, G., and Landers, W. F. (1971). Stage IV of Piaget's theory of infant's object concepts: A longitudinal study. *Child Development*, **42**, 359–372. [2]

Haddawy, P., and Suwandi, M. (1994). Decision-theoretic refinement planning using inheritance abstraction. In *Proceedings of the 2nd International Conference on Artificial Intelligence Planning Systems (AIPS-92)*. [10]

Hägerstrand, T. (1975). Space, time, and human conditions. In A. Karlqvist (ed.), *Dynamic Allocation in Urban Space*. Farnborough: Saxon House. [5]

Hall, P. G. (1992). *Urban & Regional Planning*, 3rd edition. London: Routledge. [18]

Halsall, D. N., Muhlemann, A. P., and Price, D. H. R. (1994). A review of production planning and scheduling in smaller manufacturing companies in the UK. *Production Planning and Control*, **5**(5), pp. 485–493. [7]

Hammond, K. J. (1989). Chef. In C. K. Riesbeck, and R. C. Schank (eds.), *Inside Case-Based Reasoning*, Chapter 6. Hillsdale, NJ: Lawrence Erlbaum Associates. [18]

Hari, R., and Salenius, S. (1999). Rhythmical corticomotor communication. *Neuroreport*, **10**, R1–R10. [2]

Harless, E. (1861). Der Apparat des Willens. *Zeitschrift fuer Philosophie und philosophische Kritik*, **38**, 50–73. [2]

Harlow, J. M. (1848). Passage of an iron rod through the head. *Boston Medical and Surgical Journal*, **39**, 389–393. [3]

Harlow J. M. (1868). Recovery from the passage of an iron bar through the head. *Publications of the Massachusetts Medical Society*, **2**, 327–347. [3]

Harnad, S. (1990). The symbol grounding problem. *Physica*, **D42**, 335–346. [2]

Hausman, C. R. (1993). *Charles S. Peirce's Evolutionary Philosophy*. Cambridge, England: Cambridge University Press. [5]

Hayena, R. (2001). *Onderzoek Rangeren Intelligent, fase 2*. Master's thesis in Operations Research and Management, University of Amsterdam. [16]

Hayes-Roth, B., and Hayes-Roth, F. (1979). A cognitive model of planning. *Cognitive Science*, **3**, 275–310. [3, 4, 18]

He, S., Song, R., and Chaudhry, S. S. (2000). Fuzzy dispatching model and genetic algorithms for railyard operations. *European Journal of Operations Research*, **124**, 307–331. [15]

Henke, A. (1994). Scheduling space shuttle missions: Using object-oriented techniques. *AI Expert*, **March**, 16–24. [7]

Henseler, H. (1995). REAKTION: A system for event independent reactive scheduling, In R. M. Kerr and E. Szelke (eds.), *Artificial Intelligence in Reactive Scheduling*. London: Chapman & Hall. [9]

Hentenryck, P. van (1999). *The OPL Optimisation Programming Language*. Cambridge, MA: The MIT Press. [14]

Higgins, P.G. (1999). *Job Shop Scheduling: Hybrid Intelligent Human-Computer Paradigm*. Ph.D. thesis, University of Melbourne. [6]

Hillier, F. S., and Lieberman, G. J. (1995). *Introduction to Operations Research*. New York: McGraw-Hill. [8, 16]

Hoc, J. M. (1988). *Cognitive Psychology of Planning* (C. Greenbaum, translator). London: Academic Press. (Original edition published in 1987.) [3, 4, 5, 7]

Hoc, J. M. (1989). Strategies in controlling a continuous process with long response latencies: Needs for computer support to diagnosis. *International Journal of Man-Machine Studies*, **30**, 47–67. [3]

Hoc, J. M. (1991). Effets de l'expertise des opérateurs et de la complexité de la situation dans la conduite d'un processus continu à longs délais de réponse: Le haut fourneau [Effect of operator expertise and task complexity upon the supervision of a continuous process with long time lags: A blast furnace]. *Le Travail Humain*, **54**, 225–249. [3]

Hoc, J. M. (1996). Operator expertise and verbal reports of temporal data: Supervision of a long time lag process (blast furnace). *Ergonomics*, **39**, 811–825. [3]

Hoc, J. M. (2000). From human–machine interaction to human–machine cooperation. *Ergonomics*, **43**, 833–843. [3]

Hoc, J. M (2001). Towards a cognitive approach to human–machine cooperation in dynamic situations. *International Journal of Human–Computer Studies*, **54**, 509–540. [3]

Hoc, J. M., and Carlier, X. (2002). Role of a common frame of reference in cognitive cooperation: Sharing tasks between agents in air traffic control. *Cognition, Work, & Technology*, **4**, 37–47. [3]

Hoc, J. M., and Debernard, S. (2002). Respective demands of task and function allocation on human–machine co-operation design: A psychological approach. *Connection Science*, **14**, 283–295. [3]

Hoc, J. M., and Lemoine, M. P. (1998). Cognitive evaluation of human–human and human–machine cooperation modes in air traffic control. *International Journal of Aviation Psychology*, **8**, 1–32. [3]

Hoc, J. M., and Samurçay, R. (1992). An ergonomic approach to knowledge representation. *Reliability Engineering and System Safety*, **36**, 217–230. [3]

Hoc, J. M., Amalberti, R., and Boreham, N. (1995). Human operator expertise in diagnosis, decision-making, and time management. In J. M. Hoc, P. C. Cacciabue, and E. Hollnagel (eds.), *Expertise and Technology: Cognition & Human–Computer Cooperation*, pp. 19–42. Hillsdale, NJ: Lawrence Erlbaum Associates. [3]

Hoc, J. M., Amalberti, R., and Plee, G. (2000). Vitesse du processus et temps partagé: Planification et concurrence attentionnelle [Process speed and time sharing: planning and attentional concurrence]. *L'Année Psychologique*, **100**, 629–660. [3]

Hoekert, W. (2001). *Het maken van diensten voor rangeerpersoneel* (in Dutch). Master's thesis, Erasmus University Rotterdam. [15]

Hofstede G. J. (1992). *Modesty in Modeling: On the Applicability of Interactive Planning Systems, with a Case Study in Pot Plant Cultivation*. Wageningen, the Netherlands: University of Wageningen. [7]

Holland, J. H. (1995). *Hidden Order: How Adaptation Builds Complexity*. Reading, MA: Addison-Wesley. [5]

Holland, J. H. (1998). *Emergence: From Chaos to Order*. Oxford: Oxford University Press. [5]

Homburg, V. M. F. (1999). The political economy of information management: A theoretical and empirical analysis of decision making regarding interorganizational information systems. Capelle a/d IJssel: Labyrinth. [5]

Hommel, B. (1993). Inverting the Simon effect by intention: Determinants of direction and extent of effects of irrelevant spatial information. *Psychological Research*, **55**, 270–279. [2]

Hommel, B. (1996). The cognitive representation of action: Automatic integration of perceived action effects. *Psychological Research*, **59**, 176–186. [2]

Hommel, B. (1997). Toward an action-concept model of stimulus–response compatibility. In B. Hommel and W. Prinz (eds.), *Theoretical Issues in Stimulus–Response Compatibility*, pp. 281–320. Amsterdam: Elsevier. [2]

Hommel, B. (1998a). Perceiving one's own action—and what it leads to. In J. S. Jordan (ed.), *Systems Theory and Apriori Aspects of Perception*, pp. 143–179. Amsterdam: North-Holland. [2]

Hommel, B. (1998b). Automatic stimulus–response translation in dual-task performance. *Journal of Experimental Psychology: Human Perception and Performance*, **24**, 1368–1384. [2]

Hommel, B. (2000). The prepared reflex: Automaticity and control in stimulus–response translation. In S. Monsell and J. Driver (eds.), *Control of Cognitive Processes: Attention and Performance* XVIII, pp. 247–273. Cambridge, MA: MIT Press. [2]

Hommel, B., and Eglau, B. (2002). Control of stimulus–response translation in dual-task performance. *Psychological Research*, **66**, 260–273. [2]

Hommel, B., Müsseler, J., Aschersleben, G., and Prinz, W. (2001a). The theory of event coding (TEC): A framework for perception and action planning. *Behavioral and Brain Sciences*, **24**, 849–878. [2]

Hommel, B., Müsseler, J., Aschersleben, G., and Prinz, W. (2001b). Codes and their vicissitudes. *Behavioral and Brain Sciences*, **24**, 910–937. [2]

Hommel, B., Ridderinkhof, K. R., and Theeuwes, J. (2002). (eds.). Cognitive control of attention and action. Special issue of *Psychological Research*, **66**, 4. [2]

Hsu, W. L., Prietula, M., Thompson, G., and Ow, P. S. (1993). A mixed-initiative scheduling workbench: Integrating AI, OR, and HCI. *Journal of Decision Support Systems*, **9**(3), 245–247. [9]

Hukki, K., and Norros, L. (1998). Subject-centred and systemic conceptualisation as a tool of simulator training. *Le Travail Humain*, **61**, 313–331. [3]

Hurst, E. G., and McNamara, A. B. (1967). Heuristic scheduling in a woolen mill. *Management Science*, **14**(4), 182–203. [6, 7]

Huttenlocher, P. R. (1990). Morphometric study of human cerebral cortex development. *Neuropsychologia*, **28**, 517–527. [2]

ILOG. www.ilog.com. [14]

Jackson, S. R. (2000). Perception, awareness and action. In Y. Rossetti and A. Revonsuo (eds.), *Interaction Between Dissociable Conscious and Nonconscious Processes*, pp. 73–98. Amsterdam: John Benjamins Publishing Company. [2]

Jakeman, C. M. (1994). Scheduling needs of the food processing industry. *Food Research International*, **27**, p. 117–120. [7]

James, W. (1890). *The Principles of Psychology*. New York: Dover Publications. [2]

Javaux, D., Grosjean, V., and Van Daele, A. (1991). Temporal reference systems: A particularly heuristic extension to the classical notion of time. Paper presented at the *4th Workshop of the ESPRIT MOHAWC Project*. Bamberg, October. [3]

Jeannerod, M. (1997). *The Cognitive Neuroscience of Action*. Oxford: Blackwell Publishers. [2]

Jeannerod, M. (1984). The contribution of open-loop and closed-loop control modes in prehension movements. In S. Kornblum and J. Requin (eds.), *Preparatory States and Processes*, pp. 323–337. Hillsdale, NJ: Lawrence Erlbaum Associates. [2]

Jennings, N. R. (1995). Controlling cooperative problem solving in industrial multi-agent systems using joint intentions. *Artificial Intelligence*, **75**(2), 195–240. [10]

Jennings, N. R., Sycara, K., and Woolridge, M. (1998). A roadmap of agent research and development. *Autonomous Agents and Multi-Agent Systems*, **1**, 7–38. [9]

Jensen, M. C. (1983). Organization theory and methodology. *Accounting Review*, **58**(2), 319–339. [5]

Jensen, M. C., and Meckling, W. H. (1976). Theory of the firm: Managerial behavior, agency costs and ownership structure. *Journal of Financial Economics*, **3**(4), 305–360. [5]

Jensen, R. M. (2003). The BDD-based InFoRmed planning and Controller Synthesis Tool (BIFROST) version 0.7. http://www.cs.cmu.edu/~runej. [10]

Jensen, R. M., Veloso, M. M., and Bryant, R. E. (2003). Guided symbolic universal planning. In *Proceedings of the 13th International Conference on Automated Planning and Scheduling ICAPS-03*, pp. 123–132. [10]

Jentsch, F., Barnett, J., Bowers, C., and Salas, E. (1999). Who is flying this plane anyway? What mishaps tell us about crew member role assignment and air crew situation awareness. *Human Factors*, **41**, 1–14. [3]

Johnson, M. H. (1999). Developmental neuroscience. In M. H. Bornstein and M. E. Lamb (eds.), *Developmental Psychology*, pp. 199–230. Mahwah, NJ: Lawrence Erlbaum Associates. [2]

Johnson, S. M. (1954). Optimal two- and three stage production schedules with setup times included. *Naval Research Logistics Quarterly*, **1**, 61–68. [8]

Jolicœur, P., Tombu, M., Oriet, C., and Stevanovski, B. (2002). From perception to action: Making the connection. In W. Prinz and B. Hommel (eds.), *Common Mechanisms in Perception and Action: Attention and Performance* XIX, pp. 558–586. Oxford: Oxford University Press. [2]

Jong, G. F. de (1994). Learning to plan in continuous domains. *Artificial Intelligence*, **65**, 71–141. [3]

Jong, R. de (2000). An intention–activation account of residual switch costs. In S. Monsell and J. Driver (eds.), *Control of Cognitive Processes: Attention and Performance XVIII*, pp. 357–376. Cambridge, MA: MIT Press. [2]

Jong, R. de, Liang, C.-C., and Lauber, E. (1994). Conditional and unconditional automaticity: A dual-process model of effects of spatial stimulus–response correspondence. *Journal of Experimental Psychology: Human Perception and Performance*, **20**, 731–750. [2]

Jorna, R. J. (1990). *Knowledge Representation and Symbols in the Mind*. Tübingen: Stauffenburg Verlag. [1, 4]

Jorna, R. J. (1994). Roosteren met kennis: verpleegdienstroostering in nieuw perspectief. *Tijdschrift voor Medische Informatica*, **94**, 3. (Scheduling with knowledge: Nurse scheduling in a new perspective). [4]

Jorna, R. J., and Heusden, B. van (1998). Semiotics and information-psychology: A case for semio-psychology. *Theory & Psychology*, **8**(3), pp. 755–782. [1]

Jorna, R. J., and Simons, J. L. (Red.) (1992). *Kennis in Organisaties, Toepassingen en Theorie van Kennissystemen*. Muiderberg: Coutinho (Knowledge in Organizations: Applications and Theory of Knowledge Systems). [4]

Jorna, R. J., and Wezel, W. van (1997). Objects and the world metaphor: A semiotic engineering approach. In Nöth, W. (ed.), *Semiotics of the Media*. New York: Springer-Verlag. [7]

Jorna R. J., and Wezel W. van (2002). Planning, anticipatory systems, and kinds of actors. In D. M. Dubois (ed.), *Computing Anticipatory Systems*, Casys 2001. Melville NY: American Institute of Physics Conference Proceedings, Vol. 627, pp. 411–423. [3, 7, 13, 18]

Jorna, R. J., Gazendam, H., Heesen, H. C., and Wezel W. van (1996). *Plannen en Roosteren: Taakgericht analyseren, ontwerpen en ondersteunen* (Planning and Scheduling: Task Oriented Analysis, Design and Support). Lansa: Leidschendam. [4, 5, 7, 18]

Judea Pearl, J. (1984). *Heuristics: intelligent search strategies for computer problem solving*. Boston: Addison-Wesley. [15]

Kalaska, J. F., and Hyde, M. L. (1985). Area 4 and area 5: Differences between the load direction-dependent discharge variability of cells during active postural fixation. *Experimental Brain Research*, **59**, 197–202. [2]

Kalnins, I. V., and Bruner, J. S. (1973). The coordination of visual observation and instrumental behavior in early infancy. *Perception*, **2**, 307–314. [2]

Kant, I. (1965). *Critique of Pure Reason* [originally published in German, 4th edition, 1794]. New York: St. Martins Press. [11]

Karsenty, L. (2000). Cooperative work: The role of explanation in creating a shared problem representation. *Le Travail Humain*, **63**, 289–309. [3]

Kaufmann, S. (1996). The World of Autonomous Agents and the Worlds They Mutually Create. *Lectures*. (http://www.santafe.edu/sfi/People/kauffman/Investigations.html). [11]

Keeney, R. K., and Raiffa, H. (1976). *Decisions with Multiple Objectives: Preferences and Value Trade-offs*. New York: John Wiley & Sons. [8]

Kempf, K. G. (1989). Manufacturing Planning and Scheduling: Where we are and where we need to be. *5th Conference on Artificial Intelligence Applications*, CAIA, Miami, FL. [9]

Kempf, K. G., Le Pape, C., Smith, S. F., and Fox, B. R. (1991). Issues in the Design of AI-Based Schedulers: A Workshop Report. *AI Magazine*. [9]

Kerr, R. M., and Szelke, E. (1995). *Artificial Intelligence in Reactive Scheduling*. London: Chapman & Hall. [9]

Kiewiet, D. J., and Jorna, R. J. (2005). Reasoning and inferences in the planning task: An empirical study in the NS. (in progress, to be submitted for publication). International Report, R.U. Groningen, not published. [13]

Kiewiet D. J., Jorna, R. J., and Wezel, W. van (2005). Planners are more different than we think: An analysis of domain representations using Multi Dimensional Scaling. Accepted for publication in *Applied Ergonomics*, **36**(6), 695–700. [13, 18]

Klein, G. A., Orasanu, J., Calderwood, R., and Zsambok, C. E. (1993). *Decision-Making in Action: Models and Methods.* Norwood, NJ: Ablex. [3]

Klein, M., and Methlie, L. B. (1990). *Expert Systems, a Decision Support Approach.* Reading, MA: Addison-Wesley. [4]

Klemola, U. M., and Norros, L. (1997). Analysis of the clinical behaviour of anaesthetists: Recognition of uncertainty as a basis for practice. *Medical Education*, **31**, 449–456. [3]

Klir, G. J. (1991). *Facets of Systems Science.* New York: Plenum Press. [1]

Klos, T. B. (2000). *Agent-Based Computational Transaction Cost Economics.* Capelle a/d IJssel, the Netherlands: Labyrinth. [5]

Kolmogorov, A. N. (1956). On Some Asymptotic Characteristics of Bounded Metric Spaces. *Proceedings of Academy of Sciences*, Vol. 108, No. 3 (Doklady Akademii Nauk, in Russian). [11]

Kondili, E., Pantelllides, C. C., and Sargent, R. W. (1993). A general algorithm for short-term scheduling of batch operations—I. MILP formulation. *Computers Chem. Eng*, **17**(2), pp. 211–227. [7]

Kornblum, S., Hasbroucq, T., and Osman, A. (1990). Dimensional overlap: Cognitive basis for stimulus–response compatibility—a model and taxonomy. *Psychological Review*, **97**, 253–270. [2]

Koubek, R. J., and Clarkston, T. P. (1994). The training of knowledge structures for manufacturing tasks: An empirical study. *Ergonomics*, **37**(4), 765–780. [7]

Kray, J., and Lindenberger, U. (2000). Adult age differences in task switching. *Psychology & Aging*, **15**, 126–147. [2]

Kreifelts, T., and Martial, F. (1990). A negotiation framework for autonomous agents. In *Proceedings of the 2nd European Workshop on Modeling Autonomous Agents and Multi-Agent Worlds*, pp. 169–182. [10]

Kumar, V. (1992). Algorithms for constraint-satisfaction problems: A survey. *AI Magazine*, **13**, 1. [9]

Kunde, W. (2001). Response–effect compatibility in manual choice reaction tasks. *Journal of Experimental Psychology: Human Perception and Performance*, **27**, 387–394. [2]

Kuo, W.-H. and Hwang, S.-L. (1999). The development of a human–computer interactive scheduling system. *International Journal of Computer Integrated Manufacturing*, **12**(2), pp. 156–167. [7]

Kushmerick, N., Hanks, S., and Weld, D. (1995). An algorithm for probabilistic planning. *Artificial Intelligence*, **76**, 239–286. [10]

Kutas, M., and Donchin, E. (1980). Preparation to respond as manifested by movement-related brain potentials. *Brain Research*, **202**, 95–115. [2]

Laird, J. E., Rosenbloom, P. S., and Newell, A. (1986). *Universal Subgoaling and Chunking: The Automatic Generation and Learning of Goal Hierarchies.* Boston: Kluwer. [5]

Larkin, J. H., and Reif, F. (1979). Understanding and teaching problem solving in physics. *European Journal of Science Education*, **1**, 191–203. [3]

Lauer J., Jacobs, L. W., Brusco, M. J., and Bechtold, S. E. (1994). An interactive, optimization-based decision support system for scheduling part-time, computer lab attendants. *Omega: The International Journal of Management Science*, **22**(6), 613–626. [7]

Lawler, E. L., Lenstra, J. K., Rinnooy Kan, A. H. G., and Shmoys, D. B. (eds.) (1985). *The Traveling Salesman Problem*. New York: John Wiley & Sons. [8]

Layton, C., Smith, P. J., and McCoy, E. (1994). Design of a cooperative problem-solving system for en-route flight planning: An empirical evaluation. *Human Factors*, **36**, 94–119. [3]

Lemmermann, D. (1995). *Globaler Leitstand*. Diploma thesis, Universität Oldenburg, Fachbereich Informatik. [9]

Lewin, K. (1926). Vorsatz, Wille und Bedürfnis. *Psychologische Forschung*, **7**, 330–385. [2]

Lhermitte, F. (1983). "Utilization behaviour" and its relation to lesions of the frontal lobes. *Brain*, **106**, 237–255. [2]

Lin, S., and Kernighan, B.W. (1973). An effective heuristic algorithm for the traveling salesman problem. *Operations Research*, **21**, 498–516. [8]

Lindblom, C. E. (1965). *The Intelligence of Democracy: Decision Making Through Mutual Adjustment*. New York: The Free Press. [5]

Lindblom, C. E. (1973). The science of muddling through. In A. Faludi (ed.), *A Reader in Planning Theory*, pp. 151–169. Oxford: Pergamon Press. (Original work published in *Public Administration Review*, Spring 1959.) [5]

Lingaya, N., Cordeau, J. F., Desaulniers, G., Desrosiers, J., and Soumis, F. (2002). Operational car assignment at VIA Rail Canada. *Transportation Research B*, **36**, 755–778. [8]

Littman, M. L. (1994). Markov games as a framework for multi-agent reinforcement learning. In *Proceedings of the Eleventh International Conference on Machine Learning*, pp. 157–163. San Francisco: Morgan Kaufman. [10]

Liu, J. S. and Sycara, K. P. (1993). Distributed scheduling through cooperating specialists. In *Proceedings of the IJCAI-93 Workshop on Knowledge-Based Production Planning, Scheduling, and Control*, Chambery, France. [9]

Liu, K. (2000). *Semiotics in Information Systems Engineering*. Cambridge, England: Cambridge University Press. [5]

Livesey, D. J. and Morgan, G. A. (1991). The development of response inhibition in 4- and 5-year-old children. *Australian Journal of Psychology*, **43**, 133–137. [2]

Locke, John (1993). *An Essay Concerning Human Understanding*, John W. Yolton (ed.). London: J. M. Dent, Collection. Everyman Library, 451 pages. (Original work published 1690.) [5]

Logan, G. D., and Delheimer, J. A. (2001). Parallel memory retrieval in dual-task situations: II. Episodic memory. *Journal of Experimental Psychology: Learning, Memory, and Cognition*, **27**, 668–685. [2]

Logan, G. D., and Schulkind, M. D. (2000). Parallel memory retrieval in dual-task situations: I. Semantic memory. *Journal of Experimental Psychology: Human Perception and Performance*, **26**, 1072–1090. [2]

Lotze, R. H. (1852). *Medicinische Psychologie oder die Physiologie der Seele.* Leipzig: Weidmann'sche Buchhandlung. [2]

Løvborg, L., and Brehmer, B. (1991). *NEWFIRE A Flexible System for running Simulated Firefighting Experiments.* Report No. RISØ-M-2953. Roskilde, DK: RISØ National Laboratory. [3]

Lu, C.-H., and Proctor, R. W. (1995). The influence of irrelevant location information on performance: A review of the Simon and spatial Stroop effects. *Psychonomic Bulletin & Review*, **2**, 174–207. [2]

Lübbecke, M. E., and Desrosiers, J. (2002) *Selected Topics in Column Generation.* Technical Report G-2002-64, GERAD. [15]

Lübbecke, M. E., and Zimmermann, U. T. (2003). *Shunting Minimal Rail Car Allocation.* Technical Report, Braunschweig University of Technology. [15]

Luria, A. R. (1959). *The directive function of speech in development and dissolution.* Part 1: Development of the directive function of speech in early childhood. *Word*, **15**, 341–352. [2]

Luria, A. R. (1961). *The Role of Speech in the Regulation of Normal and Abnormal Behavior.* New York: Pergamon Press. [2]

Luria, A. R. (1966). *Higher Cortical Functions in Man.* New York: Basic Books. [2]

MacCarthy, B. L., and Liu, J. (1993). Addressing the gap in scheduling research: a review of optimization and heuristic methods in production scheduling. *International Journal of Production Research*, **31**, 59–79. [6]

MacCarthy, B. L., and Wilson, J. R. (eds.). (2001). *Human Performance in Planning and Scheduling.* London: Taylor & Francis. [3]

MacKay, D. (1997). Synchronized neuronal oscillations and their role in motor processes. *Trends in Cognitive Sciences*, **1**, 176–183. [2]

Malsburg, C. von der (1981). *The Correlation Theory of Brain Function* Internal Report. Göttingen: Max-Planck Institute for Biophysical Chemistry. [2]

Mandelbrot, B. (1982). *The Fractal Geometry of Nature.* New York: Freeman. [11]

Marbe, K. (1901). *Experimentell psychologische Untersuchungen über das Urteil.* Leipzig: Engelmann. [2]

Markus, L., and Tanis, C. (2000). The enterprise systems experience—From adoption to success. In R. W. Zmud and M. F. Price (eds.), *Framing the Domains of IT Management: Projecting the Future Through the Past.* Cincinnati: Pinnaflex Educational Resources, Inc., pp. 173–207. [6]

Marsh, R. L., Hicks, J. L., and Bryan, E. S. (1999). The activation of unrelated and canceled intentions. *Memory & Cognition*, **27**, 320–327. [2]

Märtens, H., and Sauer, J. (1998). Ein Ablaufplanungssystem auf Basis neuronaler Netze, In J. Biethahn, A. Höhnerloh, J. Kuhl, M.-C. Leisewitz, V. Nissen, and M. Tietze (eds.), *Betriebswirtschaftliche Anwendungen des Softcomputing.* Wiesbaden: Vieweg. [9]

Maximov, Y., and Meystel, A. (1993). Optimum Architectures for Multiresolutional Control, *Proceedings, IEEE Conference on Aerospace Systems*, May 25–27, Westlake Village, CA. [11]

Maylor, E. A. (1996). Does prospective memory decline with age? In M. Brandimonte, G. O. Einstein, and M. A. McDaniel (eds.), *Prospective Memory: Theory and Applications*, pp. 173–197. Mahwah, NJ: Lawrence Erlbaum Associates. [2]

McCann, R. S., and Johnston, J. C. (1992). Locus of the single-channel bottleneck in dual-task interference. *Journal of Experimental Psychology: Human Perception and Performance*, **18**, 471–484. [2]

McCarthy, J. (1987). Generality in artificial intelligence. *Communications of the ACM*, **30**(1), 1030–1035. [11]

McDougall, W. (1908/1923). *An Introduction to Social Psychology*. Methuen & Co. London. [2]

McKay, K. N. (1987). *Conceptual Framework for Job Shop Scheduling*. MASc Dissertation, University of Waterloo. [6]

McKay, K. N. (1992). *Production Planning and Scheduling: A Model for Manufacturing Decisions Requiring Judgement*. Ph.D. thesis, University of Waterloo. [6]

McKay, K. N., and Buzacott, J. A. (2000). The application of computerized production control systems in job shop environments. *Computers in Industry*, **42**, 79–97. [7]

McKay, K., Pinedo, M., and Webster, S. (2002). Practice-focused research issues for scheduling systems. *Production and Operations Management*, **11**(2), pp. 249–258. [7]

McKay, K. N., Safayeni, F. R., and Buzacott, J. A. (1988). Job-shop scheduling theory: What is relevant? *Interfaces*, **18**(4), 84–90. [17]

McKay, K. N., Safayeni, F. R., and Buzacott, J. A. (1989). The scheduler's knowledge of uncertainty: The missing link. In J. Browne (ed.), *Knowledge Based Production Management Systems*. North-Holland: Elsevier Science Publishers. [17]

McKay, K. N., Safayeni, F. R., and Buzacott, J. A. (1995a). "Common sense" realities of planning and scheduling in printed circuit board production. *International Journal of Production Research*, **33**(6), 1587–1603. [6, 18]

McKay, K. N., Safayeni, F., and Buzacott, J. A. (1995b). A review of hierarchical production planning and its applicability for modern manufacturing. *Production Planning & Control*, 6(5), 384–394. [6]

McKay, K. N., Safayeni, F. R., and Buzacott, J. A. (1995c). Schedulers & planners: What and how can we learn from them. In D. E. Brown and W. T. Scherer (eds.), *Intelligent Scheduling Systems*. Boston: Kluwer Academic Publishers. [7]

McKay K. N., and Wiers, V. C. S. (1999). Unifying the theory and practice of production scheduling. *Journal of Manufacturing Systems*, **18**(4), 241–255. [6]

McKay, K. N., and Wiers, V. C. S. (2003a). Integrated decision support for planning, scheduling, and dispatching tasks in a focused factory. *Computers in Industry*, **50**(1), 5–14. [6]

McKay, K. N., and Wiers, V. C. S. (2003b). Planners, schedulers and dispatchers: A description of cognitive tasks in production control. *International Journal on Cognition, Technology and Work*, **5**(2), 82–93. [6]

McKay, K. N., and Wiers, V. C. S. (2004). *Production Control in Practice: A Survival Guide for Planners and Schedulers*. J. Ross Publishers. Fort Landerdale (FL). [6]

Messina, E., and Meystel, A. (2000). The challenge of intelligent systems. In P. Groumpos, N. Koussoulas, and M. Polycarpou (eds.), *Proceedings of the 2000 IEEE International Symposium on Intelligent Control*. Patras, Greece, July 17–19, pp. 211–216. [11]

Meyer, D. E., and Gordon, P. C. (1985). Speech production: Motor programming of phonetic features. *Journal of Memory and Language*, **24**, 3–26. [2]

Meyer, D. E., and Kieras, E. D. (1997). A computational theory of executive cognitive processes and multiple task performance: Part 1, Basic mechanisms. *Psychological Review*, **104**, 3–75. [2]

Meystel, A. (1985). Baby-robot: On the analysis of cognitive controllers for robotics. *Proceedings of the IEEE International Conference on Man & Cybernetics*, Tuscon, AZ, November 11–15, 1985, pp. 327–222. [11]

Meystel, A. (1987). Theoretical foundations of planning and navigation for autonomous robots. *International Journal of Intelligent Systems* 2, 73–128. [11, 18]

Meystel, A. (1995a). Architectures, representations and algorithms for intelligent control of robots. In M. Gupta and N. Singha (eds.), *Intelligent Control Systems*, Chapter 27, pp. 732–788. NJ: IEEE Press. [11, 18]

Meystel, A. (1995b). Multiresolutional architectures for autonomous systems with incomplete and inadequate knowledge representation. In S. G. Tzafestas and H. B. Verbruggen (eds.), *Artificial Intelligence in Industrial Decision Making, Control, and Automation*, pp. 159–223. New York: Kluwer Academic Press. [11]

Meystel, A. (1995c). *Semiotic Modeling and Situation Analysis: An Introduction.* Drexel University: Publication AdRem. [5,11]

Meystel, A. (1996). Intelligent systems: A semiotic perspective, *International Journal of Intelligent Control and Systems*, 1(1), 31–58. [11]

Meystel, A. (1997). Learning algorithms generating multigranular hierarchies. In B. Mirkin, F. R. McMorris, F. S. Roberts, and A. Rzhetsky (eds.), *Mathematical Hierarchies and Biology*, DIMACS Series in Discrete Mathematics, Vol. 37, American Mathematical Society, pp. 357–384. [11]

Meystel, A. (1998). Multiresolutional autonomy. *Proceedings of the Joint Conference on the Science and Technology of Intelligent Systems ISIC/CIRA/ISAS/'98*, pp. 516–519. Piscataway, NJ: IEEE. [5]

Meystel, A. (2000). Evolution of intelligent systems architectures: What should be measured? In A. Meystel and E. Messina (eds.), *Measuring the Performance and Intelligence of Systems*, Proceedings of the PERMIS'2000, August 14–16, 2000, Gaithersburg, pp. 361–382. [11]

Meystel, A. M., and Albus, J. S. (2001). *Intelligent Systems. Architecture, Design, and Control.* New York: John Wiley & Sons. [1,11,18]

Meystel, A., and Mironov, A. (1998). Quasi-commutative diagrams of multiresolutional systems for representation and control. *Proceedings of the Joint Conference on the Science and Technology of Intelligent Systems ISIC/CIRA/ISAS/'98*, pp. 72–77. Piscataway, NJ: IEEE. [5]

Michon, J. A. (1990). Implicit and explicit representations of time. In R. A. Block (ed.), *Cognitive Models of Psychological Time*, pp. 37–58. Hillsdale, NJ: Lawrence Erlbaum Associates. [3]

Mietus, D. M. (1994). *Understanding Planning for Effective Decision Support.* Groningen: Ph.D. thesis, University of Groningen. [4, 7, 13, 17, 18]

Miller, G. A., Galanter, E., and Pribram, K. J. (1960). *Plans and the Structure of Behavior.* New York: Holt, Rinehart and Winston. [2, 4]

Milner, A. D., and Goodale, M. A. (1995). *The Visual Brain in Action.* Oxford: Oxford University Press. [2]

Mintzberg. H. (1994). *The Rise and Fall of Strategic Planning.* Englewood Cliffs, NJ: Prentice-Hall. [4]

Mischel, H. N., and Mischel, W. (1983). The development of children's knowledge of self-control strategies. *Child Development*, **54**, 603–619. [2]

Monsell, S., and Driver, J. (eds.) (2000). *Control of Cognitive Processes. Attention and Performance XVIII.* Cambridge, MA: MIT Press. [2]

Moray, N., and Rotenberg, I. (1989). Fault management in process control: Eye movement and action. *Ergonomics*, **32**, 1319–1342. [3]

Moray, N., Dessouky, M. I., Kijowski, B. A., and Adapathya, R. (1991). Strategic behavior, workload and performance in task scheduling. *Human Factors*, **33**(6), 607–629. [7]

Morineau, T., Hoc, J. M., and Denecker, P. (2003). Cognitive control levels in air traffic radar controller activity. *International Journal of Aviation Psychology*, **13**, 107–130. [3]

Morrisons and the Office of Charles and Ray Eaems (1982). *Powers of Ten.* New York: Scientific American Library. [11]

Morton, T. E., and Pentico, D. W. (1993). *Heuristic Scheduling Systems; with Applications to Production Systems and Project Management.* New York: John Wiley & Sons. [17]

Münsterberg, H. (1889). *Beiträge zur experimentellen Psychologie*, Heft 1. Freiburg: Mohr. [2]

Murphey, M. G. (1967). Charles Sanders Peirce. In P. Edwards (ed.), *The Encyclopedia of Philosophy*, Vol. 6, pp. 70–78. New York: Macmillan/The Free Press. [5]

Murthy, V. N., and Fetz, E. E. (1992). Coherent 25- to 35-Hz oscillations in the sensorimotor cortex of awake behaving monkeys. *Proceedings of the National Academy of Sciences of the United States of America*, **89**, 5670–5674. [2]

Murthy, V. N., and Fetz, E. E. (1996). Oscillatory activity in sensorimotor cortex of awake monkeys: Synchronization of local field potentials and relation to behavior. *Journal of Neurophysiology*, **76**, 3949–3967. [2]

Myers, K. L., Tyson, W. M., Wolverton, M. J., Jarvis, P. A., Lee, T. J., and des Jardins, M. (2002). PASSAT: A User-Centric Planning Framework. *In: Proceedings of the 3rd Intl. NASA Workshop on Planning and Scheduling for Space*, Houston, TX. [7]

Müsseler, J., and Hommel, B. (1997a). Blindness to response-compatible stimuli. *Journal of Experimental Psychology: Human Perception & Performance*, **23**, 861–872. [2]

Müsseler, J., and Hommel, B. (1997b). Detecting and identifying response-compatible stimuli. *Psychonomic Bulletin & Review*, **4**, 125–129. [2]

Nagel, E. (1961). *The Structure of Science: Problems in the Logic of Scientific Explanation.* London: Routledge and Kegan Paul. [4]

Nakamura, N., and G. Salvendy, G. (1988). An experimental study of human decision-making in computer-based scheduling of flexible manufacturing system. *International Journal of Production Research*, **26**(4), 567–583. [7]

Nauta, A., and Sanders, K. (2001). Causes and consequences of perceived goal differences between departments within manufacturing organizations. *Journal of Occupational & Organizational Psychology*, **74**(3), 321–342. [6]

Neumann, O., and Klotz, W. (1994). Motor responses to nonreportable, masked stimuli: Where is the limit of direct parameter specification? In C. Umiltà and M. Moscovitch (eds.), *Attention and Performance XV: Conscious and Nonconscious Information Processing*, pp. 123–150. Cambridge, MA: MIT Press. [2]

Newell, A. (1982). The knowledge level. *Artificial Intelligence*, **18**(1), 87–127. [7,17]

Newell, A. (1990). *Unified Theories of Cognition.* Cambridge, MA: Harvard University Press. [1, 4, 5, 13]

Newell, A., and Simon, H. A. (1972). *Human Problem Solving.* Englewood Cliffs, NJ: Prentice-Hall. [3, 4, 5, 7, 13, 18]

Newell, A., and Simon, H. A. (1963). GPS, a program that simulates human thought. In E. A. Feigenbaum and J. Feldman (eds.), *Computers and Thought*, pp. 279–296. New York: McGraw-Hill. [10]

Newell, A., and Simon, H.A. (1976). Computer science as empirical enquiry: symbols and search. *Communications of the ACM*. **19**, 113–126 [4]

Newell, A., Shaw, J.C., and Simon, H.A. (1958). Elements of a theory of human problem solving. *Psychological Review*, **65**, 151–166. [4]

Neylan, T. C. (M.D.), Section Editor (1999). Frontal lobe function: Mr. Phineas Gage's famous injury. *Journal of Neuropsychiatry and Clinical Neurosciences* **11**(2), 281–283. [3]

Nicholson, T. A. J., and Pullen, R. D. (1972). A practical control system for optimizing production schedules. *International Journal of Production Research*, **16**, 219–227. [7]

Norman, P., and Naveed, S. (1990). A comparison of expert system and human operator performance for cement kiln operation. *Journal of the Operational Research Society*, **41**(11), 1007–1019. [7]

Numan, J. H. (1998). *Knowledge-Based Systems as Companions: Trust, Human–Computer Interaction and Complex Systems*. Groningen: Ph.D thesis, University of Groningen. [4]

Oddi, A., and Cesta A. (2000). Toward interactive scheduling systems for managing medical resources. *Artificial Intelligence in Medicine*, **20**(2), 113–138. [7]

Osborne, M. J., and Rubinstein, A. (1994). *A Course in Game Theory*. Cambridge, MA: MIT Press. [10]

Osman, A., Bashore, T. R., Coles, M. G. H., Donchin, E., and Meyer, D. E. (1992). On the transmission of partial information: Inferences from movement-related brain research. *Journal of Experimental Psychology: Human Perception and Performance*, **18**, 217–232. [2]

Owen, G. (1995). *Game Theory*. New York: Academic Press. [10]

Parkinson, J. S., and Blair, D. F. (1993). Does *E. coli* have a nose? *Science*, **259**(19), 1701–1702. [11]

Pashler, H. (1994). Dual-task interference in simple tasks: Data and theory. *Psychological Bulletin*, **116**, 220–244. [2]

Passino, K. M. (2000). Distributed optimization and control using only a germ of intelligence. In P. Groumpos, N. Koussoulas, and M. Polycarpou (eds.), *Proceedings of the 2000 IEEE International Symposium on Intelligent Control*, Patras, Greece, pp. P5–P13. [11]

Patalano, A. L., and Seifert, C. M. (1997). Opportunism in planning. *Cognitive Psychology*, **34**, 1–36. [2]

Pattee, H. (1987). Physical basis and origin of control. In H. H. Pattee (ed.) *Hierarchy Theory*. New York: G. Braziler. [11]

Pearl, J. (1984). *Heuristics: Intelligent Search Strategies for Computer Problem Solving*. Reading, MA: Addison-Wesley. [10]

Perenin, M.T., and Vighetto, A. (1988). Optic ataxia: A specific disruption in visuomotor mechanisms. I. Different aspects of the deficit in reaching for objects. *Brain*, **111**, 643–674. [2]

Perret, E. (1974). The left frontal lobe of man and the suppression of habitual responses in verbal categorical behavior. *Neuropsychologia*, **12**, 323–330. [2]

Pfeffer, J., and Salancik, G. R. (1978). *The External Control of Organizations*. New York: Harper & Row. [5]

Pfurtscheller, G., Flotzinger, D., and Neuper, C. (1994). Differentiation between finger, toe and tongue movement in man based on 40 Hz EEG. *Electroencephalography and Clinical Neurophysiology*, **90**, 456–460. [2]

Pylyshyn, Z.W. (1984). *Computation and Cognition*. Cambridge, MA: MIT Press. [1]

Pidd, M. (1999). Just modeling through: A rough guide to modeling. *Interfaces*, **29**, 118–132. [8]

Pierson, P. (1994). Dismantling the welfare state? (Reagan, Thatcher, and the politics of retrenchment). Cambridge, England: Cambridge University Press. [5]

Pillutla, S. N., and Nag, B. N. (1996). Object-oriented model construction in production scheduling decisions. *Decision Support Systems: The International Journal*, **18**, 357–375. [7]

Pinedo, M. (1995). *Scheduling Theory, Algorithms and Systems*. NJ, Prentice-Hall. [6]

Pinedo, M., and Yen, B.P.-C. (1997). On the design and development of object-oriented scheduling systems. *Annals of Operations Research*, **70**, 359–378. [7]

Politis, D. N. (1993). ARMA models, prewhitening and minimum cross entropy. *IEEE Transactions on Signal Processing*, **41**(2), 781–787. [11]

Popper, K. R. (1974). Unended quest: An intellectual autobiography. Glasgow, UK: Fontana/Collins, 255 pages. [5]

Posner, M. I. (ed.). (1989). *Foundations of Cognitive Science*. Boston: MIT Press. [1, 4]

Pounds, W. F. (1963). The scheduling environment. In J. F. Muth and G. L. Thompson (eds.), *Industrial Scheduling*, pp. 5–12. Englewood Cliffs, NJ: Prentice-Hall. [7]

Prablanc, C., and Pélisson, D. (1990). Gaze saccade orienting and hand pointing are locked to their goal by quick internal loops. In M. Jeannerod (ed.), *Attention and performance XIII* pp. 653–676. Hillsdale, NJ: Erlbaum Associates. [2]

Prietula, M. J., Hsu, W.-L., Ow, P. S., and Thompson, G. L. (1994). MacMerl: Mixed-initiative scheduling with coincident problem spaces. In M. Zweben and M. S. Fox (eds.), *Intelligent scheduling*. San Francisco: Morgan Kaufmann. [1, 7, 17]

Prinz, W. (1987). Ideo-motor action. In H. Heuer and A. F. Sanders (eds.), *Perspectives on Perception and Action*. Hillsdale, NJ: Erlbaum Associates. [2]

Prinz, W. (1997). Why Donders has led us astray. In B. Hommel and W. Prinz (eds.), *Theoretical Issues in Stimulus–Response Compatibility*, pp. 247–267. Amsterdam: Elsevier. [2]

Putten, J. van, Scharenborg, N., and Woerlee, A. (1993). A Generic User Interface Constructor for Planning and Scheduling Applications. *Proceedings of the HCI'93 Conference on People and Computers VIII*. [7]

Puviani, A. (1960). *Die Illusionen in der öffentlichen Finanzwirtschaft*. Berlijn: Duncker & Humblot. Original work published as Teoria dell'Illusione Finanziara, 1903. [5]

Pylyshyn, Z. W. (1984). *Computation and Cognition: Towards a Foundation for Cognitive Science*. Cambridge, MA: MIT Press. [4]

Rackovic, M., Surla, D., and Vukobratovic, M. (1999). On reducing numerical complexity of complex robot dynamics. *Journal of Intelligent and Robotic Systems*, **24**, 269–293. [11]

Raffone, A., and Wolters, G. (2001). A cortical mechanism for binding in visual working memory. *Journal of Cognitive Neuroscience*, **13**, 766–785. [2]

Raibert, M. H. (1977). *Motor Control and Learning by the State-Space Model*. Technical Report AI-TR-439. Cambridge, MA: AI Laboratory, MIT. [2]

Rasmussen, J. (1986). *Information Processing and Human–Machine Interaction: An Approach to Cognitive Engineering*. Amsterdam, the Netherlands: North-Holland. [7]

Rasmussen, J., Pejtersen, A. M., and Goodstein, L. P. (1994). *Cognitive Systems Engineering*. New York: John Wiley & Sons. [3]

Rastier, F. (1998). On signs and texts: Cognitive science faces interpretation. *Applied Semiotics*, **5**(1998.07), 305–329. [5]

Reason, J. (1990). *Human Error*. Cambridge, UK: Cambridge University Press. [3]

Reeves, C. R. (1995). *Modern Heuristic Techniques for Combinatorial Problems*. McGraw-Hill. [16]

Requin, J., Lecas, J. C., and Vitton, N. (1990). A comparison of preparation-related neuronal activity changes in the prefrontal, primary motor and posterior parietal areas of the monkey cortex: Preliminary results. *Neuroscience Letters*, **111**, 151–156. [2]

Riehle, A., and Requin, J. (1989). Monkey primary motor and premotor cortex: Single-cell activity related to prior information about direction and extent of an intended movement. *Journal of Neurophysiology*, **61**, 534–549. [2]

Riesbeck, C. K., and Schank, R. C. (1989). *Inside Case-Based Reasoning*. Hillsdale, NJ: Lawrence Erlbaum Associates. [4, 18]

Rizzolatti, G., Fadiga, L., Gallese, V., and Fogassi, L. (1996). Premotor cortex and the recognition of motor actions. *Cognitive Brain Research*, **3**, 131–141. [2]

Rizzolatti, G., Fogassi, L., and Gallese, V. (2001). Neurophysiological mechanisms underlying the understanding and imitation of action. *Nature Reviews Neuroscience*, **2**, 661–670. [2]

Robb, R. (1910). *Lectures on Organization* (Boston: private printing). [6]

Robinson, A. (1974). *Non-Standard Analysis*. Princeton, NJ: Princeton University Press. [11]

Rochat, P., and Striano, T. (1999). Emerging self-exploration by 2-month-old infants. *Developmental Science*, **2**, 206–218. [2]

Rock, I., and Palmer, S. (1990). The legacy of Gestalt psychology. *Scientific American*, **December** 84–90. [11]

Rodammer, F. A., and White, K. P. (1988). A recent survey of production scheduling. *IEEE Transactions on Systems, Man, and Cybernetics*, **18**, 841–851. [6]

Roelfsema, P. R., Engel, A. K., König, P., and Singer, W. (1997). Visuomotor integration is associated with zero time-lag synchronization among cortical areas. *Nature*, **385**, 157–161. [2]

Rosen, R. (1985). *Anticipatory Systems; Philosophical, Mathematical, and Methodological Foundations*. IFSR International Series on Systems Science and Engineering, Vol. 1. Oxford: Pergamon Press. [1]

Rosenbaum, D. A. (1980). Human movement initiation: Specification of arm, direction and extent. *Journal of Experimental Psychology: General*, **109**, 444–474. [2]

Rosenbaum, D. A. (1991). *Human Motor Control*. San Diego: Academic Press. [2]

Rosenbaum, D. A., and Kornblum, S. (1982). A priming method for investigating the selection of motor responses. *Acta Psychologica*, **51**, 223–243. [2]

Rosenbaum, D. A., Weber, R. J., Hazelett, W. M., and Hindorff, V. (1986). The parameter remapping effect in human performance: Evidence from tongue twisters and finger fumblers. *Journal of Memory and Language*, **25**, 710–725. [2]

Rossetti, Y., and Pisella, L. (2002). Several "vision for action" systems: A guide to dissociating and integrating dorsal and ventral functions. In W. Prinz and B. Hommel (eds.), *Common Mechanisms in Perception and Action: Attention & Performance XIX*, pp. 62–119. Oxford: Oxford University Press. [2]

Roth, E. M., Bennett, K. B., and Woods, D. D. (1988). Human interaction with an "intelligent" machine. In E. Hollnagel, G. Mancini, and D. D. Woods (eds.), *Cognitive Engineering in Complex Dynamic Worlds*, pp. 23–69. London: Academic Press. [3]

Rovee, C. K., and Rovee, D. T. (1969). Conjugate reinforcement in infant exploratory behavior. *Journal of Experimental Child Psychology*, **8**, 33–39. [2]

Sacerdoti, E. D. (1975). The nonlinear nature of plans. *Proceedings of the Fourth International Joint Conference on Artificial Intelligence*, pp. 206–214. [18]

Sacerdoti, E. D. (1977). *A Structure for Plans and Behavior*. New York: Elsevier. [3]

Sadeh, N., Hildum, D. W., Laliberty, T. J., McAnulty, J., Kjenstad, D., and Tseng, A. (1998). A Blackboard architecture for integrating process planning and production scheduling. *Concurrent Engineering: Research and Applications*, **6**(2), 88–100. [9]

Salenius, S., Salmelin, R., Neuper, C., Pfurtscheller, G., and Hari, R. (1996). Human cortical 40 Hz rhythm is closely related to EMG rhythmicity. *Neuroscience Letters*, **213**, 75–78. [2]

Samurçay, R., and Hoc, J. M. (1996). Causal versus topographical support for diagnosis in a dynamic situation. *Le Travail Humain*, **59**, 45–68. [3]

Samurçay, R., and Rogalski, J. (1988). Analysis of operator's cognitive activities in learning and using a method for decision making in public safety. In J. Patrick and K. D. Duncan (eds.), *Human Decision-Making and Control*, pp. 133–152. Amsterdam: North-Holland. [3]

Sanderson, P. M. (1989). The human planning and scheduling role in advanced manufacturing systems: an emerging human factors domain. *Human Factors*, **31**(6), pp. 635–666. [6, 7, 17]

Sanderson, P. M. (1991). Towards the model human scheduler. *International Journal of Human Factors in Manufacturing*, **1**(3), 195–219. [3, 6]

Sanes, J. N., and Donoghue, J. P. (1993). Oscillations in local field potentials of the primate motor cortex during voluntary movement. *Proceedings of the National Academy of Sciences of the United States of America*, **90**, 4470–4474. [2]

Sauer, J. (1993a). Meta-scheduling using dynamic scheduling knowledge. In J. Dorn and K. Froeschl (eds.), *Scheduling of Production Processes*. Chichester, England: Ellis Horwood. [9]

Sauer, J. (1993b). Wissensbasiertes Lösen von Ablaufplanungsproblemen durch explizite Heuristiken, *DISKI*, Band 37. Infix Verlag. [9]

Sauer, J. (1995). Scheduling and meta-scheduling. In C. Beierle and L. Plümer (eds.), *Logic Programming: Formal Methods and Practical Applications. Studies in Computer Science and Artificial Intelligence*, pp. 323–342. Elsevier Science. [9]

Sauer, J. (1998). A multi-site scheduling system. *AAAI's Special Interest Group in Manufacturing Workshop on Artificial Intelligence and Manufacturing: State of the Art and State of Practice*, pp. 161–168. [9]

Sauer, J. (1999). Knowledge-based scheduling techniques in industry. In L. C. Jain, R. P. Johnson, Y. Takefuji, and L. A. Zadeh (eds.), *Knowledge-Based Intelligent Techniques in Industry*, pp. 53–84. CRC Press. [9]

Sauer, J. (2000). Knowledge-based systems in scheduling, In T. L. Leondes (ed.), *Knowledge-Based Systems Techniques and Applications*, pp. 1293–1325. San Diego: Academic Press. [9]

Sauer, J., and Appelrath, H.-J. (1997). Knowledge-based design of scheduling systems. *Proceedings of "WMC97", World Manufacturing Congress*, Auckland 18.-21.11.97. Canada, ICSC Academic Press. [9]

Sauer, J., Appelrath, H.-J., and Suelmann, G. (1997). Multi-site scheduling with fuzzy-concepts. *International Journal of Approximate Reasoning in Scheduling*, **19**, 145–160. [9]

Sauer, J., and Bruns, R. (1997). Knowledge-based scheduling Systems in Industry and Medicine. *IEEE-Expert* (February), 24–31. [9]

Sauer, J., Freese, T., and Teschke, T. (2000). Towards Agent-Based Multi-Site Scheduling, In J. Sauer and J. Köhler (eds.), *Proceedings of the ECAI 2000 Workshop on New Results in Planning, Scheduling, and Design*, pp. 123–130, Berlin. [9]

Schank, R., and Abelson, R. (1977). *Scripts, Plans, Goals and Understanding*. Hillsdale, NJ: Lawrence Erlbaum Associates. [4]

Scheerer, E. (1984). Motor theories of cognitive structure: A historical review. In W. Prinz and A. F. Sanders (eds.), *Cognition and Motor Processes*, pp. 77–97. Berlin: Springer. [2]

Schmidt, K. (1991). Cooperative work: A conceptual framework. In J. Rasmussen, J. Brehmer, and J. Leplat (eds.), *Distributed Decision Making: Cognitive Models for Cooperative Work*, pp. 75–110. Chichester: John Wiley & Sons. [5]

Schmidt, R. A. (1975). A schema theory of discrete motor skill learning. *Psychological Review*, **82**, 225–260. [2]

Schoppers, M. (1987). Universal planning for reactive robots in unpredictable environments. *In: Proceedings of IJCAI-87*, pp. 1039–1046. [10]

Schraagen J. M., Chipman S. F., and Shalin V. L. (ed.) (2000). *Cognitive Task Analysis*. Mahwah, NJ: Lawrence Erlbaum Associates. [7]

Schreiber, A. T., Akkermans, J. M., Anjewierden, A. A., Hoog, R. de, Shadbolt, N. R., Velde, W. van de, and Wielinga, B. J. (2000). *Knowledge Engineering and Management: The CommonKADS Methodology*. Cambridge, MA: MIT Press. [13, 14, 17, 18]

Schreiber, G., Wielinga, B., and Breuker, J. (eds.) (1993). *KADS: A Principled Approach to Knowledge-Based System Development*. London: Academic Press. [1, 7, 13, 17, 18]

Schrijver, A. (1993). Minimum circulation of railway stock. *CWI Quarterly*, **6**, 205–217. [8]

Schuitemaker, J. (2003). *De invloed van organisatievariabelen op de kwaliteit van de planning*. Internal Report. Faculteit Bedrijfskunde; Rijksuniversiteit Groningen. [18]

Schultz, J., and Mertens, P. (2000). Untersuchung wissensbasierter und weiterer ausgewählter Ansätze zur Unterstützung der Produktionsfeinplanung—ein Methodenvergleich. *Wirtschaftsinformatik*, **42**(1), 56–65. [9]

Schumacher, E. H., Seymour, T. L., Glass, J. M., Fencsik, D. E., Lauber, E. J., Kieras, D. E., and Meyer, D. E. (2001). Virtually perfect time sharing in dual-task performance: Uncorking thecentral cognitive bottleneck. *Psychological Science*, **12**, 101–108. [2]

Shallice, T., and Burgess, P. (1998). The domain of supervisory processes and the temporal organization of behavior. In A. C. Roberts, T. W. Robbins, and L. Weiskrantz (eds.), *The Prefrontal Cortex: Executive and Cognitive Functions*. Oxford: Oxford University Press. [2]

Shallice, T. (1982). Specific impairments of planning. *Philosophical Transactions of the Royal Society London B*, **298**, 199–209. [2]

Shier, D. R. (1976). Iterative methods for determining the k shortest paths in a network. *Networks*, **6**, 205–230. [7, 17]

Simon, H. A. (1960). *The New Science of Management Decision*. New York: Harper & Row. [4]

Simon, H. A. (1962). The architecture of complexity. *Proceedings of the American Philosophical Society*, **106**, 467–482. [5]

Simon, H. A. (1981). *The Sciences of the Artificial*, 2nd edition. Cambridge, MA: The MIT Press. [1, 18]

Simon, H. A., and Newell, A. (1958). Heuristic problem solving: The next advance in operations research. *The Journal of the Operations Research Society of America*, 1–10. [4]

Simon, J. R., and Rudell, A. P. (1967). Auditory S-R compatibility: The effect of an irrelevant cue on information processing. *Journal of Applied Psychology*, **51**, 300–304. [2]

Singer, W. (1994). The organization of sensory motor representations in the Neocortex: A hypothesis based on temporal coding. In C. Umiltà and M. Moscovitch (eds.), *Attention and performance XV: Conscious and Nonconscious Information Processing*, pp. 77–107. Cambridge, MA: MIT Press. [2]

Sitter U. de, Hertog, J. F. den, and Dankbaar, B. (1997). From complex organizations with simple jobs to simple organizations with complex jobs. *Human Relations*, **50**(5), 1997. [7]

Skinner, W. (1974). The focused factory. *Harvard Business Review*, **52**(3), 113–121. [6]

Slany, W. (1996). Scheduling as a fuzzy multiple criteria optimization problem. *Fuzzy Sets and Systems*, **78**, 197–222. [9]

Smed J., Johtela, T., Johnsson, M., Puranen, M., and Nevalainen, O. (2000). An Interactive System for Scheduling Jobs in Electronic Assembly. *The International Journal of Advanced Manufacturing Technology*, **16**(6), 450–459. [7]

Smith, D. R., Parra, E. A., and Westfold, S. J. (1996). Synthesis of Planning and Scheduling Software. In Tate, A. (ed.), *Advanced Planning Technology*. Menlo Park, CA: AAAI Press. [7]

Smith, H. T., and Crabtree, R. G. (1975). Interactive planning: A study of computer aiding in the execution of a simulated scheduling task. *International Journal of Man–Machine Studies*, **7**, 213–231. [3]

Smith S. F. (1992). Knowledge-based production management: Approaches, results and prospects. *Production Planning & Control*, **3**(4), 350–380. [4, 7, 9, 18]

Smith, S. F. (1994). OPIS: A methodology and architecture for reactive scheduling. In M. Zweben, and M. S. Fox, *Intelligent Scheduling*. San Francisco: Morgan Kaufman. [7]

Smith, S. F., and Becker, M. (1997). An ontology for constructing scheduling systems. *Working Notes of 1997 AAAI Symposium on Ontological Engineering*. Stanford, CA: AAAI Press. [7]

Smith, S. F., Lassila, O., and Becker, M. (1996). Configurable, mixed-initiative systems for planning and scheduling. In Tate, A. (ed.), *Advanced Planning Technology*. Menlo Park, CA: AAAI Press. [4, 7]

Smolensky, P. (1988). On the proper treatment of connectionism. *Behavioral and Brain Sciences*, 11, 1–74. [1]

Smullyan, R. M. (1992). *Godel's Incompleteness Theorem*, Chapter 11, Self-Referential Systems. New York: Oxford University Press. [11]

Stadtler, H., and Kilger, C. (2002). *Supply Chain Management and Advanced Planning*, 2nd edition. Berlin: Springer. [4, 7]

Stamper, R. (1973). *Information in Business and Administrative Systems*. New York: John Wiley & Sons. [5]

Stamper, R. K. (2001). Organisational semiotics: Informatics without the computer? In K. Liu, R. J. Clarke, P. Bøgh Andersen, and R. K. Stamper (eds.), *Information, Organisation and Technology: Studies in Organisational Semiotics*, pp. 115–171. Boston: Kluwer Academic Publishers. [5]

Starr, M. K. (1979). Perspectives on disaggregation. In L. P. Ritzman, L. J. Krajewski, W. L. Berry, S. H. Goodman, S. T. Hardy, and L. D. Vitt (eds.), *Disaggregation. Problems in Manufacturing and Service Organizations*. Boston: Martinus Nijhoff Publishing. [1]

Staudenmayer, N. (1997). Interdependency: Conceptual, empirical, & practical issues. MIT Sloan School of Management, Working Paper 3971. [6]

Stegmann, V. (1996). *Iterative Verbesserung von Ablaufplänen*. Diplomarbeit, Universität Oldenburg, Oldenburg. [9]

Sterman, J. (1989). Modeling managerial behavior: Misperceptions of feedback in a dynamic decision making experiment. *Management Science*, **35**(3), 321–339. [6]

Sternberg, R. J. (ed.) (1982). *Handbook of Human Intelligence*. Cambridge, UK: Cambridge University Press. [11]

Stoet, G., and Hommel, B. (1999). Action planning and the temporal binding of response codes. *Journal of Experimental Psychology: Human Perception and Performance*, **25**, 1625–1640. [2]

Suchman, L. A. (1987). *Plans and Situated Actions*. Cambridge, England: Cambridge University Press. [3, 5]

Sundin, U. (1994). Assignment and scheduling. In J. Breuker and W. van der Velde (eds.), *CommonKADS Library for Expertise Modeling: Reusable Problem Solving Components*. Amsterdam: IOS Press. [7, 18]

Sutcliffe, A. (1981). *The History of Urban and Regional Planning*. London: Mansell. [18]

Tabe, T., Yamamuro, S., and Salvendy, G. (1988). An approach to knowledge elicitation in scheduling FMS: Toward a hybrid intelligent system. In W. Karwowski, H. R. Parsaei, and M. R. Wilhelm (eds.), *Ergonomics of Hybrid Automated Systems I*. New York: Elsevier Science Publishers, pp. 259–266. [6]

Tate, A. (1993). The emergence of "standard" planning and scheduling system components— open planning and scheduling architectures. In *European Workshop on Planning (EWSP '93)*. [7]

Tate, A. (ed.) (1996). *Advanced Planning Technology*. Menlo Park, CA: AAAI Press. [9]

Teahan, B. (1998). Implementation of a self-scheduling system: A solution to more than just schedules! *Journal of Nursing Management*, **6**, 361–368 [5].

Telford, C. W. (1931). The refractory phase of voluntary and associative responses. *Journal of Experimental Psychology*, **14**, 1–36. [2]

Thompson, J. D. (1967). *Organizations in Action*. New York: McGraw-Hill. [1]

Thorndike, E. L. (1913). Ideo-motor action. *Psychological Review*, **20**, 91–106. [2]

Thurley, K. E., and Hamblin, A. C. (1962). The supervisor's role in production control. *International Journal of Production Research*, **1**, 1–12. [6]

Tomii, N., and Zhou, L. J. (2000). Depot shunting scheduling using combined genetic algorithm and PERT. In *Proceedings COMPRAIL 2000*, pp. 437–446. [15]

Tomii, N., Zhou, L. J., and Fukumara, N. (1999). Shunting scheduling problem at railway stations. In *Lecture Notes in Artificial Intelligence*, **1611**, 790–797. [15]

Türksen, I. B. (1991). Fuzzy logic-based expert systems for operations management. In C. Y. Suen and R. Shinghal (eds.), *Operational Expert System Applications in Canada*. Oxford: Pergamon. [9]

Turvey, M. T. (1977). Preliminaries to a theory of action with reference to vision. In R. Shaw and J. Bransford (eds.), *Perceiving, Acting, and Knowing. Toward an Ecological Psychology*. Hillsdale, NJ: Lawrence Erlbaum Associates. [2]

Uexküll, J. von, and Kriszat, G. (1970). *Streifzüge durch die Umwelten von Tieren und Menschen*. Frankfurt: Fischer. (Original work published 1936.) [5]

Uexküll, T. von. (1998). Jakob von Uexkülls Umweltlehre. In R. Posner, K. Robering, and T. A. Sebeok (eds.), *Semiotics: A Handbook on the Sign-Theoretic Foundations of Nature and Culture*, Vol. 2, pp. 2183–2191. Berlin: Walter de Gruyter. [5]

Ulusoy, G., and Özdamar, L. (1996). A framework for an interactive project scheduling system under limited resources. *European Journal of Operations Research*, **90**(2), 362–375. [7]

Veloso, M. M. (1996). Towards mixed-initiative rationale-supported planning. In Tate, A. (ed.), *Advanced Planning Technology*. Menlo Park, CA: AAAI Press. [18]

Verbraeck, A. (1991). *Developing an Adaptive Scheduling Support Environment*. Delft: Ph.D. thesis, University of Delft. [18]

Vicente, K. J. (1999). *Cognitive Work Analysis*. Mahwah, NJ: LEA. [7]

Vicente, K. J., and Rasmussen, J. (1990). The ecology of human–machine systems II: Mediating direct perception in complex work domains. *Ecological Psychology*, **2**, 207–249. [3]

Vidal, F., Bonnet, M., and Macar, F. (1991). Programming response duration in a precueing reaction time paradigm. *Journal of Motor Behavior*, **23**, 226–234. [2]

Vlek, C. A. J., and Wagenaar, W. A. (1976). Oordelen en beslissen in onzekerheid (Judging and Deciding under Uncertainty). In J. A. Michon, E. G. J. Eijkman, and L. F. W de Klerk, (eds.), *Handboek der Psychonomie (Handbook of Psychonomics)*. Deventer: van Loghum Slaterus. [4]

Waern, Y. (1989). *Cognitive Aspects of Computer Supported Tasks*. Chichester: John Wiley & Sons. [7, 13]

Wäfler, T. (2001). Planning and scheduling in secondary work systems. In B. MacCarthy and J. Wilson (eds.), *Human Performance in Planning and Scheduling*. London: Taylor & Francis. [7]

Wagner, H. M. (1970). *Principles of Operations Research*. Englewood Cliffs, NJ: Prentice-Hall, 1970. [8]

Watson, J. S., and Ramey, C. T. (1972). Reactions to response-contingent stimulation in early infancy. *Merrill-Palmer Quarterly*, **18**, 219–227. [2]

Watson, R. (2000). Prospects for computer aided railway scheduling: perspectives from users and parallels from mass transit. *Transportation Planning and Technology*, **23**(4), pp. 303–321. [17]

Wauschkuhn, O. (1992). Untersuchung zur verteilten Produktionsplanung mit Methoden der logischen Programmierung, *IWBS Report 215*, Wissenschaftliches Zentrum, IWBS, IBM. [9]

Welford, A. T. (1952). The "psychological refractory period" and the timing of high-speed performance—A review and a theory. *British Journal of Psychology*, **43**, 2–19. [2]

Wennink, M., and Savelsbergh, M. (1996). Towards a planning board generator. *Decision Support Systems: The International Journal*, **17**(3), 199–226. [7]

Weyuker, E. (1988). Evaluating software complexity measures. *IEEE Transactions on Software Engineering*, **14**(9), 1357–1365. [11]

Wezel, W. M. C. van (1994). D*e SEC-methodiek; ontwikkelen van scheduling-applicaties.* Groningen: Internal report, University of Groningen (The SEC-methodology: development of scheduling applications). [4, 7]

Wezel, W. M. C. van (2001). *Tasks, Hierarchies, and Flexibility; Planning in Food Processing Industries*. Capelle a/d IJssel: Labyrint Publication. [4, 7, 17, 18]

Wezel, W. M. C. van, and Barten, B. (2002). Hierarchical mixed-initiative planning support. In: T. Grant, and Witteveen, C. (eds.), *Plansig 2002. Proceedings of the 21th Workshop of the UK Planning and Scheduling Special Interest Group*. Delft: Delft University of Technology. [7, 17]

Wezel, W. M. C. van, and Donk, D. P. van (1996). Scheduling in food processing industries: Preliminary findings of a task oriented approach. In Bertrand, J. W. M., Jafari, M. A., Fransoo, J. C., and Rutten, W. G. M. M. (1996). *Second International Conference on Computer Integrated Manufacturing in the Process Industries—Proceedings*, pp. 545–557. [7]

Wezel, W. van, Donk, D. P. van, and Gaalman, G. (2004). The planning flexibility bottleneck in food processing industries (forthcoming). *Journal of Operations Management*. [6]

Wezel W. M. C. van, and Jorna, R. J. (1999). The SEC-system: Reuse support for scheduling system development. *Decision Support Systems*, **26**(1), July 1999. [4, 7, 18]

Wezel W. van, and Jorna, R. J. (2001). Paradoxes in planning. *Engineering Applications of Artificial Intelligence*, **14/3**, 269–286. [1, 6, 7]

Wezel, W. M. C. van, Jorna, R. J., and Mietus, D. (1996). Scheduling in a generic perspective. *International Journal of Expert Systems; Research and Applications*, **3**(9), 357–381. [4, 7]

Wiers, V. C. S. (1996). A quantitative field study of the decision behaviour of four shop floor schedulers. *Production Planning and Control*, **7**(4), 383–392. [7]

Wiers, V. C. S. (1997a). A review of the applicability of OR and AI scheduling techniques in practice. *Omega*, **25**(2), 145–153. [6]

Wiers, V. C. S. (1997b). *Human–Computer Interaction in Production Scheduling: Analysis and Design of Decision Support Systems for Production Scheduling Tasks*. Ph.D. thesis, Eindhoven University of Technology. [6]

Wiers, V. C. S. (2002). A case study on the integration of APS and ERP in a steel processing plant. *Production Planning & Control*, **13**(6), 552–560. [6]

Williamson, O. E. (1975). *Markets and Hierarchies*. New York: The Free Press. [5]

Williamson, O. E. (1985). *The Economic Institutions of Capitalism*. New York: The Free Press. [5]

Wilson, R. A. and Keil, F. C. (1999). *The MIT Encyclopedia of the Cognitive Sciences*. Cambridge (Mass): The MIT Press. [4]

Winter, T. (1999). *Online and Real-Time Dispatching Problems*. Ph.D. thesis, Technical University of Braunschweig. [15]

Winter, T., and Zimmermann, U. T. (2000). Real-time dispatch of trams in storage yards. *Annals of Operations Research*, **96**, 287–315. [15]

Woerlee, A. P. (1991). *Decision Support Systems for Production Scheduling*. Rotterdam: Ph.D. thesis, Erasmus University Rotterdam. [7]

Wolf, G. (1994). Schedule management: An object-oriented approach. *Decision Support Systems: The International Journal*, **11**, 373–388. [7]

Wolff, P. (1987). Perceptual learning by saccades: A cognitive approach. In H. Heuer and A. F. Sanders (eds.), *Perspectives on Perception and Action*, pp. 249–271. Hillsdale, NJ: Lawrence Erlbaum Associates. [2]

Wolfram, S. (2002). *A New Kind of Science*. Champaign, IL: Wolfram Media. [5]

Wooldridge, M. (2002). *An Introduction to Multiagent Systems*. Chichester: John Wiley & Sons. [5]

Woudt, C. van't. (2001). *Zoeken naar rangeerroutes op een station* (in Dutch). Master's thesis, Erasmus University Rotterdam. [15]

Xiao, Y., Milgram, P., and Doyle, D. J. (1997). Planning behavior and its functional role in interactions with complex systems. *IEEE Transactions on Systems, Man, and Cybernetics—Part A: Systems and Humans*, **27**, 313–324. [3]

Yaniv, I., Meyer, D. E., Gordon, P. C., Huff, C. A., and Sevald, C. A. (1990). Vowel similarity, connectionist models, and syllable structure in motor programming of speech. *Journal of Memory and Language*, **29**, 1–26. [2]

Zames, G. (1979). On the metric complexity of causal linear systems: Epsilon-entropy and epsilon-dimension for continuous time. *IEEE Transactions on Automatic Control*, **AC-24**(2), 222–230. [11]

Zelazo, P. D., Reznick, J. S., and Piñon, D. E. (1995). Response control and the execution of verbal rules. *Developmental Psychology*, **31**, 508–517. [2]

Zlotkin, G., and Rosenschein, J. S. (1985). Incomplete information and deception in multi-agent negotiation. *In: Proceedings of the 12th International Joint Conference on Artificial Intelligence (IJCAI'85)*, pp. 225–231. [10]

Zwaneveld, P. J. (1997). *Railway Planning—Routing of Trains and Allocation of Passenger Lines*. PhD-Thesis Erasmus University Rotterdam, Rotterdam, NL. [15]

Zwaneveld, P. J., Kroon, L. G., Romeijn, H. E., Salomon, M., Dauzère-Pérès, S., Hoesel, S. P. M., van, and Ambergen, H. W. (1996). Routing trains through railway stations: Model formulation and algorithms. *Transportation Science*, **30**(3), 181–194. [17]

Zweben, M., and Fox, M. S. (1994). *Intelligent Scheduling*. San Francisco: Morgan Kaufman. [4, 9]

AUTHOR INDEX

Planning in Intelligent Systems: Aspects, Motivations, and Methods, Edited by Wout van Wezel,
René Jorna, and Alexander Meystel
Copyright © 2006 John Wiley & Sons, Inc.

SUBJECT INDEX

2-opt improvement, 430

A*search, 429
abstraction, 65, 82, 151, 359
  blast furnace, 96
abstraction space, 63
action automatization, 70
action control, development, 36
action features, 42
  codes, 43
  overlap, 45
action plan
  instantiation, 63
  sensimotor loops, 50
action planning, 35
  prepared reflex, 45
action plans, integrated
      assemblies, 40
action selection strategies, 316
action control, two-stage model, 31
action-effect associations, 33
actions
  effects, 28
  intelligent systems, 329
active support, 245
actor plan, 163

actors, 142, 501
  intelligent systems, 329
adapting to circumstances, 88
adjusting plans, 74
advanced logic, generalization/
      instantiation, 337
Advanced Planning and Scheduling
      systems (APS), 199
adversarial planning, 310
adversarial planning domain, 304
adversary, 307
affordance, 64
agency theory, 170
agent model, 395
aggregation, 10, 224
  generalization, 226, 359
  hierarchical planning, 229
air traffic control, 77
algorithm design, 217
algorithm of information
      organization, 334
algorithms, 220
  adversarial planning, 312
  bleuprint, 445
  closed world assumption, 14
  design, 486

Planning in Intelligent Systems: Aspects, Motivations, and Methods, Edited by Wout van Wezel, René Jorna, and Alexander Meystel